BIBLIOTHEK IN DER WISSENS-GESELLSCHAFT

Festschrift für Peter Vodosek

Herausgegeben von
Askan Blum

unter Mitarbeit von
Wolfram Henning, Agnes Jülkenbeck und Andreas Papendick

K · G · Saur München 2001

Die Deutsche Bibliothek - CIP Einheitsaufnahme

Bibliothek in der Wissensgesellschaft :
Festschrift für Peter Vodosek / hrsg. von Askan Blum.
Unter Mitarb. von Wolfram Henning . . . . - München : Saur , 2001
ISBN 3-598-11567-9

∞
Gedruckt auf säurefreiem Papier / Printed on acid-free paper

Satz: Elisabeth Messerschmidt, Stuttgart
Druck/Binden: Strauss Offsetdruck, Mörlenbach
ISBN 3-598-11567-9

Inhalt

GRUSSWORTE

AUSBILDUNG • FORTBILDUNG • WEITERBILDUNG

BIBLIOTHEKSKONZEPTE

MEDIEN- UND BIBLIOTHEKSGESCHICHTE

BERUF UND POLITIK

PERSPEKTIVEN

Christoph-E. Palmer

Grußwort

Mit der Gründung der Fachhochschule Stuttgart – Hochschule der Medien zum 1. September 2001 wird in Baden-Württemberg ein neues Kapitel der Medienbildung und Medienausbildung aufgeschlagen. Der Zusammenschluss der beiden Stuttgarter Fachhochschulen für Druck und Medien (HDM) und für Bibliotheks- und Informationswesen (HBI) ist mehr als eine Zusammenfassung der an beiden Hochschulen schon bestehenden Ausbildungsgänge in einer organisatorischen Einheit. In einer dynamisch sich entwickelnden Informationsgesellschaft schaffen wir durch den Zusammenschluss vielmehr die Voraussetzungen für etwas grundsätzlich Neues. An der Nahtstelle der Kompetenzfelder beider Hochschulen werden innovative Studienangebote möglich, mit denen die Hochschule der Medien zu einem in Deutschland bisher einmaligen Kompetenzzentrum entwickelt werden kann. Konvergenz und Vernetzung sind die zentralen Leitideen, die für den Bereich der Ausbildung das aufgreifen, was auf die gesamte Wirtschaftsbranche bezogen in der Informations- und Medientechnologie seit längerem bereits aktuell ist. Wir tragen damit nicht nur einer spezifischen Nachfrage- und Bedarfssituation bei den Unternehmen Rechnung, sondern leisten insgesamt einen wertvollen Beitrag für die Positionierung Baden-Württembergs als Standort für neue Informations- und Medientechnologien.

Es ist ein großes Verdienst der Hochschulen, dass sie auf der Grundlage von Empfehlungen der von der Landesregierung eingesetzten Kommission Fachhochschule 2000 diese Chancen erkannt und die Fusion unterstützt haben. Das ist keineswegs selbstverständlich, gehen damit doch auch über Jahrzehnte gewachsene und vertraute Strukturen, Identifikationen und Profile in einem größeren Ganzen auf, das bei aller Aufbruchstimmung und Zukunftserwartung seinen Platz doch erst noch finden muss. Mein Dank gilt deshalb in besonderem Maße den beiden Gründungsrektoren, Herrn Professor Dr. Uwe Schlegel von der HDM und Herrn Professor Dr. Peter Vodosek von der HBI. Naturgemäß war es nicht möglich, dass beide in bisheriger Verantwortung der neuen Hochschule verbunden bleiben. Umso mehr nötigt es Respekt ab, dass Professor Vodosek sich bereit gefunden hat, mit dem formellen Zusammenschluss nach 15 Jahren sein Rektoramt abzugeben.

Die Landesregierung von Baden-Württemberg hat von Anfang an keinen Zweifel daran gelassen, dass sie bereit ist, die Fusion tatkräftig zu unterstützen. Dies gilt zum einen für die Einrichtung der neuen Studiengänge Informationsdesign und Medienautor, zum anderen aber auch für die räumliche Zusammenführung an einem Standort. In der dritten Zukunftsoffensive Junge Generation, die Herr Ministerpräsident Erwin Teufel im Herbst 2000 angekündigt hat, sind als Landesanteil für die räumliche Unterbringung der neuen Hochschule in Vaihingen insgesamt 15 Mio. DM vorsehen. Damit können für den künftigen Erfolg der Hochschule entscheidende Synergieeffekte in Lehre, Forschung und Entwicklung erreicht werden. Damit sind aber auch von Seiten der Infrastruktur die Voraussetzungen gegeben für die Entwicklung eines konsistenten und einheitlichen Selbstverständnisses und einer eigenen Identität der neuen Hochschule.

}Ich bin sehr froh, dass es uns mit der Gründung der Hochschule der Medien gemeinsam gelungen ist, hier in Stuttgart einen Zukunftsentwurf Realität werden zu lassen, der bundes- und europaweit Aufmerksamkeit erzeugt und Maßstäbe setzt. Ich wünsche der neuen Hochschule eine gute und erfolgreiche Zukunft.

Uwe Schlegel

Mut zur Zukunft

Als der Rektor der HBI Prof. Dr. Peter Vodosek vor der wichtigsten Entscheidung seiner Amtszeiten stand lernte ich ihn kennen.

Die Frage für ihn war, ist es vertretbar, dass die traditionsreiche Institution HBI in der größeren Hochschule der Medien aufgeht oder nicht. Er hat sich, wissend um die damit entstehenden vielfältigen kleinen und größeren Probleme, für die neue Hochschule entschieden. Es war eine Entscheidung gegen die Institution aber eine für die Zukunft der Studierenden.

Er hat die Tür zur Hochschule der Medien, zu einem Haus, das von der Inhalterstellung über die Gestaltung, Wirtschaft und Produktion von Medien bis zur Informationswissenschaft und –beschaffung Studiengänge für alle gegenwärtigen und zukünftig denkbaren Medienberufe anbieten wird, aufgestoßen.

Die Chancen und Möglichkeiten die dieser entstehende „fullservice" Medienausbilder den Studierenden bieten wird sind enorm und bis heute noch nicht voll ausgelotet. Sie zu erkennen und zu realisieren wird die herausfordernde Aufgabe der Zukunft sein.

Das versammelte Wissen über die Medien in der europaweit einmaligen neuen Hochschule wird anspruchsvolle Forschungstätigkeiten und fundierte Entscheidungen bei der Neuausrichtung und Neugründung von Studiengängen ermöglichen.

Ein Zentrum der Medien ist im Entstehen in dem nicht nur junge Menschen hervorragend ausgebildet werden, sondern das auch ein unübersehbarer Leuchtturm in der Medienlandschaft sein wird.

In den vergangenen Jahren seit der Entscheidung für die Hochschule der Medien hat Prof. Dr. Peter Vodosek sehr viel für das Zusammenwachsen der Kulturen beider beteiligten Hochschulen getan und damit wesentliches für die so wichtige Kreativität und den erforderlichen Leistungswillen in der neuen Hochschule geleistet. Wie ich ihn kennen gelernt habe, wird er auch in Zukunft alles tun, um das entstehende Haus erfolgreich werden zu lassen.

Für all dies gehört ihm unser tiefer Dank.

Askan Blum

Einige Jahre zu früh

Festschriften werden zu runden Geburtstagen überreicht, zumeist zum 65., verbunden mit dem Ausscheiden des Geehrten aus dem aktiven Berufsleben. Peter Vodosek, Rektor der *Hochschule für Bibliotheks- und Informationswesen* (HBI)[1] erhält diese Festschrift nicht zum 65. oder 60. Geburtstag und nicht zum Ende seiner beruflichen Laufbahn, wohl aber als Würdigung für seine 15-jährige Tätigkeit als Rektor dieser Hochschule.

Mit dem Ausscheiden aus dem Rektoramt endet in mehrfacher Hinsicht eine Ära. Die HBI gibt zum 1. September 2001 ihre Selbständigkeit auf und geht zusammen mit der Hochschule Druck und Medien in der Stuttgarter *Hochschule der Medien* (HdM) auf.

Damit endet auch ein Kapitel deutscher Hochschulgeschichte. In den vergangenen Jahrzehnten waren bundesweit alle bibliothekarischen Ausbildungseinrichtungen in größere Hochschuleinrichtungen integriert worden. Die Stuttgarter Hochschule war die letzte noch eigenständige Einrichtung dieser Art in Deutschland. Diese Festschrift markiert so auch das Ende eines bedeutsamen Abschnittes bibliothekarischer Ausbildung.

Für diese Entwicklung gibt es mehrere Ursachen. Vorrangig ist es der Wandel in der Gesellschaft und damit die Veränderung auf dem Berufsmarkt und der damit verbundene Wandel in der Hochschullandschaft.

Der Wandel in der Gesellschaft ist gekennzeichnet durch die Begriffe *Informations- und Wissensgesellschaft*, der Wandel in der Hochschullandschaft durch die Verschmelzung kleinerer zu größeren Ausbildungseinrichtungen.

Hierbei stellen zwei zentrale Fragen: Verliert die bibliothekarische Ausbildung (und damit auch die Bibliothek) ihre Bedeutung? Und zum anderen: Führt die Zusammenlegung kleinerer Hochschulen zu größeren Einheiten zu einer Verschlechterung der Ausbildung?

Eine eindeutige Antwort darauf zu geben, ist nicht leicht. Eines liegt jedoch auf der Hand: die Stuttgarter Ausbildung hat sich sehr früh als maßgeblicher Teil einer Informationsgesellschaft verstanden, war dabei immer offen für neue Entwicklungen und zeigte dabei ein besonders hohes Maß an Kooperationsbereitschaft. Die Ausbildung der Bibliothekare und Informationsfachleute geriet damit nicht an den Rand unserer Gesellschaft – im Gegenteil, sie qualifizierte zunehmend für alle wichtigen Bereiche der Informations- und Wissensgesellschaft. Dabei standen und stehen nicht Worte und Begriffe im Vordergrund, sondern Inhalte, Fähigkeiten und verantwortliches Handeln. So rücken Bibliothekare und Informationsspezialisten immer stärker in die Zentren wirtschaftlichen, sozialen, kulturellen und politischen Handelns in einer weltumspannenden neuen Gesellschaft.

In der heute vielfach auch als Mediengesellschaft bezeichneten Neuen Welt ist es daher folgerichtig, beieinander liegende Fächer wie Informatik, Betriebswirtschaft, E-Commerce, Internetökonomie, Medienproduktion und -wirtschaft, Druck und Verlag in einem gesellschaftsbezogenen größeren Ausbildungskontext zu sehen und zu vermitteln, um damit den Studierenden die Chance zu bieten, konvergierende und querschnittsverzahnte Entwicklungen zu erkennen und sie richtig einordnen zu können.

---

[1] Zuvor „Fachhochschule für Bibliothekswesen" (FHB), davor „Süddeutsches Bibliothekar-Lehrinstitut" (SBL) und bei seiner Gründung im Jahre 1942 „Büchereischule Stuttgart"

Peter Vodosek hat diese Entwicklung in entscheidender Position als Rektor maßgeblich beeinflusst. Dem genaueren Verständnis seines Wirkens mögen die folgenden biographischen Angaben dienen.[2]

Peter Vodosek wurde am 20.10. 1939 in Linz (Oberösterreich) geboren. Durch seinen Vater, Konzertmeister beim Oberösterreichischen Landesorchester sowie beim Bruckner-Orchester, wurde bei ihm sehr früh die Liebe zur Musik geweckt. Das anfängliche Geigenspielen allerdings musste bald zugunsten anderer Interessen zurückstehen. In der Schule war es dann sehr bald die Geschichte, die ihn fesselte und die er später zu seinem Studienschwerpunkt machte, ergänzt durch Germanistik und Philosophie. In Graz wurde promoviert und die Magisterprüfung für das höhere Lehramt an Gymnasien abgelegt.

Berufsentscheidend wurde die Stellenausschreibung für die Besetzung des Stellvertreterpostens bei der Stadtbibliothek Linz mit der Aussicht auf ein Stipendium für ein zweijähriges Bibliothekarstudium in Deutschland. 1963 begann er mit dem Studium an der damaligen Süddeutschen Büchereischule in Stuttgart. Von der Stuttgarter Ausbildung hatte er einen weitgehend positiven Eindruck. Man war reformfreudig und bestrebt, wenn auch zunächst noch in bescheidenem Maße, der Praxis voraus zu sein. Auch durch die Praktika erfuhr er fachliche und menschliche Impulse, die ihn beruflich prägten.

Nach dem bibliothekarischen Examen (1965) nahm Vodosek die Tätigkeit des stellvertretenden Direktors in Linz auf. Dort war von Reformfreudigkeit wenig zu spüren. Als sich daher nach vierjähriger beruflicher Tätigkeit die Chance bot, eine Lehrtätigkeit in Stuttgart aufzunehmen, ergriff er diese Chance.

Zusammen mit zwei weiteren Kollegen und einer Kollegin wurde er zum Wintersemester 1969/70 als Dozent eingestellt. Damals befand sich das Institut mit 5 hauptamtlichen Lehrkräften am Beginn einer einzigartigen Expansionsphase. Der damalige Direktor Hermann Waßner hatte den Trend zur Ausweitung des Hochschulwesens nicht nur erkannt, sondern durch zahlreiche Aktivitäten auf ministerieller und politischer Ebene erfolgreich zu nutzen gewusst. So kam es zu langfristigen Ausbauplänen. Von Anfang an übernahm Vodosek neben seiner Lehrtätigkeit in den bibliothekstheoretischen Fächern und Bereichen der Literaturwissenschaft auch Aufgaben in der Hochschulverwaltung. Mit der Neuorganisation des Instituts als Fachhochschule (1977) übernahm er das Amt des Fachbereichsleiters (Dekan). Vorher hatte er schon die Leitung des Prüfungs-, des Praktikanten- und des Stundenplanamtes inne. Neben den internen Aufgaben pflegte er in den Semesterzwischenzeiten regelmäßige Kontakte zu den Öffentlichen und Wissenschaftlichen Bibliotheken. Das wirkte sich nicht nur auf die eigene Lehrtätigkeit aus, sondern band die Praktikumsplätze enger in das Unterrichtsprogramm mit ein, was wiederum die Weiterentwicklung der Studienpläne positiv beeinflusste.

1979 wurde Vodosek zum Prorektor gewählt. In diesem Amt war er eine wichtige Stütze des Rektors wie auch ein wichtiges Bindeglied zwischen Rektor, Dozentenschaft und Verwaltung. Er vermittelte loyal und erfolgreich zwischen den verschiedenen Gruppen.

Besonders gefordert wurde er in den letzten Jahren seiner siebenjährigen Amtszeit durch die häufige Vertretung des schwer erkrankten Rektors. Neben vielen anderen Aufgaben sind hier vor allem Eingliederung und Integration des Fachbereichs 7 der Fachhochschule für Öffentliche Verwaltung in die FHB als Fachbereich 3 und die Einrichtung eines selbständigen Studienganges Dokumentation (1988) zu nennen.

---

[2] Für die Angaben bis zum Ende der 80er-Jahre danke ich vor allem den Kollegen Franz Bienert und Andreas Papendieck

Eine seiner ersten Amtshandlungen war die Gründung eines Fördervereins (1987). Gleichzeitig wurde die Fortbildungsarbeit der FHB neu belebt. Vodosek erreichte, dass ein Senatsbeauftragter für die Fortbildungsarbeit ernannt wurde, dem ein klar umrissenes Aufgabengebiet übertragen wurde.

Waren in den Aufbaujahren der neuen Fachhochschule die Beziehungen zu anderen Ausbildungsinstituten und Bibliotheken auf das Inland beschränkt gewesen, so richtete man unter Vodoseks Rektorat das Augenmerk zunehmend auf die Kontaktpflege mit dem Ausland. Man nahm an internationalen Zusammenkünften teil, war Gründungsmitglied verschiedener internationaler Organisationen, so u.a. von EUCLID, schloss eine Reihe von Verträgen und traf Vereinbarungen, die den Dozenten- und Studentenaustausch förderten.

Bereits vor seinem Rektorat hatte Vodosek intensive Kontakte zu Danmarks Biblioteksskole in Kopenhagen unterhalten, Frucht seines ersten Fortbildungssemesters im Jahre 1977. Ausgebaut wurden die Beziehungen zu Hochschulen in Großbritannien, Frankreich, den Niederlanden und Schweden. Einen weiteren Schub erhielt diese Entwicklung durch die Öffnung nach Osten Anfang der 90er-Jahre und durch die Förderungsmöglichkeiten, die die EU eröffnete. So kamen Kontakte zu Hochschulen in Ungarn, der Ukraine, Russland und Weißrussland zustande. In Westeuropa taten sich Möglichkeiten der Zusammenarbeit mit Spanien und Portugal auf, vorrangig im Rahmen der BOBCATSSS-Planungen. Vodosek regte seine Kollegen dazu an, sich an nationalen und internationalen Diskussionen auf ihrem jeweiligen Fachgebiet zu beteiligen. So schuf er eine Arbeitsatmosphäre, die Grundlage für den international guten Ruf der Hochschule werden sollte. Er wurde Mitglied in zahlreichen nationalen und internationalen Organisationen und Gremien, so u.a. IFLA, American Library Association (ALA); EUCLID; Encyclopedic Dictionary of Library and Information Science (London); Europarat/Directorate of Education, Culture and Sport: expert; Library History Journal (Editorial Board); The International Centre of Information and Management Systems and Services (Universität Torun); Honorarprofessor des Staatsinstituts für Kultur in Charkow; Honorarprofessor des Staatsinstituts für Kultur in Moskau. So konnte die besondere Stellung, die die Stuttgarter Ausbildung eingenommen hatte, weiter ausgebaut werden.

Neben seiner beruflichen Tätigkeit findet Vodosek immer noch Zeit zur Pflege seiner Interessen. Dazu gehören die rege Teilnahme am kulturellen Leben, wie der Besuch von Opern, Konzerten und Kunstausstellungen, wie auch Bergwandern und Skifahren. Beruf und Hobby kann er in seiner Tätigkeit als Vorsitzender des ‚Wolfenbütteler Arbeitskreises für Bibliotheks-, Buch- und Mediengeschichte' wie als Mitglied des ‚Leipziger Arbeitskreises für Geschichte des Buchwesens' in Einklang bringen. Geschichtswissenschaft und Bibliothekswissenschaft werden hier in geglückter Weise miteinander verbunden.

Insbesondere die 90er-Jahre brachten einschneidende Veränderungen mit sich. Was mit der Einrichtung des Studiengangs ‚Dokumentation' im Jahre 1988 begonnen hatte, wurde in den 90er-Jahren zu einem Studienbereich ‚Informationswirtschaft / Informationsmanagement' erweitert, der heute mit dem bibliothekarischen Studienbereich zahlenmäßig gleichgezogen hat. Mit dem Jahreswechsel 1994/95 erhielt die FHB ihre neue Bezeichnung *Hochschule für Bibliotheks- und Informationswesen* (HBI). Gleichzeitig wurde eine umfassende Studienreform durchgeführt, die auch das Ende der Beamtenausbildung für die wissenschaftlichen Bibliotheken mit sich brachte. Weitere Reformen Ende der 90er und Anfang der 2000er-Jahre schufen neben dem bisherigen Diplomstudiengang auch Bachelor- und Masterstudiengänge mit den entsprechenden Abschlüssen, die internationalen Standards entsprechen und als wichtige Vorleistungen in die neue *Hochschule der Medien* eingebracht werden. Neben der bibliothekarisch-informationswissenschaftlichen, wurden neue informationstechnische und betriebwirtschaftliche Schwerpunkte geschaffen.

Frei werdende Stellen wurden entsprechend dieser neuen Zielsetzung besetzt und die informationstechnische Infrastruktur des Hauses zu einer der modernsten Hochschuleinrichtungen ausgebaut. In das weltumspannende Web war die HBI von Anfang an einbezogen und entwickelte eine eigene Informations- und Kommunikationskultur, die es ermöglichte, frühzeitig webbasierte Seminare und Projekte in das Studienprogramm aufzunehmen.

Die seit Mitte der 80er bewährte Zusammenarbeit mit dem Arbeitskreis für Information (AKI Stuttgart) auf dem Gebiet der Fort- und Weiterbildung erhielt eine Erweiterung durch die HBI-Akademie, die seit 1999 jährlich hochrangige mehrtägige Seminare anbietet.

Im Jahre 1999 wurde die Zusammenführung der beiden bislang noch selbständigen Stuttgarter Fachhochschulen, der Hochschule für Bibliotheks- und Informationswesen sowie die Hochschule für Druck und Medien (HDM) im Einvernehmen beider Hochschulen zusammen mit dem Ministerium für Wissenschaft, Forschung und Kunst verwirklicht, was die Schaffung des neuen Studiengangs „Informationsdesign" ermöglichte, verbunden mit einer beträchtlichen personellen Erweiterung.

Die entscheidende, von Peter Vodosek formulierte Bedingung für eine Zusammenführung der beiden Hochschulen besagt, dass dieser nur zugestimmt werden kann, wenn beide an einem gemeinsamen Standort untergebracht werden. Diese Zusage wurde zwischenzeitlich von verantwortlicher Seite gegeben, eine endgültige – vor allem finanzielle – Entscheidung steht noch aus. Alle Beteiligten gehen davon aus, dass ein Neubau in unmittelbarer Nähe zur früheren HDM im Jahre 2005 oder 2006 stehen wird.

Die Festschrift „Bibliothek in der Wissensgesellschaft" unternimmt den Versuch, das Spannungsfeld zwischen historischer und zukünftiger Orientierung zu reflektieren. In Würdigung der Verdienste von Peter Vodosek soll diese Festschrift für ihn eine Ehrung sein – für die Fachwelt ein Spiegel der Vielfalt, mit der sich die heutige Ausbildung im Informations- und Kommunikationsbereich zu befassen hat.

Die zahlreichen Veröffentlichungen[3] und das berufspolitisches Engagement sind ein beredtes Zeugnis dafür, wie sehr Peter Vodosek zeit seines Lebens daran gearbeitet hat, das Bibliothekswesen in die Gesellschaft zu integrieren, die Ausbildung zu fördern und sich gleichzeitig den Herausforderungen der Wissensgesellschaft zu stellen.

Der geschichtsbewusste und gleichzeitig zukunftsorientierte Kulturmensch und Forscher Vodosek wurde von Hermann Waßner einmal als „österreichischer Preuße" bezeichnet. Seine ihm eigene konziliante, geistreiche und großzügige Art bei gleichzeitiger gradliniger, gründlicher, pflichtbewusster und verlässlicher Arbeitsweise machen es ihm möglich, Menschen wie auch Themen zu verbinden. Seine Standpunkte und Einschätzungen boten Orientierung und ließen gleichzeitig Freiraum für Entwicklungen. Im nationalen wie internationalen Umfeld erwarb er hohes Ansehen und mit ihm die Hochschule. Die vorliegende Festschrift mag dies in ihrer Anzahl und Vielfalt der Beiträge erneut belegen.

Allen nahezu 100 Beteiligten, die am Zustandekommen dieser Festschrift mitgewirkt haben, gilt mein besonderer Dank.

Hervorheben möchte ich allein Peter Vodosek selber, dem ich für die nahezu achtjährige gute Zusammenarbeit im Rektorat zum Wohle von FHB und HBI mit dieser Festschrift in ganz besonders herzlicher Weise danke.

---

3 siehe Bibliographie

Harald Hagmann

Grußwort zum 60. Geburtstag von Peter Vodosek

Mit dem 60. Geburtstag hat es eine besondere Bewandtnis. Schon in den vorchristlichen Kulturen war er ein besonderer Tag. Die Juden wünschen sich zum Geburtstag „werde 120 Jahre alt", dem Alter, das Abraham erreichte. Und laut Altem Testament wird man ab 60 nicht mehr von Gott bestraft. In der babylonischen Kosmologie ist 60 die vollkommene Zahl und die Lebensjahre von 60 bis 70 gelten deshalb als die glücklichen Jahre. Lieber Herr Professor Vodosek, ich wünschen Ihnen gesunde und erfolgreiche glückliche Jahre! Im Namen von Herrn Minister Klaus von Trotha und auch persönlich.

Sie wurden am 20. Oktober 1939 in Linz an der Donau geboren. Ihr Vater war Konzertmeister in Linz. Sie haben an der Philosophischen Fakultät der Universität Graz Geschichte und Deutsch studiert und wurden im Jahr 1963 zum Dr. phil. promoviert.

Sie schlossen ein Studium zum Diplombibliothekar an öffentlichen Bibliotheken an und übernahmen eine leitende Stelle bei den Büchereien der Stadt Linz.

Im Oktober 1969 wurden Sie Dozent am Süddeutschen Bibliothekarlehrinstitut. Sie feiern in diesen Tagen also nicht nur Ihren 60. Geburtstag, sondern blicken auch auf eine 30-jährige Tätigkeit an dieser Fachhochschule und ihrer Vorgängereinrichtung zurück.

Im Februar 1975 wurden Sie zum Professor ernannt. Am 1. April 1979 wurden Sie zum Prorektor gewählt. Und seit dem 1. April 1986 leiten Sie als Rektor die Geschicke dieser Hochschule.

Daneben sind Sie als Vorsitzender, Vorstandsmitglied oder Mitglied in zahlreichen Arbeitskreisen und Vereinigungen engagiert, die ich hier gar nicht aufzählen kann, von denen ich aber annehme, dass zahlreiche Mitglieder heute hier mit Ihnen feiern.

Sie sind Mitherausgeber verschiedener Lehrbücher und Fachzeitschriften. Und Sie sind ein hervorragender Botschafter für Ihre Hochschule in aller Welt. In Ihrer Amtszeit wurden zahlreiche Partnerschaften mit ausländischen Hochschulen geschlossen. So gibt es Partnerschaften mit Einrichtungen in Frankreich, Italien, Israel, Russland, Österreich, Schweiz und Schweden. Sie sind Honorarprofessor der Universität für Kultur Moskau.

Herr Professor Vodosek, Sie haben die Entwicklung dieser Hochschule von Anfang an mitgestaltet. Bereits bei Ihrem Eintritt in das Süddeutsche Bibliothekarlehrinstitut, so die Aussage des früheren Rektors, Herrn Professor Waßner, sind Sie wegen Ihrer „hervorragenden Fähigkeit und uneingeschränkten Bereitschaft, sich an den Organisations- und Verwaltungsaufgaben der Fachhochschule für Bibliothekswesen zu beteiligen, unbestrittenermaßen eine der Hauptstützen der institutionellen Arbeit der Hochschule gewesen". Nach der Umorganisation des Bibliothekarlehrinstituts zur Fachhochschule übernahmen Sie das Praktikantenamt, die Ausarbeitung und die Überwachung des Stundenplans, die Herausgabe des Vorlesungsverzeichnisses und die Leitung des Fachbereichs Bibliothekswissenschaft.

1984, zwei Jahre vor Übernahme des Rektoramtes wurde der Fachbereich „Wissenschaftliches Bibliothekswesen" und „Dokumentationswesen" der Fachhochschule für Bibliothekswesen angegliedert. In die Ära „Vodosek" fiel dann die Externalisierung des Studiengangs „Wissenschaftliche Bibliotheken" und im Jahr 1995 die Umwandlung des Studiengangs „Dokumentar" zum „Informationsmanagement".

Sie haben damit konsequent und zäh die Entwicklung betrieben, die diese Hochschule einzigartig in Baden-Württemberg gemacht hat und weit über das Land hinausstrahlen lässt.

Nur eins haben Sie noch nicht erreicht:

Auch Ihre vierte Amtszeit als Rektor ist geprägt durch das Ringen um eine angemessene Unterbringung. Dieses Gebäude ist schön und geeignet, um Feste zu feiern, aber kaum als Hochschule zu nutzen. Immerhin gibt es jetzt die Lösung, im Frühjahr 2000 noch rechtzeitig zum Sommersemester alle Einrichtungen der Hochschule in den zwei, bereits seit mehreren Jahren gemieteten Gebäuden in der Wolframstraße zusammenzuführen.

Homme de lettre und Hochschulmanager: Geht das zusammen?

Wie viel kann man lesen? Das Lesen kann nur bis zu einem gewissen Grad beschleunigt werden. Dann widersetzt es sich dem Trend der Zeit. Gott sei Dank!

Aber was geht in 60 Jahren? Pro Woche ein Buch, das wären 50 pro Jahr. In 60 Jahren? Wahrscheinlich haben Sie nicht bei null angefangen, auch Sie nicht! Also rechne ich eher 50 x 50, das sind 2.500. Aber was ist dies gegenüber der weltweiten Produktion?

Sicher ergreift Sie manchmal die Sehnsucht nach den Codices der Klosterbibliotheken des Mittelalters, als die Handschriftlichkeit die Produktion bremste. Aber Buchdruck, Kopiergerät, Diktiergerät und Textverarbeitung sind nun einmal erfunden!

Die Kunst des Lesens muss durch die Kunst des Nicht-Lesens ergänzt werden. Zitat Schopenhauer: „Um das Gute zu lesen, ist eine Bedingung, dass man das Schlechte nicht lese. Denn das Leben ist kurz, Zeit und Kräfte beschränkt."

Das verbindet den Homme de lettre und den Hochschulmanager. Einerseits als persönliche Lebenskunst andererseits aber auch als Bildungsziel für die Hochschule.

Wie können wir mit der Flut von Information umgehen? Dies wird eine der wesentlichen Fragestellungen für die neue Hochschule der Medien sein, die durch Zusammenschluss der Fachhochschule für Druck und Medien einerseits und für Bibliothek und Information andererseits entstehen soll. Der Ministerrat hat am 18. Oktober, also vorgestern, das von Hochschulen und Ministerium gemeinsam entwickelte Konzept gebilligt und das Wissenschaftsministerium beauftragt, nunmehr die rechtlichen und finanziellen Voraussetzungen zu schaffen. Ich freue mich sehr, dass beide Hochschulen die Chancen erkannt haben, die in dem Zusammengehen liegen. Ich bin sicher, dass hier eine Hochschule entstehen wird, die eine wichtige Rolle im regionalen, nationalen und europäischen Markt für Medienausbildung spielen wird, die das gesamte Spektrum des Medienbereichs abdecken wird und die den Medienstandort Baden-Württemberg kennzeichnen wird.

Ich freue mich, verehrter Herr Professor Vodosek, dass Sie hieran aktiv mitwirken werden und berufe mich zum Abschluss auf Cicero, der den alten Cato sagen lässt:

> *„Wenn ihr die Geschichte fremder Völker lesen oder hören wollt, so werdet ihr finden, dass die größten Staaten von jungen Männern erschüttert, von alten hingegen aufrecht und wiederhergestellt worden sind."*

Ad multos annos!

AUSBILDUNG • FORTBILDUNG • WEITERBILDUNG

Ian M. Johnson

International development of Librarianship and information science education and the role of research

Abstract

This paper considers the role of research in international development programmes. It considers the activities that have been undertaken to establish and develop Schools of Librarianship and Information Science, and some of possible reasons why many have failed to develop once the external support was terminated. It notes that the development of a research profile rarely featured in previous activities, and contrasts this with other disciplines in which the research capacity has made university departments critical to social and economic progress. It notes the real and imaginary obstacles to research and to international cooperation, and outlines the benefits to individuals and institutions of engaging in this type of international collaborative research. Finally, it urges a combined effort to take advantage of the current global interest in information transfer to persuade the development agencies to support research efforts in the applications of librarianship and information sciences.

Introduction

During the third quarter of the last Century, there were what now appear to have been very considerable efforts:

> *„carried out among or between governmental or non-governmental organisations, groups or individuals to promote, establish, develop, maintain and evaluate library, documentation, and allied services, and librarianship and the library profession generally, in any part of the world." (Parker)*

The efforts during that period of international agencies such as UNESCO[4], the DSE (the German Foundation for International Development) [5], and the British Council[6] have been well documented, as have the efforts of the United States professional community activities supported by governmental agencies and private foundations.[7]

The Higher Education sector made a significant contribution to international development over the years. The Hochschule für Bibliotheks- und Informationswesen, played a notable part in these efforts[8], most recently in helping to found EUCLID: the European As-

---

4 PARKER, J.S. UNESCO and library development planning. 1985. London: The Library Association.

5 HUTTEMAN, Lutz. Information training for Africa: the role of the German Foundation for International Development. Information Development, 6 (2), 1990, 84-88

6 COOMBS, D. Spreading the word: the library work of the British Council. 1988. London: Mansell

7 BREWSTER, B.B. American overseas library technical assistance, 1940-1970. 1976. Metuchen, New Jersey. Scarecrow Press

8 VODOSEK, P. National and regional models of collaboration between teaching and research institutions within the field of library and information science: with the Fachhochschule für Bibliothekswesen Stuttgart (FHB) as an example. Education for Information, 12(3), September 1994, 367-78

sociation for Library and Information Education and Research and the BOBCATSSS Conferences[9] and in its participation in the LISTEN project in Hungary, funded by the European Commission.[10]

There is no doubt that these and similar activities undertaken by other Schools made a significant contribution to the establishment of education for librarianship and information sciences. Typically this involved them in releasing staff to undertake reviews and advisory visits or short periods of teaching in order to establish or develop schools of librarianship. However, it appears that some, possibly many of these activities may have had only a limited or short-term impact. It remains the case that in some countries the professional Schools remain weak and underdeveloped, with limited human and material resources, and teaching an out of date and possibly irrelevant curriculum.

We are now entering an era of rapid technological change and proliferating information resources in which information literacy is increasingly widely recognised as important. It is seen as central not only to learning, but also to decision-making, evidence-based practice, and innovation transfer. It is widely believed to have a major impact on the growth of the knowledge economy as well as the prevention of social exclusion. One conclusion that might be drawn from a simple analysis of the condition of library education in some countries or institutions would suggest that what is required is further assistance to enhance the physical resources and to guide the revision of the curriculum. Clearly some further efforts will be necessary to enable Schools of Librarianship and Information Sciences to make, and to be seen to be making, an effective contribution not only to developing the skills needed to make judgements about the relevance of information to synthesise and exploit it rather than simply the ability to identify and retrieve it, but also to promoting an appreciation of the value and impact of information.

However, in addition, it must be acknowledged that in some cases earlier efforts to develop Schools have not always failed to prevent atrophy, and there must therefore be a search for a deeper understanding of the issues that have to be confronted. People experienced in managing or developing library and information science schools and their curricula have pointed to factors likely to underpin development. There have also been studies of the management of Schools of Librarianship in the developed countries, and some analysis of recent closures of Schools in the U.S.A., but there appear to have been no critical evaluation of what contributes to the successful impact neither of external assistance on the development LIS education nor of its impact on development. The aim of this paper is to consider the state of LIS research in the developing countries, and examine the role that international collaborative research should be playing.

Some reasons for atrophy

Could it be that part of the problem may be attributable to the failure of the donor agencies to provide appropriate support? How often was external assistance introduced for political reasons by the funding agency, based on that agency's priorities, its perceptions of the

---

9 JOHNSON, I.M. The role of associations of information and library education in teaching and research: recent and potential developments in Britain and Europe. Education for Information, 18 (3/4), 2000, 201-220

10 A konyvtaros es informacios szakemberkepzes megujitasa - Renewing the education and training of librarians and information professionals: proceedings of the closing conference of the LISTEN TEMPUS JEP (1994-97); Berzsenyi College, Szombathely, Hungary, 25th to 27th June 1997. 1997. Hungary: Szombathely, Berzsenyi College. ISBN 963 9017 25 6

needs of the beneficiary institution, and its understanding of the established knowledge and capabilities of the assistance potentially available from its own country or from those institutions or individuals known to the agency's staff? In some cases, it seems fair to suggest that the purpose of the external support and the means of achieving success may not have been clearly defined and understood in advance, and the human and material resource inputs may not have matched the real requirement. In some cases, because of a change in priorities or simply pressure on limited resources, external support has not been sustained for a sufficient period of time for it to be fully effective. A recent review of the British Government's Higher Education Links Scheme (which covers a variety of disciplines) pointed to these as issues requiring attention.[11]

Could part of the problem be attributable to the characteristics of the people who become librarians and teachers of librarianship? It has certainly been suggested that students with leadership qualities may not be attracted to the profession because, in the early stages of its development in a country, it appears to offer no promising career or status, and in many cases the few qualified librarians may be being managed by older unqualified personnel, reflecting this in an atmosphere of frustration.[12]

Could part of the problem be attributable to the fact that, in effect, a consultancy service has been provided, and there are inherent limitations in the nature of consultancy activity and the *modus operandi* of consultants themselves? A consultant is recruited to carry out a specific task, and disseminates the results according to the requirements of the contract, or personal inclination and the availability of time. Consultants' reports may add to factual knowledge and point to outstanding problems, but are sometimes not readily available, even to others working with a similar remit in the same institution. For example, when undertaking a UNESCO mission to Iraq in the 1970s, Ahmed Helal (later University Librarian at Bielefeld) expressed his frustration at:

> *„the impossibility of finding the reports or knowing the recommendations which had been written by other consultants who recently visited ... "*[13]

Moreover, few published reports given any insights into the problems that the consultant may face and has to overcome to be successful, for example the internal political complexities. A rare example is a commentary written by Anand Srivastava, another UNESCO consultant of that period, who wrote openly and publicly about his experiences of developing a library school – but only some 5 years afterwards.[14]

There is also a growing belief that that the failure of many library and information sciences schools to develop to their full potential must largely be attributed to the implicit limitations of consultancy activity. A consultant is:

> *„an individual qualified by education, experience, technical ability, and temperament to advise or assist in a professional basis in identifying, defining, and solving specific*

11 ELDRIDGE, D., and others. Evaluation of the Higher Education Links Scheme: contract CNTR 99 9253. [2000. British Council/University of Manchester.] (Unpublished typescript)

12 MANZOOR, S. Trends of library users: a study in Iraqi scene. Indian Librarian, 35 (1), June 1980, 9-17

13 HELAL, A.H. Iraq: Scientific Documentation Centre; February - April 1972. Paris: UNESCO. Doc. Code. 2736/RMO.RD/DBA; FR/PP/Consultant. (Limited). 1972.

14 SRIVASTAVA, A.P. An account of expert missions of the UNESCO and the United Nations in the Middle East. Indian Librarian, 29 (1), June 1974, 33-37.

> *library problems as an impartial, objective advisor..."* [15]
> *„advising on matters within his expertise; developing new skills or knowledge on behalf of a client..."* [16]

All too often it appears that the consultants have worked within the limitations of their experience, but have failed to develop the new skills or knowledge that the beneficiary institution and its staff really need. Just as there is growing criticism of the imposition of the British models of library and information services in former colonies in Africa[17], there is equal concern about the relevance of the Anglo-American model of education for librarianship.[18,19] These concerns are neither recent nor confined to Africa. The influence of LIS educators from the United States in Latin America has been felt for over seventy years[20,21], but in the last twenty years it has been recognised some American solutions to the region's information problems were inappropriate because they did not take into account differing cultural, social, and economic conditions[22], and in the last ten years there have been reports that curricular revisions have been put in train to eliminate excessive American influence.[23] At the same time, the relevance of teaching intended primarily to meet the needs of advanced, industrialised countries materials produced has begun to be challenged by overseas students in both Britain[24] and the USA.[25] In the last twenty years, something has clearly begun to change. Whatever it is, it must be understood and incorporated it in future activities.

Research motivation

There may be other significant factors to emerge from analyses of experts' guidelines and

---

15 LOCKWOOD, J.D. Involving consultants in library change. College and research libraries, 38 (6), November 1977, 498-508

16 LIBRARY ASSOCIATION and INSTITUTE OF INFORMATION SCIENTISTS. Guidelines for consultants working in librarianship and information science. Library Association Record, 86 (4), April 1984, 174-175

17 STURGES, P. The poverty of librarianship: an historical critique of public librarianship in Anglophone Africa. Libri, 51 (1), 2001, 38-48

18 MCHOMBU, K. Which way African librarianship? IFLA Journal, 17(1), 1991, 26-38

19 TITI, M. The relationship between curriculum, learning and teaching in library and information science with special reference to the University of Transkei. 2001. PhD thesis. University of Loughborough.

20 MUELLER, S.P.M. O ensino de biblioteconomia no Brasil. [The teaching of librarianship in Brazil.] Ciencia da Informacao, 14 (1), January/June1985, 3-15

21 SOUZA, F.d.C.d. Ensino de biblioteconomia no Brasil: o modelo Norte-Americao. [Library science teaching in Brasil: a North-American model.] Informacao & Sociedade: Estudos, 3 (1), 2 1993, 1-5

22 GOLDSTEIN, E. Tranferability of American library and information science education to Mexico. in Information interaction: proceedings of the 45th ASIS Annual Meeting, Columbus, Ohio, 17-21 October 1982; edited by A.E. Petrarca, C.I. Taylor and R.S. Kohn. 1982. White Plains, New York, Knowledge Industry Publications, Inc. pp. 116-118

23 CESARINO, M.A. da N. and Vianna, M.M. O curso de graduacao em Biblioteconomia da UFMG. [The undergraduate librarianship course at Universidad Federal do Minas Gerais Library school.] Revista da Escola Biblioteconomia da UFMG, 19 (special), March 1990, 37-67

24 Conference on education of overseas students in U.K. educational institutions, London, 25-26 March 1992. Education for information, 10 (4), December 1992, Special issue

25 TALLMAN, J.I. and OJIAMBO, J.B. editors. Translating an international education to a national environment: papers presented at the international doctoral student conference sponsored by the Doctoral Guild at the University of Pittsburgh School of Library and Information Science, September 23-25, 1988. 1990. Metuchen, N.J. and London: Scarecrow Press.

comparisons with the actual patterns of development[26], but it must be acknowledged that the factors likely to be identified are those that were relevant in the circumstances that applied in the latter half of the last Century. While those efforts that were successful must be applauded, other approaches that do not appear to have been considered or attempted must also be identified and their likely utility must be evaluated. In particular, consideration must be given to what is most likely to be relevant and successful in the circumstances that will be faced in the early years of the new Millennium.

One of the features noticeably absent from most accounts of the development work that has been carried out in the past is evidence of research undertaken or any wide ranging discussion of the part that research might play in national development. It is, of course, fair comment that, in the first stages of development, the capacity for undertaking research may not have existed. There was also inevitable peer pressure to undertake research into the education and training needed by those currently employed in the profession and into its future manpower needs. These research themes were also actively encouraged by both the international professional associations and the intergovernmental agencies. For example, it was a topic in discussions on the relationship between the International Association of Technological University Libraries (IATUL) and FID (Federation Internationale de Documentation) [27], and the subject of a manual published by UNESCO.[28]

However, it is still the case that in many of the Schools of Librarianship and Information Sciences in the developing countries, there appears to be little research on other topics. The problems that this can cause are recognised in the counties concerned. In Argentina, for example, the absence of critical thought and energy within the library profession in the 1980s was attributed in part to the lack of research and the lack of journals and other publications.[29] The frustration caused to those who have studied and obtained doctoral degrees in developing countries is also significant. Various obstacles have been suggested as responsible for the lack of library and information science research. In Africa, the reasons put forward for the limited research activity have included: lack of finance; lack of time to carry out research; and a lack of primary periodicals in which to publish research results.[30]

It must be acknowledged that these obstacles are real. In many of the developing countries, the institutional budget does not make much provision for supporting research. A recent report on the situation in Tanzania indicated that the government allocates only 1 % of university budgets to support research, and almost any research must therefore be undertaken with external funds.[31] In the whole of Latin America, there are no more than about 60 journals in the field[32]; in the Arabic-speaking world there is probably no more than one

---

26 JOHNSON, I.M. Effective development of education for librarianship and information management: a preliminary analysis of critical success factors. Forthcoming paper.

27 HILL, M.W. Co-operation between FID and other organisations involved in the library and information fields. IATUL Quarterly, 3 (3), September 1989, 158-161

28 MOORE, N. Guidelines for conducting information manpower surveys. 1986. Paris: UNESCO. ref. PGI-86/WS/3

29 SABOR, J.E. The issue of librarianship in Argentina. Third World Libraries, 3 (1), Fall 1992, 40-46

30 ALEMNA, A. A. Library and information research in Africa: obstacles and opportunities. International Journal of Information and Library Research, 5 (1), 1993, 47-55

31 COUNCIL FOR INTERNATIONAL COOPERATION IN HIGHER EDUCATION. Higher education links: evaluation mission to Tanzania, Uganda, Zimbabwe; February-March 2000. 2000. London: {British Council] CICHE. Appendix 3, p.2. (Unpublished typescript)

32 MORALES CAMPOS, E. (1997) Latin America and the Caribbean in A. Large, ed. World Information Report 1997/98. Paris: UNESCO Publishing. pp.107-123. (see Table 2, p. 120)

journal published in each country[33]; and few of them are widely available outside the country of origin.

For potential researchers outside the Anglophone countries, there are additional problems arising from a limited or non-existent familiarity with English. The dominance of the English language in professional publishing acts as a barrier to external knowledge, and inhibits the dissemination of the research results. Poor coverage of non-English language journals in the major indexing/abstracting services exacerbates already limited access to bibliographic resources, although coverage of Latin American journals benefits from the efforts of CONACYT, the Mexican National Science Council[34], and the National University of Mexico's Centre for Library and Information Research.[35]

Overcoming the obstacles

Despite these obstacles there appears to be a shared belief that it is necessary to find ways of increasing the number of active researchers and improving the means of publication. To overcome the problem of limited research activity, it has been suggested that appropriate professional organisations must take steps to enhance governmental awareness of library needs, but this seems to be a forlorn hope. The experience of at least some universities in developing countries is that, paradoxically, even academics who had studied abroad and were familiar with the potential of modern library services appear to have done little to encourage library development after their return home.[36]

It has also been suggested, in Africa, that research efforts should be focus on the work that can be done by Africans themselves and the professional organisations should help them to seek the required funding.[37] If approached in the right way, this seems to offer some prospect of success. In most countries the universities are one pool of expertise to which governments and the business community can turn. Universities deliver a nation's educational aspirations, but the knowledge they develop and its application are at the heart of the economy, secure the health of the population, safeguard their culture, and underpin the democratic operation of society. Research provides evidence about existing provision, reveals gaps, highlights issues, and stimulates new ideas that may become the basis of new policies and services. By generating and disseminating knowledge, they advance thinking and create understanding. In developing countries, the universities represent the only pool of expertise readily available locally.[38] They are the national think tank. Neither governments nor businesses in such countries have the large payroll of highly qualified employees found in the industrialised countries. There is ample evidence of the involvement of other disciplines in providing research services and policy advice to governments in developing countries.[39]

---

33 Meeting of experts on the education of information specialists in the Arab region: Ecole des Sciences de l'Information, Rabat, Maroc (10-13 May 1993). Final Report. Paris: UNESCO. (ref. PGI-93/WS/13)

34 JOHNSON, I.M. Recent developments in library automation in Mexico and Venezuela. Program, 21 (4), October 1987, 379-381

35 JOHNSON, I.M. Management development for libraries and information services in Latin America and the Caribbean. International Information and Library Review, 31 (4), December 1999, 225-244

36 MANZOOR, S. Trends of library users: a study in Iraqi scene. Indian Librarian, 35 (1), June 1980, 9-17

37 OBAKA, D.N. The challenge of medical librarianship in Africa. Third World Libraries, 2 (1), Fall 1991, 14-16

38 WORLD BANK. Revitalising universities in Africa. 1997. World Bank. p.3

39 COUNCIL FOR INTERNATIONAL COOPERATION IN HIGHER EDUCATION. Higher education links: evaluation mission to Tanzania, Uganda, Zimbabwe; February-March 2000. 2000. London: {British Council] CICHE. (Unpublished typescript)

Technical cooperation

Nonetheless, there still appear to be academics in developing countries who see the opportunities for library and information science research as principally focusing inwards on library education and teaching.[40] Perhaps not surprisingly, there is also a perception that development agencies are not interested in librarianship and information science research. Given the focus on such issues by the development funding agencies, there appear to be opportunities for the Schools of Librarianship and Information Sciences in the industrialised countries to focus their expertise on researching the role of information and information services in support of relevant aspects of development. It is therefore encouraging that, despite the alleged obstacles, considerable progress has already been made in research into, for example, medical librarianship[41] and community information services.[42]

International collaborative research does present a number of challenges for the Schools in the industrialised countries. Their national research funding agencies are likely to be inward looking, and probably reluctant to support research that has no immediate application in their own country. How then can a relationship be developed, or at least a new level of interest be fostered, amongst the agencies that fund international development and research? Equally important is how to develop appropriate partnerships with Schools in the developing countries. To what extent should greater efforts be made to retain and build on the links that are established with overseas students who attend Schools in the developing countries? What is the role of international organisations such as IFLA (the International Federation of Library Associations and Institutions) in facilitating these links?

In the past, the initiative for collaboration has often been taken in the developing countries, and the needs of the Schools have often been seen as a short term updating of the curriculum and associated development of their human and material resources. How can the Schools and the development agencies be persuaded to accept that engaging in collaborative research offers them some greater hope of becoming self-sustaining in the medium term? How can research projects be identified that are likely to attract the attention of the government of the country concerned and the support of a funding agency? Do the Schools in the industrialised countries do enough to encourage overseas students to focus their research interests on topics that are relevant to their countries' needs? How often do teachers from Schools of librarianship in the industrialised countries writing their dissertations about aspects of curriculum or manpower development as it affects their School? Does this theme recur with unwarranted frequency in the work of teachers from the developing countries?

There are other problems that the Schools in the developed countries must face. How can they ensure access to appropriate sources of information? If they undertake research within their existing specialisms, they should already have the core material. How can they ensure the professional commitment of their staff? Staff will find an additional outlet for their existing research interests, the possibility of new sources of support, and perhaps some new methodological challenges and fresh insights. How can they ensure the support of their institution? Recently financial pressures on higher education in many of the indus-

---

40 ALEMNA, A. A. Library and information research in Africa: obstacles and opportunities. International Journal of Information and Library Research, 5 (1), 1993, 47-55

41 OBAKA, D.N. The challenge of medical librarianship in Africa. Third World Libraries, 2 (1), Fall 1991, 14-16

42 ABOYADE, B.O. The provision of information for rural development. Ibadan, Nigeria: Fountain Publications, 1987.

trialised countries, and the contractual constraints that the institutions are imposing on academics' time, appear to have been creating an attitude within some Universities that may be inimical to any activity that appears to subsidise international development. However, the approach discussed here should mean that the employing institution would benefit from the facilitation of the legitimate research interests of its academic staff, and from the associated staff development.[43] In short, if they concentrate on their own areas of expertise, these issues should not be a problem.

Mutual benefits

It is almost universally accepted that doing some form of research is a required activity for university teachers, not least because it provides the material they require for teaching their students. Moreover, a recent study in Britain has reported that both undergraduate and postgraduate students believe that research activity not only makes sure that their teachers are up to date and increases their credibility, but also makes them more enthusiastic.[44] In short, it helps to make them better teachers.

For those who are committed to research, whether in the developed or the developing countries, international collaboration in research offers a number of benefits. It introduces them to new opportunities for research, and develops a wider range of professional contacts with similar research interests. It may require them to adopt new, inter-disciplinary approaches and develop the range of their competences. It also attracts additional funding, which will not only attract kudos, but may provide some improvement in the resource base of the Schools in the developing countries.

For the Schools in the developing countries there are additional benefits in international collaboration. It may provide access to relevant publications, case studies, etc. produced in the developing world, and possibly assistance in overcoming any language barrier in making use of that resource. The availability of local partners may also help overcome the problems of inter-cultural communication. There is a growing understanding, at least amongst experts in communication, that interpretation often requires more than a literal translation of a text [45], and that it needs to take account of different cultural and terminological concepts. [46]

There are also particular benefits or the Schools in the developing countries in international collaboration. Their staff may have access to the richer resources of the Schools in the developed countries. Research will not only raise their awareness of the potential demand for services, the availability of relevant skills and financial resources, and a political and managerial attitudes towards the role and development of library and information services. It develops their capacity to produce accurate and timely data, to undertake analysis,

---

43 JOHNSON, I.M. Staff development in international technical cooperation programmes: the case of the TEMPUS Joint European Project 'LISTEN'. Information Development, 13 (4), December 1997, 197-202

44 UTLEY, A. Research makes you teach better. Times Higher Education Supplement, 1479, March 23, 2001.

45 WINTERS, E. Eleven commandments of localization. Active Voice (Society for Technical Communication), June 1994; republished 1996 by International Interactive Communications Society. Viewed on the Web on 25 January, 2000 at URL - http://www.bena.com/ewinters/local.html

46 GAEDE, B. Courseware and user interfaces across cultural borders (Courseware variants: content and user interfaces to provide information access for almost everybody) in Access 2000: intellectual property vs. the right to knowledge? proceedings of the 8th international BOBCATSSS symposium on library and information science, Jagiellonian University, Krakow, Poland, January 24 - 26, 2000. 2000. Copenhagen, Denmark: Royal School of Library and Information Science. pp. 161-172

and to feed back into policy making.[47] It also cannot fail to contribute to a School's clearer understanding of professional manpower requirements in the country, revisions required in their curricular content, and staff development needs in both the Schools and the nation's library and information services. These are probably the issues that are most likely to motivate and mobilise change, and help them pass new thresholds of performance.

The publication of the results of their work in the developed or the developing countries not only raises awareness of the issues, but also raises their profile and national and international standing of the collaborating institutions and the individual researchers.[48] It may also be seen as having a direct impact not only on improving library and information services, but also on the political influence of the LIS profession on society, ensuring that it is not left on the periphery of affairs.

Concluding remarks

Perhaps the most important issue that requires attention is how to capture the interest and support of the development funding agencies.

In recent years, it must be acknowledged that there appears to have been a decline in international collaborative activity, notwithstanding a short-lived engagement with the professional community in the former Soviet Union and its east European satellite states. The decline in UNESCO support in the last 5 years[49], based on its reduced budget and a lack of political support for work in this area, is well known, but the contraction of the activities of some of the other national development agencies has attracted less attention, although the causes are the same. The British Council, for example, once played a major role in leading the development of librarianship and information work world-wide, particularly by contributing to collection building in key institutions and by supporting the development of their staff to modernise services. Recent reductions in the Council's budget and the number of posts overseas for library and information specialists appear to have curtailed its developmental activities in this field at a time when they are becoming more globally significant.

However, there appears to be the beginnings of a shift in the interests of the development agencies, which may benefit library and information science education and research. The concept of the „information society" has been promoted for several years in policy statements and action plans by inter-governmental agencies such as the European Commission, the G7 group of the world's wealthiest industrialised nations, and UNESCO. Many European countries are now actively promoting information society strategies and action plans and have been thinking strategically about their information societies for some time. In addition, a report recently published by the World Bank and UNESCO has called for a decisive shift in government priorities to provide greater support for the development of higher education, arguing that increased numbers of highly skilled people are needed in the knowledge economy that is emerging largely as a result of the rapid introduction of en-

[47] COUNCIL FOR INTERNATIONAL COOPERATION IN HIGHER EDUCATION. Higher education links: evaluation mission to Tanzania, Uganda, Zimbabwe; February-March 2000. 2000. London: {British Council] CICHE. p.44. (Unpublished typescript)

[48] COUNCIL FOR INTERNATIONAL COOPERATION IN HIGHER EDUCATION. Higher education links: evaluation mission to Tanzania, Uganda, Zimbabwe; February-March 2000. 2000. London: {British Council] CICHE. p.14. (Unpublished typescript)

[49] JOHNSON, I.M. UNESCO and human resource development for the 'Information Society' Education for Information, 16 (3), September 1998, 237 - 242.

hanced Information and Communications Technologies (ICTs).[50] There also appears to be an increased willingness on the part of major private foundations such as Carnegie, Gates and Mellon to support international development activities in libraries and information services.

The underlying concept of the 'Information Society' is essentially a concern with 'information' products and services, and the way in which they are changing. However, these changes give rise to equally fundamental changes in the way information is used and its impact on every aspect of economic, educational and social activity. Effective use of information is recognised as a key success factor within a knowledge economy and within an innovation-driven society in which:

> *„learning and command of knowledge have become the key success factors of international competitiveness. 70-80 % of economic growth is said to be due to new and better knowledge..."*[51]

The challenges facing developing countries in achieving the economic and social advances that are held in prospect by these changes are not only in implementing the necessary improvements in their technical and regulatory infrastructures, but also in creating a society and workforce with the required knowledge, skills, and attitudes to make use of applications of ICTs and benefit from them. This, surely, provides ample scope for research?

It is, therefore, important that we recognise that while the activities of these agencies have declined, their influence has not diminished. When UNESCO turned its attention to the conservation of libraries and archives, through its 'Memory of the World' programme, it captured the attention of the member states. The energy that the British Council mobilised in securing the interest of the World Bank in the role of library and information services was impressive. Its support for the HEIDI project (Higher Education Investment in the Development of Information), a series of case studies of 4 countries on 4 different continents with contributions from over 100 international library and information science experts was aimed at assessing the current thinking and determining strategic policy on investment in higher education libraries and information services worldwide.[52] The associated lobbying activities were a significant influence in the establishment of the World Bank's infoDev[53] programme. It is now seeking to play a similar role in the Global Knowledge Partnership[54], a grouping of over sixty international organisations committed to ensuring that developing countries benefit from appropriate and sustainable investment in the new ICTs. The task of the LIS research community is to ensure that the role and contribution of research into librarianship and information services to economic and social development, and in moving forward the agendas of infoDev and the Global Knowledge, is fully appreciated and receives greater support.

---

50 World Bank/UNESCO, Joint Task Force on Higher Education and Society. Higher Education in Developing Countries: Peril and Promise. 2000. World Bank

51 DEPARTMENT OF TRADE AND INDUSTRY, Technology Foresight - Information, Communications and Media Panel. Point and click – learners in the ICT driving seat: a consultation document. 2000. Viewed on 27 November 2000 at URL – http://www.foresight.gov.uk

52 ILIAD (International Library and Information Action for Development). Higher education library and information service development: strategies for investment. 1995. British Library. Research and Development Department. BLRD Report 6221

53 The infoDev website was viewed on 27th March 2001 at URL http:// www.infodev.org/

54 The Global Knowledge website was viewed on 27th March 2001 at URL http://www.globalknowledge.org/

The policies of UNESCO's Division for Communication, Information and Informatics are driven by the wishes of the member states. Those of other development agencies are driven by the opinions put forward persuasively to politicians and senior government administrators, in both the developed and developing countries. It is important that IFLA's member associations and institutions contribute to that debate through their national UNESCO Commissions and appropriate government Ministries, and that IFLA engages fully in the global debate about education and research activities in the field of librarianship and information sciences. IFLA's Executive and Professional Boards now hold an annual meeting with the Presidents and Chief Executives of the member associations, and there must be an effort to ensure that international collaborative research is on the agenda of those meetings. EUCLID also has a role to play, in making representations to the relevant parts of the European Commission.

A few years ago, in a paper presented at the IFLA Conference in Copenhagen[55], this author expressed the opinion that the Schools of Librarianship in Europe were not sufficiently involved in the electronic library development programmes funded by the European Commission. At the time it provoked some comment from a member of the Commission's staff who was in the audience, and at a conference the following Spring, he presented a paper with a fairly comprehensive account of the Commission's involvement with professional education.[56] That may have been a coincidence - he certainly does not appear to have responded directly or fully to the points that had been made, - but it may be a small indication that if voices are raised they may be heard. However, if the LIS research community is to be really effective, it is important that its members not only make the case in public, but that they also do it in more private fora, and that they all say much the same thing.

55 JOHNSON, I.M. The development of education and research for the electronic library - opportunities and challenges: paper presented to the meeting of the Section on Education and Training during the I.F.L.A. conference, Copenhagen, August 1997. (I.F.L.A. Conference papers ref. 107-SET-3-E)

56 STORK, H-G. European initiatives for the professional development of librarians: paper presented to the 4th European Bielefeld Colloquium on Libraries and Publishers as Main Players in the Information Society, 10-12 February 1998. Viewed on the Web on 1 February, 2000at URL http://www.cordis.lu/libraries/en/biel-geo.html

John Feather

The domain of information studies

Information Studies: defining a discipline

What is information studies? This is surely a simple question. But it does not readily yield a simple answer. Few disciplines do. From the outside, a similar question about history or physics might seem superfluous, yet practitioners of those subjects reflect – and disagree – on the nature of the subjects, how and perhaps why they should be studied, their educational importance, their role in society, and so on. The uncertainty remains despite the fact that the traditional disciplines of the academy – the natural sciences, literature, history, language, philosophy – are as old as the academy itself, with a common origin in ancient Greece. Subjects which have developed in the last two centuries – the intellectual children of the enlightenment – have even less certainty. Among those which are now commonplace in universities throughout the world, especially in the social sciences, there is still a need felt to define and redefine themselves. Those, like Information Studies, which are less common, are even less well understood, not least by their own practitioners.

Information Studies historically derives from the study of libraries and the need to train librarians. At the same time, it is part of, or in some way related to, a cluster of other disciplines and sub-disciplines with which it shares half of its name: information science, information systems, information management, information theory, information technology and computing. How – if at all – do these disciplines relate to each other? Do they overlap? Are they indeed identical? Such a discussion is of more than merely semantic interest. It has an impact on both research and education. It has implications for academic organisation and for professional training and practice. The necessarily complex answer to the apparently simple question can be derived only from a consideration of the history and development of the discipline, its relation to other disciplines, and its place in contemporary understanding of the nature of disciplinarity.

This paper is a suggestion about how the answer might be derived, and what it might be. It begins, as the subject itself did, with the training of librarians to meet the demands of the newly created public libraries and the rapidly professionalising universities of the mid-nineteenth century. It goes forward to consider how this was transformed into an academic subject – library science – and how other subjects evolved on the periphery of the library world, which were to have a fundamental impact on how librarians worked and how they are educated. We also consider a much wider sphere: the study and growing understanding of how information and communication are used in society as a whole. Finally, we turn to defining the unique characteristics of the discipline now called Information Studies: the study of the creation, transmission, use and impact of information.

Historical background: librarian education and library science

The formal education and training of librarians was largely a product of the late nineteenth century. In the middle years of that century, there was training for archivists, notably in France at the École des Chartes, and the beginnings of librarian education in Germany. A proposal to introduce the study of *Bibliotheks-wissenschaft* into Oxford in the 1850s was abortive;[57] it was not until late in the century that properly organised training began in the United States. The tradition, which then developed in both Europe and North America, was essentially one of practical training aimed at front-line library workers. In the United States, the increasingly powerful American Library Association took the schools under its wing, and in return it took them and their graduates seriously.[58] It was nevertheless assumed that the directors of university libraries (and indeed many of their staff) would be distinguished scholars rather than professional librarians; this tradition survived until well into the second half of the twentieth century in some universities in Britain.

Despite the growth of library schools in the United States and elsewhere, it was only in the late 1920s that an academic discipline of Library Science began to be defined. This process began at the Graduate School of Library Science at the University of Chicago, under the leadership of Douglas Waples and was continued under his successors.[59] The Chicago school, founded in 1926 and located in a research-oriented private university, was a new phenomenon. Waples and his colleagues used many of techniques (and shared many of the assumptions) of the contemporary Chicago School of social scientists. They used social science methodologies, not least quantitative techniques, to analyse the functions of libraries and the patterns of behaviour of library users. Their teaching was at graduate level only. Following the Chicago example, by the 1950s a Master's level degree was regarded as the norm for professional recognition in American librarianship.

European developments were slower. In Britain, the only library school founded before World War Two was that at University College London, which opened in 1919. Although it catered only for graduates, it did not actually offer a Master's degree until 1965.[60] The schools which were founded in a number of colleges in the late 1940s and early 1950s all offered what were essentially technical training courses, producing librarians whose qualifications were professionally accredited, but who were not University graduates. It was only in the 1960s that the issue of making British librarianship a 'graduate profession' was finally resolved.[61] The practice of distinguishing between the levels of qualification obtained (such as was the case in Germany) was not followed in the UK; on the other hand, the distinction between professional and non-professional remained sharp until almost the end of the twentieth century when the Library Association finally admitted trained paraprofessional library workers to the status of Affiliate Member.

---

57 The proposal was made by Mark Pattison in his Suggestions on academical organisation with especial reference to Oxford. Edinburgh, 1869, p. 118, where he wrote that 'Bibliotheks-wissenschaft is one of the sciences which it would be desirable to naturalise in the University'. Nothing was done. For the reference, I am in debt to my former colleague Paul Morgan. The context of Pattison's suggestion is to be found in John Sparrow. Mark Pattison and the idea of a university. Cambridge: Cambridge University Press, 1967, esp. pp. 105-49.

58 There a brief account by Loriene Roy. Personality, tradition and library spirit: a brief history of librarian education. In Loriene Roy and Brooke E. Sheldon. Library and information education in the United States. London and Washington DC: Mansell, 1998, pp. 1-15; and a longer and more detailed one by Carl M. White. A historical introduction to library education: problems and progress to 1951. Metuchen, NJ: Scarecrow Press, 1976. See also the account of George W. Cole's report to the ALA's Library School Committee in 1892, in Wayne A. Weigand. The politics of an emerging profession. The American Library Association, 1876-1917. Westpoint, CN: Greenwood Press, 1986, p. 43.

59 For Waples, see John V. Richardson. Spirit of enquiry in library and information science: the Graduate Library School at Chicago 1921-1951. University of Indiana Ph.D. dissertation, 1978.

60 Gerald Bramley. Apprentice to graduate. A history of library education in the United Kingdom. London: Bingley, 1989, pp. 71-2, 188-89. This is the only book on its subject.

61 Bramley, op cit., pp. 179-87.

The complicated history of librarian education is reflected in the institutions in which it is delivered. In the United States, the accredited schools[62] are all in universities. This has been true in the United Kingdom only since 1992.[63] In France, librarian education developed in a special national institution, the École nationale superieùre des bibliothècaires. ENSB was founded in 1963.[64] There was a similar pattern in Denmark, where the Royal School of Librarianship in Copenhagen is the only school; only in the late 1990s did it transform itself into a research-based institution of higher education.[65] In Germany, a number of specialised Hochschulen took on the training role. In other countries, such as Norway, Spain and most of Eastern Europe, librarians are trained in university departments, although usually at undergraduate level. In one or two countries, notably Italy, there is in effect no professional education at all.[66] These differences reflect national traditions of higher education, of the relationship between teaching and research, and of the interactions between professional schools and the professions, which they serve. The very mixed and sometimes confusing picture had a direct impact on how the discipline developed and how it was perceived both by its own practitioners and by others in the academic world. The consequences are still with us today.

Waples and his colleagues were unequivocal in arguing they were creating a discipline called Library *Science*; the implied comparison with Social Science was deliberate, and the attempt to distance it from the sort of librarian training which had previously been offered was just as conscious.[67] The term – if not always the intellectual rigour – was widely imitated in the United States and elsewhere in the English-speaking world, but not in the United Kingdom. The distinguishing characteristic of Library Science was intended to be that it was based on data generated by research undertaken within clear methodological structures. While it was intended to train librarians, and the courses therefore included essential practical skills such as cataloguing and reference work, it was also intended to be an intellectual training like any other graduate programme. In the best of the American schools, both then and now, this ideal was largely attained, although perhaps not always

62 That is, those schools whose graduates are recognised by the American Library Association as professional librarians.

63 It was in that year that the polytechnics (and their equivalents in Scotland) were redesignated as universities; of the 17 schools then in existence, only 6 were in institutions which were universities before 1992.

64 For the earlier history of librarian education in France, see Michel Merland. The education of librarians and documentalists. In: William V. Jackson and Benjamin Whitten, eds., Library and information science in France: a 1983 overview. Austin, TX: Graduate School of Library and Information Science, 1984, pp. 143-5. In 1999, ENSB merged with the Institut de formation des bibliothécaires as the École nationale supérieure des sciences d'information et des bibliothèques. For ENSSIB, see its Web site at http://www.ennsib.fr/etudes/ index.html.

65 See the School's Web site at http://www.db.dk/.

66 Some idea of the range and scale of provision in Europe can be gained from the directory edited by Thomas A. Schröder. Information Science in Europe: a summary of institutions of education and programmes. Education for Information, 12 (1994), pp. 1 – 220. A less comprehensive listing, which is a little more up to date but certainly not current in every detail, will be found on the EUCLID web site at http://www.elt.sk/euclid/ eucdir.htm.

67 There is more than terminological interest in comparing Chicago with the school directed by Melvil Dewey at the equally distinguished Columbia University. Until the day it closed in 1991, it was called the School of Library Service. The term may have survived into the late twentieth century as a tribute to a rightly revered founder, but there is no doubt that 'service' is exactly what Dewey meant.

appreciated by the profession as a whole.[68] The strong academic and intellectual tradition which was thus embedded in the collective *psyche* of the best schools enabled them to adapt to the changing circumstances of the 1980s and to respond to insistent demands for new professional competencies.[69]

There was less clarity of purpose in Europe. The severely practical tradition, which characterised librarian education in Germany, France and the United Kingdom, sometimes even had an anti-intellectual element in it. Certainly in the United Kingdom, as late as the 1970s, there was suspicion among senior professionals that the library schools were producing theoreticians with no practical skills.[70] This perception was both wrong and ironical. Far from teaching in an ivory tower, most of the schools were teaching almost no theory and concepts. They concentrated largely on training in traditional library activities. In a few schools, however, there was a strong awareness that the great changes in the technologies of information storage and retrieval, and the potential impact of those changes on both the services and the management of libraries, could not be ignored, and a new curriculum – and arguably a new discipline – began to be forged.[71] This discipline had to confront another development, which had taken place independently of the evolution of librarian education – the emergence of information science.

The origins of information science have been well chronicled.[72] At one level, it grew out of practical necessity, as the sheer scale of scientific literature began to run out of control in the early twentieth century. From the beginning, however, there was also a concern with the 'scientific' analysis of information and information flows. The pre-war work of J. D. Bernal,[73] a distinguished scientist, found expression in a landmark conference organised in London by the Royal Society in 1948.[74] The essential problem, classically described by Bernal in terms, which are still worth reading, was the exponential growth of scientific literature, a phenomenon which had been studied since the 1920s, in terms which were themselves consciously intended to be scientific. Thus, the early students of information flows

---

68 See Evelyn H. Daniel. Library/Information Science education: the research ethos. In Charles R. McClure and Peter Hernon, eds. Library and information science research: perspectives and strategies for improvement. Norwood, NJ: Ablex, 1991, pp. 128-46.

69 Such as those detailed by José-Marie Griffiths and Donald W. King. New directions in Library and Information Science education. White Plains, NJ: Knowledge Industry Publications for ASIS, 1985, pp. 247-53. I return later to the fate of those which did not adapt.

70 I base this partly on experience. When I moved from practice to education in 1979, many of my professional colleagues talked to me along these lines. Many years later, I addressed what remained of the issue in John Feather. Creative tension or mutual misunderstanding? LIS departments and professional practice. Library Association Record, 96:1 (1994), pp. 30-31. In retrospect, I think there was fear of the academically well qualified young people who were moving into junior professional posts in the late 60s and early 70s, which largely emanated – at least in the public libraries – from the uncertainties this aroused among their typically non-graduate line managers. The reasons for disdain among some (but by no means all) academic librarians were somewhat different, and were rooted in one of the less agreeable aspects of the English social system.

71 For a characteristically trenchant analysis of the problem, and a proposed solution, which some schools adopted in whole or in part, see Blaise Cronin. The education of library-information professionals: a conflict of objectives. London: Aslib, 1982.

72 The basic texts will be found in A. J. Meadows, ed. The origins of information science. London: Taylor Graham and IIS, 1987; in this context, Meadows's Introduction (pp. 1-10) is particularly relevant. See also Brian Vickery. A century of scientific and technical information. Journal of Documentation, 55:5 (1999), pp. 476-527.

73 J. D. Bernal. The social function of science. London: Routledge, 1939, pp. 292-308.

74 Royal Society Scientific Information Conference, 21 June – 2 July 1948. Report and papers submitted. London: The Royal Society, 1948. See also Brian Vickery. The Royal Society Scientific Information Conference of 1948. Journal of Documentation, 54:3 (1998), pp. 281-83.

used the phraseology of science, conducting controlled experiments, deriving general 'laws' from their observations, and expressing some of those laws in mathematical formulae. The results of these efforts, such as the well-known work of Lotka, Zipf and Bradford,[75] are the intellectual foundation of the discipline, which came to be known as *information science*.[76]

Information science grew out of the practical problems of controlling scientific journal literature, and some of the pioneers (notably Bradford) were indeed librarians. But they seldom used the word. Bradford himself preferred the term 'documentalist', a word rarely used in English but deliberately intended to conjure up the image of the Fédération Internationale de Documentation, founded by P.-M.-G. Otlet in 1895. FID was (and is) largely concerned with the flow of scientific information, and many of those associated with it would not identify themselves with the library profession. In 1961, Jason Farradane established an academic department at the college, which was to become City University in London; this department was intended to teach the theory and practice of information science. Its graduates were to be the information intermediaries for scientists, lawyers and business people rather than the providers of books and other media to students, humanities scholars and indeed the general public.

Nevertheless, the fact was that much information science, at least in Britain and United States, was practised in libraries. The education of librarians and that of information scientists began to be identified with each other. For many library educators this was a welcome and timely development. In Britain in the late 1960s, the growth of degree programmes in the polytechnics, and the founding of new Librarianship (or Library Studies) departments in a few universities, meant that the subject was looking for intellectual respectability. Information science – even in its very name – seemed to offer a haven, but it was a step too far. Library and Information *Science* – a designation which was increasingly common in the United States and Library and Information Studies – was at odds with the essentially humanistic tradition of British and European librarianship. Library and Information *Studies* (with minor variations) became the British designation of the discipline, and the practice was imitated across Europe and some other parts of the world.

During the years when Library and Information Studies was developing as a recognised academic discipline in organisational terms, there were of course great changes afoot in what was taught and how librarians and information scientists practised their profession. In particular, the advent of computers into libraries and information agencies, which essentially dates from the late 1960s, meant that the professional practitioners needed a new range of knowledge and new skills. At the same time, the study of information flows and the impact of information was becoming a concern of many social scientists. Communications studies and media studies were products of the 1960s, building on the work of such thinkers as Habermas and Schiller who offered radical social analyses of human communi-

---

75 The key papers will all be found in Meadows, op. cit.. A colleague and I have traced these developments at slightly greater length in James Dearnley and John Feather. Wiring the World. London: Library Association Publishing, forthcoming (2001).

76 It has been argued that the 1948 conference forced a long-term rethink of LIS education, of which the founding of the department at City University is presumably to be seen as a part. (Maurice B. Line. An information world apart: the Royal Society Scientific Information Conference of 1948 in the light of 1998. Journal of Documentation, 54:3 (1998), p. 291.) But it is difficult to see the direct connection; certainly the new schools founded in the late 1940s (unfortunately, it might be felt) seemed to owe little or nothing to what was said by the contributors to the Royal Society's proceedings.

cation through the mass media. Much of what they said was very relevant to the work of information scientists, who generally ignored it.[77] In return, the work of the information scientists had little impact on the evolution of communications studies.[78] The discipline, which was increasingly coming to be referred to – at least by its practitioners – as LIS,[79] was falling into intellectual confusion and isolation before it was even fully established and defined.

Searching for an intellectual home: Information Studies

In academic terms, the marriage of library and information science was not unhappy. Certainly, it became possible to argue, with a degree of conviction, that information science provided a theoretical framework for library science, and to some extent underpinned the practice of librarianship.[80] There was a certain irony in this,[81] since the theoretical foundation of information science itself was largely based on results derived from empirical observations. It took little account of the different tradition of information theory which had been developed in United States and in Germany since 1945. This was essentially concerned with the nature of information as an entity and a concept, and how it is communicated. It had its roots in the application of probability theory to electrical, and later electronic, communications systems. The fundamental text is that of Claude Shannon and Warren Weaver, in which Shannon analysed the conceptual elements, which constitute a conversation between two people using a telephone.[82] The general principles which he derived remain valid as a basis for discussing communications between computers, machines which barely existed when he wrote. Essentially, Shannon and Weaver sought to measure the quantity and quality of information, an enterprise in which they have been followed by many others. Information theory, however, is not entirely a product of mathematicians working in the fields of telecommunications. Norbert Wiener, the originator (and baptismal godfather) of cybernetics was a distinguished contributor, as was John von Neumann, another mathematician who made fundamental contributions to the development of computing. To compound the complexity, in the 1970s and 1980s there were significant inputs from scholars who came from a tradition of cognitive psychology.[83]

Information scientists were increasingly attracted to some aspects of information theory. It offered a quantifiable scientific base too much which was of interest to them, especially in the communication and retrieval of information. So far as the LIS discipline as a whole was concerned, however, it introduced another, and seemingly arcane, element into an already complex mixture of subjects. Library Science, self-evidently a social science to its American creators, had been brought together with the more severely practical traditions of librarian training, to form an academic discipline, which could apparently hold its own. To this discipline, Information Science seemed to add universal laws derived from experimen-

---

77 Dearnley and Feather, op. cit., deal with this point at greater length.

78 I return to this point below.

79 An acronym which conveniently avoids the choice between Studies and Science.

80 I did so myself in my inaugural lecture. John Feather. Information Science and the art of librarianship. Loughborough: Loughborough University, 1989.

81 Which I did not explore at that time!

82 Claude E. Shannon and Warren Weaver. The mathematical theory of communication. Urbana, IL: University of Illinois Press, 1949.

83 On the latter point, see Nick Belkin. The cognitive viewpoint in information science. Journal of information Science, 16 (1990), pp. 11-15.

tal data and empirical observations. While information theory made sense to many information scientists, it seemed to have little to offer to Library Science which focuses on human behaviour in seeking and providing information and managing the institutions through which this is done.

It was against this background that the determinedly neutral term 'Information Studies' began to be used in Britain and elsewhere in the 1980s. Information Studies was (and often still is) understood to encompass library and information science in all its diversity. Yet, even at the most practical level, that diversity has increased in recent years, and has created a confusion which is implicit in an ambiguous terminology and continuing failure to reach a consensus on the scope and nature of the discipline. The problem has been exacerbated by some unnecessarily crude equations of one subject, or sub-discipline, with another, and by their multiplication. A few examples (in the empirical tradition of LIS!) will help to explicate the point.

Information Studies, Computer Science, and Communication and Media Studies

Among the other disciplines which have developed since the 1960s, there are two which might be thought to have a synergistic relationship with LIS. Because the computer has become an essential tool of information storage, retrieval and transmission, developments in computer science and in computing are critical to the professional practitioners who provide information to users. In a different sense, the social study of communications, and the study of the printed and broadcast mass media, would appear top share some concepts with the study of the transmission of information. Both relationships seem to be reinforced by the convergence of the technologies of communications and information which characterised the 1990s. We shall consider each in turn.

Computer Science is concerned with every aspect of computing. Computer scientists deal with hardware, software and networks. They are concerned with the mechanisms for the input, processing, storage and output of data. Computer Science, on the other hand, does not concern itself with the applications of computing in particular fields; indeed a claim to do so would effectively establish it as a meta-discipline which encompasses almost all others. Instead, its central focus is on the computer itself, its operating system, programming languages and systems architecture.[84]
A recent definition is as follows:[85]

> *Computing is concerned with the understanding, design and exploitation of computation and computing technology....It is a discipline that combines elegant theories (including those derived from a range of other disciplines such as mathematics, engineering, psychology, graphic design or well-founded experimental insight) ...with the solution of immediate practical problems...*

Clearly there is much here that Computer Science has in common with any reasonable definition of Information Studies, which is also in part concerned with the 'exploitation of

[84] For a perspective on how the academic Computer Science community understands its domain, see Association for Computing Machinery and Institution of Electrical and Electronic Engineers Joint Task Force. Computing Curricula. Report of the ACM/IEEE-CS Joint Task Force. New York: ACM, 1991.

[85] Taken from the (UK) Quality Assurance Agency for Higher Education, Benchmarking statement on computing, to be found on the agency's Web site at http://www.qaa.ac.uk/crntwork/benchmark/ computing.pdf.

computation and computing technology'. But it is also clear that Computing Science - in this definition, which has been generated by the computer scientists themselves - focuses on the design, operation and products of the computer.

There are other disciplines, which also clearly have something in common with information studies, without either encompassing it or being wholly encompassed by it. *Communication and Media Studies* is centrally concerned with the content of what is transmitted, but it is also involved with the production and reception of broadcast or printed output. It is unequivocally a social science, and has a strong and overt research base. Indeed, research is assumed to define the issues of Communication and Media Studies; educational programmes are developed around those concerns. The research, however, is empirical, and perhaps sometimes unreflective and lacking in analysis.[86] Some of the intellectual issues which arise in the literature of the discipline are not unlike those which have beset LIS: the relationship between research and education, defining the research agenda, and identifying appropriate approaches to the practice of research. Further parallels emerge when we consider the subject domain itself. There is a close and sometimes very difficult relationship with the media industry, which is looking for action research which will inform its own practices. Academics, on the other hand, are looking to make more objective, and sometimes necessarily critical, studies of how the media perform. This, in turn, is reflected in educational practice where there is a clear tension between training students to work in the media and giving them an education which enables them to be analytical, critical and objective. The apparent conflict between imparting knowledge and developing understanding on the one hand, and teaching particular skills on the other, seems to be even more acute than in LIS.[87]

The similarity of some of the conceptual problems of LIS and Communication and Media Studies arises in part from the fact that they are dealing with some of the same content and external issues. The convergence of media which characterised the 1990s has had an impact on both disciplines,[88] as the media of digital information and digital entertainment use the same storage and transmission mechanisms and to a certain extent compete with each other for the time and money of consumers.

As we consider Information Studies in the context of cognate disciplines – computer science, communications and media studies – and *their* cognate and parent disciplines – mathematics, physics, social science – can we only define Information Studies by stating what it is not? Can we actually identify a core body of knowledge and understanding which is unique to Information Studies? One approach to this problem is to define Information Studies in terms of the management of information, and by extension the management of agencies and institutions through which information is transmitted to end users. This certainly provides an important linkage with librarianship and with library science. But it still begs a question about the theoretical framework within which the discipline is located and from which it derives its intellectual strengths. It is worthwhile to attempt to

---

[86] See the criticism made by Hanno Hardt. Critical communication studies. Communication, history and theory in America. London and New York: Routledge, 1992, p. 5.

[87] See David French and Michael Richards. Theory and practice in media education. Knowing why, knowing how. In: David French and Michael Richards. Media education across Europe. London: Routledge, 1994, pp. 179-93.

[88] Ibid., p. 180, make the point in the context of media studies. For a recent LIS view, see Barbara J. Casey, Carman V. Carroll and Bertrum H. MacDonald. Convergence in information studies (archival studies, librarianship, and records management): implications for educational programs. Canadian Journal of Information and Library Science, 22:2 (1997), pp. 30-48.

define that framework a little more, and to try to identify the key issues.

The central concern is with information. Although this can be understood in a theoretical sense, in Information Studies the word typically has a more practical meaning. The classical position is to see information as something which is derived from a body of data and is processed in some way in order to achieve a greater understanding of the meaning and significance of those data. Information then becomes recorded knowledge, and thus dependent on the existence of a medium in which the record can be made and stored, and from which it can be retrieved. It is the process of making, storing and retrieving records, which constitutes the professional domain of librarians and archivists and hence provides the link which we have already noted between librarianship and information science. Indeed, it is possible to argue that Information Studies occupies precisely this centre ground where two severely practical professions confront their own theoretical base.[89]

It is, however, not necessary to accept this position in full in order to accept a broad, but still useful, definition of Information Studies. Information Studies can perhaps best be understood as a discipline which is concerned with the organisation and management of information so that it can be systematically collected, recorded, stored and retrieved. This is essentially independent of any specific application, technology or institutional base. It is also, to a great extent, independent of any analysis of content in the sense in which a sociologist in the field of media studies understands content analysis. At the same time, Information Studies encompasses the use of technologies from handwriting to computing, and the organisation and management of institutions such as libraries and archives. It also, however, allows for a far wider understanding of the theoretical base and practical applications of the discipline. All professionals depend on information to facilitate effective and accurate decision making; this too is the domain of Information Studies. This is not merely a claim for the extension and inclusiveness of the discipline; it is a recognition of the centrality of information to the decision-making process. The understanding which arises out of Information Studies, and the practical skills which derive from it, are essential constituents of the management of everything from the airline industry to zoological gardens.

Information studies and librarianship: a special relationship?

The universal applicability of the principles of information studies, derived from empirical observation, experimental practice and theoretical considerations, has historically had a close relationship with the education of librarians, if not always with the practice of librarianship. In a cultural climate in which we are more conscious than ever before of information as an entity and a commodity, does that special relationship still exist, and is it indeed helpful?

The business of librarians and archivists is to provide information for the users of their institutions. But there are many other professionals of whom that is also true. What distinguishes the librarians and the archivists from other information providers is their concern with media[90] as well as information, and their skills in the organisation and management of institutions as well as of information itself. An understanding of information is fundamen-

---

89 For the case for archives falling in the LIS domain, see Bruce W. Dearstyne and Diane L. Barlow. Archives, records management, and information management. Creating a dynamic curriculum for the next century. Journal of Education for Librarianship and Information Science, 40:3 (1999), pp. 134-41.

90 I am distinguishing here between 'media' such as books, CD-ROMs and so on (which is my meaning in this sentence) and 'the media', such as newspapers and television, which are in the domain of media studies.

tal to their work, but it is not its only foundation. The empirical foundations of both Information Science and Library Science were firmly embedded in the analysis of user need and professional practice. It follows therefore that when they change, change is required in the research and educational agendas of the disciplines. Some of the factors forcing change are economic and social.[91] Others have a technical basis, but with vast socio-economic consequences, not least the same convergence of media and technologies which has had such a profound influence on media studies in the last ten years. It has been cogently argued that one of the key reasons why so many library schools closed in the United States in the late 1980s and early 1990s was that they failed to recognise, or at least to react to, the 'paradigm shift' to an information society.[92] The schools, which have survived, not only in the United States but elsewhere in the industrialised countries, have done so because they have recognised external change, adapted to it, and in the best cases tried to lead it.[93]

In some respects, the historic relationship between Library Science and Information Science is unhelpful to the development of the academic discipline of Information Studies. The paradox is that - despite the almost universal obsession with information and the information society - information science and information theory are little regarded, and Information Studies barely recognised. This is certainly in part because of the same reluctance to change which destroyed some of the American library schools.[94] The problem is, however, wider and deeper than that, and lies in an intellectual reluctance to conceptualise the discipline. Information science always sat slightly uncomfortably in the classical model of science, despite its attempt to derive general laws from repeatable experiments or observable phenomena. Similarly, library science became so inter-twined with the teaching of the skills of librarianship that its research agenda was often stifled by practical necessity. The intellectual problem lies in the fact that information is not a physical object,[95] a difficulty to which post-modern scientific epistemology is argued to offer a solution.[96] The practical problem lies in the essentially inward-looking tradition of the Information Studies discipline. It is fundamental to postmodernism that disciplines, activities and intellectual products define themselves.[97] The self-definition of information studies has always been practical, linking itself to other disciplines from librarianship to management, and always seemingly lacking the confidence to claim its own ground.

Yet the ground is there to be claimed, and it is distinctive. There are three essential ingredients:

– Information Studies seeks to understand information and the processes by which it is

---

91 See, for example, Thomas A. Childers. Undoing business as usual in Information Studies. Journal of Education for Librarianship and Information Science, 37:2 (1996), pp. 148-53.

92 Larry J. Ostler, Therri C. Dahlin and J. D. Willardson. The closing of American library schools. Problems and opportunities. Westport, CN: Greenwood, 1995, pp. 25-29.

93 For a useful, if somewhat mechanistic, summary of the UK position, see Ian M. Johnson. Challenges in developing professionals for the 'information society': and some responses by the British schools of librarianship and information studies. Library Review, 47:3 (1998), pp. 152-59.

94 See, for example, Harry Bruce. A new perspective on information education for Australia. Education for Information, 17:3 (1999), pp. 187-98.

95 Gernot Wersig. Information science: the study of post-modern knowledge. Information Processing and Management, 29 (1993), pp. 229-39.

96 Ron Day. LIS, method, and post-modern science. Journal of Education for Librarianship and Information Science, 37:4 (1996), pp. 317-24.

97 A point made by Day (see note 40), who links it to the seminal work of Jean-François Lyotard. The postmodern condition: a report on knowledge. Minneapolis, MN: University of Minnesota Press, 1984.

created, stored, analysed, retrieved and transmitted. Information, despite its lack of physical properties, is a definable entity; it is an assemblage of data which can be linked with other such assemblages to formulate knowledge. It is this fact, generally acknowledged, that gives the discipline access to a sound conceptual framework which is related to other disciplines but independent of them.
- *Information Studies is concerned with the wider social and economic dimension of information.* It engages with such concepts as information overload, information deprivation and information richness. It is seeking a relationship with other social sciences, which deal with other aspects of these and other phenomena, including sociology and economics.
- Information Studies offers a framework within which professional providers of information can gain a greater understanding of the principles which underpin their professional practice. These professionals include information mangers, librarians, archivists and records managers, but the profession is becoming less exclusive as more and more people in many professions and occupations process information as an essential element in their work.

The extent to which the discipline defined in the previous paragraph is actually researched and taught is questionable. Indeed, it is far from fully developed. Information Studies academics have fought shy of the political dimension of their subject, unlike their colleagues in media studies with their intellectual home in the politically engaged social sciences.[98] For more than thirty years, information studies academics have tried to shake off the traditionally fustian image of librarianship by clinging to the coat-tails of computer science and information technology. Too many of them in the 1970s equated this with information science, which they barely understood and certainly failed to absorb into their intellectual universe. Even computing was taught in library schools only as a mechanistic tool, an electronic card index drawer for a library catalogue.[99]

As a result, a great opportunity was lost. The world moved on. It created an information society without consulting the self-proclaimed experts in information. They themselves consistently failed to define an agenda which had any apparent relevance outside the narrow world of information-providing agencies. As a consequence, the 'information society' is too often simply equated with the applications of computing.[100] The analyses of sociologists, insightful as they are at their best, do not really come to grips with the nature of the 'information' which they see at the heart of a global paradigm shift. Even the most profound sociological study, that by Manuel Castells, makes only a brief reference to Porat's 'classic' definition ('data that have been organised and communicated') and then moves on to information technology which is assumed thereafter to be the driver of a new social and economic order.[101] The loss of historical perspective has led to some strange assumptions

98 This criticism is true even of some of the most acute analysts, such as Dave Muddiman. Towards a post-modern context for information and library education. Education for Information, 17:1 (1999), 1-19, a rare attempt to engage with these issues containing many valuable insights, and which has influenced my own thinking on the matter. For the media studies approach to the political question, see Hardt, op. cit., p. 9, where he writes that research in the subject helps 'to formulate a political agenda'

99 The same criticism is made by Ostler, Dahlin and Willardson, op. cit., p. 32.

100 Spectacularly and expensively so by the European Commission in the Delors Report (1993) and the Bangemann Report (1994), an error only gradually being corrected. For an analysis, see Dearnley and Feather, op. cit.

101 Manuel Castells. The rise of the network society. Oxford: Blackwell, 1996, pp. 17 (and n. 27 quoting Porat), 29 et seqq.

about the nature of this allegedly 'new' society in which we are living.

The future of information studies lies in making an aggressive claim to its own ground. It lies in recognising the unique nature of the contribution which it can make. It lies in engaging with the external intellectual world, and bringing from that world the concepts, ideas and insights which can transform it. The professions, which the discipline has traditionally served, will not suffer because of this. They too can undergo an intellectual transformation as their practitioners learn to value themselves more highly and are more highly valued by others. The claim made for the role of information professionals in the information society will ring a little less hollowly when information itself is better understood and Information Studies takes it proper place in the spectrum of knowledge.

Dietmar von Hoyningen-Huene

Positionierung der Fachhochschulen auf einem globalen Bildungsmarkt

1. Situationsanalyse

Wir verfolgen gegenwärtig die dramatischen Auswirkungen der Globalisierung der Wirtschaft auf die Unternehmensstrukturen und -strategien bis hin zu den Konsequenzen, die wir alle unmittelbar durch Veränderungen in den sozialen Sicherungssystemen zu spüren bekommen. Wir sehen die Schwierigkeiten, mit denen Deutschland und Europa als Ganzes im internationalen Wettbewerb zunehmend konfrontiert sind. Die Staaten der Europäischen Union stehen im Wettbewerb mit sich rasch entwickelnden Ländern, insbesondere in Südostasien, die hohe Wachstumsraten bei gleichzeitig niedrigen Arbeitslosenzahlen ausweisen. Diese Länder sind heute in der Lage, die vollständige Kette von Forschung, Produktentwicklung, Produktion und Vertrieb genauso qualifiziert zu beherrschen wie wir, aber oft zu wesentlich niedrigeren Kosten und günstigeren Rahmenbedingungen. Die Folgen sind Wettbewerbsnachteile für den Standort Europa und oft Verlust auch von qualifizierten Arbeitsplätzen. In Deutschland ist die Situation insofern besonders problematisch, als sich zu Beginn der 90er-Jahre in Folge der Wiedervereinigung eine spezifische Binnenkonjunktur ergeben hat, die uns die dramatischen Auswirkungen der zunehmenden Globalisierung der Wirtschaft und der Liberalisierung der Märkte erst zeitverzögert, aber dann umso drastischer vor Augen geführt hat. Damit hat sich ein Reformstau ergeben, der von der Reform der Steuergesetzgebung, der sozialen Sicherungssysteme bis hin zum Bildungswesen reicht und der zu zunehmender Unruhe und teilweise Resignation in der Gesellschaft geführt hat. Diese deutsche Befindlichkeit steht in einem bemerkenswerten Gegensatz zu dem Optimismus, dem Engagement und auch der Bereitschaft zur Gestaltung der eigenen Zukunft, die man auf eindrucksvolle Weise in den Ländern Asiens und zunehmend auch Südamerikas erlebt.

Man hat oft den Eindruck, dass die Debatte um den Wirtschaftsstandort zu einer reinen Kostendebatte verkommt. Unterschätzt wird nach meinem Dafürhalten die Bedeutung, die dem Bildungs- und Wissenschaftssystem mit wachsender wirtschaftlicher Globalisierung und beim Wandel der Industrie- zur Wissens- und Dienstleistungsgesellschaft zukommt.

Nach der Globalisierung der Wirtschaft folgt jetzt die Globalisierung der Bildungssysteme.

Wir haben einen globalen Markt in dem Feld Bildung und Ausbildung. Im Vergleich zu anderen Ländern hat Deutschland auf diesem internationalen Bildungsstandort dramatisch an Attraktivität verloren:

Die Gesamtzahl der ausländischen Studierenden ist in deutschen Hochschulen in den letzten Jahrzehnten ständig gestiegen. Die für 1998 ausgewiesene Zahl von rd. 166.000 ausländischen Studierenden[102] bedarf jedoch der Erläuterung. Etwa 40 % sind sog. „Bildungsinländer". Demgegenüber stagniert die Zahl der „echten" ausländischen Studierenden seit längerem.

[102] Bundesmin. für Bildung und Forschung, Grund- und Strukturdaten, 1999/2000, Bonn, 2000, S. 194/195

Ausländische Studierende kommen überwiegend aus wenigen Herkunftsländern:

Türkei	23.689
Iran	7.867
Griechenland	7.800
Polen	7.015
Italien	6.363
Österreich	6.300
Frankreich	6.146
VR China	5.355
Marokko	5.255
Russ. Förderation	4.930

In dieser Gruppe befinden sich auf den ersten Plätzen die Staaten mit dem größten Anteil der (bisher im Einzelnen statistisch nicht ausgewiesenen) Bildungsinländer. Die Zahl der Studierenden aus den USA ist vom Höchststand von 4.436 im Jahre 1992 auf 3.719 im Jahre 1998 gesunken. Die Zahl westeuropäischer Studierender im Rahmen der EU-Mobilitätsprogramme hat sich von 28.008 (1992) auf 43.479 (1998) gut entwickelt. Ein stärkerer Zustrom zeigt sich auch in letzter Zeit aus den mittel-, ost- und südosteuropäischen Staaten. Von 1992 bis 1998 hat sich die Zahl afrikanischer Studierender auf 16.500 verdoppelt, wobei Marokko (5.255) und Kamerun (2.966) den größten Anteil an dieser Gruppe stellen. Demgegenüber verharrt der Anteil der Studierenden aus Asien (16.310; ohne Iran, China, Korea) und Lateinamerika (4.468) insgesamt auf einem niedrigen Stand. Die Zahl indonesischer Studierender ist in den letzten zehn Jahren zurückgegangen. Insbesondere Studierende aus den Wachstumsregionen des asiatisch-pazifischen Raums gehen zu Studien- und Ausbildungszwecken vornehmlich in die USA, nach Australien und teilweise nach Japan.

Nachdenklich stimmt auch die Tatsache, dass Deutschland in Bezug auf den Austausch von wissenschaftlichem Nachwuchs mit den führenden Industrieländern eher ein Export- als ein Importland geworden ist. Die Zahl der deutschen Nachwuchswissenschaftler, die sich im Ausland weiterqualifizieren, ist inzwischen höher als die Zahl ausländischer Nachwuchswissenschaftler, die zu uns kommen.

Im Ergebnis kann man also festhalten, dass es zunehmend weniger Studenten aus den sich dynamisch entwickelnden Regionen in Südostasien und aus Südamerika gibt und damit zu wenig Multiplikatoren in diesen rasch wachsenden Märkten vorhanden sind. Als Exportnation ist Deutschland im besonderen Maße im internationalen Geflecht aus Wettbewerb und Kooperation auf partnerschaftliche Beziehungen und Kontakte zu diesen Ländern angewiesen. Offensichtlich funktionieren belastbare Partnerschaften in der Praxis vor allem dann, wenn die Partner vergleichbare Bildungserfahrungen teilen und die jeweils andere Kultur schon in ihrer Ausbildung kennen gelernt haben.

Von daher ist es wichtig, Gründe für diese Probleme zu identifizieren und Instrumentarien und visionäre Modelle für deren Lösung im Kontext der Diskussion um die Hochschulstrukturreform zu entwickeln und zu erproben.

2. Gründe für die mangelnde Akzeptanz des Studienstandards in Deutschland

Damit ein Studium in Deutschland für junge Leute aus Asien nicht zum Auslaufmodell und auch für unsere deutschen Studienbewerber wieder attraktiver wird, muss an einer ganzen Reihe von Stellen gegengesteuert werden.

Sprachbarrieren

Zunächst muss man die Sprachbarrieren als ein wesentliches Hindernis anerkennen. Die lingua franca der modernen Gesellschaft ist sowohl in der Wirtschaft als auch in der Wissenschaft Englisch. Englisch beherrschen Studieninteressenten in der Regel schon, bevor sie ein Studium in den USA aufnehmen wollen. Die Kandidaten, die in Deutschland studieren wollen, müssen Deutsch erst lernen und selbst, wenn sie die sechsmonatigen Deutschkurse der Goethe-Institute mit Erfolg absolviert haben, können sie den Vorlesungen i.d.R. noch nicht folgen. Es dauert erfahrungsgemäß rund ein Jahr, bis Ausländer genug Deutsch können, um den Lehrveranstaltungen folgen zu können. Deutschland ist darüber hinaus gegenwärtig nicht in der Lage, das Erlernen der deutschen Sprache im Ausland attraktiver zu machen. Das System der deutschen Auslandsschulen, in denen neben Kindern deutscher Diplomaten und Kaufleute, zunehmend auch die Kinder der Eliten dieser Gastgeberländer lernen, wird nicht ausgebaut. Zahlreiche Einrichtungen der „Goethe-Institute zur Pflege der deutschen Sprache im Ausland und zur Förderung der internationalen kulturellen Zusammenarbeit" - so der vollständige Titel - werden gegenwärtig geschlossen.

Insofern ist es nur konsequent, dass das Bundesministerium für Bildung und Forschung im Rahmen eines Sonderprogramms Modellversuche zur Entwicklung international ausgerichteter Studiengänge fördert. Diese Studiengänge sollen bestimmte Rahmenbedingungen erfüllen und je zur Hälfte mit Deutschen und Ausländern besetzt werden und neben Deutsch auch in einer weiteren Fremdsprache, in der Regel Englisch, angeboten werden.

Auf einer Tagung des Ministeriums für wirtschaftliche Zusammenarbeit in Bonn, einigten sich der Präsident der brasilianischen Bildungskommission, Baeta Neves, sowie der Präsident der Pädagogischen Hochschule Yaoundè in Kamerun, Ndong, noch am Leichtesten darauf, dass Sprachschwierigkeiten gern bewältigt würden, wenn nur die Motivation und die Begeisterung, in Deutschland zu studieren, vorhanden sei. Wenn die Begeisterung nicht ausreicht, obwohl ein deutscher Hochschulabschluss nach wie vor hohes Ansehen genießt und oft Tür und Tor öffnet, muss es offenbar noch eine Reihe anderer Hindernisse geben.

Unterschiedliche Bildungssysteme

Die größte Schwierigkeit liegt in den Unterschieden im Schul- und Hochschulsystem. Hier geht es zum einen um die unterschiedliche Zielsetzung der Bildungssysteme und zum anderen um unterschiedliche Strukturen und Abschlussgrade. In Deutschland - zumal an den Universitäten - legen die Deutschen mehr Wert auf Selbsterkenntnis, Selbsterziehung und zweckfreie Forschung. Dagegen richten Studenten, insbesondere Studenten aus Entwicklungsländern, das Augenmerk auf den Nutzen, den sie in gut organisiertem Lernen und bei zweckdienlicher Forschung schneller und direkter zu finden hoffen. Entsprechend haben sich gut strukturierte Studienstrukturen mit einer vertikal differenzierten Undergraduate Basis und einem Postgraduate Aufbau, mit den Abschlussgraden Bachelor, Master und PhD, eingebürgert.

Wir haben dagegen in Deutschland ein horizontal differenziertes System von Universitäten und Fachhochschulen, die Abschlussgrade verleihen, die gleichwertig aber andersartig sind. Dieses System - und das noch viel kompliziertere französische System - ist international weitgehend unbekannt. Das angelsächsisch strukturierte Modell ist in Japan, in Australien und inzwischen auch in Asien, das vorherrschende System. Ergebnis ist die restriktive gegenseitige Anerkennung und Einstufung von Studienleistungen und die mangelhafte Anerkennung deutscher Studienabschlüsse im Ausland. Hinzu kommen vergleichsweise lange und nicht kalkulierbare Studienzeiten, die als nachteilig und nicht erforderlich angesehen werden.

Fehlendes internationales Bildungsmarketing

Zu lange sind die deutschen Hochschulen im Stil nachgeordneter Behörden behandelt und alimentiert worden. Ein Wettbewerb um die besten Studierenden und die qualifiziertesten Mitarbeiter sowie um Mittel, war lange Jahre allenfalls Gegenstand einer sehr akademisch geführten Diskussion. Die primär an quantitativen Parametern festgemachte staatliche Alimentierung, das Fehlen privatwirtschaftlicher Elemente führte dazu, dass die deutschen Hochschulen im nationalen und erst recht im internationalen Geschäft des Bildungsmarketing unerfahren sind. Für ausländische Hochschulen ist der Erfolg im Wettbewerb um ausländische Studierende eine Einnahmequelle. Deshalb bieten sie neben aktiver Information und Repräsentanz „vor Ort“ auch die direkte Ansprache einzelner Studierender als potenzielle Kunden sowie spezielle Arrangements für Studienbedingungen und Betreuung an.

Auf dem internationalen Bildungsmarkt besteht ein harter Wettbewerb um die besten Stipendiaten. Dieser Markt wird durch die USA, Großbritannien, Australien, die Niederlande und Japan beherrscht. In den USA werden allein die Einnahmen aus der Ausbildung ausländischer Studenten mit 10 Mrd DM veranschlagt. Dabei sind diese direkten Einnahmen nicht einmal das Wichtigste. Um Größenordnungen ertragreicher, wenn auch schwer messbar, sind die indirekten Effekte, die sich aus dem zeitweiligen oder dauerhaften Aufsaugen hochkarätiger Nachwuchspotenziale aus aller Herren Länder ergeben, die die Listen amerikanischer Nobelpreisträger schmücken. Vor allem aber sind die vielen intensiven Verbindungen zu Führungseliten im Ausland, die so als ein „big boys network” aufgebaut werden, von unschätzbarem Wert.

Man kann festhalten:
Es gab über lange Zeit an den deutschen Hochschulen keine leistungsorientierte Veränderungskultur als Reaktion auf einen sich ändernden Bildungsmarkt und auf sich ändernde Anforderungen in Wirtschaft und Gesellschaft.

Studienumfeld

Daneben ist in Deutschland für Ausländer die Haltung der Ausländerbehörden, die eine primär an der Abwehr von Wirtschaftsflüchtlingen orientierte Politik betreiben und mit ihren restriktiven bürokratischen Methoden auch für Studieninteressenten nahezu unüberwindliche Hürden aufbauen und auch eine nicht ausländerfreundliche Grundstimmung ein ernstes Hindernis. Auch die Lebenshaltungskosten in Deutschland sind hoch. Sie werden auch nicht dadurch aufgewogen, dass in Deutschland keine Studiengebühren bezahlt werden.

Wenn man aufgrund der vorstehenden Überlegungen erkennt, dass zwar die deutschen Hochschulen und Forschungseinrichtungen noch einen international guten Ruf genießen, aber eben nicht mehr, wie in der Vergangenheit, das Mekka für den wissenschaftlichen Nachwuchs aus aller Welt sind und die Problematik des Bildungsstandortes direkt auch mit der Entwicklung des Wirtschaftsstandortes zusammenhängt, ist es dringlich erforderlich Maßnahmen zu ergreifen, damit Deutschland seine Konkurrenzfähigkeit in diesem globalen Bildungsmarkt wiedergewinnt.

3. *Maßnahmen zur Verbesserung der Attraktivität des Bildungsstandortes Deutschland*

In dem Papier „Hochschulen für das 21. Jahrhundert“[103] führte der damalige Bundesminister für Bildung, Wissenschaft, Forschung und Technologie, Dr. Rüttgers aus:

> *„Das deutsche Hochschulsystem muss aus internen Gründen der Effizienz, des Wettbewerbs und der Selbststeuerung nach Leistungskriterien strukturell und inhaltlich reformiert werden.*
> *Hierzu treten wichtige Gründe der internationalen Entwicklung, die ebenfalls Anpassungen im Hinblick auf kürzere Studienzeiten bis zum ersten (berufsqualifizierenden) Abschluss, auf die Anerkennung von Studienleistungen und die internationale Kompatibilität von Abschlussgraden nahelegen. Diese Anpassungen sollen im Detail nicht staatlich verordnet werden, sondern sich im Wettbewerb aller Hochschulen entwickeln. Staatliche Gesetzgebung muss diesen Wettbewerb um Studierende, qualifiziertes Personal, Finanzmittel und Leistungsanerkennung aber möglich machen und anstoßen.*
> *Es ist wahrscheinlich nicht sinnvoll, die in den 70er-Jahren unter dem Stichwort „Kurzstudiengänge" lange Zeit, aber fruchtlos geführte Debatte über ein neues staatlich verordnetes und „auf einen Schlag" einzuführendes Gesamtsystem erneut aufzulegen. Allen Hochschulen sollte aber im Wettbewerb ermöglicht werden, kürzere Studiengänge von mindestens 3-jähriger Dauer (Bachelor) zu entwickeln und für hierauf aufbauende Studiengänge von bis zu 2-jähriger Dauer (Master) Abschlussgrade zu verleihen, die sich am internationalen Standard orientieren. Die deutsche Hochschulgesetzgebung käme damit einem offensichtlichen Bedarf durch Ausgestaltung in einem eigenen Rechtsrahmen entgegen und würde Interessenten nicht mehr auf den bereits stark frequentierten Nebenweg verweisen, sich solche Abschlussmöglichkeiten durch Inanspruchnahme von nicht immer in erster Linie qualitätsorientierten ausländischen Kooperationspartnern zu verschaffen. In einem international, auch durch Entwicklungen der modernen Informations- und Medientechnik zunehmend offenen System, in dem ausländische Grade zudem durch internationale Vereinbarungen auch in Deutschland anzuerkennen sind, würde ein Verzicht auf diese Möglichkeit einen Wettbewerbsnachteil für deutsche Hochschulen bedeuten."*

Es zeigt sich, dass diese Überlegungen zu einem der Angelpunkte bei der Änderung des Hochschulrahmengesetzes geworden sind.

- Wesentliche Leitelemente in dem neuen Hochschulrahmengesetz, das inzwischen in einer Reihe von Hochschulgesetzen der Länder konkretisiert wurde, sind:
- Stärkung der Autonomie der Hochschulen durch Veränderung der Leitungsorgane und Einführung eines Hochschulrates
- Leistungsorientierte Zuweisung staatlicher Haushaltsmittel im Rahmen eines Globalhaushaltes
- Einführung einer Kosten-Leistungsrechnung und interne Verteilung der Ressourcen auf die Fachbereiche nach Leistungs- und Qualitätsgesichtspunkten

---

103 Hochschulen für das 21. Jahrhundert, Grundsatzpapier zur Novelle des HRG, Dr. J. Rüttgers, Bonn, 1997

Neben der Änderung der hochschulorganisatorischen Randbedingungen, die zu umfangreichen und oft schmerzlichen Veränderungsprozessen in den Hochschulen geführt haben, ist vor allem bedeutsam, dass im §19 des neuen Hochschulrahmengesetzes ausgeführt wird:

> *„Zur Erprobung können Studiengänge eingerichtet werden, die zu einem Bachelor- oder Bakkalaureusgrad und zu einem Master- oder Magistergrad führen."*

In einem Beschluss der Kultusministerkonferenz vom 05. März 1999 wird ergänzend festgehalten:[104]

- Bachelor- und Masterstudiengänge können sowohl an Universitäten und gleichgestellten Hochschulen als auch an Fachhochschulen eingerichtet werden, ohne die unterschiedlichen Bildungsziele dieser Hochschularten in Frage zu stellen.
- Die Regelstudienzeiten für Bachelor- und Masterstudiengänge ergeben sich aus § 19 Abs. 2 bis 5 HRG und betragen mindestens drei und höchstens vier Jahre für die Bachelorstudiengänge und mindestens ein und höchstens zwei Jahre für die Masterstudiengänge.
- Der Bachelor ist ein eigenständiger berufsqualifizierender Abschluss. Bachelorstudiengänge können daher auch dann eingerichtet werden, wenn an der Hochschule kein entsprechender Masterabschluss erworben werden kann.
- Zugangsvoraussetzung für einen Masterstudiengang ist in jedem Fall ein berufsqualifizierender erster Studienabschluss. Darüber hinaus kann das Studium im Masterstudiengang von weiteren besonderen Zulassungsvoraussetzungen abhängig gemacht werden. Die Länder können sich die Genehmigung der Zulassungskriterien vorbehalten.
- Das Diplom (FH) entspricht im internationalen Vergleich dem vierjährigen Bachelor honours, Diplom- und Magisterabschlüsse an Universitäten dem Master.
- Masterabschlüsse an Universitäten und Fachhochschulen berechtigen grundsätzlich zur Promotion.

Diese neuen Möglichkeiten haben dazu geführt, dass bereits Ende 2000 rund 600 derartige international orientierte Studiengänge an den deutschen Hochschulen etabliert waren. Sie differenzieren sich in 382 Studiengänge mit Bachelorabschluss und 217 mit Masterabschluss. Nach Fächergruppen differenziert, liegt der Schwerpunkt eindeutig im Bereich die Ingenieurwissenschaften mit 215 Studiengängen und den Rechts-, Sozial- und Wirtschaftswissenschaften mit 204 Studiengängen.[105] Nach Angaben des Statistischen Bundesamtes studierten im WS 1999/2001 bereits 6.702 Studierende in Bachelor- oder Masterstudiengängen, wobei Baden-Württemberg mit 1.346 Studierenden knapp vor Nordrhein-Westfalen mit 1.307 Studierenden den Spitzenplatz einnimmt.[106]

In der Zwischenzeit zeigt sich, dass die Richtung der Hochschulreformen in den Ländern der EU ähnlichen Trends folgt. In einer gemeinsamen Erklärung der EU-Bildungsminister vom 19. Juni 1999 in Bologna wurden folgende interessante Entwicklungsziele vereinbart:[107]

---

[104] Beschluss der 285. KMK vom 05.03.1999: „Strukturvorgaben für die Einführung von Bachelor-/Bakkalaureus- und Master-/Magisterstudiengängen, Bonn 1999".

[105] Angaben nach dem HRK-Hochschulkompass (www.hochschulkompass.de).

[106] Statistisches Bundesamt, VII C Hochschulstatistik „Studierende mit angestrebtem Abschluss „Bachelor" oder „Master" im Wintersemester 1999/2000 nach Bundesländern, 23.10.2000"

[107] Der Europäische Hochschulraum. Gemeinsame Erklärung der Europäischen Bildungsminister, 19. Juni 1999, Bologna

„Wir bekräftigen unsere Unterstützung der in der Sorbonne-Erklärung dargelegten allgemeinen Grundsätze und wir werden unsere Maßnahmen koordinieren, um kurzfristig, auf jeden Fall aber innerhalb der ersten Dekade des dritten Jahrtausends, die folgenden Ziele, die wir für die Errichtung eines europäischen Hochschulraumes und für die Förderung der europäischen Hochschulen weltweit für vorrangig halten, zu erreichen: ....
Einführung eines Systems, das sich im Wesentlichen auf zwei Hauptzyklen stützt: einen Zyklus bis zum ersten Abschluss (undergraduate) und einen Zyklus nach dem ersten Abschluss (graduate). Regelvoraussetzung für die Zulassung zum zweiten Zyklus ist der erfolgreiche Abschluss des ersten Studienzyklus, der mindestens drei Jahre dauert. Der nach dem ersten Zyklus erworbene Abschluss attestiert eine für den europäischen Arbeitsmarkt relevante Qualifikationsebene. Der zweite Zyklus sollte, wie in vielen europäischen Ländern, mit dem Master und/oder der Promotion schließen."

Damit ergibt sich folgende Situation:

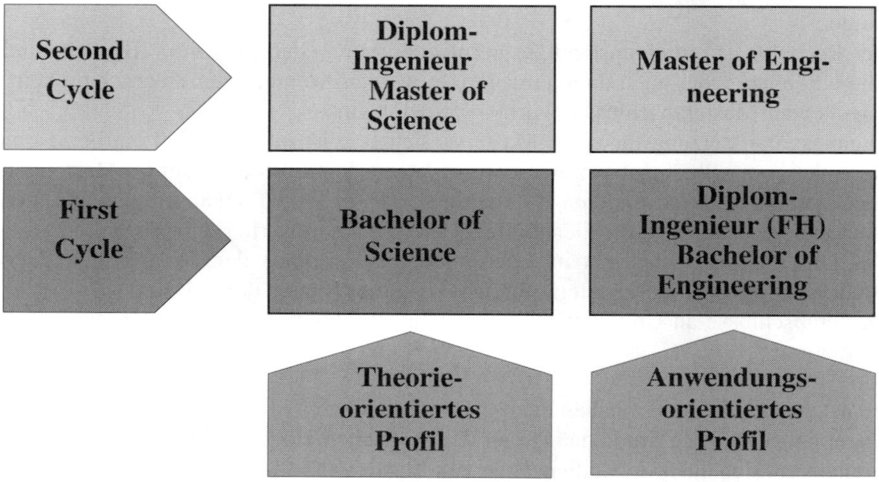

Qualifikationsniveaus und –profile in der Ingenieurausbildung

Im Einzelnen ergeben sich für die unterschiedlichen Hochschularten folgende Probleme:

- Universitäten müssen erhebliche Studienreformprozesse unternehmen, wenn sie einen vom Arbeitsmarkt akzeptierten berufsqualifizierenden Bachelorabschluss einführen.
- Die Fachhochschulen müssen erhebliche Anstrengungen unternehmen, wenn sie einen Masterstudiengang einführen, da dieser Abschluss ein höheres Niveau hat, als die bisher in den Fachhochschulen angebotenen Diplomstudiengängen. Gerade die Fachhochschulen in Baden-Württemberg haben eine hohe Qualität und damit das Potenzial, in Schwerpunktbereichen erfolgreich solche Studiengänge z.T. auch in Kooperation mit anderen Hochschulen zu entwickeln.

Neben der Verbesserung der internationalen Kompatibilität durch die Einführung dieser neuen Studienstrukturen und Abschlüsse und damit der Verbesserung der Studentenmobilität verfolgt man damit folgende Ziele:

- Einleitung von Studienreformprozessen, Modularisierung, Einführung von Credit Point Systemen, interdisziplinäre, interfakultative Orientierung
- möglichst vielen jungen Menschen mit einem ersten berufsqualifizierenden Abschluss wissenschaftliche Grundlagen für einen erfolgreichen Berufseinstieg zu vermitteln
- realistische Einhaltung von Verweil- und Fachstudienzeiten an den Hochschulen, Verkürzung der Studienzeiten, Verkleinerung der Zahl der Studienabbrecher
- mit einem zweiten Abschluss - bei entsprechender Eignung und Motivation - Optionen zur weiteren fachlichen Vertiefung oder auch zu einer Verbreiterung des Wissens und einer forschungsorientierten Qualifikation zu geben
- Neuorganisation der Schnittstelle Studienabschluss/Weiterbildung durch geeignete Konstruktion der Masterstudiengänge.

So wird klar, dass es bei der Einführung neuer gestufter Abschlüsse nicht nur darum geht, die internationale Kompatibilität herzustellen - dabei spreche ich von Kompatibilität und nicht, was viele offenbar verwechseln, von Kopie - sondern es sind damit eine ganze Reihe notwendiger Studienreformprozesse verbunden, die ich skizziert habe.

Die Hochschule für Bibliotheks- und Informationswesen Stuttgart hat unter der bewährten Leitung ihres langjährigen Rektors, Prof. Dr. Peter Vodosek, mit großem Engagement erfolgreich die Chancen, die diese neuen Möglichkeiten eröffnet haben, genutzt und bietet alternativ zu den Diplomabschlüssen in den Studiengängen Informationswirtschaft sowie Bibliotheks- und Medienmanagement den Bachelorabschluss an. Daneben wurden die Masterstudiengänge Bibliotheks- und Medienmanagement sowie Informationswirtschaft eingerichtet. Damit hat die Hochschule sowohl auf das Interesse der Studienanfänger als vor allem auch auf die Anforderungen eines rasch wachsenden Marktes der multimedialen Internet- und Intranetanwendungen reagiert und sich damit ihre herausragende Stellung gesichert. Besonders bemerkenswert sind auch umfangreiche studienorganisatorische Innovationen. So wird z.B. der Masterstudiengang Bibliotheks- und Medienmanagement in Teilzeit angeboten und ist modular aufgebaut. Ein attraktives Studienangebot ist auch im Masterstudiengang Informationswirtschaft angelegt. Im ersten Studienjahr finden praxisorientierte Seminare statt, die in 7 Module gegliedert sind.

Schlussbemerkung

Gegenwärtig laufen an den deutschen Hochschulen umfangreiche Veränderungsprozesse ab, die durch die neue Hochschulgesetzgebung ausgelöst wurden. In diesem Zusammenhang wird in der Öffentlichkeit auch die Frage intensiv diskutiert, wie der Studienstandort Deutschland verstärkt für ausländische Studenten und Wissenschaftler attraktiver gemacht werden kann. Hintergrund dieser Debatte ist die Tatsache, dass die Anzahl ausländischer Studierender aus einer Reihe von Ländern, vor allem aus denen der wirtschaftlich boomenden asiatisch-pazifischen Region, unterrepräsentiert und stark zurückgegangen ist.

Im Zuge der Novellierung der Hochschulgesetzgebung wurde den deutschen Hochschulen nun die Möglichkeit gegeben, gestufte Studiengangkonzepte mit Bachelor- und Masterabschlüssen zu entwickeln. Dies bietet vor allem den Fachhochschulen, deren Strukturen große Ähnlichkeiten mit dem amerikanischen Studiensystem aufweisen, große Chancen, sich im zunehmenden globalen Wettbewerb der Hochschulen erfolgreich zu positionieren und auch im nationalen Kontext das Verhältnis zu den Universitäten konstruktiv weiterzuentwickeln. Die Hochschule für Bibliotheks- und Informationswesen hat diese

Chancen unter der langjährigen kompetenten Leitung von Herrn Prof. Dr. Vodosek genutzt und damit hervorragende Entwicklungsperspektiven für die bestehenden Studiengänge und hervorragende Berufschancen für die Absolventen in einem sich rasch verändernden Berufsfeld eröffnet.

Franz Berger

Auf dem Weg zu einer europäischen Kooperation bei der Ausbildung der Bibliothekare:

Prolog zu einem Artikel

Die Geschichte begann wie solche Geschichten häufig beginnen. Anfang des Jahres erhielt ich einen Brief des Prorektors der HBI Stuttgart, Prof. Dipl.-Ing. Askan Blum, mit der Ankündigung einer Festschrift für den langjährigen Rektor Prof. Dr. Peter Vodosek, verbunden mit der Einladung, dazu einen Beitrag zu schreiben. Abgabetermin für den Artikel wäre Ende März. Obwohl ich mir noch nicht im klaren war, wie mein Beitrag aussehen sollte, fiel es mir schwer, „Nein“ zu sagen. Denn die Fachhochschule in Stuttgart war im Laufe meiner langjährigen Tätigkeit im Dienst der Südtiroler Bibliotheken zu einem unverzichtbaren Partner bei der Aus- und Fortbildung unserer BibliothekarInnen und bei der Anwerbung von Diplom-BibliothekarInnen aus Deutschland geworden. Außerdem hatte ich Rektor Vodosek bei verschiedenen Anlässen sehr schätzen gelernt. Und schließlich lag der Abgabetermin für den Artikel ja noch in beruhigender Ferne. Bis Ende März würde mir schon etwas einfallen, dachte ich. Und sagte zu.

Dann begann das Brainstorming, das Sammeln, Verfolgen, Abwägen und Verwerfen von Ideen, das zu einem ordnungsgemäßen festschriftwürdigen Beitrag hätte führen sollen. Die Betonung liegt auf „hätte“, denn bis heute - drei Tage vor der Abgabefrist - hat sich das gewünschte Ergebnis noch nicht eingestellt.

Von Anfang an war mir klar, dass ich für diese Festschrift keinen wie immer gearteten gelehrten oder wissenschaftlichen Artikel beisteuern würde, sondern eher einen Beitrag mit Impulscharakter. Ein paar *Thesen* könnte ich formulieren, dachte ich mir. Thesen im Sinne von Postulaten bzw. von Forderungen. Thesen zu einer mehr europäischen Dimension bibliothekarischer Studiengänge und Curricula. Thesen, die auffordern sollten, die bibliothekarische Ausbildung weniger landesbezogen und mehr international als bisher anzulegen. Thesen, die an die steigende länderübergreifende Mobilität von BibliothekarInnen erinnern sollten. Oder an den Bedarf nach qualifizierten mehrsprachigen Fachkräften bei uns und anderswo in Europa. Ich wollte darauf hinweisen, dass neben Auslandspraktika verstärkt auch das Erlernen einer dritten oder vierten europäischen Sprache gefördert werden sollte. Ich wollte sagen, dass eine europäische Landkarte der bibliothekarischen Studiengänge auf Hochschul- und Universitätsebene wünschenswert wäre oder - um eine Modewort zu gebrauchen - ein entsprechendes Portal im Internet. Weiters: SOCRATES-Programme für Studierende im Bereich des Bibliothekswesens, Kooperationsabkommen mit Universitäten und Hochschulen in anderen europäischen Ländern, spezielle Jobbörsen für mehrsprachige und an Auslandsaufenthalten interessierten BibliothekarInnen usw.

Die Idee mit den Thesen hielt nicht lange. Denn schon bald wurde mir klar, dass ich einfach nicht den Überblick hatte, um zum Bereich der bibliothekarischen Ausbildung in Europa etwas einigermaßen Repräsentatives und Zukunftsweisendes sagen zu können. So schwächte ich die Idee ab und überlegte mir, ob es nicht besser wäre, einfach nur ein paar *Überlegungen oder Vorschläge zu einer engeren europäischen Kooperation* auf dem genannten Gebiet zu formulieren, und zwar *auf dem Hintergrund der diesbezüglichen Ent-*

wicklungen und Bestrebungen in Italien. Ich wußte, dass in Italien aufgrund der 1999 beschlossenen einschneidenden Universitätsreform überall an einer Neuordnung der Studiengänge gearbeitet wird. Eine gute Gelegenheit - dachte ich mir -, um an einigen Universitäten, die auch Studiengänge im Bereich des Bibliothekswesens anbieten, nachzufragen, in welcher Weise bei der Konzipierung der neuen Studiengänge eine europäische Orientierung ins Auge gefasst würde. Ich besprach diese neue Idee mit einer Kollegin, die an der Università della Tuscia in Viterbo Bibliothekswissenschaften studiert hatte, wurde von ihr in diesem Vorhaben bestärkt und erbat von einigen bekannten Professoren der italienischen Bibliotheksszene, tätig an den Universitäten La Sapienza/Rom, Viterbo und Venedig, Auskünfte und Meinungen zu dieser Thematik. Alle antworteten schnell und ziemlich einheitlich auf meine Mail: „Wir sind gerade dabei, im Sinne der Universitätsreform die neuen Studienordnungen für die verschiedenen Studiengänge zu erarbeiten. Im Bereich Bibliothekswesen planen wir dreijährige Laureatsstudiengänge in Archiv- und Bibliothekswissenschaften (d.h. Grundstudiengänge, die zur ‚laurea' führen) sowie – darauf aufbauend – zweijährige Fachlaureatstudiengänge (‚laurea specialistica')." Fallweise werden – so wurde mir vermittelt - auch Studiengänge für das Forschungsdoktorat geplant sowie universitäre Masterkurse, die gemäß Universitätsreform in Italien nicht zu einem akademischen Grad führen, sondern den Rang von berufsspezifischen Fortbildungsmaßnahmen haben. Wie die Studienpläne konkret aussehen werden, ist noch unklar, wird sich aber an den meisten Studienorten bis zum Sommer klären, da ab diesem Herbst die Reform greifen soll. Eines wurde mir bei meinen Recherchen klar: Die Universitätsreform führt einerseits zu einer stärkerer didaktischen Planungsautonomie der Universitäten und Fakultäten. Andererseits erscheint durch die Vorgabe von Laureatsklassen mit teilweise verbindlichen Disziplinen in manchen Fällen der Spielraum für innovative arbeitsmarktorientierte Studiengänge doch sehr eingeschränkt. Dies gilt vor allem für die bibliothekarischen Grundstudiengänge, die in der Laureatsklasse Wissenschaften der Kulturgüter angesiedelt sein werden und sich daher schwer tun dürften, wichtigen neuen Fächern in den Bereichen Management, Neue Medien und Informationstechnologien gebührend Raum zu geben. Anders sieht es auf der Stufe der Fachlaureatsstudiengänge (auch Studiengänge der zweiten Ebene genannt) aus. Hier bietet u.a. die Laureatsklasse Techniken und Methoden für die Informationsgesellschaft ein verheißungsvolles Zuhause für moderne Informations- und Bibliotheksmanagement-Studiengänge. Und der größte Gestaltungsfreiraum wird bei den Masterkursen gegeben sein, sowohl hinsichtlich der Inhalte als auch der Kooperationsformen. Und hier dürften italienische Universitäten, wie sich schon ankündigt, auch ihr ganzes kreatives Potential für universitäts- und länderübergreifende Projekte ausspielen.

Damit aber zurück zu meiner Geschichte. Ich musste erkennen, dass die bibliothekarischen Ausbildungsstätten an italienischen Universitäten zur Zeit ganz mit der Umsetzung der Universitätsreform im eigenen Hause beschäftigt sind und sich daher derzeit nicht große Gedanken über Kooperationen auf europäischer Ebene machen können. Ich verstand aber auch, dass sie dabei sind, ein durch und durch europäisch geprägtes System einzuführen, mit dem Stufenmodell 3+2, mit der Einführung von Studienguthaben und mit einer stärkeren didaktischen Autonomie – alles ganz im Sinne der Gemeinsamen Erklärung der Europäischen Wissenschaftsminister vom 19. Juni 1999 in Bologna. Und schließlich begriff ich, dass es noch verfrüht ist, in einem Beitrag für eine Festschrift auf dem Hintergrund der noch unübersehbaren Entwicklungen in Italien konkrete Vorschläge und Überlegungen für eine europäische Kooperation bei der bibliothekarischen Ausbildung auf Hochschulebene zu formulieren. Und so musste ich auch diese Idee fallen lassen.

Inzwischen stand die Studienfahrt der HBI Stuttgart nach Südtirol vor der Tür, in deren Rahmen für den 21. März 2001 vormittags auch ein Besuch der Freien Universität Bozen und insbesondere der Universitätsbibliothek sowie ein Gespräch über Möglichkeiten einer künftigen Zusammenarbeit auf dem Programm standen. Diese Begegnung würde mich sicher auf die rettende Idee für meinen Beitrag bringen, so dachte ich. Und so war es auch. Das Wiedersehen mit Professoren, die auf Fortbildungsseminaren und Ausbildungslehrgängen in Südtirol im Einsatz waren (Prof. Nagl und Prof. Jülkenbeck), das Gespräch mit Rektor Vodosek, Dekanin Jülkenbeck, Prof. Hütter und Verwaltungsdirektor Marquardt, in dem Visionen und Pläne für kurz- und mittelfristige Kooperationen entworfen wurden, weckte in mir Erinnerungen und Träume. Und so war ich gar nicht überrascht, als mir nach der anschließenden Bahnfahrt nach Florenz, auf der ich die neuesten Informationsmaterialien der HBI durchgelesen und Strategien für eine künftige intensivere Zusammenarbeit angedacht hatte, folgende kühne Idee kam: Schreib doch für diese Festschrift eine *Chronik über 50 Jahre Bibliotheksachse Bozen – Stuttgart bzw. Südtiroler Bibliothekswesen und HBI Stuttgart*! Beginn mit dem Jahr 1976, in dem du auf deiner bibliothekarischen Einstiegs-Rundreise durch Deutschland das erste Mal die „Villa“ auf der Feuerbacher Heide besucht hast, und ende mit dem Jahr 2025, in dem die Freie Universität Bozen und die Hochschule der Medien Stuttgart (oder ihre Nachfolgeinstitution) zusammen mit ihren europäischen, amerikanischen und japanischen Partnern das fünfjährige Bestehen von OSOLEMIO (**O**nline **S**chool **O**f **L**ibrarianship **E**diting **M**edia **I**nformation & Communication.) feiern! Die Idee einer „Chronik“ über 25 vergangene Jahre und ebensoviel Zukunft reizte mich. Was sollte da hineinkommen? Natürlich die Besuche in Stuttgart, allein und mit Südtiroler Studiengruppen, die HBI-Studienfahrten nach Südtirol, der Einsatz von Professoren der HBI bei unseren Seminaren – insbesondere bei den Seminarblöcken im Rahmen des Lehrganges für Bibliothekare und Buchhändler - , dann als wichtige Station das Studium von Südtiroler StudentInnen an der HBI ab 1993, damit verbunden die Zusammenarbeit mit dem Praktikantenamt, die Kontakte mit der HBI-Akademie, die Mails an die HBI-Jobbörse zwecks Anwerbung von Diplom-BibliothekarInnen u.a. Und dann vor allem auch die künftigen Stationen der Zusammenarbeit aufgrund einer Kooperationsvereinbarung zwischen der Freien Universität Bozen und der HBI Stuttgart: ab Herbst 2001 absolvieren mehrere StudentInnen ihr Praktikumssemester an der UB Bozen; die Hochschule der Medien Stuttgart wirbt ab 2002 mit einem Stand in geeignetem Rahmen (z.B. Open day der Universität) in Bozen; ab 200x gemeinsamer Masterstudiengang; ab 200y Kooperation bei Grundstudiengängen; ab 200z weitere Schritte...

Nach der Rückkehr von der Academic-Press-Tagung in Florenz trat die Ernüchterung ein. Wie sollte ich eine Chronik schreiben, wenn ich die meisten Daten nicht mehr genau wusste? Ich hatte ja diese Unterlagen vor zwei Jahren im Amt für Bibliothekswesen zurückgelassen. Zum genauen Recherchieren brauchte ich Zeit, die ich jetzt nicht hatte. Und an die Zukunft mit der Arbeitsweise eines Chronisten herangehen? Nein, das ist doch nicht zielführend!

So fasste ich Mut und warf auch diese dritte Idee eines Beitrages für die Festschrift zu Ehren von Rektor Vodosek in den Papierkorb. Es war mir nun klar, dass nie ein ordentlicher Artikel zustande kommen würde. Daher setzte ich mich hin und schrieb einfach nur diesen *Prolog*. Und die frei gewordene Zeit verwendete ich, um für die Universitätsleitung einen Bericht über den HBI-Besuch und Überlegungen zur Kooperation zwischen Freier Universität Bozen und HBI-Stuttgart zu schreiben, um den Rektor auf eine Kooperationsvereinbarung mit der HBI einzustimmen, um die rechtlichen Voraussetzungen für die Zusammenarbeit bei Studiengängen zu studieren...

Schreiben ist gut, Handeln ist besser. Lang lebe die Kooperation mit der HBI Stuttgart (oder wie immer sie in Zukunft heißen mag) und mit ihrem geschätzten bisherigen Rektor Prof. Dr. Peter Vodosek!

Mihály Pálvölgyi and Mária Kovács

Twelve years of co-operation HBI Stuttgart - BDF KIT Szombathely

The Stuttgart inspiration

The aim of this contribution is to give a brief summary of the 12-year relationship between HBI and the LIS Department in Szombathely, to analyse the development of the ties between the two colleges. Special attention is honoured to Professor Dr. Peter Vodosek, who has always been an initiator and supporter of this bilateral relationship that grew into multilateral co-operation between 1994-97 in the frames of the LISTEN TEMPUS JEP.

How did it start?

As Professor Vodosek put in his article (Vodosek, 1997) after the collapse of regimes in Eastern Europe it came to a number of exploration tours from East to West to make contacts to LIS schools in Western Europe. The relationship between the two colleges started through the visit of Dr. Maria Kovács to Stuttgart in June 1989, which was returned by Prof. Vodosek visit to Szombathely on 7-11 October 1990. In November 1990 it came to signing a bilateral contract by the heads of partner schools, Prof. Dr. Peter Vodosek and Dr. Gyula Tóth.

The bilateral contract

According to the contract the German partner undertook supplying Hungarian colleagues with information, publications, and professional guidelines as regards Western European, and German LIS developments, providing information on FHB - Fachhochschule für Bibliothekswesen curricula, and allowing access to their teaching materials.

It was decided to help Hungarian staff and students in order to adapt to European standards of LIS training and education. Stuttgart undertook offering support to Hungarian staff and students in applying for DAAD scholarships, too.

The Hungarian partner undertook studying the German LIS curriculum, and working on preparing a proposal for TEMPUS support, organising study trips of German staff and students to Hungary, as well as writing surveys about Hungarian LIS development issues in German to inform the German partners. It was decided that joint projects and exchange of publications be promoted.

Following the contract

The first support from FHB came right in December 1990, when Professor Vodosek offered expert advice on the curriculum development, contributing to the implementation of a new curriculum in Szombathely in 1992. From 1991 on it came to visits by many professors from Stuttgart (Peter Vodosek, Andreas Papendieck, Wolfram Henning, Ingeborg

Spribille, Susanne Krüger ...) to Szombathely to give guest lectures, or participate in conferences and in return Hungarian staff and students were hosted through study tours. In 1994 Mária Kovács received a one-month scholarship from HBI to investigate the topic „social work in library".

The first study trip ...

Invited by HBI to visit the partner school in Stuttgart, a group study tour was organised in June 21-27 1992 by 3 professors and 8 students from Szombathely, to strengthen the relationships, and visit selected libraries and other institutions in Stuttgart and Stuttgart region: Stadtbücherei Stuttgart, Universitätsbibliothek, Zentralbibliothek IBM Deutschland, Bibliothek des Amerikahauses, Rechenzentrum und AV-Medienzentrum der Hochschule, Württembergische Landesbibliothek, Einkaufszentrale für Bibliotheken. Professional discussions with German colleagues was integrated in the programme too.

Another one-week study trip by 10 Hungarian students and one professor was supported later by DAAD, which was strongly supported intellectually by the German partner, focusing on school library and media centres in Germany. This trip in 1997 helped acquainted with new models of school library and media centres to become a tool of pedagogical repertoire.

The first joint seminar

The contacts culminated in a seminar organised in October 3 - to 7 1994 in Szombathely with the generous support of the Stuttgart college about the incorporation of new information technology into the LIS training. A team of 6 dedicated German colleagues was organised by Prof. Askan Blum to share their knowledge in database searching, online searching, and CD-ROM, and also donated a number of professional materials.

EUCLID AND BOBCATSSS - together in the big family of LIS schools

Through HBI Szombathely was integrated into the foundation of such international cooperation scheme as EUCLID, and also BOBCATSSS that meant the co-operation of Budapest, Oslo, Barcelona, Copenhagen, Amsterdam, Tampere, Stuttgart, Sheffield and Szombathely. The annual BOBCATSSS symposia organised in Budapest by the Dutch partners offered a wonderful opportunity for exchanging training, research and education results for both students and staff of European LIS schools.

The memorable years of TEMPUS

Based on close co-operation with the Hochschule für Bibliotheks- und Informationswesen (Stuttgart), Royal School of Librarianship (Copenhagen), The Robert Gordon University, School of Information and Media (Aberdeen) De Montfort University (Leicester), and with the LIS Department of Nyíregyháza, and 3 Hungarian libraries (in Budapest, Veszprém and Zalaegerszeg) a TEMPUS proposal was submitted by BDTF in 1994, and approved by Brussels.

The 4 major aims of the project (1994-97) were to build up basic computer infrastructure for LIS training at the LIS departments in Szombathely, and Nyíregyháza, integrate modern IT into LIS course teaching, to modernise the programme of education, develop a new curriculum that is in harmony with European requirements, furthermore to introduce new special courses in business information, and user education.

An important aspect of the LISTEN TEMPUS programme was the East-West mobility for students and staff of the participating institutions.

Its aim was to create the basic infrastructure needed for the education and training of librarians and information professionals, to modernise the programme of education, to facilitate the effective use of information technology in education,

TEMPUS project intensified staff and student mobility; e.g. teachers from Stuttgart came to Szombathely, (Margaret Payer.) offer expert advice in teaching methods, and course development. Hungarian teachers had the opportunity to spend one week to visit HBI, and libraries in and around Stuttgart to study curriculum and courses in action, the learning environments, the work placement co-operation schemes between HBI and libraries

The study tours of Hungarian staff members to Stuttgart in 1996 proofed to be very successful, and German staff kept on providing professional advice, e.g. Prof. Margarete Payer in 1997 in issues of the bibliographic description of electronic documents.

The new curriculum developed at Stuttgart in 1995 was translated into Hungarian, and in addition to British and Danish partners's ideas it served as a model reflected in the new LIS curriculum implemented in 1997 in Szombathely and Nyíregyháza.

Student mobility was carried out in the third year of the project, covering 15 months mobility grant for East-West mobility and 5 months mobility grant provided for West-East mobility.

Out of the 11 students 5 went to Germany: Hajnalka Czimondor), Hajnalka Vécsei and Andrea Vaskó spent one month in the Stuttgart area in practical training, Tímea Makrai had a 4-week work placement at Stuttgart UNI-Bibliothek, and Gabriella Magyar went also to Germany to gathered materials for her thesis about Beutel books. The other 6 Hungarian students went either to Copenhagen, Aberdeen, or Leicester. As regards West-East mobility out of the 5 Western students it was Sonia Schmidt from Stuttgart to come Hungary to have her practical training in Spring 1997 at Kôszeg Town Library, and also Vas County Library (both libraries with good German collections).

The TEMPUS project culminated in June 1997 an international closing conference held in Szombathely, with 130 participants, an East-West forum for exchanging thoughts and experiences concerning the development of the education and training of librarians and information professionals.

Hungarian students to study in Stuttgart from 1993/1994 to 2000/2001

Through the generous support from HBI and DAAD it became possible for Szombathely to send one or more students to Stuttgart for studying there for autumn semesters. Hungarian students had to prepare applications for the scholarships, and the best and happy ones were selected based on earlier study achievements, LIS skills, German language skills, as well as on the quality of study plans in Stuttgart. On a whole linguistic capabilities of most Hungarian students were satisfactory, as in addition to passing at least a medium level state exam, they had thorough preparation in a Special German for Librarians course having its roots back in the 1980s. (Pálvölgyi, Mihály - Tóth, Györgyi)

Study Year	Names of Hungarian students to study at HBI
1991/92	Hajnalka Németh, Thyra Takács
1992/93	-
1993/94	Anita Belovári, Hajnalka Stenger
1994/95	Zoltán Balogh, Emese Pluhár
1995/96	Hajnalka Czimondor, Judit Fazekas, Márta Pöcze, Hajnalka Vécsei
1996/97	Zsuzsa Garisa, Tímea Makrai, Krisztina Németh
1997/98	Anna Forgó
1998/99	Katalin Bagi
1999/2000	Bettina Daka, Hajnalka Mátyás
2000/2001	Ágnes Bognár, Ildikó Szabó

The major study aims formulated by Hungarian students in their proposals included getting acquainted with German library practice and theory, updating computer skills, developing German language skills, studying courses up to their interests or not taught in Hungary, and last but not least, working on their projects and theses.

The practicalities of scholarship

After approving the scholarship usually in June, the Hungarian students had to apply for and receive their visa. In right time they got all the necessary preliminary information as regards accommodation and contact information from Stuttgart. On arriving to Stuttgart (usually by overnight buses) in early Octobers they were received, accompanied to hostel by a HBI student. Most of them still had one week prior to starting the semester, and could explore the city of Stuttgart and surroundings, supplied with a package they got (including scholarship, guide to lectures and seminars, city map, with interesting sights).

Our students were mostly accommodated in Stuttgart- Vaihingen, in a student hostel, in an area with nice parks, lakes about, and the friendly and familiar atmosphere at the hostel was reflected in their study reports as comfortable, memorable. (as Bettina Daka puts in her final report). One week or so before the studies started, they could very well feel at home in the hostel, each student having a room of her/his own, but gathering at kitchen for cooking, chatting, watch TV, play cards, etc. (Katalin Bagi)

In getting adjusted to the quite new environment it was good to have a student of Hungarian origin there for many years - Ferenc Becker - with a kind and helpful attitude.

The introductory orientation programme

The introductory week for first year students was very positively reflected in the reports, of Hungarian students, being greeted by HBI leaders Prof. Vodosek, Prof. Spribille, Prof. Roos, Prof. Blum, Prof. Kuhlemann, and also by senior LIS students, to have a clear, straightforward, and motivating information as regards important aspects of study and student life. All the reports refer to the good organisation emphasise helpfulness, and friendly atmosphere of the introductory week for college freshmen.

The Hungarians were integrated into the foreign students group, the number of students varying year by year from 7 to 14 and could study and have fun together with students from other parts of Europe: South Tyrol, Italy, France, Greece, Russia, Latvia, and sometimes also from other continents, like Brazil. To have a get-acquainted evening at the very beginning, and have talks with each other.

The introduction of the new „reformed" curriculum in Stuttgart and the growth of the college and participating in an international conference

4 Hungarian students (Hajnalka Vécsei witnessed the transition period 95/96 from the old curriculum to the new one, new reformed curriculum, that characterised new media, new information technology use which was very useful from the point of Hungarian students.

It was the first years basic study, with about 80 % computer application, (as Judit Fazekas put in her report). Hajnalka Vécsei emphasised how much she liked Information technology Informationstechniken. (Prof. Blum)

Four of our students could witness (Hajnalka Czimondor, Hajnalka Vécsei, Judit Fazekas, Márta Pöcze) the landmark international *conference „Informationsspezalisten zwischen Technik und gesellschaftlicher Verantwortung"* organised in HBI, by Prof. Blum and Prof. Spribille, and a number of devoted students. December 4-5 1995 with lots of interesting lectures and forums. They realised the tremendous work invested into the one year of preparation, and emphasise its importance in strengthening the links between students, teachers, and theoretical and practical professionals. Hajnalka Vécsei remembers the „*Podiumsdiskussion*", where among other participants she could speak about her possible future job opportunities, problems of and new opportunities for Hungarian libraries in the new circumstances, and had to answer three questions from the audience.

Our students could witness the growth of the college in students' numbers, and in growing diversity of course offers. The emphasis on self-motivation in course seledtion and participation made a real effect on the Hungarian students.

Cultural touring of Germany

> *„Studieren an der HBI. Ein fach- und landeskundliches Seminar für ausländische und interessierte deutsche Studierende (mit Exkursion)"*

„Prof. Kuhlemann took care of us" - is a standard ingredient of each Hungarian student's study report. In fact, Prof. Kuhlemann and other staff did their best for our students to make feel them well, including organising a get-acquainted dinner for the members of foreign student group, giving presentations about German culture, organising excursions to wonderful cities in South Germany. Munich, Reutlingen (EKZ Einkaufszentrale für Bibliotheken), Heidelberg (the university town, old town, university library), Tübingen. Nürnberg, Freiburg and Strasbourg and other cities are also mentioned with living memory. These study tours were very well organised, always having a guide (often HBI-alumni), to make the programme interesting, useful, and concise. The idea of organising a tour to the Frankfurt Book Fair in 1999 (with Hungary in focus) was warmly reflected in Hungarian reports.

Our students could see libraries in action, admire the treasures of museums and galleries, or and be involved in fascinating sight-seeing.

The courses Hungarian students took

„It was difficult for me, to compile a plan because there were so many interesting courses and many of them were offered at the same time". It was not easy, but Hugarian students tried. There were altogether 42 different courses Hungarian students took part (including both core courses and electives!)

They included „standard" courses, all of them participated in („Studieren an der HBI. Ein fach- und landeskundliches Seminar für Ausländische Studierende") or visited by many of them (Einführung in Studium und Praxis, Einführung in die Praxis - including visits to public and scientific libraries, Multimediale Kommunikation: Informationstechnische (IT Grundlagen Textverarbeitung und Gestaltung - Word for Windows, Netzwerkmanagement, Arbeits-, Lern- und Präsentationstechniken etc.), English as foreign language, and courses up to the special interests of individual students (Frauenbilder im Film, Einführung in HTML, CD-ROM Angebote in Grossstadtbibliotheken, Medium in Jugendalltag (Jugendkulturen, Kunst- und Museumsbibliotheken etc.)

Although Hungarian students appreciated the efforts of lecturers to make their lectures inviting, and interesting, the most living memories are from learning by doing. The seminars and lab sessions supplied a lot of experiences for them.

Work, study and presentations techniques was very popular, because it was found application oriented, and they could test all methods, classes were very interesting, sometimes they even forgot they are at class. In fact, practically oriented dynamic courses, offering lots of practical experiences, e.g. in solving problems in Information Retrieval, were found memorable. Courses integrating visits to libraries were referred to as lively, and memorable, e.g. Periodicals in the library, Bibliotheksarbeit mit Jugendlichen and other courses also conveyed new impulses, instructions, and experiences to students.

The seminars and sessions they participated in were a good combination of theory and practice, with a lot of application, presentation and evaluation.

Hajnalka Vécsei appreciated that students were also involved into holding seminars, e.g. about Netzwerkmanagement (in Prof. Payer's class)

The Hungarian students appreciated that they were treated as „normal" students, and were also challenged to contribute. In fact, they were actively involved, in seminars, e.g. Bettina Daka and Hajnalka Mátyás, studied and presented an Italian language teaching CD for the Study with new media, theories, concepts, and examples course taught by Prof. Kuhlemann.

Or Hajnalka Mátyás gave a presentation about the system of school system in Hungary, LIS training, and school library situation in Prof. Papendiecks seminar.

Although Hungarian students did not get marks at Stuttgart, the work they invest into seminars, and lab sessions will be awarding, and it is much easier to complete the related course in Hungary.

Work placement

The very efficient work placement system was often referred to by Hungarian students, as Hajnalka Mátyás was amazed by the German way of taking work placement very seriously, noting that German students are very well motivated for that and are aware of the fact, that is a very important step in building their future careers. In fact, they have a separate semester for that. They have to sit for job interview, writes a letter, present them. The libraries also take it very serious, in hoping to find the best applicants for a given period. It was a great experience for Ildikó Szabó and Ágnes Bognár to take their work placement in the College Library in the autumn semester 2000.

Training materials and access to information and learning resources

Our students appreciated the student and study-centred approach of the College, supplying students with *scripts, course materials* (Bettina Daka) Scripts were always supplied, thus we could have a logical, structured approach to follow the lectures, and seminars (Hajnalka Mátyás)

Drawing our attention that on the Intranet all documents can be accessed, and downloaded, and printed free of charge. (Katalin Bagi), We got all materials of all topics, and copies of related literature, Popular Genres of the Media (Populäre Genren der Medien) ... (Tímea Makrai)

They appreciated the very *strong media presence in education.* Media in youth everyday life/youth culture, integrated a lot of diverse activities, where a lot of media were presented, films projected, etc., and I also could prepare a presentation on the importance of computer, strengths, weaknesses, and use with young people. (Bettina Daka)

The IT-element was found very intensive:

E-mailing was great, all the necessary information was circulating via e-mail, and one could find a place for that in the lab with 15 PCs for especially that purpose (Katalin Bagi). It helped me be up-to-date with important developments at College, and keep contact, and discuss everything important with my group mates and friends (she adds). A rapid communication medium for students and teachers as well, questions can be asked via e-mail, as well (Bettina)

We spent about 60 % of our time with computers, studied word processing intensively during the very first week (Bagi)

Opportunity for online learning was heartily welcome. The whole subject is available, online, and can be printed. The students selected topics for working on, elaborating, and adding to hypertext, with literature, and links, was written as referring to the Informationsnetze, Kommunikationstechnik, Netzwerkmanagement course. It was very nice, too, to have Hungarian language version of the Stuttgart homepage, due to the fact that there has always been Hungarian students there.

Joining libraries, individual study

The library is mentioned by most students are the Frauenbibliothek, always open, no librarian is watching, everybody can get in, check out, or just read about. Reliability, familiarity are keywords, books are on open access, there is a copying machine in the corridor you can take books out and copy if you want (Katalin Bagi). Absolutely confidence (writes Bettina Daka, too)

Many Hungarian students mention joining other libraries, too to work on their individual projects, and thesis. Many of them became being library members in Stuttgart at many libraries for the time of their studies (Stadtbücherei, Württembergische Landesbibliothek, Uni-Bibliothek, (e.g. Tímea Makrai, Bettina Daka)

Relaxation and free time activities

The *spacious club area* in the ground floor in Wolframstraße, where you can sit down, read about, acquire a lot of information about theatre, cinema, concerts, travelling, job opportunities, etc. and select was memorable (Katalin Bagi) Opportunity for relaxed communication, ad nice place

They could join *facultative associations,* lively friendly companies - in the area of films, philosophy, women, periodicals. Katalin Bagi also participated in editing of HBI-ZAK, Zeitung Angewandter Kreativität, and wrote about her experiences at the college and Stuttgart, (Bagi, Katalin, Als Gaststudentin an der HBI, 1998. January) *Cultural events, and parties* were also found exciting: „I loved book presentations, literature evenings, lectures about libraries" (Bettina Daka).

„Out of the student parties many students mentioned was by many Hungarian students was the memorable Film Nacht the Villa, where films were projected the whole night. It was a phantastic epxerience to see films films projected for fans for 12 hours of time in three different rooms simultaneously". (Katalin Bagi)

Most Hungarian students opened up in hearts and made good friends both at *the hostel and the school,* participated in communication events, parties, tasted foods of different nations, and had also lots of fun: cooking, table football, billiard championships, different parties (goulash party etc., birthday party, farewell party etc) in the hostel, in different Stuttgart restaurants, (e.g. the Griechisches Restaurant), and pubs (e.g. the Irish pub) (Tímea Makrai)

The *Wanderlust* was motivated in many Hungarian students, and they set for trips on weekends to explore Ludwigsburg, and small towns about, to gather experiences and memories of beautiful churches, castles, cloisters, old town halls, square, old roads, etc. (Katalin Bagi). The special atmosphere of the Stuttgart *Weihnachtsmarkt* is also reflected in her study report.

A summary of the inspirations and experiences our students got from Stuttgart

What have been the greatest experiences in Germany? What did our students emphasise in their report?

The positive human attitude

As Hajnalka Czimondor put: the German students were friendly, they talked to us willingly, and it was nice to communicate, teachers were also very helpful and supportive.

The helping attitude of students and teachers is often referred to. „Good group atmosphere, good organisation, helpful, and friendly people, and wonderful places. Got in friendship, with quite a few students, and also teachers, and also outside, and still keep contact. Anna Forgó,

Being involved

The fact that they were intensively involved in courses, and test their growing professional and language skills in presentations, too. In fact they left a „part of themselves" in Stuttgart, e.g. Tímea Makrai by developing a personal homepage, (http://machno.hbi.stutttgart.de/~babo), and helping in building up a server (Babylon). For many of our students it was an inspiring experience to see modern media centre in action, to see an Internet connection in a library (at a time it was still not possible in Hungary) and get involved in activities. In addition being involved in cultural experiences (cinema, theatre, and opera) was very memorable (Ildikó Szabó, Ágnes Bognár).

Growing personally

One thing we could realise at once the change in their attitude, they have become more independent in behaviour, and selection, more self-confident. „ I could gather a lot of professional and personal experiences." (Anna Forgó)

Being dropped into another culture

„It was exciting and interesting to be dropped into another culture, and compare experiences, and knowledge with new impressions. I have become more tolerant, more self-confident, made friends. The experiences I could gather are unforgettable from both professional and human point of view" (Hajnalka Mátyás)

Thank you very much, HBI, DAAD, and LIS Department for the support, for the best period of my life. I could become more independent and gather experiences for lifetime. The 4 months in Stuttgart allowed me to grow both professionally and also personally. Thank you (Katalin Bagi).

Adaptation and dissemination of „Stuttgart experiences" in Hungary

Experiences have been adapted both by Hungarian staff and students. In the frames of the LISTEN TEMPUS project (1994-97) the LIS curriculum at HBI was reviewed, and some major study documents translated. In fact, the new Hungarian LIS curriculum introduced in 1997 in Szombathely and Nyíregyháza can owe a lot to EU partners, (Copenhagen, Aberdeen, Leicester and Stuttgart). Some major features of the Stuttgart model were adapted, including the concept of information management, the incorporation of media into the curriculum, the idea of having a basic module, introducing students into study and work techniques and methods, professional practice, the idea of having an Information and society module, and a Management module, and introduce specialisations, in Szombathely we have now the offer in public librarianship, school librarianship, information management and information brokerage. (Information management, 1999)

In addition, some major articles written by German partners have been translated into Hungarian to appear in leading LIS periodicals. (Vodosek, 1991) (Vodosek,1992) (Papendieck, 1999). giving new inspirations to Hungarians in different aspects of library and information science education and practice. The linguistic inspiration (developing multilingual skills) and the humanistic inspiration (integration of classic and modern values) are especially worth mentioning.

Professor Vodosek invited us to write articles either in German or English to appear in leading LIS periodicals in Germany. (Tóth, 1992) (Pálvölgyi, 2000).

Elaboration and dissemination of study experiences through students

A number of ideas were raised by our students after returning home, including

- „It would be good if DAAD could support a whole study year, so that we could test our knowledge sitting for a real exam" (Tímea Makrai).
- „It would be fine to start a help-desk service at our school in Hungary, too" (Hajnalka Czimondor).
- „It would be fine to have a separate practical semester in Hungary, too" (Hajnalka Mátyás).
- „It would be good to have open computer labs, where you can stay and work" (Katalin Bagi.

Some of these ideas could be realised (new lab, help-desk), some are unfortunately not possible because of the double-major system in Hungary (separate practical semester), and some we have got to try in the future (to spend a whole study year or a whole semester in each other's schools).

The students coming back shared their experiences in Stuttgart through presentations to other students in Szombathely, including also the Students day, that is held once a year and always had a lot of impact on the audience, and through articles to appear either in college media, or even published in national LIS periodicals, like that of Katalin Bagi's very impressive report of her staying in Stuttgart.

It was mentioned that Hungarian students - as a part of their duties - worked also on their projects and theses in Stuttgart. Some of the most successful theses having been prepared so far are:

- Hajnalka Vécsei: German, English-Hungarian terminology of Librarianship.
- Hajnalka Czimondor (Information sources and services of German language study on the Internet.
- Bettina Daka: German-English-Hungarian Web-dictionary of library and information terminology, also paying attention to student life, studies and IT terminology in hope of intensify European student mobility.
- Katalin Bagi: Access to German language LIS electronic periodicals.

Student mobility perspectives

Efforts have to be made now in Hungary to offer inviting study programmes for students from our partner schools in the frames of the ERASMUS project. We are in the process of compiling professionally and personally rewarding programmes, in close co-operation with other departments of Berzsenyi College, with major libraries, and European information and documentation centres, to allow students from partner schools to get acquainted with Hungarian library/information and media sector.

Dear partners in Stuttgart, dear Professor Vodosek. Thank you for your partnership!

Bibliography

(Pálvölgyi, 1996) Deutschkurs für Bibliothekarstudenten. Experimentelles Lehrbuch. /Mihály Pálvölgyi. Szombathely, Berzsenyi Dániel Tanárképző Főiskola, Könyvtár Informatikai Tanszék, 1996.

(Papendieck, 1999) Papendieck, Andreas : Az iskolai könyvtárügy Németországban. Translated by Mihály Pálvölgyi. In: Az elmélet és valóság kontrasztja. Az iskolai könyvtári konferencia előadásai. Edited by Mária Kovács. Szombathely: Berzsenyi Dániel Főiskola, 1999. 60-68.p. (School librarianship in Germany).

(Tóth, 1992) Tóth Gyula: „...nicht nur sehr früh gestorben, sondern auch zu früh geboren Erwin Szabó (1887-1918) : Anwalt eines modernes öffentlichen Bibliothekwesens in Ungarn / Tóth Gyula ; ford.- In: Buch und Bibliothek ISSN 0340-0301. - Bd. 44. Hft.Nr. 3. (1992), p. 221-229.

(Vodosek, 1991) Vodosek, Peter: A német könyvtárügy történeti gyökerei, jelenlegi helyzete, távlatai / Peter Vodosek ; Transl by Mihály Pálvölgyi. In: Könyvtáros ISSN 0450-7886. - 41. évf. 4. sz. (1991), p. 225-229. (Historic roots, present situation and perspectives of German librarianship)

(Vodosek, 1992) Vodosek, Peter. „Képzés - európai keretben" / Peter Vodosek ; ford. - In: Tudományos és műszaki tájékoztatás ISSN 0041-3917. -39. évf. 9. sz. (1992), p. 384-387. (Bildung im Europäischen Rahmen)

(Vodosek, 1997) Vodosek, Peter: Leistungsfähige Computer für ungarische Hochschulen. In: HBI Aktuell, Ausgabe 2/1997.

(Vodosek, 1997) Vodosek, Peter: Renewing the Education and Training of Librarians and Information Professionals. In: Closing Conference of LISTEN TEMPUS JEP (1994-97). Edited by Péter Murányi. Szombathely, Berzsenyi Dániel Teacher Training College, 1997.

Ole Harbo

Von der Fachhochschule zur Universität

Die Entwicklung der Dänischen Bibliothekshochschule
Übersetzung: Dr. Ursel und Ulrich Bracher

1. Einleitung

Der erste Kursus für dänische Volksbibliothekare wurde im Sommer 1909 in der Volkshochschule von Vejlby bei Aarhus abgehalten. Er stand in Verbindung mit der sogenannten „Landesausstellung", in der unter anderem eine Musterbibliothek für einen Ort mit Eisenbahnanschluss gezeigt wurde und auch das erste dänische allgemeine Bibliothekstreffen stattfand.

Der wichtigste Lehrer des Kurses war Andreas Schack Steenberg (1845 - 1929), der große Pionier des Volksbibliothekswesens, der sein ganzes Erwachsenenleben hindurch für die Sache der Volksbibliotheken eintrat. Er war als Sohn dänischer Eltern in Altona geboren, das damals noch zum dänischen Königreich gehörte, und machte seine erste Bekanntschaft mit den englischen und amerikanischen Volksbibliotheken beim Lesen des Buches des österreichischen Pioniers Edw. Reyers über Volksbibliotheken von 1893.

1899 wurde er Mitglied des „Komitees zur Unterstützung der Büchersammlung für die Volksbibliotheken", das die geringen staatlichen Zuschüsse an die Volksbibliotheken verteilte, und ab 1910 wurde er zum Leiter des Unternehmens eingesetzt, das jetzt „Staatliches Komitee für die Büchersammlung" hieß.

Er hielt in den darauffolgenden Jahren Kurse auf privater Basis ab, oft mit Unterstützung seiner Tochter Jeanette. Sie war die erste Dänin, die 1908 - 09 eine amerikanische Bibliothekarausbildung erhielt. Am 1.12.1917 beschloss das Büchersammlungs-Komitee die Errichtung einer eigentlichen Bibliotheksschule, deren Aktivität vor allem vom Staat finanziert wurde. Als durch das erste Volksbibliotheksgesetz 1920 die staatliche Bibliotheksbehörde entstand, wurde die Schule dieser unterstellt. Ihr erster Leiter wurde Sven Dahl (1887 - 1963), damals Bibliotheksinspekteur, aber seit 1943 der erste Reichsbibliothekar des Landes.

Von 1920 bis 1956 unterstand die Schule der Bibliotheksbehörde, in der die Unterrichtsaufsicht beim Bibliotheksinspekteur lag; das war von 1925 bis 1946 Robert L. Hansen und von 1946 bis 1956 Erik Allerslev Jensen. Der Unterricht war ausschließlich für die Volksbibliothekare vorgesehen. Die Ausbildungszeit stieg von 3 Monaten Schule und 4 Monaten Praxis im Jahre 1918 auf 4 Jahre im Jahre 1938 an; davon waren 3 Jahre Praxis und 1 Jahr Theorie an der Schule.

Im Bereich der wissenschaftlichen Bibliotheken gab es keine formalisierte Ausbildung; man lernte von den älteren Kollegen an der Bibliothek.

2. Die Dänische Bibliotheksfachhochschule (Danmarks Biblioteksskole) 1956 bis 1995

Als die Dänische Bibliotheksschule als selbständige Institution errichtet wurde, umfasste sie den Unterricht für Volks- wie für wissenschaftliche Bibliotheken.

Zum ersten Rektor der Schule wurde Preben Kirkegaard (geb. 1913) ernannt, der aus dem Bereich der Volksbibliotheken kam und zuletzt Leiter der Zentralbibliothek in Vejle gewesen war. Es war sowohl sein Ziel als auch das vieler anderer, dass die Schule zu einer Universität des Bibliothekswesens werden sollte. Daher gab es während dieses ganzen Zeitraums auf vielen Gebieten Bestrebungen, dieses Ziel zu erreichen, und zwar durch Inhalt und Form des Unterrichts, durch den Aufbau von Forschungsaktivitäten, hinsichtlich der Leitung der Schule und der Einstufung der Dienstränge sowie durch alle jene Insignien, die an Universitätseinrichtungen geknüpft sind.

Insofern ist es nicht abwegig, die Entwicklung der Schule unter diesem übergeordneten Gesichtspunkt zu sehen, auch wenn es Perioden mit wenig neuer Entwicklung gab. Andererseits kann man nicht von wirklichen Rückschlägen sprechen.

Bei Beginn der Volksbibliothekars-Ausbildung 1956 standen 1½ Jahre theoretischer Ausbildung 2½ Jahren Praxis gegenüber; die Ausbildung zum wissenschaftlichen Bibliothekar dagegen umfasste 2 - 300 Stunden Theorie, weil die Ausbildung hier solchen Personen galt, die bereits angestellt waren, während man bei Volksbibliotheken von Auszubildenden sprach.

Der Hauptinhalt der schulischen Unterweisung der künftigen Volksbibliothekare bestand in Buchkenntnissen; man erwartete von den Schülern, dass sie sich während ihres Aufenthalts an der Fachhochschule mit dem Inhalt eines großen Teils der schönen und der Fachliteratur vertraut machten, doch gab es schon ab 1960 Diskussionen darüber, dies zu ändern und statt dessen freie Wahl zwischen kleineren Bereichen der Literatur einzuführen.

Die ständigen Lehrer kamen sowohl von den Volksbüchereien (d.h. mit Ausbildung durch die Schule selbst) als auch von den wissenschaftlichen Bibliotheken, wo der Hintergrund für die Ausbildung akademisch, sehr häufig humanistisch war.

In dem Abschnitt über die Ziele der Schule gab es eine etwas unklare Bestimmung über Forschung: „für theoretische Studien tätig zu werden". Doch wurde diese Bestimmung bei Änderung des Schulgesetzes 1965 dahingehend präzisiert, dass die Schule „die Forschung zu fördern" habe.

Für die wissenschaftlichen Bibliotheken wurde eine vierjährige Ausbildungszeit für die Auszubildenden eingeführt mit einer Vergütung, die höher war als diejenige, die andere Studierende erhielten, und einer Verteilung auf je 2 Jahre Theorie und 2 Jahre Praxis, während die Ausbildung zum Volksbibliothekar 3 Jahre Theorie und 1 Jahr Praxis umfasste.

In den 60er-Jahren sprach man von einer großen Zunahme der Teilnehmerzahl, so dass die Schule jetzt sowohl den quantitativen als auch den qualitativen Herausforderungen zu entsprechen hatte. Das bedeutete viele Neueinstellungen, nun auch von Akademikern ohne Bibliothekserfahrung. Die Gehaltseinstufung der Lehrer wurde ein wachsendes Problem, wenn man sie mit derjenigen der Universitätslehrer verglich, denn die Lehrer der Schule hatten eine wöchentliche Pflichtstundenzahl von 14 - 16 Stunden oder doppelt so viele Stunden wie die Universitätslehrer.

1971 - 73 wurde der nächste Vorschlag für eine Gesetzesänderung vorgelegt, wonach es möglich sein sollte, Abteilungen der Schule in Verbindung mit den neuen Universitätszentren (Odense, Roskilde und Aalborg) einzurichten. Hier sollten Professuren geschaffen werden, Rektor und Prorektor sollten wie an den Universitäten wählbar sein, schließlich war eine gemeinsame vierjährige Grundausbildung für alle Bibliothekare vorgesehen.

Der Gesetzesvorschlag wurde nicht angenommen, doch erhielt die Schule 1973 ihre Abteilung in Aalborg zur Lösung der quantitativen Probleme. Seit 1971 gab es eine liberalisierte Verwaltungsordnung, die Studierenden und Angestellten größeren Einfluss auf die

Leitung der Schule zugestand; es war aber keine Rede von einer gewählten Leitung. Hier müsste man einfügen, dass es Professorenstellen in Dänemark nur an Universitäten und den anderen höheren

Lehranstalten gibt, und dass damit eine fachliche und forschungsmäßige Spitzenstellung bezeichnet wird, die man erst erreicht, wenn man sich durch mehrjährige Forschung als Adjunkt und Lektor qualifiziert hat.

An dänischen Universitäten gibt es verhältnismäßig wenige Professoren im Vergleich zu anderen wissenschaftlichen Stelleninhabern, und die Ernennung geschieht nach fachkundiger Einschätzung durch Kollegen und häufig in Konkurrenz mit mehreren gut qualifizierten Bewerbern.

In den 70er-Jahren gab es neue Entwicklungen auf dem pädagogischen Sektor. Eine fachübergreifende Grundausbildung an den Universitätszentren in Roskilde und Aalborg mit Projektarbeit als wesentlicher Studientätigkeit färbte auf die Dänische Bibliotheksschule ab, so dass die Forderungen nach Eigenaktivität der Studierenden gewaltig zunahmen und sich das Gewicht vom Auswendiglernen und Zusammenfassen auf Theoriebildung und Analyse verschob.

Das bedeutete, dass die wöchentliche Stundenzahl der Studierenden von über 20 auf 16 verringert wurde, so dass mehr Zeit für häusliche Arbeit, für Feldstudien und für eine Zusammenarbeit unter den Studierenden übrig blieb.

Ebenso kam es zu einer wesentlichen Verstärkung der Forschungsarbeit der Schule, was sich unter anderem darin ausdrückte, dass ihre Lehrer mit Vorträgen auf internationalen Konferenzen auftraten und die nordische Zusammenarbeit zwischen den Bibliotheksschulen ausgebaut wurde. Im Unterricht gab es im Lauf der Zeit auch fremdsprachiges Material, besonders in englisch, und in verschiedenen Fächern tauchten ausländische Gastdozenten auf, nachdem allmählich Absprachen mit anderen Hochschulen getroffen worden waren, darunter die erste, mit der Hochschule für Bibliothekswesen in Stuttgart, auf Initiative von Peter Vodosek. 1978 wurde dasselbe Ausbildungsmuster für beide Linien eingeführt, so dass alle Studierenden (jetzt hießen sie nicht mehr Auszubildende) 3 Jahre Theorie an der Schule und 1 Jahr Praxis in einer Bibliothek erhielten.

Ab 1979 wurde die Besetzung von Lehrerstellen an der Schule durch ein Gremium von Gleichgestellten vorgenommen, so wie es auch an den Universitäten geschieht.

1983 schied Preben Kirkegaard aus Altersgründen als Rektor aus und wurde durch Ole Harbo (geb. 1943) abgelöst, der bis dahin die Leitung der Bibliothek der Handelshochschule in Kopenhagen innegehabt hatte, aber zuvor Lehrer an der Schule gewesen war.

Die nächste Gesetzesänderung erfolgte 1985, und damit wurde ein grosser Schritt hin zur akademischen Entwicklung getan.

Die Schule war in den Jahren zuvor vom Finanzministerium ins Visier genommen worden, das von der Einführung weiterreichender Ausbildungen an der Bibliotheksfachhochschule abgeraten hatte; doch die damalige Kultusministerin, Mimi Jacobsen, trat dafür ein, dem Gesetz einen Passus einzufügen, dass diese nach Verhandlungen mit dem Unterrichtsministerium eingeführt werden könnten. 1961 war das Kultusministerium errichtet worden, und das Bibliothekswesen samt der Schule war vom Unterrichtsministerium auf das neue Ministerium übertragen worden. Das bedeutete eine zweckmäßige Platzierung der Schule im Verhältnis zu ihren Benutzern, gab aber Anlass zu vielen Schwierigkeiten in Verbindung mit der Akademisierung, da die Universitäten grundsätzlich gegen die Errichtung konkurrierender Einrichtungen waren und auf mancherlei Weise die Entwicklung zu hindern suchten, welche die Schule und Teile der Bibliothekswelt wünschten.

Inhaltlich wurde die Ausbildung verbreitert, indem auch die Informationsdienstleistungen des privaten Sektors einbezogen wurde, so wie die Schule ihre eigene Konsulentenabteilung einrichtete, um Kurse und Beratung anzubieten für Bibliotheken und andere Informationsbetriebe.

Die internationale Zusammenarbeit wurde weiter ausgebaut mit europäischen Aktivitäten, Gastlehrern und Studentenaustausch.

In der internen Organisation kam es zur Reduktion der Anzahl der Fachbereiche von über 20 bis auf letztlich 10, so dass die fachlichen Milieus größer wurden, und man richtete eine Vizechef-Stelle für einen Unterrichtsleiter ein, die mit Niels Ole Pors (geb. 1948) besetzt wurde, der von der Abteilung der Fachhochschule in Aalborg herkam.

Nachdem die neue Grundausbildung gut eingeführt war, ging die Schule an die Kandidatenausbildung und erhielt die Genehmigung des Kultministeriums, 1990 eine zweijährige Ausbildung zum Master in Bibliotheks- und Informationswissenschaft zu beginnen als Oberbau über die vierjährige Grundausbildung. Die beiden Ministerien verhandelten darüber, und das Kultusministerium konnte seinen Vorschlag gegen den Willen des Unterrichtsministeriums durchsetzen.

Die Kandidatenausbildung wurde 1991 von einem dänischen und einem finnischen Professor bewertet; beide gaben ein sehr günstiges Urteil ab. Daraufhin wurde die Ausbildung vom Ministerium als ständige Einrichtung genehmigt.

Im Gesetz von 1985 war außerdem eine Bestimmung enthalten, wonach die Schule Forschung zu betreiben habe, was damit zu einem Hauptziel der Schule neben dem Unterricht erklärt wurde.

Auf dem pädagogischen Sektor wurden solche Studienformen weiterentwickelt, durch die man die Studierenden aktivierte: Übungen, Seminare, Projektaufgaben usw., wodurch auch inhaltlich der Fortschritt von Theorie und Methode auf Kosten von Beschreibung und Praxis gefördert wurde.

Der Anteil an ausländischem Unterrichtsmaterial wuchs ständig, und in der Kandidatenausbildung waren über 75 % des Stoffes in englisch.

Nach 1992 hatten wir die barocke Situation, dass die Schule eine vierjährige Ausbildung besaß, die zum Diplom führte, aber formell keine Bachelorausbildung. Zudem gab es eine zweijährige Ausbildung zum Master, aber danach keine Ph.D.-Ausbildung. Die Schule hatte ihre allmählich gut eingespielte wissenschaftliche Tätigkeit, aber keine Professoren, und die verschiedenen Arbeitsplätze an ihr waren nicht so hoch bezahlt wie die entsprechenden Stellen an der Universität.

Die Dänische Bibliotheks-Fachhochschule war eine der größten, wenn nicht die größte Anstalt für die Ausbildung von Bibliothekaren in der Welt (über 70 vollbeschäftigte Lehrer mit Forschungsaufgaben), und es war für die Umwelt unbegreiflich, dass man sich nicht an sie wenden konnte, um einen Doktorgrad in Bibliotheks- und Informationswesen zu erwerben.

So war die Lage gegen Ende der 90 er-Jahre reif für eine schliessliche Gleichstellung zwischen der Fachhochschule und den Universitäten; doch dauerte dieser Vorgang mehrere Jahre, und zunächst musste eine ganze Reihe von Hindernissen aus dem Weg geräumt werden.

3. Vorbereitung und Durchführung des Gesetzes von 1998

Wenn ein Ausbildungsgesetz geändert werden soll, gibt es viele Interessenten, die ihre Gesichtspunkte gerne durchsetzen möchten. Als das Gesetz von 1965 vorbereitet wurde, schrieb Rektor Preben Kirkegaard auf Grund von Gesprächen und Anhörungen eine Stellungnahme an das Ministerium. Das Gesetz von 1985 wurde geprägt von einer großen und allseitig zusammengesetzten Kommission, in der alle interessierten Gruppen vertreten waren, und es gab ein Gutachten über den Mehrheits- und den Minderheitsvorschlag.

Gegen Ende der 1990er-Jahre war das Vorgehen mehr vom Ministerium gelenkt, und die Vorschläge wurden von Seiten der Leitung der Schule und von den Beamten des Ministeriums ausgearbeitet. Inzwischen wurde die Gesetzesvorlage mit einigen der wichtigsten Interessenten besprochen, und der schließliche Vorschlag wurde allen betroffenen Parteien, Einrichtungen und Organisationen zur Anhörung zugeleitet.

In dem Verlauf bis zum Gesetz von 1998 gab es zwei Hauptgegner der Akademisierung, die von ganz verschiedenen Voraussetzungen ausgingen. Auf der einen Seite waren es noch immer das Unterrichtsministerium und die Universitäten, die keine Konkurrenz haben wollten, während auf der anderen Seite der Landesverband der Gemeinden (KL) stand, der fürchtete, eine Akademisierung könnte bedeuten, dass alle sich bis aufs Master-Niveau ausbilden lassen und damit zu einer Erhöhung des Bibliothekarsgehalts beitragen würden.

Den Einwendungen der Universitäten konnte man damit begegnen, dass es sich bei einer Dänischen Bibliothekshochschule um ein Fachgebiet handelte, das es an keiner anderen Lehranstalt im Lande gab und das deshalb hier gepflegt werden musste. Man musste dabei bis zum höchsten wissenschaftlichen Niveau gehen, eine Definition, die offiziell für einen Unterricht auf Universitätsniveau steht.

Den Einwänden des Landesverbands der Gemeinden (KL) wurde entgegengehalten, dass Ausstiegsmöglichkeiten bestehen, sowohl nach 3 Jahren Bachelor-Studien als auch nach einem weiteren halben Jahr mit einem sogenannten erwerbsorientierten Projekt, das den Titel Bibliothekar D.B. (Bibliotekar D.B.) verleiht, der bisher für Bibliothekare mit der vierjährigen Diplomausbildung verwendet wurde. Indem man von der vierjährigen Ausbildung zu 3 oder 3,5 Jahren überging, wurde auch ein „Gleichgewicht" im Verhältnis zu anderen Universitäten hergestellt, indes die Dänische Bibliotheksfachhochschule in den Jahren 1990-98 praktisch die längste Kandidatenausbildung des Landes mit 4 plus 2 Jahren besaß.

Die übrigen interessierten Parteien unterstützten im großen und ganzen die Änderungen im Gesetz.

Ein Gebiet, auf dem sich die Bibliotheks-Hochschule von den Universitäten unterscheidet, ist die Frage der Leitung. An den Universitäten werden die leitenden Kräfte, sowohl der Rektor und Prorektor als auch die Dekane, gewählt. In den Unterrichts- und Forschungseinrichtungen des Kultusministeriums gibt es sowohl gewählte als auch ernannte Leiter, und das Ministerium wünschte in der Bibliothekshochschule das System der ernannten Leiter beizubehalten. Als Gegenleistung forderten Organisationen, welche die angestellten Lehrer vertreten, eine Änderung der Leitung. Diese Frage wurde von den Parteien des Parlaments behandelt. Das Ergebnis war eine ernannte Leitung; doch setzten sich viele Redner für eine Wahl ein. Ole Harbo gab im Herbst 1998 das Rektorat ab; ihm folgte in der Leitung der Schule Leif Loerring (geb. 1945), der zuvor die Leitung der Dänischen Pädagogischen Bibliothek innegehabt hatte.

Die Organisation, welche die an der Schule Angestellten vertritt, interessierte sich natürlich auch für die Arbeitsbedingungen an der Hochschule. Die zu gut 20 % eigenfinanzierte Forschung, die an der Hochschule Tradition ist, beträgt nur halb soviel wie das Forschungsvolumen der Universitäten, und man wünschte sich diesen Forschungsanteil erhöht. Das wird wohl allmählich so kommen, ist aber kein Anliegen der Gesetzgebung und hängt sehr von der künftigen finanziellen Situation der Hochschule ab.

Ein anderes Kapitel ist die Frage der Gehaltseinstufung, d.h. sowohl die Frage der Einrichtung von Professuren als auch die der Bedingungen der Gehalts- und Arbeitsverhältnisse für neue und bereits ernannte Lehrer. Es ist dies ein Verhandlungsgegenstand zwischen dem Ministerium und der Leitung der Hochschule auf der einen und den Organisationen der Arbeitnehmer auf der anderen Seite und insofern keine Frage der Gesetzgebung.

Nachdem die verfassungsmäßigen Stufen des Gesetzgebungsprozesses durchlaufen waren, wurde das neue Gesetz über die Dänische Bibliothekshochschule vom dänischen Parlament im Dezember 1997 angenommen und von der Königin am 14. Januar 1998 unterschrieben. Es trat mit dem 1. September 1998 in Kraft. Allerdings wurden zwei Bestimmungen - über das Ziel der Hochschule und über Studien zum Ph.D. - ausgesetzt, bis eine Bewertung der Forschungstätigkeit der Schule stattgefunden hatte.

Die Bewertung der Forschungsarbeit erfolgte 1999 durch eine Gruppe von 5 Spezialisten, 3 nordischen und 2 dänischen, die Interviews abhielten, Forschungsberichte lasen und die Pläne des Instituts beurteilten. Die Beurteilung war sehr positiv und empfahl ohne Einschränkung, die oben genannten Paragraphen des Gesetzes in Kraft zu setzen. Das tat das Kultusministerium mit seiner Bekanntmachung vom 17. März 2000, wonach das neue Gesetz denn in Kraft ist.

Darauf begann die Schule im Sommer 2000 mit den ersten vier Ph.D.-Studierenden in eigener Regie, so dass auch dieser wichtige Teil des Akademisierungsprozesses vorliegt.

Die nächste Etappe war die Regelung der Stellung der Professoren, und hier gab es zwei Probleme; teils in der Gehalts- und Anstellungsfrage, weil das neue staatliche Besoldungssystem von einem Grundlohn ausgeht, der zentral abgesprochen ist, sowie einer

Zulage, die mit der lokalen Anstalt abgesprochen und von ihr finanziert wird. Das Finanzministerium war natürlich der Auffassung, dass zentral so wenig wie möglich bezahlt werden sollte. Die Einstellung wurde zeitlich begrenzt, wie es mehr und mehr üblich geworden ist für Leute in leitenden staatlichen Stellungen und für sogenannte Forschungsprofessoren an den Universitäten.

Das war zum Teil ein Problem mit den Gewerkschaften, welche die Errichtung von Professuren an die Lösung der Frage der ganzen üblichen Stellenstruktur knüpften. Dadurch wurde die - im einzelnen betrachtet - untergeordnete Sache der gehalts- und Arbeitsverhältnisse einiger weniger mit weit größeren Problemkreisen vermischt, und während des Verhandlungsverlaufs gab es des öfteren große Schwierigkeiten, eine annehmbare Lösung zu finden. Doch gelang dies nach endlosem Tauziehen, so dass der erste Professor, Peter Ingwersen, am 1. Januar 2001 sein Amt antreten konnte und der zweite, Birger Hjoerland, am 1. Februar, und es hat sich eine grundsätzliche Lösung für die künftige Stellungsstruktur für neue und alte Lehrer gefunden.

All dies bedeutet, dass die verschiedenen Teile des neuen Gesetzes funktionieren. Das einzige, wofür keine Regeln festgesetzt sind, ist der Erwerb des Doktorgrads, eines Grads, der über dem Ph.D.-Grad liegt; doch gibt das Gesetz auch dafür eine Möglichkeit.

4. Mögliche Zukunftsaussichten für die Dänische Bibliothekshochschule

Die Hochschule untersteht dem Kultusministerium, war aber in Verbindung mit Regierungsumbildungen auf dem Weg zum Unterrichts- und Forschungsministerium. Diese Möglichkeit könnte sich immer noch in der Zukunft realisieren; doch würde eine solche Veränderung der Zugehörigkeit heute im Gegensatz zu früher der Hochschule nicht so viele Schwierigkeiten bereiten, weil sie jetzt den Universitätsstatus erhalten hat.

Es gibt auch die Möglichkeit, dass die Schule mit einer anderen Universität zusammengelegt wird. Das würde vermutlich mehr Probleme schaffen insofern, als die möglichen Partner viel größer sind als die Bibliothekshochschule, die bei einer derartigen Zusammenlegung kein großes Gewicht haben könnte, was wiederum ein Problem für das traditionell gute Verhältnis zwischen der Bibliotheksschule und ihren Hauptabnehmern, den Volks- und den wissenschaftlichen Bibliotheken, darstellen kann.

Eine andere strategische Möglichkeit wäre, die Bibliothekshochschule zur Universität des Kultusministeriums für Bibliotheken, Archive und Museen zu entwickeln. Das hängt damit zusammen, dass es in Dänemark keine allgemeine Ausbildung für das Archivwesen oder Museologie gibt. Das gibt es nur im Bibliothekswesen, ebenso wie akademische Spezialisten.

Schließlich kann man sich vorstellen, dass die Hochschule so wie bisher weiterbesteht, also als unabhängige Einrichtung, die nach internationalem Maßstab eine bedeutende Größe und ein großes Forschungsvolumen hat. Sie hat ihre besondere Konsulenten- und Fortbildungstätigkeit, welche ihren Klienten gute fachliche Beziehungen vermittelt und viele andere Aktivitäten, die unter der jetzigen Konstruktion am besten gedeihen.

Es wird - unabhängig von der künftigen Struktur - genug Aufgaben und Herausforderungen für die künftige Schule geben. Das gilt so auch für die ständige Anpassung der Ausbildungsformen an den Bedarf der Gesellschaft, und hier ist das Entscheidende, dass das Typische der Schule als Dänemarks höchster fachlicher Institution innerhalb der Bibliotheks- und Informationswissenschaft ausgebaut und entwickelt wird, so dass sie nicht nur zu einer unter vielen Einrichtungen mit Unterricht und Forschung in allgemeinen humanistischen und gesellschaftswissenschaftlichen Fächern wird.

Literaturangaben

Mogens Iversen Bibliotekaruddannelserne i Danmark 1918 - 1979 (Bibliothekarsausbildungen in Dänemark 1918 - 1979), Kopenhagen 1982

Ole Harbo Bibliotekaruddannelse i Danmark i 75 aar 1918 - 1993 (75 Jahre Bibliothekarsausbildung in Dänemark 1918 - 1993), Kopenhagen 1993

Ole Harbo Towards a Danish LIS University, in: Journal of Documentation, vol. 56, No.1, Januar 2000, Seite 5 - 11

Lov om Danmarks Biblioteksskole, Lov nr.17 af 14. januar 1998 (Gesetz über die Dänische Bibliothekshochschule, Gesetz Nr. 17 vom 14. Januar 1998)

Bekendtgoerelse om ikrafttraeden af lov om Danmarks Biblioteksskole, Bekendtgoerelse nr.181 af 17. mars 2000 (Bekanntmachung über das Inkrafttreten des Gesetzes über die Dänische Bibliothekshochschule, Bekanntmachung Nr. 181 vom 17. März 2000)

C. Olivia Frost

Schools of information in an information age: meeting the challenges through evolution and revolution

Introduction

Am Beginn meines Vortrags möchte ich einige Worte in Ihrer Sprache an Sie richten. Es ist mir eine Ehre, Ihnen Grüße aus den Vereinigten Staaten zu überbringen. Dafür gibt es mehrere Gründe:

Für eine Professorin der Bibliotheks- und Informationswissenschaften von einer amerikanischen Universität ist es eine große Freude, zu jungen Absolventen und Absolventinnen meiner wissenschaftlichen Profession am Tage ihrer Graduierung zu sprechen. Ich sehe wesentliche Gemeinsamkeiten zwischen unseren beiden Schulen was die Visionen unserer Profession anbelangt, und auch in dem, was wir in unseren akademischen Programmen zu erreichen versuchen.

Weiterhin denke ich, dass wir die zukünftige Richtung der Entwicklung unserer Wissenschaft übereinstimmend einschätzen. Schließlich gibt es auch noch einen persönlichen Grund. Als Austauschstudentin habe ich vor einiger Zeit in Berlin Germanistik studiert. Auch deshalb ist es für mich von besonderer Bedeutung heute hier zu sein um mit Ihnen diesen Tag zu verbringen.

The theme of my talk is challenges for information schools at a time of both evolution and revolution. My premise is that the practice of our information field is undergoing change of a revolutionary nature. At the same time, I strongly believe that this revolutionary change does not mean that we discard our past, but instead that we are building upon a proud foundation to create our future. Within the last decade, the field of library and information science has been profoundly altered. As a result of those fundamental changes, schools in the United States which prepare library and information professionals have undergone major change as well. Are these changes revolutionary or evolutionary? I think both. I would like to talk to you about some of the challenges in education for library and information professionals, and how the Michigan experience and other schools like it have reflected these changes.

My talk will describe how our education and profession has changed from the following perspectives: First, What is our vision of the field? How are the vision and the changes in the profession reflected in the academic program? Who are the students who are entering the field and will form its future? Who are the educators? What is the research of our new field and the research done by the faculty who teach at our schools? What is the curriculum and courses that our students are taking? Finally, how is the professional practice evolving? What are the jobs that our students are going out to, and how do they reflect the changing profession?

I will be addressing these questions in the context of the program at the University of Michigan School of Information. While the School of Information is in many ways unique in its approach, at the same time it can be considered a barometer of change in the profession. We are noticing that new schools of information are emerging which are based on our model. I think the University of Michigan reflects both the successes as well as the challenges that we face in the profession at large. In describing our program, I will ask you to think of how these developments compare with the German and European information professions and especially with your own program here at Stuttgart.

First, a little background about the University of Michigan. Michigan is one of about 56 graduate schools in the U. S. and Canada whose programs include library and information science and are accredited at the national level by the American Library Association. Our school began about 75 years ago as a school of library science, and five years ago we changed our mission and broadened our curriculum to provide a broader spectrum of information studies. In recognition of the broadening of our school, we changed our name from the School of Information and Library Studies to the School of Information. We have 25 faculty and about 250 students, most of whom are studying for a degree of Master of Science in Information, a two-year program. We also have about 30 students in the doctoral program. We are located in a large research university, considered among the top public research universities in the United States.

What is the vision of the profession that underlies our school?

At the Michigan School of Information, we have a vision which underlies our programmatic activities at all levels. At our school, we embrace a vision in which information systems and services improve the quality of life. Our mission is to discover the principles and concepts that will enable society to realize this vision, to design the technologies, systems, services and practices that will substantiate the vision, and to educate new generations of professionals who will put that vision into practice. We believe that information professionals will play an increasingly vital role in empowering individuals, communities, and organizations to capture the promise of the information age.

The School of Information is dedicated to investigating the fundamental role of information in society. Its field of study is information: how it is created, identified, collected, structured, managed, preserved, accessed, processed, and presented. Also, we are concerned with how information is used in different environments, with different technologies, and over time. In general, our research, teaching and service are focused on the interplay between information, technology, and people.

We see revolutionary change in our information society in many ways. We strongly believe that recent technologies have resulted in unprecedented change in the use of information which is reshaping our communities, institutions, and individual lives. We believe that in managing these transformations, society must focus on more than just the technology. Our school is founded on the premise that the study of information must encompass a broad array of fields to address information problems. We believe that there are unifying principles which requires that these fields be explored from an integrated approach – an approach which views information problems from a broad perspective encompassing many disciplines.

Our approach is *revolutionary* in its recognition of the fundamental changes in the information society. It is also *revolutionary* in the way it provides an integrated interdisciplinary approach to the study of information. At the same time, it adopts an *evolutionary* model which builds upon the existing knowledge base of the disciplines of library science and archives which we feel are essential to information study.

We feel that to be a successful information professional of any kind, it will be important to have an understanding of and competency in a variety of fields. To understand the people and societies which are consumers or users of information, we as information professionals must be knowledgeable in fields such as cognitive psychology, social organizations, economics, and public policy. To understand recorded knowledge, we need to know how information becomes knowledge, how knowledge is created, structured, disseminated, and used. We need to know about information behavior, the different structures and types of recorded knowledge, and the different forms of knowledge production, and how to translate those structures, types and forms into usable resources. Information professionals also address key issues regarding the content of knowledge, the medium in which it is communicated, its authenticity, validity, selection and collection, organization, and description. It is also critical to have a deeper understanding of the technologies by which information and knowledge are stored, disseminated, retrieved, and preserved – from the printing press to the latest computer technology. Social issues of a legal and ethical nature are also critical to our understanding.

We see these principles applying to the practice in many kinds of information settings. The School of Information began as a school of library science, and we still continue to prepare librarians, but our mission has broadened to include a number of information professions, including archives, information economics, management and policy, human-computer interaction, and many more. Within any one of these fields we believe it is important that people have broad knowledge in a number of related disciplines. For example, we think today's librarians need to have an understanding of economics in the pricing of information goods and services. We see information policy as critical for librarians to make decisions on access to information, and involving issues such as intellectual property or copyright, and privacy.

At the same time, we see that librarians have their own contributions to make to other fields. For example, principles of the organization of information are critical in the management and control of knowledge. The librarians' focus on the content of information, and on the user of information, provide an approach critical to the understanding of many new information environments in the digital age. In the United States, a basic philosophical premise of the library profession is the support of communities and improvement of social welfare. Libraries played an important role in bringing literacy, learning and information to people who had no other means of access to these. At the School of Information, we believe that the values imbedded in the core beliefs of librarianship are also central to the information age.

Who are the students who are now entering the profession?

In many respects, we are seeing a new influx of people entering our profession, and there have been revolutionary changes in the composition of our student body. Because our field encompasses a wide array of areas, and offers opportunities to practice in many arenas, we draw students from a wide spectrum of subject areas. Librarianship has always attracted students from many different fields, and this is even more true today. This gives us a diverse student population, and students find it stimulating to study with people from other backgrounds. We feel it important that information professions be drawn from various disciplines. We want both the humanists and the scientists, the technicians and the social scientists, the artists and the lawyers.

Students from our program come from no fewer than 50 different disciplines, including business, art, history, literature, law, medicine, nursing, economics, psychology, computer science, the biological and physical sciences. The field of information has become broadly diversified and offers many new opportunities; the field has gained new prominence with the emergence of the information age and the recognition that the types of skills that librarians' have are valuable in the new digital environment. At the same time, one of the factors that have attracted people to the library profession is its focus on service to people. We are finding that this still remains attractive to prospective students, and that this extends to other information areas in our program. Students are attracted to our program in part because of the variety of interesting and socially relevant jobs that this profession offers that enable people to make a difference in the society in which they work and live. We see computer scientists entering our program because it offers them an opportunity to do work that is user-centered, that serves society, and has interesting human challenges. We see humanists attracted to us because of the potential to use technology to serve humanistic ends.

Who are the faculty who are educating the new information professionals?

To offer a multidisciplinary program to address information problems requires that we have a faculty from many disciplines. A revolutionary change has occurred in our faculty composition. When I first began teaching at Michigan in what was then called the School of Library Science, the faculty were almost entirely from backgrounds in that field. At the School of Information, we now have faculty with doctorates in fields such as library science, psychology, economics, political science, history, computer science, engineering, management, and organizational theory. When we look for new faculty members, we require that the individual be able to apply their expertise to more than one area of the curriculum.

Throughout the University of Michigan and the American university system, faculty who teach in research institutions such as ours are expected to maintain an increasingly rigorous research agenda, and this means that faculty must spend much of their time on their research. However, we try to incorporate our research into our teaching, and to have our students involved in carrying out the research. Typically, a research project will involve faculty from diverse fields within our school and also faculty from other parts of the university or other universities. It involves a collaborative effort, is usually applied to problems faced by society. It is typically user-centered and relies on human feedback to evaluate systems and services.

The funding for the research comes from national agencies, private foundations, and corporations. It reflects the growing recognition of information problems in our society, and the growing importance attached to research in these areas. Research used to play only a small role in our school and in other programs of library studies. Today, at our school, research accounts for about one third of our budget, and helps pay for student tuition fees among other things. The School of Information is one of the smallest schools in the University of Michigan system. We have only 250 students out of a total of 35,000. But of the 17 schools in the University we rank 7th in the amount of research funding we bring in. In functional size, we are much bigger than our actual numbers, and this is in large part through the partnerships that we have created in the research, private, and public sectors.

What is the intellectual core content of the profession, and how is it reflected in the curriculum that we teach?

As the intellectual core of our profession has broadened and evolved, so has the curriculum of our school. Some areas are entirely new, others continue but with a new focus on the digital environment. Our school offers a degree with five different options.

Students can pursue a degree focusing on library and information studies. This builds upon our traditional program which we have been offering for over 75 years. We have also been offering a program in Archives and Records Management for several decades. These reflect evolutionary changes. Our newer programs include the specializations of Human Computer Interaction, and Information Economics, Management and Policy. There is also a fifth specialization which allows a student to design their own specialization by selecting courses to pursue a program of study which encompasses many areas, or which does not currently exist as a formal specialization. In addition, there are other options which are not formal specializations but which have emerged as newly developing areas, such as Information Architecture, and Community Information Technology.

These options reflect the emerging profession in a number of ways. First, the field of information has broadened to include a wide array of discipline areas. In today's information world, students can practice information management in several arenas, of which libraries are one of the most important, but not the only venue. Second, these discipline areas can be integrated in several ways. For example, a student planning on a career in libraries will need to know about information policy, information management, how people interact with computers, as well as the economics of information service, especially with digital formats. Students will need to have a basic understanding of how computers work so as to be able to make informed decisions on the purchase and management of information systems. They will need to have an understanding of how to assess the information needs of their users. Assessing the needs of information users is one of the areas that we feel all information professionals will need to know. To make sure that all of our students have knowledge in these areas, our integrated approach to the study of information requires that all students regardless of specialization must take four foundations courses. These courses include areas such as economics, computer science, library science, archival science, psychology, and organizational study.

What are the most active areas of our curriculum? Without a doubt, the ones that are generating the most excitement in the information profession: namely, the areas relating to digital information management. Students with skills in these areas are landing jobs as webmasters, usability engineers, and information architects. They are applying these skills in venues which span universities, government and non-profit organizations, large corporations, as well as start-up companies. E-commerce is one of the most rapidly growing areas of the information profession, and this technology and its related issues affect just about all aspects of society. We see e-commerce as an area focused not only on business and technology but on information, and Michigan is one of only a handful of universities in the United States offering programs in this new field. This interdisciplinary course of study draws on principles of information and library science, economics, management, organizational theory, psychology, and computer science to propose answers to the tough new questions confronting the networked society. For example, When does it make economic sense to give away information products for free? What business models work for information commerce, and how should information goods be priced? Our program gives students an in-depth understanding of core information issues, such as creating, measuring, managing, pricing, and sharing information in both nonprofits and for-profit environments.

How do we teach the curriculum?

How is our curriculum delivered? Increasingly, schools of information in the U.S. as well as throughout higher education in the U.S. are developing programs and courses which are independent of distance. Our school does not have a distance education program for our masters degree. However, we are using many of the information technology tools in distance learning to enhance the education. We have a seminar which brings together students from SI, American University, and the Universities of Fort Hare and Witwatersrand in South Africa. The course explores the socio-economic, political and cultural implications of globalization in a knowledge-based Information Society, and employs a suite of web-based tools to create a globally networked collaborative learning environment. Students work in virtual teams across continents to create group projects. Our use of virtual curriculum delivery is not to displace the physical delivery, but to radically alter and enhance classroom instruction.

Group project work is an important part of our curriculum delivery style in most of our courses. Students are assigned projects in class which require them to work with other students. We are finding that employers – whether they come from libraries or the corporate sector, all affirm the critical importance of having team skills in the workplace. Another key skill that employers value is the ability to assess the needs of the client in developing an information service or product, and the ability to evaluate the effectiveness of the service or product. We incorporate this is in both the theory and practice of our courses.

It is critical that professionals have hands-on experience, and this is something that we build upon from our previous curriculum. What is new is the way in which our students have been taking the skills they have learned and applying them to meet the needs of information organizations across a broad spectrum of information environments. This creates new venues of practical internship, and the service roles that our students play. Many organizations value the technology skills that our students bring to the workplace, and see our students as change-agents. In workplaces that are already technology-intensive, our students often contribute an approach that is more user-centered.

We are particularly proud of the internship efforts that our students have undertaken in under-served areas in the U. S and in South Africa. At the University of Fort Hare, over the past three years, SI students have assisted Library staff with arrangement and description of African National Congress materials and have helped to make these materials accessible online. In this remote and under-developed area of South Africa, SI students also provided basic computer training to local community groups and, developed e-commerce strategies for a woman's craft collective, and helped to develop plans for a distance education program for student teachers in the Eastern Cape.

Other outreach activities for our students included internship projects in the Navajo Nation, and Native American communities in the Upper Peninsula. In the Detroit area, students developed an information system that allows community service agencies to share information using a common platform. My own project work with students involves use of the Web to broaden the reach of cultural heritage content. My students work with primary and secondary school teachers and learners, museums, and regional and virtual communities to develop tools and services to capture and disseminate cultural materials. This type of project work reflects new roles for the professionals participating in the projects, as well as changes in the mission of their organizations and professions. These courses and activities exemplify the value that we attach to service which shows up in both our teaching and research. They exemplify as well the emphasis we place on putting users at the center of our work.

Employment opportunities for graduates

What are some of the jobs that our students are going out to and how do they reflect the changing information environment? There has been some evolutionary change, and some of the jobs are similar but with a new digital emphasis. For example, some of our recent graduates have found jobs as digital information systems librarian, digital archives researcher, and electronic resources information specialist. Students from all five of our specializations have found jobs in the emerging field of information architecture, which is one of the most rapidly growing areas in our profession.

Other new job titles include Video Indexer/researcher, Web Research Specialist, Webmaster, Human Factors Specialist, Usability Engineer, and User Interface Design Consultant. Our students in Information Economics, Management and Policy have found positions in e-commerce consulting, and as information policy specialists. These jobs are in corporate venues – for Microsoft, Intel, Amazon.com, as well as in universities, schools, non-profit and other community organizations. Some of our students envisioned and design their own jobs, and convinced potential employers of the need for these skills.

Many of these jobs did not exist at the time our new school was founded five years ago and in the early stages of our program we were developing curriculum to prepare students for jobs that were yet to be created.

We are finding that information professionals are moving from one type of profession to another. A student may graduate from our program and take a job as a webmaster for a non-profit corporation, and then move into the position of electronic content manager at a private corporate firm, and then move into a position as content specialist at a university. Or, they may begin their career at a public library, and then assume a position at a university library, and then to a corporate information environment.

Conclusion

In conclusion, these are times of both revolutionary change- in which we are seeing new information fields, new content in our curriculum, different types of students and faculty, and different types of jobs for our graduates. At the same time, these changes are also evolutionary in nature, building upon rather than replacing some of the foundations of information theory and practice. The basic mission of information practice is still to create and use information content, systems and services to help people with their information needs. What has changed is the way in which we are achieving this goal as well as the broader venues in which information practice take place. I congratulate you upon the completion of your academic program, and wish you every success for the future. I am convinced that, like our students in Michigan, you are learning the skills that will make you critical players in the new information age.

Ingeborg Spribille

„in order to survive“: Amerikanische Bibliotheken als unverzichtbare Partner für Lehrende und Lernende - ein Reisebericht

Angesichts der zunehmenden Digitalisierung von Informationen sowie ihrer Zugänglichkeit durch das Internet – und damit von Zuhause aus - haben die Bibliotheken die Aufgabe, sich neu positionieren[108]. Ein Blick in die USA - das gelobte Land für Bibliotheken - macht deutlich: Auch hier steht man offensichtlich unter Legitimationszwang. „How must libraries evolve with technology in order to survive?“[109] lautet eine der wesentlichen derzeitigen Fragen in Komitees und auf Konferenzen.

Bei der Rollen-Neudefinition gewinnt die Funktion der Bibliothek als Partner für Lehrende und Lernende in den letzten Jahren eine neue Bewertung, wie zahlreiche amerikanische Veröffentlichungen und Programme[110] belegen.

Da sich auch die deutschen Bibliotheken – die wissenschaftlichen wie die öffentlichen - immer mehr auch als Vermittler von Informationskompetenz einerseits[111] und als Lernort andererseits[112] profilieren, gilt es zu prüfen, inwieweit Modelle und Erfahrungen amerikanischer Bibliotheken für uns möglicherweise nützlich sein können. Voraussetzung ist allerdings, man lässt das K.O.-Argument „Geld“ einmal beiseite und konzentriert sein Augenmerk auf die Kreativität der amerikanischen Bibliothekare, sich als unverzichtbare Partner in der digitalen Welt für Lehrende und Lernende zu profilieren.

Eine Studienreise im Rahmen eines Fortbildungssemesters bot die Gelegenheit, verschiedene Konzepte vor Ort kennenzulernen. Dabei galt das Interesse sowohl den Schulungsangeboten der Bibliotheken als auch weiteren Dienstleistungen für Lernende und Lehrende, durch die die klassischen Funktionen der Bibliothek – beschaffen, erschließen, vermitteln - eine zeitgemäße Neudefinition erfahren.

Im Folgenden werden exemplarisch die entsprechenden Konzepte zweier Universitätsbibliotheken – der Texas Woman's University Library in Denton sowie der Moffitt Undergraduate Library der University of California in Berkeley – vorgestellt. Universitätsbibliotheken haben per se die Aufgabe, das Studium und die Lehre zu unterstützen. Die ausgewählten Beispiele variieren das Thema Bibliothek als Partner für Lehrende und Lernende auf jeweils eigene Weise.

---

108 vlg. Hobohm, Hans Christoph: Was Bibliotheken wert sind. Die wirtschaftliche Bedeutung der Bibliothek und ihre Ausrichtung auf die Informationsgesellschaft, in: BuB, 51(1999)1, S. 36 - 43

109 s. Metropolitan Coperative Library System (MCLS): Public Perception of Public Libraries. Draft Research Report. MetaResearch September 1999. Sacramento, CA 1999 (unveröffentlichtes Papier), S. 2

110 vgl. Wittkopf, Barbara: Current Trends in User Education in the United States, in : booklet 7, ifla '95, S. 119 – 129;

111 vgl. u.a. Schultka, Holger: Benutzerschulung: ein Serviceangebot an Universitätsbibliotheken, in: Bibliotheksdienst, (1999)12, S. 2063 – 2073; Bunke, Christa: Benutzerschulung. Konzept und Erfahrung an der Zentral- und Landesbibliothek Berlin, in Bibliotheksdienst (2000)9, S. ; Homann, Benno: Informationskompetenz als Grundlage für bibliothekarische Schulungskonzepte, in: Bibliotheksdienst (2000)6, S.

112 vgl. die Konzepte zu den Lernateliers der Bibliothek 21 in Stuttgart, s. Link „Druckfrisch“, in: http://www.stuttgart.de/stadtbuecherei

Beispiel 1: Texas Woman's University-Library in Denton / Texas

Die Texas Woman's University in Denton[113] ist mit ca. 10.000 Studierenden (davon 90 % weiblich) die größte Frauenuniversität in den USA und zählt zu den mittelgroßen amerikanischen Universitäten. Zur Universität gehört auch die School of Library and Information Studies. Für die insgesamt 11 Fakultäten gibt es eine zentrale Universitätsbibliothek. Auf das prachtvolle neue Gebäude der Bibliothek[114], seine besonderen Medienbestände[115] und seinen Reference Service soll an dieser Stelle nicht eingegangen werden.

Schulungen und Unterstützung von Lehrveranstaltungen

Was für deutsche Bibliotheken eher die Ausnahme sein dürfte, aber in großen amerikanischen Bibliotheken schon sehr verbreitet ist: Die Bibliothek verfügt[116] für ihre Schulungen über eigene Unterrichtsräume: einen IT-gestützten Unterrichtsraum - die „Library Lecture Hall" - ausgestattet mit einem Lehr- / Präsentationscomputer, Fernsehanschluss sowie mit einem Beamer, sowie über einen großen EDV-Unterrichtsraum. Dieser *„Library Academic Computing Lab"* bietet 24 modernste multimediale, Internetvernetzte PC-Einzelplätze.

Hier führen die Bibliothekarinnen des Reference Service nach einem festgelegten Semester- und Wochenplan folgende Kurse durch:

- allgemeine Datenbankschulungen: Einführung in 75 Datenbanken
- Faculty Workshops: Einführungen in das fachbezogene Medien- und Informationsangebot für Angehörige einzelner Fakultäten
- Internet-Recherche-Kurse

Mit diesem Angebot fällt diese Bibliothek jedoch nicht aus dem Rahmen des an amerikanischen Universitätsbibliotheken üblichen Schulungsprogramms. Eine Besonderheit dieser Bibliothek sind jedoch die Dienstleistungen ihres „Media Services & S.I.T.E. Lab" (Software & Instructional Technology Exploration). Das S.I.T.E. Labor existiert seit 1996. Es war ursprünglich eingerichtet worden, um Professoren dabei zu unterstützen, ihre Kursmaterialien zu entwickeln, d.h. herzustellen. Neben einem ausleihbaren Video- und CD-ROM-Bestand umfasst die Ausstattung

- die technische Ausrüstung für Großveranstaltungen
- die Hard- und Software zur digitalen Produktion von Fotos, Grafiken und Videofilmen
- vor allem jedoch die Hard- und Software-Ausstattung (für Macintosh und Windows) zur Verarbeitung und Herstellung von multimedialen Produkten: 6 Workstations (4 weitere für 2001 geplant) und 6 Internet-Arbeitsplätze

Mit dieser Ausstattung unterstützt das informationstechnologische Fachpersonal[117] Studie-

---

[113] Denton liegt ca. 40 km nördlich von Dallas und hat ca. 70.000 Einwohner.

[114] s. http://www.twu.edu/library

[115] Die Bibliothek umfasst insgesamt über 1 Million Medieneinheiten; bemerkenswert sind in der Woman's Collection vor allem die Archive der amerikanischen Pilotinnen aus dem 2. Weltkrieg sowie der amerikanischen Soldatinnen inklusive der Teilnehmerinnen am Persischen Golf Krieg

[116] neben den ca. 20 Benutzer-PCs zur OPAC-, CD-ROM- und Internetrecherche im Auskunftsbereich der Bibliothek sowie neben einem Library Computer Lab mit 20 PCs für das ungestörte Arbeiten der Studierenden

[117] es sind keine Bibliothekare sondern EDV-Spezialisten mit dreijähriger Ausbildung oder Berufserfahrung

rende und Hochschullehrer bei der Durchführung von universitären Großveranstaltungen, bei Projekten sowie bei der multimedialen Präsentation von studentischen Arbeitsergebnissen. Die Schulungsinhalte für Studierende und Professoren sind u.a.

- „How to scan materials (Adobe PhotoShop) and import them into presentations"
- „How to capture video clips (using Adobe Premiere) and import them into presentations"
- „How to create a web page (using MS FrontPage)"
- „How to use a digital camera"...

Das Trainingsangebot wird informell organisiert – für Studierende in kleinen Gruppen bis zu sechs Teilnehmern; es gibt keinen Lehrplan und keinen Stundenplan. Das heißt, die Mitarbeiter des Labors, ergänzt durch studentische Assistenten, bieten ihre Unterstützung und Schulung auf aktuelle Nachfrage hin an. Je nach Bedarf wird der Umfang und die Art der Schulungen und der weiteren Hilfen gemeinsam mit den Studierenden und den Professoren geplant. Ziel ist die Befähigung zum selbständigen Arbeiten mit den Programmen.

Die Erfahrung zeigt, dass die meisten Professoren zunächst Einzelschulungen benötigen, die sie in ihren eigenen Büros bevorzugen. Diesem Wunsch wurde entsprochen.

Alle Schulungen sind absolut kostenlos. Das Labor ist 96 Stunden wöchentlich geöffnet. Das Angebot wird gut genutzt, obwohl die Schulungen nicht Teil des offiziellen Lehrplans der Studierenden sind. Die Studierenden besuchen sie freiwillig, zusätzlich. Jede Wochen nehmen ca. 6 – 12 Studierende diese Trainings- und Hilfsangebote in Anspruch. D.h. insgesamt werden wöchentlich zwischen 12 und 24 Stunden Schulungen durchgeführt.

Dienstleistungen für die Fakultäten

Um die Zusammenarbeit mit den Professoren optimal zu planen und zu gestalten, haben alle 12 Bibliothekarinnen der Universitätsbibliothek jeweils ca. 20 Professoren/innen zu betreuen. Art und Umfang der Betreuung werden durch ein „Collaborative Assignment Program" vor Semesterbeginn mit jedem Professor, der Interesse an der Unterstützung durch die Bibliothek hat, neu vereinbart.

Die Bibliothekarinnen wollen auf diese Weise erfahren, welche neuen Themengebiete im kommenden Semester relevant sein werden, um sich rechtzeitig auf entsprechende fachspezifische Recherche - Unterstützung und fachspezifische Recherchekurse für die Studierenden vorzubereiten; außerdem sind sie daran interessiert, die „Information Literacy" von Studierenden und Professoren angesichts ständig neuer Informationstechnologie und neuer Informationsquellen fortlaufend zu aktualisieren.

Folgende Dienstleistungen bietet das F.I.R.S.T (Faculty Information Research Support Team) für jedes lehrende Fakultätsmitglied an,

- regelmäßig und aktuell die Inhaltsverzeichnisse der persönlich relevanten Fachzeitschriften per E-Mail zuzuschicken;
- bei Bedarf Zeitschriftenartikel auch online zu beschaffen;
- nach vorgegebenen Themen und Schlagwörtern wöchentliche Recherchen in Zeitschriften - Datenbanken durchzuführen;
- Recherchehilfen bei der Suche nach Stipendien und Stiftungen
- fach- bzw. themenbezogene Rechercheschulungen für Lehre und Forschung des jeweiligen Semesters – für die Lehrenden und für die Studierenden (s.o.)
- Beschaffung von benötigten Büchern über den Lehrverkehr bis zu Beginn des Semesters
- Die Beschaffung bzw. Digitalisierung von kostenfreien Texten sowie deren HTML-Präsentation im Intranet zur Unterstützung von web-based-training

Alle diese Dienstleistungen sind für Fakultätsangehörige kostenfrei.

Die Kundenorientierung der TWU-Library

Dieser Katalog an Dienstleistungen zeigt das hohe Niveau an Kundenorientierung, das im folgenden noch einmal verdeutlicht werden soll.

Selbstverständlich profitiert diese Universitätsbibliothek finanziell von den hohen Studiengebühren und Sponsorengeldern. Doch gleichzeitig steht die Bibliothek damit unter dem Druck, sich als unverzichtbare Einrichtung permanent zu profilieren. Die studentischen Kunden, die viel bezahlen – und dafür meistens auch noch nebenbei arbeiten müssen –, erwarten etwas für ihre Investition. Die Professoren, die selbst unter Leistungsdruck stehen, erwarten eine Infrastruktur, die ihnen die Konzentrierung auf ihre eigentlichen Lehr- und Forschungsarbeiten ermöglicht. Die Sponsoren, meist inzwischen reich gewordene Alumni, investieren auch nur in nützliche, erfolgreiche und damit angesehene Einrichtungen.

Das hohe Maß an Kundenorientierung zeigt sich auf verschiedenen Ebenen:

1. Der Kunde „Professor/in" bekommt genau die Dienstleistungen, die er oder sie persönlich benötigt, und dort, wo sie gewünscht wird – wenn es sein muss als Einzelschulung im eigenen Büro. Zwar dienen auch hier die Schulungen als Hilfe zur Selbsthilfe. Trotzdem fühlen sich die Bibliothekare auch für die Informationsrecherche und Medien- und Informationsbeschaffung und sogar auch für die Digitalisierung von Texten und ihrer Präsentation im Intranet auch zuständig und verantwortlich.
2. Alle Dienstleistungen werden in Zusammenarbeit mit den Kunden – Professoren wie Studierenden – entwickelt. Dafür gibt es verschiedene Methoden:
   - das „Collaborative Assignment Program" (s.o.)
   - Slogans auf allen möglichen Handouts, die immer wieder zur Kooperation auffordern, wie

     „Share your ideas with the staff"

     „This is *Your* lab ... make us to make it work."

     „Your Suggestions: ..."
   - „Library Instruction Request"-Formulare, auf denen Professoren die Schulungsanforderungen für ihre Studenten sehr differenziert benennen können.
3. Bei der Planung von Dienstleistungen zeigen die Bibliothekare ein Höchstmaß an Flexibilität: die Dienstleistungen werden für jedes Semester neu geplant und es gibt neben feststehenden Trainingskursen auch Schulungskurse, die „on demand" angeboten werden, ohne feststehende Stundenpläne.
4. Die Mitarbeiter präsentieren sich als nach wie vor wichtigste Informationsquelle der Bibliothek, die man ohne Scheu jederzeit nutzen kann. So wird z.B. in der Informationsbroschüre des S.I.T.E. Lab bei den Ressourcen an erster Stelle „a friendly and helpfull staff" genannt, und dann erst die technologische Infrastruktur.
5. Die Mitarbeiter verpflichten sich in der „library's mission" nicht nur zur ständigen Bereitschaft, Fragen zu beantworten und jegliche Art von Hilfe zu leisten; sie versprechen auch, dass die informationstechnologische Unterstützung immer auf dem neuesten Stand ist – sowohl von der Ausstattung als auch von der fachlichen Kompetenz her.
6. Die Bibliothek ist sehr am Feedback ihrer Benutzer interessiert.
   - Alle Schulungen werden ständig durch die Teilnehmer evaluiert; bewertet werden u.a. der Umfang der Schulung, die Qualität der Schulungsmaterialien sowie die Schulungskompetenz der Bibliothekarinnen.

– Jeder Benutzer wird ermuntert, seine Meinung über die Bibliothek, ihr Medienangebot, ihre Dienstleistungen und die Mitarbeiter zu äußern. Entsprechende „Library Service Opinion Survey" – Karten sind an die Bibliotheksdirektorin persönlich adressiert. Sie werden persönlich beantwortet, wenn gewünscht, auch telefonisch.

Neben diesem hohen Grad an Benutzerorientierung ist das besondere Merkmal dieser Bibliothek ihr Verständnis von „information literacy". Dazu gehört hier mehr als Recherchekompetenz, nämlich die Kompetenz, Informationen multimedial zu gestalten und zu vermitteln.

Beispiel 2: The Teaching Library der University of California in Berkeley

Die University of California in Berkeley hat auf ihrem Campus neben einer Reihe von Spezialbibliotheken zwei zentrale Universitätsbibliotheken: die Doe Library für „graduates" und die Moffitt Library für die Erstsemester bzw. „undergraduates". Hier in der Moffitt Undergraduate Library ist die sogenannte Teaching Library eingerichtet worden. Das besondere an diesem Konzept ist, dass hier ein schon vorhandenes Dienstleistungsangebot – die üblichen Benutzerschulungen - weiterentwickelt und unter einem eigenen Etikett besonders öffentlichkeitswirksam herausgestellt wurde und nun als Teaching Library vermarktet wird.

Die Teaching Library gibt es seit 1993. Das von ihr propagierte Anliegen ist es, angesichts der zunehmenden Digitalisierung der Informationen dem veränderten Schulungsbedarf der Bibliotheksbenutzer zu entsprechen.

Der Schulungsbedarf wurde durch eine Studie 1994 konkretisiert[118]; ein Test von graduierten Studierenden der politischen und soziologischen Fakultät ergab: weniger als 50 % der Befragten waren in der Lage

- eine korrekte Online-Recherche nach Medien der Bibliothek durchzuführen
- Bücher und Zeitschriftenartikel richtig zu zitieren
- Online-Recherche-Ergebnisse einzugrenzen
- wesentliche Informationsquellen ihres Fachgebietes zu benennen
- wesentliche elektronische Quellen ihres Themenschwerpunktes zu benennen.

Die Befragung machte auch deutlich: die Teilnahme an Bibliotheksschulungen ist die wesentliche Voraussetzung für die Kenntnis der relevanten fachlichen Quellen und für die Kompetenz der Recherche in Fach-Datenbanken. Von den Studierenden, die bei diesem Test die meisten Punkte gemacht hatten, hatten 87 % an Schulungen der Bibliothek teilgenommen.

Bei diesen Defiziten der Studierenden und dem entsprechenden Schulungsbedarf setzt die Teaching Library mit ihrem Konzept an. Die Teaching Library beschreibt sich als „Gateway to Information Literacy"[119], definiert als die Fähigkeit, Informationen zu finden, zu bewerten und auszuwählen; dabei geht es vorwiegend um den Umgang mit elektronischen Informationen. Es ist das Ziel der Teaching Library, allen Studierenden Information Lite-

---

118 vgl. Maughan, Pat D.: Early results, Spring 1994: Teaching Library information literacy survey, in: CU News. The Weekly Newsletter of the Library. University of California, Berkeley 49(30. Juni 1994)26, S. 1, 3-4

119 s. Information Literacy Competencies for Students. Unveröffentlichtes handout der Teaching Libary der University of California, Berkeley. o.J.

racy zu vermitteln – jedoch nicht nur für das momentane Studium; angesichts der ständigen Weiterentwicklung der elektronischen Informationen sollen die Studierenden außerdem Selbstlernkompetenzen erwerben, um ihre Information Literacy im Lebenslangen Lernen ständig aktualisieren zu können[120].

Trainingsangebote für die Universität

Das Trainingsangebot der Teaching Library - das in Zusammenarbeit mit Hochschullehrern erarbeitet wird - zeichnet sich durch eine besondere Differenzierung der Inhalte und Schwierigkeitsgrade sowie durch seinen Umfang aus; das Angebot besteht aus

- „Drop-In-Workshops" für Studierende zur Nutzung von OPAC, Datenbanken und Internet, wie
  - Ersteinführung in die Bibliothek und ihre elektronischen Informationsquellen
  - Einführung in das Internet
  - Einführung in die Nutzung von Suchmaschinen
  - Methoden zur Bewertung und zum Zitieren von Webseiten
  - Einführung in die „California Digital Library" der Universität: Datenbanken im Netz und auf CD-ROM
  - Online-Recherche nach Online-Zeitschriften
  - Online-Recherche nach Büchern
  - Online-Recherche nach Zeitschriftenartikeln
  - Recherche in der Online-Datenbank LEXIS-NEXIS
  - Datenbankaufbau zur Erstellung einer eigenen Literatur-Datenbank
- „Faculty Seminars on Electronic Research Resources" für Professoren/innen, graduierte Studierende und andere wissenschaftliche Mitarbeiter/innen, wie
  - Effektives Recherchieren und Bestellen im Online-Katalog der Bibliothek
  - Effektive Recherche und die Nutzung von „document delivery" in Datenbanken für Fortgeschrittene
  - Effektive Suche nach wissenschaftlichen Quellen im Internet
  - Einführung in die Elektronischen Quellen des eigenen Fachgebiets
  - Web-Design-Kurse für Anfänger und für Fortgeschrittene

Die Teaching Library ist für diese Schulungen mit drei PC-Pools ausgestattet. Die Schulungen werden von neun Bibliotheksmitarbeiterinnen durchgeführt, die sich dafür – als willkommene Abwechslung – freiwillig gemeldet haben. Sie finden zum Teil während des Semesters statt, z.T. während der Sommerakademien. Ergänzt werden sie durch web-based-training.

Die Orientierung nach draußen:
Medien- und Schulungsangebote für Schulen und Kindergärten

Die Teaching Library fühlt sich auch dafür verantwortlich, die Studierenden von morgen zu erreichen und zu fördern, d.h. sie an die Informationsquellen der Universitätsbibliothek heranzuführen. Sie tut dies in Zusammenarbeit mit Lehrern und Erziehern mit einem populären Medienangebot der Universität, der großen Sammlung an historischen Fotos zur Ge-

---

[120] vgl. The Teaching Library. Transforming Education, in: Bene Legere. Newsletter of the Library Associates. (Spring 1997)47, S. 1-3

schichte Kaliforniens. Diese Fotos werden Lehrern und Erziehern digital per Internet zur Verfügung stellt. Das „California Heritage Project“ sorgt für die Digitalisierung und Archivierung der großen historischen Fotosammlung sowie für die Schulung der Pädagogen bei der Nutzung des Internets zur Präsentation dieser Fotos in ihren Kindergärten und Schulklassen. Außerdem werden Schulklassen zu Bibliotheksführungen eingeladen, bei denen sie die Originale der Fotos besichtigen können.[121]

Weitere Dienstleistungen der Teaching Library

Zum Zuständigkeitsbereich der Teaching Library zählt auch die Gestaltung des benutzerfreundlichen Leitsystems, die Gestaltung von Werbepostern sowie die Veröffentlichung von Lernmaterialien zur Begleitung der Kurse; dabei wird sie unterstützt durch das Graphic-Office der Bibliothek.

Für Studienanfänger stellt die Teaching Library als Sommer-Semesterferien-Lektüre jedes Jahr eine Liste mit ca. 25 Buchtipps zusammen. Die annotierten Titel sind von Berkeley-Professoren verfasst; sie dienen der Allgemeinbildung und dem Vergnügen; dabei sind preisgekrönte Titel und Titel mit aktuellen bzw. gesellschaftlich wichtigen Themen – Fachbücher, Romane und Lyrik.

The Teaching Library: Ein Marketinginstrument

Die Teaching Library ist nicht nur ein Dienstleistungskonzept sondern auch ein Marketinginstrument für die Moffitt Undergraduates Library – und so wird es auch von den Mitarbeitern der Teaching Library gesehen. Mit Hilfe der Benutzerschulungen wird Werbung gemacht für die Mediensammlungen, die Informationszugänge, für die Professionalität der Mitarbeiter.

Das heißt, mit dem Angebot der Teaching Library stellt die Bibliothek unter Beweis, dass die zunehmende Digitalisierung der Informationen und ihre zunehmende Verfügbarkeit durch das Internet für Hochschulangehörige[122] eben nicht die Bibliotheken und die Bibliothekare überflüssig machen, sondern dass sie notwendiger denn je sind:

> *„.... computers don't ever replace librarians. ... the undergraduate learning experience is being transformed by the digital revolution. The Library is at the forefront of this transformation – offering a dazzling array of opportunities for students, faculty, and general public.“*[123]

Durch die Teaching Library positioniert sich die Universitätsbibliothek auch künftig als unverzichtbarer Partner der Lehrenden und Lernenden. Zum Marketinginstrument „Teaching Library“ gehören

- das Label „Teaching Library“
- das sehr differenzierte, ganz am konkreten Bedarf orientierte Schulungsangebot
- der Test zur Erfassung und Dokumentierung des Defizits und Bedarfs an Informationskompetenz

---

[121] Dieses Projekt dient außerdem der Förderung benachteiligter Bevölkerungsgruppen – Indianern und Afroamerikanern -, in dem es die historische Bedeutung der heute randständigen Gruppen dokumentiert und sie selbst, d.h. die Kinder dieser benachteiligten Gruppen, mit ihren historischen Wurzeln bekannt macht.

[122] Der Anteil der privaten Internet-Zugänge ist unter den amerikanischen „post graduates“ im Zeitraum von 1998 bis 2000 von 53 % auf 69,9 % angestiegen; vgl. Percent of U.S. Households with Internet Access by Education of Householders, 1998 and 2000, in: Falling Through the Net, a.a.O. S. 11

[123] s. Profile of the Teaching Library. Scholarly Research Can Now Be Done Anny Time, Any Place, in: Bene Legere. Newsletter of the Library Associates. (Spring 1997) 47, S. 2-3

- die Erarbeitung des Schulungsangebots in Zusammenarbeit mit den Hochschullehrern
- die zusätzlichen imagefördernden Dienstleistungen, die auf pfiffig gestalteten Faltblättern bekannt gemacht werden.

Benutzerschulungen sind nichts Neues in Bibliotheken. Wichtig ist jedoch offensichtlich, dass ihre Bedeutung für alle erkennbar und spürbar wird. Hier in Berkeley werden sie sogar zum wichtigen Marketinginstrument der gesamten Universitätsbibliothek.

Amerikanische Beispiele: Modelle für deutsche Universitätsbibliotheken?

Die beiden vorgestellten amerikanischen „Antworten" haben beeindruckt, man kann, man sollte von ihnen lernen.

- Lernen kann man, was man schon immer und nicht nur in diesen beispielhaften Universitätsbibliotheken in den USA lernen konnte, nämlich, wie man sich als Bibliothek vor allem durch Dienstleistungen – und zwar hochgradig benutzerorientierten Dienstleistungen - unverzichtbar machen kann und wie man diese Unverzichtbarkeit auch selbstbewusst nach außen darstellt.
- Man lernt, dass man angesichts der dynamisch fortschreitenden Digitalisierung der Information mehr tun kann als neben den Printmedien immer mehr Computer aufzustellen und den Zugang zu Online-Datenbanken zu organisieren.
- Man lernt, dass es nicht genug ist, am Auskunftsplatz der Bibliothek zu sitzen und auf fragende Besucher zu warten.
- Lernen kann man vor allem, diese Entwicklung als Herausforderung zu begreifen und sie nach außen hin auch als solche darzustellen und nicht als Problem. Probleme haben die anderen, die Studierenden ohne Informationskompetenz, die überforderten Hochschullehrer, die Gefahr laufen, den Anschluss zu verpassen in der Informationsgesellschaft. Das muss deutlich gemacht werden gegenüber den Kunden und gegenüber den Geldgebern der Bibliothek.
- Und lernen kann man schließlich, wie man diese Dienstleistungen durch eine entsprechende Öffentlichkeitsarbeit so bekannt macht, dass jedem der persönliche Nutzen klar wird, um seine eigene Arbeit zu optimieren.

Die Entwicklung und Vermarktung der vorgestellten Dienstleistungen erfordern natürlich Zeit – aber sie setzen auch eine „Dienstleistungshaltung" voraus, eine Bereitschaft, die Bibliothekskunden dort abzuholen, wo ihre Probleme, Bedürfnisse oder Interessen sind - und sie erfordern Kreativität. Diesen Luxus leisten sich die amerikanischen Kollegen. Natürlich lässt sich dies nicht einfach in Deutschland einführen – aber ist es wirklich nur das fehlende Geld und Personal, was uns daran hindert? Sollte man sich nicht auch in unseren Bibliotheken mehr von diesem diesen Luxus leisten - „in order to survive"

Paul Sturges

Research on records management in Africa: a basis for programmes of professional education

Introduction

This article argues the value of a research-based approach to records management in Africa. Records management is frankly the least fashionable of the information professions, and this is as true or more true in Africa as elsewhere. Most of what the article says is fully applicable anywhere in the world, but, as it is based on a conference paper given at an African conference (SCECSAL 2000, Windhoek, Namibia, 10t^{h} - 15th April 2000), and all the examples are drawn from Africa, it has been left as addressed to Africa. The article is based on the premise that good management of documentation can achieve important results in a comparatively inexpensive way, and the penalties of neglect can be considerable. Disasters can overcome the organisation or individual if record keeping is not effective and poor management of records results in long-term damage to the organisation. At the very least, time is wasted in painstakingly extracting information from inadequately organised files, or effort and money is wasted in repeating work that has not been documented in properly retrievable form. African institutions, and many African nations, exist with such a vulnerable financial base that this line of argument is compelling. They cannot afford to reinvent the wheel, especially if blueprints of the wheel have been forgotten somewhere at the back of a shelf in a dusty cupboard in a backroom.

Poor records management also leads inevitably to unjustifiable risk-taking. As Mchombu put it in 1992,

> *One of the hallmarks of a good African civil servant or manager is the ability to take decisions without having all of the relevant information.*[124]

Even more outspoken was the Ghanaian Secretary of Education, K.B. Asante, who in 1989 suggested that,

> *The major factor to gross inefficiency and lack of continuity in the policies, procedures, and measures of many African governments is not, as is commonly supposed, frequent changes in governments, but bad management of records.*[125]

It is easy to illustrate poor records management in small ways from personal experience. For instance, whilst employed by an African university the author was asked to contact the former students of a programme so as to obtain feedback to be used in redesigning the programme content. On asking for access to the student records he was directed to a gallery in which he found the documents in an incomplete and miss-filed mess. As a result, an im-

---

124 Mchombu, Kingo. Information management in Africa: an uncharted terrain. FID News Bulletin, 42, 1992. p.187.

125 Speech to the Second West African Regional Workshop on the Management of Semi-Current Records, Accra, August 1989, quoted in Wamukoya, Justus. Records: a neglected information resource in Africa. Records Management Journal, 5, 1, 1995. 15-22. p.19

portant, but comparatively simple, strategic exercise became unnecessarily difficult and could not cover the complete body of former students. Worse examples than this would be easy to find. For instance, in some cases the organisation may not be able to establish claim to property and rights for which contracts and other agreements have been inadequately documented. What is also sometimes forgotten is that poor records management can also adversely affect the ordinary citizen.

A few years ago when the author was in a waiting room before an appointment with a government official in Zimbabwe, a woman who was also waiting asked about his purpose. On being told that it was connected with information work, her response was to say 'Our biggest information problem here in Zimbabwe is the state of our records'. She then described the plight of veterans of the freedom struggle who were unable to draw the pensions and allowances to which they were entitled because of the chaotic state of the relevant official records. The roots of the veterans' desire for land, that began to disrupt the country during 1999, may be seen as partially rooted in this government neglect and inefficiency. Similar difficulties also exist in Zimbabwe with the records of the registration of births, which are vital for matters such as the issue of passports and the establishment of eligibility for entry to the schools system. Although this is generally extremely damaging, one highly successful administrator with a Zimbabwean municipality tells how in his youth it was turned to his advantage. He neglected his schooling and was expelled. The family set him to work on their farm, but the painfully hard work soon made him long to be back in the system. Fortunately for him an uncle was able to exploit the gaps in the records and obtain him a birth certificate which showed him as still of an age for school entry. After studying hard this time his career blossomed and he has never had to look back with regret, but for the majority the poor state of the official records only brings misery.

Despite the strong case that can be argued for its importance, it is much harder to make the practice of records management seem more attractive. However, various current tendencies are influencing opinion in a more positive direction. First, the drive for efficiency in business and in public administration, which derives from the Economic Structural Adjustment Programmes (ESAPs) imposed on debtor governments by the international financial institutions, has forced organisations to look very closely at the effectiveness of their procedures and practices.[126] Second, the fact that many records are now kept in computerised form has given the issue a more contemporary, less dusty, appearance. Finally, there is the fashionable attention now paid to knowledge management. Since much of the knowledge to which the term refers is actually in the form of the organisation's records, the vogue for knowledge management should carry records management along with it. Perhaps, at last, records management is about to have its day. If this is true, it could have a significant effect, because records management is the easiest of the form of information work in which to make improvements and the one most likely to produce immediate dividends for the organisation.

The need for research

Any area of professional practice requires an organised body of specialised knowledge that can be used as a basis for development. There is very little African professional literature on records management, which in itself confirms the impression that only a low level of

[126] Sturges, Paul. Social intelligence for developing countries: the role of grey literature. Collection Building, 18, 3, 1999. 114-125.

interest and activity exists. McIlwaine's very thorough *Writings on African archives*[127] seeks to cover a wide range of material on archives, broadly defined, from the earliest writings on the topic through to 1995. However, it lists little more than 100 articles, reports and theses on records management. A search for items that have appeared since that year does not reveal great numbers of new publications. Some of the material listed by McIlwaine, such as copies of unpublished conference papers, is very rare and probably only traceable in a few collections. Only four countries (Kenya, Nigeria, South Africa and Zimbabwe) have produced a reasonable number of items. Much of the material only relates to circumstances in a single country and may not have much general significance. The nature of the literature does seem to suggest that in most countries, continent-wide, records management is not a major interest of information professionals.

Nevertheless, the writings that have appeared do show that interest has increased and that this has been prompted, in part at least, by organisations like the International Council on Archives (ICA) and the International Records Management Council (IRMC). The ICA was a sponsor, with UNESCO, of a survey of the archival situation in Africa in the early 1990s by Mazikana, which naturally revealed a good deal about the state of records management.[128] The ICRM held its Third Congress in Harare in September 1993, and a keynote paper addressed the information management problems peculiar to Africa, dealing in particular with access to information resources.[129] This international interest has continued, and, for instance, in 1996 the biannual meeting of the East and Southern Regional Branch of the ICA, held in Zambia, took strategic planning and the role of information in the achievement of organisational objectives as its theme.

During the 1990s a very small number of general discussions of the state of records management in Africa have appeared in the English language. It is also worth remembering that attention has been paid to the problem in the Francophone countries for at least as long, and even somewhat longer. The concept of records management, translated as *gestion des dossiers*, was discussed in relation to Francophone West Africa in 1984 by Mbaye[130]. More recently, Mnjama[131] summed up the problem as revealing itself in chaotic document stores with few controls on the movement of documents. This he put down to ineffective tools and techniques, as a consequence of under-funding of services, unsuitable personnel, and bad management. Wamukoya located the problem at policy level, suggesting that in Africa 'The acceptance of a records management policy organisation-wide, is rather rare and only very few organisations are beginning to appreciate its benefits.'[132] Thurston does, however detect a new awareness by senior public officials of the importance of records management in public sector reforms, which has the potential to effect change and improvement.[133] Furthermore, in one or two countries there is some positive

127 McIlwaine, John. Writings on African archives. London, Hans Zell, 1996.

128 Mazikana, Peter. The role of records management in business during market reform programmes. Janus, 1, 1996. p.43.

129 Njovana, Samuel. The International Records Management Council in Zimbabwe. Information Development 10, 1, 1994. 23-24.

130 Mbaye, Saliou. Problèmes des archives et de la gestion des dossiers en Afrique de l'Ouest Francophone. Gazette des Archives, 127, 1984. 287-298.

131 Mnjama, Nathan. Archives and records management in Africa. Information Development, 9, 17, 1993. 83-86.

132 Wamukoya, Justus. Records: a neglected information resource in Africa. Records Management Journal, 5, 1, 1995. 15-22. p.17

133 Thurston, Anne. Records management in Africa: old problems, dynamic new solutions. Records Management Journal, 6, 3, 1996. 187-199.

development. Akussah actually reported an embarrassment of success in 1996 Ghana, saying that,

> *Today almost all financial institutions, corporations and parastatals have functional records management systems. The unfortunate consequence of this development is the high turnover of professional and semi-professional staff in the National Archives.*[134]

Shafts of light in the gloom such as this, however, do not justify discussion of records management in Africa as other than a problem. Something of the structure and dimensions of the problem and the way in which research can illuminate it can be illustrated in the form of studies using different research techniques.

Research studies

Information and library science is a comparatively new discipline in African universities and its practitioners often have little time or encouragement to do research. When they do, they lack models and have insufficient guidance as to worthwhile topics or appropriate techniques. This is especially true of new entrants to the profession who must do small pieces of research for bachelor's or master's degrees. In some cases they seem only to be aware of techniques that involve finding and reading documents, or which obtain information and opinion from people via questionnaires. They seem not to have been made aware of the limitations of these techniques, and the wide range of other valuable techniques that can be used. Some examples of slightly different approaches to technique which work well in African circumstances were suggested by Sturges and Chimseu in 1996.[135] The studies which follow were deliberately chosen because they illustrate the use of three different research methods: the information audit, participant observation, and a programme of semi-structured interviews. A few words about these techniques are necessary as introduction to the studies.

The information audit is a technique perhaps most commonly used within the management of organisations, but it is also an excellent technique for the outside researcher, if the necessary level of co-operation can be obtained. Through drawing up an inventory of an organisation's information resources, and exploring the way in which information flows throughout the organisation, it seeks to enable managers to ensure the optimum exploitation of information for the organisation's benefit. For the researcher the information audit provides an anatomy of information in action. In the case described here, research for a master's dissertation was used to create an unusually detailed and informative inventory of the information resources held by the chosen organisation and also those that it did not hold. From this it is possible to infer the way in which it satisfied, or failed to satisfy, its information requirements.

Participant observation is a technique whereby an investigator seeks to gain membership of, or a close association with, a human group that is to be studied. It requires the investigator to take up the social usages of the group, whilst retaining a critical objectivity. It

---

[134] Akussah, Harry. Records management in Ghana: an overview. African Journal of Library, Archives and Information Science, 6, 2, 1996. 101-106. p.103.

[135] Sturges, Paul and Chimseu, George. Qualitative research in information studies: a Malawian study. Education for Information, 14, 1996. 117-126.

is extremely open to the dangers of bias, either in favour of the group or of the outside perspective that the investigator brings to the study. Despite this, it offers enormous potential for deep insights into the social practices of groups, and the rationale for these. Student professional placement reports, such as those used here, offer excellent opportunities for the insights obtained through induction into the work practices of the organisation offering the placement. Placements, just like all other participant research, involve ethical dilemmas about how far the information obtained from associates, even temporary associates, can decently be used as research data. Anonymised and presented in as neutral a manner as possible, the findings of participant observation are an important, though admittedly controversial source.

Semi-structured interviews are a more familiar technique than the two already discussed. The interview, as such, is often referred to as a conversation with a purpose. That purpose is to obtain relevant information that will allow the measurement of something. It is also worth mentioning that a questionnaire is effectively an interview that can take place without the presence of the interviewer. In both the formal interview and the questionnaire the structure and phrasing of the interviewer's contribution to the conversation is crucial. Yet despite all the effort that is put into interview and questionnaire design, the results generally disappoint or, at least partly, mislead. The semi-structured interview accepts the problem of validity and hands part of the initiative back to the interviewee. This may possibly increase the danger of misleading or irrelevant response, but it increases the scope for obtaining the interviewee's experience, feelings and opinions. The interviews used here were based on a loosely structured schedule, but the interviewees were encouraged to express themselves freely on the topics covered.

The ADDIS ABABA WATER AND SEWERAGE AUTHORITY: an information audit[136]

The Authority (AAWSA) is a public institution with the responsibility for supplying water to the city of Addis Ababa for drinking and other domestic purposes, protection of underground water resources, and disposal of sewage. All of its administrative departments, service units, branch offices and divisions use information to manage human resources, finance and facilities, and to plan and monitor a host of different activities.

In addition to information resources acquired from outside the organisation, AAWSA generates information internally both in graphical form and as extensive files of written text. More specifically there are maps, drawings and engineering documents which represent the water and sewer network and the various structures and installations connected to it. There are substantive documents produced in the course of major construction and maintenance projects; research and study reports; and procedural and operations manuals. There are also technical specifications and manuals relating to the various pumps, meters, valves and other installations that have been purchased over the years. There are planning and management reports, intended for fairly limited circulation. There are records of installation, maintenance, testing, and retirement of parts of the system, and there are measurement records of water production, consumption, pressure and flow. There are also customer records and other finance-related documentation.

---

136 Derived from a Master of Information Science dissertation An information support system for water and sewerage service management with particular reference to Addis Ababa Water and Sewerage Authority, Addis Ababa University, 1995, by kind permission of the author Abera Melese Tefera.

Documentation in all forms, including maps, engineering documents and reports was scattered among a large number of locations within the organisation. Retrieval was difficult; once documents were circulated there was little control over their whereabouts; and there was no means to cross reference, extract and manipulate data from the various forms of documentation to produce new reports on any topic. AAWSA has a Library and a Computer Information Service, both of which are specifically provided to perform information functions. The Library is at the Head Office and is run by one librarian. In 1995 it had less than 3,000 documents, not adequately catalogued or otherwise listed. The stock did not include any of AAWSA's internally-generated documentation. The Computer Information Service was intended to carry out system analysis, design and implementation; data collection, storage and processing; and the dissemination of information. In 1995 it had one minicomputer and three PCs with no commercial application software. It performed mainly financial housekeeping activities, using programs developed in-house, and did no information handling activity relating to AAWSA's core water distribution and sewage disposal functions. There was no organisation-wide network.

The consequences of this were apparent in the running of AAWSA. Planned preventative maintenance was non existent: failures were corrected when they occurred. Planning for expansion of the system was hampered because the trends in water consumption and details of new installations already put in place could not be effectively matched. Some components of the system, both under and over-ground, could only be located with difficulty, and accurate information on crucial installations such as valves which control water flow to different subdivisions of the city was lacking. Most of these problems stemmed from inability to locate documentation that existed, or should have existed, somewhere within the organisation. What is more, large quantities of vital information on matters such as the location of mains, water meters and manholes, seemed never to have been recorded, existing only in the memories of long-serving employees. The extent to which these employees passed on their knowledge before they retired governed whether some matters were known to AAWSA or not. Strategic planning for water and sewerage provision in Addis Ababa was often obliged to rely on guesswork and intuition rather then facts. There was quite simply no effective information and records management within the organisation to provide the necessary support.

Records management in Kenyan institutions: participant observation studies[137]

The organisations in which the observation took place included an NGO, a major hospital, a private clinic, law courts and a university faculty office. All had systems for the management of records, but these varied from the rudimentary, to an elaborate system intended to provide for all aspects of storage, retrieval and tracking of file movements. The least developed system was one which was contributed to and used by all members of the organisation, but which does not appear to have had staff whose work was dedicated specifically to its management. In other cases, records management was one function of an administrative office where staff shared duties including filing and retrieval. Other organisations had more than one registry, each dealing with records generated and used by a different admin-

[137] Based on student placement reports by Joseph Gakuo, Alphonce Juma, Mercy Kalunge, Stephen Macharia, Jackson Mwanza, and Hellen Ndegwa, By kind permission of the Dean of the Faculty of Information Science, Moi University, Kenya, 1998.

istrative section. Finally, one organisation did have a designated central records department.

The types of material which were stored included, in some of the organisations, vital personal records such as medical patient records, legal case records and student records. In addition to this, all the organisations kept administrative material of various kinds. It is hardly necessary to stress the importance of the documentation relating to people. People's health, freedom, finances, careers and a multitude of related matters, often depend on accurate and easily retrieved personal records. It is therefore worth mentioning that medical records were found filed in chronological order, requiring a searcher to browse in the most likely date area of the files, with second records created when an original could not at first be found. It was also the case that legal records might be hard to trace between courtroom, registry and court archive, sometimes even being destroyed after as little as three years. In general, this type of confusion was to be found across the whole range of records, personal and administrative.

The observers found that most of the organisations had systems that were imperfectly designed and implemented, though it was true that there was one well-organised exception. Current, semi-current and inactive records were mixed together, stored chaotically and filed according to no coherent system in one example. In another, filing was often by date even though documents were allocated identifying numbers for filing, and misfiling was common. There was frequently no obvious way of drawing together related files, such as the in-patient and out-patient records which a medical institution often created for the same patient. In particular the means used for tracking the movement of records removed from store was very frequently inadequate. In these cases there were sometimes no well-established rules as to who could remove files and how those who had the right were supposed to record what they had done.

The storage of records was generally less than adequate. Space was short in most cases, and even where there was plenty of space, it was poorly used. Files were kept on shelves, in cupboards and cabinets, as well as on the floor or work surfaces, generally without much system. Files suffered damage and deteriorated in such conditions, with the filing numbers becoming rubbed away from the covers in one institution. Records themselves might be illegibly written and be in the process of disintegration from frequent handling. Specialist staff were not always provided, and if they were, their numbers tended to be insufficient, and their educational level and training scarcely adequate for the problems with which they had to deal. As stated earlier, the observers found considerable variation amongst the organisations observed, but the positive examples were exceptions to the rule that the management of the records was extremely poor across the range. A general consequence of this was that most of the organisations were unable to generate accurate operational statistics, and were not in a position to exploit valuable data which existed in a raw state in their files.

Opportunitiesfor information professionalsin Zimbabwe: interviews with employers[138]

To assist the National University of Science and Technology (NUST), Bulawayo, Zimbabwe, in assessing the market for the information professionals who might be educated in a pro-

138 Based on research carried out by the author for the National University of Science and Technology, Bulawayo, Zimbabwe, in October and November 1996.

posed Department of Library Science, a small programme of interviews with senior representatives of major employers was carried out in late 1996. In all, representatives of seven employing organisations (two government ministries, two parastatals, two financial institutions and a city council) were interviewed on the basis of a loosely structured interview schedule. Each interviewee was sent an outline of the topics to be discussed. This listed some of the main occupations that might be considered information professions (librarians, information officers, database managers, records managers, archivists and others) and also set out some of the tasks which might make up the work of information professionals, whatever their job title. The actual interviews only followed this in a broad way, allowing the interviewee considerable discretion as to which aspects were emphasised and which given less attention.

Even though some of the interviewees expressed doubts as to whether they could provide useful information, all responded fully and helpfully. Some of them already employed librarians, and the others recognised that the publications that they all acquired would benefit from professional attention. However, most were clear that employing librarians was beyond their scope, desirable though it might be in principle. Several organisations employed information officers of one kind or another to disseminate information from, or about, the organisation. The kinds of qualifications they saw such professionals as requiring were generally in relevant subjects such as agriculture or finance, or in the skills of journalism. Whilst none of the organisations currently used computers and networks for more than a few routine administrative functions, two (a parastatal and an insurance company) were in the process of creating computerised management information systems. Both saw the need this created for computer professionals, but did not see the running of the systems as particularly a role for information professionals.

What was much more universal amongst the organisations in this sample group was the sense that professionals were needed to organise their paper records. The responses on the subject of records management were particularly interesting. None of the interviewees expressed complete satisfaction with their state of affairs. One government ministry, in response to this sense of ill-ease had done much to improve the situation, introducing a new system of organisation for their files. Other organisations reported attitudes varying from qualified satisfaction through to embarrassment and distress at their records management performance. Much of this related to the fact that records were usually in the care of employees with clerk status, who might keep files in good order, but who did not have a grasp of how to exploit the content of files for the organisation's benefit. Thus, one parastatal was able to show the interviewer round a tidy and well-kept storage area that nevertheless did not have a system or personnel capable of more than simple retrieval of specified files. The main conclusion from the programme of interviews was that they suggested the existence of widespread employment potential for information professionals. This potential was not yet fully perceived within the institutions themselves, although there was surprisingly strong awareness of the need for better records management.

Conclusions

Taken together, the three studies give out a strong message. Organisations that need to be intense users of information, if they are to function well, are all too often incredibly neglectful of the information resources that they actually possess. The problems that the information audit of AAWSA revealed were so overwhelming that they should be characterised as issues of total information management, with poor records management only a component of the scene. Computerisation, networking, management of intellectual capital and the provision of a research library seem to be needed just as much as implementation of a simple but robust system for the organisation and retrieval of records. The latter might seem to be the easiest of these to implement, calling only for the introduction of methods and procedures to make the most of existing and new internally-generated resources.

It is clear from the Kenyan participant observation, however, that if records management might be easier than other forms of organisational information upgrade, it is still not all that easy to get it right. Each of the organisations observed had systems in place, but only one or two were reasonably effective. In the others, records were vulnerable to the essential imperfections of the systems used, and to the careless and inefficient administration of those systems. Where the records were vulnerable, the organisations themselves and also their clients were vulnerable too. To complete the sequence, the Zimbabwean interviews revealed something that might be a dawning consciousness of the significance of good records management. The organisations concerned were not about to bring in major changes immediately. It did sound, however, as though they might be persuadable. This evidence, incomplete though it certainly is, generates a series of questions. Is there really an opportunity to persuade organisations to improve their records management? If there is, who should persuade them? How should these persuaders set about doing it? What would the consequences be for the information professions?

First of all, it is clear that organisations are persuadable. The Zimbabwean interviews suggested this, but the study was much too small to be a basis for confident generalisations about Zimbabwe, let alone other, less advanced, countries. Evidence from South Africa supports the idea that employers are certainly interested in improving records management in a more advanced economy. An unpublished survey by Mavis Titi of the University of Transkei (which will be included in her PhD submission at Loughborough University), found that 50 % of employers she contacted saw records management as a high priority for the core of professional education for information work. A further 38 % of her respondents felt that there was a need for its development as a specialisation. Even better than these expressions of opinion has been the success of graduates from Moi University in Kenya and from the University of Botswana in finding posts in the broad area of information management, many of which include major records management elements.

Maybe the argument which actually convinces employers to upgrade their records management activities is that by doing so they are activating an existing resource, not investing in a new, capital-intensive venture. The best reason for good records management is, after all, just common sense. As suggested earlier, records management is most attractive when seen as part of an information management, or knowledge management package. This principle that the records manager is a member of one of a group of information professions, not some isolated practitioner of a set of administrative routines, is central to the argument of this paper. It is a principle that has been argued out in some detail by Walters[139] who supports the development of graduate level programmes in what he calls the nonbibliographic information professions. The implication for the information professions is clearly that of increasing convergence, with records management fully included.

Convergence of the professions needs to be rooted in convergence of professional education. This is something that is welcomed by progressive schools of library science. Witness the title of the University of Namibia's School of Information and Communication

139 Walters, Tyler. Rediscovering the theoretical base of records management and its implications for graduate education. Journal of Education for Library and Information Science, 36, 2, 1995. 139-154.

Studies, whose programmes also include substantial elements of records management. The survey by Titi, mentioned earlier, suggests that South African academics also appreciate the possibilities. Interestingly, however, her survey of academics shows them as less committed than her employer respondents. Only 36 % of academics regarded records management as core to the information science curriculum, whilst 57 % saw it as an important specialisation. She also cites a Fort Hare University 'Seminar on Curriculum Development' which saw records management as important to the information science curriculum because of its significance to organisations. Such trends introduce problems of professional territory in large, highly developed educational systems such as those of North America and Europe: schools of archive science, information management and others are often in competition with schools of library science for programme areas like records management. For a forward-looking African school, the professional territory is often there for the taking. More difficult is for educators to come terms with the specific needs in their own locality, and to match their response closely to these needs.

This requirement to understand the precise needs that arise from particular situations (different types of organisation, different forms of governance, different business and financial environments) is what creates the need for research. The techniques used in the studies described above are amongst an interesting range that can be used for this purpose. When the precise nature of need is established, library associations and other professional bodies can encourage organisations to take specific measures to introduce or upgrade records management services. What are needed at this stage are personnel capable of administering and developing records management. This places the key responsibility firmly with educators. The programmes they devise and offer should be designed to take advantage of a research-based awareness of the professional environment.

Maria Biener

Das bibliothekarische Wissensdefizit in rechtlichen Fragen

Bemerkungen zu Methoden und Möglichkeiten der Vermittlung bibliotheksrechtlicher Kenntnisse an Fachhochschulen[140] - gleichzeitig ein Plädoyer für integratives Lernen -

Am 30. und 31. Oktober 2000 hielt die Rechtskommission des EDBI ihre letztjährige „Herbstsitzung“ ab. Der Bericht ist im Dezember-Heft 2000 des „Bibliotheksdienst“ nachzulesen[141]. U.a. heißt es dort[142]:

> *... In diesem Zusammenhang werden auch Anfragen einzelner Bibliotheken erwähnt, die Videokassetten unnötigerweise mit Ausleihrechten kaufen. Hierin zeigt sich wieder ein nicht selten zu beobachtendes Wissensdefizit in rechtlichen Fragen, das auch auf unzureichende Ausbildung an den Fachhochschulen zurückzuführen ist. Die Rechtskommission beschließt daher, über die „Konferenz der Informatorischen und Bibliothekarischen Ausbildungseinrichtungen“ (KIBA) an die Fachhochschulen zu appellieren, um die Ausbildung in Rechtsfragen zu verbessern.*

Es bleibt zu hoffen, dass es der Rechtskommission gelingt, damit eine umfassende Debatte anzustoßen, die längst hätte geführt werden müssen. Allerdings scheinen die Voraussetzungen dafür nicht besonders günstig; es scheint sich eine gewisse Resignation breit gemacht zu haben.

Von der Schwierigkeit, ein Lehrgebiet „Bibliotheksrecht“ zu etablieren

Ganz offensichtlich gibt es unter den hauptamtlichen Dozenten der bibliothekarischen Ausbildungseinrichtungen nur wenige Voll-Juristen – noch nicht einmal an jedem Institut einen (wenngleich es immer wieder gelungen zu sein scheint, qualifizierte - und pädagogisch begabte! - Juristen als Lehrbeauftragte für einzelne Lehrveranstaltungen zu gewinnen)[143].

Wenn ein Nicht-Jurist über die in Bibliotheken auftretenden Rechtsfragen doziert, so ist er vielleicht mit einem Blinden, der von der Farbe redet, vergleichbar! Ähnliches könnte aber auch für einen Juristen gelten, der das Bibliothekswesen nicht kennt und mit den tatsächlich dort auftretenden Problemen nicht vertraut ist.

Gibt es ein „Bibliotheksrecht“?

Warum hat sich das „Bibliotheksrecht“ als Lehrgebiet nur ansatzweise etabliert, und warum haben bisher nur wenige bibliothekserfahrene Juristen den Weg an eine bibliothekarische Ausbildungsstätte gefunden?

---

140 Aus Termingründen wurde dieser Aufsatz Mitte März 2001 abgeschlossen. Erkenntnisse aus einschlägigen Veranstaltungen des 91. Deutschen Bibliothekartags (2.-5. April 2001 in Bielefeld) konnten leider nicht mehr abgewartet werden!

141 Rösner, Helmut: „Rechtskommission des EDBI, Herbstsitzung in Berlin“ // in: Bibliotheksdienst 34 (2000), H. 12, S. 2036-2041.

142 Rösner, Helmut: „Rechtskommission ...“ // in: Bibliotheksdienst 34 (2000), S. 2038.

143 Ich räume ein und bitte gleichzeitig dafür um Nachsicht, dass ich so manches aus der (vielleicht etwas einseitigen?) Sicht meiner eigenen an der HBI Stuttgart gemachten Beobachtungen und Erfahrungen darstelle!

Eine vorläufige Antwort auf diese Fragen findet man sicherlich auch darin, dass das „Bibliotheksrecht" keine eigene Rechtsmaterie[144] ist. Sich mit dem „Bibliotheksrecht" zu beschäftigen, heißt: aus ca. 80.000 Vorschriften[145] aller nur denkbaren Rechtsgebiete diejenigen herauszusuchen, die vielleicht im Bibliotheks-Alltag irgendwann und irgendwo relevant werden könnten, wobei die Rechtslage im einzelnen auch von der Rechtsform des Bibliotheksträgers abhängen und für zahlreiche Bibliotheken u.a. auch die (in 16 Bundesländern vielleicht unterschiedlich ausgestalteten?) Landesvorschriften von Belang sein können. Kommt hinzu, dass insbesondere die Gemeinden im Rahmen ihrer Satzungsbefugnis einen beträchtlichen Spielraum hinsichtlich der Ausgestaltung des Benutzungsverhältnisses haben, wobei sie zwischen öffentlich-rechtlichen und privatrechtlichen Benutzungsordnungen wählen können.

Ein hauptamtlicher Dozent des „Bibliotheksrechts" sollte nach Möglichkeit das gesamte Recht überblicken und mit dem Bibliotheksalltag in allen Sparten vertraut sein – und wer kann dies heutzutage noch für sich in Anspruch nehmen?

Vieles ist strittig!

Da außerhalb der (in der Normen-Hierarchie ziemlich weit unten rangierenden) Bibliotheksbenutzungs-Ordnungen kaum spezielle bibliotheksrechtliche Vorschriften existieren, so verwundert es wahrscheinlich nicht, dass die Anwendbarkeit von Gesetzen und Verordnungen im Einzelfall vielfach strittig ist.

Beispiel: hat eine Gemeinde-Bibliothek eine öffentlich-rechtliche Benutzungs-Ordnung, so gilt für die Rechtsbeziehungen zwischen Bibliothek und Benutzer das BGB *nachrangig* nach den Verwaltungs-Vorschriften. Des öfteren aber scheint es recht zweifelhaft zu sein, ob die existierenden Verwaltungs-Vorschriften für den jeweiligen konkreten (Streit-)Fall „einschlägig" sind. – Oder: gemäß § 832 BGB haften Erziehungsberechtigte für Schäden, die ihre minderjährigen Kinder bzw. Schutzbefohlenen angerichtet haben, *nur dann*, wenn sie nachweislich ihre Aufsichtspflicht verletzt haben. Umstritten ist, ob die in kommunalen öffentlichen Bibliotheken allgemein bekannten „Haftungs-Erklärungen" daran etwas ändern. Monika Rasche hielt eine solche Erklärung zumindest in einer 1993 erschienenen Publikation für wirksam[146] - anders jedoch Thomas Clemens in einem etwa gleichzeitig erschienenen Aufsatz:

> *Die Rechtsstellung der Bibliothek bzw. der Gemeinde ließe sich nur dadurch verbessern, dass bei der Begründung des Benutzungsverhältnisses eine Bürgschafts-*

---

144 Bereits ausführlich dargestellt von Hildebert Kirchner in: Bibliotheks- und Dokumentationsrecht. - Wiesbaden: Reichert, 1981. - (Elemente des Buch- und Bibliothekswesens ; Bd. 8). - S. 1-7.

145 Es soll hier nicht der Eindruck erweckt werden, als gäbe es die höchst verdienstvolle Sammlung „Rechtsvorschriften für die Bibliotheksarbeit" nicht, die in 3 verschiedenen Auflagen 1992, 1994 und 1998 als „DBI-Materialien"-Band Nr. 117, 137 bzw. 172 erschien. Doch gerade diese Sammlung macht ja deutlich, dass die bibliotheks-relevanten Vorschriften aus den unterschiedlichsten Rechtsgebieten zusammengetragen werden müssen, - und es fragt sich, ob ihre weitere Aktualisierung nach der in Gang befindlichen Abwicklung des DBI und der bereits erfolgten Schließung der Publikations-Abteilung überhaupt noch gewährleistet ist!

146 Rasche, Monika: „Zulassung von Kindern und Jugendlichen zur Bibliotheksbenutzung" // in: Rossoll, Erika: Die Benutzungsordnung einer Öffentlichen Bibliothek : Formulierungsvorschlag – Materialien – Beispiele / [erarb. von Erika Rossoll ...] - Berlin : Deutsches Bibliotheksinst., 1993. - (Arbeitshilfen / Deutsches. Bibliotheksinstitut). - S. 21-23, bes. S. 23. - Clemens, Thomas: „Rechtsfragen der Öffentlichen Bibliotheken: Das Bibliotheks-Benutzungsverhältnis : Teil II des überarbeiteten Referats, gehalten auf der Fortbildungstagung der Staatlichen Beratungsstellen Nürnberg und Würzburg am 1.7.1992 in Neustadt a.d. Aisch" // in: DIE NEUE BÜCHEREI 1993, H. 2, S. 121-127, Zitat von S. 123. Vorsorglich sei darauf hingewiesen, dass eine Bürgschaftserklärung mit einer Haftungserklärung keineswegs verwechselt werden darf.

erklärung der Eltern abverlangt wird. Von diesem sicheren Weg ist aber abzuraten; denn er könnte dazu führen, dass gerade sozial schwächere Schichten von der Bibliotheksbenutzung abgeschreckt werden.

Probleme in der Lehre

Solche (hier bei weitem noch nicht ausgeloteten!) Komplikationen sollen Studierenden vermittelt werden, die im allgemeinen der Rechtswissenschaft kein besonders großes Interesse entgegenbringen – die vielleicht sogar ein Jura-Studium abgebrochen oder sich bewusst gegen ein solches entschieden haben, ehe sie ihre bibliothekarische Ausbildung begannen.

Neben umfassenden juristischen Kenntnissen und einer gewissen Vertrautheit mit dem Bibliothekswesen müsste also ein Dozent des Bibliotheksrechts auch noch eine besondere pädagogische Begabung mitbringen – vielleicht sogar noch die Fähigkeit, neben dem Bibliotheksrecht ein zweites Fach zu unterrichten, da sich das relativ umfangreiche Lehr-Deputat eines Fachhochschul-Professors mit den für angehende Bibliothekare relevanten juristischen Inhalten (in einer für die Studierenden „verträglichen" Menge) vielleicht nicht erfüllen ließe.

Die (hoffentlich noch in Gang kommende) Debatte um die Vermittlung juristischer Kenntnisse an künftige Bibliothekarinnen und Bibliothekare wird, so ist zu befürchten, nicht so ohne weiteres damit enden, dass sich an den Ausbildungsstätten ein umfassendes Lehrgebiet „Bibliotheksrecht" (mit den dazu gehörigen Dozenten-Stellen!) etabliert.

Die besonderen Kalamitäten des Urheberrechts

Wenn hier von Komplikationen die Rede ist, so lohnt sich ein kurzer Blick auf das für Bibliothekare unentbehrliche Urheberrecht, das ja immerhin eine relativ geschlossene Rechtsmaterie darstellt. Im Urheberrecht ist nicht nur (wie auf vielen anderen Rechts-Gebieten) so manches umstritten, sondern auch vieles im Fluß und die künftige Entwicklung ungewiss.

Man denke an den fast 7-jährigen Rechtsstreit des Börsenvereins gegen die Technische Informationsbibliothek (TIB) Hannover (resp. das Land Niedersachsen), den der Bundesgerichtshof am 25.2.1999 dadurch beendete, dass er auf eine „durch die technische und wirtschaftliche Entwicklung entstandene Gesetzeslücke"[147] erkannte und (sicherlich zur Überraschung und zum Ärger vieler Bibliothekare und Wissenschaftler) den Kopien-Direkt-Versand der TIB und anderer größerer Bibliotheken für vergütungs-pflichtig im Sinne des Urheberrechtes erklärte – was im September 2000 einen zwischen Bund und Ländern auf der einen und den Verwertungsgesellschaften auf der anderen Seite geschlossenen Vertrag (der im übrigen noch einige Fragen offen lässt!) zur Folge hatte.

Man denke ferner an die seit vielen Jahren kontrovers diskutierte EU-Richtlinie zur „Harmonisierung bestimmter Aspekte des Urheberrechts ...", die am 14. Februar 2001 – entgegen anders lautender Prophezeiungen verschiedener Beobachter – vom Europäischen

---

[147] zitiert nach: Urheberrechtliche Zulässigkeit des Kopienversands öffentlicher Bibliotheken / Pressestelle des Bundesgerichtshofs. – (Mitteilung der Pressestelle / Bundesgerichtshof ; Nr. 16). – S. 1. – Das ausführliche Urteil ist nachzulesen in: Entscheidungssammlung zum Bibliotheksrecht / hrsg. von der Rechtskommission des Deutschen Bibliotheksinstituts und der Kommission für Rechtsfragen des Vereins Deutscher Bibliothekare. [Erarb. von ... : Jürgen Christoph Gödan ... Red. Helmut Rösner]. - Stand: April 2000. - Berlin : Ehem. Dt. Bibliotheksinst., 2000. - (Dbi-Materialien ; 197). - S. 348-370 ; in dem vorl. Zusammenhang bes. zu beachten: S. 368.

Parlament doch noch verabschiedet und nicht nochmals auf die lange Bank geschoben wurde, wobei 188 von 197 Änderungsanträgen auf der Strecke und viele Fragen ungeklärt blieben. (Die Mitgliedsstaaten müssen die Richtlinie nach deren offenbar nahe bevorstehendem Inkrafttreten innerhalb von 18 Monaten in nationales Recht umsetzen, nach weiteren 18 Monaten soll überprüft werden, ob die neuen Regelungen praktikabel sind)[148].

Wer in der bibliothekarischen Ausbildung Lehrveranstaltungen zum Urheberrecht anbietet, muss nicht nur die (vom Kampf konträrer Interessen und vom Druck der Lobbyisten stark beeinflusste) Entwicklung besonders genau beobachten – er muss auch Studierenden, die der Rechtswissenschaft ziemlich fern stehen, erklären, dass und warum sie sich mit einer Rechtslage befassen sollen, die in einigen Jahren (also vielleicht schon bei Abschluss des Studiums!) mit einiger Wahrscheinlichkeit überholt sein wird.

Es bleibe dahingestellt, ob es eine Erleichterung oder eine besondere Erschwernis bedeutet, dass die mühselige Vermittlung des Urheberrechts möglicherweise nur ca. 15 % der Dienstaufgaben eines hauptamtlichen Dozenten ausmachen würde.

Was vielleicht Aussicht auf Erfolg hätte

Dass die Vermittlung rechtlicher Kenntnisse in der bibliothekarischen Ausbildung ungeachtet aller bestehenden Schwierigkeiten und Probleme ein absolutes Muss darstellt, sei hiermit ausdrücklich anerkannt.

Der Praxisbezug

Wenn an einer Fachhochschule Konzepte zur Vermittlung des Lehrstoffes zu entwickeln sind, so stellt die mutmaßliche Akzeptanz bei den Studierenden nicht unbedingt eine zu vernachlässigende Größe dar. Ohne mit neuesten Umfrage-Ergebnissen aufwarten zu können, glaube ich in einer mehr als 18-jährigen Lehrtätigkeit beobachtet zu haben, dass Lehrinhalte bei den Studierenden auf umso größeres Interesse stoßen, je deutlicher der Praxisbezug dabei in Erscheinung tritt. Nicht zuletzt sehe ich meine Beobachtungen durch Ergebnisse von Umfragen gestützt, die bereits Ende der 60er-Jahre an acht nordamerikanischen Universitäten unter Studierenden der Sozialarbeit/Sozialpädagogik durchgeführt wurden. Einer der Projektbetreuer gab seine Erkenntnisse 1974 in einer deutschsprachigen, in der Bundesrepublik Deutschland erschienenen Publikation folgendermaßen wieder[149]:

> *Die Studenten sprachen sich eindeutig dafür aus, dass nur eine Verbindung von theoretischen und praktischen Lehr-, Lernangeboten das Curriculum effektiv macht und dass, wenn ein Praxisbezug von Ihnen nicht gesehen wird, sie auch große Schwierigkeiten haben, motiviert und lernaufnahmebereit zu sein.*

Konventionelle bibliothekarische Arbeitsfelder wie Erwerbung/Bestandsaufbau, Öffentlichkeitsarbeit/Programmarbeit und Informationsvermittlung/Benutzerschulung/Benutzerberatung spielen denn auch bei der Gliederung des Lehrstoffes immer noch eine gewisse

---

148 „Private Kopien in der EU bleiben straflos (Update) : Meldung vom 14.02.2001, 15:25" // in: Heise News-Ticker. – http://www.heise.de/newsticker/data/jk-14.02.01-004/(10.03.01). – Rösner, Helmut: „Der Kampf um Brüssel : Copyright-Richtlinie beschlossen" // in: Bibliotheksdienst 35 (2001), H. 3, S. 321-328.

149 Lowy, Louis: „'Integrative Learning and Teaching' Projekt (ILTP) und ‚Lehrplanentwicklungsprojekt'„ // in: Lehrplanentwicklung für Sozialarbeiter und Sozialpädagogen : zur Auseinandersetzung um Berufsauftrag u. Berufsausbildung / Teresa Bock; Louis Lowy u. a. Hrsg. von d. Kath. Fachhochschule Nordrhein-Westfalen. - Freiburg (im Breisgau) : Lambertus-Verlag, 1974. - S. 292-294, Zitat von S. 294.

Rolle, wenn sie auch durch moderne Begriffe wie „Kulturmanagement“ oder „Informationsdesign“ bzw. den ebenso schlichten wie vieldeutigen Begriff „Medien“ (samt so manchen dazu gehörigen Komposita) überlagert werden. In letzter Zeit wieder neu eingeführte Fächerbezeichnungen wie „Betriebswirtschaftslehre“ sind anwendungsbezogen zu sehen, die Psychologie, die 1995 an der HBI Stuttgart angeblich abgeschafft wurde, lebte in Seminaren zu Gesprächsführung und Kommunikation weiter.

Es sei in diesem Zusammenhang angemerkt, dass der Anwendungs- und Praxis-Bezug überhaupt als ein wesentliches Merkmal des Fachhochschulstudiums gilt, und dass die Fachhochschulen sich gerade dadurch von den Universitäten unterscheiden. Abgesehen von der Erwartung der Studierenden und dem Selbstverständnis der Institutionen darf und muss hier auf Vorgaben des Gesetzgebers zurückgegriffen werden, deren Inhalt hier der Einfachheit halber nach Creifelds‘ Rechtswörterbuch zitiert sei[150]:

> *Fachhochschulen sind Einrichtungen des Bildungswesens, die durch praxisbezogene Lehre eine auf wissenschaftlicher oder künstlerischer Grundlage beruhende Bildung vermitteln, die zu selbständiger Tätigkeit im Beruf befähigt.*

Ob daraus nicht vielleicht folgt, dass die Vermittlung rechtlicher Kenntnisse vorrangig und jeweils punktuell in praxisfeld-orientierte Lehrveranstaltungen eingebaut werden muss?

Die Beteiligung Außenstehender

Wenn obige Frage zu bejahen ist, dann sollten künftig

- mehr Seminare mit jeweils 2 Dozenten stattfinden können,
- hauptamtliche Dozenten die Möglichkeit haben, sich bei der Behandlung juristischer Fragen von rechtskundigen Spezialisten auf Kosten der Fachhochschule beraten zu lassen,
- rechtswissenschaftliche Crash-Kurse für hauptamtliche Dozenten von den Fachhochschulen (bzw. den zuständigen Fachbereichen) organisiert und finanziert werden.

Ohne eine vermehrte Beteiligung Außenstehender ist dies natürlich nicht zu bewerkstelligen. Ein neuralgischer Punkt ist dabei die Honorierung der beteiligten (und nicht der Fachhochschule als hauptamtliche Dozenten angehörenden) Juristen; so sind z.B. die Honorare, die eine Fachhochschule ihren Lehrbeauftragten zugestehen darf, in ihrer bescheidenen Höhe nicht gerade verlockend.

Integratives Lernen

Es sind besonders die folgenden Tätigkeitsfelder, in denen sich das Bibliothekspersonal immer wieder mit rechtlichen Fragen konfrontiert sieht:

- die Erwerbung von Medien,
- die Planung und Durchführung von Veranstaltungen,
- (fast) alle Tätigkeiten, die irgend etwas mit dem großen Komplex der Bibliotheksbenutzung zu tun haben.

Die letzteren seien hier einer näheren Betrachtung unterzogen. Dass zwischen einer Bibliothek und ihren Benutzern bzw. Kunden vielfältige Rechtsbeziehungen bestehen, dürfte

---

[150] Rechtswörterbuch / begr. von Carl Creifelds. Hrsg. von Klaus Weber. Bearb. von Dieter Guntz .... - 16., neubearb. Aufl.. - München : Beck, 2000. – S. 444.

dem Personal überwiegend erst im Konfliktfall bewusst werden. Konfliktsituationen aber bewältigt man bekanntlich nicht nur mit einer (oft sehr schwierigen!) Abklärung der Rechtslage, sondern auch mit Diplomatie und psychologischem Feingefühl. Das letztere gilt heutzutage nicht mehr allein als eine Begabung, die man entweder besitzt oder nicht besitzt. Vielmehr gelten kommunikative Fähigkeiten bis zu einem gewissen Grade als erlernbar, und in einem der wohl meist verbreiteten Bücher, die jemals von einem Wissenschaftler zur Psychologie der Kommunikation verfasst wurden, heißt es[151]:

> *... hat die Psychologie etwas anzubieten, um die zwischenmenschliche Kommunikation nicht nur wissenschaftlich zu erhellen, sondern auch „besser" zu machen? Sie hat.*

Was läge da näher, als dass man (im Sinne eines „integrativen Lernens") versucht, die Vermittlung rechtlicher Kenntnisse in einem praxis-orientierten Seminar mit derjenigen kommunikationspsychologischer Grundbegriffe zu verbinden? Ich habe dies an der HBI Stuttgart in Seminaren zum Thema „Konflikte zwischen Bibliothek und Benutzer" mehrfach praktiziert, wobei die bisherigen Seminare mehr oder minder eindeutig dem Studiengang „Öffentliche Bibliotheken" zugeordnet waren. Der Verlauf des bisher letzten Durchgangs, der im Wintersemester 2000/2001 erfolgte, sei hier kurz vorgestellt:

Vorstellung eines Beispiels

In der ersten Sitzung konfrontierte ich die Teilnehmer/innen mit einer Reihe von schriftlich fixierten Konfliktsituationen, die zunächst spontan aus der Sicht des gesunden Menschenverstandes und bei den Teilnehmern evtl. bereits vorhandener Vorkenntnisse und Vorerfahrungen analysiert wurden. In einigen nachfolgenden Sitzungen war die Vorstellung ausgewählter Gesetzestexte an der Reihe. Dass ich als Nicht-Juristin die „einschlägigen" Gesetze überhaupt ausfindig machen und in der Lehrveranstaltung zumindest ansatzweise kommentieren konnte, verdanke ich nicht nur dem „DBI-Materialien"-Band „Rechtsvorschriften für die Bibliotheksarbeit"[152] und der Lektüre juristischer Kommentar-Werke, sondern auch der vorangegangenen Zusammenarbeit mit zwei juristisch kompetenten Lehrbeauftragten, nämlich:

- Herrn Dr. Thomas Clemens, der in den 90er-Jahren dreimal den juristischen Part in einem von mir angebotenen Seminar übernahm[153], und
- Herrn Dipl. Bibl. Günther Thomas, der im Wintersemester 1999/2000 ein einschlägiges Seminar im Alleingang durchführte und hierzu ein fast 60-seitiges Skriptum erstellte[154].

Auf die Gesetzestexte folgten einige Gerichtsurteile (die ich den Studierenden allerdings

---

151 Schulz von Thun, Friedemann: Miteinander reden. - Orig.-Ausg.. – Reinbek bei Hamburg : Rowohlt. - [1]. Störungen und Klärungen : Psychologie d. zwischenmenschl. Kommunikation. - 1981. - (rororo ; 7489 : rororo-Sachbuch). – Später noch häufig neu erschienen und durch weitere Bände ergänzt. Hier zitiert nach dem 450.-499. Tsd. – Nov. 1994. – Bd. 1, S. 11.

152 Rechtsvorschriften für die Bibliotheksarbeit / hrsg. von der Rechtskommission des Deutschen Bibliotheksinstituts. - 3., überarb. und erw. Ausg.. - Berlin : Dt. Bibliotheksinst., 1998. - (Dbi-Materialien ; 172).

153 Herrn Dr. Clemens verdanke ich u.a. auch wertvolle Hinweise auf nützliche Formulierungen, wie sie in Benutzungs-Ordnungen nach Möglichkeit vorkommen sollen!

154 Thomas, Günther: Seminar „Umgang mit Konflikten", HBI, Wintersemester 1999/2000. – [Stuttgart, 2000]. – [unveröffentlichtes Skriptum.

nur in einer gewissermaßen „filtrierten" Form und nicht etwa im Volltext zumutete[155]) und ausgewählte Benutzungsordnungen, sodann die Vermittlung grundlegender kommunikationspsychologischer Kenntnisse anhand von (eher praxis-orientierter) psychologischer Fachliteratur. All das geschah unter möglichst häufiger Bezugnahme auf die in der ersten Sitzung vorgestellten Konfliktsituationen. Zur Kontrolle für beide Seiten sollten die Studierenden nach einigen Wochen ausgewählte Konfliktsituationen in einer kleinen Hausarbeit schriftlich analysieren, wobei

a) Bemerkungen zur Rechtslage
b) Vorschläge für die Benutzungsordnung
c) Vorschläge für das Verhalten des Bibliothekspersonals

zu machen waren. Diese Analyse hätte ich mir eigentlich folgendermaßen vorgestellt:

1. Ein Benutzer behauptet ziemlich empört, bei ihm seien Bücher angemahnt worden, die er niemals ausgeliehen habe.

a) Die Beweispflicht liegt bei der Bibliothek (die Bibliothek muss im Ernstfall beweisen, dass der Benutzer die Bücher ausgeliehen hat – nicht der Benutzer, dass er sie nicht ausgeliehen hat). – Für einen etwaigen Missbrauch seines Ausweises würde der Benutzer nur in sehr engen Grenzen haften (beinahe unabhängig davon, was die Benutzungsordnung bez. einer etwaigen Haftung vorsieht!)[156].

b) Folgendes würde die Beweislage merklich verbessern: für jeden Ausleihvorgang wird ein Beleg (mit dem spätest-möglichen Rückgabe-Datum!) ausgedruckt. Jeder Benutzer ist laut Benutzungsordnung verpflichtet, den Beleg sofort zu überprüfen und etwaige Unstimmigkeiten unverzüglich zu reklamieren. – Der Benutzer hat nicht nur eine Ausweis-Nummer, sondern auch eine PIN (Geheim-Ziffer), die er bei jedem Ausleihverbuchungs-Vorgang über eine Tastatur eingibt, und/oder die Ausweise sind mit einem Lichtbild versehen. – Der Benutzer ist lt. Benutzungsordnung verpflichtet, den Ausweis (getrennt von der PIN!) sorgfältig zu verwahren und einen etwaigen Verlust sofort zu melden.

c) Am Verbuchungs-PC den Ausleihstatus der angemahnten Bücher überprüfen, ggf. im Regal nachsehen, ob die Bücher dort stehen. — Falls der Verbleib der Bücher auf diesem Weg ermittelt wird, ist vielleicht eine höfliche Entschuldigung fällig. -- Die Bücher, falls sie nicht aufgefunden werden, auf ein Vermisstkonto buchen, damit die EDV-Anlage nicht noch weitere Mahnungen erstellt. – Bisher angefallene Mahngebühren evtl. erlassen (dies insbesondere bei Verdacht auf einen Fehler der Bibliothek!). – Den Benutzer höflich bitten, dass er zu Hause nochmals nachsieht, ob er (oder ein Familien-Mitglied) die Bücher nicht vielleicht doch ausgeliehen hat; fragen, ob er seinen Ausweis zeitweilig vermisst hat oder jetzt immer noch vermisst. – Notfalls den Ausweis sperren (wenn Ausweis-Verlust zu befürchten!).

2. Ein Benutzer verweigert die Zahlung von Mahngebühren.
Seine Begründung: er habe keine Mahnung erhalten!

---

155 Die Gerichtsurteile betreffen vielfach nicht Bibliotheken, sondern z.B. Gastwirte oder Supermärkte. Der bibliothekarischen Fachwelt müssen die aus solchen Urteilen zu ziehenden Konsequenzen durch kompetente Juristen vermittelt werden. Die einschlägige und teilweise hier zitierte Fachliteratur habe ich dankbar benutzt.

156 Vgl. Haager, Michael: „Bank und Bibliothek : wer haftet bei Missbrauch von Leseausweisen?"// in: Buch und Bibliothek 52 (2000), H. 10/11, S. 619-620, zu einem Urteil des Amtsgerichts Duisburg gegen die Stadt Duisburg.

a) Aus §130 BGB („Wirksamwerden der Willenserklärung gegenüber Abwesenden") wäre ableitbar, dass die Mahnung erst wirksam wird, wenn sie zugegangen ist – dass der Benutzer sie also u.U. nicht zu bezahlen braucht![157] – Dass der Benutzer die Mahnung nicht erhalten habe, ist eine Aussage, deren Wahrheitsgehalt die Bibliothek nicht überprüfen kann, zumal sie ja noch nicht einmal die Mahnungen selbst zur Post bringt, sondern über das städtische Versandamt verschickt (dort könnten die Mahnungen sogar u.U. liegen geblieben sein!).
b) Am besten auf Mahngebühren verzichten und statt dessen die Säumnisentgelte/Säumnisgebühren entsprechend höher ansetzen. Die Mahnung wird dann zu einem kostenlosen Service, der nachlässige Benutzer davor bewahrt, dass sie einzelne Medien versehentlich mehrere Jahre lang behalten und dann horrende Säumnisentgelte/Säumnisgebühren bezahlen müssen[158]. Eine Situation wie die o.g. kann dann gar nicht erst eintreten. – Oder: den Weg der Benutzungsordnung der Württembergischen Landes-Bibliothek wählen (die Mahngebühren werden fällig, sobald das EDV-Programm die Mahnung erstellt bzw. eingetragen hat. Das Versandrisiko trägt nicht die Bibliothek).
c) Höflich und bestimmt auf die Benutzungsordnung verweisen – oder, wenn die Benutzungsordnung in diesem Fall nichts „hergibt", notfalls einen Gebührenerlass durchführen (da ja der Benutzer im Recht sein könnte!)

U. U. könnte sich folgender Dialog abspielen:

> Bibliothekar/in *(verbalisierend, paraphrasierend)*[159]*: „Sie haben keine Mahnung bekommen?"*
> Benutzer *(ungehalten): „Nein – und ich zahle auch nicht!"*
> Bibliothekar/in *(nach wie vor ruhig und höflich): „Sie sehen nicht ein, dass Sie bezahlen sollen?"*

Vielleicht überlegt der zahlungsunwillige Benutzer sich die Sache dann anders!? (Nach Möglichkeit den Gebühren-Erlass nicht vorschnell durchführen!)

3. Ein Benutzer kommt nach längerer Pause (nach mehr als 6 Monaten!) mal wieder in die Bibliothek und will Bücher ausleihen. Das Ausleihverbuchungssystem verweigert die Ausleihverbuchung mit dem Hinweis „Gebührenlimit überschritten". Eine nähere Prüfung der Sachlage ergibt: bei seinem letzten Besuch in der Bibliothek ist der Benutzer DM 30.00 schuldig geblieben, wobei es sich um Säumnisentgelte für die damals zurückgegebenen Bücher gehandelt hätte.

a) Der Ausdruck Säumnis*entgelte* lässt auf eine privatrechtliche Benutzungsordnung schließen. Gem. §§ 558, 606 BGB gilt eine 6-monatige Verjährungsfrist ab dem Tag, an dem die Bibliothek die entliehenen Medien zurückerhalten hat. Ob Miete (§ 558) oder

---

157 Für Bibliotheken mit öffentlich-rechtlichen Benutzungs-Ordnungen ließen sich wohl vergleichbare Verwaltungsvorschriften finden, doch sei eingeräumt, dass all diese Ableitungen letzten Endes strittig sind.

158 Dass durch eine Mahnung der Benutzer „in Verzug gesetzt" werden müsste, trifft wohl in den meisten Bibliotheken nicht zu, da es üblich ist, bei der Entleihung von Medien Ausleihquittungen mit Angabe des Fälligkeitsdatums oder wenigstens Fristzettel auszuhändigen. (§ 284, II BGB: „... eine Zeit nach dem Kalender bestimmt ..."

159 Zur Gesprächsführung vgl. man z.B.: Beraten will gelernt sein : ein praktisches Lehrbuch für Anfänger und Fortgeschrittene / Sabine Bachmair .... - Weinheim ; Basel : Beltz, 1999. - (Beltz-Taschenbuch ; 30 : Psychologie). -- Lizenz der Psychologie-Verl.-Union., Weinheim. (auch frühere Aufl./Ausg. evtl. brauchbar!

Leihe (§ 606) vorliegt, braucht in diesem Zusammenhang nicht geprüft zu werden, da für beides die gleiche Verjährungsfrist gilt! -- Allerdings wird die Verjährung nur dann wirksam, wenn der Schuldner sie geltend macht. Das Bibliothekspersonal muss den Benutzer zunächst höflich um die Entrichtung der Entgelte bitten.

b) Bei einer öffentlich-rechtlichen Benutzungsordnung wäre die Verjährungsfrist wesentlich länger (wahrscheinlich 5 Jahre ab Rückgabe gem. § 3 I Nr. 5a Kommunalabgaben-Ordnung BAW, in Verb. mit § 228 Bundes-Abgabenordnung) – und damit das Risiko, dass die oben beschriebene Situation eintritt, wesentlich geringer! Eigentlich liegt in einem solchen Fall auch ein Versäumnis der Bibliothek vor, die rechtzeitig vor Verstreichen der Verjährungsfrist eine Meldung an die zuständigen Stellen der Gemeinde-Verwaltung machen müsste, um eine „Festsetzung" durch Mahnbescheid / Vollstreckungsbescheid / Gerichtsurteil zu erreichen. (Eine Mahnung der Bibliothek hätte keine verjährungs-unterbrechende Wirkung, ebenso wenig ist es Sache der Bibliothek, einen Mahnbescheid zu erwirken!) Erst nach einem Gerichtsurteil würde § 218, I BGB (30 Jahre!) greifen.

c) Gegenüber dem Benutzer muss jeglicher Vorwurf oder vorwurfsvolle Tonfall vermieden werden. Es könnte sein, dass er geneigt ist, mit „Beziehungs-Ohren" (Schulz von Thun[160]) zu hören und aus dem vorwurfsvollen Ton eine Abwertung seiner Person herzuleiten. Dann würde er sich wahrscheinlich damit zur Wehr setzen, dass er ein Versäumnis der Bibliothek zu entdecken sucht und auf die Idee kommt, dass die Bibliothek nichts mehr von ihm fordern kann, wenn sie so lange nichts unternommen hat. (Abwehrmechanismus!)

4. Eine Benutzerin berichtet aufgeregt, ihr Mantel sei von der Garderobe verschwunden (m.a.W.: gestohlen!). Die Garderobe ist unbewacht und befindet sich in der Nähe der Verbuchungstheke.

a) Selbst ein Schild „Für Garderobe wird nicht gehaftet" entbindet die Bibliothek in diesem Zusammenhang nicht von jeglicher Sorgfalts- und Fürsorgepflicht. Entscheidend wichtig ist dabei die Tatsache, dass die Bibliotheksbenutzer im allgemeinen nicht die Möglichkeit haben, während ihres Aufenthalts in der Bibliothek die Garderobe im Auge zu behalten. (Letzteres lässt sich aus verschiedenen Gerichtsurteilen gegen Gastwirte ableiten, bei denen es um gestohlene Mäntel ging![161]) – Ableitbar aus Art. 34 GG liegt die Haftung beim Bibliotheksträger, das Personal haftet höchstens (über „Rückgriff") bei Vorsatz oder grober Fahrlässigkeit. – Hat die Benutzerin einen besonders wertvollen Mantel an die unbewachte Garderobe gehängt und musste sie aufgrund langjähriger und/oder häufiger Bibliotheksbenutzung wissen, dass die Garderobe nicht bewacht wird, dann muss sie sich zumindest teilweise ein eigenes Mit-Verschulden zurechnen lassen (ihr Haftungsanspruch verringert sich dadurch, vgl. § 254 BGB).

b) Über die Benutzungsordnung lässt sich dieses Problem nicht lösen (es sei denn, es wären abschließbare Garderobenschränke in ausreichender Zahl vorhanden, dann könnten die Benutzer verpflichtet werden, von diesem Angebot Gebrauch zu machen.)

c) Ruhe bewahren, suchen helfen, *nicht* behaupten, dass das Theken-Personal nicht auch

---

160 Schulz von Thun, Friedemann: Miteinander reden / Friedemann Schulz von Thun. - Orig.-Ausg.. – Reinbek bei Hamburg : Rowohlt. - [1]. Störungen und Klärungen : Psychologie d. zwischenmenschl. Kommunikation. - 1981. - (rororo ; 7489 : rororo-Sachbuch). – Später noch häufig neu erschienen und durch weitere Bände ergänzt.

161 Sander, Mareike: „Haftung des Wirts für die Garderobe der Gäste : Urteile und Tipps ..." / [Mareike Sander], in: SWR4 – Recht so! – http://www.swr.de/swr4rp/rechtso000814.html (7.11.00.

noch die Garderobe beaufsichtigen könne. Die relevanten Fakten eruieren und notieren, für den Fall, dass die Benutzerin beim Bibliotheksträger Schadenersatz geltend macht.

5. Ein Benutzer schimpft heftig, weil er schon wieder Säumnisgebühren entrichten soll, wo er doch auswärts wohnt und nicht in so kurzen Abständen den Bibliotheksort aufsuchen kann (bzw. zwar am Bibliotheksort arbeitet, aber immer unabkömmlich ist, wenn die Bibliothek gerade geöffnet hat).

a) Laut § 10 der Gemeinde-Ordnung BAW hätten nur Personen, die in einer Gemeinde wohnen oder dort ein Grundstück besitzen bzw. ein Gewerbe betreiben, einen Rechtsanspruch darauf, zur Benutzung der Gemeindebibliothek zugelassen zu werden. Insofern stellt es schon ein gewisses Entgegenkommen der Gemeinde bzw. der Bibliothek dar, wenn ein auswärtiger Benutzer Bücher u.a. Medien ausleihen kann. – Als Härtefall (mit Gebühren-Erlass!) könnte der Benutzer eigentlich nur dann eingestuft werden, wenn er sich in einer finanziellen Notlage befände und noch zusätzliche Erschwernisse vorhanden wären. (vgl. § 59, Abs.1, Nr. 3 der LHO-BAW und weitere einschlägige Verwaltungs-Vorschriften!). Als ein zusätzliches Erschwernis könnte man vielleicht die vom Benutzer geschilderte Situation betrachten; eine finanzielle Notlage müsste er erst noch nachweisen oder glaubhaft machen.

b) „Die Bibliothek steht allen Einwohnern der Gemeinde ... etc. [Formulierung in Anlehnung an die Gemeinde-Ordnung] offen. Die Bibliotheksleitung kann auch andere Personen zur Benutzung zulassen. Deren Benutzungsrecht kann von vornherein beschränkt oder mit Auflagen verbunden werden.“ – Damit erhält die Bibliothek z.B. die Möglichkeit, die Zulassung Auswärtiger zeitlich zu befristen und Benutzern, die unangenehm aufgefallen sind, die Verlängerung des Benutzungs-Verhältnisses zu verweigern. Der Eindruck willkürlicher Entscheidungen muss dabei vermieden werden.

c) „Ich kann Ihren Ärger verstehen [Verständnis besänftigt vielleicht den wütenden Benutzer!], aber ich darf Ihnen die Gebühren nur dann erlassen, wenn Sie mir eine finanzielle Notlage nachweisen oder wenigstens glaubhaft machen.“ – „Ich möchte Ihnen solchen Ärger gerne künftig ersparen[162]. Darf ich Sie auf Möglichkeiten der Leihfristverlängerung hinweisen ...“

6. Eine Benutzerin, die schon einmal beim „Klauen“ erwischt wurde, verläßt mit prall gefüllter Tasche die Bibliothek, ohne etwas verbuchen zu lassen. Die Sache ist höchst verdächtig.

a) Bei begründetem Diebstahls-Verdacht wäre eine Taschenkontrolle juristisch unbedenklich. Es könnte sogar geltend gemacht werden, dass das Öffentliche Interesse an der Bewahrung des Bibliotheksguts stärker wiegt als das evtl. verletzte Persönlichkeitsrecht der verdächtigen Benutzerin[163]. Trotzdem sollte sich die Bibliothek um die Vermeidung von Peinlichkeiten bemühen! – Nicht jedes unbefugte (unverbuchte) Mitnehmen von Medien aus der Bibliothek ist ein Diebstahl; denn zum Diebstahl gehört die Absicht der

---

162 Zur Bedeutung von Ich- Botschaften vgl. man u.a. Gassner, Burghard: „Ursachen kennen, Signale richtig deuten : über den Umgang mit schwierigen Besuchern in Bibliotheken“ // in: BUB 52 (2000), H.12, S. 718-724, bes. 722

163 Vgl. Holland, Claudia: „Taschenkontrollen im Supermarkt – Taschenkontrollen in Bibliotheken, eine vergleichbare Situation?“ // in: Bibliotheksdienst 29 (1995), H. 6, S. 967-971

rechtswidrigen Zueignung (§ 242 StGB), die im „Ernstfall" bewiesen werden muss![164]

b) „Mitgebrachte Taschen – ausgenommen kleine Handtaschen – sind beim Betreten der Bibliothek in die dafür vorgesehenen Schränke einzuschließen" [zusätzlich entsprechender Aushang – evtl. höflicher formuliert! – im Eingangsbereich der Bibliothek!]. – „Das Bibliothekspersonal kann – auch ohne konkreten Diebstahlsverdacht – Einblick in mitgebrachte Gegenstände und die Überbekleidung nehmen."

c) „Ich bin verpflichtet, gelegentlich Routine-Kontrollen durchzuführen. <Auch die Benutzungsordnung sieht dies ausdrücklich vor.> Dürfte ich bitte in Ihre Tasche sehen?" – Nach Möglichkeit jeden Eindruck eines Diebstahlsverdachts vermeiden! Selbst, wenn man unverbuchte Medien in der Tasche findet, nicht von Diebstahl oder ähnlichem sprechen, sondern: „Dürfen wir das bitte verbuchen?"

7. Ein Dreizehnjähriger hat in o.g. Bibliothek ca. 15 (relativ neuwertige) Bücher (alle auf einmal!) ausgeliehen und sie auf dem Heimweg verloren (z.B.: Fußball gespielt, die Tasche mit den Büchern irgendwo abgestellt). Die Eltern des Jungen verweigern jeglichen Schadenersatz. Der Junge selbst behauptet, er bekomme nicht genug Taschengeld, um für die verlorenen Bücher Ersatz leisten zu können.

a) Gem. § 832 BGB haften die Eltern nur dann, wenn sie die Aufsichtspflicht verletzt haben. Daran ändern auch die von den Bibliotheken üblicherweise geforderten „Haftungs-Erklärungen" wahrscheinlich nichts! – Eine Verletzung der Aufsichtspflicht kann man hier kaum unterstellen, da man doch wohl nicht erwarten darf, dass die Eltern ihren 13-jährigen Sohn in die Bibliothek und wieder nach Hause begleiten, damit er die entliehenen Bücher auf dem Heimweg nicht verliert. – Den 13-Jährigen aufgrund des „Deliktsrechts" (BGB §§ 823, I bzw. 828, I und II) in späteren Jahren, wenn er eigenes Geld verdient, zu belangen, kann wahrscheinlich nicht in Erwägung gezogen werden, da ein 13-Jähriger vielleicht doch noch nicht die nötige Einsicht besitzt, um den Verlust der Bücher vorherzusehen, wenn er irgendwo spontan die Tasche abstellt und sich ablenken lässt. –Eine wirksame Schadensbegrenzung ist nur über eine Ausleihbeschränkung für Minderjährige möglich. Ob dies bibliothekspolitisch wünschenswert ist (Ausleihzahlen!), bleibe dahingestellt.

b) „Die Bibliotheksleitung kann für bestimmte Benutzer- bzw. Mediengruppen die Ausleihe begrenzen". – „Wenn Medien nach Ablauf der Leihfrist nicht zurückgegeben worden sind und/oder Gebühren/Entgelte und/oder Schaden-Ersatzforderungen nicht erfüllt sind, kann die Bibliothek die Ausleihe weiterer Medien ganz oder teilweise ablehnen."

c) Den Benutzer sperren (nur den 13-Jährigen, nicht seine Eltern!), was evtl. auch ohne entsprechenden Passus der Benutzungs-Ordnung aufgrund des Zurückbehaltungsrechts (§ 273 BGB) möglich wäre. Dem 13-Jährigen erklären, dass er erst wieder ausleihen kann, wenn er Schadenersatz für die verlorenen Bücher geleistet hat. – Ihn bei dieser Gelegenheit vielleicht nochmals fragen, ob er wirklich nicht aus eigener Tasche zahlen kann (vielleicht hat er ein ansehnliches Sparkonto? Einsicht vorausgesetzt, würde er mit diesem evtl. haften). – Evtl. die Eltern bitten, zu prüfen, ob sie eine Haftpflichtversicherung haben, die den Schaden ggf. übernimmt (nicht besonders aussichtsreich, zwingt aber die Eltern, sich nochmals mit der Angelegenheit auseinander zu setzen).

---

[164] Man vgl. dazu u.a. Böhm, Peter P.: „Bücherentwendungen aus Hochschulbibliotheken als Rechtsproblem" / Peter P. Böhm u. Günter F. Paschek // in: Zeitschrift für Bibliothekswesen und Bibliographie 28 (1981), H.2, S. 90-100.

Es sei eingestanden, dass die meisten Hausarbeiten meiner Seminar-Teilnehmer/innen ziemlich weit hinter meinen hier skizzierten Vorstellungen zurückblieben, weshalb anhand weiterer Fallbeispiele insbesondere die Verknüpfung von rechtlichen und psychologischen Aspekten noch einmal eingeübt werden musste!
Das Seminar (das im übrigen vier Semester-Wochenstunden umfasste) war damit noch nicht zu Ende. Die weiteren Themen waren:

- wesentliche Unterschiede, die zwischen einer Benutzungsordnung einerseits und einer Benutzungsanleitung (einem Bibliotheksführer) andererseits (und zwar nicht zuletzt in der Formulierung!) bestehen,
- die Konzeption und Erstellung von Benutzungs-Anleitungen, Bibliotheksführern und verschiedenen Quick-Guides.

Die Unterschiede, die im Sprachduktus zwischen einer Benutzungsordnung und einer Benutzungsanleitung/einem Bibliotheksführer bestehen, hervorzuheben, halte ich für besonders wichtig; denn ich habe in den Jahren, in denen ich selbst noch als Bibliothekarin tätig war, viele Bibliotheksführer und Benutzungsanleitungen gesehen, in denen es z.B. hieß:

> *Mitgebrachte Taschen sind beim Betreten der Bibliothek in die dafür vorgesehenen Schränke einzuschließen.*

Eine solche Formulierung ist in einer Benutzungsordnung durchaus angebracht, in einem Bibliotheksführer (einer Benutzungsanleitung) dagegen sollte es heißen:

> *Bitte schließen Sie mitgebrachte Taschen beim Betreten der Bibliothek in die im Eingangsbereich aufgestellten Schränke ein!*

Höflichkeit, direkte Ansprache und konkrete Handlungsanweisungen sind in einem Bibliotheksführer (einer Benutzungsanleitung) ein absolutes Muss, in einer Bibliotheksordnung sind sie dagegen eher fehl am Platz. Damit die Studierenden solche Unterschiede begreifen, sollten Benutzungsordnung und Bibliotheksführer nach Möglichkeit Gegenstand ein und derselben Lehrveranstaltung sein.

Defizite und ihre Minimierung

Das integrative Lernen mit Fallbeispielen, die unter möglichst vielen theoretischen und praktischen Aspekten beleuchtet werden (bereits in der Gründungsphase der Fachhochschulen für das Studium der Sozialarbeit/Sozialpädagogik vereinzelt ins Auge gefasst[165]) scheint immer noch entscheidende Vorteile zu haben – auch und gerade in der bibliothekarischen Ausbildung. Doch seien Defizite dieses Konzepts eingeräumt:

- Man kann nicht alles, was im Berufsalltag irgendwie zusammenhängt, in ein und dieselbe Lehrveranstaltung packen (so ist es mir z.B. noch nie so recht gelungen, nennenswerte Rollenspiel-Anteile in eines der hier beschriebenen Seminare zu integrieren!). Eine organisatorisch und personell bedingte Zersplitterung wird dem integrativen Lernen

[165] Lowy, Louis: „'Integrative Learning and Teaching' Projekt (ILTP) und ‚Lehrplanentwicklungsprojekt'„ // in: Lehrplanentwicklung für Sozialarbeiter und Sozialpädagogen : zur Auseinandersetzung um Berufsauftrag u. Berufsausbildung / Teresa Bock; Louis Lowy u. a. Hrsg. von d. Kath. Fachhochschule Nordrhein-Westfalen. - Freiburg (im Breisgau) : Lambertus-Verlag, 1974. – S. 292-294, bes. S. 393.

immer gewisse Grenzen setzen.
- Es fehlt dem integrativen Lernen sowohl an Systematik, als auch vielleicht an wissenschaftlicher Differenzierung (möglicherweise aus der Sicht vieler Juristen ein entscheidendes Manko!)
- Ein Dozent, der juristische (oder auch psychologische) Kenntnisse berufsfeld-orientiert im Selbststudium erworben hat, um sie an Studierende weiterzugeben, wird sich zumindest schwer tun, diese Kenntnisse immer rechtzeitig zu aktualisieren.

Doch solche Defizite lassen sich bis zu einem gewissen Grad minimieren. Neben der bereits erwähnten Beteiligung externer Experten sei auf Möglichkeiten, die sich in neuen Masterstudiengängen eröffnen, verwiesen.

Die neuen Masterstudiengänge sind Aufbaustudiengänge, die auf anspruchsvollere berufliche Aufgaben (z.B. Leitungs- und Management-Aufgaben) vorbereiten sollen.

Benutzungsordnungen zu formulieren, deren Verabschiedung auf den Weg zu bringen, mit dem zuständigen Rechtsamt über strittige Rechtsfragen und über Konflikte, die zwischen der Bibliothek und ihren Benutzern aufgetreten sind, zu diskutieren, wird zumindest in mittleren und größeren Bibliotheken eher die Aufgabe der (mit höheren Studienabschlüssen ausgestatteten) Bibliotheksleitung, als diejenige einer „gewöhnlichen" (Diplom-) Bibliothekarin sein.

Hinzu kommt die der Bibliotheksleitung obliegende Verantwortung für einen arbeitsrechtlich und tarifrechtlich korrekten Dienstbetrieb, für die ordnungsgemäße Verwendung der Finanzmittel (bei wachsender Eigenverantwortung im Rahmen der Budgetierung), für die juristisch korrekte Gestaltung der in der Bibliothek verwendeten Formulare (Beispiel: Hervorhebung der Einwilligung zur Verarbeitung personenbezogener Daten im Anmeldeformular), für eine (datenschutz-)rechtlich korrekte EDV-Anwendung, wobei relevante Entscheidungen vielfach schon bei der Planung bzw. auf der Ebene der Systemverwaltung zu treffen sind – nicht zu vergessen die immer komplizierter werdenden Aspekte des Urheberrechts und des Jugendschutzes (und diese Aufzählung ist keineswegs vollständig).

Je größer die Bibliothek, desto größer ist auch die Verantwortung – und je anspruchsvoller der Studienabschluss, desto größer dürften auch die Erwartungen der jeweiligen Verwaltung in die rechtlichen Kenntnisse des Bibliotheksleiters sein. Diese Kenntnisse müssen bei einer sich ständig wandelnden Rechtslage ein Berufsleben lang aktuell gehalten werden, was einschlägige methodische Fertigkeiten (und nicht nur bibliothekarisch-bibliographische!) voraussetzt und vielleicht während des Aufbau-Studiums eine eher systematische, als nur punktuelle Beschäftigung mit ausgewählten Rechtsgebieten erfordert bzw. sinnvoll erscheinen lässt.

Nennenswerte, mit mehr wissenschaftlicher Akribie zu behandelnde juristische Anteile an den Lehrinhalten der Aufbaustudiengänge würden denn auch die eingangs skizzierten personellen Probleme in einem anderen Lichte erscheinen lassen.

Schlussbemerkung

Es liegt mir fern, irgendwelche Patentrezepte anpreisen zu wollen. Vielmehr läge mir daran, eine Diskussion anzustoßen. Dem Einwand, dass rechtliche Kenntnisse z. B. in Öffentlichen Bibliotheken nicht so wichtig seien, weil es ja bei den Kommunen und Landkreisen Rechtsämter gebe, möchte ich von vornherein mit einem Zitat aus der Zeitschrift „Buch und Bibliothek" vom Februar 1999 begegnen[166]:

Nach aller Erfahrung sind die Rechtsämter im Zeitalter des Lean-Management und des Downsizing stark belastet. Außerdem liegen keine oder nur wenige Fachkenntnisse im Bereich Bibliothek vor. Anfragen können meist nicht schnell genug beantwortet werden und entsprechen nicht immer den Bedürfnissen.

Die Notwendigkeit eigener rechtlicher Kenntnisse und die Zusammenarbeit mit anderen Ämtern können nicht gegeneinander ausgespielt werden.

Zitierte Literatur

Beraten will gelernt sein : ein praktisches Lehrbuch für Anfänger und Fortgeschrittene / Sabine Bachmair .... - Weinheim ; Basel : Beltz, 1999. -- (Beltz-Taschenbuch ; 30 : Psychologie). - Lizenz der Psychologie-Verl.-Union., Weinheim.

Böhm, Peter P.: „Bücherentwendungen aus Hochschulbibliotheken als Rechtsproblem" / Peter P. Böhm u. Günter F. Paschek // in: Zeitschrift für Bibliothekswesen und Bibliographie 28 (1981), H.2, S. 90-100.

Clemens, Thomas: „Rechtsfragen der Öffentlichen Bibliotheken: Das Bibliotheks-Benutzungsverhältnis : Teil II des überarbeiteten Referats, gehalten auf der Fortbildungstagung der Staatlichen Beratungsstellen Nürnberg und Würzburg am 1.7.1992 in Neustadt a.d. Aisch" // in: DIE NEUE BÜCHEREI 1993, H. 2, S. 121-127.

Entscheidungssammlung zum Bibliotheksrecht / hrsg. von der Rechtskommission des Deutschen Bibliotheksinstituts und der Kommission für Rechtsfragen des Vereins Deutscher Bibliothekare. [Erarb. von ... : Jürgen Christoph Gödan ... Red. Helmut Rösner]. - Stand: April 2000.. - Berlin : Ehem. Dt. Bibliotheksinst., 2000. - (Dbi-Materialien ; 197).

Gassner, Burghard: „Ursachen kennen, Signale richtig deuten : über den Umgang mit schwierigen Besuchern in Bibliotheken" // in: BUB 52 (2000), H.12, S. 718-724.

Haager, Michael: „Bank und Bibliothek : wer haftet bei Missbrauch von Leseausweisen?"// in: Buch und Bibliothek 52 (2000), H. 10/11, S. 619-620.

Haager, Michael: „Meist gratis, nie umsonst : Rechtsberatung für Bibliotheken" // in: Buch und Bibliothek 51 (1999), H.2, S. 128-131.

Holland, Claudia: „Taschenkontrollen im Supermarkt – Taschenkontrollen in Bibliotheken, eine vergleichbare Situation?" // in: Bibliotheksdienst 29 (1995), H. 6, S. 967-971.

Kirchner, Hildebert: Bibliotheks- und Dokumentationsrecht. - Wiesbaden : Reichert, 1981. - . (Elemente des Buch- und Bibliothekswesens ; Bd. 8).

Lowy, Louis: „'Integrative Learning and Teaching' Projekt (ILTP) und ‚Lehrplanentwicklungsprojekt'„ // in: Lehrplanentwicklung für Sozialarbeiter und Sozialpädagogen : zur Auseinandersetzung um Berufsauftrag u. Berufsausbildung / Teresa Bock; Louis Lowy u. a. Hrsg. von d. Kath. Fachhochschule Nordrhein-Westfalen. - Freiburg (im Breisgau) : Lambertus-Verlag, 1974. – S. 292-294.

„Private Kopien in der EU bleiben straflos (Update) : Meldung vom 14.02.2001, 15:25" // in: Heise News-Ticker. – http://www.heise.de/newsticker/data/jk-14.02.01-004/ (10.03.01)

Rasche, Monika: „Zulassung von Kindern und Jugendlichen zur Bibliotheksbenutzung" // in: Rossoll, Erika: Die Benutzungsordnung einer Öffentlichen Bibliothek : Formulierungs-

[166] Haager, Michael: „Meist gratis, nie umsonst : Rechtsberatung für Bibliotheken" // in: Buch und Bibliothek 51 (1999), H.2, S. 128-131, Zitat von S. 130.

vorschlag – Materialien – Beispiele / [erarb. von Erika Rossoll ...] - Berlin : Deutsches Bibliotheksinst., 1993. - (Arbeitshilfen / Deutsches. Bibliotheksinstitut). – S. 21-23.

Rechtsvorschriften für die Bibliotheksarbeit / hrsg. von der Rechtskommission des Deutschen Bibliotheksinstituts. - 3., überarb. und erw. Ausg.. - Berlin : Dt. Bibliotheksinst., 1998. - (Dbi-Materialien ; 172).

Rechtswörterbuch / begr. von Carl Creifelds. Hrsg. von Klaus Weber. Bearb. von Dieter Guntz .... - 16., neubearb. Aufl.. - München : Beck, 2000.

Rösner, Helmut: „Der Kampf um Brüssel : Copyright-Richtlinie beschlossen“ // in: Bibliotheksdienst 35 (2001), H. 3, S. 321-328.

Rösner, Helmut: „Rechtskommission des EDBI, Herbstsitzung in Berlin“ // in: Bibliotheksdienst 34 (2000), H. 12, S. 2036-2041.

Sander, Mareike: „Haftung des Wirts für die Garderobe der Gäste : Urteile und Tipps ...“ / [Mareike Sander], in: SWR4 – Recht so! – http://www.swr.de/swr4rp/rechtso000814.html (7.11.00).

Schulz von Thun, Friedemann: Miteinander reden. - Orig.-Ausg.. – Reinbek bei Hamburg : Rowohlt. - [1]. Störungen und Klärungen : Psychologie d. zwischenmenschl. Kommunikation. - 1981. - (rororo ; 7489 : rororo-Sachbuch). – Später noch häufig neu erschienen und durch weitere Bände ergänzt.

Thomas, Günther: Seminar „Umgang mit Konflikten“, HBI, Wintersemester 1999/2000. – [Stuttgart, 2000]. – [unveröffentlichtes Skriptum].

Urheberrechtliche Zulässigkeit des Kopienversands öffentlicher Bibliotheken / Pressestelle des Bundesgerichtshofs. – (Mitteilung der Pressestelle / Bundesgerichtshof, Pressestelle ; Nr. 16)

Frank Thissen

Merkmale effektiven Lernens

Virtuelle Lehrveranstaltungen - neue Formen des Lehrens und Lernens

Neuere Untersuchungen zur Lernforschung beschreiben den menschlichen Wissenserwerb als aktiven, selbstregulativen und konstruktiven Prozess, der weniger durch äußere Anregungen, als durch interne Befindlichkeiten, Vorerfahrungen und Erwartungen eines Lerners beeinflusst wird. Wissen entsteht in der intensiven Auseinandersetzung mit Situationen, Frage- und Problemstellungen. Wissen entsteht dann, wenn es in eine konkrete Situation eingebunden ist und dem Lerner nicht einen Algorithmus zur Beantwortung einer Fragestellung anbietet, sondern es ihm zunächst intensiv ermöglicht, die Fragestellung selbst zu verstehen und sich mit ihr auseinander zu setzen (GALLIN).

Der Anfang des Wissens ist die Haltung des Nichtwissens, die Sokrates beschrieben hat. Eine offene Haltung, die Unsicherheiten zulässt und wünscht. Eine Haltung, sich nicht für das »Ja« oder »Nein« entscheidet, sondern das »sowohl – als auch« zulässt. Und das »vielleicht«. Diese Haltung ermöglicht es, offen für Situationen, Menschen, Fragestellungen zu sein. Sie ermöglicht es, sich selber immer wieder infrage zu stellen und immer wieder hinzuzulernen, umzulernen, auch zu verlernen.

Diese Haltung der Offenheit – sowohl kognitiv als auch emotional – führt unweigerlich zur Kommunikation. Sie bleibt nicht bei sich stehen, sondern sucht ein Gegenüber, um mit ihm Ideen zu teilen, mit Gedanken zu spielen, zu experimentieren und auch zu reflektieren. Es ist das »dialogische Prinzip« (BUBER), ein kreatives Prinzip, denn »in einem Dialog versuchen [...] die Gesprächsteilnehmer nicht, einander gewisse Ideen oder Informationen *mitzuteilen*, die ihnen bekannt sind. Vielmehr könnte man sagen, dass die beiden *etwas gemeinsam machen*, das heißt, das sie zusammen etwas Neues schaffen.« (BOHM, S. 27)

Durch den Dialog entsteht eine neue Qualität im Umgang mit den Themen des Dialogs. Diese werden nicht mehr unter der Perspektive des »Habens« gesehen, sondern unter der Perspektive des »Seins« (FROMM). Kein »ich weiß«, d.h. ich besitze ein bestimmtes Wissen, sondern das »ich lerne« steht dabei im Vordergrund. Es ist ein anderes Wissen, eines, das Psychologen mit dem Begriff der kognitiven Karten (DOWS) beschrieben haben und das die moderne Hirnforschung bei der Untersuchung und Visualisierung von Prozessen im menschlichen Gehirn sichtbar machen kann. Wissen ist keine Ablagerung von materialisierten Informationen, sondern der Aufbau eines flexiblen Netzwerkes, das permanent angepasst wird. Es ist die Konstruktion, die Re-konstruktion, De-konstruktion – die permanente Veränderung (KÖSEL).

Im Gegensatz dazu steht das Paradigma des Wissenserwerbs gemäß der »Nürnberger Trichter«-Methode. Hier ist Wissen ein Sammeln und Anhäufen von Informationsmaterial, ohne eine tiefere kognitive und emotionale Verarbeitung. Es ist ein relativ emotionsloses Aneignen von »Stoff«, der in einer Prüfung nützlich sein soll. Diese Form der Wissensaneignung führt nach MANDL u.a. zu verschiedenen Problemen. Zum einen erzeugt sie sehr häufig ein sogenanntes »träges Wissen« (ARZBERGER, S. 43), d.h. ein Wissen, das zwar prinzipiell vorhanden, aber in Anwendungssituationen nicht anwendbar ist. Außerdem ist oft ein »mangelnder Wissenstransfer« zu beobachten (ARZBERGER ebd.): das Wissen kann nicht auf eine konkrete Situation, die nicht mit der Lernsituation identisch ist, angewendet werden.

Um diese Probleme zu reduzieren, werden folgende Merkmale für Lernumgebungen gefordert (ARZBERGER / GERSTENMAIER / REINMANN-ROTHMEIER):

- Die Lernsituation sollte *problemorientiert* sein. D.h. das Thema sollte ausgehend von einer konkreten und realistischen Problemlage erschlossen werden. Hierbei sollte es die Möglichkeit geben, sich zunächst intensiv mit der Fragestellung selber auseinander zu setzen, bevor Lösungsmöglichkeiten nachgegangen wird. Problemorientierte Lernumgebungen können ein exploratives Lernen ermöglichen, bei dem der Lerner Lösungsmöglichkeiten eigenständig entdecken und entwickeln kann. Das Lernsystem und der »Lehrer« bieten dabei Hilfestellungen, sie sind Anreger im Sinne der Mäeutik.
- Eine effektive Lernumgebung sollte *authentisch* sein. Nicht abstrakte, konstruierte Situationen, sondern Anwendungsfälle aus der Praxis bieten Lernern komplexe und realistische Lernerfahrungen. Diese Fälle sind *situiert*, sie integrieren Probleme oder Aufgaben in einen komplexen Kontext. Situiertheit ermöglicht es Lernern, sich besser an den Kontext zu erinnern, es werden kognitive Anker gesetzt.
- Ein weiteres Merkmal sind die *multiplen Kontexte und Perspektiven*, in denen die Auseinandersetzung mit der Thematik stattfindet. Durch unterschiedliche Blickwinkel gewinnt die Lernsituation eine Vielschichtigkeit, die es ermöglicht, ein differenziertes Verständnis zu erwerben und die Komplexität vielfältig wahrzunehmen.
- Ebenso spielt der *soziale Kontext* eine wesentliche Rolle. Menschen sind Lebewesen, die in Gemeinschaften, d.h. sozialen Beziehungen zu anderen Menschen stehen und sich darüber definieren. Aus diesem Grund ist Lernen immer auch ein sozialer Prozess. Gemeinsames Handeln ist eine Form des menschlichen Orientierungsverhaltens (LUHMANN / MATURANA), es ist eine Form der permanenten Abgleichung und Kommunikation darüber, wie Welt, wie Wissen von der Gemeinschaft interpretiert werden kann – es ist die Kultur.
- Außerdem stellen Faktoren, die positive *Emotionen fördern*, eine weitere wichtige Voraussetzung für Lernerfolge dar. Wie GOLEMAN, CIOMPI und DAMASIO gezeigt haben, ist unser kognitives System wesentlich durch emotionale Komponenten beeinflusst. Eine Lernbedingung, in der sich ein Lerner wohlfühlt, verspricht wesentlich größeren Lernerfolg als eine emotional negativ bestimmte Umgebung, die lernbehindernd ist (VESTER).

Virtuelle Seminare als Ermöglichungsformen des aktiven, selbstgesteuerten Lernens

Virtuelle Lernformen stellen zunächst grundsätzlich per se eine Reduktion des Lernens im Vergleich zu Präsenzveranstaltungen dar. Die soziale Kommunikation ist durch das Medium Computer stark eingeschränkt, nonverbale Kommunikation der Teilnehmer untereinander ist unmöglich, die asynchrone Form der Kommunikation (Newsgroups etc.) ist stark gewöhnungsbedürftig. Selbstgesteuertes Lernen erfordert zudem ein hohes Maß an Eigenmotivation und Engagement. Technische Probleme erschweren die Situation zusätzlich.

Trotz dieser Schwierigkeiten erscheinen mir virtuelle Lernveranstaltungen effektiv und sinnvoll zu sein, wenn sie didaktisch angemessen gestaltet sind und die oben beschriebenen Merkmale der aktivierenden Lernkontexte berücksichtigen. In einer virtuelle Propädeutik-Veranstaltung im Wintersemester 2000/2001 an der Hochschule für Bibliotheks- und Informationswesen wurden die ca. 140 Teilnehmer zu Beginn aufgefordert, eine ganz individuelle Lerngeschichte aufzuschreiben. Diese Geschichten wurden gesammelt und auf einer Web-Seite für alle Teilnehmer veröffentlicht. In einem zweiten Schritt bekam jeder Teilnehmer die Aufgabe, die drei Beiträge, die in der Liste nach dem eigenen Beitrag aufgelistet worden sind, zu kommentieren, d.h. den Autoren eine Rückmeldung zur Lerngeschichte zu geben. Hieraus entstand eine intensive Diskussion über Lernerfahrungen, es kristallisierten sich (zunächst subjektiv wahrgenommene) lernfördernde bzw. lernbehindernde Merkmale heraus und jeder Teilnehmer hatte den Einstieg in ein Thema gefunden, das mit seiner individuellen Situation zu tun hatte. Erst danach wurden die Teilnehmer mit Material zum Thema Lernen konfrontiert, das ihnen die Möglichkeit gab, mehr darüber zu erfahren, eigenes Erleben zu reflektieren und weitere Anregungen zur Optimierung des eigenen Lernprozesses zu erhalten.

In einem Seminar zum Thema *Digitales Informationsdesign* erhielten die Teilnehmer zu Beginn die Aufgabe, ein digitales Lexikon zum Thema Informationsdesign zu erstellen. Die Gruppe sammelte zunächst Stichworte und definierte die grundsätzliche Struktur eines Lexikonartikels. Danach erarbeiteten Kleingruppen die einzelnen Beiträge, die von einem Koordinationsteam gesammelt und in das Netz gestellt wurden. Die Arbeitsgruppen sollten dann die Hyperlinks, d.h. die Beziehungen zwischen ihren Artikeln und denen der übrigen Beiträge festlegen und integrieren. Dadurch musste jede Gruppe die Beiträge der anderen Gruppen lesen und sich Gedanken über die Zusammenhänge machen.

Ein ähnliches Projekt ist für das Wintersemester 2001/2002 geplant. Unter dem Thema Interkulturelle Kommunikation wird eine Gruppe der neuen Hochschule der Medien zusammen mit einer Gruppe türkischer Studenten der Anadolu-Universität (Türkei) ein multimediales Informationssystem zum türkisch-deutschen Kulturvergleich erstellen. Die Basis hierfür ist zunächst die Auseinandersetzung mit dem Strategiespiel ECOTONOS, das es den Teilnehmern ermöglich, kulturelle Verschiedenheiten zu *erleben*. Danach werden die Teilnehmer mit Hilfe der Kommunikationsmöglichkeiten des Internets gemeinsam und dialogisch das Thema erarbeiten und visualisieren. Dabei wird sowohl das Thema als auch die Auseinandersetzung mit der anderen Kultur selbst auf einer Metaebene eine große Rolle spielen und zum Lernerfolg beitragen.

Virtuelle Lernumgebungen bieten vielfältige Möglichkeiten. Entscheidend zum Erfolg scheint mir dabei zu sein, die aktivierenden, kommunikativen Komponenten in den Vordergrund zu stellen. Das Netz *allein* als multimediales Materiallager zu verwenden, ist wenig effektiv und führt wieder zum oben beschriebenen *trägen Wissen*, diesmal auf einem technisch höheren Niveau, aber ebenso unbefriedigend.

Literatur

Arzberger, Heinz / Brehm, Karl-Heinz: Computerunterstützte Lernumgebungen. Erlangen 1994

Bohm, David: Der Dialog. Das offene Gespräch am Ende der Diskussionen. Stuttgart 1998

Buber, Martin: Das dialogische Prinzip. Darmstadt 7. Aufl. 1994

Ciompi, Luc: Die emotionalen Grundlagen des Denkens. Entwurf einer fraktalen Affektenlogik. Göttingen 1997

Damasio, Antonio R.: Ich fühle also bin ich. Die Entschlüsselung des Bewusstseins. München 2000

Downs, Roger M. / Stea, David: Kognitive Karten. Die Welt in unseren Köpfen. New York 1992

Fromm, Erich: Haben oder Sein. Die seelischen Grundlagen einer neuen Gesellschaft. Stuttgart 1996

Gallin, Peter / Ruf, Urs: Sprache und Mathematik in der Schule. Auf eigenen Wegen zur Fachkompetenz. Zürich 1990

Gerstenmaier, Jochen / Mandl, Heinz: Wissenserwerb unter konstruktivistischer Perspektive. Forschungsbericht Nr. 33. März 1994

Goleman, Daniel: Emotionale Intelligenz. München 11. Aufl. 1999

Kösel, Edmund: Die Modellierung von Lernwelten. Ein Handbuch zur Subjektiven Didaktik. Elztal-Dallau 3. Aufl. 1997

Luhmann, Niklas: Soziale Systeme. Grundriß einer allgemeinen Theorie. Frankfurt/M. 1987

Maturana, Humberto: Biologie der Realität. Frankfurt/M. 1998

Reinmann-Rothmeier, Gabi / Mandl, Heinz: Wissensvermittlung. Ansätze zur Förderung des Wissenserwerbs. Forschungsbericht Nr. 34. März 1994

Vester, Frederik: Denken, lernen, vergessen. Stuttgart 1998

Gabriele Ott-Osterwold

Theorie und Praxis der Kunstvermittlung

Den Betrachtungen, die Herrn Professor Dr. Peter Vodosek gewidmet sind, liegt ein Motto zugrunde, das künstlerische und kunstvermittelnde Aktivitäten charakterisiert, die im Rahmen des Kulturmanagements an der Hochschule für Bibliotheks- und Informationswesen in Stuttgart praktiziert werden: „Kunst im Gange" geht von einem Kunstbegriff aus, der sich in Bewegung befindet, dessen Kriterien zeitbewusst, gegenwartsbezogen und perspektivisch sind. Das Motto „Kunst im Gange" bezeichnet zyklische Ausstellungs-Aktivitäten innerhalb der Hochschule, es zielt auf den konkreten Ortsbezug. Thematisiert werden Arbeitsräume, die auffälligen und unauffälligen Neben- und Zwischenräume: Gänge, die von den ‚Bewohnern' der Hochschule innerhalb ihrer Arbeitsrhythmen ‚begangen' werden. „Kunst im Gange" versteht sich als temporärer Eingriff in ‚gängige' Bewegungsabläufe, sie stimuliert architektonische Gegebenheiten, sie reflektiert infrastrukturelle Funktionen; sie befragt und bereichert die Räume.

Das Lehrprogramm geht von folgenden Prämissen aus: Interdisziplinäre Seminare mit den Studenten/innen während der Projektierungsphase, intermediale Darstellungsform innerhalb der Ausstellung und offene Teamarbeit bei der Realisierung. Ein Hauptanliegen dabei ist die Kooperation mit weiteren kulturellen Institutionen in der Region Stuttgart, die zukünftigen Bibliothekaren zugute kommen kann. Hier hat die Zusammenarbeit mit der Staatlichen Akademie der Bildenden Künste in Stuttgart - insbesondere mit der Klasse Professor Holger Bunk - eine besondere Bedeutung. Der gegenseitige Gedankenaustausch mit Mitarbeitern und Studenten der Kunstakademie bereichert die pädagogische Arbeit im Bereich Kulturmanagement der HBI. Ziel dabei ist, mit den komplexen theoretischen und praktischen Erfahrungen in der Auseinandersetzung mit Kunst und Kunstvermittlung die beruflichen Perspektiven der beteiligten Studenten/innen zu erweitern und damit auf die gesamten Aktivitäten der Hochschule sowie auf ihre Ausstrahlung in die Öffentlichkeit einzuwirken.

Die aktuellen Installationen in dem Hochschulbereich Wolframstrasse rekrutieren sich aus einem Entwicklungsprozess, der 1994 mit „Kunst in der Villa" - in der Feuerbacher Heide - begann. Die projektbezogene Arbeit hatte zum Ziel, das Fach Kulturmanagement in bestimmten Zeitrhythmen (ein Semester theoretische Vorbereitungsphase, ein Semester Projekt-Realisierung) auf ein orts- und raumbezogenes Ausstellungs-Szenarium zu beziehen. Dabei ging man von unterschiedlichen Themen aus, die mit den Studenten/innen unter der Leitung der Dozentin (Gabriele Ott-Osterwold) erarbeitet wurden. Als Beispiele seien genannt: „Die Pose" - eine Spiegelung spezifischer Formen der Verhaltensstruktur, persönlicher Klischees und Imagewerbung anhand von künstlerischer Photographie, Graphik und Plakatkunst.

„Andy Warhol: Schwarz auf weiß" Werkbetrachtungen und die Analyse seiner Arbeitsmethoden mündeten in Kreationen seitens der Studenten ein, die sich in technisch modifizierten Darstellungsformen artikulierten.

„Portrait - vier Standpunkte": In der Ausstellung zum Thema „Das Portrait im Zeitalter der Photographie" Korrespondierten photographische Selbsterfahrungen der Studenten mit Kunstgeschichtlichen Positionen.

Die Vorbereitung und Realisierung einer Kunstausstellung ‚in der Villa' mit der Photo-Künstlerin Beate Reinecke und dem Multimedia-Künstler Herbert Moser gab den Beteiligten einen unmittelbaren, nachhaltigen und offenen Einblick in den Arbeitrhythmus zweier Künstlermentalitäten. Jenes Konzept, innerhalb der Seminare mit Künstlern direkt zu kooperieren und ihr Werk vor Ort zu installieren, gab dem Ausstellungszyklus „Kunst in der Villa" eine besondere Prägung. Diese Aktivitäten erzeugten eine lebhafte Kommunikation der Projektgruppen im Bereich Kulturmanagement sowie eine vielschichtige Diskussion innerhalb des Hochschulkomplexes (Lehrkörper, Studentenschaft, Verwaltung). Fachspezifische und fachübergreifende Argumente berührten sich in ihren jeweiligen Kompetenzen.

Jener interdisziplinäre Hintergrund motivierte die umfangreichen ortsbezogenen Aktivitäten in dem Hochschulkomplex Wolframstrasse. Thema war „Stuttgart 21 - ‚der urbane Blick'" - ein differenzierter ‚Blick' aus dem Fenster der Hochschulräumlichkeiten auf das entleerte, unbebaute, vieldiskutierte und teilweise auch umstrittene ehemalige Bahnterrain. Die Intensität und Komplexität der künstlerischen Reaktionen seitens der Beteiligten, die im Hause sichtbar vermittelt wurden, und die konkrete Präsenz der installierten Objekte erzeugte eine offen und durchaus positiv gestaltete Kommunikation. Dieser Erfolg ermutigte zu der herausfordernden, innovierenden und intensiven Zusammenarbeit ist der Kunstakademie. Hier entwickelt sich eine kooperative Perspektive der HBI. Heterogene installative Gestaltungsmedien zu motivieren, die Arbeitsmodelle und Zielvorstellungen der Hochschule für Bibliotheks- und Informationswesen mit künstlerischen Initiativen zukunftsweisend zu verbinden. Herr Professor Dr. Peter Vodosek und das Rektorat haben die Projekte „In der Villa" und „Kunst im Gange" mit persönlichem Engagement unterstützt. Dafür sei ihm sehr herzlich gedankt. Einbezogen in den Dank ist Herr Professor Wolfram Henning, die Hochschulverwaltung und der Förderverein.

Andreas Papendieck

Fortbildung war immer eine Herausforderung Eine FHB/HBI Bilanz nach 35 Jahren

Fortbildung gab es schon immer. Als Adam seinen Job als Paradies-Parkwächter durch fristlose Kündigung verlor, blieb ihm nichts anderes übrig als Fortbildung, um Frau und Kinder ernähren zu können. Es ist nicht überliefert, wie er das zuwege brachte – aber ganz offensichtlich mit Erfolg. Schließlich verdankt die heutig Menschheit ihre Existenz ausschließlich seinem Fortbildungswillen zum Agrarökonomen.

Wann Fortbildung für Bibliothekare eingeführt wurde, ist nicht überliefert. Wann in der FHB/HBI hingegen sehr wohl. Und diese Geschichte war äußerst abwechslungsreich. So lohnt es sich, im Rahmen dieser Festschrift Rückschau zu halten. Eine Rückschau auch deshalb, weil im beruflichen Aufgabenfeld von Peter Vodosek Fortbildung eine besondere Stellung einnahm und zwar auf verschiedenen Ebenen, vorrangig in der Hochschule, gleichfalls aber auch auf Verbands- und überregionaler Kommissionsebene.

Erste Überlegungen hinsichtlich der Institutionalisierung einer geregelten Fortbildungsarbeit wurden am vormaligen Süddt. Bibliothekar-Lehrinstitut bereits 1965 angestellt, niedergelegt in einem Grundsatzpapier, das Grundlage für die darauf folgenden Beratungen wurde.[167] Ein erster Gedankenaustausch mit Vertretern der Berufspraxis fand am 9. Februar 1966 im Volkshochschulheim Waldhof in Freiburg-Littenweiler statt.[168] Die Chancen für eine kontinuierliche und geregelte Fortbildungsarbeit waren insofern nicht schlecht, als das damalige Kultusministerium an dieser neuen Aufgabenstellung großes Interesse zeigte und sich auch dafür einzusetzen versprach, die notwendigen Mittel im Staatshaushalt einzuwerben. Wenn auch keine Mittel für die Teilnehmer in Aussicht gestellt wurden, so doch immerhin Honorar- und Fahrtkosten für die Referenten. Damit war zumindest ein Anfang gemacht.

Die beginnende Fortbildungsarbeit basierte auf der engen Zusammenarbeit mit den Großstadtbibliotheken Stuttgart, Mannheim und Karlsruhe, den staatlichen Büchereistellen und dem damaligen Berufsverband der „Volksbibliothekare“. Die inhaltliche Zielsetzung war – gemessen an heutigen Anforderungen – sicherlich bescheiden, spiegelte sie doch nichts weiter wider als das, was das Büchereiwesen zu der Zeit war: eine öffentliche Leseanstalt. Die angedachten Themenkomplexe (Sachliteratur, Schöne Literatur, die Bücherei im öffentlichen Leben, Büchereipraxis, Jugendbüchereiwesen und Jugendliteratur, Musikbüchereiwesen) gingen nicht über das hinaus, was bereits Alltagspraxis war. Angedacht wurde eine Fortbildung von Praktikern für Praktiker, wenngleich auch die Arbeitsformen sicherlich didaktisches Geschick verrieten. Vorgesehen waren je nach Themeninhalt Wochenendseminare, Tagungsserien an unregelmäßig aufeinander folgenden Wochenenden und längerfristige seminaristische Veranstaltungen für kleinere Gruppen.

Dass auf diese Absichtserklärung ziemlich postwendend die ersten Veranstaltungen an-

167 Grundsatzprogramm zur Regelung der beruflichen Fortbildung von Diplom-Bibliothekaren für den Dienst an Öffentlichen Büchereien. 1965. Maschinenschriftlich

168 Ergebnisprotokoll Dr. Waßner: Beratungssitzung zur Fortbildungsarbeit des Süddt. Bibliothekar-Lehrinstituts mit Anhang. Maschinenschriftlich

gekündigt und auch durchgeführt wurden, ließ Hoffnung aufkommen.[169] Den Anfang - gleichsam den Start der Fortbildungsarbeit - machte vom 21.-24. April 1966 eine Musik - bibliothekarische Tagung, womit nicht nur die Bedeutung der musikbibliothekarischen Ausbildung für die Stuttgarter Schule betont wurde, sondern die Themen, die angeschnitten wurden zeigten, dass in diesem Bereich durch das Aufwerfen gesellschaftspolischer Fragen der übliche bibliothekarische Rahmen bereits gesprengt wurde.

Immerhin stellte auch die erste angekündigte Seminarreihe zum Thema „Verwaltung" den bescheidenen Versuch dar, den angehenden oder auch bereits praktizierenden Bibliotheksleitern mehr zu vermitteln als den im Pflichtstudium vermittelten Stoff im Bereich „Verwaltungskunde". Allerdings wird man aus heutiger Sicht mutmaßen müssen, dass Themen wie „Die finanzielle Situation des Landes" und „Die gegenwärtige Finanzlage der Städte", jeweils dargeboten von erfahrenen Verwaltungspraktikern, mehr informativen Inhalts waren und eher Hinweise für die Mangelverwaltung enthielten, als dass neue finanzpolitische Ziele angedacht wurden. Dass im November des gleichen Jahres (1966) an zwei Wochenenden eine Fortsetzung dieser Reihe stattfand, für die der populäre Oberbürgermeister von Ulm Dr. Pfizer gewonnen werden konnte, war an sich ein gutes Zeichen, wenn auch erstaunt, dass für das unspektakuläre Thema „Die Stellung der öffentlichen Bücherei im Verwaltungsaufbau der Kommune" zwei volle Fortbildungstage angesetzt wurden.

Die Reihe fand allerdings nach der 5. Sitzung, entgegen den geplanten 8 Sitzungen, im Februar 1967 ein vorzeitiges Ende, da die Initiatoren sich ausschließlich auf den Referentenstamm stützten, der ihnen im Großstadtbereich zur Verfügung stand. Ambitioniert war der Versuch, das Thema „Kybernetik" zu behandeln, da erkannt wurde, dass die Öffentlichen Büchereien im Bereich Naturwissenschaft und Technik einen enormen Nachholbedarf hatten. Als Referent sprach zum ersten Mal ein in der Materie bestens bewanderter Fachmann aus dem universitären Bereich: Prof. Dr. Helmar Frank. Allerdings blieb diese Form der Referentengewinnung zunächst eine Einzelerscheinung.

Keineswegs zufriedenstellend hingegen verlief die Veranstaltungsreihe „Überörtliche Referatsarbeit". Zwar hatte man die Notwendigkeit erkannt, einen Überblick über neuere Entwicklungen vor allem in den Bereichen zu geben, bei denen der Bestandsaufbau aufgrund des Personalbestandes schwierig war, so besonders in den Gebieten Mathematik, Physik, Wirtschaft, Maschinenbau, Fertigungstechnik, Bauwesen, Recht und Medizin,[170] aber die traditionelle bibliothekarische Form eines Literaturberichtes erwies sich alsbald doch als sehr spröde. Da kaum auf Entwicklungstendenzen innerhalb der einzelnen Wissenschaftsgebiete eingegangen wurde, vielmehr es sich um eine Aufzählung neuerer Titel handelte, traten angesichts der Fülle der vorgestellten Titel, immerhin wurden jeweils 4 - 5 Gebiete an einem Tag abgehandelt, bei den Teilnehmern leichte Ermüdungserscheinungen auf.

Ende der 60er, Anfang der 70er-Jahre erfolgte durch die Umwandlung des Lehrinstituts in eine Fachhochschule eine Zäsur, die sich auch auf die Fortbildungsarbeit nachhaltig auswirken sollte. Zweifelsohne band der Umwandlungsprozess mit der Errichtung neuer Hochschulgremien und mit der Berufung einer Reihe neuer Kollegen die planerischen Kräfte, auch wenn es zunächst mit einem Haushaltstrick gelang, den Zugriff auf die Fortbildungsmittel zu behaupten, die trotz des Wechsels des Lehrinstituts vom Ressort des Kultusministeriums zum Wissenschaftsministerium bei ersterem verblieben waren. Der

169 Süddeutsches Bibliothekar-Lehrinstitut: Berufliche Weiterbildung von Bibliothekaren an Öffentlichen Bibliotheken. Ankündigungsprogramm. Vorwort: Dr. Joseph Epp u. Dr. Willi Wendling

170 Süddeutsches Bibliothekar-Lehrinstitut: Veranstaltungsreiche: Überörtliche Lektoratsarbeit. Maschinenschriftlich

neue Status einer Fachhochschule brachte allerdings auch Verpflichtungen mit sich, denen man sich nicht entziehen konnte. Zum einen war es das Erfordernis einer Standortbestimmung, zum anderen die Besinnung auf die eigenen Möglichkeiten.

Thema Standortbestimmung: Was sich vom 12. – 14. Oktober 1972 im Rahmen einer offiziell angekündigten „Fortbildungstagung" abspielte, war mehr als das. Es war für die frisch zu Ehren gekommene FHB hinsichtlich ihrer Stellung als neu definierte Ausbildungsstätte eine Frage der Reputation, entschieden nach den theoretischen Grundlagen einer modernen Bibliothekswissenschaft zu fragen. So war die Tagung „Bibliothekswissenschaft und Öffentliche Bibliothek" im Kern ein hochrangiger Gedankenaustausch, ein Colloquium mit der Ambition, eine inhaltliche Abgrenzung und eine methodische Fundierung für eine Wissenschaft zu finden, die erst im Entstehen war. „Hauptaspekt der Fragestellung soll die Arbeit der kommunalen Öffentlichen Bibliothek bzw. die dieser Arbeit zugrunde zu legende Theorie sein" - so im Einladungsschreiben.[171]

Die aufgeworfenen Fragen waren in der Tat von völlig neuer Qualität. Nicht mehr Zustandsbeschreibungen wurden offeriert, sondern alle vorgetragenen Referate zeigten einen erstaunlich weitsichtigen Blick nach vorn.

Emunds dreigeteilte Bibliothek wurde von ihm selber im Kontext einer bibliothekswissenschaftlichen Propädeutik vorgetragen. Die Benutzerforschung wurde in Verbindung mit bibliothekssoziologischen Fragen gesehen (König-Kurowski), die Bibliothek im Kontext einer weitgefassten sozialen Kommunikation definiert (Henning). Erstmalig wurden betriebswirtschaftliche Überlegungen im Zusammenhang mit der Bibliotheksorganisation angestellt (Beyersdorff) und letztlich auch die Bibliothek als Bestandteil wissenschaftlicher Betrachtung definiert (Langenbucher).

Für die Fortbildungspraxis allerdings blieben diese Ansätze ohne Folgen. Neu war, dass jetzt verstärkt auf eigene Kräfte zurückgegriffen wurde, die sich mit methodischem und didaktischem Geschick der Themen annahmen, die in der Berufsöffentlichkeit neu an Inter -esse gewonnen hatten. Dazu zählte vorrangig der an angelsächsischen Vorbildern definierte und ausgerichtete ‚Auskunftsdienst'. Mit den nicht nur in Stuttgart, sondern auch in Weinheim, Biberach und Heidelberg durchgeführten Tagesveranstaltungen im Oktober 1972 und September 1973 kam die FHB inhaltlich wie organisatorisch einem weitverbreiteten Wunsch der Berufsöffentlichkeit entgegen. Diese methodisch ausgefeilten, am praktischen Bedarf orientierten Seminare erhielten ihr Sahnehäubchen mit einer bundesweit ausgeschriebenen, im Oktober 1973 durchgeführten Tagung mit dem für diese Zeit aktuellen Titel ‚Information oder Aufklärung? Die Öffentliche Bibliothek als Informationszentrum'. Damit hatte man eine Thematik aufgegriffen, die die bibliothekspolitische Diskussion jener Zeit nachhaltig beschäftigte. Die Bibliothek als Instrument gesellschaftlichen Wandels. Horst Ernestus (Wuppertal), Hermann Glaser (Nürnberg), Udo Becker (Herder Verlag Freiburg), Wolfram Henning und Andreas Papendieck versuchten, jeder aus einem anderen Blickwinkel, die Facetten auszuleuchten, die deutlich machten, dass Auskunftstätigkeit in der Bibliothek mehr war als lediglich Informationsvermittlung.

Im November 1974 wurde dann der Versuch unternommen, die gewonnenen theoretischen Erkenntnisse und praktischen Ansätze auf Bundesebene in ein verbindliches einheit-

[171] Fachhochschule für Bibliothekswesen Stuttgart: Einladung zur Fortbildungstagung Bibliothekswissenschaft und Öffentliche Bibliothek. Maschinenschriftlich

liches Unterrichtsprogramm einzubinden.[172] Es gelang zwar, die Vertreter fast aller bibliothekarischer Ausbildungsinstitute an einen Tisch zu bringen, aber mehr auch nicht. Die Rahmenbedingungen in den einzelnen Instituten waren doch zu unterschiedlich, als dass ein gemeinsames Konzept hätte zustande kommen können.

Die tastenden, pragmatischen Versuche hatten zu der Einsicht geführt, dass es wünschenswert wäre, eine Tagungsstruktur anzustreben, die durch eine logische Abfolge bestimmt wird: gute theoretische Fundierung, verbunden mit aus der Praxis gewonnenen Erfahrungen. Grenzen allerdings zeigten sich auch hier sehr bald. Nicht jedes Thema bot genügend theoretische Grundlagen, die es opportun erschienen ließen, hierfür jeweils ein Grundlagenseminar anzubieten.

Andererseits wurde immer deutlicher, dass es notwendig war, Themen anzubieten, deren Bedeutung für das Bibliothekswesen sich erst in Umrissen abzeichnete. Darunter fielen zunächst Themen wie ‚AV-Medien in Bibliotheken' (November 1973) – dann das Thema ‚Schulbibliotheken', (Oktober 1974), ein Thema, das durch das 1973 veröffentlichte neue KGSt-Gutachten für die Bibliotheken absolute Priorität gewann. Die Thematik war in der Bibliothekslandschaft ein Novum. Entsprechend war die Resonanz. Die Teilnehmerzahl lag bei über 90. Das schon damals zentrale Thema der Tagung, die Einbindung der Bibliothek in den Lernprozess, hat bis heute nichts an Aktualität verloren. Auch in den späteren Tagungen wurde es immer wieder aufgegriffen und von den verschiedensten Seiten her beleuchtet.

Nachdem ab 1974 in den Kommunen das neue Haushaltsrecht mit den veränderten Bestimmungen für den Vermögenshaushalt, dem neu eingeführten Finanzplan verbunden mit dem Investitionsprogramm langsam zu greifen begann, bestand auch für die FHB Handlungsbedarf. Bereits im Mai 1975 wurde unter dem Thema „Kommunalhaushalt und Öffentliche Bibliothek" eine 1½-tägige Tagung durchgeführt, bei der ausschließlich Referenten aus der kommunalen Finanz- und Kulturverwaltung zu Worte kamen (Stuttgart, München, Regensburg, Hannover). Referate und Diskussionen waren sachbezogen und problemorientiert gleichermaßen. Die gewünschte Zielsetzung, Verwaltungshandeln aus dem Blickwinkel der Verwaltung selber zu verstehen, konnte vermittelt werden.

Gleichzeitig rückte ein zweiter Themenkomplex jetzt stärker in das Blickfeld der Bibliothekare und gewann damit für die Fortbildung eine besondere Bedeutung: die Betriebswirtschaft. War drei Jahre zuvor im Rahmen der Frage nach den Grundlagen einer Bibliothekswissenschaft zum ersten Mal überhaupt das Problem einer Kostenrechnung angeschnitten worden, so stellten sich jetzt bereits Fragen über Personalführung, Personalrecht, Mitarbeiterbeurteilung, Personaleinsatz, Motivation, Betriebsorganisation und Führungstechnik. Dieses breitgefächerte Themenangebot konnte der Berufsöffentlichkeit vorgestellt werden, weil mit der Besetzung einer betriebswirtschaftlichen Dozentenstelle die fachliche Kompetenz von FHB-Seite gewährleistet war.

Mitte der 70er-Jahre wurde das Thema Fortbildung berufspolitisch immer virulenter. Obwohl Baden-Württemberg, speziell der Stuttgarter Raum, bundesweit nach Nordrhein-Westfalen und Berlin die beste Versorgungsdichte aufwies, fühlte man sich hier keineswegs auf einer Insel der Seligen. Vielmehr sah man in den Stuttgarter Möglichkeiten auch eine Verpflichtung, der nachzukommen der damalige Rektor, Dr. H. Waßner, und später sein Nachfolger, Dr. Peter Vodosek, ständig bemüht waren. In allen wichtigen regionalen

---

172 Bibliographie und Auskunftsdienst als Lehrfach an Ausbildungsstätten für Bibliothekare. Fortbildungstagung der FHB Stuttgart am 21. U. 22. November 1974. Programm maschinenschriftlich

und überregionalen Gremien wurden von ihnen regelmäßig die Stuttgarter Erfahrungen eingebracht. Die immer wieder beklagte Tatsache, dass die Fortbildungsangebote in der Bundesrepublik in keiner Weise flächendeckend waren und dringend Abhilfe nötig war,[173] konnte die FHB allerdings auch nicht aus der Welt schaffen.

Eine Intensivierung der Fortbildungsarbeit an der FHB stand regelmäßig auf der Tagesordnung, zumal das Problem einer Fortbildung für die zeitweise nicht im Beruf stehenden Kolleginnen stärker ins Bewusstsein rückte. Die Aktivitäten zielten in drei Richtungen:

a) Die Sondervortragsreihen, die in unregelmäßigen Abständen für die Studierenden als praxisrelevante Ergänzungen zum offiziellen Unterrichtsstoff durchgeführt wurden, wurden der Berufsöffentlichkeit zugänglich gemacht bzw. die mitgeschnittenen Tonkassetten zum Selberhören angeboten.
b) Der intensive Ausbau der musikbibliothekarischen Zusatzausbildung ging einher mit einem verstärkten Angebot an musikbibliothekarischen Fortbildungsveranstaltungen.
c) Erstellung von Unterrichtsmaterialien für ein Fernstudienprogramm, als gemeinsames Projekt von FHB und DBI (Berlin). Das Projekt, finanziert vom Bundesministerium für Bildung und Wissenschaft, erstreckte sich auf die Jahre 1975 bis 1979 und betrat für den bibliothekarischen Berufsstand Neuland. Basierend auf Lehrbriefen wurden zur Ergänzung multimediale Medien erstellt, was die didaktischen Spielräume nicht unerheblich erweiterte. Erstellt wurden ausschließlich in der Verantwortung von FHB-Dozenten je ein Fortbildungspaket zum Thema ‚Auskunftsdienst'; ‚Regeln für die alphabetische Katalogisierung' und ein Lehrbriefprogramm als Begleitmaterial für das musikbibliothekarische Zusatzstudium. Später folgte ein Lehrbrief- und Medienprogramm zum Thema ‚Schulbibliothek'.

Außerdem wurde ein umfängliches Gutachten zum Thema ‚Fortbildungsplan' erstellt.[174]

So gesehen waren die 70er-Jahre trotz sehr geringer Mittel durchaus von Erfolg gekrönt. Ende des Jahrzehnts allerdings, als der FHB die Zugriffsmöglichkeit auf die Fortbildungsmittel, die bei den Fachstellen etatisiert waren, endgültig genommen wurde, sah sich das Rektorat außerstande, weiterhin ein kontinuierliche Fortbildungsarbeit anzubieten. Das bis dato gut angenommene Angebot erlosch. Der vom Ministerium unterbreitete Vorschlag, kostendeckende Teilnehmergebühren zu verlangen, wurde seitens der Hochschule als inakzeptabel abgelehnt. Um überhaupt Flagge zeigen zu können, wurden FHB-Dozenten verstärkt bei Verbandstagungen u.ä. aktiv.

Dieser unbefriedigende Zustand wurde von Peter Vodosek, der am 1. April 1983 zum neuen Rektor der FHB gewählt worden war, bereits in der 1. Senatssitzung am 7. Mai 1986 durch die Wahl eines Senatsbeauftragten für Fortbildungsangelegenheiten beendet. Gleichzeitig wurde ein Senatsausschuss für Fortbildungsfragen gebildet, der dem Fortbildungsbeauftragten beratend zur Seite stand. Ein umfangreiches Rahmenkonzept wurde vorgegeben: Analyse des Fortbildungsbedarfs; Entwicklung eines Fortbildungskonzepts; Planung

[173] so besonders: Hans Peter Thun: Lifelong Learning? Bibliothekarische Fortbildung ist Notstandsgebiet. In: BuB 25 (1975), S. 164-166
Ders.: Die Koordinierung bibliothekarischer Fortbildungsarbeit in der Bundesrepublik Deutschland. Bericht über acht frustrierende Jahre. In: BuB 29 (1977), S. 143-161

[174] Fortbildungsplan. Entwurf der Grundsatzplanung zur Fortbildung der Bibliothekare. Empfehlungen zur Fortbildung im Bereich der öffentlichen Bibliotheken und Vorschläge zu einer Gesamtplanung für ein bibliothekarisches Fernstudium. Berlin: Deutsches Bibliotheksinstitut 1980. 201 S. (dbi-materialien; 3)

von Fortbildungsveranstaltungen; Kontakte zu anderen Anbietern; Mitarbeit in überörtlichen Gremien.

An der finanziellen Situation allerdings änderte sich nichts. Das anzuwendende Rezept hieß schlicht: Bündelung von Ressourcen.

Bereits im folgenden Jahr 1987 wurde ein Jahresprogramm erstellt, das Kontinuität zu versprechen schien. Die Fachhochschule meldete sich endlich wieder zurück, auch wenn der Neuanfang am 9. Februar 1987 kläglich misslang.

Das Rezept selber machte durchaus Sinn. Das Jahresprogramm konnte zusammengestellt werden mit der Unterstützung einer Reihe von FHB-Professoren, dem im Juni 1987 neu gegründeten Arbeitskreis für Information (AKI) und den einzelnen Berufsverbänden. Auf diese Weise konnte bereits im Herbst des gleichen Jahres eine von allen bibliothekarischen Berufsverbänden gemeinsam getragene Veranstaltung realisiert werden, für die in der Nachbarregion Bayern sogar eine abgespeckte Wiederholung stattfand (Tagungsthema: Ausstellungen in Wissenschaftlichen und Öffentlichen Bibliotheken).

Die Zusammenarbeit mit dem Arbeitskreis für Information sollte sich für die Fortbildungsarbeit der FHB auch in Zukunft als die gegenseitig fruchtbarste und ergiebigste erweisen, wobei man sich selbst in Krisenzeiten gegenseitig zu stützen verstand. Sehr bald kam auch das DBI (Berlin) als Geldgeber und Mitveranstalter mit ins Boot, was wesentlich dazu beitrug, den Handlungsspielraum bei der Tagungsplanung zu erweitern.

Finanziell gesehen wurde weitgehend ohne Netz gearbeitet. Trotz der Kooperationsbereitschaft waren doch alle Partner zwangsläufig daran interessiert, ohne finanzielle Einbußen über die Runden zu kommen. Die Veranstaltungen mussten sich wirtschaftlich einigermaßen tragen, wobei die FHB/HBI das technische Equipment und die Räumlichkeiten kostenlos zur Verfügung stellte.

Ein Überblick über die seit 1987 in den Rektoratsberichten regelmäßig veröffentlichten Jahresbilanzen zeigt im nachhinein, wie nah immer am Ball geblieben wurde. Alles was auf Neuentwicklung und Veränderung hindeutete, wurde früh aufgegriffen und als Angebot umgesetzt. Waren es am Anfang Datenbanken und Retrievalsprachen, so musste sich die Fortbildung sehr bald um die verschiedenen auf den Markt drängenden Bibliothekssysteme kümmern. Es folgten die neuen CD-ROM-Produkte, das neue Betriebssystem dBase, die Textverarbeitungsprogramme WordPerfect und später WinWord mit allen verbesserten Versionen. Die ganze Angebotspalette des World Wide Web wurde ins Programm aufgenommen, Excel-Schulungen durchgeführt, multimediale elektronische Dokumente beschrieben, das Programmieren und Gestalten mit HTML geschult und Provider-Projekte vermittelt. Es gab so gut wie keine IT-Thematik, die nicht im Fortbildungsangebot auftauchte, wobei eine akzeptable Arbeitsteilung sich eingespielt hatte. Fühlte sich der Arbeitskreis für Information vorrangig für die Programmgestaltung verantwortlich, wurde vom Rektorat und der Verwaltung zielstrebig der notwendige technische Geräteausbau vorangetrieben, sodass die Stuttgarter Hochschule sich mit dem Etikett schmücken konnte, die technisch am großzügigsten ausgebaute bibliothekarische Ausbildungsstätte in der Bundesrepublik zu sein.

Die Angebotsstruktur war gestuft und entsprach entfernt dem Konzept, das bereits in den 60er-Jahren entwickelt worden war und den Bedürfnissen und Wünschen der Berufsöffentlichkeit am ehesten gerecht wurde: Abendveranstaltungen, Halbtagesveranstaltungen, Wochenendseminare und mehrtägige Seminare. Letztere entwickelten sich zu Jahrestagungen, da der finanzielle und personelle Aufwand ein mehrfaches Angebot im Laufe eines Jahres verbot. Dabei erwiesen sich die Kooperationspartner nicht nur als verlässliche Partner, vielmehr konnte auch bei der Planung auf deren Know-how zurückgegriffen werden. Was war in? Behandelt wurden die Themen: Werbung und PR im Marketingkonzept (1988); Kulturmanagement (1991); Schulbibliothek und Lernprozeß (1992); Beruf: Literaturveranstalter (1994); Verwaltungsreform (1995); Multimedia Online (1996); Storytelling (1997);

Von der Schulbibliothek zur Mediothek: Internet, Multimedia, CD-ROM (1999); Multimedia im schulischen Lernprozess (2000).

In den letzten Jahren trat dann verstärkt das von Prof. Heidtmann gegründete Institut für angewandte Kindermedienforschung (Ifak) als Tagungsveranstalter auf, das mit seinen bundesweit ausgeschriebenen Kongressen weithin hohe Beachtung fand. Thema der 1998 durchgeführten Tagung: Mediengesellschaft – Klassengesellschaft. Ebenfalls in diesem Kontext muss auch Frau Prof. Krüger genannt werden, die mit Themen aus dem Kinder- und Jugendbibliotheksbereich hier eine Lücke zu schließen verstand.

Zu diesen auf mehrere Schultern verteilten Fortbildungsangeboten zählen in letzter Zeit auch die von Rafael Capurro organisierten und geleiteten Symposien und Workshops zum Thema Informationsethik, die international Beachtung finden.

Damit aber nicht genug. Nach einer Reihe von Vorplanungen und von Gesprächen mit der Berufsöffentlichkeit wurde 1998 der Gedanke der HBI-Akademie geboren, mit der Peter Vodosek die Chance erkannte, ein Fortbildungsprogramm bereitzuhalten, das sich inhaltlich und vom zeitlichen Umfang her von den bisherigen Angeboten deutlich abhob. Orientiert an der Idee der angelsächsischen Summer school wurde der Gedanke aufgegriffen, dass Fortbildung eingebettet in einen gemeinschaftlichen Lernprozess sein sollte – mit gemeinsamen Mahlzeiten und gemeinsamen Abendveranstaltungen. Die Idee kam bei der ersten einwöchigen Tagung voll zum Tragen. Das Tagungsthema „Bibliotheksmanagement im Neuen Steuerungsmodell" befasste sich nicht nur theoretisch mit den neuen Entwicklungstendenzen, die durch die Verwaltungsreform auf die Bibliotheken ausstrahlten, sondern schloss die Schulung praktischer Handhabung mit ein. Wenn auch die beiden nachfolgenden Tagungen zeitlich reduziert werden mussten, so waren doch mit den Themen „Selbstgesteuertes Lernen" und „Wissensmanagement" Felder besetzt worden, die für das bibliothekarische Berufsfeld Neuland waren. Die wichtigste Erfahrung, die gewonnen wurde war, dass Bibliotheken im Prozess des Lifelong Learning als Gesprächspartner nur dann interessant bleiben werden, wenn sie in diesen Bereichen die erforderliche Professionalität erwerben.

Auf der Habenseite des Akademiekonzeptes steht, dass es gelungen ist, neue Interessentengruppen anzusprechen und für die Arbeit des Hauses zu gewinnen. Das gleiche gilt auch bezüglich der Gewinnung neuer Referenten. Die bisherige positive Entwicklung lässt hoffen.

Das Fortbildungsangebot wurde so im letzten Jahrzehnt vielfältiger und anspruchsvoller. Der Kreis der Kooperationspartner wurde größer, das Teilnehmerspektrum vielfältiger. So gesehen sieht die Bilanz, die hier zu ziehen war, erfreulich aus. Erfreulich deshalb, weil von Peter Vodosek ein Neuanfang gewagt wurde, von dem zugegebenermaßen niemand am Anfang wusste, ob dieser Versuch klappen würde. Es hat geklappt.

Henner Grube

Schöne Formen und andere.

Denken - vermitteln

1998 erschienen im verdienstvollen Eichborn-Verlag die *„Essais"* von Michel de Montaigne in einer neuen Übersetzung von Hans Stilett, die den zeitgenössischen deutschen Leser erstmals wieder ahnen lässt, dass Montaignes Essays vielleicht doch nicht nur aus literarhistorischen und geistesgeschichtlichen Gründen gepriesen werden; und diese Ausgabe der *„Essais"* ist auch buchbinderisch-handwerklich und drucktechnisch-formal äußerst ansprechend. Anlässlich seines siebzigsten Geburtstages, Ende 1999, wurde Hans Magnus Enzensberger unter anderem wegen seiner luziden Essays gelobt, mit denen er schon Anfang der Sechzigerjahre große Aufmerksamkeit gewann (und uns Schüler Mitte der Sechziger faszinierte). Christian Schärf, Privatdozent an der Universität Mainz, veröffentlichte Ende 1999 *„Geschichte des Essays. Von Montaigne bis Adorno"* bei Vandenhoeck und Ruprecht - über dreißig Jahre lang gab es (nach den Monographien von Bruno Berger und Ludwig Rohner) eine solche Bemühung nicht mehr. --- Neue Aufmerksamkeit für eine (einflussreiche) literarische Gattung? so fragte ich mich vor einiger Zeit in einer Mußestunde.

*

In wunderschöner, breiter und gelehrter Weise legt Christian Schärf die Geschichte der Gattung dar. Er spricht zunächst über Essay und Essayismus. Dann widmet er sich sehr ausführlich dem ersten Auftreten des Essays bei Montaigne und Bacon. Hierbei macht er deutlich, welch' Spannweite durch diese doppelte Wurzel schon angelegt ist. Ebenso ausführlich behandelt er aus dem achtzehnten und neunzehnten Jahrhundert Voltaire, Diderot, Schlegel, Novalis, Emerson und Nietzsche. Und im zwanzigsten Jahrhundert gilt seine Aufmerksamkeit Hugo von Hofmannsthal, den Manns, Musil und Broch und schließlich Benjamin und Adorno.

Zu Montaigne schreibt Schärf scharfsinnig: „An Montaigne läßt sich studieren, wie das neuzeitliche Individuum und seine zunächst geistigen Herrschaftsansprüche aus einem Schreibakt heraus entspringen, wie das Schreiben zum Medium subjektiver Autonomie wird und wie in diesem Akt die revolutionären Kräfte der Zukunft in einem Kern angelegt sind, der durch äußerliche Einwirkung unzerstörbar scheint."

Anhand einer literarischen Gattung wird hier - wie in der gesamten Monographie - in nuce eine (perspektivische) Geistesgeschichte über mehrere Jahrhunderte entwickelt. Das ist äußerst anregend und zeigt Gelehrsamkeit in einem fast schon verloren geglaubten Sinne. Texte scheinen auf, Autoren werden in ihren Bestrebungen verdeutlicht, die jeweilige Zeitgenossenschaft wird beleuchtet, Entwicklungstendenzen, in denen wir selbst stehen, werden verständlich gemacht, Philosophisches wird in seiner engen Verknüpfung zum Literarischen und zu dieser Gattung in Sonderheit ungescheut thematisiert, die Geschichte der Intellektuellen und des intellektuellen Lebens tut sich auf. Die Publikation ist so gedrängt in ihrer Fülle, dass ich die Lektüre über vier Tage strecken musste, obwohl es sich nur um 280 Seiten handelt.

Aber bin ich zufrieden?

„Essay - so Schärf am Anfang seiner *‚Geschichte des Essays‘* - bezeichnet auf diesem Terrain den immer wieder offenen, immerfort schwierigen Raum, in dem das Subjekt und der Wille zum Ausdruck zusammenstoßen.“ Das ist recht vage und kryptisch; es wird zwar im Laufe der Darlegung glücklicherweise durchaus viel heller, aber sehr klar wird trotzdem nicht, was die Gattung denn selbst ausmacht. „Essay und Essayismus beherbergen als Begriffe die energetischen Potentiale, durch die die alten Gattungsgrenzen aufgesprengt werden konnten und das autoritäre Phantasma der Regelwerkspoetiken überwunden wurde.“ „Es geht also in der vorliegenden Darstellung um eine Gattung ebenso wie um ein Syndrom, und zwar deshalb, weil die Gattung oft nur als Syndrom in Erscheinung trat.“ Ja, aber ... darin steckt schon das Dilemma.

Es ist richtig, es sind Zuckerbäckerkünste, eine Gattungsgeschichte rein durch strukturelle Formwandlungen geben zu wollen. Es ist gut, sie in ihrem Produktionskontext zu sehen; und der ist hier zunächst einmal der Essayismus. Es ist unbezweifelt, dass die alten Gattungsgrenzen aufgesprengt wurden und dass der Essay dazu seinen Teil beigetragen hat. Aber!

Sollte ich mich - will heißen: Schärf sich - als Literaturwissenschaftler nicht trotzdem bemühen, die morphologischen Wandlungen zu erkennen und nachzuzeichnen? Denn da ist doch ein Etwas, was bei aller historischen und individuellen Unterschiedlichkeit einheitlich als „Essay“ bezeichnet wird. Was ist das? Und wie sieht es aus? Was wandelt sich? Was bleibt? Oder gibt es gar keinen Kern? (Das muss ja kein Wesen sein, beileibe nicht - igitt, bewahre! - Und selbst der Kern muss nicht unwandelbar sein. Es geht nicht um überzeitliche, ahistorische Merkmale. Da sei Klaus W. Hempfers *„Gattungstheorie“* vor, und davor bewahre uns ebenso der Nominalismus beispielsweise eines Richard Rorty.)

Werden nicht längst entschiedene Kämpfe und Einsichten reproduziert, in der (doch gar nicht angezweifelten) Behauptung vom Ende der Regelwerkspoetiken? Ich muss mir selbstverständlich Klarheit über die verschiedenartigen gestalterischen und inhaltlichen Ansätze, die bei den einzelnen Autoren zur Arbeit mit dem Essay geführt haben, verschaffen. Aber muss ich - und darf ich - wegen der produktionsästhetischen Perspektive (so reizvoll sie auch sein mag) auf die gestaltästhetischen Fragestellungen verzichten? Ich brauche ja durchaus nicht dem „literaturwissenschaftlichen Irrglauben“ verfallen, man könne eine rein formale Geschichte einer Gattung als sinnvoll betrachten. Und kann ich heute wirklich noch so ungestraft die literatursoziologische und vor allem die wirkungsästhetische Fragestellung außer Acht lassen oder völlig marginalisieren? Was könnten wir über uns selbst alles erfahren, wenn wir darüber forschten, warum Montaigne für uns noch interessant ist ... und warum er andererseits so schrecklich obsolet zu sein scheint. Und könnte die wirkungsästhetische Perspektive nicht eine sein, die in wunderbarer Weise die Frage nach den formalen Wandlungen und den auktorialen Intentionen zu einem sinnvollen Forschen umschlösse?

Und wenn denn Partei genommen wird für Montaigne und gegen Bacon und gegen Hermann Grimm und Rudolf Kassner, die Manns und Musil und Broch und so weiter - all das mag als beherzt erscheinen und sich gegen die Beliebigkeit stemmen und zum populären Interesse beitragen, doch bekomme ich so tatsächlich die Gattung unverstellt in den Blick? Wundert es wirklich, dass am Ende wieder die Höhenkammliteratur (oder: eine - einseitig gesetzte - Höhenkammliteratur) sichtbar wird - und anderes wie die kulturkonservative Essayistik und beispielsweise das umfangreiche essayistische Werk Kassners eher in Nebenabsätzen aufscheint? Klar, der Beliebigkeit müssen wir begegnen und dem kulturgeschichtlichen Positivismus müssen wir nicht mehr frönen und „philologische Vollständigkeit“ müssen wir nicht zum Nonplusultra erklären und im Wust wollen wir auch nicht ersaufen - gleichwohl, wo bleibt das Bemühen um kulturgeschichtliche Gerechtigkeit? Auf jeden Fall können wir so die Erfolgsgeschichte der Gattung Essay doch keineswegs fassen, jedenfalls nicht als Erfolgsgeschichte einer intellektuellen oder auch einer bürgerlichen Schreib- (und Denk-)weise. Geschichte - auch Literaturgeschichte - besteht eben nicht nur aus Innovationen, Verblüffungen und Zaubereien. Was macht heute die Faszination des Essays aus und wie war es früher? Wer unter den Essayisten hatte hohe Auflagen? Wer schrieb nur für die Schublade? Und bergen die Archive vielleicht neben den Kriegspostkarten und autobiographischen Notizen der vielen Unbekannten auch Essays von Unbekannten?

Ebenso: Kann ich heute ernsthaft über den literarischen Essay schreiben und erwähne nur einmal eben am Rande den Radio- oder Fernsehessay? Wenn es sich hier gar nicht um Essays handelt, wäre das nicht ausführlich zu klären? Was sagte eine solche begriffliche Usurpation - oder Mauersetzung - aus? Andererseits: Warum kann ich das Essayistische im Roman goutieren, den Versessay so gerade eben noch akzeptieren, aber nicht den Rundfunkessay und nicht den Fernsehessay?

„Eine besondere Art der Versuchung nämlich, das Versprechen auf ein Surplus an Erfahrung, die erotische Spannungslage zwischen Denken und Form in einer existentiellen Entscheidungsszene.“ Ja, richtig. Aber das gilt vielleicht nicht nur für das, was ich schätze, sondern vielleicht auch für das, was ich hasse - und eben anderen als von mir geliebten Ausdruck gefunden hat.

Am 4. Januar 2000 schrieb Heinz Schlaffer, Professor der Literaturwissenschaft an der Universität Stuttgart, in der *„Frankfurter Rundschau“* in einer kurzen Klage über die universitären Studien: „In einem Seminar über den *Essay* hat noch keiner der dreißig Teilnehmer die Namen Adorno und Benjamin gehört. Auch die Gattung *Essay* wird - da man die Zeitungen, Zeitschriften und Bücher, in denen Essays zu finden wären, nicht liest - mit anderen Formen verwechselt.“ --- Ist vielleicht nicht nur die wohlfeile Klage über die Lesefaulheit und das fehlende Selbststudium der Studenten in Erwägung zu ziehen, sondern auch die Engführung akademischer Forschung zu beklagen, die zwar zu anregenden, gelehrten Publikationen führt, dem Lesebereiten (mag er nun Student sein oder nicht) auch vieles vermittelt, ihn jedoch mit der Frage zurücklässt, was für ein Ding denn das nun letztlich sei, um das es ging - hier: der Essay?

*

Wie auch immer. Die verdienstvolle Publikation Christian Schärfs zeigt auch die Nähe dieser Gattung zur Philosophie. Was weiß aber die Philosophie selbst - die es natürlich nicht gibt - über diese Textgattung? In einer weiteren Mußestunde befragte ich Philosophie-Lexika auf meinem Regal. - Ach, Gott, hätt‘ ich nur nicht.

Es schweigen dazu, haben keinen entsprechenden Artikel, keinen Eintrag in den Registern: *„Philosophisches Wörterbuch“* begründet von Heinrich Schmidt (Kröner), *„Philosophie“* herausgegeben von Alwin Diemer und Ivo Frenzel (Das Fischer Lexikon), *„Philosophisches Wörterbuch“* herausgegeben von Georg Klaus und Manfred Buhr (das europäische Buch; 2 Bände), *„Philosophisches Wörterbuch“* von Alois Halder und Max Müller (Herder), *„Enzyklopädie Philosophie“* herausgegeben von Hans Jörg Sandkühler (Meiner; 2 Bände), *„Metzler Philosophie Lexikon“* herausgegeben von Peter Prechtl und Franz-Peter Burkard.

Einen positiven Befund bietet nur - und rettet das Ansehen der philosophischen Lexika - das *„Historische Wörterbuch der Philosophie“*, begründet von Joachim Ritter, das seit

1971 bei der Wissenschaftlichen Buchgesellschaft erscheint und es bis jetzt auf zehn Bände gebracht hat. Der zweite Band bietet zum Essay drei Spalten mit Literaturangaben. L. Černý skizziert in dem Artikel die Geschichte der Gattung, sagt etwas zu häufigen Inhalten und auktorialen Haltungen. Und führt unter anderem aus: „Dem E. geht es um die *vérité des faits*. Er macht Schluss mit der Philosophie als Wissenschaft und Schule und kehrt zurück zu ihrem Eigentlichen, das ihr Name ausdrückt: zur Liebe der Weisheit nämlich, zur Weisheit, die der Lebenserfahrung entspringt und nicht der Gelehrtenstube." „Der E. siedelt zwischen der Theorie und der Praxis, zwischen Philosophie und Politik." Und Černý beendet den Artikel mit: „Es nimmt also nicht Wunder, dass die Essayistik jeweils aufblüht, wenn sich die philosophischen Systeme lockern und die Freiheit der Rede garantiert ist. Vielleicht erklärt dies, warum der E. in Frankreich und England seine Heimat hat und in Deutschland erst spät heimisch wurde." Klar, das hört sich alles hausbackener und schlichter als bei Schärf an; dass es so aber in einem Lexikon der Philosophie von diesem Gewicht steht, ist schon beachtlich.

Jetzt war ich neugierig geworden und prüfte Lexika der Philosophie nach anderen literarischen Gattungen ab, deren sich Philosophen bedienen, als da sind: *Aphorismus* (einschließlich *Maxime, Reflexion, Sentenz*), *Fragment, Brief, Dialog*. Fast alle Lexika boten etwas - natürlich auf unterschiedlichem Niveau und mit unterschiedlicher Ausführlichkeit - zum *Dialog*. Dies wundert ja nicht, da doch die Philosophiegeschichte aus Anmerkungen zu Platon besteht (ich glaube, George Edward Moore hat es gesagt) und von Platon - sieht man von den wenigen Briefen ab - ausschließlich dialogische Texte tradiert sind. (Von dem - wie kürzlich anlässlich seines hundertersten Geburtstags - hochgelobten Meister des philosophischen Gesprächs, dem Hermeneutiker Hans-Georg Gadamer, ist dabei natürlich nicht die Rede.) *Aphorismus* und *Fragment* tauchen hingegen nur vereinzelt auf - was aber angesichts des Schweigens zum *Essay* schon phänomenal wirkt. Die Begriffe *Maxime* und - vor allem - *Reflexion* sind häufiger verzeichnet, allerdings nicht im Hinblick auf die Textsorte. Selbstverständlich bei diesem Befund - die Suche nach anderen literarischen Gattungen, in denen wichtige philosophische Veröffentlichungen geschrieben sind, wie *Gedicht* oder *Autobiographie* hätte ich mir schenken können (immerhin *Allegorie* taucht einmal auf).

Aber um die Berücksichtigung der gängigen - sozusagen nicht-ästhetischen, nichtliterarischen - Textsorten der akademischen Philosophie steht es nicht besser. Die erwähnten Lexika verzeichnen nicht Darstellungsweisen wie *Abhandlung, Traktat, Vorlesung* (oder: *Lesung*); im Hinblick auf die noch unspezifischeren, gleichwohl in der Philosophie völlig üblichen Publikationsformen wie *Aufsatz, Rezension, Dissertation, Forschungsbericht, Lehrbuch, Einführung, Lexikon, Wörterbuch* schweigen sie gleichfalls. (Immerhin sind nicht alle genannten Philosophielexika an der *Enzyklopädie* vorbeigegangen. Das wäre nun aber auch wirklich „ein Hammer".)

Es fehlen damit ebenfalls Hinweise darauf, dass bestimmte Darstellungsformen in bestimmten Epochen typisch waren - wie in der Antike das *dialektische Gespräch*, die *geschlossene Argumentation*, die *Allegorese* und das *philosophische Gedicht* oder beispielsweise im Mittelalter *disputatio, commentarius, summa* oder *lectio*.

Dies drängt den Verdacht auf, der sich weitgehend mit meiner Erinnerung an mein Philosophiestudium deckt: Die Reflexion auf die eigene Darstellungsform gehört - im Allgemeinen - nicht zum Metier (bestallter, will heißen: universitärer) Philosophen. (Der Befund ist übrigens auch nicht nur eine Frage des Erscheinungsjahrs der genannten Lexika, denn mehrere stammen aus den neunziger Jahren... Huch: Eben fällt mir ein, ich muss ja noch herauskehren, dass ich nicht ganz so naiv bin, wie ich scheine. Also, es sei hiermit bekannt: Es gibt mehr Lexika der Philosophie, als in meinem Bücherschrank vorhanden sind - und selbst dort finden sich noch einzelne spezielle Lexika, die ich für philosophische Fragen heranziehe und hier nicht genannt habe. Es mag also alles gar nicht so schlimm sein, wie ich wähne.)

Aber die Darstellungsform ist doch niemals äußerlich, philosophischer Erkenntnisgewinnung und -vermittlung sowie studierender Erkenntnisaneignung akzidentiell. Sie vermittelt etwas, das den Inhalt stärkt oder ihn konterkariert, sie gibt ein Surplus, der mehr ist als ein ästhetischer Schein. Und die Wahl der Textsorte dürfte doch für die Darstellung nicht ganz unerheblich sein. Sollte sie vielleicht eine Funktion haben? Folgt gar etwas aus der Wahl der Gattung, was der Autor zunächst nicht beabsichtigte? Hat die Gattungswahl vielleicht am Ende Einfluss auf das Denken und das Gedachte? Kann die gewählte Gattung den Leser nicht vielleicht in seiner Aufmerksamkeit und seinem Urteil lenken (und ablenken)? An all dem können doch auch philosophiegeschichtliche Würdigung und Forschung nicht vorbeigehen. Oder doch? Sind das nur Fragen der Muße von Laien?

Gab es im zwanzigsten Jahrhundert nicht einige philosophische Publikationen, die (auch) durch ihre Form herausragten - wie beispielsweise Adornos essayistische *„Minima Moralia"*, Wittgensteins an romantische Fragmente gemahnende *„Philosophische Untersuchungen"* oder Alains, nämlich Emile-Auguste Chartiers, Füllhorn der Propos? Haben nicht auch Philosophen des zwanzigsten Jahrhunderts auf literarische Formen reflektiert - wie Adorno auf den Essay oder Hans Blumenberg auf die Metapher? Aber das alles hat sich ja wohl nicht bis in die Lexika der Philosophie niedergeschlagen.

*

Wie glücklich war ich daher, als ich plötzlich und ganz zufällig - aber was ist wirklich kontingent - den Titel *„Literarische Formen der Philosophie"*, herausgegeben von Gottfried Gabriel und Christiane Schildknecht, Stuttgart: Metzler, 1990, entdeckte. Hat mein Entsetzen über die Unreflektiertheit der Philosophen glücklicherweise etwas mit meiner Unkenntnis der laufenden philosophiegeschichtlichen Forschungen zu tun? Das wäre erfreulich - für die Philosophiegeschichte.

Also: Der Band stammt von 1990. Die angehängte Literaturliste veranlasst eine Modifikation meiner Anwürfe und Fragen: Die philosophiegeschichtliche Reflexion auf die Darstellungsformen philosophischer Texte gibt es, wenn sie auch sicher eher randständig ist. Die letztere Einschränkung wird nicht nur durch die Kürze jener Liste gestützt, sondern auch durch die Tatsache, dass der Sammelband in den zehn Jahren seit seinem Erscheinen erst eine Auflage erlebt hat, mehr aber verdiente.

Wenn in der Einleitung des Sammelwerks von der „häufig übersehenen methodischen Bedeutung literarischer Formen der Philosophie" die Rede ist, kann das nur als eine stolze Untertreibung, als eine Verkennung der Tatsachen oder als eine (vielleicht zur Vermeidung des Vorwurfs der Nestbeschmutzung und der folgenden akademischen Isolation oder mindestens Stigmatisierung) gewollte Schönfärberei wirken.

*

Erfreulich nicht allein, dass die Frage nach den Darstellungsformen philosophischer Texte aufgenommen wird. Erfreulich, dass die Aufsatzsammlung *„Literarische Formen der Philosophie"* bereits gleich über die literarischen Gattungen, die Textsorten, hinausgeht. Der erste Aufsatz, von dem einen der Herausgeber, Gottfried Gabriel, beginnt mit dem (nicht nur für diesen Aufsatz) programmatischen Satz: „Gegenstand dieser Untersuchung ist, ganz allgemein gesprochen, die Philosophie als Literatur." Die Philosophie als Literatur ... ja.

Gabriel untersucht die Texte mehrerer Philosophen. Harald Fricke beschäftigt sich mit philosophischen Aphoristikern. Nach der Struktur und Zielsetzung platonischer Dialoge fragt Thomas Alexander Szlezák. Dieter Teichert thematisiert die Briefe Senecas an Lucilius. Thomas Rentsch widmet sich der mittelalterlichen Kultur der quaestio. Die zweite Herausgeberin, Christiane Schildknecht, erörtert die literarische Form bei Descartes. Mit den Dialogen Humes setzt sich Bernd Gräfrath auseinander. Catherine Wilson analysiert die Darstellungsform von Kants Transzendentaler Methodenlehre. Herders Abhandlung über den Ursprung der Sprache nimmt sich Ulrich Gaier vor. Und Soraya de Chadarevian beobachtet die Auflösung der cartesianischen Begriffswelt bei Merleau-Ponty.

Erhellende, jedenfalls für mich wirklich erhellende Beiträge allesamt! - Ganz besonders hat es mir der Beitrag Schildknechts, *„Erleuchtung und Tarnung. Überlegungen zur literarischen Form bei René Descartes“*, angetan. Da liest man schon im Eingangskapitel den für diese Aufsatzsammlung zentralen Gedanken: „Wird die Interpretation eines philosophischen Autors um die hermeneutische Komponente der literarischen Form reduziert, so hat dies oftmals Missverständnisse und Verkürzungen des Inhalts zur Folge.“

Schildknecht geht zunächst von den autobiographisch-kontemplativ gefärbten Texten *„Discours“* und *„Meditationes“* aus, wechselt dann zur dialogisch Wissen bildenden und vermittelnden *„Recherche de la Vérité“*. In letzterer sieht sie eine inhaltliche Deckungsfähigkeit zu den *„Meditationes“*, aber eben auch formale Veränderungen: Die monologische Meditation wird durch den Dialog ersetzt. Und diesen Dialog versteht sie als einen Schaukampf - denn die Synthese oder finale Einsicht wird von den Dialogpartnern nicht gemeinsam erarbeitet, sondern von einem Dritten gesetzt; Zweck des Schaukampfs ist die (wie sich zeigen wird: vorsichtige) Popularisierung der Erkenntnis. Schildknecht thematisiert dann die Beschäftigung Descartes mit der Optik und seine Metaphorik des Lichts: Theorie des Lichts, geometrische Optik und Sinnesphysiologie machen das Herzstück der Philosophie Descartes aus.

Schließlich fragt Schildknecht, warum Descartes zu seiner Schreibweise kommt. Das halte ich für spannend. - Diese Schreibweise sieht sie als Maskerade zum Zwecke der Tarnung. Descartes will nicht wie Campanella im Gefängnis oder wie Bruno auf dem Scheiterhaufen landen. Daher zieht er aus Vorsicht nicht nur erste Schriften zurück, sondern er sichert die späteren mehrfach ab. Dafür wählt er bestimmte Argumentationsstrukturen, seine Intentionen verunklarende Termini und bestimmte literarische Formen, verfasst Widmungsschreiben an die Sorbonne, fordert die Leser auf, ihm mögliche Einwände mitzuteilen. Er verweist darauf, dass es sich zunächst um seine subjektive Ansicht handelt; er greift gern zur Form des Als-ob, zu hypothetischen Formulierungen, zu autobiographischen Stilisierungen, nimmt scholastisches Gedankengut auf, verschweigt einiges. Harmlos erscheinende Prämissen werden vorsichtig entwickelt, die schwerwiegenden Implikationen der Zerstörung der Aristotelischen Prinzipien aber bleiben im Hintergrund - eben: implizit. Durch Zitate aus persönlichen Äußerungen Descartes sichert Schildknecht ab, dass dies alles mehr als Unterstellungen und Vermutungen ihrerseits sind.

Im Schlusskapitel Schildknechts heißt es: „Der Leser Cartesischer Schriften wird dadurch, dass die Widersprüche innerhalb des Cartesischen Oeuvre nicht aufgelöst werden, verunsichert und desorientiert. Das Ausbleiben einer eindeutigen Perspektivierung wirft ihn auf sich selbst zurück. Auch auf diese Weise kann eine in systematischer und tarnender Absicht entworfene monologische Form literarischer Darstellung zu einer Auseinandersetzung mit dem Text und in der Auseinandersetzung mit diesem zu selbständiger Wissensbildung aufseiten des philosophischen Subjekts beitragen.“ Und schließlich transzendiert sie ihre unmittelbare Fragestellung und generalisiert. Es gibt für sie zwei Weisen des Umgangs mit philosophischen Texten: Es wird - erstens - das philosophische System als Netz von Propositionen angenommen, die und deren Verbindung es aufzudecken und gegebenenfalls zu verbessern gilt. Es ist - zweitens - die Weltsicht des philosophischen Subjekts zu er- und vermitteln. Zu letzterem ist es wichtig, Implizites und Indirektes - eben auch die literarische Form philosophischer Texte - heranzuziehen. (Nicht nur das halte ich für ganz erheblich und erfreulich.)

Dieses mehr andeutende Kurzreferat eines Artikels macht - über meine Begeisterung und Genugtuung hinaus - vielleicht etwas deutlich, was fast alle Beiträge auszeichnet: Es wird nicht nur gestaltästhetisch gefragt (Wie ist die Form der Texte?). Es wird auch nicht nur produktionsästhetisch nachgedacht (Was wollte der Philosoph mit dieser Form?). Es taucht auch - und zwar nicht marginalisiert - die rezeptionsästhetische Perspektive auf: Was bedeutet die spezifische Form für den Leser? Das freut mich ganz besonders, halte ich doch erst eine Interpretation, die allen drei Fragerichtungen nachgeht, für gelungen. Angesichts des akademischen Herkunftsortes der meisten der hier vereinten Philosophiegeschichtler - Konstanz - nimmt die Berücksichtigung des Aspekts der Wirkung allerdings nicht besonders wunder, ist dies doch der Universitätsort, an dem in den siebziger Jahren von Wolfgang Iser und Hans Robert Jauß die westdeutsche Variante der literaturtheoretischen Wirkungsästhetik entwickelt wurde.

Allerdings --- ich meine: Die Rezeption müsste die alles organisierende Perspektive sein, von ihr müsste ganz bewusst ausgegangen werden. Denn wir Leser - auch die privilegierten, weil in der Lektüre, Analyse und Interpretation geschulten und ständig geforderten Philosophiegeschichtler - sind nicht Götter, die voraussetzungslos den Text als solchen wahrnehmen oder dem Autor über die Schulter schauen, sondern zunächst einmal lesende Menschen in einer bestimmten historischen Situation.

Sehr merkwürdig bleibt für mich darüber hinaus eine Vermutung, die bis zum Ende des Bandes nicht weichen will. Die hier versammelten Philosophiegeschichtler scheinen die Vorstellung zu haben, es gäbe so etwas wie einen ästhetisch merkmalfreien propositonal-argumentativen Text. Den ästhetisch merkmallosen Text kann es aber doch nur im philosophisch-platonischen Himmel der anti-septisch immunisierten abstrakten Ideen geben, also allenfalls als methodisch-heuristische Kontrast-Idee.

Aber krittel ich nicht schon gleich wieder, bleibe ich doch einfach - auch wenn nicht alle meine Eingangs- und Zwischenfragen beantwortet werden - bei meiner Freude! Es ist einfach schön und zugleich sehr nützlich und sollte eigentlich selbstverständlich sein, dass auf die Formen des Vermittelns von Gedanken reflektiert wird - nicht allein aus ästhetischen oder pädagogischen Gründen.

*

Peter Vodosek verfügt nicht nur über ein immenses Wissen, er kennt nicht nur verborgene Details der Geschichte unserer bibliothekarischen Profession und der weiteren Kulturgeschichte, er fühlt sich nicht nur der wissenschaftlichen Wahrheit verpflichtet.

Als Rektor hat er es verstanden, der Hochschule für Bibliotheks- und Informationswesen ein internationales Renommee zu verschaffen. Nicht nur in dieser Rolle zeichnete er sich als ein Modernisierer aus, der die Tradition nicht aus den Augen verloren hat.

Als akademischer Lehrer lenkt er die Aufmerksamkeit der Studierenden immer wieder auch auf die Form der Vermittlung - wie ich häufig höre, sogar im Hinblick auf das Verfassen von Semesterarbeiten. Und er schätzt die schöne Form - auch die literarisch schöne Form, die schöne Form des Sagens. Selbst spielt er gerne mit dem gelehrten Zitat und seiner gewitzten Platzierung. Sein Publikum ist - er weiß es und freut sich drüber - schon auf das Bonmot und die blitzartig erhellende Anekdote eingestimmt. Und seine Leser und Zuhörer schätzen es - keineswegs nur in Mußestunden -, dass hier einer im wissenschaftlichen Lehr- und Konferenzbetrieb Humor, Schönheitssinn und Freude an der Kunst des Vermittelns nicht verloren hat.

Rafael Capurro

Ethik im Bilde

Einführungsbeitrag zum IV. Internationalen HBI-Workshop zur Informationsethik: „Ethik als Wirklichkeitskonstruktion. Ansätze zu einer konstruktivistischen Informationsethik", 18. - 19. November 1999.*

1. „Geister-Zitierung"

Raffael von Urbino (1483-1520) malte zwischen 1509 und 1511 eine Reihe von Fresken im Auftrag des Papstes Julius II. im Vatikanpalast, darunter ein 577 x 814 cm großes Fresko, das in der Kunstgeschichte als „Schule von Athen" bekannt ist und über die Jahrhunderte eine außergewöhnliche Faszination auf seine Betrachter ausgeübt hat (Löhneysen 1992). Julius II. bezog nach dem Tode seines Vorgängers Alexander VI. Borgia (1492-1503) drei neue Gemächer und einen Saal, die als „Stanzen Raffaels" (*stanza* = Zimmer) berühmt geworden sind. Die „Stanza della Segnatura" in der sich die „Schule von Athen" befindet, war vermutlich als Bibliothek und Lesezimmer bestimmt. Diese *stanza* wurde später so genannt, weil dort Urkundenunterzeichnungen und Siegelungen vorgenommen wurden.

---

* Der Text ist verfügbar unter http://www.capurro.de/raffael.htm. Außerdem können die Beiträge zum Workshop als Video im Netz angesehen werden unter: http://v.hbi-stuttgart.de/Workshop/infoet~1.htm

In seiner Raffaels-Biographie schreibt Wilhelm Kelber:

> *„Eine Bibliothek war damals etwas anderes als heute. Das Buch war noch heilig, noch unentweiht. Es gab noch keine Kritik und keine Ursache dazu. Man las mit Devotion. Der Herzog von Urbino empfand ein gedrucktes Buch als unwürdig. Er duldete keines in seiner Bibliothek. Seine Bücher mussten durch die menschliche Handschrift die Würde des Inhalts wahren. Man ließ sich auch keine Bücher kommen, weder ins Haus noch gar von auswärts, sondern man reiste hin, wo sie waren, rückte seinen Stuhl vor das Pult, wo der Foliant an einer Kette an seinem festen Ort lag. Genau wie man heute Galerien besucht. Wo Bücher waren, war Weihe. Und das Lesen selbst ein vernehmlicher Umgang mit dem Schreiber, eine Art Geister-Zitierung. Man las mit der Seele und erlebte mehr als blasse Gedanken. Dieser inneren Situation entsprach es, den Geist der Autoren in Gemälden zu vergegenwärtigen, den der Leser erfühlte. Man „zitierte" den Autor." (Kelber 1993: 18)*

Ich möchte diesen Hinweis über die „Geister-Zitierung" als Leitfaden für eine Interpretation oder, besser gesagt, als Einladung zu einer je eigenen Auseinandersetzung mit Raffaels Bild aufgreifen. Unversehens sind wir schon mitten beim Thema unseres Workshops. Denn wenn wir dieses Bild anschauen, dann sind wir mit einer vielschichtigen Komposition konfrontiert, bei der wir den Eindruck haben, dass jeder Versuch ihren Sinn zu erfassen nur als eine Rekonstruktion aus der einen oder anderen Perspektive bedeuten muss. Wir sind, mit anderen Worten, Teil des Bildes und nicht ein objektiver Betrachter. Es ist so, und das ist bereits eine mögliche Stellungnahme, dass wir, wenn wir von den Texten zu ihren Autoren vorgehen, feststellen, dass diese wahre Art der Zitierung, diese „Geister-Zitierung" also, uns vor eine viel größere Herausforderung stellt als der Versuch, Geschriebenes oder Gedrucktes auszulegen.

Wie sollen wir in dieser komplexen Situation miteinander umgehen? Wen sollen wir zuerst zitieren, d.h. zuhören oder zuschauen? Davor wüssten wir natürlich zu gern who is who. In welcher Reihenfolge sollen wir vorgehen? Dürfen wir uns überall einmischen? Wo befinden wir uns eigentlich, wenn wir in diesem Bild sind? Wir haben offenbar ein großes Informationsdefizit, aber wir sind uns auch im klaren, dass eine isolierte Deutung einzelner Figuren oder Gruppen uns vor die Frage nach dem Zusammenhang, oder in der Hypertext-Sprache übersetzt, nach den vielfältigen möglichen sinnvollen und weniger sinnvollen *links* stellt. Die Situation selbst erscheint uns vielleicht als eine Momentaufnahme, die in mehrere räumliche und zeitliche Richtungen weist, sowohl im Bild selbst, als auch in ihrem Bezug zu den anderen Fresken dieser stanza.

Diese Hypertext-Annäherung an die „Schule von Athen" ist zunächst eine Einladung, uns selber ein Netz von Bedeutungs- und Verweisungszusammenhängen aufzubauen, das zwar aus einem beliebigen subjektiven Interesse zu entstehen scheint, in Wahrheit aber als eine mögliche Antwort auf ein Angesprochen-werden zu verstehen ist. Das bedeutet, dass der Leser dieses Bildes zunächst glaubt, die hier zitierten Geister nach eigenem Gutdünken verlinken zu können, während aber in Wahrheit er selbst derjenige ist, der zu einer Teilnahme, in welcher Form auch immer, eingeladen wird. Unser Beobachterstatus, der zugleich der Status eines unbeteiligten Konstrukteurs zu sein scheint, entpuppt sich als eine Chimäre: Es gibt kein Beobachten, das nicht zugleich ein Mitmachen bedeutet. Wie aber mitmachen? Nach welchen Regeln? Und was sollen wir dabei tun? Worauf läuft das Gespräch mit der einen oder anderen Person hinaus? Und was ist, wenn jemand nur da sitzt oder liegt, völlig losgelöst von einer Kommunikationsgemeinschaft, in die eigenen Gedanken versunken oder dem, was um ihn herum stattfindet, nicht die Spur einer Aufmerksamkeit widmet? Und wie stellt sich das Verhältnis zu Personen dar, die in so unterschiedlichen Aktivitäten beschäftigt sind, dass sie in sich geschlossene Teilgemeinschaften bilden oder zu bilden scheinen, während andere wiederum mit Freude aufeinander zugehen oder einem anderen gebannt zuhören? Und wie steht es um das Verhältnis zwischen Menschen verschiedenen Alters und, was in diesem Bild zumindest auf den ersten Blick kaum ins Gewicht fällt, zwischen den Geschlechtern?

Das Bild bezieht uns auch in ein dynamisches Geschehen oder in einen Durchgang ein, der in verschiedene Richtungen führt. Wir befinden uns dabei mitten in einer Halle oder in einer tempelartigen Anlage. Die göttliche und die menschliche Welt, die sich das Bild horizontal teilen, bilden eine Einheit. Diese konstruierte Welt, die der Gespräche und die der Bauwerke und Bildnisse, lässt eine von sich aus aufgehende Natur durchscheinen. Diese überragt die massive aber offene Konstruktion der Halle. Links ist eine Tür, eine wirkliche Tür sollten wir sagen, die von einer *stanza* in die nächste führt. Fast ist es aber so, als ob wir durch diese Tür in die Welt gelangen könnten, in der wir schon sind, wenn wir uns in das Bild 'ein-bilden' und dabei den Unterschied zwischen Bild und außenstehendem Beobachter aufgeben. In diesem Fall stehen wir mitten in einer vorgegebenen von anderen konstruierten und uns tradierten Welt der Gespräche und der Bauwerke und fragen uns, was für Möglichkeiten des Mitmachens uns diese Konstruktionen und Traditionen zulassen, in welche Verhältnisse sie uns einführen, und wie wir uns auf sie einlassen können.

2. Who is who?

Schauen wir uns die Sachverhalte etwas näher an. An der Decke dieser *stanza* befinden sich vier symbolische weibliche Gestalten, welche Theologie, Philosophie, Jurisprudenz und Poesie darstellen. Ferner befinden sich zwischen diesen Medaillons folgende Szenen: das „Urteil Salomos" zwischen Philosophie und Jurisprudenz, „Adam und Eva" zwischen Jurisprudenz und Theologie, „Apollo und Marsyas" zwischen Theologie und Poesie, und „Astronomie" zwischen Poesie und Philosophie. Auf der gegenüberliegenden Wand malte Raffael ein anderes Fresko, die „Disputa", in der eine Fülle von Teilnehmern über die Hostie auf dem Altar disputieren. An den beiden anderen Wänden sind die Fresken „Parnass" und die drei Kardinaltugenden (Stärke, Weisheit, Mäßigung) dargestellt. Über der „Schule von Athen" steht das Medaillon der Philosophie umgeben vom „Urteil Salomos" und von der „Astronomie". Die Bezeichnung „Schule von Athen" stammt von Giovanni Pietro Bellori (ca. 1615-1696) (Kelber 1993: 463).

Who is who in der „Schule von Athen"? Mit dieser Frage hat sich zuletzt Glenn Most (Most 1999) auseinandergesetzt. Es besteht die Gefahr zu glauben, so Most, alle Rätsel dieses Bildes wären gelöst, wenn wir einige oder sogar alle Namen der hier dargestellten Personen genau wüssten (Most 1999: 10). Gleich zu Beginn standen sich zwei konkurrierende Interpretationen dieses Bildes gegenüber. Giorgio Vassari (1511-1574) nannte Raffaels Fresko eine *storia* und sah in ihm den Versuch einer Harmonisierung von Theologie, Philosophie und Astrologie. Er identifizierte zwei Arten von Personen bzw. Personengruppen, nämlich, auf der einen Seite, historische Gestalten wie Platon mit seinem kosmologischen Dialog „Timaios" und Aristoteles mit einem allgemein gekennzeichneten Werk „Ethica", Diogenes mit seiner Tasse, Zoroasther und den Hl. Matthäus, sowie, auf der anderen Seite, zeitgenössische Personen wie Federico II., Herzog von Mantua, Bramante und Raffael selbst (Most 1999: 12). Demgegenüber behauptete Pietro Bellori (ca. 1615-1696), das Fresko stelle keine Geschichte, sondern lediglich einen Disput zwischen Philosophen,

Rhetoren, Poeten, Mathematikern und Gelehrten aus anderen Disziplinen dar. Er identifizierte ferner weitere Personen wie Sokrates, Pythagoras, Empedokles, Archimedes und Alkibiades. Most selbst teilt die 58 dargestellten Personen in drei Kategorien ein:

a) Personen, die aufgrund der dargestellten Attribute unverwechselbar sind. Das betrifft sechs oder sieben Figuren, nämlich: Platon, Aristoteles, Diogenes, Ptolemaios (im rechten Vordergrund, mit dunklem Mantel, erkennbar am Erdglobus), Pythagoras (im linken Vordergrund, vor einer Schreibtafel auf dem ein pythagoreisches Problem erkennbar), Sokrates (an seinem unverwechselbaren Gesicht erkennbar) sowie schließlich Raffael selbst (im rechten Vordergrund, neben Ptolemaios).
b) Figuren, die aufgrund ihrer Attribute einer bestimmten Kategorie von Personen zugeschrieben werden können, so z.B. den Geometer (Archimedes oder Euklid) im rechten Vordergrund.
c) Die restlichen 46 Figuren, die trotz ihrer Aktivitäten unbestimmt bleiben und eher wie Komparsen rund um einen Star wirken.

Das zeigt, so Most, dass hier die Philosophie anhand dessen dargestellt wird, was Philosophen gewöhnlich tun, nämlich lesen, schreiben, lehren, argumentieren, demonstrieren, fragen, zuhören und nachdenken (Most 1999: 20-27). Unser Bild steht zwar in der Tradition ikonographischer Darstellungen der Philosophie, Raffael bricht aber u.a. mit der Tradition der Sieben Freien Künste, als er hier nicht nur sieben allegorische Gestalten, sondern eine Fülle von wirklichen 'Geistern' zitiert.

Mehrere Gruppen sind in bezug auf das Thema unserer Tagung bemerkenswert: darunter der Nachrichtenüberbringer am linken oberen Rand, der freudig gegrüßt wird, die aufmerksamen Zuhörer um Sokrates, Platon und Aristoteles, die als Paar sich gegenseitig anschauen und ansprechen. Ich möchte aber die Aufmerksamkeit auf die zwei Gruppen vorne links und rechts richten. Die rechte Gruppe auf der Seite von Ptolemaios mit dem Erdglobus und der neben ihm stehenden Gestalt mit dem Himmelsglobus stellt nach Most:

> *„ein anschauliches Modell für die erfolgreiche Vermittlung von Wissen dar: Der Lehrer scheut keine Mühen und kniet unbequem, damit die Tafel, auf der er mit seinen Zirkel Strecken abgreift, für die vier seiner Demonstration folgenden Studenten gut erkennbar ist; und diese letzteren verkörpern vier aufeinanderfolgende Stufen des Erkenntnisprozesses, von schmerzlicher Verwirrung über wilde Mutmaßung und hoffnungsvolles Fragen bis hin zu befriedigter Gewißheit." (Moos 1999: 56-57)*

Diese Gruppe kontrastiert wiederum mit der Gruppe am linken Rand um Pythagoras herum, der das Thema des Verbergens von Wissen verkörpert. Pythagoreer pflegten zu sagen, es dürfe nicht alles allen mitgeteilt werden, denn sie, die Pythagoreer, verfolgen das Gute auf der Grundlage ihres Wissens, das den Gegnern nicht zugänglich sein sollte. Diogenes Laertius berichtet, dass Pythagoras' Schüler ihr Vermögen zum gemeinsamen Besitz zusammenlegten, denn Pythagoras war der erste der sagte,

> *„daß unter Freunden alles gemeinsam und daß Freundschaft Gleichheit sei."*

Fünf Jahre lang mussten die Schüler schweigen und den Lehrvorträgen ausschließlich als Hörer folgen, ohne den Meister zu Gesicht zu bekommen,

> *„bis sie sich hinreichend bewährt hätten; von da ab gehörten sie zu seinem Hause und durften ihn sehen."*

Pythagoras erstmals habe das Himmelsgebäude *kosmos* genannt und die Erde als rund bezeichnet (Diogenes Laertius 1967: 115, 133). Die Bezeichnung *Philosoph* geht auf Pyhagoras zurück. Die Pythagoreer teilten sich in zwei Richtungen, die *Akousmatiker* (Hörer) und die *Mathematiker* (Schüler):

> *„Mathematiker hießen jene, welche4 mehr in den besonderen und im Hinblick auf Exaktheit gepflegten Lehren seiner Wissenschaft unterrichtet worden waren, Akousmatiker jene, welche nur die kurzgefassten Vorschriften ohne exakte Begründung vernommen hatten." (Diels/Kranz 18.2)*

Pythagoreer und Ptolemeer stehen bei Raffael in einem scharfen informationsethischen Kontrast.

3. Zu Besuch bei Protagoras

Gab es eine literarische Vorgabe, fragt sich Most, für diese eindrucksvolle Darstellung eines philosophischen Kongresses bei dem Bücher - elf sind dargestellt - eine wichtige Rolle spielen? Most glaubt einen solchen Inspirationstext im Platonischen Dialog „Protagoras" entdeckt zu haben. Sokrates und der junge Hippokrates machen sich auf den Weg, um im Haus des Kallias, im größten und prächtigsten Haus Athens, den Sophist Protagoras zu treffen.

Der Text lautet:

> *„Als wir nun eingetreten waren, trafen wir den Protagoras in dem vorderen Säulengange herumwandelnd. Neben ihm aber gingen auf der einen Seite Kallias, der Sohn des Hipponikos, und sein Bruder von mütterlicher Seite, Paralos, der Sohn des Perikles, und Charmides, der Sohn des Glaukon, auf der anderen aber der andere Sohn des Perikles, Xanthippos, ferner Philippides, des Philomelos Sohn, und Antimoiros von Mende, der am meisten im Ruf steht von den Schülern des Protagoras und als eigentlicher Kunstjünger bei ihm lernt, um selber Sophist zu werden. Andere aber zogen hinterdrein und hörten dem, was gesprochen wurde, zu, und von diesen schien der größte Teil aus Fremden zu bestehen, welche Protagoras aus allen Städten, durch welche er auch kommen mag, hinter sich herzieht durch den Zauber seines Mundes, wie Orpheus, so dass sie alle willenlos diesem Zauber nachfolgen; es waren aber auch einige von den Einheimischen in diesem Reigen. An dem Anblicke dieses Letzteren nun hatte ich am meisten meine Freude, nämlich darüber, wie hübsch diese stummen Zuhörer sich davor in acht nahmen, dem Protagoras vorne in den Weg zu treten, vielmehr, sooft er und die, die mit ihm gingen, sich umdrehten, sich sittig und wohlgeregelt auf beide Seiten verteilten, kehrtmachten und sich dann hinten in der schönsten Ordnung wieder anschlossen.*
>
> *Jenem zunächst erblickt' ich, wie Homeros sagt, den Hippias aus Elis, welcher in dem gegenüberliegenden Säulengange sich auf einen Throm gesetzt hatte; um ihn herum aber saßen auf Bänken Eryximachos, des Akumenos Sohn, Phaidros aus Myrrinus, Andron, des Androtion Sohn, und von Fremden mehrere Landleute des Hippias und einige andere, und man konnte bemerken, dass sie ihm gerade Fragen aus der Erd- und Sternkunde, nämlich über die Natur des Alls und die Himmelserscheinungen vorlegten, und wie er von seinem Thron aus einem jeden von ihnen Auskunft über das Gefragte gab und es mit ihnen durchging.*
>
> *Auch des Tantalos ferner schauet' ich. Denn es war wirklich auch Prodikos aus Keos da und befand sich in einem Gemache, welches vordem Hipponikos als Vorratskammer benutzt hatte; jetzt aber hat wegen der Menge der Einkehrenden*

Kallias auch dieses ausgeräumt und zur Aufnahme von Fremden eingerichtet. Prodikos nun lag noch im Bette, eingehüllt in Pelze und Decken, und zwar in nicht wenige, wie der Augenschein lehrte; ihm zur Seite aber saßen auf den nahestehenden Ruhebetten Pausanias aus Kerameis und neben diesem ein noch sehr junger Mensch, von schönen und trefflichen Anlagen, wie es mir vorkam, jedenfalls aber von Gestalt überaus schön. Wenn ich mich recht erinnere, so hörte ich, dass sein Name Agathon sei, und es sollte mich nicht wundern, wenn er der Geliebte des Pausanias wäre. Dieser junge Mensch also war dort zugegen, und die beiden Adeimantos ferner, den Sohn des Kepis und den des Leukolophides, und noch einige andere erblickte man daselbst. Worüber sie aber sprachen, konnte ich von draußen nicht verstehen, so dringend ich auch wünschte, den Prodikos zu hören - denn gar hochweise und göttlich scheint mir der Mann zu sein -, sondern der dumpfe Widerhall, welchen der tiefe Ton seiner Stimme in dem Gemache gab, machte seine Worte unvernehmlich." (Prot. 314e-316a)

4. Raffael und wir

So wie Plato im „Protagoras" eine Fülle von Personen zu einem Stelldichein zitiert, so gestaltet Raffael seinen Kongress in dessen Mittelpunkt Welt und Mensch, Kosmologie und Ethik, Platon und Aristoteles stehen. Ethik ist im Bilde im doppelten Sinne des Wortes: Sie wird als Disziplin und als Handlung versinnbildlicht. Die nach vorne und nach unten weisende Hand des Aristoteles - in einem braunen und hellblauen an Erde und Wasser, so scheint es mir zumindest, hinweisenden Gewand - steht im Spannungsverhältnis zum erhobenen Finger des Platon, der sowohl von seinem roten Gewand als auch von der Form seines Körpers her an eine Flamme erinnert und somit an Feuer und Luft. Mit beiden Gesten und in beiden Gestalten wird das Verhältnis zwischen dem Göttlichen und dem Menschlichen ‚angemessen', ‚ausgemessen' und ‚angespannt'. Ethik ist überall dort, wo Menschen miteinander sprechen, forschen, in scheinbarer Isolation nachdenken, alles akribisch festhalten, auf neue Nachrichten freudig reagieren, sich von einem Meister alle Argumente aufzählen lassen, Himmel und Erde in den Händen zu haben glauben. Menschsein heißt leben in einem Feld von spannungsreichen Alternativen.

Ethik im Bilde bedeutet aber auch, dass sie über die Situation in der sie steht Bescheid weiß aber nicht im Sinne von Besserwisserei oder als bloße historische Forschung, sondern als „Geister-Zitierung", bei der Alte und Neue, antiqui et moderni, sich versammeln, wo der Zitierende zum Zitierten mutiert und seine scheinbare neutrale Position aufgibt. Fünf Figuren in verschiedenen Altersstufen - auf der linken Seite zwei Kinder sowie der weiß gekleidete junge Mann (vielleicht eine Anspielung auf Francesco Maria della Rovere, Herzog von Urbino) sowie eine stehende Figur am rechten Rand und Raffael selbst - blicken den Betrachter an und laden ihn zur Teilnahme am Mitteilungsgeschehen ein.

Alle Verständnisbemühungen sind umsonst, solange wir nicht selbst in ein Gespräch involviert sind. Raffaels Bild bleibt uns deshalb ein Rätsel und es geht uns dabei wie Sokrates und Hippokrates, die nur die dumpfen Töne des Prodikos und das Gemurmel der Gespräche zu hören vermögen, bis sie sich Protagoras persönlich zuwenden und ihm sagen:

„Du bist es, Protagoras, den aufzusuchen wir hierher gekommen sind.
Wollt ihr mich, erwiderte er, allein sprechen oder im Beisein der anderen?
Uns, versetzte ich, soll das gleich sein. Vernimm denn den Zweck unseres Kommens und prüfe selbst." (Prot. 316 a)

In diesem Sinne wünsche ich den Teilnehmern unseres Workshops ein konstruktives Disputieren und Nachdenken nach dem Beispiel von Raffaels „Schule von Athen."

Literatur

Diogenes Laertius: Leben und Meinungen berühmter Philosophen. Hamburg 1967.
Kelber, W.: Raphael von Urbino. Leben und Werk. Stuttgart 1993 (2. Aufl.)
Löhneysen, W. v.: Raffael unter den Philosophen - Philosophen über Raffael Berlin 1992.
Most, G.W.: Raffael und die Schule von Athen. Frankfurt a.M. 1999

BIBLIOTHEKSKONZEPTE

Arend Flemming

Partnerschaften Öffentlicher Bibliotheken

Einleitung

Im Internationalen Expertennetzwerk Öffentliche Bibliotheken, einem Projekt der Bertelsmann Stiftung, (http://www.bertelsmann-stiftung.de/INOEB) verfasste Glen E. Holt eine Analyse der Partnerschaftsarbeit von Öffentlichen Bibliotheken in den USA unter Einbezug von weltweiten Erfahrungen. Die Umsetzung dieser Arbeit in die deutsche Bibliothekspraxis bot sich an, da die Städtischen Bibliotheken Dresden bereits zahlreiche Kommunikationsbeziehungen aufgebaut haben, auf der anderen Seite jedoch die Möglichkeiten der Dezentralen Ressourcenverantwortung noch nicht ausgeschöpft scheinen. Gerade um zur Aufgabenerfüllung bei knappen Eigenfinanzen systematisch und zielgerichtet Partner zu gewinnen, sollten die amerikanischen und internationalen Erfahrungen untersucht und neben den eigenen Konzepten beispielhaft umgesetzt werden.

Motivation und Bedeutung von Partnerschaften

Als Motivation zur Strukturierung der Kommunikationsbeziehungen der Öffentlichen Bibliothek liegt die steigende Bedeutung von Bibliothekspartnerschaften unter den gegenwärtigen gesellschaftlichen Bedingungen der bibliothekarischen Arbeit zu Grunde. Folgende sechs Gründe lassen sich erkennen:

- die Computervernetzung schafft neue technologische Möglichkeiten und Notwendigkeiten der Zusammenarbeit,
- die politischen Gremien drängen auf vernetzte Dienstleistungen,
- die Notwendigkeit, finanzielle Lücken durch Partner zu überbrücken,
- die Bibliotheksnutzer erwarten komplexe Dienstleistungen, welche eine Bibliothek allein nicht mit höchster Qualität anbieten kann,
- um einen Beitrag zum demokratischen Grundrecht auf Informationsfreiheit leisten zu können, müssen alle Bürgerinnen und Bürger erreicht werden,
- die Bibliotheken wollen beweisen, dass sie ernst zu nehmende Partner in der Informationsgesellschaft darstellen.

So motiviert sollte ein Geflecht an Partnerschaften aufgebaut werden, welches vor allem davon geprägt ist, dass es auf gegenseitigem Nutzen basiert. Sehr richtig und wichtig ist die Betonung, dass jeder Partner einen Vorteil aus einer Zusammenarbeit erwarten kann und dieser Nutzen auch darstellbar sein muss.

Auftragsorientierung

Der Nutzen für die Bibliothek besteht in der größtmöglichen Nähe zur Aufgabenerfüllung. Partnerschaften sollten ausschließlich der Zielerreichung der Bibliothek dienen. Voraussetzung ist natürlich das Selbstverständnis und der eindeutige politische Auftrag für die bibliothekarischen Dienstleistungen.

So können Bibliothekspartnerschaften die Leistungen steigern helfen, finanzielle Hilfe sein und Innovation ermöglichen. Erfolgreiche Partnerschaften und ihre Darstellung führen zur Verbesserung des Image sowohl der Bibliothek als auch des Partners.

Fernhalten sollte man sich von Partnern, die nichts zur Partnerschaft beitragen, unrealistische Forderungen stellen oder politisch nicht akzeptiert werden.

Organisation von Partnerschaften

Das Funktionieren einer Partnerschaft hängt neben der deutlichen Erkennbarkeit des beidseitigen Nutzens von der Professionalität ihrer Organisation und Kommunikation ab. Dabei sind klare Absprachen zum Management der jeweiligen Partnerschaft sowie bei großen Projekten eine vertragliche Vereinbarung zu empfehlen.

Bei der professionellen Verwaltung der Partnerschaften findet man in den Öffentlichen Bibliotheken die größten Veränderungspotentiale. Unverzichtbar sind die Kommunikationsfähigkeiten von Leitung und Belegschaft der Bibliothek. Eine weitere Erfolgsvoraussetzung ist die gute Kenntnis der Partner und ihres Umfeldes.
Die bei der Organisation einer Partnerschaft zu beachtenden Fallstricke sind:

- die falsche Auswahl des Partners durch Missachtung der Priorität der Aufgabenerfüllung,
- die Missachtung oder Fehleinschätzung des zu erwartenden Nutzens für alle Partner,
- die ungenügende Qualifikation des mit der Organisation der Partnerschaft betrauten Personals,
- die ungenügende Kenntnis des Partners und der damit verbundene falsche Ansatz für die Initialkommunikation.

Um den Fallstricken zu entgehen, sollte die Evaluierung der Partnerschaften und eine intensive Schulung des Bibliothekspersonals zum Kommunikationsmanagement gehören. Es kommt jedoch stets darauf an, dass jede Mitarbeiterin und jeder Mitarbeiter sich bewusst ist, am Image der Bibliothek maßgeblich mitverantwortlich zu sein. Die für das Image der öffentlichen Bibliothek maßgeblichen Elemente:

- Dienstleistung,
- Professionalität in
  - traditioneller Bildungsarbeit,
  - innovativer Informationsvermittlung sowie
  - Unterhaltung und Kultur,
- breitestes Kunden- (= Bürger-) (= Wähler-) spektrum

entstehen nicht von selbst, sind viel schneller zerstört als aufgebaut und müssen mit viel Engagement und Liebe zum Beruf gepflegt werden.

Aus unseren Erfahrungen lassen sich folgende Voraussetzungen für erfolgreiche Partnerschaftsarbeit zusammenfassen:

- gute professionelle Öffentlichkeitsarbeit der Bibliothek,
- positive Einstellung der Mitarbeiter zur Partnerschaft und zum Partner,
- positives Image der Bibliothek und ihrer Leistungen,
- klare Zielvorstellungen,
- Schnittstelle zu Unternehmenszielen des Partners,
- attraktive Projektidee und gute Strategie inklusive deren Beschreibung,
- klarer und verbindlicher Kostenplan.

Partnerschaften der Städtischen Bibliotheken Dresden

Strukturierung der Partnerschaften

Die Städtischen Bibliotheken Dresden haben natürlich zahlreiche Partner, welche mit wirtschaftlichen Verträgen gebunden sind. Die bestehende Kommunikation erleichtert oft die Diskussion auch eine Projektzusammenarbeit neben der Produzent-Kunde-Beziehung aufzubauen.

Darüber hinaus ergaben sich aus der Umsetzung der bibliothekspolitischen Ziele zahlreiche Notwendigkeiten vor allem aber Möglichkeiten, ganz andere Partner an die Bibliothek zu binden.

Diese Partner mit verschiedener Motivation sind am Ende dieses Beitrags mit folgender an Holt angelehnten Struktur verknüpft:

- Partnerschaften zur Aus- und Fortbildung,
- Finanzierungspartnerschaften,
- Partnerschaften zur Informationsverbreitung und Programmentwicklung für ein gemeinsames Publikum,
- Partnerschaften für Forschungs- und Entwicklungsprojekte,
- Politische Allianzen.

Aus der Tabelle wird deutlich, dass sich einige Partner auch auf verschiedenen Gebieten binden lassen.

Der Ausgangspunkt aller unserer Partnerschaften sind die Bibliotheksentwicklungsplanungen. Sie stellen den Kontrakt mit dem Stadtrat dar, welcher sowohl Aufgaben- als auch Budgetsicherheit bieten soll. Aus den vereinbarten Zielen und Aufgaben erwachsen die Ideen zum Anknüpfen von Partnerschaften. Die Vereinbarungen zum Mitteleinsatz zeigen Deckungslücken und geben Klarheit zu den möglichen Eigenanteilen bei der Finanzierung partnerschaftlicher Projekte.

In Deutschland ist es nach wie vor keine Ausnahme, dass gute Partnerschaftsideen von Bibliotheken daran scheitern, dass sie der Genehmigung von Dienststellen der Stadtverwaltung oder von Bürgermeistern bedürfen, diese aber nicht bekommen, weil das Verständnis für die Notwendigkeit und die Chancen fehlt.

Neben der quantitativ zu bewertenden Etatsituation spielt daher auch die dezentrale Ressourcenverantwortung und die Budgetierung im Rahmen der Verwaltungsmodernisierung eine wichtige qualitative Rolle. Die Bibliothek kann aktuell sowohl inhaltliche als auch finanzielle Prioritäten im Rahmen des vereinbarten Kontraktes, auf Basis der Eigenverantwortung und eben gemeinsam mit den Partnern flexibel festlegen.

Beispiele neuer Partnerschaften

Auch anlässlich der Beschäftigung mit der Strukturierung der Partnerschaften führten wir in den letzten zwei Jahren eine Reihe von Projekten durch, welche bestehende Partner mit neuen zusammenführte. Diese Projekte sollen beispielhaft vorgestellt werden.

Design-Wechsel Fahrbibliothek

Die Fahrbibliothek fand in ihrer früheren Gestaltung keine große Beachtung im Stadtbild. Ein pfiffiges, ansprechendes Design würde jedoch nur unter Einsatz nicht unbeträchtlicher finanzieller Mittel möglich.

Daraus entstand die Idee, den Sprayern, die sonst nur illegal arbeiten, ein bewusstes, für sie und für die Bevölkerung akzeptables Angebot zu machen. Außerdem sollte zumindest ein Teil der Mittel für Farbe, Lack und Arbeitslohn durch Sponsorengelder abgedeckt werden.

Wir wandten uns an den in Dresden ansässige Jugendklub ABC, welcher jährlich einen Graffitiwettbewerb international ausschreibt und vereinbarten bei einem ersten Treffen: Der Wettbewerb wird wie immer ausgeschrieben, als Hauptpreis darf der Sieger ein Bibliotheksfahrzeug nach einem eigenen, von uns vorher begutachteten Entwurf gestalten.

Die entsprechenden Firmen waren überraschend schnell gefunden: eine Lackiererei, welche die anfallenden vor- und nachbereitenden Arbeiten übernahm und ein Farbenhersteller, welcher die Grundfarbe und den für die Konservierung der Graffiti notwendigen Klarlack zur Verfügung stellte.

Durch die ausgezeichnete Zusammenarbeit aller Beteiligten, die zuvor in dieser Form noch nichts miteinander zu tun hatten, konnten trotz äußerst ungünstiger Witterung alle Arbeiten termingerecht fertiggestellt werden.

Ihren Abschluss fand diese Aktion bei der Präsentation des Wagens auf einem Fest zum 70-jährigen Jubiläum der Dresdner Fahrbibliothek.

Sanierung der Plastik „Lesendes Mädchen"

Die lebensgroße Plastik des „Lesenden Mädchens" vom Bildhauer Heinz Mamat wurde vom Rat des Stadtbezirkes Süd 1958 vor der Stadtteilbibliothek Südvorstadt aufgestellt. Die Plastik war mehr als 30 Jahre eine Art Wahrzeichen und Orientierungspunkt für alle Anwohner und Besucher in der Südvorstadt. Wie selbstverständlich lenkte sie die Blicke der Vorübergehenden auf die Bibliothek.

1989 wurde die Figur mutwillig zerstört, vom Sockel gestürzt, Kopf und Beine abgebrochen. Die Mitarbeiter der Bibliothek und Bewohner des Hauses bargen die Einzelteile im Keller der Bibliothek in der Hoffnung, einmal finanzielle Unterstützung für die Restaurierung zu erhalten. Auf Grund der nicht vorhandenen Mittel schlugen jedoch alle Bemühungen fehl.

Viele Nachfragen über das Schicksal des „Lesenden Mädchens" und das Interesse, diese kleine Figur der Öffentlichkeit wieder zugänglich zu machen, bewogen uns zum Aufruf einer Spendenaktion in der Stadtteilbibliothek Südvorstadt. Laut eines Kostenvoranschlages mussten 3.146,00 DM erbracht werden.

Das 40-jährige Bibliotheksjubiläum der Stadtteilbibliothek erschien als günstiger Anlass, denn dadurch machte auch die Presse auf das Anliegen aufmerksam.

Die „Überreste" stellten wir im Eingangsbereich der Bibliothek auf, damit waren sie praktisch nicht zu übersehen. So gelang es, das Interesse bei den Benutzern zu wecken.

Ein Drittel des gesamten Spendenaufkommens erbrachten die Leserinnen und Leser. Es waren auch die ganz kleinen Pfennigbeträge, die mit geholfen haben, dem Ziel näher zu kommen. Entscheidend war nicht nur der finanzielle, sondern auch der ideelle Wert.

Um die Spendenfreudigkeit wach zu halten, bedurfte es aber immer wieder vieler Gespräche mit den Benutzern. Durch die Informationen über den Spendenstand waren sie stets mit einbezogen.

Die örtliche Zweigstelle der Stadtsparkasse Dresden und ein im Wohngebiet tätiges Projektierungsbüro wurden zusätzlich als Partner gewonnen.

Mit einem Steinmetz- und Bildhauermeister, der das „Lesende Mädchen" noch vor der Zerstörung kannte, fanden wir einen Fachmann als Partner, der Verständnis für unsere Situation hatte. Er führte die Leistung zum Materialpreis aus.

Zum Welttag des Buches konnte die restaurierte Figur in Anwesenheit des Kulturbürgermeisters, der Partner, vieler Benutzer, Gäste und der Presse der Öffentlichkeit wieder übergeben werden.

Absicherung des Bücherhausdienstes

Bibliotheksarbeit mit Senioren hat in den Städtischen Bibliotheken Dresden eine fast 30-jährige Tradition. In Senioren- und Pflegeheimen gibt es kleine, von der Sozialen Bibliotheksarbeit betreute Bibliotheken, die von den alten Menschen bis vor wenigen Jahren rege genutzt wurden.

Inzwischen ist eine Trendwende zu beobachten: Seniorenheime entwickeln sich immer mehr zu Pflegeheimen. Alte Menschen, aber auch jüngere Körperbehinderte, bleiben so lange wie möglich in ihren Wohnungen und lassen sich ambulant versorgen. Für diese Menschen, die den Weg in die öffentliche Bibliothek nicht mehr allein bewältigen können, wurde 1996 von den Städtischen Bibliotheken Dresden ein Bücherhausdienst eingerichtet.

Als wichtigste Arbeit zu Beginn des Projektes erwies sich das Bekanntmachen des neuen Bibliotheksangebotes in der Öffentlichkeit und die Suche nach Projektpartnern. Werbeblätter an ca. 100 Multiplikatoren wurden verteilt.

Nach telefonischer Nachfrage seitens der Bibliothek erfolgte ein Rücklauf von ca. 30 Einrichtungen in 2 Formen:

- Weitervermittlung des Angebotes an entsprechende Einzelpersonen,
- Einladung zu Informationsveranstaltungen, in denen die Bibliothek das Projekt vor Mitarbeitern oder potentiellen Nutzern vorstellen konnte.

Mit 15 der 100 angeschriebenen Einrichtungen gab es auch Kontakte über den Bücherhausdienst hinaus (z.B. Literaturveranstaltungen in Seniorentreffs, Teilnahme an Weiterbildungsveranstaltungen der Seniorenarbeit, Verteilung von Werbeblättern der Einrichtungen in der Bibliothek).

Das führte wiederum zur ständigen Vermittlung von Lesern für den Bücherhausdienst - zur Zeit werden 130 Behinderte und hochbetagte Senioren betreut.

Neben den ständigen Bemühungen um personelle Absicherung der Arbeitsbeschaffungsmaßnahmen erwies sich das Fahrzeug zu Beginn des Jahres 2000 als Problem. Seit Beginn des Projektes mussten die Mitarbeiter ihren Privat-Pkw für die täglichen Touren zur Verfügung stellen. Es ist sehr schwer, geeignete ABM-Kräfte mit eigenem Fahrzeug zu finden.

Vor der Entscheidung stehend, entweder fachlich und sozial geeignetes Personal ohne eigenes Fahrzeug oder weniger der Sache aufgeschlossene Personen mit eigenem Auto zu beschäftigen, war, auch um das Stammpersonal der Sozialen Bibliotheksarbeit sowie Praktikanten und Zivildienstleistende in die Bücher-Hausversorgung einzubeziehen, ein bibliothekseigenes Fahrzeug notwendig.

Dazu beschritten wir zwei Wege:

- Beteiligung an einem Wettbewerb „Bürger stiften Zukunft" bei der Dresdner Bürgerstiftung: Die Bibliothek wurde in einen „Projektmarkt" aufgenommen, d.h. bei geeigneten Sponsoren wurden wir in Betracht gezogen, außerdem verdoppelt die Stiftung das gespendete Geld.
- Kontakt mit Autohäusern mit dem Angebot, ein zur Verfügung gestelltes Fahrzeug sowohl für Transportaufgaben im Rahmen des Projektes als auch zu Werbezwecken zu nutzen.

Nach einigen Bemühungen (neben sofortigen Absagen und Vertröstungen auch mehrerer Gesprächsangebote) fanden wir ein Autohaus, welches uns einen für unsere Zwecke gut geeigneten Gebrauchtwagen zum halben Preis anbot.
Nun erwiesen sich die gleichzeitigen Bemühungen bei der Bürgerstiftung als richtige Entscheidung. Die Stiftung bestätigte uns die Finanzierung der anderen Hälfte des Autopreises. So gelang es tatsächlich, sowohl ein Auto eigens für den Bücherhausdienst einzusetzen, als auch die Dienstleistungen personell hochwertig abzusichern.

Bestseller-Präsentation in der Haupt- und Musikbibliothek

Bücherwand „Belletristik-Bestseller"

Mit dem Umzug in das World Trade Center Dresden eröffneten sich für die Haupt- und Musikbibliothek viele neue Möglichkeiten in der Einrichtung und Nutzung.
Erstmals war es u.a. möglich, auf einer stark erweiterten Nutzungsfläche neue Varianten der Präsentation für Medien zu finden. Zahlreiche Aufsteller und Präsentationswände werben nun für Neuerscheinungen, Ausstellungen und Bestseller.
Im Bereich der Belletristik werden in drei Wandregalen die Bestseller, die in TV-Programmen besprochenen Titel und Bücher für zukünftige Bibliothekslesungen ausgestellt. Die Regale heben sich mit ihren grünen Rückwänden von der üblichen Wandgestaltung ab. In großer Beschriftung wird auf diese Sonderausstellung aufmerksam gemacht.

Durch die attraktive Gestaltung und die getrennte Aufstellung ergab sich die Idee, diesen Buchbereich einer ortsansässigen Buchhandlung zur Verfügung zu stellen. Die Attraktivität wird erhöht durch die große Besucheranzahl. Täglich nutzen durchschnittlich 2.500 Besucher die Bibliothek.

Die Suche nach einem geeigneten Partner konnte schnell beendet werden, da eine bereits vorhandene Partnerbuchhandlung zur gleichen Zeit im Begriff war, sich neu zu profilieren. Die vorhandenen Ideen konnten nach einigen Gesprächen sofort konkretisiert und in die Tat umgesetzt werden.

Die ausgestellten Bücher (16 Exemplare) werden der Bibliothek kostenfrei zur Verfügung gestellt. Zusätzlich erhält die Bibliothek ein zweites kostenfreies Exemplar zur sofortigen Ausleihe. Bei jedem Ausstellungswechsel werden pro Titel erneut zwei Exemplare von der Buchhandlung geliefert.

Die Buchhandlung wirbt mit ihrem Logo an der Präsentationswand. Weiterhin erscheint in jedem Buch der Hinweis, dass es sich um ein Geschenk der Buchhandlung an die Bibliothek handelt.

Die ausgestellten Titel werden gemeinsam mit der Buchhandlung ausgewählt, da von beiden Einrichtungen entsprechende Fachleute zur Entscheidung herangezogen werden. Die Bibliothek sorgt selbstverständlich für die fachgerechte und attraktive Präsentation.

CD-Charts TOP 100

In der Haupt- und Musikbibliothek besteht mit einer CD-Präsentation „Charts 100" eine stark genutzte Möglichkeit für die Bibliotheksbenutzer, die von der Gesellschaft „Media Control" wöchentlich ermittelten 100 Bestseller-CDs des Musiktonträgermarktes in der Bibliothek anzuhören. Dieser Informationsservice der Bibliothek entspricht sehr stark den Benutzerinteressen, unabhängig von der Entleihung und ohne Kaufabsicht eine freie Informationsmöglichkeit über diese CDs zu nutzen.

Anfangs wurden die CDs zur Bestückung bzw. für die wöchentlichen Platzierungsveränderungen der Wand aus dem Medienetat der Bibliothek angekauft, mit dem Nachteil, dass diese nicht zur Entleihung zur Verfügung standen. Eine vertragliche Regelung mit einem Musiktonträgergeschäft erlaubt nun, dass das Geschäft die entsprechenden CDs an die Bibliothek ausleiht um dafür entsprechende Werbefläche bei den „Charts 100“ zu nutzen. Die Bibliothek kann ihren Etat damit effektiver nutzen und bei Bedarf die Präsentations-CDs nach Ausscheiden aus den „Charts 100“ sehr preiswert kaufen.

Jugendprojekte Bibliothek und Kunst
Die Städtischen Bibliotheken Dresden starteten 1999 ein Gemeinschaftsprojekt mit dem Theater Junge Generation und der Bertelsmann Buch AG München unter dem Motto „Theaterexkurse”.

Ausgangspunkt war die Überlegung, eine beidseitig nutzbringende Kooperation zwischen der Großstadtbibliothek und dem örtlichen Kinder- und Jugendtheater aufzubauen, da wir

- beide städtische Einrichtungen mit vergleichbarem Auftrag sind,
- die gleiche Hauptzielgruppe mit unseren Angeboten erreichen wollen,
- dazu jeweils spezifische Methoden und Möglichkeiten nutzen, deren Vernetzung sinnvoll und effektiv ist,
- durch geeignete Angebote Brücken bauen wollen zwischen Literatur, Bibliothek und Theater,
- ständig auf der Suche nach neuen Wegen in der Medienvermittlung sind,
- dem Veranstaltungsprofil in der Haupt- und Musikbibliothek einen weiteren wichtigen Akzent hinzufügen wollten.

Das Projekt setzte sich aus zwei Teilen zusammen, dem Werbekonzept und dem Veranstaltungskonzept. Beide Teile wurden gemeinsam mit dem Theater der Jungen Generation konzipiert und umgesetzt.

Das Theater konnte über einen Zeitraum von einem halben Jahr in unserem Haus für seine Programme, Aufführungen und Premieren kostenlos werben. Dazu wurde ein gemeinsames Werbekonzept erarbeitet, um eine attraktive Gestaltung der Bibliothek sicherzustellen und eine Überfrachtung mit reiner Theaterwerbung zu vermeiden. Durch raumhohe Sichttafeln, befestigt an vorhandenen Säulen, wurde besonders auf jene Stücke und Aufführungen aufmerksam gemacht, die auch im Mittelpunkt der angebotenen Theater-Workshops standen. Im Gegenzug und dank der finanziellen Unterstützung durch die Bertelsmann Buch AG war es uns möglich, mit Hilfe von erfahrenen Theaterpädagogen und Schauspielern des Theaters ein attraktives Veranstaltungsprogramm für Kinder und Jugendliche zu entwickeln und durchzuführen.

Durch speziell hergestellte Faltblätter und Flyer mit den Logos der drei beteiligten Partner, wurden die Veranstaltungsangebote in Bibliotheken, Schulen und im Theater bekannt gemacht und beworben.

Ziel des Veranstaltungskonzeptes war es, Kinder und Jugendliche durch szenische Lesungen, Gespräche, Spiele mit und ohne Requisiten sowie Improvisation innerhalb einer Reihe von spezifischen Veranstaltungsangeboten zum kreativen Umgang mit Texten anzuregen und auf diesem Weg auf Bücher und Theater neugierig zu machen.

Durchgeführt wurden zahlreiche Veranstaltungen mit einem Theater-Projekttag als Höhepunkt.

Für uns war es in diesem Zusammenhang wichtig, besonders jenen Jugendlichen Angebote zu unterbreiten, die nur selten oder gar nicht Bibliotheken nutzen. Dies ist über anfängliche Schwierigkeiten (die jeweiligen Berufsschulklassen mussten für den entsprechenden Vormittag aus dem normalen Schulbetrieb ausgeplant werden) im Verlauf des Projektes immer besser gelungen. Inzwischen haben sich so gute Beziehungen zu den umliegenden Berufsschulen herausgebildet, dass es Nachfragen nach weiteren Veranstaltungen und Reihen seitens der Lehrkräfte gibt.

Die Kooperation mit dem Theater Junge Generation ermöglichte uns qualitativ hochwertige, von Fachkräften professionell durchgeführte Werkstatt-Veranstaltungen, die für uns aus eigener Kraft so nicht realisierbar gewesen wären. Wichtig war dabei auch der Effekt, dass die Bibliothekarinnen der Hauptbibliothek die Gelegenheit hatten, neue Formen und Varianten des spielerischen und kreativen Umsetzens von Texten in ein anderes Medium mitzuerleben und selbst zu erlernen, die sie an anderer Stelle nachnutzen können. Ferner entfielen eigene aufwendige Vorbereitungen.

Ein weiterer positiver Effekt ist das gegenseitige Kennenlernen von Ansprechpartnern und Kontaktpersonen. Aus der großen Resonanz auf die Theaterlesung konzipierten wir als erste gemeinsame Aktion nach Ablauf des Projekts eine Lesenacht, die in der Haupt- und Musikbibliothek aus Anlass des 50. Geburtstages des Theaters Junge Generation durchgeführt wurde. In vier Vorabend- und einer Abendveranstaltung kamen Autoren zu Wort, die die Geschichte des Theaters mitgeprägt haben und als Buchautoren und Dramatiker namhaft sind. Für uns als Partner, Mitorganisator und Gastgeber der Veranstaltungen brachte diese Aktion viel Publikumszuspruch (ca. 350 Besucher) und eine positive Presse, ohne Honorarmittel in Anspruch genommen zu haben.

Inzwischen gibt es auch ein Nachfolgeprojekt, das sich unter dem Titel „Anstiftung zur Kunst" mit bildender Kunst für Kinder beschäftigen soll und ebenfalls von der Bertelsmann Buch AG durch die Übernahme der Honorarmittel gefördert wird. Dies ermöglicht uns die Zusammenarbeit mit einer jungen Künstlerin, die diese Veranstaltungen in zehn verschiedenen Bibliotheken des Stadtnetzes durchführen wird.

Arbeitsanalyse Haupt- und Musikbibliothek

Grundlage für das Entstehen einer Partnerschaft mit der Hochschule für Technik und Wirtschaft Dresden war die Überprüfung der Zweckmäßigkeit der vorhandenen Mitarbeiter-Einsatzplanung. Es stand u.a. die Frage, ob mit den verfügbaren Personalressourcen eine bessere Anpassung der Arbeitsabläufe in der Bibliothek an die Besucherzahl möglich ist.

Die Optimierung des Einsatzes der Mitarbeiter im Verbuchungsbereich spielte eine besondere Rolle, da durch Urlaub und Krankheit mehrfach zu wenig Verbuchungsschalter geöffnet werden konnten. Ziel war somit sowohl eine Verbesserung des Service für die Benutzer als auch eine Entlastung der Mitarbeiter.

Mit einer Schilderung der Sachlage wurden verschiedene regionale Hochschulen befragt, ob Interesse an einer Zusammenarbeit in Form einer Diplomarbeit besteht. Die Hochschule für Technik und Wirtschaft Dresden, Fachbereich Wirtschaftswissenschaften, Studiengang Betriebswirtschaftslehre reagierte sehr schnell mit einer positiven Rückmeldung.

In Form einer Seminararbeit arbeiteten acht Studenten, betreut durch Ihren Professor, im Studienschwerpunkt Produktionslogistik an diesem Thema in folgenden vier Komplexen:

- Dienstleistungsqualität und Benchmarking,
- arbeits- und tarifrechtliche Grundlagen des Zeitmanagements,
- Analyse des Ist-Zustandes,
- Erarbeitung eines Soll-Konzeptes.

Regelmäßige gemeinsame Beratungen und eine Mitarbeiterumfrage gewährleisteten, dass die vorgeschlagenen Lösungen den Vorstellungen der Praxis entsprachen.
Mit der abschließenden Übergabe der Seminararbeit an die Bibliothek wurden wichtige Vorschläge und Hinweise gegeben.

Die Erarbeitung der Projektarbeit hat in viele Richtungen neue Denkanstöße vermittelt. Gespräche und Diskussionen innerhalb des Bibliotheksteams folgten und zeigten, wie wichtig die Auseinandersetzung mit dem Problem war.

Inzwischen wurden zahlreiche Ideen verwirklicht und haben erste Erfolge gebracht. Die Partnerschaft hat neue Anstöße gegeben, weiterhin ständig die von unsteten Faktoren beeinflussten Arbeitsabläufe zu optimieren.

Qualitätsindikatoren

Die Städtischen Bibliotheken arbeiten seit 1996 mit einem vertraglich vereinbarten Produktplan. Zur Bemessung der Produkte existieren Indikatoren, welche die Quantität, die Qualität und die Kosten der zu erbringenden Dienstleistungen beschreiben. Während zur Definition von quantitativen Indikatoren die Controlling-Erfahrungen seit 1993 sowie zahlreiche Betriebsvergleichs- und Statistikprojekte heranzuziehen waren und sich die Kostenkennzahlen aus der seit 1998 existierenden Kosten- und Leistungsrechnung ergeben, erfolgte die Definition und Erfassung der Produktqualität bisher eher spontan.

Um auf diesem Gebiet eine gesicherte Basis herzustellen, erwies sich die Suche nach einer Partnerschaft mit Kommunikationsprofis als notwendig. Als Ergebnis führten die Städtischen Bibliotheken Dresden im Februar 2000 gemeinsam mit dem Institut für Kommunikationswissenschaft der Technischen Universität Dresden eine repräsentative Benutzerbefragung im Rahmen einer Magisterarbeit zum Thema „Qualitative Leistungsmessung Öffentlicher Bibliotheken" durch.

„Qualität" ist ein hypothetisches Konstrukt, das selbst nicht messbar ist. Aufgabe der Magisterarbeit war es deshalb zunächst, messbare Indikatoren für Qualität zu erarbeiten. Darauf aufbauend sollte dann ein Instrument zur Messung der bibliothekarischen Qualität entwickelt werden, das - kontinuierlich angewandt - den Städtischen Bibliotheken einen Qualitätsvergleich über die Zeit hinweg möglich macht.

Die Untersuchung beschäftigte sich zunächst mit einem Modell zur Qualitätsmessung Öffentlicher Bibliotheken. Dabei wurde von einem subjektiven Qualitätsbegriff ausgegangen. Qualität ist demnach nichts statisches, sondern bemisst sich immer als subjektiver Vergleichsprozess jedes einzelnen Benutzers zwischen seinen Erwartungen und den wahrgenommenen Bibliotheksleistungen.

Das Projekt folgte in seiner Strategie dem Modell zur Qualitätsmessung. Zunächst wurde geklärt, wer die Benutzer der Städtischen Bibliotheken Dresden sind (soziodemographische Merkmale), mit welchen Erwartungen, Wünschen und Medieninteressen sie in ihre Bibliothek kommen und welche Faktoren diese Erwartungen beeinflussen. Erst dann folgten die Erfahrungen der Benutzer und ihre Bewertung der durch die Bibliotheken angebotenen Leistungen. Der Vergleich der Erwartungen der Benutzer mit ihren Aussagen zur Zufriedenheit ließ abschließend Empfehlungen zur Qualitätsverbesserung zu. Dabei hatten diejenigen Qualitätskriterien die höchste Priorität zur Verbesserung, die den Benutzern sehr wichtig, mit denen sie jedoch nicht zufrieden sind.

Insgesamt kamen 670 ausgefüllte Fragebögen zurück. Die Rücklaufquote betrug damit 75 Prozent. Angesichts der für eine Bibliotheksbefragung ungewöhnlichen Länge und der Tatsache, dass der Fragebogen nicht mit nach Hause genommen werden durfte, sondern gleich vor Ort ausgefüllt werden musste, ist die Rücklaufquote als sehr gut zu bewerten.

Die Fragebögen wurden in der Universität per Scanner eingelesen und mit einer Statistik-Software ausgewertet. Ein schriftlicher Bericht fasst die wesentlichen Ergebnisse zusammen. Er geht nicht auf die Angaben zu den einzelnen Zweigbibliotheken aufgrund der zu kleinen Fallzahl für jede einzelne Bibliothek ein. Möglich ist jedoch ein Vergleich zwischen der Haupt- und Musikbibliothek und dem Stadtnetz.

Ein ergänzender Tabellenband enthält den Fragebogen, die Häufigkeitsauszählungen aller Fragebogen-Items sowie die Anmerkungen und Verbesserungsvorschläge der Benutzer bezüglich der Städtischen Bibliotheken insgesamt und zu den einzelnen Bibliotheken.

Nach der Präsentation der Studie und der Umfrageergebnisse im Rahmen einer für alle Mitarbeiter offenen (Fortbildungsveranstaltung) Leitungsberatung durch die Fachleute der TU Dresden erfolgte die Auswertung gründlich in der Bibliothek.

Auf der einen Seite werden die Erkenntnisse bezüglich der Qualitätsindikatoren in das Kontraktmanagement ab 2002 einfließen, auf der anderen Seite wurden sofort mit Beginn des 2. Halbjahres 2000 Maßnahmen zur Steigerung der Qualität der bibliothekarischen Dienstleistungsangebote erarbeitet und umgesetzt.

Zusammenfassung, Schlussfolgerungen

Ohne unsere aktive Partnerschaftsarbeit wäre die Aufgabenfülle kaum zu bewältigen, die Qualität bibliothekarischer Arbeit auf einem niedrigeren Niveau.

Neben dem wirtschaftlichen und inhaltlichen Nutzen hat der Imagegewinn höchste Bedeutung. Dieser resultiert aus dem Beweis der professionellen Kommunikationsfähigkeit der Bibliothek und ihrer Leitung. Dieser Imagevorteil wirkt auf die Partner zurück und zieht weitere Partner an. Er wirkt aber auch nach Innen, ist Motivationsmotor für die Mitarbeiterinnen und Mitarbeiter und trägt zur Sicherung des Budgets bei, da die öffentlichen Mittel schwerer kürzbar sind, wenn auf ihrer Basis Drittmittel eingeworben wurden.

In der Kommunikation mit den Partnern gilt es, die Klischees des öffentlichen Dienstes (Betulichkeit, Langatmigkeit, Umstandskrämerei, Unzuverlässigkeit und Inkompetenz) zu bekämpfen. Entscheidend sind die kommunikativen Fähigkeiten der Mitarbeiterinnen und Mitarbeiter. Die Partner der Bibliothek lieben eine effektive Kommunikation, Entscheidungsfreude und Zuverlässigkeit.

Die Partnerschaftsarbeit lässt sich kaum in die hierarchischen Strukturen der traditionellen Behörde integrieren. Sie sollte Teil eines neuen mitarbeiterorientierten Gesamtverständnisses des Bibliotheksmanagement sein.

Formen / Partner	**Partnerschaften zur Aus- und Fortbildung**	**Finanzierungs-partnerschaften**	**Partnerschaften zur Informationsverbreitung und Programmentwicklung für ein gemeinsames Publikum**	**Partnerschaften für Forschungs- und Entwicklungsprojekte**	**Politische Allianzen**
Stadtrat		Budgetbeschluss	Wähler = Nutzer		SR-Beschlüsse sind Aufgabengrundlage
Stadtverwaltung	Nutzung städtischer Fortbildungsangebote	Budgetverhandlungen interne Verrechnungen	Bürger = Nutzer Auslage von Informationsmaterial dresden.de		
EU, Bund, Land	Ausbildungsberatung Prüfungswesen Nutzung der Angebote der Landeszentrale für politische Bildung	Fahrbibliothek Sanierungsfördermittel Stadtteilbibliothek Pieschen EU-Projekt zum Jahr der Sprachen 2001	Basis-Info-Dienst für: Bundes- und Landeszentralen für politische Bildung und gesundheitliche Aufklärung		bibliothekspolitischer Einfluss auf Gesetzgebung und Förderprogramme (Kulturraumgesetz)
DBV, BDB, Berufsverbände	Nutzung der Fortbildungsangebote des VdDB				DBV-Vorsitz als bibliothekspolitische Verantwortung Vizepräsidentschaft AIBM, LG Deutschland
Fachstellen für ÖB	Abstimmung Fortbildung	Unterstützung bei Förderprogrammen	Vorträge in Fachstellenveranstaltungen		
DBI (EDBI)	Nutzung von Fortbildungsprogrammen	gemeinsame Fortbildungsfinanzierung	DBS	Kommissionsarbeit (Kinder- und Jugendbibliothek)	Beirat
bibliothekarische Ausbildungseinrichtungen	Ausbildungskoordinierung: Fachangestellte für Medien und Informationsdienste Nutzung Fortbildungsangebote		Vorträge in HTWK Leipzig	Betreuung von Praktikanten und Diplomarbeiten	
Bibliotheken	SLUB: überbetriebliche Lehrunterweisungen abgestimmte Fortbildungsprogramme	Bildung Konsortien zu Lizenzverträgen	SLUB: gemeinsamer Bibliothekenführer vernetzte Informationsangebote Leihverkehr Absprache Bestandsprofile	Ermittlung Leistungsindikatoren	Abstimmung kommunaler Bibliothekspolitik in Großstadtsystemen

Formen / Partner	**Partnerschaften zur Aus- und Fortbildung**	**Finanzierungs-partnerschaften**	**Partnerschaften zur Informationsverbreitung und Programmentwicklung für ein gemeinsames Publikum**	**Partnerschaften für Forschungs- und Entwicklungsprojekte**	**Politische Allianzen**
ekz	Teilnahme an Workshops		Entwicklung Informationsdienst Lektoratskooperation		Interessenabstimmung in und außerhalb BDB
(lokale) Weiterbildungsinstitute	Nutzen Fortbildungsprogramme				
VHS	Fortbildungswoche		Vorträge von Lektoren im Fortbildungsprogramm gegenseitige Werbung		Vorstandsarbeit im VHS e.V.
Schulen		Betreibervertrag für Öffentliche Schulbibliotheken	jede Schule hat Partnerbibliothek Klassenführungen Projektwochen Kindermedienprojekt Ausleihstellen in Förderschulen	Schülerbefragungen	
TU				Qualitätsindikatoren	
HTW				Arbeitsuntersuchung Haupt- und Musikbibliothek	
Buchhandlungen	Vorstellung von Neuerscheinungen Ausbildungspraktika	Bestseller Haupt- und Musikbibliothek gemeinsame Veranstaltungen Werbekostenpauschale	gemeinsame Veranstaltungsreihen gemeinsame Werbung: Veranstaltungsplakate		
Archive	Lehrunterweisungen gemeinsame Fortbildungsveranstaltungen				
Verlage		Veranstaltungen Vermarktung Schaufenster	Verlagsausstellungen (Käufer = Nutzer) Bertelsmann-Buch-AG: - Theaterprojekt - Kunstprojekt		
Schriftstellervereinigungen			Werbung für Lesereihen Veranstaltungsreihen		Mitarbeit Förderkreis für Literatur in Sachsen e.V.

Formen Partner **Medien**	**Partnerschaften zur Aus- und Fortbildung**	**Finanzierungs-partnerschaften**	**Partnerschaften zur Informationsver-breitung und Pro-grammentwicklung für ein gemeinsames Publikum** Pressearbeit	**Partner-schaften für For-schungs- und Ent-wicklungs-projekte**	**Politische Allianzen**
(Stadtteil) Kulturein richtungen			Auslage Informati-onsmaterial und Aus-hang Plakate Theaterprojekt gemeinsame Werbung **Theater der Jungen Generation** Hygienemuseum abgestimmte Veran-staltungsprogramme		
Jugendein-richtungen		Graffiti Fahrbib-liothek	medien@age: Jugendbibliothek & Jugendinformations-stelle Werbung Projektwochen		
Senioren - Vereini-gungen			Führung von Senio-rengruppen Veranstaltungsreihe Bücherhausdienst		politische Lob-by
Stiftungen	Nutzung Veran-staltungsangebote: Bertelsmann, A-denauer, Ebert	Bertelsmann Stif-tung: Filialpro-jekt Stiftung Lesen u.a. : Veranstal-tungen Bürgerstiftung: Fahrzeug Bücherhaus dienst	Bertelsmann Stiftung: Filialprojekt	Bertels-mann Stif-tung: Interna-tionales Experten-netzwerk	Bertelsmann Stiftung: BIX
Werbe-firmen		Vermarktung von Werbeträgern			
(lokale) Wirtschaft		Sponsoring	Veranstaltungsreihe mit Krankenkasse		
örtlicher Handel		Sponsoring	Stadtteilfeste und Bibliotheks-veranstaltungen		
regionale & lokale Ver-einigung	ÖTV: Fortbil-dungsprogramme		Vermittlung & Aus-lage von Informati-onsmaterial Veranstaltungen Ausstellungen Projektwoche Aus-länderrat		
Banken		Sponsoring	Stadtteil- und Biblio-theksfeste		

Formen / Partner	**Partnerschaften zur Aus- und Fortbildung**	**Finanzierungs-partnerschaften**	**Partnerschaften zur Informationsver-breitung und Pro-grammentwicklung für ein gemeinsames Publikum**	**Partner-schaften für For-schungs- und Ent-wicklungs-projekte**	**Politische Allianzen**
Arbeitsamt & Personalver-mittlungsein-richtungen	Betreuung von Praktikanten und Umschülern	ABM : EDV-Einführung Arbeit & Lernen: Möbel-anfertigung	ABM: Bücher-Haus-Dienst	ABM: Bib-liotheks-geschichte ABM: Ar-chivierung	
Vermieter		Sponsoring	Veranstaltungen, Ausstellungen		
Mieterbund		Medienbe-schaffung	Informationsveran-staltungen		

Elmar Mittler

Die Göttinger Forschungsbibliothek

Konzeption und praktische Umsetzung im Historischen Gebäude der Niedersächsischen Staats- und Universitätsbibliothek Göttingen

1.1 Die Forschungsbibliothek in Deutschland

Der Begriff der Forschungsbibliothek (engl. research library) ist in Deutschland seit Bernhard Fabians[175] 1983 erschienener Studie „Buch, Bibliothek und Geisteswissenschaftliche Forschung“ in Fachkreisen intensiv diskutiert und in der Öffentlichkeit teilweise geradezu inflationär verwendet worden.[176] Mit der Förderung fünf großer Bibliotheken durch die Volkswagenstiftung, die sich in der Arbeitsgemeinschaft Sammlung Deutscher Drucke zu einer Art segmentierter Nationalbibliothek zusammengeschlossen und inzwischen auch Die Deutsche Bibliothek in ihren Kreis aufgenommen haben[177] sowie mit dem Erscheinen des Handbuchs der Historischen Buchbestände[178] sind wesentliche Forderungen Fabians zur Ergänzung des historischen Buchbestandes und der Information über seine Standorte erreicht worden.

Die Idee der Forschungsbibliothek, deren wesentliche Elemente Knoche 1993[179] noch einmal zusammengefasst hat, ist in Berlin und anderswo über Planungen noch nicht wesentlich hinausgekommen. In Göttingen aber konnte im Jahre 2000 durch Sanierung eines Teilbereichs des Historischen Gebäudes ein wesentlicher Schritt zu der Realisierung des Konzeptes getan werden, über das hier berichtet werden soll.

1.2 Die Göttinger Universitätsbibliothek Ausgangspunkt der modernen Forschungsbibliothek

Goethes oft zitierte Bemerkung von der Göttinger Bibliothek als Kapital, das lautlos unberechenbare Zinsen spendet, die er bei seinem ersten Besuch spontan formulierte, wurde vor allem bei seinem längeren Forschungsaufenthalt in Göttingen 1801[180] bestätigt: Gab er doch eine umfangreiche Liste von Literatur zur Geschichte der Farbenlehre ab, die er anderswo nicht hatte finden können. Zu seiner Verblüffung legte man ihm nicht nur die gewünschten Titel vor, sondern noch weitere, die er noch nicht kannte. Damit hatte sich das Konzept der Göttinger Biblio-

---

175 Bernhard Fabian: Buch, Bibliothek und geisteswissenschaftliche Forschung. Göttingen 1983

176 Vgl. Michael Knoche: Die Forschungsbibliothek. In: Bibliothek 17 (1993) S. 291 - 300 hier S. 292 f.

177 1450 - 1600 Bayerische Staatsbibliothek München, 1601 - 1700 Herzog August Bibliothek Wolfenbüttel, 1701 - 1800 Niedersächsische Staats- und Universitätsbibliothek Göttingen, 1801 - 1870 Stadt- und Universitätsbibliothek Frankfurt, 1871 - 1912 Staatsbibliothek Preußischer Kulturbesitz Berlin. Arbeitsgemeinschaft Sammlung Deutscher Drucke: Das deutsche Buch. Die Sammlung Deutscher Drucke 1450 - 1912. Hrsg. von Bernhard Fabian und Elmar Mittler, Wiesbaden 1995. Kulturen im Kontext. Zehn Jahre Sammlung Deutscher Drucke. Berlin 1999

178 Fabian, Bernhard (Hrsg.): Handbuch der historischen Buchbestände in Deutschland. Hildesheim, 1992 -

179 Knoche, Anm. 2, S. 294

180 Vgl. hierzu: Mittler, Elmar (Hrsg.): „Der gute Kopf leuchtet überall hervor“. Goethe, Göttingen und die Wissenschaft. Göttingen 1999. insbes. S. 56 ff.

thek mit ihrer weltweiten Erwerbungspolitik und ihrer für die damalige Zeit perfekten systematischen Aufstellung einmal mehr glänzend bewiesen[181].

Doch Forschungsansprüche wechseln schnell. Das ist nicht nur in den Naturwissenschaften mit ihrer schnell veralternden Literatur der Fall. Auch die Geisteswissenschaften haben wechselnden Literaturbedarf. Beim Symposium „Forschung in der Bibliothek“[182] hat Fabian das systematische Dilemma von Forschung und Bibliothek herausgearbeitet, das selbst scheinbar so perfekte Sammlungen wie die der Göttinger Bibliothek für das 18. und frühe 19. Jahrhundert schon wegen der Auswahlprinzipien (in diesem Fall z. B. die strikte Beschränkung auf Literatur, die einen Erkenntnisfortschritt dokumentierte[183]) für neue Forschungsbereiche wie Alltagsgeschichte oder „gender studies“ weniger ergiebig macht.[184] In Göttingen werden heute im Rahmen der Sammlung Deutscher Drucke z. B. zeitgenössische Übersetzungen von wichtigen ausländischen Titeln des 18. Jahrhunderts ins Deutsche erworben, die heute von hohem kulturhistorischen Interesse (Erkenntnistransfer, inhaltliche Überarbeitung usw.) sind - Heynes Auswahlkriterien aber zu seiner Zeit nicht standhalten konnten.

Eine der wesentlichen Forderungen der Wissenschaftler, die sich aus dieser Forschungssituation mit immer neuen Aspekten und Fragestellungen ergibt, ist die nach direktem Zugang zu den Buchbeständen.[185] Durch das direkte Durchsuchen der Bestände sind z. B. Funde auch für Fragestellungen möglich, die früher bei der systematischen Erschließung nicht berücksichtigt worden sind (und werden konnten). Die Erfüllung dieses Wunsches der Leser bedeutet natürlich ein großes bibliothekarisches Dilemma: historische Bibliotheksbestände frei zugänglich zu machen, birgt vielfältige Risiken für den Bestand. Neben der stärkeren Belastung des Materials durch die Nutzung und der Gefahr des Verstellens sind Vandalismus durch Heraustrennen von Seiten und letztlich Verlust durch Diebstahl ernst zu nehmende Risiken. Deutsche Universitätsbibliotheken haben mit freiem Magazinzutritt teilweise schlechte Erfahrungen gemacht und den Magazinzugang abgeschafft. Im angelsächsischen Raum wird den Forschern aber weiterhin das Arbeiten am systematisch aufgestellten Bestand erlaubt. Im traditionell benutzerfreundlichen Göttingen hat man sich deshalb entschlossen, freien Zugang auch für größere Teile des älteren Bestandes in der „Forschungsbibliothek“ für einen ausgesuchten Benutzerkreis zu ermöglichen.

2. Bauliche Konzeption und Realisierung in Göttingen

Mit Bezug und Eröffnung des Neubaus der SUB Göttingen 1992/1993 stehen dort den Benutzern der Bibliothek über 600 Arbeitsplätze in zwei Lesebereichen mit rund 450.000 Bänden Freihandbestand und weitere ca. 800.000 Bände in einem Freihandmagazin frei zugänglich zur Verfügung. Das neue Gebäude ist aber nicht so groß ausgelegt, dass es die

---

181 Vgl. Bernhard Fabian: Göttingen als Forschungsbibliothek im 18. Jahrhundert. In: Öffentliche und private Bibliotheken im 17. und 18. Jahrhundert. Bremen 1977, S. 209 - 233

182 Vgl. hierzu Bibliothek und Wissenschaft BuW 30 (1997)

183 Bernhard Fabian: Forschung und Bibliothek. In: BuW (Anm. 8) S. 12-25, hier insbes. S. 20f

184 Christian Gottlob Heyne. In: Göttingische Gelehrte Anzeigen 1810, II., S. 252f.

185 Vgl. hierzu die Ausführungen von Helen Watanabe-O'Kelly: Literaturwissenschaft im späten 20. Jahrhundert und die Erforschung der Literatur der Frauen 1500-1800. In: BuW (Anm. 8) S. 41-49 und Dieter Breuer: Konfessionelle Vorbehalte in der Frühneuzeitforschung und ihre Folgen für die bibliothekarische Sammlung und Erschließung. BuW (Anm.8) S. 50-58 sowie die Zusammenfassung von Elmar Mittler: Forschung in der Bibliothek. BuW (Anm.8) S. 1-4, hier insbes., S 2f.

Gesamtbestände der Bibliothek aufnehmen könnte. Schon bei der Programmplanung wurde deshalb vom Wissenschaftsrat empfohlen, im Historischen Gebäude die Sondersammlungen der Bibliothek unterzubringen. Im Rahmen der Sanierungsplanung wurde seit 1990 daraus das Konzept der Göttinger Forschungsbibliothek entwickelt.[186]

2.1 Das Bibliotheksviertel Prinzenstraße - Papendiek - Paulinerstraße

war von Anfang seiner Nutzung an ein Ort geistiger Konzentration und Ausstrahlung: die erste Bebauung erfolgte durch die Dominikaner, denen das Gelände am Leinekanal am 14.03. 1294 urkundlich von Herzog Albrecht II. von Braunschweig und Lüneburg überlassen wurde[187]. Der Auflösung der Ordensniederlassung in der Reformationszeit folgten Nutzungen insbesondere als Pädagogium (1542- 1545 und 1586 - 1734).[188] Die Vorbereitung für die Nutzung durch die 1737 gegründete Universität führte praktisch zum Neubau der Klostergebäudlichkeiten bis auf die Kirche.[189] Anbauten im 18. Jahrhundert dienten insbesondere der Erweiterung der Flächen für die schnell wachsende Bibliothek, die 1812 auch das neu eingezogene Obergeschoss der Paulinerkirche zur Aufstellung der Bestände zur Geschichte übernahm.[190] Durch Erweiterungsbauten nach Süden (1787) und nach Norden (1887) sowie nach Südwesten (Magazinbau 1916) entstand das jetzige Bibliotheksensemble, das bis 1992 Hauptstandort der Niedersächsischen Staats- und Universitätsbibliothek Göttingen (SUB) war.[191]

Es war nach dem Bezug des Neubaus nicht immer leicht, die Nutzung des Historischen Gebäudes für Bibliothekszwecke zu sichern, da in der Öffentlichkeit der Eindruck entstanden war, dass das - mit entsprechend verringerter Nutzungsfrequenz - für einige Sondersammlungen, Handschriften und wertvollen Drucke sowie Karten (seit 1998 auch für die Asien- und Afrikabestände) im Rahmen der gegebenen Raumstruktur kontinuierlich weitergenutzte Gebäude leer stehe und veräußert werden könne. In ihrer Antwort auf die Anfrage des Abgeordneten Trittin stellte sich die Regierung des Landes Niedersachsen - auch aus Kostengründen - entschieden hinter die Konzeption der Weiternutzung des Gebäudes für die SUB Göttingen.[192]

Der Eindruck der Nichtnutzung wurde in dieser Zeit dadurch verstärkt, dass aus Sicherheitsgründen der Haupteingang von der Prinzenstraße in den Papendiek verlegt werden

---

186 Elmar Mittler: Die Forschungsbibliothek im Altbau der Niedersächsischen Staats- und Universitätsbibliothek Göttingen. In: Georgia Augusta 58 (1993) S. 55-58 sowie Elmar Mittler: Auf dem Wege zu einem bibliothekarischen Gesamtkonzept: Neubau und historisches Gebäudeensemble der Niedersächsischen Staats- und Universitätsbibliothek Göttingen. In: Bibliotheksbauten in der Praxis Wiesbaden 1994. S. 223-241, bes. S. 237ff. Elmar Mittler: Die Göttinger Forschungsbibliothek – Tradition und Bauaufgabe. In: 700 Jahre Paulinerkirche. Göttingen 1994, S. 156-159

187 Peter Aufgebauer. Die Mendikanten in Göttingen. In: 700 Jahre Paulinerkirche (Anm. 12) hier: S. 43

188 Eva Schlotheuber: Die Auflösung der Bettelordensklöster in der Reformation, In: 700 Jahre Paulinerkirche (Anm. 12) S. 35 - 39 und S. 71 - 74 sowie Berthold Michael: Die beiden Pädagogien im Paulinerkloster. In: 700 Jahre Paulinerkirche (Anm. 12), S. 111 - 144

189 Reimer Eck: Vom Pädagogium zur Keimzelle von Universität und Bibliothek, In: 700 Jahre Paulinerkirche (Anm. 12), S. 145 - 149, hier S. 146

190 Heinz Fuchs: Die Paulinerkirche als Teil der Universitätsbibliothek (19. und 20. Jahrhundert), In: 700 Jahre Paulinerkirche (Anm. 12), S. 149 - 153

191 vgl. insbesondere Werner Seidel: Baugeschichte der Niedersächsischen Staats- und Universitätsbibliothek in Göttingen. Göttingen 1953, S. 21 f.

192 Antwort auf eine Kleine Anfrage des Abg. Trittin (Drucksache 13/523) betr. Nutzung der Paulinerkirche in Göttingen als Teil der Göttinger Universitätsbibliothek (Niedersächsischer Landtag, 13. Wahlperiode, Drucksache 13/677)

musste. Damit wurde zugleich die erstmals vom Verfasser im August 1990 (noch vor seinem offiziellen Dienstantritt in Göttingen) in einer Bausitzung vorgeschlagene Neuorientierung der Eingangssituation in (noch völlig unzulänglicher Form) verwirklicht, die im Rahmen der Kostenvorermittlung Bau von den damit betrauten Architekten Venneberg und Zech (Hannover) mit Engagement aufgegriffen wurde.[193]

2.2 Kernstück der neuen Forschungsbibliothek

ist der Prinzenstraßenbau des späten 19. Jahrhunderts. Er wurde als Magazingebäude errichtet, durch das man über ein Treppenhaus in den damals mit Oberlicht versehenen Lesesaal im Zentrum des Gebäudes gelangte. Diese ehemals geschlossenen Magazinbereiche werden als Forschungslesebereiche mit den am intensivsten gebrauchten älteren Beständen den Benutzern zugänglich gemacht. Im Zuge eines ersten Sanierungsabschnitts konnte 1999/2000 dieses Ziel für die in historischer Form erhaltene doppelstöckige Anlage des 2. Obergeschosses mit der offiziellen Eröffnung am 8. Dezember 2000 durch Minister Oppermann erreicht werden.[194]

In diesem „Forschungslesesaal" 18. Jahrhundert und „Wissenschaftsgeschichte" (2. Obergeschoss des Prinzenstraßenbaus) wurde Kernliteratur wie wichtige Zeitschriften und Reihen, aber auch Sachgruppen z. B. mit der biographischen Literatur aufgestellt. Insbesondere stehen damit ca. 150.000 Bände von Literatur aus dem Zeitraum 1601 - 1900 bereit.

2.3 Im zweiten Sanierungsabschnitt

wird das jetzt als Handschriften- und Raralesesaal benutzte 1. Obergeschoss ebenfalls wieder eine zweistöckige Regalanlage erhalten, aber weiterhin auch den Lesebereich für die Handschriften und wertvollen Drucke sowie für das Universitätsarchiv aufnehmen.

Die Kapazität wird durch Kompaktmagazinierung in den Zwischengeschossen des Hauptgebäudes und Ausbau des unteren Kirchenbereiches wesentlich erhöht. Im Zwischengeschoss für die Aufstellung auch der Archivalien des Lesebereichs werden Arbeitskabinen für Wissenschaftler geschaffen. Der schon jetzt eingerichtete Asien-Afrika-Lesesaal im Obergeschoss des Westflügels (am Papendiek) bleibt mit dieser Funktion erhalten. Die Kartensammlung erhält Räumlichkeiten im Erdgeschoss (NO) des Prinzenstraßenbaus. Als ergänzende technische Abteilungen werden die Fotostelle (NW-Bereich des EG im Prinzenstraßenbau) und das Digitalisierungszentrum (NW-Bereich des EG am Papendiek) sowie die Restaurierungswerkstatt (EG im SO des Gebäudeteils an der Paulinerstraße) untergebracht.

Ergänzend sei darauf hingewiesen, dass in den neueren Räumlichkeiten des Hauses interne Dienststellen oder in ihrer Forschung stark auf die Bibliotheksbestände bezogene Forschergruppen der Universität sowie der Akademie der Wissenschaften und die Genealogische Gesellschaft untergebracht sind. So werden das Mittelhochdeutsche Wörterbuch, der Zeitschriftenindex 18. Jahrhundert und die Ausgabe der naturwissenschaftlichen Schriften Lichtenbergs im Hause erarbeitet.

---

[193] 700 Jahre Paulinerkirche (Anm. 12), S. 153 - 155 und 169 - 170; Herrn Reimer Eck danke ich für die Bereitstellung von aktuellen Materialien zu den verschiedenen Eingängen des Gebäudes, die mir erlaubten, auch als (noch) Außenstehender eine Neukonzeption für ein Gebäude vorzubereiten, das ich vorher nur aufgrund der Literatur kannte.

[194] Pressebericht vom 09.12.2000 z. B. im Göttinger Tageblatt über die Homepage der SUB (http://www.sub.uni-goettingen.de, Pressespiegel, erreichbar)

2.4 *Informationszentrum für den wissenschaftlichen Benutzer*

der Forschungsbibliothek 18. Jahrhundert und Wissenschaftsgeschichte wird der derzeit als Standort der Bereichsbibliothek Physik (Umzug nach dem Abschluss des 1. Bauabschnittes des Neubaus der Physik im Nordbereich der Universität ca. 2003) genutzte, nach dem Zweiten Weltkrieg als Kataloglesesaal ausgestaltete westliche zentrale Gebäudebereich zwischen Paulinerkirche und Prinzenstraßenbau, dessen Ostteil als Schulungs- bzw. Multimediaraum verwendet wird.

2.5 *Der meistbesuchte Gebäudeteil in der Forschungsbibliothek*

aber ist schon jetzt der Ausstellungs- und Veranstaltungsraum im Obergeschoss der Paulinerkirche. Er konnte im ersten Sanierungsabschnitt in optisch enger Anlehnung an die Neugestaltung aus dem Jahre 1812 saniert werden. Dazu wurde

- der Kirchenraum (anders als beim Wiederaufbau nach dem Zweiten Weltkrieg) durchgängig weiß (bei den Pfeilern war ein helles Grau der Kompromiss) gestrichen;
- die Regale wurden auch in der Detailaufteilung analog zur alten Regaleinteilung gebaut;
- in guter Sichthöhe wurden in die Regale Vitrinen eingebaut (bei denen Erfahrungen der Heidelberger Palatinaausstellung 1986 eingebracht werden konnten). In Greifhöhe wurden unter und über die Vitrinen eine Schutzverglasung eingebaut; die eingebaute Innenbeleuchtung verhindert dabei störende Verspiegelungen;
- die Kombination Vitrine / beleuchtete Regale wurde auch im Chorbereich als neu entwickelte Bibliotheksvitrine eingesetzt;
- durch entsprechende Verblendung im oberen Bereich der Regale war es möglich, auch eine indirekte Beleuchtung über die Decke zu erreichen, die - wie auch Fotos deutlich zeigen - in beeindruckender Weise der historischen Beleuchtungssituation entspricht.

Zum Gesamtbild in der Kirche tragen auch andere Details bei, die dem Besucher sicher nicht immer im Einzelnen auffallen, aber den Gesamteindruck des Raumes beeinflussen. So waren die alten Dielen in Regalnähe längs und im übrigen Raum quer angeordnet. Bei der Sanierung gelang es, diesen Raumeindruck zurückzugewinnen. Dabei wurde der Holzboden wie im 18. Jahrhundert nur geölt, nicht in moderner Weise versiegelt. Erwähnt sei in diesem Zusammenhang auch die Farbgebung der Fenster an der Paulinerkirche und am Prinzenstraßenbau, die sich bewusst an nachweisbaren alten Farben orientiert.

Eine weitere Besonderheit des Kirchenraums stellt das Schatzhaus als voll klimatisierte und hochgesicherte Großvitrine dar, bei der eine passive Klimatisierung ohne Luftverwirbelung im Bereich der internen Ausstellungskästen realisiert werden konnte.[195]

[195] Vitrinenhersteller bieten heute – sozusagen standardmäßig – Einzelklimatisierung jeder Vitrine an. In der British Library (London) oder der Bibliothèque nationale de France (Paris) werden derartige Konstruktionen eingesetzt. In diesen Vitrinen wird ein permanenter Luftzug erzeugt, der kontinuierlich die Verwirbelung von Mikrostäuben mit sich bringt. Um einen derartigen Effekt möglichst auszuschließen, wurde eine Konstruktion realisiert, bei der die Ausstellungsboxen im Schatzhaus von klimatisierter Luft (außer an der Schauseite) umflossen sind und sich damit in einem stabilen Klima befinden. Für den ergänzenden notwendigen (minimalen) Temperatur- und Feuchtigkeitsausgleich gibt es an den Vitrinen noch kleinere Einlässe. Messungen zeigen, dass damit eine Stabilität der Klimawerte in den Vitrinen und dem gesamten Schatzhaus erreicht wird. Ähnlich erfolgt die Klimatisierung im Schautresor im Manesse-Raum der Universitätsbibliothek Heidelberg. Vgl. Elmar Mittler: Bibliothek im Wandel. Heidelberg 1989, S. 24

2.7 Ausstellungs- und Veranstaltungsmöglichkeiten

sind ein wesentlicher Teil der Konzeption der Göttinger Forschungsbibliothek, die nicht nur ideale Arbeitsmöglichkeiten, sondern auch Kommunikations- und Präsentationsmöglichkeiten für die Forschungsarbeit und ihre Ergebnisse bieten will. Ergänzend wird die Sanierung des Heynehauses (Heyne hat als Direktor der Bibliothek 1760 - 1812 entscheidenden Einfluss auf ihre Konzeption und internationale Ausstrahlung gehabt) zu einem wesentlichen Teil des Gesamtkonzeptes der Neugestaltung des Bibliotheksviertels. Das Fachwerkgebäude wird im Rahmen der Sanierung seinen historischen Eingang wiedererhalten, der direkt gegenüber dem Papendiekeingang der Bibliothek am Lichtenberghof liegt. Im Erdgeschoss des Heynehauses werden zwei (teilbare) Veranstaltungsräume für je ca. 40 Personen das Angebot in der Paulinerkirche für 100 bis über 200 Personen bzw. im Schulungsraum der Forschungsbibliothek (ca. 80 Personen) in idealer Weise ergänzen. Sollte sich der Plan verwirklichen lassen, im derzeit von Studierenden bewohnten neueren Annex des Heynehauses Suiten für Stipendiaten und andere längerfristig in der Forschungsbibliothek arbeitende Wissenschaftler zu schaffen, wäre in Göttingen ein ideales geisteswissenschaftliches und wissenschaftshistorisches Zentrum entstanden, das durch seine Ausstellungen und Veranstaltungen, aber auch für breitere Kreise der interessierten Öffentlichkeit ein besonderer Anziehungspunkt sein wird.

Exkurs: Zur Wegeführung im Gebäude

Bei der ersten großen Ausstellung im Gutenberg- und Expojahr 2000 hat sich die neue Konzeption insbesondere auch der Eingangsregelung aufs Beste bewährt: durch den Lichtenberghof zwischen Paulinerkirche und Informationszentrum (derzeit Bereichsbibliothek Physik) werden die Besucher der Ausstellungen und/oder Veranstaltungen ebenso wie die Benutzer der Forschungsbibliothek durch einen repräsentativen Eingang des 18. Jahrhunderts in den Westflügel des ehemaligen Dominikanerklosters geführt. Ein Seitenweg ermöglicht auch den problemlosen Zugang für Behinderte. Über Aufzug oder das Treppenhaus gelangt man in das 1. Obergeschoss. Hier ist der zentrale Verteiler und Aufsichtsbereich: die Besucher der Paulinerkirche finden leicht den Weg nach Süden, die Benutzer der Forschungsbibliothek werden nach Norden geführt.

Es ist leicht erkennbar, dass die Wegeführung des späten 19. Jahrhunderts vom (baulich stark hervorgehobenen) Portal in der Prinzenstraße für die neuen Funktionen nicht mehr verwendbar ist. Es würden sonst die vielen Ausstellungs- und Veranstaltungsbesucher (allein die Gutenbergausstellung lockte in 5 Monaten über 27.000 Menschen an) mitten durch Bereiche führen, in denen besonders schützenswerte Bestände einem überschaubaren Kreis von Forschern in relativ freizügiger Weise zu konzentrierter wissenschaftlicher Arbeit bereitgestellt werden. Das ließe sich weder aus Sicherheits- noch unter Arbeitsgesichtspunkten vereinen. Demgegenüber ermöglicht der zentrale Aufsichtspunkt für Paulinerkirche und Forschungsbibliothek die Dauerausstellung oder weniger frequentierte Sonderausstellungen in den gut gesicherten Vitrinen und dem Schatzhaus in der Paulinerkirche ohne zusätzlichen Personalaufwand zugänglich zu machen.

Es bleibt natürlich eine Herausforderung, den Prinzenstraßeneingang in einer angemessenen Weise zu aktivieren. Spontane Zustimmung findet dabei immer wieder der Gedanke, ihn für Multimediapräsentation in die Prinzenstraße hinein zu benutzen. Damit würde zusätzliches Leben in diesen etwas tot wirkenden Abschnitt des Weges vom Bahnhof zum Stadtzentrum gebracht. Der Charakter der Bibliothek als traditionsbewusstes Archiv wissenschaftlicher Literatur und hochmodernes Zentrum digitaler Informationsmedien würde erkennbar. Durch eine 3D-Simulation können Funktion und Wegeführung im Gebäude verdeutlicht werden; entsprechende Bilder und Texte würden die Attraktivität von Ausstellungen und Veranstaltungen erhöhen. Es ist zu hoffen, dass sich diese Konzeption im 2. Bauabschnitt realisieren lässt.

Es sind aber nicht nur praktische Gesichtspunkte, die sich bei der neuen Wegeführung als positiv erweisen. Für den aufmerksamen Besucher des Gebäudekomplexes wird beim Besuch die alte Struktur des Paulinerklosters deutlich; wer dann in die Forschungsbibliothek geht, durchschreitet Teile des ersten Bibliotheksraums des 18. Jahrhunderts und seiner Erweiterung aus dem 19. Jahrhundert. Im oberen Foyer aus dieser Zeit findet er die historischen Bandkataloge. Sein Weg führt ihn weiter in die Forschungslesebereiche des Prinzenstraßenbaus, in denen er im 2. Obergeschoss die historische Regalanlage bewundern und an den modernen Arbeitsplätzen auch mit Funk-LAN optimal arbeiten kann. So führt der Weg vom 14. bis ins 21. Jahrhundert.

Der Rückweg aus den wertvollen Beständen, die alle technisch gesichert sind, ist auch aus psychologischen Gründen ziemlich lang. Er führt durch zwei Buchsicherungsanlagen, die auch mit Personal ausgestattet sind. Verbunden mit der dauerhaften Speicherung der Aufenthaltsdaten aller Besucher sind so möglichst gute Voraussetzungen für die Sicherheit der Bestände geschaffen.

3. Die Konzeption der Forschungsbibliothek - Realisierung und neue Aspekte

Michael Knoche[196] hat in seinen Überlegungen zur Forschungsbibliothek 12 Aspekte für ihre Konzeption zusammengestellt; diese Checkliste ist von der Ausrichtung auf die Geisteswissenschaften über Qualität und Quantität der Bestände und ihre Erschließung bis hin zur Präsenzhaltung der Bücher für die Forscher und die Ausrichtung auf bestandsorientierte Forschungsprojekte in Göttingen ebenso erfüllt, wie bei der Organisation und Aufnahme von Kongressen und Veranstaltungen.

Das Göttinger Beispiel kann dabei zeigen, dass nicht nur alte Fürstenbibliotheken, wie die Herzog August Bibliothek Wolfenbüttel, sondern auch (und gerade) eine auf eine Universität ausgerichtete Bibliothek ihre Dienstleistungen für die geisteswissenschaftlichen und wissenschaftshistorischen Forscher in einer auf deren Bedürfnisse speziell ausgerichteten bibliothekarischen Einrichtung zusammenfassen kann, die natürlich auch den Studierenden höherer Semester zur Verfügung steht.

Über Knoches Konzeption hinaus ist in Göttingen die Bereitstellung auch historischen Materials in größerem Umfang mit freiem Zugang realisiert. Ein weiterer neuer Akzent ist die bewusste Ausrichtung auf die Bereitstellung von Forschungsergebnissen auch in größeren Ausstellungen. Schließlich wird mit dem Konzept der Digitalisierung wichtiger Bestände eine neue Dimension des wissenschaftlichen Arbeitens mit den Beständen über die rein lokale Nutzung und den Zugriff über Online-Kataloge hinaus ermöglicht. Die Bibliothek kann damit dem auswärtigen Wissenschaftler den direkten Zugriff auf besonders wichtige und viel gebrauchte Bestände auch von überall in der Welt ermöglichen.
Sie realisiert damit die Konzeption der virtuellen Forschungsbibliothek, in der neue Formen des technisch unterstützten Arbeitens aber auch der wissenschaftlichen Kommunika-

[196] Knoche (Anm. 2) S. 294

tion ermöglicht werden.[197] In Göttingen hoffen wir, dass uns im Jahre 2001 ein Service für den Forscher von heute gelingt, der vor 200 Jahren (1801) nach Goethes Zeugnis erfolgreich war: dass die Bibliothek mit ihren neuen Serviceleistungen mehr bieten kann, als der Leser erwarten konnte.

197 vgl. dazu auch: Elmar Mittler: Verteilte digitale Forschungsbibliothek – ein neues Paradigma für das Verhältnis von Bibliothek und Forschung? In BuW (Anm. 8) S. 141-149

Helmut Gamsjäger

Bibliotheken als Dorfbrunnen der Informationsgesellschaft

Konzept für den Neubau der Hauptbibliothek und der Volkshochschule in Linz

Bereits im 18. Jahrhundert finden wir in Zukunftsromanen das Ende des Buchzeitalters als Motiv. In der zweiten Hälfte des 20. Jahrhunderts wird das Ende des Gutenberg-Zeitalters prognostiziert. In Ray Bradburys Roman „Fahrenheit 451" steht das Buch für Individualität, Geistigkeit, ja Menschlichkeit überhaupt in einer Welt der unbegrenzten Einflussnahme elektronischer Medien.[198] Waren für Leibniz Bibliotheken noch Schatzkammern des menschlichen Geistes, so berichtet in Marie Luise Kaschnitz' Text „Das letzte Buch" ein Kind, es hätte im Museum das letzte Buch ausgestellt gesehen.[199] Sind Bibliotheken Auslaufmodelle im Informationszeitalter? Wozu noch Bibliotheken bauen, wenn sie in naher Zukunft überflüssig sein werden?

Modell der Hauptbibliothek und der Volkshochschule in Linz

1. Leitgedanken für die Planung der Hauptbibliothek

Von Heinrich von Kleist stammt der Satz „Nirgends kann man den Grad der Kultur einer Stadt und überhaupt den Geist ihres herrschenden Geschmacks schneller und zugleich

---

[198] Vgl. dazu: G. Ruppelt: „Das letzte Buch", In: BuB, 53(2001), S. 199 ff. Bad Honnef 2001

[199] M. L. Kaschnitz: Das letzte Buch, In: Gesammelte Werke, Bd 3, S. 408, Frankfurt/M. 1982

richtiger kennen lernen als in den Lesebibliotheken". Am 2. März 2000 hat der Gemeinderat der Stadt Linz den Kulturentwicklungsplan beschlossen, in dem sich die Stadt dazu bekennt, die Grundlagen für eine positive und permanente Kulturentwicklung zu sichern und durch geeignete Maßnahmen immer wieder den aktuellen Anforderungen und Entwicklungen anzupassen. Mit diesem Kulturentwicklungsplan wurde auch die Errichtung eines Kompetenzzentrums für kulturelle Bildung beschlossen. Neue, zukunftsweisende Konzepte für eine synergetische Gemeinschaftsnutzung durch Volkshochschule und Bibliothek und der Vernetzung mit anderen Kultur- und Bildungseinrichtungen sollen entwickelt werden. Von der Bibliothek wurden vier Leitgedanken für diesen Neubau formuliert:

1.1 Dorfbrunnenfunktion

Wolf Rauch schrieb in seinem Referat „Bibliothek – Wozu" beim Österreichischen Bibliothekartag 2000 den Bibliotheken eine „Dorfbrunnenfunktion" in der Informationsgesellschaft zu. „Information und Kommunikation sind zutiefst soziale Aktivitäten. Soziale Aktivitäten brauchen reale Orte des Austausches – je virtueller und unpersönlicher die Kommunikation wird, desto wichtiger werden soziale Ergänzungen werden".[200]

Bereits 1988 hatte Robert Jungk vor der Vereinsamung gewarnt und gesagt, der Mensch „geht mit Geräten mehr um als mit den Mitmenschen" und gefordert „Es muss Plätze geben, wo Menschen zusammenkommen und sich treffen, wo Menschen tatsächlich wieder miteinander ins Gespräch kommen. Eine öffentliche Bibliothek der Zukunft sollte ein solcher Platz der menschlichen Kommunikation sein."[201]

> *„A well-used public library will make a significant contribution to the vitality of an urban area and be an important learning and social centre and meeting place".*[202]

1.2 Leseanimation

Renate Möhrmann schrieb 1994 „Die neuen Armen von morgen werden die Lesefaulen von heute sein". Lesen ist eine wichtige Kulturtechnik. Wer komplexe Texte nicht mehr erfassen kann, wird das untere Drittel der Pyramide in der Informationsgesellschaft besetzen. Er wird besonders bedroht sein durch die Rationalisierungs- und die Globalisierungsfalle und keinen qualifizierten Beruf ausüben können. Lesekompetenz ist die unabdingbare Voraussetzung, um Medienkompetenz zu erwerben. Dieses Ziel entspricht voll den IFLA-Guidelines for Public Libraries in the 21st Century:

> *„The public library should actively support literacy campaigns, as literacy is the key to education and knowledge and to the use of libraries and information services. Newly literate people need easy access to appropriate reading materials to maintain and develop their skills".*[203]

1.3 Erlebnisbibliothek

Die Funktionalität einer Bibliothek ist wichtig, die Akzeptanz durch die KundInnen wichtiger. Eine gut funktionierende Bibliothek, die von den KundInnen nicht angenommen

---

200 W. Rauch: Bibliothek – Wozu?, In: B.I.T. online 3(2000), S. 401 ff. Wien 2000
201 R. Jungk auf einer Tagung f. Bibliothekare in der Evangelischen Akademie Bad Boll 1988
202 Ph. Gill u.a.: Revision of IFLA's Guidelines for Public Libraries, 2000, S. 11
203 s. 5, S. 7

wird, ist eine Fehlplanung. Eine Bibliothek, die ihre Besucher nicht unmittelbar fasziniert, wird bald unter Besucherschwund leiden. Die neue Hauptbibliothek soll keine Verwahrungsanstalt für Medien werden, sondern eine Erlebnisbibliothek. Sie soll ein Ort der Begegnung, ein Ort, an dem alle sozialen Gruppen Medienerlebnisse haben können, werden. Warum sollen unsere KundInnen ihre eigenen vier Wände verlassen, sich auf den Weg in eine Bibliothek machen, wenn sie doch zu Hause viele unserer Angebote in wesentlich gemütlicher Weise benützen können? Die Tendenz zu einer neuen Häuslichkeit, einem neuen Biedermeier ist ein gesellschaftliches Phänomen, dem Bibliotheken nur durch die Qualität ihrer Angebote und ihr Ambiente entgegen wirken können. Einrichtung einer Bibliothek soll zum Besuch animieren. Gefragt ist die Bibliothek der kurzen Wege. Die Trennung der Medien nach Datenträgern, d.h. die Trennung von Printmedien und AV-Medien ist ein Anachronismus, für den nur allzu oft räumliche Unzulänglichkeiten als Vorwand angeführt werden. Wenn wir eine Reise plane, möchten wir in unserer Bibliothek Bildbände, Reiseführer aber auch Reisevideos nahe bei einander finden.

1.4 Flexibilität

Seriöse Vorhersagen über die Entwicklung der Informations- und Kommunikationstechnologie können höchstens mittelfristig erfolgen. Bedenkt man, dass im Normalfall zwischen Planung und Fertigstellung eines Bibliotheksbaus mindestens fünf Jahre liegen, dann wird das Dilemma der Vorhersagen evident. Die Bibliothek soll aber auch noch in zwanzig Jahren funktionell sein und den Bedürfnissen ihrer KundInnen entsprechen. In den IFLA-Guidelines steht daher die Forderung: „They (libraries) should be designed to reflect the functions of the library services and be sufficiently flexible to accommodate new and changing services".[204]

2. Historischer Rückblick

Im Jahre 1939 übernahm die Stadt Linz die Buchbestände (ca. 13.000 Bände) des aufgelösten Oberösterreichischen Volksbildungsvereines, um eine eigene städtische Bücherei zu betreiben. Neben der Hauptbücherei, die im Gebäude der Studienbibliothek untergebracht wurde, bestanden noch zwei Zweigstellen. Mit Kriegsende geriet die städtische Bücherei in eine trostlose Situation. Die Räume der Hauptbücherei waren durch Bombenschäden unbenutzbar geworden, eine Weiterverwendung der Bibliothekare, die entweder Reichsdeutsche oder Nationalsozialisten waren, kam nicht in Frage und von den ca. 14.000 Bänden mussten ca. 4.000 Bände NS-Literatur ausgeschieden und ca. 3.000 als Kriegsverlust abgeschrieben werden. Erst ein Jahr später konnte der Büchereibetrieb in einem Notquartier wieder aufgenommen werden. Mit der Übersiedlung aus dem Provisorium in das Haus Museumstrasse 15 wurde der kontinuierliche Aufstieg der städtischen Büchereien zum zweitgrößten öffentlichen Bibliothekssystem Österreichs eingeleitet.[205]

3. Zur Ausgangssituation:

Volkshochschule wie Hauptbibliothek sind in Gebäuden untergebracht, die ursprünglich für eine andere Nutzung errichtet worden sind und daher nur sehr bedingt für ihre gegenwärtige Verwendung geeignet sind. So war das Gebäude, in dem die Hauptbibliothek situiert ist, ursprünglich die oberösterreichische Filiale der Österreichischen Nationalbank. Da

---

[204] s. 5, S. 7

[205] M. Schimböck: Volksbüchereien in Linz, In: Historisches Jahrbuch der Stadt Linz, 1997, S. 353 ff.

erstmals im Jahre 1989 der Plan diskutiert wurde, die Hauptbibliothek mit der Oberösterreichischen Landesbibliothek in der ehemaligen Bundesstaatlichen Studienbibliothek zu vereinigen, wurden über ein Jahrzehnt die notwendigen Sanierungsarbeiten immer wieder hinausgeschoben. Die Studienbibliothek war im Zuge der maria-theresianischen Bibliotheksreform als wissenschaftliche Allgemeinbibliothek 1774 gegründet worden. Das Gebäude war der einzige selbständige Bibliotheksbau in Österreich in der Zwischenkriegszeit und daher von großer Bedeutung. Das Bundesministerium für Wissenschaft und Forschung plante eine Zerschlagung dieser Bibliothek aus Kostengründen. So sollten die wertvollen Handschriften und Inkunabeln, die im Zuge der Klosteraufhebungen unter Kaiser Joseph II. in ihren Besitz gekommen waren, der Österreichischen Nationalbibliothek übergeben werden, die rechts- und sozialwissenschaftlichen Werke der Universitätsbibliothek und die restlichen Bücher an Interessierte abgestoßen werden. Sowohl das Land Oberösterreich wie die Landeshauptstadt Linz wollten diese durch Jahrhunderte gewachsene Einheit erhalten und durch Vereinigung mit den Beständen der Hauptbibliothek in Kooperation eine wissenschaftliche und öffentliche Bibliothek führen. Um diesen Plan zu verwirklichen, sollte anschließend an das historische Bibliotheksgebäude ein Zubau errichtet werden, der den Anforderungen an eine moderne Bibliothek entsprach, und der Altbau behutsam mit so wenig Eingriffen in die historische Bausubstanz wie möglich restauriert werden. In allen inhaltlichen Fragen, wie Systematik, Software, Kompetenzabklärung usw. konnte das Einvernehmen hergestellt werden. Letztendlich scheiterte das Vorhaben 1998 an der Finanzierung.

Größtmögliche Nutzung von Synergieeffekten war das Zauberwort, das die verantwortlichen Politiker (Bürgermeister und Kulturstadtrat) bewog, einen geeigneten Standort für den gemeinsamen Neubau für die Hauptbibliothek und die Volkshochschule zu suchen. Im Bereich des Hauptbahnhofes besitzt die Stadt ein unverbautes Areal. Die Anbindung an den öffentlichen Nahverkehr, die zentrale Lage und die städtebauliche Herausforderung direkt an der Einfahrt in das Stadtzentrum sind ideale Voraussetzungen.

Die beiden Institute wurden aufgefordert, ein Raum- und Funktionsprogramm zu erstellen, das vor allem die räumlichen, personellen und logistischen Synergien optimal nutzen sollte. Vom Architektenteam (Kneidinger/Stögmüller) wurde dieses Programm unter Berücksichtigung der oben erwähnten Herausforderungen des Bauplatzes umgesetzt. Diese Planung wurde nach einigen Korrekturen vom Gestaltungsbeirat der Stadt Linz akzeptiert.

Ein wichtiges bauliches Signal für die städtische Kultur- und Bildungspolitik an einem prominenten Platz konnte somit in Angriff genommen werden. Für die Volkshochschule ist ein markanter, transparenter 16-geschossiger Turm mit elliptischen Grundriss und für die Hauptbibliothek ein zweigeschossiger Riegel geplant. Ein gemeinsamer Sockel mit einer zweigeschossigen Halle verbindet die beiden Gebäudeteile. Der Gestaltungsbeirat betonte in seiner abschließenden Beurteilung, dass das Projekt durch eine fantasievolle und städtebaulich sensible Formulierung besticht und die drei ineinander verschränkten Gebäudeteile eine gut nachvollziehbare Komposition darstellen. Diese Planung ermöglicht auch die optimale Realisierung der Vorgabe, Synergien weitgehend zu nutzen. Diese räumliche Nähe von Volkshochschule und Hauptbibliothek erfüllt eine zentrale Forderung der IFLA: „They (libraries) should be located close to other community activities e.g. shops and cultural centres. Wherever possible the library should also be available for community use, for example for meetings and exhibitions and in larger buildings for theatrical, musical, audio-visual and media performances“.[206]

---

[206] s. 5, S. 11

4. Ist-Analyse der Stadtbibliothek

4.1 Besucherfrequenz

Durch die Einführung der Jahreskarte, die Vernetzung aller Standorte und dem damit gegebenen Zugriff auf den Gesamtbestand der Stadtbibliothek von jedem Standort aus konnte im Jahr 2000 eine Steigerung der Entlehnzahlen von 800.502 auf 912.469 oder um 14 % erreicht werden. Bei den im Haus Museumstrasse untergebrachten drei Bereichen (Hauptbibliothek, Mediathek, Notenabteilung) betrug die Steigerung das Doppelte:

	1999	2000	+ %
Hauptbibliothek	164.997,-	174.518,-	5,5*
Mediathek	87.633,-	148.209,-	40,9
Notenabteilung	6.442,-	8.972,-	28,2
Summe	259.072,-	331.699,-	28,0

* Geringere Steigerungsrate, da keine AV-Medien entlehnt werden

Nach internationalen Schätzungen nimmt jeder Besucher durchschnittlich drei Medien/Besuch mit. Auf Grund der kundenfreundlichen Jahreskarte ist diese Zahl für die Stadtbibliothek höher und zwar mit fünf anzusetzen. Daraus ergibt sich für das Haus Museumstrasse eine Kundenfrequenz von ca. 66.400 im Jahr 2000. Dazu kommen noch die Benützer der Internetkioske und jene Kunden, die die dezentralen Bürgerservice-Angebote in Anspruch nehmen (insgesamt ca. 40.000 im Jahr 2000). Diese 106.400 Besucher dividiert durch die 248 Öffnungstage ergibt eine tägliche Besucherfrequenz von ca. 430 bzw. eine stündliche von 55 Besuchern.

4.2 Bedarfsanalyse

Die oben angeführten Zahlen beweisen deutlich die Bedeutung der Stadtbibliothek für die Versorgung nicht nur der Linzer Bevölkerung (ca. 20 % der KundInnen sind Nicht-Linzer) mit Information. Vor allem das Angebot an neuen Medien (CD-ROM, DVD), bzw. der kostenlose Internet-Zugang wird in einem signifikant steigendem Ausmaß genutzt. Da die anderen Linzer Bibliotheken in diesen Bereichen auch nicht annähernd an den Standard der Stadtbibliothek heranreichen, ist dieses Angebot z.Z. konkurrenzlos. Mit Beginn des Jahres 2001 wird der Katalog der Stadtbibliothek im Internet recherchierbar sein. Damit ist eine weitere Steigerung der Entlehnungen zu erwarten, vor allem für die Kunden der Notenabteilung wird dieser Service von größter Bedeutung sein. Die Notenabteilung besitzt Musikalien, die in keiner anderen Bibliothek vorhanden sind. Ihre Bestände werden europaweit im Wege der Fernleihe benützt. Für die Kunden aus anderen europäischen Ländern sind daher Katalogrecherchen im Internet eine wesentliche Serviceverbesserung, da an die Recherche sofort die Bestellung des Notenmaterials elektronisch angeschlossen werden kann.

4.3 Qualität der Leistungserbringung

Mit 39 Öffnungsstunden/Woche liegen die Hauptbibliothek und die Mediathek österreichweit an der Spitze. Die Stadtbibliotheken Wien, Graz und Innsbruck haben jeweils nur 30 Stunden/Woche geöffnet und Salzburg 32 Stunden (siehe Beil. 1). Die Kundenfreundlichkeit der Öffnungszeiten, die Qualität des Medienangebotes und die Kundenorientierung der MitarbeiterInnen haben in einem Ranking des „Standards" für die Stadtbibliothek den *1. Platz* gebracht. Durch die Verleihung des Gütesiegels des „Erwachsenenbildungs-Forums OÖ" wurden die Leistungen der Stadtbibliothek ebenfalls ausgezeichnet.

4.4 Kostenschätzung

Durch die Zusammenlegung von Zweigstellen können finanzielle und personelle Ressourcen erschlossen werden, die einen kostenneutralen Betrieb der Hauptbibliothek im Neubau erlauben.

Eine Zusammenlegung der Zweigstellen Neue Heimat, Froschberg und Spallerhof mit den benachbarten Zweigstellen Auwiesen oder Keferfeld/Oed, Hauptbibliothek und Einsteinstrasse würde folgende Einsparungen bringen:

Standort	Personal	Sachaufwand	Reinigung
Neue Heimat	638.000,-	111.000,-	
Froschberg	754.000,-	225.000,-	155.000,-
Spallerhof	400.000,-	63.000,-	
Summe	1,792.000,-	399.000,-	155.000,-

Gesamteinsparung 2,346.000,-
ohne Personal 554.000,-

5. Räumliches und inhaltliches Konzept für den Neubau

5.1 Inhaltliche Zielvorgaben

In ihrem Manifest von 1994 fordert die UNESCO die Entscheidungsträger auf nationaler und lokaler Ebene auf, die Prinzipien ihres Manifestes zu verwirklichen und formuliert die Ziele einer Öffentlichen Bibliothek.

> *„Freiheit, Wohlstand und die Entwicklung der Gesellschaft und des Einzelnen sind menschliche Grundwerte. Sie werden nur erreicht durch die Fähigkeit gutinformierter Bürger, ihre demokratischen Rechte auszuüben und aktiv in der Gesellschaft mitzuwirken. Konstruktive Teilnahme und die Entwicklung der Demokratie hängen von einer zufrieden stellenden Bildung genauso ab wie von freiem und ungehindertem Zugriff auf Wissen, Gedanken, Kultur und Informationen.*
> *Die Öffentliche Bibliothek, der lokale Zugang zum Wissen, liefert eine Grundvoraussetzung für lebenslanges Lernen, unabhängige Entscheidungsfindung und kulturelle Entwicklung des Einzelnen und der gesellschaftlichen Gruppen."*

Dieses Manifest bekundet die Überzeugung der UNESCO, dass die Öffentliche Bibliothek eine lebendige Kraft für Bildung, Kultur und Information und ein wesentliches Handlungselement für die Förderung von Frieden und geistiger Ausgewogenheit im Denken von Männern und Frauen darstellt.

Die UNESCO fordert deshalb nationale und lokale Regierungen auf, die Entwicklung von Öffentlichen Bibliotheken zu unterstützen und sich dabei aktiv zu engagieren.

Ziele der Öffentlichen Bibliothek
Die folgenden Schlüsselziele, die sich auf Information, Lesefähigkeit, Bildung und Kultur beziehen, sollten zu den Kernaufgaben der Öffentlichen Bibliothek gehören:

- Lesegewohnheiten bei Kindern von klein aufwecken und unterstützen;
- individuelles Lernen und Selbststudium ebenso fördern wie staatliche Bildung auf allen Ebenen;
- Gelegenheit für die kreative persönliche Entwicklung bieten;
- Fantasie und Kreativität bei Kindern und Jugendlichen anregen;
- Bewusst machen des kulturellen Erbes, Wertschätzung der Künste, der wissenschaftliche Errungenschaften und Neuerungen;
- Zugang ermöglichen zu kulturellen Ausdrucksweisen aller darstellenden Künste;
- Pflegen von interkulturellen Dialogen und Fördern kultureller Vielfältigkeit;
- Unterstützen der mündlichen Überlieferung;
- den Zugriff der Bürger auf alle Arten von Informationen sicherstellen, die das Gemeinwesen betreffen;
- adäquate Informationsdienste für lokale Initiativen, Verbände und Interessengruppe; anbieten;
- Entwicklung der Fertigkeiten der Informationsbeschaffung und Nutzung von Computern;
- Unterstützung und Teilnahme an Lese-Aktivitäten und –Programmen für alle Altersgruppen und Einführung solcher Aktivitäten, wenn nötig

5.2 Räumliche Zielvorgaben

Beispiele in anderen Städten (z. B. München) zeigen, dass die optimale Anbindung an das öffentliche Verkehrsnetz zu einer enormen Steigerung der Besucherfrequenz führen kann. Die Realisierung von Synergieeffekten zwischen Volkshochschule und Stadtbibliothek erlaubt einen personalsparsamen und kostengünstigen Betrieb. Räumliche Synergien (Foyer, Mehrzwecksaal, gemeinsame Infothek, Kinderbetreuung u.ä.), personelle (Sekretariat, Kraftfahrer, Hausdienst u.ä.) wie auch in der Logistik (Belieferung der Zweigstellen) sind nur bei einem räumlichen Nahverhältnis beider Einrichtungen realisierbar. Bei der Erstellung des Raum- und Funktionsprogramms wurde daher darauf geachtet, dass Synergiebereich von KundInnen beider Einrichtungen problemlos benützt werden können. Durch den Einsatz eines Mediensicherungssystems wird eine großzügige Offenheit dieser Bereiche ermöglicht. Es kann nicht Aufgabe dieses Beitrages sein, hier alle Planvorgaben an die Architekten aufzulisten. Erwähnung sollen daher nur die Synergievorgaben finden.

5.3. Synergien

5.3.1 Medien- und Selbstlernzentrum

In diesem Zentrum für „lebenslanges Lernen" sollen die Medienkompetenz der Bibliothek sowie die Strukturen und Erfahrungen der Volkshochschule gebündelt werden. Für die berufliche Weiterbildung gibt es zahlreiche Einrichtungen; dagegen stellt die allgemeine, persönliche Weiterbildung ein Nischenprodukt dar. Soziales Lernen, Erwerb von Medienkompetenz und professionelle Nutzung des Informationsangebotes dienen der Persönlichkeitsentwicklung. Öffentliche Bibliotheken können bei diesen Faktoren eine wesentliche Rolle spielen, wie ein Projekt der IFLA (International Federation of Library Associations) zeigt.

Dieses Projekt wird von öffentlichen Bibliotheken und Institutionen der Erwachsenenbildung in Schweden und Kanada unter Mitbeteiligung von Tschechien, Spanien und Chile im Zeitraum 2000 – 2003 durchgeführt.

„Life long learning contains of various forms of education and training, formal and informal, e.g. the school system from primary to tertiary level, the free adult education, informal search and training, individually, in a group setting or within the framework of social movements. Within all these forms of education and training, there is a necessity of working methods developing the ability to search for information and develop knowledge actively and independently. The classroom and the traditional textbook must therefore be supplemented by archives, libraries and museums, institutions offering a broad choice of different media and professional guidance in information search.
Public libraries and lifelong learning
In a society of lifelong learning - whether of a formal or informal nature - public libraries will be nodes connecting the local learning setting with the global resources of information and knowledge. Public libraries must therefore be allowed to play a role of fundamental importance in the development of future systems of lifelong learning. The development of the information and communication technology has already laid the basis for the creation of information networks, giving users even of small local public libraries access to the world wide sources of information. The public libraries also offer guidance and training in information search and quality rating of information sources. Thus, public libraries are necessary if not sufficient prerequisites for a democratic knowledge society."[207]

Ziele dieses Projektes sind öffentliche Bibliotheken eine strategische Rolle im Bereich des lebenslangen Lernens zu zuordnen, BibliothekarInnen auf *ihre* Rolle als „Pfadfinder im Informationsdschungel" vor zu bereiten und die Zusammenarbeit zwischen Bibliothek und Einrichtungen der Erwachsenenbildung zu fördern. Mit dem Medien- und Selbstlernzentrum wollen Volkshochschule und Stadtbibliothek erstmalig in Österreich die Ergebnisse aus diesem IFLA-Projekt umsetzen.

5.3.2 Kinderbetreuung
Viele der KundInnen der Volkshochschule aber auch der Stadtbibliothek klagen, dass eine Teilnahme an Kursen der Volkshochschule wie an Veranstaltungen beider Einrichtungen für sie auf Grund eines Kindes nur schwer organisierbar ist. Durch das Angebot einer qualitativ hochwertigen Kinderbetreuung soll ein wertvoller Beitrag zur Chancengleichheit und zur qualifizierten Weiterbildung vor allem für Mütter geboten werden. Die räumlichen und personellen Voraussetzungen dafür wurden eingeplant. Gleichzeitig soll damit die Kreativität von Kindern gefördert und diese mit den vielfältigen Medien-angeboten der Bibliothek vertraut werden. Wenn Kinder rechtzeitig und gezielt mit der Benützung einer öffentlichen Bibliothek in Kontakt treten können, wird ihre Beziehung zur Bibliothek gefestigt und sie bleiben auch als Erwachsene als KundInnen erhalten.

5.3.3 Kundenbereich
Die Vermutung, dass viele KursbesucherInnen der Volkshochschule gleichzeitig KundInnen der Stadtbibliothek sind, ist berechtigt. Diese Personengruppe wird im Neubau beide Funktionen in Anspruch nehmen können. Darüber hinaus wird es aber auch möglich sein, Interessenten der jeweils anderen Einrichtung gezielt auf die eigenen Angebote aufmerksam zu machen. Die zu erwartende Steigerung der Kundenfrequenz stellt auch eine wirtschaftliche Größe dar.

Durch die für den Mehrzwecksaal im Erdgeschoss notwendige Raumhöhe erstreckt sich

207 The Role of Public Libraries in Lifelong Learning – a Project under the Section of Public Libraries, IFLA

das Foyer über zwei Stockwerke mit einer Galerieverbauung. Unmittelbar bei der Eingangszone ist eine Infothek geplant. Hier sollen die KundInnen Erstinformationen über beide Einrichtungen erhalten, sich für Kurse der Volkshochschule anmelden können und alle Funktionen des dezentralen Bürgerservices der Stadt nützen können. Eine Aufwertung würde diese Infothek erfahren, wenn es bis zur Fertigstellung des Neubaus gelingen sollte, die Voraussetzungen für ein „Ticket-Corner" zu schaffen. Die Möglichkeit an diesem zentralen Punkt der Stadt in unmittelbarer Nähe der Nahverkehrsdrehscheibe Hauptbahnhof, Eintrittskarten für die verschiedensten Institute nicht nur der Stadt (Brucknerhaus, Stadtmuseum, Lentos-Museum, Posthof)) sondern auch des Landes Oberösterreich (Landestheater, Landesmuseum) sowie privater Einrichtungen (z.B. Theater Phönix) an einer Stelle kaufen zu können, würde den BesucherInnen dieser Einrichtungen viele Wege ersparen. Selbstverständlich sollte es sein, an dieser Infothek alle für Touristen relevanten Daten (z.B. Hotelreservierungen) hier zu erhalten. Um diese Einrichtung sinnvoll nutzen zu können, müssten ihre Öffnungszeiten über jene der Hauptbibliothek hinaus gehen.

5.3.4 Organisatorische Synergien

Gemeinsame Nutzung der Infrastruktur, Zusammenführung von Controlling und Rechnungswesen bringen Einsparungen in der Ausstattung und im Personaleinsatz. Die Vermarktung des Hauses als Bildungs- und Kompetenzzentrum, seine Positionierung im Bereich der Erwachsenenbildung setzten eine gemeinsame Öffentlichkeitsarbeit und Corporate Design voraus. Dabei sollen die Unterschiede zwischen Volkshochschule und Stadtbibliothek nicht nivelliert, die vielen Gemeinsamkeiten jedoch sinnvoll unterstrichen werden.

Sowohl Stadtbibliothek wie Volkshochschule betreiben eine flächendeckende Versorgung der Linzer Bevölkerung im Rahmen ihres Zweigstellensystems. Eine Zusammenführung dieser Doppelstruktur brächte qualitative Verbesserungen und ökonomischeren Mitteleinsatz.

Das Zweigstellensystem der Stadtbibliothek (insgesamt existieren z. Z. 15 Standorte) mit gravierenden Unterschieden in der Besucherfrequenz soll im Zuge einer von externer Seite begleiteten Organisationsentwicklung optimiert werden. Durch Auflassungen, bzw. Zusammenlegung von Standorten sollen personelle und finanzielle Mittel frei werden, die die höheren Aufwendungen für den Betrieb des Neubaus kostenneutral egalisieren werden.

5.3.5 Personelle Synergien

Da die finanzielle Situation der Stadt Linz, insbesondere im Bereich der Kulturverwaltung die größtmögliche Sparsamkeit und Effizienz beim finanziellen und personellen Ressourceneinsatz erforderlich macht und Verbesserungen der Situation mittelfristig nicht zu erwarten sind, sollen Personal und Budget beider Institutionen als Einheit gesehen werden. Damit werden hohe Flexibilität in Zeiten der Spitzenauslastung (z.b. Semesterbeginn in der Volkshochschule) und Finanzierungsmöglichkeiten für aufwendige Veranstaltungen geschaffen. Eine entsprechende Kompetenzregelung der Verantwortlichkeiten der Direktionen soll verhindern, dass diese Flexibilität auf Dauern zu Lasten einer Einrichtung realisiert wird.

5.3.6 Räumliche Synergien

Die gemeinsame Nutzung von Foyer mit Infothek und Cafeteria, Veranstaltungssaal, Kinderbetreuung und Medien- und Selbstlernzentrum vermindern den Raumbedarf und verbessert die Auslastung der Infrastruktur. Die Direktionen beider Einrichtungen werden benachbart situiert, um im Urlaubs- oder Krankheitsfall, bzw. bei erhöhtem Arbeitsanfall wechselseitige Unterstützung zu ermöglichen.

6. Öffnungszeiten

Wenn auch die Hauptbibliothek mit 39 Öffnungsstunden/Woche österreichweit an der Spitze liegt, müssen an diesem Standort die Öffnungszeiten erweitert werden. Das Raum- und Funktionsprogramm nahm darauf Bedacht, dass für bestimmte Bereiche der Stadtbibliothek verschiedene Öffnungszeiten möglich sind. Die Analyse der Verlaufskurven der Entlehnfrequenz ergab eine Spitzenauslastung der Hauptbibliothek und der Mediathek zwischen 14.00 und 17.00 Uhr. Diese drei Tagesstunden sind ca. 30 % der wöchentlichen Öffnungszeiten und bringen eine signifikant höhere Entlehnfrequenz von über 40 % der wöchentlichen Entlehnungen. Diese Ist-Analyse beleuchtet das Kundenverhalten im derzeitigen Gebäude besitzt aber geringe Aussagekraft über die Spitzenauslastung im Neubau. Wir denken daran, die besonders frequentierten Freihandbereiche wie Belletristik, Sachbücher und Zeitungs- und Journalauslage Montag bis Freitag von 9.00 bis 21.00 und am Samstag von 9.00 bis 13.00 offen zu halten. Die Infothek sollte an diesen Tagen bereits ab 7.00 besetzt sein. Andere Bereiche wie die Notenabteilung werden bereits um 17.00 geschlossen werden, bzw. an Samstagen nicht geöffnet sein. Um auf ein eventuell geändertes Kundenverhalten adäquat und rechtzeitig reagieren zu können, muss die Anordnung der Freihandbereiche flexibel sein.

Da mit keiner Aufstockung des Personalstandes gerechnet werden kann, sind organisatorische und räumliche Voraussetzungen erforderlich, um den Betrieb der Kernzonen zu den oben angeführten Zeiten mit höchstens drei MitarbeiterInnen aufrecht halten zu können.

„Fortschritt ist ein anderer Name für Risiko des Irrtums, und weil das so ist, tut man gut daran, die Richtung, in der man gehen will, vorher abzustecken, um sich nicht im Chaos zu verlieren“.[208] Klare Zielsetzungen sind für die weitere Entwicklung der Stadtbibliothek Linz ein Gebot der Stunde. Wie fast alle NPOs (Nonprofit-Organisationen) haben auch wir einige Schwierigkeiten mit dieser Forderung. Der rasante Wandel der Informations- und Kommunikationstechnik macht Aussagen über die zukünftige Rolle der Bibliothek in der Wissensgesellschaft fast unmöglich. Die Diskrepanz zwischen der realen Alltags- und Medienkultur auf der einen Seite und unserem Angebot an Medienprodukten ist augenscheinlich. Da unser Angebot hauptsächlich von jenen Bevölkerungsschichten angenommen wird, für die das Lesen von Büchern zu ihrer Medienkultur gehört, hat diese Diskrepanz noch zu keinem dramatischen Sinken der Entlehnzahlen geführt. Im Gegenteil verzeichnete die Stadtbibliothek Linz im Jahr 2000 ein Rekordergebnis. Das ist aber kein Grund zufrieden zu sein und am Status quo fest zu halten. Das Interesse Jugendlicher am traditionellen Angebot der öffentlichen Bibliotheken ist alarmierend. Wir brauchen einen Attraktivitätsschub, um bisherige Benützer zu halten und künftige zu gewinnen. Wir hoffen, mit unseren Überlegungen und unseren Zielvorgaben für den Neubau dieses Attraktivitätsschub zu bewerkstelligen.

---

[208] H. Pross: „Informationsgesellschaft als globaler Tele-Zoo, In: Gewerkschaftliche Monatshefte, 41 (1990), S 54

Alfred Pfoser

Wien bekommt eine neue Hauptbibliothek

Stadtpolitik, Stadtplanung und Bibliotheksbau

Die jetzige Hauptbücherei in der Skodagasse

Das Zweigstellennetz der Wiener Städtischen Büchereien geht auf das Rote Wien zurück, das mit seinem Wohnbauprogramm eine in ganz Europa beachtete Form der Sozialpolitik betrieb. Die „Arbeiterbüchereien" der 20er und 30er-Jahre gehörten zur kulturellen Infrastruktur der damals errichteten Superblocks; noch heute ist ein Teil der Büchereien in den gleichen Räumlichkeiten untergebracht wie in der Ersten Republik. Über die Zeiten hat sich die Kleinteiligkeit des Wiener Büchereinetzes erhalten; 1999 werden von den Wiener Städtischen Büchereien 54 Zweigstellen betrieben, überwiegend in den Außenbezirken außerhalb des Gürtels und jenseits der Donau gelegen.

Im Austrofaschismus und im Nationalsozialismus wurden die „Volks- und Arbeiterbüchereien" kommunalisiert. Es gab zwar Pläne, das Filialnetz stärker zu zentralisieren, aber in die Realität umgesetzt wurden diese Vorhaben nicht. Auch nach 1945 bildete die literarische Nahversorgung für die einkommensschwächere Bevölkerung das Herzstück städtischer Bibliothekspolitik. Die Büchereien, meist in Gemeindebauten oder „Häusern der Begegnung" (hier zusammen mit Volkshochschulen, Musikschulen und anderen Gemeindeeinrichtungen) untergebracht, verteilten sich über die ganze Stadt; neue Siedlungsgebiete verlangten nach neuen Filialen. Übergeordnete urbanpolitische Gesichtspunkte spielten eine sehr geringe Rolle. Die Zweigstellen waren auf das unmittelbare Einzugsgebiet orientiert. Erst in den 90er-Jahren kamen Filialtypen zum Zuge, die in/ nahe bei Einkaufszentren oder Einkaufsstraßen situiert sind, die auf gesamtstädtische Verkehrsströme achten und bei denen die Anbindung an das öffentliche Verkehrsnetz von Bedeutung ist. Bezeichnenderweise unterhalten die Wiener Städtischen Büchereien im Zentrum der Stadt oder rund um den Ersten Bezirk, wo die meisten wichtigen Kulturbauten der Bundeshauptstadt stehen und wo sich auch die größte Kulturbaustelle der Zweiten Republik Österreich, das so genannte „Museumquartier", befindet, nur eine Bücherbushaltestelle.

Der Wunsch nach einer Hauptbücherei wurde über Jahrzehnte nachgereiht. Erst in den 60er-Jahren wurde mit dem Bau an der Ecke Laudongasse/ Skodagasse, am Platz des abgerissenen, geschichtlich bedeutsamen Bürgertheaters, begonnen. Allerdings gelang es dem damaligen Leiter der Städtischen Büchereien Rudolf Müller nicht, die Stadtverwaltung zu einem eigenen repräsentativen Neubau zu bewegen. So dient ein Teil des Gebäudes bis heute als Studentenheim, und nur der einstöckige Vorbau sowie ein Teil des Haupttraktes (mit Untergeschoss insgesamt vier Ebenen) stehen den Städtischen Büchereien zur Verfügung. Die Hauptbücherei liegt im Inneren des 8. Gemeindebezirks, der Standort Skodagasse ist im innerstädtischen Verkehrsstrom als etwas versteckt zu bezeichnen.

Die neue Hauptbücherei, 1970 eröffnet, bot immerhin Möglichkeiten, die alle bis dahin in Wien bestehenden Potenziale der Büchereiarbeit weit übertrafen. Als Spezialabteilung hatte das neue „Haus des Buches" eine Musikabteilung mit Plattenabspielung zu bieten. Ein großer Veranstaltungsraum war ebenfalls integriert; die Hauptbücherei war damit in der Anfangszeit ihres Bestehens einer der wenigen Anbieter von Kulturveranstaltungen in der Stadt.

Bereits wenige Jahre nach der Eröffnung waren allerdings die verfügbaren Räume zu eng geworden. Die Nachfrage überstieg alle Erwartungen. Die Zahl der Nutzer verdoppelte sich innerhalb eines Jahrzehntes (1970: 5.219, 1980: 11.479) und steht 1999 bei etwa 20.000 eingeschriebenen Lesern. Gegenwärtig frequentieren an Spitzentagen mehr als 2.000 Personen die Hauptbücherei in der Skodagasse, es herrscht Gedränge, Sitzplätze und OPAC-Bildschirme zur Recherche sind permanent ausgebucht. Die Kapazitäten des Gebäudes sind restlos ausgeschöpft, zeitgemäßen Anforderungen kann nicht mehr entsprochen werden.

Die Hauptbücherei begann 1970 mit einem Buchbestand von 67.799 Einheiten, 1980 war dieser bereits auf 95.374 Medien angestiegen. 1999 verfügt die einzige allgemein zugängliche, in Freihand geführte Großbibliothek Wiens ohne Spezialisierung über mehr als 200.000 entlehnbare Medien. Die Hälfte des Bestandes wird aus Platzgründen im Keller magaziniert und steht dem Benutzer nur über die Recherche in OPAC-Schirmen zur Verfügung. Auch das Magazin hat mittlerweile die Grenze seiner Kapazität erreicht. Zwei Internet-Arbeitsplätze, noch dazu im Foyer des Veranstaltungssaales gelegen, sind ein Hinweis darauf, dass die Hauptbücherei zwar bemüht ist, bei den virtuellen Informationsmöglichkeiten mitzuhalten, aber räumlich gefesselt ist.

Zum traditionellen Sammelschwerpunkt Bücher kamen nach und nach die neuen, auch entlehnbaren audiovisuellen Medien (Tonkassetten, CDs, CD-ROMs, Videos) hinzu. Eine vernünftige Präsentation dieser in ihrer Informationsfunktion immer wichtiger werdenden Medien ist derzeit nicht möglich; der Aufbau und Ausbau des Medienbestandes wird durch die räumliche Beengtheit genauso limitiert wie ein Ausbau des Zeitschriften- und Zeitungsangebotes.

Die bestehende Hauptbücherei wie auch die übrigen Zweigstellen der Städtischen Büchereien arbeiten nach dem einst gültigen Konzept von Entlehnbibliotheken. Dieses ignoriert, dass bis zu 50 Prozent der Nutzer heute die Bibliothek aufsuchen, um ihre Potenziale vor Ort zu nutzen. Die Leser suchen an den Regalen, recherchieren an den Bildschirmen, wollen moderne Arbeitsplätze (mit PCs, mit Anschlussmöglichkeiten für den Laptop) in Anspruch nehmen und ein leistungsfähiges Kopierservice vorfinden. Eine moderne Öffentliche Bibliothek erfüllt zumindest eine Doppelfunktion: Sie ist nach wie vor eine im Freihandsystem präsentierte Entlehnbibliothek wie in den vielen Jahrzehnten zuvor; gleichzeitig werden vom Publikum immer mehr Qualitäten einer Arbeitsbibliothek mit ansprechendem Service gefordert. Darüber hinaus strebt die zeitgemäße Öffentliche Bibliothek an, Wissen zum Raumerlebnis zu machen und mit ihrem Ambiente ein real erfahrenes Medium des „Edutainments" zu werden. Seit Jahren definiert sich die Öffentliche Bibliothek auch als Kultur- und Veranstaltungszentrum, zu dem selbstverständlich ein Café oder Restaurant gehört. Zusammengefasst lässt sich die zeitgemäße Bibliothek als eine große Wissens- und Freizeitmaschine fassen, als besonderer Ort in der Stadt definieren, an den alle Bevölkerungsteile, mit sehr unterschiedlichen Vorstellungen, gerne hingehen. Die zukünftige Hauptbibliothek soll diesem umfassenden Anforderungsprofil entsprechen.

Die Standortsuche - Die Stadt bevorzugt den Gürtel

Die Forderung nach einer neuen Hauptbibliothek geht bereits auf die späten 80er-Jahre zurück; seit damals wurde dieser Wunsch regelmäßig von der Leitung der Städtischen Büchereien an die Stadtpolitik herangetragen, kam aber innerhalb der gesamtstädtischen Planung nicht zum Zug. Trotz des von den Architekten Laurids/ Ortner vorgesehenen Büchertурmes wurden die Städtischen Büchereien bei den Planungen für das „Museumquartier", die größte Kulturbaustelle Wiens, nicht berücksichtigt. Und dies, obwohl das große Areal der ehemaligen Hofstallungen ein idealer Standort gewesen wäre.

Seit Mitte der 90er-Jahre beschäftigte das Projekt „Neue Hauptbibliothek" die Stadtverwaltung erstmals konkret. Erste Standorte auf der so genannten „Platte" der Donauuferautobahn, am Gumpendorfer Gürtel, in Michelbeuern, aber auch am Neubaugürtel wurden überprüft. Entsprechend dem Schwerpunkt der Stadtplanung lagen alle diese Standorte nicht in oder um die City, sondern in den Brennpunkten der kommunalen Stadtpolitik. Die in bester U-Bahn-Anbindung gelegene „Platte", ursprünglich als Terrain für eine von Budapest und Wien gemeinsam getragene, aber nach einer Volksbefragung abgesagte EXPO im Jahr 1994 entwickelt, sollte nicht nur mit Büro- und Wohnbauten besiedelt, sondern auch mit Kultur- und Bildungsprojekten (neben der neuen Hauptbibliothek auch mit einer viel diskutierten Dependance des Guggenheim-Museums) aufgewertet werden. Mehrere Komponenten haben zusammengespielt, wieso schließlich der verkehrstechnisch neuralgische Urban-Loritz-Platz am Gürtel zum Standort für die neue Hauptbibliothek gewählt wurde.

Seit den 90er-Jahren hat der Gürtel, die große kreisförmige Verkehrsader der Stadt, im stadtplanerischen und stadtpolitischen Diskurs höchste Aufmerksamkeitswerte. Planungsstadtrat Hannes Swoboda bezeichnete 1995 den Gürtel als „offene Wunde in der Stadt".[209] Eine dreispurige Straße auf jeder Seite der ehemaligen Stadtbahn, nunmehr U 6, machte und macht den Gürtel zur Stadtautobahn. Die beinahe 100.000 Autos, die tagtäglich über den Gürtel fahren, nehmen die ehemalige Prachtstraße total in Besitz und schneiden die inneren von den äußeren Bezirken ab. Die radialen Verbindungen von der Innenstadt in die Vororte bringen abermals Automassen in die Gürtelzone. Staus auf und rund um den Gürtel gehören zum alltäglichen Wahnsinn der mobilen Gesellschaft, die regionale und überregionale Durchzugsstraßen durch die Stadt braucht und alle lokalen Bedürfnisse niederwalzt.

Durch die Verkehrslawine und die daraus resultierenden Lärm- und Abgasemissionen ist in den vielen Jahren der Gürtel zu einer urbanen Problemzone geworden. Geschäfte am Gürtel sperrten zu oder siedelten ab. An ihrer statt dominierten mehr und mehr Sexshops und Bordelle, nächtens wurde die anonyme Masse der Autofahrer unübersehbar mit dem Straßenstrich konfrontiert. Der Gürtel bekam das Image eines Rotlichtdistrikts, umgeben von Zinshäusern aus der Gründerzeit, in denen türkische oder jugoslawische Arbeitsimmigranten mit ihren Familien wohnen. In den umliegenden Quartieren (wienerisch: „Grätzeln") waren der Wohnungsstandard niedrig, der Mangel an Grünflächen drastisch, der Ausländeranteil sehr hoch. Spekulation ließ Häuser verkommen, füllte kleine Wohnungen mit großen Familien und presste selbst aus desolaten Räumen Wucherpreise. Die Gürtelzone wurde zu einem sozialen Spannungsgebiet; Stadtplaner sprachen von „Verslumung".

> *Dabei ist in Vergessenheit geraten, dass der Gürtel lange Zeit als Prachtstrasse gehandelt wurde.*[210] *Die alte habsburgische Haupt- und Residenzstadt Wien war als monozentrische Stadt angelegt. Zwei kreisförmige Linien prägen noch heute den Stadtkörper, die Ringstraße umschließt den Ersten Bezirk, die Gürtelstraße umgibt die rund um die Innenstadt gelegenen Vorstädte (Bezirke 3 - 9) in einem von der*

---

209 Der Falter, Nr. 22, 1995, S.13.

210 Madeleine Petrovic: Der Wiener Gürtel. Wiederentdeckung einer lebendigen Prachtstraße. Wien 1998.

Ringstraße ein bis zwei Kilometer entfernten Bogen. Bis 1890 verlief an dieser Stelle die Stadtgrenze; der die Stadt hier umschließende Linienwall diente einerseits militärischen Zwecken, andererseits hatte er die Funktion einer Zollgrenze und Mautstelle. Die Lebenshaltungskosten außerhalb des Linienwalls waren günstiger als innerhalb der Stadt, sodass sich viele zuziehende Arbeiter hier ansiedelten. Die Industrie fand hier unbebaute Flächen vor, sodass sich das Industriegebiet innerhalb des Gürtels (u.a. der Brillantengrund am Schottenfeld) über den Linienwall nach Rudolfsheim und Ottakring hinaus ausdehnte. Weil in Wien eine Verzehrungssteuer eingehoben wurde, siedelten sich Gasthäuser, Heurige und Vergnügungsetablissements außerhalb der Stadtgrenze an.

Sowohl die Ringstraße wie der Gürtel sind Produkt der Gründerzeit in der zweiten Hälfte des 19. Jahrhunderts. Die Gürtelzone kann es zwar nicht mit der Opulenz der Ringstraßenpalais aufnehmen, allein die ästhetische Qualität der von Otto Wagner im Jugendstil konzipierten Stadtbahnstationen deutet auf den Ehrgeiz und Anspruch der Stadtplanung hin, dass der Gürtel auch repräsentative Funktionen in der Stadt erfüllt und erfüllen kann. Diese gingen verloren und verkamen durch den Massenverkehr. Es gibt aber seit etwa einem Jahrzehnt heftige öffentliche und private Bemühungen, das atmosphärisch starke Ambiente des Gürtels wieder hervorzukehren und ihm zumindest einen Teil von seiner alten Schönheit wieder zu geben.

Um auf die architektonische Schönheit der ehemaligen Stadtbahn zu verweisen, wurden im Zuge der Umstellung auf den U-Bahn-Betrieb alle Stationsgebäude generalsaniert. Nach und nach entdeckte auch die prosperierende Gastronomieszene die Gürtelzone als interessanten Standort. MacDonalds nutzte die Gürtelbögen zur Selbstinszenierung; das Firmenlogo schreibt die alte Architektursprache weiter. Das „Chelsea", eine Szenetreff der Rock- und Technomusik, war genauso ein Vorreiter in der Belebung des Biotops Gürtel wie das „Blaustern" (ehemals Café Grillparzer), dessen Vorplatz sich bei schönem Wetter in einen belebten Treffpunkt von Schülern und Studenten verwandelt. Diese und weitere Szenelokal-Gründungen waren ein Indikator dafür, dass der Gürtel als Durchzugsstraße und Verkehrshölle ein junges Publikum nicht mehr abstieß, sondern geradezu in Ergänzung zu alten Lokalen, etwa dem Weinhaus Sittl (mit seinem Garten und dem auch für Veranstaltungen genutzten Pavillon) oder dem Café Carina in der Stadtbahnstation Josefstädterstraße oder dem Café Westend vis-a-vis vom Westbahnhof, magisch anzog. Große Hotels wie „Wimberger" oder „Astoria" zogen Neubauten am Gürtel auf. Der neu angelegte, über den gesamten Westgürtel geführte Fahrradweg, zwischen Autofahrstreifen und U-Bahn gelegen und überschattet von den Baumreihen, war eine weitere infrastrukturelle Maßnahme, die neue Schichten an den Gürtel brachte. Der Fahrradweg war nicht nur ein Instrument der innerstädtischen Mobilität, sondern auch eines für die Freizeitnutzung der Bewohner in den angrenzenden Bezirken.

In dem angedeuteten Spannungsfeld zwischen „Verslumung" und Belebung wurde der Gürtel zum besonderen Objekt der Stadtplanung und Stadtsanierung. Das von der Stadt betriebene und von der EU geförderte Gürtel-Plus-Projekt (Start 1995; Gesamtfördermittel: über 400 Millionen Schilling) machte es möglich, dass der Gürtel ins Zentrum der öffentlichen Aufmerksamkeit rückte. Inspiriert durch die Gelder, die Brüssel zur Verfügung stellte, präsentierten nun Architekten, Künstler, Unternehmer und Initiativen ihre vielfältigen, miteinander konkurrierenden Projekte. Im Sommer 1996 widmete sich das 7. Wiener Architekturseminar der Zukunft der Gürtelstraße, bei dem Stadtplanern aus aller Welt der Gürtel als exemplarisches Beispiel der Stadtmeliorisierung vorgestellt wurde.

Der Urban-Loritz-Platz

Der Urban-Loritz-Platz war jahrzehntelang eine urbane Wüste, dabei hat er im Öffentlichen Verkehr große Bedeutung. Er ist von zwei kleinen Parks umgeben, die Stadthalle, seit den 60er-Jahren die größte Veranstaltungs- und Sporthalle in der Stadt (Fassungsraum: mehr als 10.000 Personen), ist in der Nähe. In seinen Dimensionen ist der Urban-Loritz-Platz sehr weitläufig; an seiner Nordseite ist eine U-Bahnstation, zwei Straßenbahnlinien haben hier ihre Endstation und ihre Umkehrschleife, zwei weitere Linien queren den Platz. Geschätzte 30.000 Personen steigen täglich hier ein und aus. Trotzdem gab es jahrzehntelang keine bewusste Platzgestaltung. So nahm sich ein Wildwuchs von Kiosken und Leuchttafeln des Platzes an. Gefährliche Überschneidungen des Straßenbahnverkehrs mit dem Fußgängerstrom taten ein Übriges, um den Platz zum „Unort" zu machen..

Arch. Silja Tillner, die mit ihren Initiativen große Verdienste um die Belebung der gesamten Gürtelmeile hat, legte Mitte der 90er-Jahre einen Plan zur urbanen Aufwertung des Urban-Loritz-Platzes vor, der dann nach und nach auch realisiert wurde. Der Straßenbahnverkehr wurde neu organisiert, mit einer zeltartigen Überdachung sollte ein wettergeschützter Aufenthaltsraum geschaffen werden. Mit Herbst 1999 wurden diese Projekte abgeschlossen.

Die vielen Aktivitäten rund um den Gürtel inspirierten auch Baumeister Richard Lugner, sich in die Gestaltung der Zone einzuklinken. Mitte der 80er-Jahre hatte Lugner, nur eine Straßenzeile vom Gürtel entfernt, in der Gablenzgasse ein Einkaufszentrum errichtet. Nun plante er nicht nur eine Erweiterung des Shopping-Centers, sondern präsentierte ein medial Aufsehen erregendes Projekt: die „Wolkenspange". Lugner war nie verlegen, wenn es galt, große öffentliche Auftritte zu inszenieren. Zuerst waren es die Opernballauftritte mit internationalen Stars, dann folgte die „Wolkenspange", ermuntert durch seine Erfolge lockten ihn politische Auftritte (Bundespräsidentenwahlkampf 1998, Nationalratswahlen 1999). Lugner hatte sein Einkaufszentrum von der Gürtelseite mittels Parkgarageneinfahrt erschlossen. Bis zum Jahr 2000 ist die Erweiterung bis zum Gürtel hin geplant. Die im Frühjahr abgerissenen Gürtelhäuser werden ersetzt durch eine Multiplex-Kinocenter für rund 2400 Personen in neun Sälen; ihnen angeschlossen sollen Gastronomie- und Unterhaltungsbetriebe und weitere Teile des Einkaufszentrums werden.

Zur Abrundung der Shopping-Mall plante Lugner einen Übergang über den Gürtel zur U-Bahnlinie. Dort, wo jetzt die Hauptbibliothek gebaut wird, sollte nach seinem Plan ein auf Stützen schwebender Glasbau mit etwa 4000 bis 5000 Quadratmeter entstehen, der über der Gürtelfahrbahn direkt an die Lugner-City angebunden ist. Die Planung für den exponierten Pavillon, der bald als „Wolkenspange" in den Zeitungen von sich reden machte, kam von einem der bekanntesten Wiener Architekten, Adolf Krischanitz.

In den Verhandlungen mit dem damaligen Planungsstadtrat Hannes Sowoboda wurde der rein kommerzielle Charakter der Nutzung kritisiert. Den Jugendlichen dürften, so die Antwort der Stadt, nicht nur Spielhallen und eine Diskothek, sondern müssten auch andere Freizeiteinrichtungen wie ein Jugendklub oder ein Internet-Café angeboten werden. Der Fachbeirat für Stadtplanung stieß sich nicht nur an der geschäftlichen Verwertung, vor allem an der spektakulären Gürtelüberbrückung im Dienste einer Firma, sondern monierte generell, dass es keine Eingriffe in die alte Stadtbahn-Anlage geben sollte. Stadtrat Sowoboda versprach trotzdem Unterstützung für das Lugner-Projekt, verlangte Umplanungen und verwies darauf, dass schon manche Projekte trotz Ablehnung durch den Beirat realisiert worden wären.

In der zweiten Jahreshälfte 1997 tauchte in der Stadtplanung, in Konkurrenz zum Lugnerschen Projekt, erstmals die Idee auf, dass die Kommune selbst an dieser exponierten Stelle einen öffentlich genutzten Bau realisieren könnte. Diverse Standorte einer neuen Hauptbibliothek wurden zu diesem Zeitpunkt gerade überprüft. Als bestätigt wurde, dass ein Bau an dieser Stelle auch größere Flächen vertragen und die Mindeststandards einer zukünftigen Hauptbibliothek erfüllen würde, wurde der Leitung der Wiener Städtischen Büchereien vorgeschlagen, die künftige neue Hauptbibliothek inklusive einer neuen Zentrale der Städtischen Büchereien am Urban Loritz-Platz errichten. Franz Pascher, der damalige Leiter, nahm den Vorschlag mit Begeisterung auf. Weitere Beratungen über die Möglichkeiten des Standortes folgten. Planungsstadtrat Bernhard Görg legte sich schließlich im Februar 1998 erstmals öffentlich fest, wenn er der öffentlichen Nutzung Priorität vor der privaten einräumte: „Die Planungen für den Bibliotheksneubau haben vorerst einmal Vorrang."[211]

Das Zitat zeigt aber auch, dass sich die Stadtpolitik noch nicht endgültig fixieren wollte. Die Politiker waren in den medialen Äußerungen vorsichtig, das Projekt einer Hauptbibliothek am Urban-Loritz-Platz war umstritten wie schon das Lugner-Projekt zuvor. Innerhalb der Architektenschaft, der Stadtplaner und Magistratsbeamten war die Meinung über das Vorhaben keineswegs eindeutig positiv. Diese Gespaltenheit bzw. der Wettbewerb zwischen „Wolkenspange" und Hauptbibliothek wurde auch medial kommuniziert. Richard Lugner versuchte über Zeitungsartikel sein Projekt zu retten, indem er die von seiner Seite kommenden privaten Investitionen hervorstrich und die Attraktivität einer Bibliothek bezweifelte. Im Zentrum seiner Attacken standen die geringen Bibliotheksöffnungszeiten. Viele aus der Buchbranche oder aus der Stadtverwaltung äußerten Bedenken wegen des extremen Standortes für die Bibliothek und brachten andere Varianten ins Spiel. Der Architekturbeirat der Stadt hielt an seinem Beschluss fest, dass die in der Tiefe gelegene, denkmalgeschützte U-Bahnstation, die einst von Otto Wagner errichtet wurde, nicht überbaut werden sollte. Ein Beispiel für die Gespaltenheit der Meinung bot auch die grüne Oppositionspartei. Während sich die grüne Wiener Stadträtin Friedrun Huemer für den Bau aussprach, setzte sich die grüne Klubobfrau im Parlament, Madeleine Petrovic, Autorin eines Buches über den Gürtel, für Richard Lugners „Wolkenspange" ein und titulierte das neue Stadtprojekt als „Wolkenkuckucksbibliothek".

Der Architekturwettbewerb

Um etwaige Zweifel über die Sinnhaftigkeit des Projektes zu zerstreuen, die Meinungsbildung zu vertiefen und die Gegner zu überzeugen, wurde ein zweistufiger, EU-weit offener, baukünstlerischer Architekturwettbewerb „Hauptbibliothek und Zentralverwaltung der Wiener Städtischen Büchereien" initiiert, um die beste stadtplanerische und architektonische Lösung zu erhalten. Im Magistrat wurde auf rasche Abwicklung gedrängt. Die Strittigkeit des Projekts zeigte sich noch bei der Besetzung der Jury, aus der sich Architekten, noch ehe sie ihre Aufgaben begonnen hatten, wieder zurückzogen.

In den Ausschreibungsunterlagen eingefügt war ein Umgebungsplan mit der genauen Markierung des Planungsgebietes. Dadurch war allen Entwürfen von vornherein ein enger Rahmen vorgegeben. Die Neuregulierung des Straßenbahnverkehrs und das Zeltdach über den Urban-Loritz-Platz waren bereits in Bau; dadurch kam der Platz vor der U-Bahnstation für die neue Hauptbibliothek nicht mehr in Frage. Als Planungszone war der eingeschränk-

211 Roman Freihsl: Bücher statt Wolkenspange, in: Der Standard 6.2.1998, S.7.

te Bereich zwischen der U-Bahnstation Urban-Loritz-Platz und der Station Burggasse ausgewiesen, wobei ein Respektabstand zum Otto-Wagner-Bau der U-Bahnstation Burggasse eingehalten werden sollte. Weil die Baumreihen entlang der U-Bahn und den Gürtel-Fahrbahnen möglichst wenig tangiert werden sollten, war auch die Maximalbreite des Baus einigermaßen vorgegeben.

Ab 14. August 1998 wurden die Unterlagen ausgegeben, Abgabeschluss für die 1. Wettbewerbstufe war der 12. Oktober 1998. Bei der ersten Jurierung des Preisgerichts am 3./4. und 10./11. November 1998 wurden unter den 121 Entwürfen von Architekturbüros aus ganz Europa zehn ausgewählt. In der Folge wurden die Architekten dieser Projekte zur weiteren Bearbeitung, unter Berücksichtigung der Kritik der Jury, aufgefordert. Am 14./15. Januar 1999 entschied das Preisgericht über den Sieger des Wettbewerbs. Am 15. Januar 1999 wurde in einer Pressekonferenz vom Juryvorsitzenden, Universitätsprofessor Ernst Stracke, und den das Projekt betreibenden Stadträten, Vizebürgermeisterin Grete Laska (SPÖ) und Vizebürgermeister Bernhard Görg (ÖVP) der Wiener Architekt Ernst Mayr als Gewinner den Medien präsentiert.

Ausschlaggebend in der Bewertung waren mehrere Dimensionen: die bautechnische Bewältigung des Vorhabens, der Beitrag zur Stadtgestaltung, die baukünstlerische Qualität, die Umsetzung des bibliothekarischen Konzepts und, last but not least, die Kosten. In einer von der BAWAG, einer großen Bank, gesponserten Ausstellung wurden vom 27. Jänner bis zum 13.Februar 1999 sämtliche Projekte des Wettbewerbs der Öffentlichkeit zugänglich gemacht, um die ganze Fülle der Ideen, die in den Architekturwettbewerb eingeflossen sind, zu präsentieren. Lang gestreckte Kuben konkurrierten mit unkonventionellen skulpturalen Gebilden, Bahnhofs-Hallen standen gegen kühne Tragkonstruktionen, klassische Hochhäuser wetteiferten mit futuristisch anmutenden Baukörperakkumulationen.

Die Vorgaben für die Bibliothek im Wettbewerbsausschreibungstext waren einigermaßen deutlich, die Vorgaben für die Gestaltung der Beziehung zwischen U-Bahnstation und Bibliothekseingang blieben allerdings bewusst offen. Die Jury war gespannt auf die kreativen Lösungsvorschläge der Architekten. In der Beurteilung der Projekte wurden die diesbezüglichen Ideen genau studiert.

Schon mit und erst recht nach dem Architekturwettbewerb überlappte die positive Grundstimmung für das Projekt alle kritischen Stimmen. Die Gegner gaben sich geschlagen oder zogen sich zurück; Skeptiker wechselten die Position. Die Stimmung in den Medien war gekippt. Statt Zweifel über eine Bibliothek generell und den Standort im besonderen überwog jetzt Euphorie über „Wissenstempel, Büchersammlung, Aufbruch ins Medienzeitalter“(Die Presse).[212] Das Lugner-Projekt war endgültig gefallen und im Abseits des Vergessens. Noch wenige Monate zuvor hatten sich wichtige Medien skeptisch gegeben bzw. wie „Kurier“[213] („Rückschlag der Gürtelsanierung“, „Ende für größte private Investitionsvorhaben am Gürtel“), „Falter“ und „Profil“ gegen das Projekt positioniert. Auch der Gestaltungsbeirat machte einige Wochen später keine neuen Anstrengungen, das Projekt durch öffentliche Stellungnahmen zu Fall zu bringen.

---

212 Die Presse 16.1.1999, S.17.

213 Kurier

Rasche Realisierung des Siegerprojektes - Der Prozess bis zum Spatenstich

In der Textierung durch die Jury lautete die Begründung, wieso Ernst Mayrs Modell einer „Treppenbibliothek" den ersten Preis errungen hatte:

> *„Eine groß dimensionierte Freitreppe, die im Sommer einen zwanglosen, urbanen Treffpunkt bilden könnte, gibt dem Bauwerk seine besondere, unverwechselbare Charakteristik. Sie nimmt auf zwei Ebenen die Hauptzugänge in die Bibliothek und die U-Bahnstation auf und führt vom Urban-Loritz-Platz zu einer Dachterrasse, der das Bibliothekscafé in Form einer Rotunde aufgesetzt ist. - Die Fassaden entlang der lärmenden Gürtelfahrbahnen sind weitgehend geschlossen, wobei aber das Gebäude über dem offenen Schacht der U-Bahnstation Burggasse-Stadthalle aufgeständert wird und somit die Blickbeziehungen quer über den Gürtel und aus der Station heraus gewährleistet. - Im Inneren erwarten uns große, ruhige Bibliothekssäle, deren kontemplativer Charakter durch ein raffiniert geführtes Oberlicht unterstrichen wird. Die Übergänge zwischen den einzelnen Bibliotheksbereichen sind fließend; auch ergeben sich durch räumliche Zäsuren und Oberlichten Blickbeziehungen zwischen den beiden Bibliotheksgeschossen."*

Bei der Pressekonferenz am 15. Januar 1999 wurde auch öffentlich der politische Wille bekundet, das Projekt innerhalb eines sehr kurzen Zeitraumes zu realisieren. Als Eröffnungstermin wurde der Herbst 2001 genannt; dieser Zieltermin stand in Zusammenhang mit den zur gleichen Zeit anstehenden Gemeinderats- und Landtagswahlen. Etwa zwei Wochen nach der Pressekonferenz nahm die Projektstruktur Gestalt an, mit der die weitere Planung und Errichtung der Hauptbibliothek abgewickelt werden sollte. Die Projektkoordination wurde von der MA 24 - Hochbau übernommen, im konkreten durch Dr. Peter Marchart. Der Architekt Ernst Mayr wurde zusammen mit seinem Statiker zum Generalplaner bestellt.

Schon beim Architekturwettbewerb, dann in der ersten Planungsphase stellte sich heraus, dass die geplante Eingangssituation in die U-Bahnstation und in die Bibliothek eine hochkomplexe Konstellation erzeugt. Die Wiener Linien brachten in den Verhandlungen ihr ganzes Gewicht an Fachwissen und Wichtigkeit ein und drängten auf ihnen geläufige Lösungen; erst in einer langen Kette von Sitzungen schälten sich die Lösungen heraus, die beide Partner zufrieden stellten. Der Zwang zu einer konfliktuösen Zusammenarbeit, so zeichnete sich ab, wird vermutlich den ganzen Bauprozess und wahrscheinlich auch die Betriebsführung nach der Eröffnung stark beeinflussen.

Schnell stellte sich heraus, dass das Projekt in zwei Baustellen und in zwei Einreichverfahren zu unterteilen ist. Durch das „Eisenbahnrechtliche Verfahren" ist die Genehmigung für den Tiefbau einzuleiten, das baubehördliche Verfahren betrifft den Hochbau. Die Bauabwicklung wurde in der Folge entsprechend in zwei Teile separiert, dem siegreichen Architekt Ernst Mayr gesellte sich das langjährig im U-Bahnbau tätige Ingenieursbüro Pauser (Ing. Poszt) bei, das die Planung tätigte und die Ausführung des Tiefbaus überwacht. Vorerst galt es, für beide Verfahren die Planungsarbeiten bis zur Einreichung voranzutreiben. Ein wesentlicher Schritt bei diesem Prozess war, vor der Einreichung einen Vorentwurf nochmals auf seine Wirtschaftlichkeit zu prüfen. Erst nach der so genannten „Wirtschaftlichkeitsprüfung"(19.Mai 1999) wurde von der Stadtpolitik Grünes Licht für die Einreichung gegeben und im Gemeinderat ein Baubudget von 360 Mill. öS beschlossen. In Rekordzeit konnten die rechtlichen Verfahren in der ersten Oktoberhälfte 1999 abgeschlossen werden. Die Angebotsabgabe und -eröffnung vom 27. Oktober 1999 für das erste Baulos

(U-Bahn) durch die Wiener Linien war die Voraussetzung, dass der Baubeginn tatsächlich noch im Herbst 1999 angesetzt werden konnte. (Spatenstich 29. November 1999)

Vor allem über die Sommermonate wurde vom Leitungsteam der Bibliothek und dem Architekten energisch an der Überarbeitung des Wettbewerbsentwurfes gearbeitet und Varianten des bibliothekarischen Funktionsprogramms (Hinführung zur Bibliothek, Geschossfunktionen, Abfolge der Räume) in der Anwendung auf das konkrete Projekt diskutiert und in Einbeziehung von Haustechnik, baupolizeilichen Vorgaben, Brandschutztechnik, natürlich immer unter Berücksichtigung der Kosten, entschieden, um - wie gefordert - im September 1999 die Einreichpläne fertig stellen zu können.

Die Besonderheiten der zukünftigen Hauptbibliothek Wien

Die Treppe

Vom Urban-Loritz-Platz aus wird der Beginn des Gebäudes in Form einer Treppenanlage, die sich von hier aus gleichmäßig über alle Geschosse entwickelt, prägnant interpretiert. Die riesige Freitreppe gibt dem Gebäude etwas Monumentales und hebt es im Gürtelbereich als neues Wahrzeichen der Stadt deutlich hervor. Das Membrandach des Urban-Loritz-Platzes (Arch. Silja Tillner) wird verlängert und in das Projekt einbezogen. Die Treppe, die auch der Hinführung zum Bibliothekseingang dient, stellt den Kontakt zur Stadt her und soll an dieser belebten Stelle als Kommunikations- und Sitzbereich dienen. Am oberen Ende der Treppenanlage befindet sich eine öffentlich zugängliche großzügige Terrassenlandschaft, die als Platz zum Lesen im Freien, für Ausstellungen und als Caféstandort genutzt werden soll. In der Treppe drückt sich eine starke Geste des Einladens aus. Sie gibt sich weltoffen, macht durch die Eingangszonen im Erdgeschoss und im zweiten Geschoss neugierig und öffnet den Weg der Aufmerksamkeit in den Himmel. Zugleich schließt sie das Gebäude deutlich ab.

An der Längsseite ist das Gebäude relativ geschlossen. Das erste Stockwerk, das Bürogeschoss, hat Fenster zur Gürtelfahrbahn, während das Gebäude in den beiden Bibliotheksgeschossen nach außen fast gänzlich abgeschottet ist. Nur an wenigen Stellen ist der Blickbezug zu den Gürtelfahrbahnen durch kleine punktartigen Fenster (Büros und Lese-Erker) gegeben. Die Tageslichtführung im Bibliotheksinneren erfolgt zum Teil indirekt durch Oberlichtsheds und die großen verglasten Zäsuren in der Gebäudemittelachse. Immer wieder aber eröffnet sich dem Besucher in großzügigen zweigeschossigen Bereichen auch der Blick auf den Himmel, wird das „Draußen“ durch die Lichtführung von oben erfahrbar. Somit schafft es die Architektur, trotz der langen axialen Gebäudeerstreckung und der nach außen fast gänzlich geschlossenen Fassade durch interessante Blickbeziehungen zwischen den Geschossen und durch eine spektakuläre Lichtführung offene und großzügige Innenraumeindrücke zu erzielen. Darüber hinaus werden die gesamten Bibliotheksbereiche in ihrer Introvertiertheit der besonders exponierten Lage des Standortes Rechnung tragen und durch erlebnisreiche Räume die Verweilqualität erhöhen.

Während die Gürtelseiten eine pure Keramikfassade nach außen kehren, dominiert im Norden der Anlage dagegen Glas. Hier haben die Benutzer einen weiten Blick über die Stadt, von den dort gelegenen Arbeitsplätzen und Leseecken wird man über den Gürtel bis zu den Hügeln des Wienerwalds sehen können.

Gemeinsame Erschließung von Bibliothek und U-Bahn

Der Bibliotheksbau erstreckt sich in Längsrichtung über den Bahnsteigbereich zur Otto Wagner-Station Burggasse. Das Gebäude ist abgesehen vom Kopfbereich der großen Eingangshalle und der dahinterliegenden U-Bahn/Bibliotheksliftgruppe zum größten Teil aufgeständert. Der Architekt übernimmt dabei das Achsmaß Otto Wagners (jeweils 8,10 m) und reagiert damit in seinem Gebäudeaufbau auf das unmittelbare Umfeld. Die Aufständerung lässt den dreigeschossigen Baukörper über dem U-Bahnbereich „schweben" und ermöglicht die Blickbeziehung zwischen den beiden Gürtelseiten, aber auch die Sicht auf den historischen Perronbereich der ehemaligen Stadtbahnstation vom Erdgeschossniveau aus. Der gesamte Bereich der Otto Wagner-Station mit den Bahnsteigen bleibt in Mayrs Projekt unverändert.

Im Planungsprozess gelang es, eine Eingangslösung zu finden, die die Wiener Linien zufrieden stellt, also dem U-Bahnbetrieb adäquat ist, und gleichzeitig die Erschließung der Bibliothek optimal löst. Sowohl beim Haupteingang als auch beim Lifthaus ist die Hinführung zur Bibliothek mit den Anforderungen des Öffentlichen Verkehrs optimal verknüpft. Einmal wird das vorhandene Stationsgebäude der U6 am Urban-Loritz-Platz durch ein neues Bauwerk, das in den Kopfbereich der Bibliothek integriert wird, ersetzt. Die beiden, von den Bahnsteigen aufwärts führenden seitlichen Stiegen werden bis zum Zwischenpodest erhalten und münden dann über Quersteigen symmetrisch in die Halle ein. Der zentrale U-Bahn-Abgang wird von den beiden Bibliothekszugängen (Stiegenanlagen in Kombination mit Rolltreppen) flankiert.

Das im Bibliothekskörper integrierte Lifthaus ist der Ausgangsort für den Zugang zur U-Bahn wie zur Bibliothek; der Benutzer braucht keine langen Wege zurücklegen, um vom einen Lift zum anderen umzusteigen. Von der gemeinsamen Lifthalle wird die Bibliothek in allen Stockwerken bis zur Dachterrasse erschlossen.

Die Hinführung zur Bibliothek

Von der Halle der U6 führen die beiden Treppen/Rolltreppenanlagen direkt in die Eingangshalle der Bibliothek im 2. Obergeschoss. Den zweiten Eingang (Sommereingang) erreicht man über die Freitreppe. Dieser liegt ebenfalls im 2. Obergeschoss und mündet wie der Haupteingang in die Eingangshalle. Diese kann auch für kleinere Ausstellungen und Informationsveranstaltungen genutzt werden. In diesem „bibliotheksexternen" Bereich (d.h. noch außerhalb der Buchsicherungsanlage) sind die notwendigen Garderoben und Sanitäranlagen, die große Empfangs- und Buchrückgabetheke, aber auch der Zeitungslesebereich frei zugänglich gelegen. Von der Eingangszone aus erreicht man auf kurzem Weg den multifunktionellen Veranstaltungsbereich im Geschoss darüber (Internetbereich, Ausstellungsfläche und Veranstaltungssaal), auch das (unabhängig vom Bibliotheksbetrieb erreichbare) Café, dessen Glasrotunde prominent die vordere Treppenkante der mehr als 2.000 m² großen Dachterrasse bestimmt.

Die innere Organisation - das College-System

Die alte Hauptbücherei wird weitgehend nach einem zentralisierten System geführt. Um die Verantwortung für die jeweiligen Arbeitsbereiche zu erhöhen und die Motivation zu stärken, um für die Kunden klare Ansprechpartner in der Unübersichtlichkeit der Bibliothek zu schaffen, sieht die Organisation der neuen Hauptbibliothek eine Restrukturierung des Betriebes vor, die sich am international erfolgreichen Vorbild der „fraktalen Bibliothek" orientiert. Folgende „Colleges" sind organisatorisch geplant:

- Allgemeine Information/Schnelle Bibliothek/Abendöffnungszone
- Kindermedienzentrum
- Musikbibliothek
- College I: Sachbuch I
- College II: Sachbuch II
- College III: Literarisches Zentrum

Bei der Planung zeigte sich sehr bald, dass die architektonische Umsetzung des Konzepts „Fraktale Bibliothek“ durch die Längsausrichtung des Gebäudes nur begrenzt möglich ist. Organisatorisch ist eine Dezentralisierung möglich, nicht aber das gebaute Nebeneinander von Bibliotheksabteilungen und Büroräumlichkeiten, um die Kompaktheit und Eigenständigkeit eines Colleges zu betonen und eine Sichtbeziehung zwischen Verwaltung und Publikumsbetrieb zu haben. Große Büroräume, die allen MitarbeiterInnen der Colleges einen Arbeitsplatz geben, würden in der schmalen, sehr langen Kubatur die Publikumsbereiche zu sehr einschnüren. - Standort, Planungsfeld und Baukörper haben also unmittelbaren Einfluss auf das Bibliothekskonzept.

Bibliothekskonzept, Organisation, Personal und Bau

Der Bau einer neuen Hauptbibliothek fordert nicht nur die Baufachleute, sondern stößt den ganzen Betrieb in eine heiße Umbruchsphase. Bauplanung und Bauausführung beschäftigen vorerst nur die Leitung, werden aber von allen MitarbeiterInnen mit größter Aufmerksamkeit verfolgt. Bei der Reorganisation des Betriebes, bei der Verlängerung der Öffnungszeiten, bei der Personalentwicklung sind von Anfang an alle 250 MitarbeiterInnen der Wiener Städtischen Büchereien mehr oder weniger intensiv involviert, weil sich bei ihnen Fragen über Fragen aufdrängen. Über den komplexen Prozess, der schon längst begonnen hat und in den wir mitten drin stecken, wird bei anderer Gelegenheit berichtet werden.

Ingrid Bussmann

Die Bibliothek als Atelier des innovativen Lernens

1. Wissen schafft Zukunft

> *„Bildung spielt in der Wissensgesellschaft von morgen eine zentrale Rolle. Die Zukunft des Einzelnen sowie die gesellschaftliche und wirtschaftliche Entwicklung hängen entscheidend davon ab, ob es uns gelingt, heute das Wissen zu erschließen und zu vermitteln, das morgen gebraucht wird. Hierfür benötigen wir eine Neugestaltung des Lehrens und Lernens."* [214]

Die zukünftige Wissensgesellschaft ist nicht nur Schlagwort, sondern eine wesentliche Herausforderung für die Zukunft. Auf diese Herausforderung zu reagieren ist Chance und Anforderung an Bibliotheken. Bibliotheken können Zukunft gestalten. Sie können zur Entwicklung einer innovativen Lernkultur beitragen, um eine nachhaltige und verantwortungsbewusste Partizipation am gesellschaftlichen Wandel zu unterstützen. In der Dynamik und Fülle des zunehmenden weltweiten Wissens muss der Einzelne neue Qualifikationen zur Auswahl, Bewertung und Umsetzung von Information in Erkenntnisprozesse und verantwortungsbewusstes Handeln entwickeln.

Bildung – so das Forum Bildung – wird zum lebenslangen Prozess, der nicht nur in den klassischen Bildungsinstitutionen stattfindet. Neue Lernorte sind ebenso gefordert wie neue Lernwege und neue Qualifikationen:

- „Zunehmender Bedarf an Methoden-, Orientierungs-, Bewertungs-, und Gestaltungskompetenzen, um Wissen zu erschließen und anzuwenden
- personale und soziale Kompetenzen: höhere Anforderungen an Eigenverantwortung und Gemeinschaftsfähigkeit, aber auch an Kreativität und Innovationsfähigkeit, Fähigkeit zur Orientierung im Wandel
- Verzahnung von Leben und Arbeiten, zunehmende Bedeutung des informellen Lernens sowie des lebenslangen Lernens."[215]

Der Trendforscher Mathias Horx beschreibt „Die acht Sphären der Zukunft", die Soziosphere, die BodySphere, MindSphere, KnowledgeSphere, TechnoSphere, CosumerSphere, EconoSphere, PolitoSphere[216], deren Zusammenspiel die Zukunft bestimmt. In der „Knowledgesphere"[217] entstehen grundlegende Veränderungen. Lernen ist nicht mehr ein linearer Prozess, in dem „der Wissende dem Nicht-Wissenden etwas vermittelt", sondern ein vernetzter Prozess, in dem „nicht nur neue, soziale Skills, sondern auch ein Selbst- und Menschenbild, das von Kooperation und gemeinsamen Lernprozessen geprägt ist" eine zentrale Rolle spielen.

Wissen ist die Fähigkeit, Informationen in Sinnbezüge zu stellen, die Handeln prägen,

---

214 „Wissen schafft Zukunft" – Forum Bildung, in: http://www.forum-bildung.de/forum, S. 1
215 s.o., S. 1
216 Mathias Horx, Die acht Sphären der Zukunft, Hamburg 1999, s. 48f
217 s.o., s. 153 ff

sei es im beruflichen, im sozialen, im familiären, im gesellschaftlichen und politischen Kontext. Wissen ist der persönliche Orientierungsrahmen, nicht die Fakten, die man kennt, sondern die Leitlinien, Werte, Ziele, die Handeln prägen.

Wissen ist die Voraussetzung für verantwortungsbewusstes Handeln und damit für die friedliche Bewältigung des gesellschaftlichen, wirtschaftlichen und technischen Wandels.

An dieses ganzheitliche Zusammenspiel knüpft die Bibliothek als neuer Lernort an.

2. Selbstgesteuertes Lernen schafft Zukunft

Lebenslanges Lernen ist sicher keine neue Forderung - aber sie stellt sich neu, angesichts des technologischen Wandels und der Anforderungen an neue Lernwege. Neben das organisierte Lernen in Kursen, tritt das selbstorganisierte Lernen im Sinne einer Selbststeuerung - ich habe ein konkretes Problem und versuche, schnell die Lösung zu finden, indem ich Experten im Hause frage, zu Büchern oder Medien greife oder einfach Neues ausprobiere. Neben das bewusst geplante Lernen tritt das Lernen aus der konkreten täglichen Erfahrung. Notwendig werden Strukturen, dieses Erfahrungslernen bewusst zu machen und Handlungskonsequenzen daraus zu ziehen. Das formelle Lernen in organisierten Lernstrukturen verknüpft sich mit dem informellen, offenen Lernen in unterschiedlichen Lebenszusammenhängen.

Lernen erfordert die Begegnung mit anderen Menschen, den Austausch der Erfahrung, die Begegnung mit Experten, Künstlern, um neues zu entwickeln. Das kognitiv gesteuerte Lernen, das gezielt Antworten auf Fragen sucht, verbindet sich mit dem innovativen Lernen, das neue Sinnbezüge entwickelt und so kreative Ideen ermöglicht.

„Zukunftschance Lernen“ so nannte der Club of Rome seinen „Bericht für die achtziger Jahre“.[218] In der Studie heißt es:

> *„Lernen erfordert ein umfangreiches Reservoir an Bezügen. Innovatives Lernen muss deshalb die Fähigkeit des Individuums, neue Sinnbezüge zu finden, aufzunehmen und zu schaffen, fördern - kurz es muss den Bestand an Sinnbezügen bereichern.“*

Dieses Netz verschiedener Lernwege wird das Lernen der Zukunft bestimmen. Und die Selbststeuerung besteht darin, die Steuerung der Lernprozesse selbst in die Hand zu nehmen, sich seine Lernwege selbst zu suchen. In diesen Kontext der Selbststeuerung positioniert sich der Lernort Bibliothek.

3. Lernsetting Bibliothek

Bereitstellen

Was eine Bibliothek traditionell zum Lernort prädestiniert ist ihr Mediensortiment - denn der lernende, suchende Mensch findet zunächst einmal seine Antworten in den Büchern und Medien der Bibliothek. Die Aufgabe der Bibliothek ist es, Wissen transparent zu machen, Zugänge zu schaffen, die Bereitstellung und Erschließung des Medienangebots, Zugang zum Internet, zu CD-ROM-Datenbanken, PC-Arbeitsplätze für diejenigen, die zu Hause noch nicht die notwendige Ausstattung haben, die Erprobung neuer Technologien, was immer sich noch entwickelt.

---

[218] CLUB OF ROME, Zukunftschance Lernen. Bericht für die achtziger Jahre, hrsg. von Aurelio Peccei, München 1983, S. 50.

Die Bibliothek stellt die Angebote bereit, die für die Zukunftsqualifikation der Menschen erforderlich sind. Soweit ist die Rolle der Bibliothek in den Lernprozessen der Menschen die eines Anbieters, der auf Nachfrage reagiert.

Dass dies den Erwartungen der Besucher entgegenkommt, belegen die Ergebnisse einer Besucherumfrage in der Stadtbücherei Stuttgart Anfang 2000 im Rahmen des Projektes „EFIL – Entwicklung und Förderung innovativer Lernarrangements“ des Deutschen Instituts für Erwachsenenbildung (DIE).[219]

Für eine optimale Lernumgebung brauchen die Besucher Ruhe und viele Medien.

Und auf die Frage, in welcher Umgebung man am liebsten lernt, vorausgesetzt, die Ausstattung sei optimal, liegt die Bibliothek als Lernort an zweiter Stelle. Am liebsten natürlich lernt man zu Hause.

Neue Sinnbezüge schaffen

Doch die Bereitstellung des Medienangebots allein reicht für die Unterstützung zukunftsorientierter Lernprozesse nicht aus.

Die Bibliothek kann ein Ort sein, der nicht nur Wege zu Antworten auf Fragen aufzeigt, sondern selbst Fragen aufwirft, das Entdecken und Finden inszeniert – neue Sinnzusammenhänge präsentiert, Themen gestaltet.

Dazu gehören neue Arrangements des Medienangebots. In der Stadtbücherei Stuttgart heißen diese Arrangements Lernateliers. Sie präsentieren das Medienangebot in thematischen Zusammenhängen, die sich von den traditionellen systematischen Strukturen der Klassifikation lösen. Sie verbinden alle Medienarten vom Buch über die Zeitschrift, die CD-ROM, das Video bis hin zum PC-Arbeitsplatz und zur Interneterschließung.

Die Ateliers basieren auf genau definierten Bestandsprofilen, in denen zukünftige Entwicklungen ebenso berücksichtigt sind, wie die Zielgruppen und die Ist-Analyse der bestehenden Angebote anderer Einrichtungen in der Stadt.

Die Nachhaltigkeit der Angebote – auch eine zentrale Forderung des Forums Bildung an die zukünftigen Qualifikationen – spielt eine neue und besondere Rolle. Die Schnelllebigkeit des Medienmarktes erfordert ein Umdenken bei den Sortimentsprofilen. Mindestens in einer großstädtischen Zentralbücherei sind relevante Medien längerfristig anzubieten, unabhängig von der reinen Markt- und Nutzungsorientierung.

Agieren – Themen gestalten

Doch der Gestaltungsspielraum der Bibliothek als Ort des innovativen Lernens geht über die Medienbereitstellung in thematischen Sinnzusammenhängen hinaus. Die Bibliothek agiert, in dem sie Themen gestaltet.

Vor vielen Jahren präsentierte die Stadtbücherei Stuttgart eine Ausstellung zum Thema Lyrik und stellte fest, dass sich die Menschen danach mit Lyrik beschäftigten.

Das Europäische Jahr der Sprachen in Stuttgart hätte kaum Beachtung gefunden, ohne ein von der Stadtbücherei initiiertes Sprachfestival über das gesamte Jahr, das den Blick auf die Bedeutung von Sprachkenntnissen und Interkultureller Kompetenz legt. Medienpräsentationen, Ausstellungen, Veranstaltungen, Workshops rücken Themen ins Bewusstsein der Menschen und fördern so neue Lern- und Erkenntnisprozesse.

Auch für die digitale Welt gilt, dass die Bibliothek Inhalte gestaltet. Als content provi-

---

[219] EFIL siehe: http://www.die-frankfurt.de/efil/

der kann sie virtuelle Plattformen schaffen, die von den Lernateliers mit Inhalten gefüllt werden - interessante News, neue Trends im Medienmarkt, Newsletter, Content, der im Rahmen der Veranstaltungsarbeit entsteht, beispielsweise ein Web-Forum zum Europäischen Jahr der Sprachen.

So entsteht ein aktiver Beitrag, den gesellschaftlichen Wandel zu gestalten.

Mit der Präsentation der Medien in thematischen Sinnzusammenhängen und der bewussten Gestaltung von Themen werden mehrere Ziele im Prozess des selbstgesteuerten Lernens erreicht:

- Die Bibliothek bietet dem Lernenden durch die Inszenierung der Angebote Hilfestellung, seine Antworten einfacher zu finden.
- Die Bibliothek bietet dem Lernenden Angebote, seine Fragen zu entdecken und zu strukturieren.
- Das medienübergreifende Arrangement fördert den selbstverständlichen Umgang mit verschiedenen Medien und vermittelt im Tun Medienkompetenz.
- Der Lernende wird von Wissensangeboten umgeben und entdeckt neue Kontexte zu seinen Fragen.

Lernen und Beratung

Über 80 % der Besucher in der Zentralbücherei und in den Stadtteilbüchereien in Stuttgart erwarten von den Mitarbeitern der Stadtbücherei fachlich- inhaltliche Beratungskompetenz. Es geht dabei nicht um die Frage, wo man welche Information mit welchen Suchwegen findet, sondern es geht um inhaltliche Kompetenz.

Welchen Sprachkurs wähle ich, wenn ich Portugiesisch als Anfänger lernen möchte? Wie steige ich ein, wenn ich mich mit Lyrik beschäftigen will? Wie baue ich ein Bewerbungsschreiben richtig auf? Beispiele aus dem Alltag, die zeigen, das neue Erwartungen an die Mitarbeiter gestellt werden.

Die Zahl der Haushalte, die Internetanschlüsse haben und damit die Möglichkeit zu Hause zu recherchieren, nimmt zu. Aber je mehr Informationen zugänglich werden, desto mehr steigt der Bedarf an fachlich-inhaltlicher Unterstützung.

Im Prozess des selbstgesteuerten Lernens spielt die Begegnung mit Menschen, die Bescheid wissen, eine zentrale Rolle. Dies wird auch von den Bildungseinrichtungen der Erwachsenenbildung beobachtet.

Im Rahmen des Projektes EFIL hat die Stadtbücherei Stuttgart in Zusammenarbeit mit der Volkshochschule ein sehr erfolgreiches Pilotprojekt zur Lernberatung Englisch durchgeführt. Wissenseinstufung, Kursberatung, Beratung über Selbstlernmedien und computerunterstütztes Lernen erfolgte durch Experten der Volkshochschule und der Stadtbücherei.

Im Rahmen des „Markts der Sprachen" zum Europäischen Jahr der Sprachen wurde dieses Angebot für weitere Sprachen auch in Zusammenarbeit mit privaten Sprachschulen mit Erfolg wiederholt.

Die Beratungskompetenz der Bibliothek ist eine einmalige Qualität für die Zukunft, die durch virtuelle und digitale Entwicklungen nicht ersetzbar ist.

Allerdings kann die Bibliothek mit ihren Personalressourcen den Beratungsbedarf nicht allein erfüllen. Die Kooperation mit anderen Bildungs- und Kultureinrichtungen und der Aufbau von Expertennetzwerke, auch mit zukünftigen Lernberatern, sind erforderlich.

Lehren

Nicht nur die individuelle Lernberatung gehört zu den besonderen Zukunftsqualitäten der Bibliothek. Bibliotheken sind Experten in der Aufbereitung, Erschließung und Bewertung von Information in unterschiedlichen Medien. Diese spezielle Kompetenz befähigt die Bibliothek, auch die Rolle der Lehrenden, Unterstützenden zu übernehmen. In der Förderung von Medienkompetenz ist die Bibliothek aktiver Partner in der Wissensvermittlung.

Medienrallyes für Kinder, Workshops zur Nutzung des Internets, Einführungen in das gezielte Auffinden von Informationen gehören zu den gefragten Angeboten.

„Open Mind"

Die kognitive Wissensverarbeitung ist nur eine Facette des Wissenszeitalters. Ideen, Individualität und Kreativität, ein Bewusstsein des Open Mind, emotionale und spirituelle Intelligenz zählt Mathias Horx zu den Schlüsselbegriffen des Wissenszeitalters.

> *„Das Unbewusste ist es, das die höchsten Formen von Komplexität verarbeiten kann – und nicht das kognitive Bewusstsein."* [220]

Die Besucherumfrage in der Stadtbücherei Stuttgart hat bestätigt, dass die Besucher die Bibliothek als Anregungsraum wahrnehmen.

Aber worin liegt die Anregung?

Die Anregung liegt in dem Zusammenspiel zwischen Ordnung und Verblüffung, Medienpräsentationen, die unerwartete Themen aufgreifen, Ausstellungen, die Blickweisen in Frage stellen. Warum steht ein Wohnwagen vor der Stadtbücherei, hängt wochenlang ein Lenin-Porträt im Foyer im Rahmen einer Ausstellung mit dem Titel „Kurskorrektur – Qualitätssicherung" – beides Teile eines ungewöhnlichen künstlerischen Prozesses, der Fragen aufwirft, Verblüffung hervorruft, oft auch nur in der unterbewussten Wahrnehmung. Denn die Besucherbefragungen haben auch gezeigt, dass die gerade laufende Ausstellung vom Besucher, den das Thema nicht direkt anspricht, gar nicht wahrgenommen wird. Aber die Besucher wünschen sich Ausstellungen, weil sie das Anregungspotential spüren und wahrnehmen, dass dies dem Ort Bibliothek eine besondere emotionale Qualität verleiht, aus der eine Atmosphäre der Inspiration entsteht, ein bewusst nicht unbedingt beschreibbarer, aber emotional wohl wirksamer Prozess.

Das Lernen der Zukunft sieht Mathias Horx als „die Frage nach einem neuen Menschenbild, im dem Lernen kein „Erwerbsakt" mehr ist, sondern mit geistigem und sozialem Wachstum zu tun hat" – zu diesem geistigen und sozialen Wachstum kann die Bibliothek einen wesentlichen Betrag leisten, denn sie löst das Lernen aus dem Kontext rein kognitiver Wissensaneignung und integriert es in einen Kontext künstlerischer Impulse – durch die Begegnung mit Künstlern, künstlerische Schaffensprozesse im und mit dem Haus, durch Begegnungen mit Experten, Wissenschaftlern, Literaten. – im realen Ort Bibliothek ebenso wie in der virtuellen Welt, wie die literarischen Experimente des „Futuristischen Lesesalons" der Stadtbücherei Stuttgart.[221]

Die emotionale Qualität solcher Begegnungen fügt sich in den ganzheitlichen Lernprozess, der die Gesamtpersönlichkeit des Einzelnen umfasst.

---

[220] Horx, Die acht Sphären der Zukunft s. 165

[221] siehe: „Futuristischer Lesesalon" http://stuttgart.de/stadtbuecherei

4. Die lernende Organisation

Um die Bibliothek zu einem inspirierenden Lernort für die Besucher zu entwickeln, muss die Organisation selbst offen und lernbereit sein. Sie muss Wandel wahrnehmen, annehmen und gestalten. Das setzt Achtsamkeit und Sensibilität für Veränderungsprozesse voraus und fordert eine Organisationsstruktur, die offen ist für Experimente und die Erprobung neuen Handelns.

Dazu gehört eine Gesprächskultur, die gemeinsames Nachdenken ermöglicht, und die entsprechenden Plattformen wie Braintrusts, Moderationstage, Workshops.

Daneben ist eine formale Informations- und Kommunikationsstruktur erforderlich, die Partizipation an den Alltagsentwicklungen ermöglicht und permanente Optimierungsprozesse sichert. Neben den üblichen Besprechungen gewinnt das Intranet hier eine immer größere Bedeutung.

Eine zentrale Säule der lernenden Organisation ist die permanente Qualifizierung der Mitarbeiter. Neben der Medien- und Technologiekompetenz, die das Fortbildungs- und Schulungsangebot der letzten Jahre geprägt hat, wird immer deutlicher, dass die inhaltliche Kompetenz für einen optimierten Beratungs- und Auskunftsdienst mehr und mehr gefördert werden muss.

Bei einer Zukunftswerkstatt im Rahmen des EFIL-Projektes der Stadtbücherei Stuttgart formulierte eine Mitarbeiterin auf die Frage, welche Kompetenzen die Mitarbeiter in Zukunft erfüllen müssen, sie sehe sich in Zukunft vor allem als Reiseleiterin in der Wissenslandschaft, als Moderatorin, die Wege aufzeigt und zu Zielen hinführt. Gute Reiseleiter verfügen über großes Fachwissen über das Land, in dem sie reisen. So sind auch Bibliothekare – mindestens in großen Zentralbibliotheken - gefordert, immer mehr zu fachlichen Spezialisten und Experten für ihre Fachgebiete zu werden. Allerdings sind auch die Grenzen für die Lernberatung deutlich zu ziehen, denn es macht wenig Sinn, wenn Bibliothekare zu Schmalspurpädagogen werden, um inhaltliche Lernberatung zu machen. Die Reiseleiter durch die Wissenslandschaft müssen auch zu den Experten führen, die über die notwendigen inhaltlichen Kompetenzen verfügen. Das heißt auch neue Wege der Zusammenarbeit mit dem Experten der Erwachsenenbildung. Und das heißt - Entgrenzung der Institutionen und die Gestaltung neuer Lern- und Bildungsnetze in der Stadt, in der Region oder darüber hinaus.

Diese sich abzeichnenden Zukunftsperspektiven haben Rückwirkungen auf die Ausbildung, heißt dies doch, dass für die Zukunft der Bibliothek als Lernort Experten gefordert sind, die inhaltliche Kompetenz, Beratungskompetenz, Managementkompetenz und Zukunftsoffenheit sowie Kreativität miteinander verbinden.

Horst Heidtmann

Multimedia in Kinder- und Jugendbibliotheken

Bestandserhebungen und Nutzerbefragungen in ausgewählten Bibliotheken

1995 kamen die ersten Edutainment-CD-ROMs für Kinder in Deutschland auf den Markt, „Multimedia" war in diesem Jahr das „Wort des Jahres. Obwohl die ersten Kindertitel sich auf schlichte Animationen, kleine interaktive Spiele und überschaubare Grafiken beschränkten (Heidtmann, 1995), stieß das neue Medium sofort nachhaltiges Interesse bei seinen Zielgruppen. Kinder und Jugendliche wollen die gesamte Bandbreite der zur Verfügung stehenden Medien nutzen, vor allem wollen sie Zugang zu den Technologien haben, die als besonders fortschrittlich und als die für die Gesellschaft wichtigsten gelten. Kinder wachsen in einer audiovisuell und multimedial geprägten Umwelt heran. In praktisch allen Haushalten sind Fernseh- wie Audiogeräte mehrfach vorhanden. Etwa die Hälfte aller deutschen Haushalte besitzt Anfang des Jahres 2001 mindestens einen Personalcomputer. Haushalte mit schulpflichtigen Kindern weisen eine überdurchschnittliche Ausstattung mit Medienhardware auf.

Nach der letzten „Kids Verbraucher Analyse KVA 2000" (Egmont Ehapa Verlag, 2000) und anderen Studien nutzt mehr als die Hälfte der 6- bis 17-Jährigen den PC häufig bis regelmäßig, von den 12 bis 17-Jährigen nutzen ihn mehr als 50 % sogar täglich; jeder Dritte im Alter zwischen 6 und 17 Jahren surft bereits häufiger im Internet. Immer jüngere Kinder wünschen sich heute einen Computer, ein Drittel der Jungen im Alter zwischen 6 und 9 Jahren will einen eigenen PC, möglichst mit Internetzugang.

Mit dem immer rascher werdenden Wandel der gesellschaftlichen Kommunikation haben sich in den vergangenen Jahrzehnten auch die Medienpräferenzen von Kindern und Jugendlichen entsprechend verändert. Die Kinder- und Jugendbibliotheken in Deutschland haben auf Veränderungen der Medienlandschaft zumeist nur sehr verhalten reagiert. Kritische Bestandsaufnahmen aus den vergangenen Jahrzehnten (König, 1986; Heidtmann, 1989; Heidtmann/Nagl, 1995; u.a.) resümieren wiederkehrend die – wachsende – Diskrepanz zwischen der Medienzusammensetzung von Bibliotheksbeständen und dem Medienalltag, den Medieninteressen der jugendlichen Nutzer. Nach der Einführung der kompakten MusiCassette als preiswertes und robustes Massenmedium 1965 hat es mehr als 30 Jahre gebraucht bis etwa die Hälfte der Öffentlichen Bibliotheken Tonträger für Kinder in ihren Beständen führt (Schmitt, 1999). Nachdem der kommerzielle Videomarkt in den frühen 1980er-Jahren mit nicht gerade kindgerechten Sujets prosperierte, wurden kindgemäße Videobestände von Bibliotheken im Regelfall nur auf Druck der kommunalen Träger eingerichtet; bis 1992 hatten insgesamt gerade 100 Öffentliche Bibliotheken in der BRD nennenswerte Videobestände vorzuweisen (Heidtmann, 2000); 1997 bieten immerhin 30 % der deutschen Bibliotheken Videos für Kinder und Jugendliche an (Schmitt, 1999).

Bibliothekarinnen und Bibliothekare verstanden sich über lange Zeit mehrheitlich als ‚Hüter der Buchkultur', sie orientierten sich vorrangig an ihrer eigenen medialen Sozialisation, was die Akzeptanz neuer Medien erschwerte. Einrichtungen der bibliothekarischen Aus- und Fortbildung haben darauf nach und nach in notwendiger Weise reagiert. Als erste

Institution hat die damalige Fachhochschule für Bibliothekswesen (FHB) in Stuttgart 1986 eine Professur für neue Medien und Kinder- und Jugendbibliotheken eingerichtet, neu ausgeschrieben und wenig später um eine zweite Professorenstelle in diesem Bereich ergänzt. An der Stuttgarter Hochschule für Bibliotheks- und Informationswesen (HBI) ist dann 1997 - mit Unterstützung der Hochschulleitung und der zentralen Gremien - ein Institut für angewandte Kindermedienforschung (IfaK) eingerichtet worden, das seinen Arbeitsschwerpunkt im Bereich der neuen, der digitalen und interaktiven Medien hat. In der Aus- wie auch in der Fortbildung bietet die HBI - allein und mit anderen Trägern - für Kinder- und Jugendbibliothekarinnen seit etlichen Jahren Veranstaltungen über Nonbook-Medien und seit 1995 auch über Multimedia an.

Der Multimedia-Markt in Deutschland

Nach einer ersten Euphorie 1995 und anfänglichen Höhenflügen (Heidtmann, 1996, A) sind die Umsätze mit der CD-ROM als Trägermedium von Multimedia-Programmen in den späten 1990er-Jahren wieder spürbar zurückgegangen. Der prognostizierte Boom ist ausgeblieben. Die CD-ROM hat Bücher weder verdrängt noch ersetzt. Multimedia ist als neues Medium ergänzend neben die bisherigen getreten, im Jahr 2000 ist der Umsatz mit Kinder- und Jugendbüchern hierzulande sogar überproportional gestiegen - *Harry Potter* sei Dank.

In Deutschland zeichnet sich ein ähnlicher Trend ab wie schon seit längerem in den USA oder in Großbritannien, wo sich die großen Publikumsverlage wie HarperCollins oder Penguin bereits wieder von der CD-ROM verabschiedet haben. Hierzulande hat die Bertelsmann Electronic Publishing Mitte 1997 ihre Aktivitäten fast vollständig eingestellt. Microsoft produziert keine Kindersoftware mehr, die größeren deutschen CD-ROM-Produzenten haben sich in den vergangenen Jahren zu wenigen Unternehmensgruppen zusammengeschlossen.

Inhaltlich und ästhetisch ambitionierte Multimedia-Projekte sind drastisch zurückgenommen worden. Die Ravensburger Tochter Interactive produziert jetzt fast nur noch interaktive Spielgeschichten mit Motiven der Kinderserienliteratur oder „Moving Puzzles" mit zerschnittenen Videosequenzen. Der wichtigste deutsche Kindersoftware-Entwickler, der Berliner Tivola-Verlag, erzielt gegenwärtig die höchsten Verkaufszahlen mit interaktiven *TKKG*-Spielgeschichten (nach Stoffen aus der gleichnamigen Kinderbuchserie), von denen innerhalb weniger Monate bis zu 100.000 CD-ROMs verkauft werden.

Für die Vermarktung von Multimedia-CD-ROMs lässt sich eine übergreifende Tendenz beobachten, die für alle Kindermedien charakteristisch ist: Figuren, Stoffe, Spielsszenarien, die in einem Medium erfolgreich waren, werden in medialen Verbünden, in Medienverbundsystemen vermarktet. Kinder als Kunden verbinden mit den Produkten dann bereits positive Vorerwartungen, sie können angenehme Medienerlebnisse in einem anderen Medium mit Variationen wiederholen.

Die inhaltliche Umorientierung der Softwareanbieter auf weniger anspruchsvolle Kinderunterhaltung ist vom Markt angenommen worden. Bei niedrigeren Produktionskosten und höheren Umsätzen sind zudem die Preise für CD-ROMs binnen weniger Jahre drastisch gefallen. Allein von 1998 auf 1999 ging - nach Angaben der GfK - der Durchschnittspreis von DM 40,88 auf DM 27,60 für einen Kindertitel zurück. Der Kindersoftwaremarkt hat 1999 insgesamt kräftig zugelegt. Die Zahl der verkauften Titel hat sich verdoppelt, das Umsatzvolumen (Verkauf an private Haushalte) ist 1999 um etwa ein Viertel auf ca. 115 Millionen Mark gestiegen. Im Vergleich dazu: die Umsätze im seit einigen Jahren boomenden Kindertonträgermarkt lagen 1999 noch doppelt so hoch, mit Kinder- und Jugendbüchern wurde 1999 sogar ein Umsatzvolumen von annähernd 800 Millionen Mark erzielt, etwa siebenmal so viel wie mit Kindersoftware.

Gleichwohl: für die deutschen Softwareanbieter hat das Segment Kinderunterhaltung mittlerweile eine zentrale Bedeutung gewonnen. Das dürfte auch auf absehbare Zeit so bleiben. Von Jugendlichen werden Multimedia-Anwendungen auf CD-ROM als Lern- oder Lexikonprogramme genutzt, ansonsten dient ihnen die CD-ROM fast ausschließlich als Trägermedium von Computerspielen. Wie bereits seit längerem in den USA zu erkennen ist, suchen deshalb auch hierzulande die CD-ROM-Anbieter ein immer jüngeres Publikum, denn lediglich Kinder im Vorschulalter und wenig darüber sind „dazu bereit..., sich dieselbe Geschichte immer wieder anzusehen." (Negroponte, 1997)

CD-ROMs in Kinder- und Jugendbibliotheken

1995 haben erste Kinderbibliotheken einige Multimedia-Programme für Kinder angeschafft, zunächst nur zur Präsenznutzung. Nach einer vom Deutschen Bibliotheksinstitut (dbi) durchgeführten Erhebung über Medienangebote in Kinder- und Jugendbibliotheken verfügte 1997 gerade jede zwanzigste Bibliothek über CD-ROMs für Kinder. 1998 konnten bereits 258 Bibliotheken (13,7 %) Software für Kinder anbieten. „Sie besaßen im Durchschnitt 50 CD-ROMs bzw. Software auf Diskette" (Schmitt, 1999).

Das IfaK der HBI Stuttgart bemüht sich nach „Abwicklung des dbi" darum, Erhebungen zur Nutzung und Funktion von Kindermedien in Öffentlichen Bibliotheken exemplarisch fortzusetzen, soweit dies dem IfaK mit den vorhandenen Ressourcen möglich ist. Studierende der Hochschule für Bibliotheks- und Informationswesen haben im Rahmen eines Projektseminars im Winter 2000/2001 (bis einschließlich Januar 2001) Erhebungen in etwa 30 öffentlichen Kinder- und Jugendbibliotheken durchgeführt; zudem wurden in diesen Bibliotheken knapp 300 Kinder und Jugendliche zur Nutzung von Multimedia-CD-ROMs interviewt. Bei den untersuchten Bibliotheken handelt es sich um sechs (zentrale) Großstadtbibliotheken sowie um sieben Zweigstellen in Großstädten, ferner um neun Mittelstadtbibliotheken sowie eine -zweigstelle und um mehrere Kleinstadtbüchereien, die fast alle im südwestdeutschen Raum liegen. Diese Erhebungen sind nicht repräsentativ, erlauben aber verallgemeinerbare Aussagen zur Nutzung dieses Mediums.

Die Anzahl der Medieneinheiten in den befragten Kinder- und Jugendbibliotheken liegt zwischen 4.000 und 32.000, im Durchschnitt um 20.000 Einheiten. In einigen Klein- und Mittelstädten erreichen Nonbookmedien am gesamten Kinderbibliotheksbestand lediglich Anteile von 1 bis 2 %. Durchschnittlich erreichen die Nonbookmedien einen Bestandsanteil von etwa 10 %, in einer Mittelstadt- und zwei Großstadtbibliotheken kommen sie auf einen Anteil von 20 % oder mehr. Diese Bestandszusammensetzung entspricht den vom dbi 1997 ermittelten Daten. Printmedien dominieren die Kinderbibliotheksbestände also nach wie vor.

Bei den Entleihungen von Kinder- und Jugendbüchern liegt die durchschnittliche Frequenz bei 4,5 Ausleihen pro Buch im Jahr. Von den untersuchten Bibliotheken bieten lediglich 3 keine Videokassetten für Kinder an, in den anderen erreichen Videos (auch bei sehr großen Beständen) im Durchschnitt deutlich höhere Ausleihquoten als Printmedien, im Einzelfall bis zu 26-mal pro Kassette und Jahr. Im Durchschnitt kommen die Videos in den befragten Kinder- und Jugendbibliotheken auf 11,7 Ausleihen pro Jahr.

Die CD-ROM-Bestände für Kinder sind innerhalb weniger Jahre erkennbar gewachsen. Alle untersuchten Kinder- und Jugendbibliotheken bieten ihren Nutzern heute auch Software! Nur drei von ihnen haben Bestände mit weniger als 100 CD-ROMs (16 und 76 bzw. 77), an vier Orten finden sich bereits Bestände zwischen 500 und 1.000 Einheiten, die durchschnittliche Bestandsgröße liegt Anfang des Jahres 2001bei 279 CD-ROM-Titeln. Das entspricht einem durchschnittlichen Anteil von zwei bis drei % am Gesamtmedienbestand; gelegentlich kommen CD-ROMs auf fünf oder sogar auf über sechs % Anteil am gesamten Bestand der Kinderbibliothek. 1997 lag der Bestandsanteil von Kinder-CD-ROMs im statistischen Mittel noch bei 1,2 Promille (Schmitt, 1999).

Kriterien für den Bestandsaufbau werden von den Bibliotheken eher uneinheitlich gehandhabt. Mancherorts stehen pädagogische Aspekte im Vordergrund, teilweise scheint man sich vor allem an den aus der Kinderliteratur vertrauten Stoffen, Figuren- und Autorennamen zu orientieren. Fast überall sind Lernsoftware und Edutainmentprogramme vorhanden; kaum weniger häufig werden Kinderspielprogramme und Sachinformationen (Infotainment u.ä.) auf CD-ROMs angeboten. Nur die Hälfte aller Bestände enthält nennenswerte Anteile von interaktiven Geschichten (*Living Books*) oder Lexika (z.B. *Duden*). Andere spezifische Multimedia-Gattungen, wie z.B. Kreativitätsprogramme, sind noch seltener vorhanden.

Bewusst verzichten die meisten Bibliotheken auf gängige Computerspielsoftware, auf Action-, Jump and Run-, Sport- oder selbst Strategie-Spiele (oder machen diese erst Nutzern ab 16 Jahren zugänglich). Gewaltorientierte Software, Horror- oder Gruselmotive sind ohnehin kein Thema und auch Konsolenspiele (Playstation etc.) werden von fast allen Büchereien dezidiert abgelehnt.

Ausleihe von CD-ROMs in Kinder- und Jugendbibliotheken

Praktisch überall stehen die CD-ROMs für Kinder und Jugendliche mittlerweile zur Ausleihe zur Verfügung, nur selten noch mit verkürzten Ausleihfristen, nur im Einzelfall mit einer gesonderten Ausleihgebühr (z.B. DM 1,- pro CD). Einige Büchereien stellen kleine Teilbestände (unterrichtsbegleitende Lernsoftware oder interaktive Nachschlagewerke) generell oder zeitlich befristet nur für die Präsenznutzung bereit. Lediglich eine Bibliothek (Mediothek in Stuttgart) bietet aufgrund ihres Gesamtkonzeptes auch die gesamte Kindersoftware ausschließlich zur Nutzung vor Ort an. Ansonsten werden heute überall die CD-ROMs überdurchschnittlich oft entliehen, selbst wenn populären Genres oder Bestseller in den Beständen nicht vorhanden sind. Auf alle untersuchten Kinderbibliotheken bezogen kommt jede einzelne CD-ROM auf durchschnittlich 12,8 Entleihungen pro Jahr (bei einem mittelgroßen Bestand sogar auf 25 Ausleihen p.a.), etwas mehr also als die Videokassetten, die bislang eindeutig am beliebtesten waren. Bezogen auf den Umsatz sind CD-ROMs gegenwärtig also das gefragteste Kindermedium.

In den meisten Bibliotheken beginnen Kinder im Alter von fünf oder sechs Jahren die CD-ROMs selbst zu entleihen, mehrfach wird - von Mitarbeiterinnen - sogar die Altersgruppe der Drei- bis Vierjährigen genannt. Die jugendliche Kernnutzerschaft wird meist zwischen acht und 12 Jahren eingeordnet. Für kleinere Kinder wählen allerdings häufig die Eltern Software aus und entleihen diese dann auch. Bei der geschlechtsspezifischen Zusammensetzung können die meisten Büchereien keine Unterschiede ausmachen, Mädchen und Jungen interessieren sich gleichermaßen für Multimedia-Anwendungen. Bei einem Viertel der befragten Bibliotheken liegt der Anteil der Jungen bei der CD-ROM-Nutzung etwas höher (das Verhältnis wird auf drei zu zwei geschätzt); in einer einzelnen Mittelstadtbibliothek leihen dagegen doppelt so viel Mädchen wie Jungen Kindersoftware aus.

In der Mehrheit der befragten Bibliotheken stehen für Kinder und Jugendliche PCs zur Präsenznutzung von Programmen zur Verfügung, manchmal müssen sich die Kinder die Rechner allerdings mit anderen Bibliotheksbenutzern teilen. Nur in wenigen Orten ist die Präsenznutzung - aus Kostengründen oder aufgrund „schlechter Erfahrungen“ – grundsätzlich nicht möglich. Mehrere Bibliotheken bieten vorinstallierte Programme an: gefragte Lernsoftware, z.B. aus der *Alfons*-Reihe, wird fest installiert; fünf oder sechs neue CD-ROMs stehen monatlich wechselnd in der Kinderbücherei auf einem PC zur Verfügung; auf einem „Spielecomputer“ sind 15 attraktive Spiele fest installiert; auf mehreren PCs werden gattungsbezogen Programme kompiliert und den Kindern als „Lern-PC“, „Forschungs-PC“ oder „Geschichten-PC“ angeboten. Alle diese Angebote zur Präsenznutzung haben sich in der Praxis offenkundig gut bewährt.

Die Nutzung des CD-ROM-Angebotes ist von der Zusammensetzung der Bestände abhängig. Die von den Kindern in fast allen Bibliotheken (nach Ausleihstatistik oder Beobachtung der Mitarbeiterinnen) mit deutlicher Präferenz genutzte Gattung ist Edutainment, mit erkennbarem Abstand folgen Lernsoftware und Spiele. Die am stärksten gefragten Einzeltitel erreichen durchweg 18 bis 20 Ausleihen pro Jahr, gelegentlich sogar 30. Allerdings ist die Nachfrage in den Bibliotheken ebenso facettenreich wie mittlerweile das Angebot. Von knapp 30 Bibliotheken werden mehr als 60 Titel genannt, die aktuell (je nach Statistik 1999 und/oder 2000) am häufigsten entliehen und nachgefragt worden sind. So entfallen auch auf deutlich vorn in den „Charts“ liegenden Titel nicht sehr viele Nennungen:

CD-ROM-Bibliotheks-Charts:

Die am häufigsten entliehenen Einzeltitel

1. Fritzi Fisch und der verschwundene Schatz (Ravensburger)
2. Das Geheimnis der Burg (Bibliogr. Institut)
3. Pettersson und Findus (Terzio)

Die am häufigsten entliehenen Reihen

1. Löwenzahn (Terzio)
2. Max.../ Max und Marie.. (Tivola)
3. ADDY (Coktel/Havas Interactive)
4. Willy Werkel (Terzio)
5. TKKG (Tivola)

Die Stadtbücherei Stuttgart hat für alle ihre an die zentrale EDV angeschlossenen Zweigstellen folgende Hitliste der am häufigsten entliehenen Kinder-CD-ROM-Titel für das Jahr 1999 erstellt:

CD-ROM-Ausleihcharts Stuttgart 1999

1. Fritzi Fisch und der verschwundene Schatz (Ravensburger)
2. TKKG, Teil 2 (Tivola)
3. Max und das Schlossgespenst (Tivola)
4. Schneewittchen und die sieben Hänsel (Tivola)

5. Max und Marie gehen einkaufen (Tivola)
6. Pettersson und Findus (Terzio)
7. Elroy auf Ganovenjagd (Ravensburger)
8. Fritzi Fisch 2 (Ravensburger)
9. Max und die Geheimformel (Tivola)
10. Die Zahlenstadt (Ravensburger)

Bei den in den Kinder- und Jugendbibliotheken gegenwärtig am meisten nachgefragten CD-ROMs dominieren als Produzenten die wichtigsten Anbieter von Edutainment, nicht alle gehören zu den Marktführern bei kommerzieller Kindersoftware:

1. Tivola
2. Ravensburger
3. Terzio
4. Havas Interactive

mit etwas Abstand gefolgt von

5. BI Brockhaus
6. Disney
7. LEGO

Mehr als drei viertel der befragten Bibliotheken bieten den Kindern und Jugendlichen nicht nur Multimedia auf der CD-ROM, sondern auch einen Zugang ins Internet. Meist steht allerdings noch kein eigener Internetanschluß in der Kinderbücherei bereit, sondern Kinder und Jugendliche teilen sich mit den Erwachsenen die vorhandenen Netzzugänge. Auf den meisten PCs ist Internet-Filtersoftware installiert, trotzdem wird mehrfach erst Jugendlichen ab 14 Jahren der Netzzugang gestattet. Immerhin bieten bereits gegenwärtig drei Kinderbüchereien eigene Internetarbeitsplätze für ihre Klientel, 10 planen dies für die nahe Zukunft. (Die von Kindern und Jugendlichen in Bibliotheken am häufigsten aufgerufenen Websites sind durch diese Befragung nicht systematisch ermittelt worden, sehr häufig genannt werden die *Pokemon*- und *Big Brother*-Seiten.)

Etwa ein Drittel der befragten Bibliotheken nutzt die interaktiven und digitalen Medien mittlerweile auch in der Programmarbeit für Kinder und Jugendliche, z.B. für Bilderbuchkino, Quiz- und Suchspiele. Ein Teil bietet Einführungen in die Nutzung des PCs, des Internets oder sogar regelmäßige Internetkurse an. Nur sehr wenige Bibliothekarinnen lehnen es ab, die neuen Medien weitergehender in ihre Programmarbeit zu integrieren.

Medienausstattung jugendlicher Bibliotheksbenutzer

Zusätzlich zu den statistischen Erhebungen sind in den Bibliotheken insgesamt 295 Kinder und Jugendliche im Alter zwischen vier und 17 Jahren interviewt worden, mehr als drei Viertel von ihnen sind zwischen neun und 14 Jahren alt gewesen. Der Anteil der Jungen liegt mit 56 % höher als üblich. Bei den Interviews sind Kinder im Vorschul- und Kleinkindalter in Begleitung der Eltern oder älterer Geschwister, die mit den oder für die Kleinen antworten. Ein Drittel der Befragten besucht das Gymnasium, 25 % die Grundschule, 20 % die Hauptschule, etwas weniger die Realschule.

Von den Befragten verfügt kaum weniger als die Hälfte allein oder zusammen mit Geschwistern bereits über einen eigenen PC, dabei handelt es sich überproportional oft um Kinder, die ein Gymnasium besuchen. Bei Gymnasiasten ohne eigenen PC kommt zudem sehr häufig der Hinweis: „Aber demnächst bekomme ich einen eigenen PC“. Für die große

Mehrheit der Kinder und Jugendlichen steht alternativ - vielfach auch ergänzend – mindestens ein PC zur Nutzung durch alle Familienmitglieder zur Verfügung. Kaum mehr als 10 % der befragten Kinder und Jugendlichen haben in der Familie keinen Zugriff auf einen PC. Aus der Norm fallen einige Mädchen, wie eine 12-jährige Gymnasiastin, der der Vater nur gelegentlich die Benutzung des PCs zum Schreiben eines Briefes gestattet.

Fast alle Kinder und Jugendlichen, die daheim einen PC benutzen können, besitzen selbst auch eigene CD-ROMs, 50 % von ihnen allerdings nur 10 Stück oder weniger. Jeweils 10 % (vorwiegend Jugendliche) besitzen bis zu 20 Stück und bis zu 50 Stück und sechs Jugendliche (ältere Gymnasiasten) geben an, mehr als 50 CD-ROMs zu besitzen. Kaum mehr als fünf % der Befragten verfügen über keine eigenen Multimedia-Programme. Bei diesen privaten Medienbeständen handelt es sich vermutlich überwiegend um Spielessoftware, ein Drittel der Befragten besitzt außerdem (oder statt dessen) Lernsoftware und Lernspiele (wobei diese oft „von den Eltern gekauft" worden sind, von den Jugendlichen aber nicht genutzt werden).

Bei etwa 40 % der Bibliotheksbenutzer zwischen vier und 17 Jahren ist zuhause bereits ein eigener Internetanschluß vorhanden (der allenfalls von den Kleinsten aus Kostengründen nicht oder nur eingeschränkt genutzt werden darf). Die große Mehrheit der befragten Gymnasiasten kann ab Sekundarstufe I, fast alle von ihnen können ab 18 Jahren auf das Internet zugreifen. Im Gegensatz dazu sind besonders oft in nicht deutschstämmigen (türkischen) Familien weder ein PC noch ein Internetzugang vorhanden.

Nutzung von CD-ROMs durch Kinder- und Jugendliche

In allen untersuchten Bibliotheken stehen zwar CD-ROMs für Kinder und Jugendliche im Bestand, doch auf die Frage: „Entleihst Du CD-ROMs in dieser Bibliothek?" antworten 40 % mit „nein". Auf Nachfragen stellt sich dann heraus, dass ihnen vielfach unbekannt ist, dass ihre Bibliothek CD-ROMs im Bestand hat, weil diese ungünstig, nicht sofort auffindbar gestellt sind. Knapp 10 % der Befragten, ausschließlich Mädchen, haben offenkundig nur ein geringes oder gar kein Interesse am Medium CD-ROM. Einige ältere Mädchen lesen oder spielen lieber mit ihren Freundinnen: „CD-ROMs verblöden nur". Mädchen im Grundschulalter, die die Nutzung von CD-ROMs dezidiert verweigern, sogar für „schädlich" halten, reproduzieren erkennbar Vorgaben und Meinungen ihrer Eltern. Einem 12-jährigem Gymnasiasten verbieten die Eltern sogar das Ausleihen von CD-ROMs. Etwa 10 % leihen gar nicht oder nur selten aus, weil die interessanten (neuen) Titel immer gerade verliehen seien oder weil sie auf andere Öffentliche Bibliotheken ausweichen, die größere CD-ROM-Bestände anbieten. Und mehrere ältere, vorrangig an PC-Spielen interessierte Jungen kaufen „lieber gleich selbst".

Die Mehrheit der Befragten kann CD-ROMs auch in der jeweiligen Kinder- und Jugendbücherei benutzen, macht davon aber nur teilweise Gebrauch, hat diese Möglichkeit z.T. bisher nicht zur Kenntnis genommen. Ein Viertel gibt an, dass Präsenznutzung oder Antesten von CD-ROMs nicht möglich seien und zeigt sich darüber - manchmal - spürbar enttäuscht.

Knapp die Hälfte der jungen BibliotheksbesucherInnen ist mit dem vorhandenen CD-ROM-Angebot zufrieden, bei diesen „Zufriedenen" stellen allerdings Mädchen, die nicht zu den Intensivnutzern des Mediums zählen, einen besonders hohen Anteil. Ein Viertel ist dezidiert unzufrieden mit dem Bestand, weil insgesamt zu wenige Titel vorhanden sind oder weil sie die Bestände für veraltet halten, weil Neuerscheinungen fehlen. Kleinere

Kinder beklagen mehrfach, dass zu wenig Edutainment-Programme angeboten werden, ältere Jungen klagen über „zu viele Lernprogramme“. Insgesamt kritisieren ältere Kinder und Jugendliche unabhängig vom Geschlecht, dass die Bestände „zu kindisch“ seien, dass vor allem Spiele fehlten. Dabei vermissen sie jedoch nicht vorrangig, wie manche Realschüler, die „Ballerspiele“: „Scheiß CD-ROMs, überhaupt keine Action, nur für Kinder!“ (14-jähriger Realschüler). Die Zufriedenheit ist naturgemäß besonders groß bei den Beständen von Großstadtbibliotheken, z.B. bei der Mediothek in Stuttgart, und altersbezogen bei den Nutzern im Grundschulalter.

Nutzungspräferenzen

Bei den bevorzugten Gattungen und Genres auf der CD-ROM liegen auch bei jungen Bibliothekskunden - wie bei Kindern und Jugendlichen überhaupt - Computerspiele deutlich vorn (etwa bei 50 %). Bei der Spielesoftware sind nach eigenem Bekunden - unabhängig vom Geschlecht - 15 % besonders an Adventure-Games interessiert, 12 % an Sportspielen und -simulationen (Jungen u.a. an Autorennen, Mädchen u.a. an *Barbie Super Sport*), 11 % schätzen besonders die Jump and Run- und etwas weniger die Strategie-Spiele. Vor allem bei männlichen Haupt- und Realschülern (und vereinzelt auch Schülerinnen) sind „Ballerspiele“ am beliebtesten, die von Mädchen andererseits fast genau so häufig dezidiert abgelehnt werden: „Es ist sinnlos, Raumschiffe oder Menschen abzuschießen!“ Mädchen schätzen statt dessen Quizspiele wie *Wer wird Millionär?*

Die Liebhaber von Computerspielen finden ihre Bedürfnisse in Öffentlichen Bibliotheken nur eingeschränkt berücksichtigt; von ihnen entleiht daher dort kaum mehr als die Hälfte Spiele auf CD-ROM, sie weichen vielfach auf kommerzielle Videotheken aus, um Spielesoftware zu bekommen.

Lernsoftware und Lernspiele sind für ein Viertel der Befragten die bevorzugte Gattung. Hier sind Bibliotheksbestände deutlich besser bestückt, mehr als 30 % der Kinder und Jugendlichen haben entsprechende Titel bereits (z.T. häufiger) ausgeliehen. Bei den bevorzugten Gattungen stehen an dritter Stelle (bei knapp 20 %) Edutainment-Programme, besonders bei jüngeren Kindern, in deutlichem Abstand gefolgt von interaktiven Geschichten und interaktiven Lexika. Andere Gattungen wie Sachinformations- und Kreativprogramme oder interaktive Puzzles werden nur selten präferiert.

Viele Kinder können auf Nachfragen keine Lieblings-CD-ROM nennen, sie suchen meist auch im Bibliotheksbestand nicht gezielt nach bestimmten Titeln, sondern nach Gattungen, Genres, Themen. Bei der Zusammenstellung der insgesamt genannten Lieblingstitel ist auffällig, dass sich keine eindeutigen, herausragenden Hits ausmachen lassen; die Diversifikation der Interessen und Präferenzen ist bei Multimedia-CD-ROMs noch erheblich größer als die bei früheren Erhebungen zu anderen Kinder- und Jugendmedien erkennbar gewordene breite Streuung. (Heidtmann, 1996, B). Von knapp 250 Kindern und Jugendlichen werden insgesamt 109 Titel als „beliebteste CD-ROM“ genannt, davon etwa 60 % Spiel-, 30 % Edutainment- und 10 % Lernprogramme. Allerdings werden die meisten Titel nur von einem, zwei oder drei Kindern und Jugendlichen als „Hit“ eingestuft. An der Spitze liegen mit deutlichem Abstand zwei Computerspiele, *LEGO Racers* (mit 16 Nennungen, gut 5 %) gefolgt von *Age of Empires* (Erwachsenenspiel mit 9 Nennungen). Alle anderen genannten Titel sind Reihen, Folgen oder neue Versionen vorliegender Spielmotive, die zumeist zwischen 10- oder 20-mal, bei den beiden Spitzenplätzen über 20-mal genannt worden sind:

Horst Heidtmann

Hitliste der beliebtesten CD-ROMs

Beliebteste Einzeltitel

1. LEGO Racers (LEGO)
2. Age of Empires (Microsoft)

Beliebteste Reihen

1. LEGO (LEGO)
1. Löwenzahn (Terzio)
2. ADDY (Havas)
3. FIFA (EA Sports)
4. TKKG (Tivola)
5. Tomb Raider (Eidos)
6. Pettersson & Findus (Oetinger)
7. Willy Werkel (Terzio)
8. Die Siedler (BlueByte)
9. Command and Conquer (Electronic Arts)
9. Sim City (Electronic Arts)
10. Fritzi Fisch (Ravensburger)
10. Fünf Freunde (Ravensburger)

Die meisten Kinder und Jugendlichen haben heute immer breiter aufgefächerte Medieninteressen, dies benennen sie vielfach sehr dezidiert. Die Präferenzen gehen auch bei Multimedia geschlechtsspezifisch auseinander, aber nicht so deutlich wie bei den Printmedien (Bischof / Heidtmann, 2000). Bei kleineren Mädchen und Jungen besteht ein vergleichbares Interesse an Edutainment und Spielgeschichten, ältere Kinder und Jugendliche bevorzugen eindeutig - weitgehend unabhängig vom Schultypus – Spielesoftware, Jungen etwas stärker Adventures, Sport und Simulationen, Mädchen insgesamt eher Geschicklichkeits- und Strategiespiele (aber auch etliche jüngere wie ältere Mädchen sind von Lara Croft aus den *Tomb Raider*-Spielen begeistert. Auf die Frage, welche CD-ROMs (Art, Themen) in der jeweiligen Bibliothek vermisst werden, erfolgt als häufigste Antwort „es fehlen Spiele für Jugendliche“, als zweithäufigste „zu wenig Spiele für ältere Kinder“. Zur Anschaffung gewünscht werden dementsprechend häufig Action- und Adventurespiele sowie Sportspiele und Simulationen (mehrfach auch Playstation- und Konsolenspiele). Lediglich einer Reihe von älteren Jugendlichen (meist Gymnasiasten) fehlt es an unterrichtsbegleitender Lernsoftware (vorrangig für Englisch, Deutsch, Mathematik). Insgesamt werden selten detaillierte Wünsche geäußert, da die meisten offenkundig keinen Überblick über das Marktangebot haben, aus der Presse oder den Kinder- wie Jugendzeitschriften nur über neue, aufwendiger beworbene Spiele Bescheid wissen.

Bei der Frage nach den im Bestand fehlenden Titeln werden daher überwiegend gängige Erwachsenen-PC-Spiele genannt (*Tomb Raider, Quake, Resident Evil* u.a.) sowie Edutainment-Programme mit Figuren aus dem Medienverbund (*TKKG, Pokemon, Sailormoon*). Am häufigsten wünschen sich die Befragten jedoch, dass populäre Titel gestaffelt werden: „man muß auf die guten Spiele zu lange warten.“

Funktionen und Gratifikationen von Multimedia

Um die Funktionen im Medienalltag von Kindern und Jugendlichen und um die spezifische Gratifikation von Multimedia-Programmen für die jugendlichen Rezipienten differenzierter ermitteln zu können, sind zusammenhängend mehrere Fragen gestellt worden:

- Warum benutzt Du CD-ROMs?
- Was gefällt Dir besonders an einer CD-ROM?
- Was ist für Dich bei einer CD-ROM anders als bei einem Buch, bei einem Video oder bei sonstigen Medien?

Erwartungsgemäß fällt es Kindern und Jugendlichen zum Teil recht schwer ihr Medienverhalten zu reflektieren oder zu verbalisieren. Dennoch ergeben sich aus den Antworten in der Gesamtheit eindeutige und verallgemeinerbare Befunde.

Multimedia wird demnach von den meisten Kindern wie Jugendlichen zunächst pauschal - vorrangig oder ausschließlich - als Unterhaltungsmedium gesehen, das Spaß und Zeitvertreib besser zu bieten vermag als alle oder zumindest die meisten anderen Medien:

„Macht halt Spaß." (Realschüler, 11 J.)

„Lustig, nicht so grau." (13-jähriger Junge)

CD-ROMs sind „Tausend mal spannender als ein Buch." (Realschüler, 11 J.)

„Weil sie so toll sind und weil da drin so schöne Sachen vorkommen." (5-Jähriger)

Etwa 40 % der Befragten setzen Multimedia mit Spielprogrammen gleich oder sehen in erster Linie das Spielmedium:

„Gut zum Spielen...abwechslungsreich...spannend."

„Am coolsten sind Spiele so mit 3-D." (10-jähriger Grundschüler)

Spiele auf der CD-ROM, besonders Simulationen, Autofahren oder Flugsimulator, Autorennen oder Sportwettkämpfe wirken auf viele Nutzer authentischer; sie können sich bei den Spielen „abreagieren" (13-jährige Gymnasiastin). Die inszenierte Gewalt wirkt realistisch, wenn man bei einem Eishockey-Spiel die Spieler „gegen die Bande fahren lassen" kann, „dann schlagen sie sich ihre Scheißfressen auf, das sieht man in der Großaufnahme und überall ist Blut zu sehen. Voll geil, ehrlich." (Realschüler, 14 J.)

Bei den PC-Spielen gibt es Erfolgserlebnisse, wer sich anstrengt, kann „sich mit der Zeit immer mehr verbessern und Rekorde aufstellen." „Es gibt verschiedene Level und Schwierigkeitsstufen." Und bei *Tomb Raider* z.B. sieht zudem „die Frau...so geil aus und `s iss superschwierig ins nächste Level zu kommen." (13-jähriger Realschüler)

Ein Drittel der Befragten schätzt, mehr oder minder differenziert ausformuliert, an der CD-ROM besonders Multimedialität und Interaktivität. Multimediaprogramme sind abwechslungs- und variantenreicher, sie bieten durch die Interaktion mit dem Programm „mehr Ebenen und Möglichkeiten als bei anderen Medien", es gibt „mehr Action". Als besonders wichtig wird gesehen, dass man „in das Geschehen eingreifen", „den Handlungsverlauf mitbestimmen", „mit der Maus selbst herumlaufen" oder (bei *TKKG*-Krimis) „den Fall selber lösen" kann. „Man schaut nicht nur zu," sondern „kann Tieren helfen" (10-jähriges Mädchen) und „Tore schießen". „Im Buch geht alles ohne dich, aber im Computer nichts."(11-jähriger Hauptschüler)

Ältere wie Jüngere betonen besonders die kreativen Aspekte des Mediums, „man kann selbst etwas gestalten", z.B. Briefpapier mit *Sailor Moon*-Motiven, man kann bei Spielen selbst aktiv sein oder „selbst etwas bauen" (8-Jähriger), nach Auffassung kleiner Jungen sogar mehr als mit ihren sonstigen Spielzeugen.

Die Möglichkeiten zur Interaktion mit dem Programm, zur Steuerung von Figuren durch ausgestaltete Szenarien können zudem die Intensität der Rezeption verstärken („Man kann Geschichten besser erleben," 12-jähriges Mädchen) oder die Identifikation mit den Figuren (z.B. bei Jungen mit den Action-Helden) erleichtern. Dass die vom Programm vorgegeben Aufgaben oder Spielziele nur durch eigene Aktivität und / oder Kreativität zu lösen oder zu erreichen sind, wirkt motivierend: „Weil es Spaß macht, das Ende zu entdecken." (Realschüler, 13 J.)

20 %, mehrheitlich ältere Kinder und Jugendliche, schätzen Multimedia besonders als Lern- und Informationsmedium. Edutainment- und Infotainment-Programme bieten eine Einheit von Spielen und Lernen, man lernt daher mit Spaß. Bei Lernprogrammen wird man belohnt, wenn man etwas richtig gemacht hat, „außerdem kann man hundert mal nachfragen, wenn man etwas nicht verstanden hat. Bei meinen Lehrern kann ich das nicht, die erklären das zwei oder drei mal höchstens und dann wird man gleich Idiot genannt." (11-Jährige, Gymnasium) Schulbegleitende Lernprogramme „erklären Englisch besser verständlich als die Lehrer", Schulanfänger und Grundschüler ziehen multimediale Lernprogramme ihren Schulbüchern vor, weil sie (z.B. bei *Rayman*) „verschiedene Levels" bieten, dadurch „bleibt" es „spannend und man lernt was."(9-Jährige). Jugendliche nutzen Lernsoftware, „um Lernstoff der Schule zu wiederholen." (15-jähriger Realschüler). Nur in einem Einzelfall wird das Lernen mit der CD-ROM für schwieriger gehalten als das mit Buch: „Man kann sich den Stoff schlechter merken. „ (18-Jährige, Gymnasium)

Vor allem bei älteren Jugendlichen gilt die CD-ROM als komfortables Informationsmedium, das eine besonders schnelle und bequeme Suche nach den benötigten Informationen ermöglicht. „Man muß nicht ewig in einem Buch blättern."

Man kann „wirklich stundenlang die CD-ROM nutzen..., sich sofort zu den Infos über bestimmte Länder oder Städte klicken... Man hat einfach so viele Möglichkeiten. Außerdem ist alles übersichtlich gemacht und Dinge, für die man sich nicht interessiert, kann man schnell überspringen. Beim Buch würde das viel länger dauern und man findet kaum so ein umfangreiches Buch." (17-jährige Gymnasiastin über den *Encarta Weltaltlas*). Von zwei Jugendlichen wird sogar auf kognitive Aspekte hingewiesen, dass nämlich ein Multimedia-Programm eine andere Struktur oder Didaktik der Informationsvermittlung nutzt: „man denkt anders bei der CD-ROM."

Beim Vergleich der CD-ROM mit dem Buch lassen sich die Einschätzungen der Kinder und Jugendlichen in drei etwa gleichgroßen Gruppen zusammenfassen. Am größten ist davon die Gruppe derjenigen, die die CD-ROM für besser halten als das Buch. Vor allem Jungen lesen nicht gern oder allenfalls Comics, was aus neueren Erhebungen ohnehin bekannt ist (Bischof / Heidtmann, 2000). Bücher lesen gilt als anstrengender, „Lesen ist Scheiße" (11 J., Hauptschüler) oder „dauert zwei Tage". Dem Buch fehlt die Interaktivität, „man ist nur passiv", „es gibt keine Action". Bei einer CD-ROM „muß weniger gelesen werden als in einem Buch", es gibt wenig Schrift, mehr Bilder. Die grafische Gestaltung insgesamt sowie grafisch gestaltete Anleitungen und Benutzerführungen werden wiederholt als besonderer Vorteil der CD herausgestellt. Zudem wird dort oft fast alles mündlich erklärt, was besonders kleinere Kinder lieben: „weil die Figuren sprechen" (Mädchen, 5 J.). Der Phantasieaufwand ist bei der Rezeption einer CD-ROM - wie bei anderen visuellen oder audiovisuellen Medien auch - geringer: „Man kann die Figuren sehen, man muß sie sich nicht vorstellen." (11-jährige Gymnasiastin)

Das unterschiedliche Gewicht der Medien wird allerdings nur von einem Realschüler (14 J.) für wichtig gehalten: „Buch ist schwer zum Rumtragen."

Die zweite große Gruppe hält Buch und CD-ROM für „gleich gut, aber irgendwie anders“, denn „beim Lesen muß man die Phantasie anstrengen und beim PC-Spielen nachdenken und lernen“, beides gefällt vorrangig Mädchen (zu den Jungen mit dieser Einschätzung gehört ein überproportionaler Anteil von Waldorfschülern).

Für die dritte, etwas kleinere Gruppe (fast ausschließlich Mädchen im Alter zwischen 10 und 14 Jahren) ist Lesen besser, „weil man sich da alles allein vorstellen kann“, „weil man da nicht verliert“, „nichts machen muß“ und weil man „beim Lesen...nicht so müde wie am PC“ wird. Für diese Mädchen sind Bücher nicht zuletzt deswegen spannender als eine CD-ROM, „da man da über Gefühle lesen kann“ und „weil sie besser Gefühle beschreiben können.“

Im Vergleich mit den AV-Medien schneidet die CD-ROM ähnlich ab. Eine große Gruppe von Jungen und Mädchen findet TV und Video weniger interessant, „schneller langweilig“, empfindet es als weniger angenehm, dass man nur passiv rezipieren kann: „In einem Video kann man nicht eingreifen. Man ist an die Geschichte gebunden.“ (9-Jähriger) Das Medium Video ist „zu nah am Fernsehen“, die „CD-ROM ist neuer“ und damit offenkundig „trendiger“. Für die zweite Gruppe sind Video und CD-ROM „gleich gut“, Videos werden gern genutzt, wenn man „zu müde ist für eine CD-ROM“. Die dritte, kaum kleinere Gruppe, schätzt Videos als angenehmen Zeitvertreib mehr als Multimedia, insbesondere, weil „man nichts tun muß“.

Für einige kleinere Kinder die originelle, an gängigen Cartoonfiguren orientierte Gestaltung der Charaktere, z.B. bei *Fritzi Fisch*, oder die Bekanntheit der Figuren aus dem Medienverbund gewichtige Motivation zur Nutzung einer CD-ROM: „Weil, da ist doch der Benjamin und den kenn‘ ich von den Kassetten.“

Weniger als fünf % der befragten Jungen und Mädchen verweisen auf die kommunikativen und sozialen Aspekte der Multimedianutzung: man kann „mit Freundinnen zusammen spielen“ und mit Freunden oder „es ist super, mit Papi am Computer zu spielen“ (6-Jähriger).

Nutzungsgewohnheiten

Nur 20 % der befragten Kinder und Jugendlichen geben an, dass sie die CD-ROMs gemeinsam mit Freunden oder Geschwistern nutzen, und nur Kinder im Vorschulalter oder darunter spielen zusammen mit den Eltern. Die meisten spielen daheim, überwiegend allein am PC, jüngere Kinder am Nachmittag, die älteren eher abends. Ein Drittel der Befragten nutzt CD-ROMs auch in der Bibliothek, wer zuhause keinen PC hat, spielt manchmal ausschließlich dort.

Gerade in einer einzigen Schule (Stuttgart-Vaihingen) können Kinder Spiele oder Edutainment-Programme außerhalb des Unterrichts an Schul-PCs nutzen. In den meisten Schulen finden Multimedia-Programme jedoch weder im noch außerhalb des Unterrichtes regelmäßig Verwendung. Etwa ein Drittel der Befragten gibt sogar an, dass sie für den Schulunterricht keine Multimedia-PCs zur Verfügung stehen haben, dass CD-ROMs im Unterricht nie verwendet werden. Ein weiteres Drittel sagt, dass an ihren Schulen PCs mit entsprechender Software zur Verfügung stehen, dass aber nur sehr oder zu wenige vorhanden und auch diese nur eingeschränkt, häufig „nur für höhere Klassen“ nutzbar seien. „Wir haben einen Computer im Klassenzimmer, da fehlen allerdings die Lautsprecher und er steht nur herum.“ (Grundschüler, 9 Jahre) An einigen Hauptschulen werden PCs gerade zum Schreiben von Diktaten genutzt, an Realschulen lediglich zur Einführung in den Umgang mit einer Textverarbeitung.

Allenfalls für das letzte Drittel, vor allem an Realschulen und an der gymnasialen Oberstufe, findet regelmäßig IT-Unterricht statt, werden Internet- oder IT-AGs angeboten, ist der Umgang mit Multimedia schon weitergehender in den Unterricht integriert. Und lediglich eine Grundschule (2. Klasse, Heilbronn) hat für jedes Klassenzimmer zwei Computer, an denen täglich einige Kinder während des Unterrichtes arbeiten, während gleichzeitig die restlichen Schüler mit anderen Arbeiten befasst sind.

Resümee

Selbst wenn kleine Bibliotheken gelegentlich noch keine Software für Kinder oder nur sehr kleine Bestände bieten können, so sind Multimediaprogramme mittlerweile fast überall akzeptiert und vorhanden. Multimedia hat sich damit wesentlich schneller und umfassender als die bisherigen neuen Medien in den bundesdeutschen Kinder- und Jugendbibliotheken durchgesetzt. Die Ursachen hierfür liegen zum einen darin, dass sich die CD-ROM als digitales Trägermedium für Datenbanken (Bibliographien u.ä.) vielerorts in den Bibliotheken bereits bewährt hatte. Zum anderen verknüpfen Multimedia-Anwendungen alte und neue Medien mit einander, nutzen Schrift und Standbilder, arbeiten mit Texten, sind also näher an den Printmedien als die audiovisuellen Medien. Und nicht zuletzt findet auch an Öffentlichen Bibliotheken ein kontinuierlicher Generationswandel statt, jüngere Mitarbeiterinnen sind selbst medial anders sozialisiert, haben sich während des Studiums mit audiovisuellen wie mit digitalen Medien auseinandergesetzt, haben in Seminarprojekten - nicht nur an der HBI, Stuttgart - die Leistungsfähigkeit von Multimediaprogrammen oder die Einsetzbarkeit interaktiver Medien in der Bibliotheksarbeit mit Kindern erprobt.

CD-ROMs sind gegenwärtig das beliebteste, das am stärksten nachgefragte und sich am schnellsten umsetzende Kinder- und Jugendmedium. Das hängt zwar auch damit zusammen, dass das Medium noch relativ neu ist, dass die Bestände im Regelfall kleiner sind als bei den traditionellen Medien sind. Die Attraktivität von Multimediaanwendungen liegt aber besonders in ihren medienspezifischen Leistungsmöglichkeiten begründet, die von Kindern wahrgenommen und entsprechend geschätzt wird. Programme reagieren auf Anweisungen, die jungen Nutzer können in Interaktion treten, Handlungsverläufe ändern, Figuren führen, selbst Aufgaben lösen. Multimedia verlangt Aktivität und Kreativität, fördert die Individualität von Rezeptionsprozessen, entspricht damit auch hochgradig der Segmentierung von Medieninteressen bei den nachwachsenden Generationen.

CD-ROMs können Bücher nicht ersetzen oder verdrängen, aber sie können bestimmte Funktionen von anderen Medien substituieren. Wünsche nach Aktion, nach abwechslungsreicher Unterhaltung, nach möglichst enger Einbindung des Rezipienten in das Geschehen werden zunehmend durch Computerspiele, Spielprogramme oder Spielgeschichten befriedigt. Diese arbeiten mit vergleichbaren narrativen Strukturen wie die erzählende Literatur, sind aber attraktiver, weil der Gang der Narration beeinflusst und gesteuert werden kann. Kinder und Jugendliche nutzen jedoch gleichzeitig die traditionellen Erzählmedien weiter, denn spezifische Funktionen der Erzählliteratur, wie z.B. Gefühle, innere Bewegung, Beziehungen einfühlsam auszugestalten, können über Multimediaprogramme nicht in vergleichbarer Weise rzipiert werden. PC-Programme bieten zwar mehr Eigenbeteiligung, fordern aber auch mehr Engagement des Nutzers, sind oft anstrengender zu rezipieren. Video und andere filmische Medien gestatten unaufwendigere, eher passive Formen der Rezeption von Geschichten. Kinder und jugendliche nutzen heute mehrheitlich differenziert und situationsbezogen das Spektrum aller zur Verfügung stehenden Medien.

Computerspiele im engeren wie im weiteren Sinne sind auch bei jugendlichen Bibliotheksbenutzern die bevorzugte Gattung. Spielesoftware wird jedoch beim Bestandsaufbau nicht hinreichend berücksichtigt oder sogar von Bibliotheksmitarbeiterinnen mancherorts als seichte Unterhaltung abgelehnt. Hier hat sich vielleicht die vor Jahrzehnten kultivierte „untere Grenze" für „bibliotheksgeeignete" Kinderbücher auf ein neues Medium verlagert. Unübersehbar ist zumindest die Diskrepanz zwischen den Ausleihcharts, den in den Bibliotheken am meisten ausgeliehenen und am intensivsten genutzten Titeln und Gattungen auf der einen Seite, und den bei Kindern und Jugendlichen bevorzugten Gattungen, den tatsächlich beliebtesten und meistgewünschten Titeln auf der anderen Seite. Wenn aktuelle Spielesoftware oder populäre Spiele nicht im Bestand vorhanden sind, wählen sich Kinder oder Jugendliche notgedrungen andere Programme mit spielerischen Komponenten aus, Edutainment oder Lernspiele.

Kinder- und Jugendmedien vernetzen sich immer enger mit den Popularmedien für Erwachsene. Für Spielsoftware lassen sich keine strikten Trennungen zwischen Kinder-, Jugend- und Erwachsenentiteln aufrecht halten. Kinder greifen - wie auch bei den AV-Medien - immer früher auf bisherige Jugendthemen zu, Jugendliche rezipieren immer früher Erwachsenthemen und -formate. Kinder- und Jugendbibliotheken sollten auf die zentrale Bedeutung von Computerspielen im Medienalltag ihrer Kunden reagieren, sollten vermehrt (aktuelle) Spielesoftware in ihre Multimediabestände integrieren. Das Marktangebot ist keineswegs mehr von gewaltverherrlichenden oder sexistischen Titeln geprägt, es gibt etliche Institutionen, die Spielesoftware sichten und empfehlen, auch die Annotationsdienste der ekz befassen sich differenziert mit Spielenovitäten. Kinder- und Jugendliche, die sich für Computerspiele begeistern, werden in ihren Belangen von Öffentlichen Bibliotheken unzureichend berücksichtigt. Sie müssen auf andere Institutionen ausweichen, bleiben aus der Bibliothek weg.

Bibliotheken sollten aber auch ihren gesellschaftlichen Aufgaben, wie der Sicherung des Zugangs zu Bildung und Information nachkommen. Obwohl bei einer Befragung jugendlicher BibliotheksbenutzerInnen überproportional besser gebildete Kinder aus den Mittelschichten erreicht werden, so bestätigen sich in den IfaK-Befragungen die aktuellen Warnungen der Wissenskluft-Forschung (GMK, 1999): eine große Gruppe von Kindern und Jugendlichen nutzt Medien ausschließlich zur Unterhaltung, eine andere Gruppe nutzt CD-ROMs als Lernmedien und Informationsträger. Kinder- und Jugendbibliotheken sollten beide Möglichkeiten des Leistungsspektrums von Multimedia berücksichtigen, auch für vorrangig an Unterhaltung Interessierte problemlose Zugriffsmöglichkeiten auf Bildung und Information bereit stellen, den eher Bildungsbeflissenen intelligent konzipierte Spielesoftware bieten.

Die Umfrage zeigt zudem am Rande, dass geschlechtsspezifische Sozialisationsmuster bei der Nutzung neuer Medien tradiert werden, vorrangig wohl vom Elternhaus gefördert. Kleinere Mädchen gehen heute offen und interessiert mit Computermedien um, nutzen kompetent Multimediaanwendungen. Ältere distanzieren sich wieder vom Medium. Es fehlen Programme mit positiven, weiblichen Identifikationsfiguren, es fehlen die spezifischen Stoffe und Themen, die Kinder- und Jugendbibliotheken für Mädchen mit Selbstverständlichkeit in ihren Jugendliteratur- oder Videobeständen offerieren.

Auch wenn die Haushaltsausstattung mit Computerhardware schneller voran schreitet als den aktuellen Statistiken zu entnehmen ist, haben immerhin noch 10 % der Jungen und Mädchen im familiären Umfeld keinen Zugang zu PCs. Und selbst dort, wo in den Familien mehrere Rechner genutzt werden können, fehlt es an kindgerechter Software. Insgesamt ein Drittel der befragten Kinder und Jugendlichen nutzt die Möglichkeit, in der Bibliothek Multimediaprogramme einsehen oder durchspielen zu können, ein größerer Anteil würde gern davon Gebrauch machen. Kinderbibliotheken sollten nicht zuletzt deswegen mehr PC-Arbeitsplätze anbieten, weil diese offenkundig in den Schulen immer noch nicht bereit gestellt werden können.

Literatur:

Bischof, Ulrike u. Horst Heidtmann (2000): „Warum sind Film- und Fernsehbücher so erfolgreich? Das Ifak forscht zur Kinder- und Jugendliteratur im Medienverbund“, in: Buch und Bibliothek H. 6/7, 2000, S. 414-417.

Egmont Ehapa Verlag (Hg.) (2000): Kids Verbraucher Analyse KVA 2000. Junge Zielgruppen 6 bis 17 Jahre, Stuttgart.

GMK Gesellschaft für Medienpädagogik und Kommunikationskultur (Hg.) (1999): Mediengesellschaft - neue ‚Klassengesellschaft‘? Medienpädagogik und sozio-kulturelle Unterschiede, Bielefeld (= Themen. Rundbrief Nr. 42, Redaktion: Ulrike Bischof).

Heidtmann, Horst (1989): „Überlegungen zur Bibliotheksarbeit für Jugendliche“, in: Informationen Jugendliteratur und Medien H. 4, S. 170-179.

Heidtmann, Horst (1995): „Multimedia für Kids“, in: Arbeitskreis für Jugendliteratur (Hg.): Das Buch der Jugend 1995-1996, München 1995, S.4-5.

Heidtmann, Horst (1996, A): Kinder- und Jugendliteratur multimedial und interaktiv. Multimedia-Anwendungen auf CD-ROM (= Beiträge Jugendliteratur und Medien, 7. Beiheft), Weinheim.

Heidtmann, Horst (1996, B): „Bibi, Pippi, Benjamin - die Medienfreunde der Kinder. Ergebnisse einer Umfrage an Bibliotheken“, in: Buch und Bibliothek H. 6/7, 1996, S.554-556.

Heidtmann, Horst (2000): „Der Videomarkt für Kinder. Angebote - Nutzung - Perspektiven“, in: Kinder- und Jugendfilmzentrum in Deutschland/StadtBibliothek Köln (Hg.): KiViF special. Die Videothek für Kinder und Jugendliche. Erfahrungen aus einem Modellversuch, Köln 2000, S. 8-13.

Heidtmann, Horst u. Manfred Nagl (1995): „‚Nütze die Jugend nicht: sie vergeht!‘ Öffentliche Bibliotheken, Jugendkultur und Jugendbibliotheksarbeit“, in: Buch und Bibliothek H. 6, 1995, S. 562-569.

König, Johann-Günther (1986): Institutionen für fiktive Adressaten. Zur Funktion der Kinder- und Jugendbibliotheken im Kommunikationsprozeß, Bad Honnef.

Negroponte, Nicholas: Total digital. Die Welt zwischen 0 und I oder Die Zukunft der Kommunikation, München 1997 (überarbeitete Taschenbuchausg.)

Schmitt, Rita (1999): „Angebote für Kinder und Jugendliche in Öffentlichen Bibliotheken. Eine Bestandsaufnahme“, in: Giraffe. Bibliotheken für Kinder und Jugendliche im Blick H. 1, 1999, S. 20-24.

Konrad Umlauf

Die Warengruppen-Systematik des Buchhandels

Abstract

Die Warengruppen-Systematik des Buchhandels wird auf dem Hintergrund der bibliothekarischen Beschäftigung mit dem Thema Sacherschließung in den Zusammenhang der Erschließung durch Klassifikationen versus verbaler Sacherschließung gestellt. Sie wird strukturell und ihrer Funktion für den Buchhandel sowie hinsichtlich möglicher Anwendungen in Bibliotheken analysiert. Mängel der gegenwärtigen Anwendung auf der VLB-CD-ROM werden aufgezeigt und Lösungswege angesprochen.

Einleitung

Nach dem Scheitern der Einheitsklassifikation in den 70er-Jahren des vorigen Jahrhunderts[222] stand die Beschlagwortung im Mittelpunkt des bibliothekarischen Interesses am Thema Sacherschließung. Klassifikationen wurden als Instrument der Freihandaufstellung angesehen, bei der man fast ein Vierteljahrhundert lang meinte, mit unbefriedigenden und uneinheitlichen Lösungen leben zu können. Zwischen der akademischen Beschäftigung mit der klassifikatorischen Sacherschließung[223] und der Praxis der Bibliotheken klaffte eine beträchtliche Lücke.

Erst in den 90er-Jahren gewann das Thema Klassifikation eine neue Bedeutung. 1994 wurde gefordert, dass die verbale Sacherschließung in Online-Katalogen durch eine klassifikatorische Erschließung ergänzt werden solle.[224] Wo sie angeboten wird, nehmen die Nutzer sie allerdings kaum zur Kenntnis: Nach einer Untersuchung Andreas Zartls[225] an Wiener wissenschaftlichen Bibliotheken erfolgt die Recherche in OPACs außerordentlich selten mithilfe der Notation. Allerdings erfordert eine klassifikatorische Recherche in den untersuchten OPACs die Eingabe der Notation.

Nur sehr komfortable Lösungen, wie sie etwa mit der Online-Fassung der RVK (Regensburger Verbundklassifikation[226]) angeboten werden - wenn auch noch ohne Verknüpfung mit dem online verfügbaren Register – scheinen in der Lage zu sein, für Nutzer wirklich attraktiv zu werden: Über die Stichwortsuche in Klassenbeschreibungen kommt der Nutzer in die Klassifikation, kann sich dort voran- und schließlich zu den Titeln einer Klasse weiterklicken.

In den 90er-Jahren wurden einige in Öffentlichen Bibliotheken mehr oder minder ver-

---

222 Einheitsklassifikation : die Geschichte einer fortwirkenden Idee / Armin Müller-Dreier. - Wiesbaden : Harrassowitz, 1994. - (Beiträge zum Buch- und Bibliothekswesen; Bd. 35)

223 Beispielsweise: Einführung in die Inhaltserschließung (1990). 3. Aufl. Begr. von Winfried Gödert, bearb. von Holger Nohr. Hamburg: Fachhochschule, FB Bibl.wes. (Materialien zur Inhaltserschließung, H. 1) - Einführung in die Inhaltserschließung (1990). 3. Aufl. Begr. von Winfried Gödert, bearb. von Holger Nohr. Hamburg: Fachhochschule, FB Bibl.wes. (Materialien zur Inhaltserschließung, H. 1)

224 Sacherschließung in Online-Katalogen (1994). Berlin: Dt. Bibliotheksinstitut (Dbi-Materialien. 132).

225 http://info.uibk.ac.at/sci-org/voeb/za.html.

226 http://www.bibliothek.uni-regensburg.de/Systematik/rvk_onl.htm.

breitete Klassifikationen, u.a. die SfB (Systematik für Bibliotheken[227]) und die ASB (Allgemeine Systematik für Bibliotheken[228]) aktualisiert. Demnächst soll die KAB (Klassifikation für Allgemeinbibliotheken[229]) modernisiert, vor allem in einigen Bereichen, z.B. beim Thema EDV, differenziert werden. Handlungsbedarf auch für Klassifikationen in Universitätsbibliotheken wurde ebenfalls festgestellt.[230] Dies mündete Ende der 90er-Jahre in Überlegungen zur Anwendung der DDC (Dewey Decimal Classification[231]) in Verbundkatalogen. Im März 2000 hat die Arbeitsgruppe Klassifikatorische Erschließung der Konferenz für Regelwerksfragen eine Machbarkeitsstudie[232] vorgelegt, in der die Voraussetzungen und Möglichkeiten einer Anwendung der DDC in Deutschland, Österreich und der Schweiz erörtert und ihre Anwendung im deutschen Sprachraum empfohlen werden. Die Bedingungen, auch in Hinsicht der erforderlichen Ressourcen und der Arbeitsschritte, werden in der Machbarkeitsstudie genannt. Im Rahmen des Bezugs von Fremddaten aus USA und Großbritannien sind bereits jetzt in den deutschen Verbünden Titeldaten mit DDC-Notationen vorhanden, allerdings i.d.R. nicht nach den Notationen recherchierbar.

In der Informationswissenschaft und –praxis weitete sich das Thema Klassifikation zur Entwicklung von Systemen des Wissensmanagements.[233]

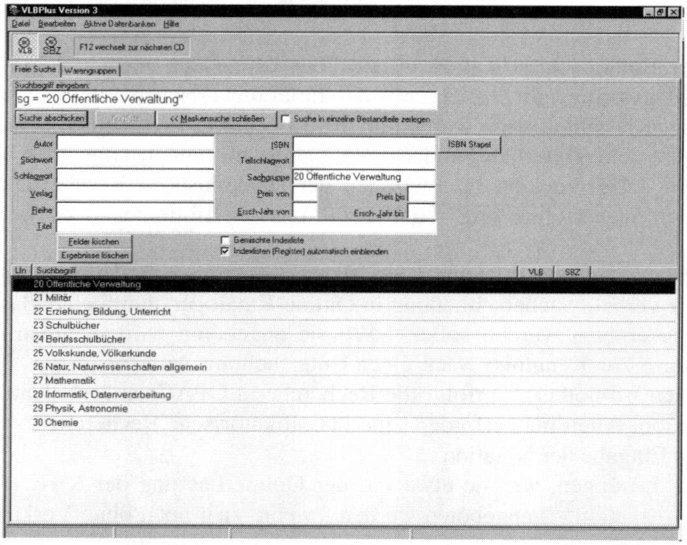

Abbildung 1: Ausschnitt aus den Sachgruppen des VLB

227 Systematik für Bibliotheken SfB (1997). München: Saur.

228 Allgemeine Systematik für Öffentliche Bibliotheken ASB (1999). Ausg. 1999. Berlin: Dt. Bibliotheksinst. - Umlauf (2000a), Konrad: Zur ASB 1999. Allgemeine Systematik für Öffentliche Bibliotheken, Grundsätze, Strukturmerkmale, Umklassifizieren. Berlin: Institut für Bibliothekswissenschaft der Humboldt-Universität zu Berlin (Berliner Handreichungen zur Bibliothekswissenschaft. 77) = http://www.ib.hu-berlin.de/~kumlau/handreichungen/h77/.

229 Klassifikation für Allgemeinbibliotheken KAB (1993). Sachliteratur und Belletristik (KAB/E). Berlin: Dt. Bibliotheksinst.

230 Klassifikationen für wissenschaftliche Bibliotheken. Berlin: Dt. Bibliotheksinstitut (Dbi-Materialien. 175).

231 Dewey, Melvil (1996): Dewey Decimal Classification and relative Index. Ed. 21. Albany, N.Y.: Forest Press.

232 http://www.ddb.de/aktuell/fachforum/machbarkeit.pdf.

233 Classification, data analysis and data highways (1998).. Balderjahn, Ingo ...(eds.) Berlin: Springer (Proceedings of the ... Annual Conference of the Gesellschaft für Klassifikation. 21).

Interessanterweise vollzog sich eine in manchen Punkten ähnliche Entwicklung in Buchhandelsdatenbanken. Auch dort setzte man lange Zeit auf die verbale Sacherschließung. Erst Ende der 90er-Jahre wurde dem eine differenzierte klassifikatorische Sacherschließung zur Seite gestellt, wenn man von der rudimentären Erschließung durch Zuordnung der Titel zu 66 mehr oder minder breiten, gleichgeordneten Sachgruppen des VLB (Ausschnitt siehe Abbildung 1) absieht.

Im Folgenden soll die Warengruppen-Systematik des Buchhandels, wie sie auf der VLB-CD-ROM angeboten wird, dargestellt und erörtert werden.

1. Die Warengruppen-Systematik des Buchhandels

1.1 In welchem Zusammenhang steht die Warengruppen-Systematik?

Die Kenntnis der Waren des Buchhandels steht im Mittelpunkt der buchhändlerischen Qualifikation. Sie ist gewissermaßen die eine Hälfte der Beratungskompetenz. Die andere Hälfte der buchhändlerischen Beratungskompetenz besteht in der Kenntnis der Kundschaft und der Fähigkeit, in der richtigen Weise auf die Kunden ein- und zuzugehen. Der Sortimentsbuchhandel vermittelt zwischen dem Warenangebot und den Kundenwünschen. Darüber hinaus erfordert ein erfolgreiches Handeln des Buchhändlers/der Buchhändlerin auch betriebswirtschaftliche Kompetenz und spezielle Branchenkenntnisse.

Weitere zentrale Erfolgsbedingungen für den Sortimentsbuchhandel sind:
- vor allem ein individuelles Profil und unverwechselbares Gesicht, damit die Kunden motiviert werden, nicht irgendwo oder über anonyme Großversandhandlungen zu kaufen, sondern gerade in einer bestimmten, ihren Interessen und Wünschen angepassten Sortimentsbuchhandlung,
- kompromisslos guter Service, denn zufriedene Kunden sind treue Kunden,
- höchste Beratungskompetenz, denn die Informationsmöglichkeiten der Kunden über Internet und aus Zeitschriften sind heute so umfassend, aber auch so verwirrend vielfältig wie nie zuvor,
- eine wirtschaftlich außerordentlich effiziente, konsequent auf die Kundenwünsche ausgerichtete Betriebsführung, denn nur so sind Service und permanente Weiterbildung für das Personal finanzierbar.

Es kommt maßgeblich darauf an, eine Brücke zwischen diesen beiden Zielbereichen – individuelles Profil sowie guter Service einerseits und wirtschaftliche Betriebsführung andererseits - zu bauen. Das scheint kaum möglich zu sein, denn eine wesentliche Quelle wirtschaftlicher Betriebsführung sind Konfektionierung und Standardisierung statt stets erneuter Einzelfallbehandlung und individueller Bearbeitung.

1.2 Was ist die Warengruppengruppen-Systematik?

Die Warengruppen-Systematik des Buchhandels ist ein Baustein für diese Brücke: Ein individuelles Profil und unverwechselbares Gesicht werden aus flexibel verwendbaren, konfektionierten Elementen aufgebaut.

Die Warengruppen-Systematik gruppiert die Waren des Buchhandels (Bücher, CD-ROMs, Hörbücher u.v.a.m.) unter Gesichtspunkten
- des Inhalts, des Themas, z.B. Kunstgeschichte oder Thermodynamik,
- der Zielgruppe und des Verwendungszwecks, z.B. Lernhilfen / Abiturwissen oder Bilderbücher,

- der Darstellungsform, z.B. Nachschlagewerke oder Bildbände,
- der Editionsform, z.B. Taschenbuch oder Video.

Damit macht die Warengruppen-Systematik die Orientierung in der Warenfülle unter den Gesichtspunkten möglich, die den Fragestellungen der Kunden entsprechen.

Sie wurde entwickelt von den Barsortimenten *Georg Lingenbrinck, Koch, Neff & Oetinger* sowie *Koehler & Volckmar* und ist abgestimmt mit den Barsortimenten *Könemann, Umbreit* und *Wehling*.
Die Barsortimente ordnen jeden Titel, den sie in ihr Programm aufnehmen, einer Warengruppe zu. Die Warengruppenziffer ist auf der VLB-CD-ROM sowie auf den Barsortiments-CD-ROMs enthalten und wird auf den Klebeetiketten, mit denen die Barsortimente die ausgelieferte Ware versehen, ausgedruckt. Die Beschränkung der Warengruppenzuordnung auf Barsortimentstitel ist nicht von Nachteil, denn andere Titel werden im Großen und Ganzen aufgrund genauer Angaben des Kunden bestellt, wobei die Warengruppenzuordnung keine Funktion hätte. Freilich ist gegenwärtig die Zuordnung etlicher Themen und Titel zu den Warenuntergruppen noch nicht ganz einheitlich. So kommt es wiederholt vor, dass die Hardcover-Ausgabe eines Titels einer anderen Warenuntergruppe zugeordnet ist als die Taschenbuch-Ausgabe desselben Titels. Das ist zur Zeit noch nicht optimal, fällt aber nicht so störend ins Gewicht, dass die Anwendung der Warengruppen-Systematik sinnlos würde. Im Kapitel 4 werden diese Mängel vertieft anhand von Beispielen dargestellt.

Im Einzelnen ist die Warengruppenziffer folgendermaßen aufgebaut:

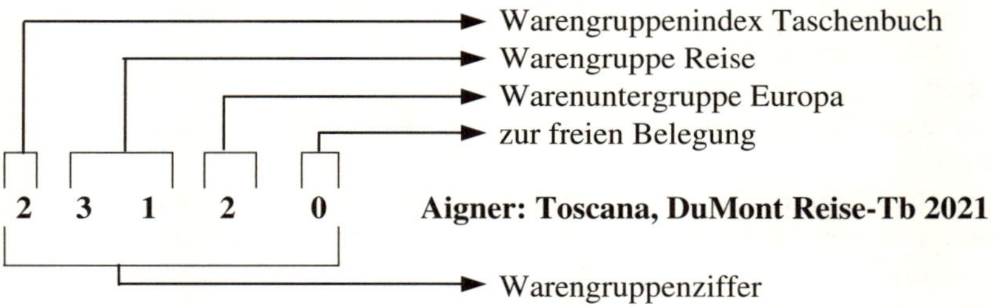

Der Warengruppenindex steht am Anfang der Warengruppenziffer, kann aber je nach Warenwirtschaftssystem der einzelnen Sortimentsbuchhandlung auch an die letzte Stelle gerückt werden.

1.3 Wie wird die Warengruppengruppen-Systematik verwendet?

Die Warengruppe ist als sekundäres Merkmal recherchierbar und verbessert wesentlich die Qualität der Recherche auf den bibliografischen CD-ROMs. Sie wird angezeigt, nachdem die sekundäre Recherche nach Warengruppen erfolgte. Wenn ohne Warengruppe recherchiert wurde, wird diese auch nicht angezeigt.

Die Abbildungen 2 und 3 zeigen das Vorgehen am Beispiel der Suche nach Toskana-Reiseführern: Mit dem Stich-/Schlagwort tos?an* findet man 324 Treffer (VLBPlus-CD-ROM, Ausgabe August 2000); mit Hilfe der Warengruppe als sekundärem Suchmerkmal stellt man fest, dass 56 davon Reiseführer sind. Man erspart sich also das Durchmustern einer großen Zahl von nicht in Frage kommenden Titeln. Demselben Kunden kann der Buchhändler gleich gezielt einen Krimi für sein Urlaubsgebiet empfehlen (Abbildung 4).

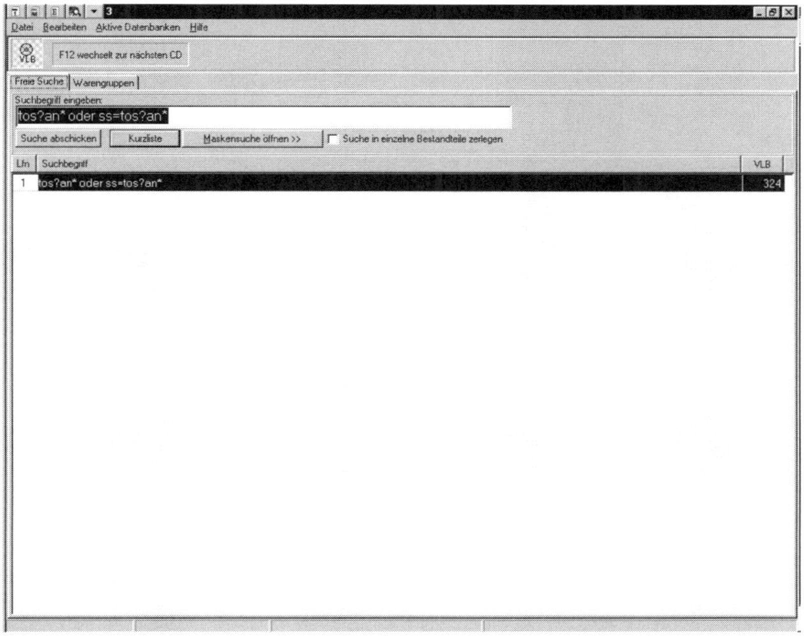

Abbildung 2: Suche auf der VLBPlus-CD-ROM mit Stich-/Schlagwort

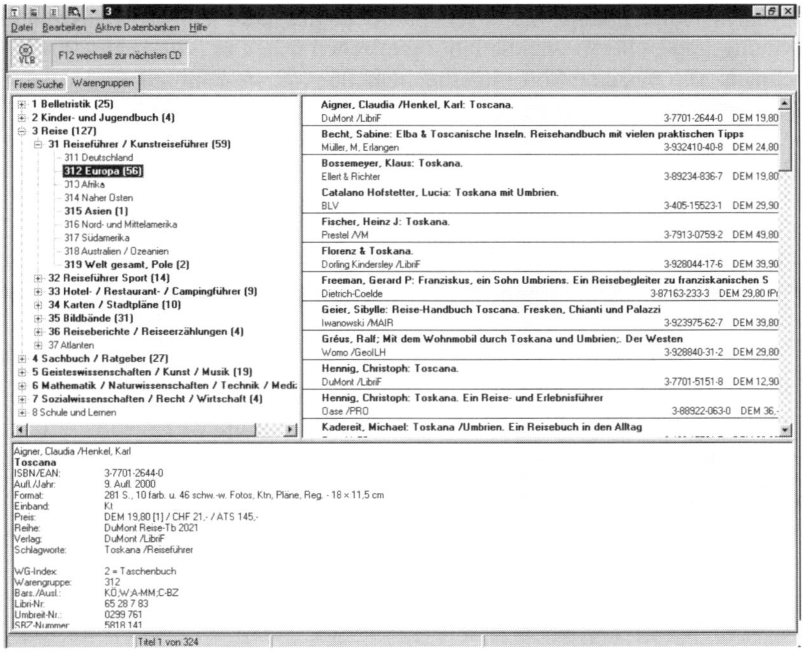

Abbildung 3: Sekundäre Suche anhand der Warengruppe *31 Reiseführer*

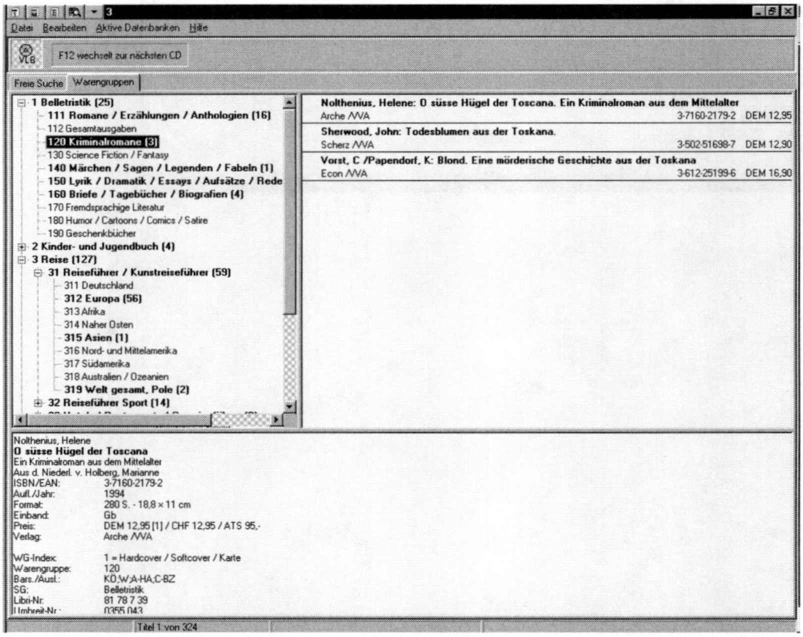

Abbildung 4: Sekundäre Suche anhand der Warengruppe. *120 Kriminalromane*

Die Sortimentsbuchhandlung kann die Warengruppenziffer oder einzelne Bestandteile, z.B. nur die Warengruppe, ebenso wie die bibliografischen Daten in ihr Warenwirtschaftssystem übernehmen. Die einzelne Sortimentsbuchhandlung kann dann auf Basis der Warengruppen-Systematik

- in der Kundenberatung eine sonst nicht mögliche Transparenz des Warenlagers erreichen,
- die Entwicklung ihres Lagers unter vielfältigen Gesichtspunkten beobachten, z.B. das Warenlager und den Umsatz nach einzelnen Warengruppen genau feststellen,
- auf dieser Grundlage gezielt Lagerergänzungen bzw. Remissionen vornehmen
- und den weiteren Ausbau des Lagers effizient steuern,
- ferner sehr leicht entscheiden, an welcher Stelle des eigenen Lagers neue Titel präsentiert werden können.

1.4 Warengruppengruppen-Systematik und Lagerpräsentation

Das Lager der Sortimentsbuchhandlung könnte wie die Warengruppen-Systematik gegliedert sein. Das hätte einige Vorteile:

Klarer und logischer Aufbau des Warenlagers.

- Leichte Orientierung für die Kunden und für das Buchhandelspersonal. Insbesondere kurzfristig beschäftigten Hilfskräften fällt es leicht, die neu gelieferte Ware anhand der Warengruppe, die auf dem vom Lieferanten mitgelieferten Etikett ersichtlich ist, an der richtigen Stelle ins Regal zu stellen.

Die Nachteile überwiegen aber:

- Die an sich klare und logische Abfolge der Warengruppen im Ladengeschäft ist nur für den nachvollziehbar, der die ganze Warengruppen-Systematik überblickt. Die meisten Kunden tun das nicht und interessieren sich nur für bestimmte Themen, nicht für das ganze Themenspektrum.

- Andere Gesichtspunkte als die Warengruppen-Systematik müssten bei der Warenpräsentation unberücksichtigt bleiben, beispielsweise die Intensität der Nachfrage oder jahreszeitlich schwankende Nachfragen.
- Eine Raumgliederung würde nur einen Sinn machen, wenn die neun Warengruppen ungefähr gleich stark vertreten würden. Das ist im Allgemeine Sortiment meistens nicht so. Kleine Warengruppen würden zwischen mit vielen Titeln vertretenen Warengruppen untergehen.
- Vor allem würde eine strikt an der Warengruppen-Systematik orientierte Aufbau des Ladengeschäfts die Chance verschenken, Titel, Themen und Artikel gemeinsam zu präsentieren, die in der Erwartung der Kunden zusammengehören (beispielsweise Toskana-Reiseführer und Krimis, die in der Toskana spielen), die aber nach der Systematik in verschiedene Warengruppen gehören.
- Ein individuelles Erscheinungsbild der Sortimentsbuchhandlung wäre nur noch begrenzt möglich – aber gerade der individuelle Auftritt ist eine der wichtigsten Strategien im Konkurrenzkampf.

Im Ergebnis soll betont werden: Die Warengruppen-Systematik ist ein wertvolles Instrument bei der Recherche und bei der Sortimentspflege – für die Sortimentspräsentation ist sie nur hinsichtlich der Zuordnung neuer Titel zu der eigenen Gliederung des Lagers hilfreich.

Sie ist aus denselben Gründen auch für kleinere Öffentliche Bibliotheken bis zu einem Bestand von etwa 30.000 Medieneinheiten anwendbar, aber dort sollte man wohl eine Klassifikation bevorzugen, für die man qualifizierte klassifikatorische Fremddaten bekommt, also die ASB, die SfB oder die KAB, auch wenn diese für kleine Öffentliche Bibliotheken in Teilen zu differenziert zu schein scheinen. Aber sind nicht auch klassifikatorische Fremddaten nach der Warengruppen-Systematik erhältlich? So wie die ekz.bibliotheksservice GmbH für die Bibliotheken klassifiziert, so klassifizieren die Barsortimente für ihre Kunden, die Buchhandlungen – und Bibliotheken könnten diese Daten ebenso übernehmen und auf Signaturschildern und an der Regalbeschilderung anbringen. Darauf ist im Kapitel 4 einzugehen.

2. Strukturmerkmale der Warengruppen-Systematik

Klassifikationstheoretisch stellt sich die Warengruppen-Systematik des Buchhandels als eine Mischung von Klassifikationen dar, die an Wissenschaftssystematiken orientiert sind – bibliothekarische Beispiele sind die RVK und die DDC –, und Klassifikationen vom Typ Reader Interest Classfication[234].

Der Umfang beträgt etwa 1.000 Klassen. Die Klassenbenennungen sind knapp, Klassenerläuterungen fehlen. Freilich haben die Barsortimente der gedruckten Fassung der Warengruppen-Systematik ein Register beigegeben, das etwa 3.400 Eintragungen umfasst. Zum Vergleich: Das gedruckte Register zur ASB 1999 hat einen Umfang von ca. 18.000 Eintragungen. Die Notationen der Warengruppen-Systematik sind hierarchieabbildend und

[234] Umlauf (1989), Konrad: Angebotspräsentation und Aufstellungssystematik in der Öffentlichen Bibliothek. In: Das Buch in Praxis und Wissenschaft. Hrsg. von Peter Vodosek. Wiesbaden: Harrassowitz (Buchwissenschaftliche Beiträge aus dem Deutschen Bucharchiv München. Bd. 25), S. 512-540.

bestehen aus einer dreistelligen Zahl, die um den Warengruppen-Index sowie um eine fünfte Stelle ergänzt wird, die der einzelnen Buchhandlung eine Untergliederung der Warenuntergruppen erlauben soll.

Freilich unterscheidet sich naturgemäß jede Medienklassifikation von Wissenschaftssystematiken, weil ihr Bezugspunkt nicht Wissen, sondern in Form von Medien publiziertes Wissen, publizierter kultureller Ausdruck usw. ist. In der Hierarchie der Entitäten von Dokumenten gemäß den *Functional requirements for bibliographic records* der IFLA arbeiten Medienklassifikationen, wie sie in Bibliotheken traditionell zur Anwendung kommen, auf der Ebene der *expressions*:

Entität	*Beispiel*
Work: a distinct intellectual or artistic creation	Beethovens Sinfonie Nr. 1 in C-Dur
Expression: the intellectual or artistic realization of a work in the form of alpha-numeric, musical, or choreographic notation, sound, image, object, movement, etc., or any combinations of such forms	Der Mitschnitt der Aufführung von Beethovens Sinfonie Nr. 1 in C-Dur, gespielt von den London Classical Players mit Norrington, Roger (Dir.), London 1987
Manifestation: the physical embodiment of an expression of a work	Beethovens Sinfonie Nr. 1 in C-Dur, gespielt von den London Classical Players mit Norrington, Roger (Dir.), London 1987, auf CD von EMI-Electrola 1992
Item: a single exemplare of a manifestation	Das Exemplar mit der Zugangsnummer 92/12345 im Deutschen Musikarchiv Berlin

Dieser Aspekt wird mit Hilfe des Warengruppenindex abgebildet; diese Kennziffer steht am Anfang der Warengruppenziffer und kennzeichnet die Editionsform (so die Terminologie der Warengruppen-Systematik):

1 Hardcover / Softcover / Karte
2 Taschenbuch
3 Zeitschrift
4 Video
5 Audio CD / Cassette (Literatur / Musik / Sprache)
6 CD-ROM / Diskette (Software)
7 Kalender
Im Sortimentsbuchhandel dominieren

Wandkalender mit Bindung am oberen Rand und
Buchkalender mit Bindung am linken Rand,
die mehr als das Kalendarium und Raum für Eintragungen (Nutzkalendarium) enthalten, etwa Bilder, Sprüche, Textauszüge. Aber es gibt nahezu unendlich viele Kalenderformen bis hin zu Mousepad-Kalendern und Kalendern auf CD-ROM oder in Form einer Audio-CD. Weitere Kalenderformen werden vor allem über den Schreibwarenhandel, ggf. auch im PBS-Bereich von Buchhandlungen (Papier, Bürobedarf, Schreibwaren) geführt, der insbesondere bei kleineren Buchhandlungen ein wichtiges wirtschaftliches Standbein darstellt: Abreißkalender, Adresskalender, Arbeitskalender, Notizkalender, Querterminer, Schreibtischkalender, Steckkalender, Taschenkalender, Terminkalender,

Terminplaner, Umlegekalender, Umsteckkalender, Vormerkkalender.

8 Nonbook / PBS
Nonbook als Bezeichnung für diesen Warengruppenindex ist zwar prägnant, aber auch ungenau, denn bestimmte Nonbooks wie Audio-CDs oder Zeitschriften sind hier nicht gemeint. PBS ist die Abkürzung für Papier, Bürobedarf, Schreibwaren. Der Warengruppenindex soll auch Waren, die gar keine Medien sind, klassifizieren. Der Warengruppenindex *8 Nonbook / PBS* umfasst im Sortimentsbuchhandel vor allem:
- Arbeitstransparente (bedruckte Overheadfolien),
- Bildpostkarten,
- Diaserien,
- Geschenkartikel,
- Gesellschaftsspiele,
- Kunstpostkarten,
- Mikroformen,
- Spielkarten,
- Spielzeug,
- Stofftiere,
- T-Shirts,
- Tarotkarten,
- Weine (das Barsortiment Koch, Neff & Oetinger, Stuttgart, ergänzt sein Wein- und Kochbuchsortiment mit einer Kollektion italienischer Weine, die über die branchenüblichen Bestell- und Lieferwege laufen),
- Zauberstäbe (jedenfalls solange Harry Potter Kinderherzen begeistert).

Für Globen und Kartenzubehör sieht die Warengruppen-Systematik je eine eigene Warengruppe vor (*380* für Globen und *390* für Kartenzubehör).

9 Loseblatt-Ausgabe.

Ein Taschenbuch-Ratgeber über Wirbelsäulengymnastik erhält die Warengruppenziffer *24640* (*464* ist die Warenuntergruppe *Fitness / Aerobic / Bodybuilding / Gymnastik*), ein Video zum selben Thema die Warengruppenziffer *44640* und eine Audio-CD *54640*.

Der Reader-Interest-Ansatz kommt vor allem in der Bildung der Hauptwarengruppe *4 Sachbuch / Ratgeber* zum Ausdruck (Überblick siehe Abbildung 5). Sie enthält vor allem Sachbücher, Ratgeber, Anleitungen und Bildbände für Freizeit- und Hobbythemen, für Essen und Trinken, Lebensführung und gesundes Leben, ferner allgemeine Nachschlagewerke und Wörterbücher. Sie enthält Fach- und wissenschaftliche Bücher fast nur bei den Themen, für die es in den Hauptwarengruppen *5 Geisteswissenschaften / Kunst / Musik*, *6 Mathematik / Naturwissenschaften / Technik / Medizin* und *7 Sozialwissenschaften / Recht / Wirtschaft* keine eigenen Warengruppen gibt. Das ist z.B. bei den Themen Sport (sportwissenschaftliche Fachliteratur), Foto- und Fahrzeugtechnik, Ernährungswissenschaft und Gastronomie (Fachliteratur für das Gastgewerbe) der Fall, während zahlreiche andere Themen sowohl in der Hauptwarengruppe *4* wie auch in einer der Hauptwarengruppen *5*, *6* oder *7* verortet sind. Hier einige Beispiele:

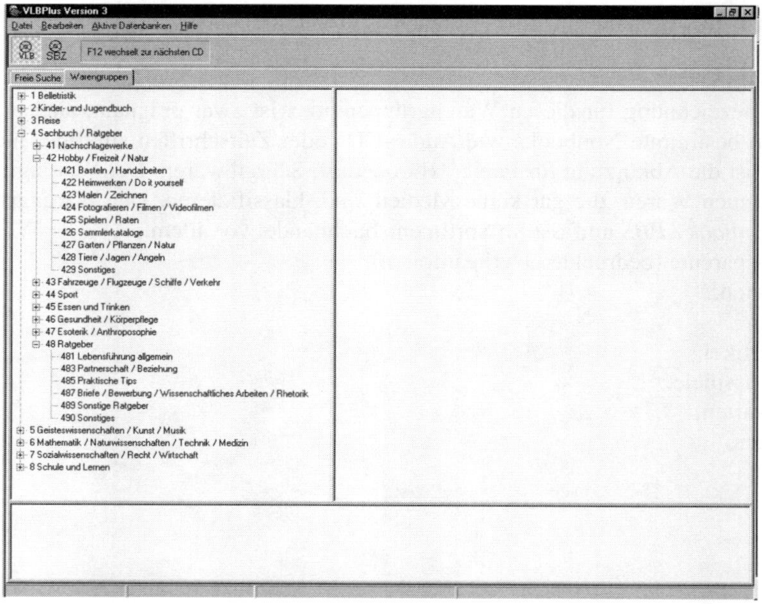

Abbildung 5: Hauptwarengruppe *4 Sachbuch / Ratgeber*. Auch die hier nicht geöffneten Warengruppen *41 Nachschlagewerke*, *43 Fahrzeuge* usw. sind untergliedert.

Thema	*verortet in den Warenuntergruppen*	
Wirbelsäulen-Gymnastik	*464 Fitness / Aerobic / Bodybuilding / Gymnastik*	*696 Medizin / Pharmazie – Andere Fachgebiete*
Bewerbung	*487 Briefe / Bewerbung / Wissenschaftliches Arbeiten / Rhetorik*	*786 Werbung / Marketing*
Hausbau	*422 Heimwerken / Do it Yourself*	*686 Bau- und Umwelttechnik*

Hier geht es um die Trennung der Ratgeber von der Fachliteratur, der Sachbücher von den wissenschaftlichen Monografien. Allerdings liegt es in der Natur der Sache, dass die Unterscheidung oft beliebig erscheint, wie das folgende Beispiel zeigt:

- Warenuntergruppe *686 Bau- und Umwelttechnik*: Riedl, Bernhard /Schoberth, Gerhard: Checklisten für den selbstorganisierten Hausbau. Baugenehmigung, Baudurchführung ohne Bauleiter, Angebote einholen und prüfen, Rechnungsprüfung, Abnahme, Mängelbeseitigung, Haftung und Gewährleistung, Musterverträge, mvg
- Warenuntergruppe *422 Heimwerken / Do it yourself*: Grosses Checklisten-Handbuch für Bauherren. Die 2000 wichtigsten Fragen und Antworten rund um den Hausbau, Compact (Compact-Checkliste).

Weitere Merkmale, die dem Reader-Interest-Ansatz nahe stehen und sich aus dem Anwendungsbereich ergeben, sind vor allem

- die Warenuntergruppe *190 Geschenkbücher*:
  Sie umfasst solche Bücher, die eigentlich nur als Geschenk gekauft werden. Typische Inhalte sind kurze Texte in Kombination mit Illustrationen nach Gemälden, Aquarellen, Cartoons, Porträt-, Landschaftsfotos. Viele Titel sind in Titelformulierung und Inhalt auf typische Geschenkanlässe bezogen, etwa Ehejubiläen, Firmung, Geburtstag, Gene-

sung, Hochzeit, Jahresfeste, Kommunion, Konfirmation, Partybesuch, Taufe. Andere Geschenkbücher sprechen den Beschenkten in sozialen Rollensituationen oder -wechseln an, als Geschäftspartner, Großmutter, -vater, Kollege, Lebens-, Beziehungspartner, Mutter, Taufpate, Vater, Ruheständler. Wieder andere Geschenkbücher nehmen auf Vorlieben, Hobbies, Sternzeichen oder den Glauben Bezug.

– die Hauptwarengruppe *3 Reise*.
  Sie enthält Bücher, Karten und andere Medien, die man zur Reisevorbereitung und -durchführung braucht, ferner verwandte Warengruppen, nämlich Bildbände, Reiseberichte, Atlanten und Globen. Geowissenschaftliche Literatur findet man in der Warengruppe *66 Geowissenschaften*. Im Einzelnen ist die Hauptwarengruppe 3 Reise in folgende Warengruppen untergliedert:

  31 Reiseführer / Kunstreiseführer
  32 Reiseführer Sport
  33 Hotel- und Restaurantführer / Campingführer
  34 Karten / Stadtpläne
  35 Bildbände
  36 Reiseberichte / Reiseerzählungen
  37 Atlanten
  380 Globen
  390 Kartenzubehör

Die weitere Untergliederung der Warengruppen 31 bis 36 erfolgt einheitlich nach Ländern und Kontinenten.

Die Hauptwarengruppe *8 Schule und Lernen* deckt sich thematisch mit nahezu alle anderen Hauptwarengruppen, ist aber nach dem Kriterium Zielgruppe / Verwendungszweck gebildet. Inhalt und Untergliederung gehen aus Abbildung 6 hervor.

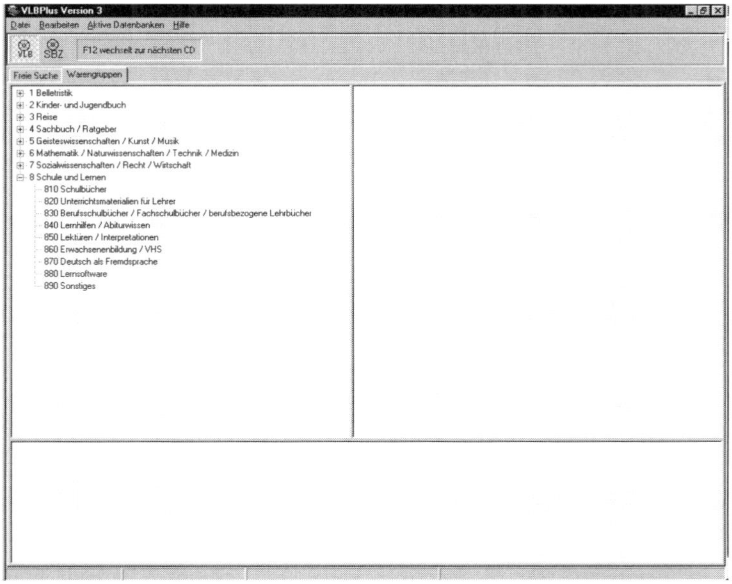

Abbildung 6: Hauptwarengruppe *8 Schule und Lernen*

Die Kombination der Aspekte Inhalt, Zielgruppe und Verwendungszweck zur Erzeugung der Warengruppen-Systematik ist indessen uneinheitlich. Nach der Klassifikationstheorie[235] darf jeweils nur ein einziges Kriterium zur Zergliederung einer Klasse (hospitality in array) angewendet werden. Daran hält sich die Warengruppen-Systematik ebenso wenig wie die meisten Bibliotheksklassifikationen. In der Folge entstehen Unklarheiten in der Zuordnung.

So beginnen die meisten Warengruppen mit den beiden Warenuntergruppen *Populäre Darstellungen* (Zergliederungskriterium: Zielgruppe) und *Allgemeines, Lexika, Geschichte, Berufe* (Zergliederungskriterien: Inhalt, Darstellungsform) bzw. mit einer dieser beiden Klassen, bevor die weiteren Warenuntergruppen Teilgebiete auflisten (Zergliederungskriterium: Inhalt). Die gleichzeitige Anwendung mehrerer Zergliederungskriterien führt regelmäßig zu Überschneidungen zwischen Klasseninhalten, weil die Klassen nicht disjunkt sind. Die unklaren Zuordnungen schlagen sich darin nieder, dass beispielsweise das *Lexikon der Abwassertechnik* in der 6. Auflage 2000 der Warenuntergruppe *682 Technik allgemein / Nachschlagewerke / Geschichte* zugeordnet ist (Abbildung 7), derselbe Titel in der 5. Aufl. 1993 aber der Warenuntergruppe *686 Bau- und Umwelttechnik*. Entsprechende Beispiele lassen sich in nahezu beliebiger Anzahl finden.

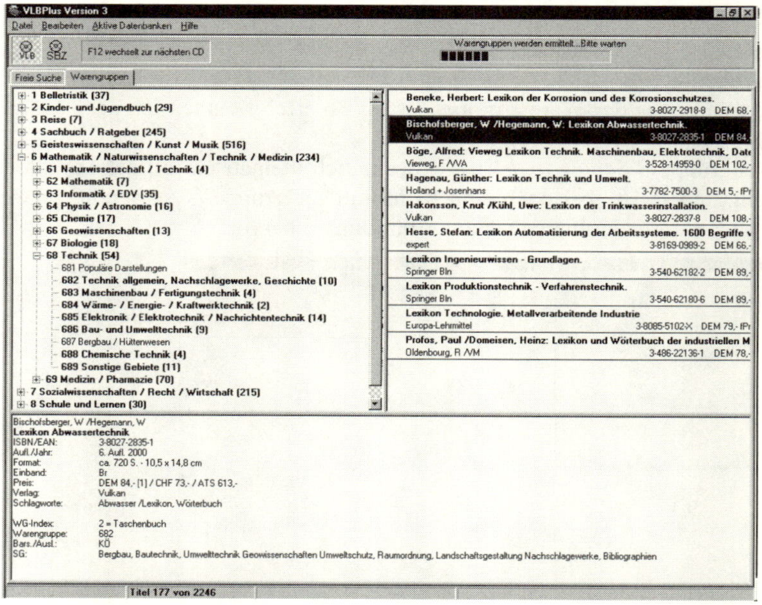

Abbildung 7: Inkonsistente hospitality in array

3. Inkonsistente Anwendung der Warengruppen-Systematik

Im Folgenden sollen weitere Fälle inkonsistenter Anwendung der Warengruppen-Systematik beispielhaft aufgeführt werden.

– *552* Geschichte – *Allgemeines, Lexika, Nachschlagewerke*: Lehnert, Gertrud: Frauen

[235] Buchanan (1989), Brian: Bibliothekarische Klassifikationstheorie. München: Saur.

machen Mode. Coco Chanel, Jil Sander, Vivienne Westwood. Modeschöpferinnen vom 18. Jahrhundert bis heute, edition ebersbach. Richtig wäre Warenuntergruppe *586 Innenarchitektur / Design*, dort auch andere Titel über Bekleidungsmode und Biografien über Modeschöpferinnen.

- Vornamen-Lexika sind folgenden Warenuntergruppen zugeordnet, ohne dass sachliche Unterschiede zwischen den Vornamen-Lexika dies rechtfertigen würde:
  411 Lexika / Nachschlagewerke / Chroniken / Jahrbücher
  415 Adressbücher / Telefonbücher / Kursbücher / Einkaufsführer
  419 Nachschlagewerke – Sonstiges (hier die meisten, das Register verweist auf diese Warenuntergruppe)
  481 Lebensführung allgemein
  483 Partnerschaft / Beziehung.

Nährwert- und Kalorientabellen findet man gleichermaßen in den Warenuntergruppen

461 Gesundheit / Körperpflege – Allgemeines / Lexika
462 Ratgeber Gesundheit
463 Gesunde Ernährung
452 Essen und Trinken – Ernährungswissenschaft / Gastronomie / Hotellerie

- Bücher über Qigong stehen in der Warenuntergruppe 465 Entspannung / Yoga / Meditation / Autogenes Training, Videos über dasselbe Thema in der Warenuntergruppe 464 Fitness / Aerobic / Bodybuilding / Gymnastik.
- Störig, Hans J.: Kleine Weltgeschichte der Philosophie: Die Ausgabe im Kohlhammer-Verlag ist der Warenuntergruppe 521 Philosophie – Populäre Darstellungen zugeordnet, die Fischer-Taschenbuchausgabe 522 Philosophie – Allgemeines / Lexika / Nachschlagwerke. In zahllosen Fällen sind verschiedene Ausgaben desselben Werkes verschiedenen Warenuntergruppen zugeordnet. In manchen Fällen sind beide Zuordnungen plausibel, in anderen Fällen ist mindestens eine Zuordnung nicht nachvollziehbar.
- Stadler, Friedrich: Studien zum Wiener Kreis. Ursprung, Entwicklung und Wirkung des Logischen Empirismus im Kontext, Suhrkamp, ist falsch der Warenuntergruppe 423 Philosophie – Antike zugeordnet. Richtig wäre 527 Philosophie – 20./21. Jahrhundert.
- DuBosque, Doug: Perspektive. Zeichnen Schritt für Schritt, Taschen, ist falsch der Gruppe 582 Kunst allgemein zugeordnet, richtig wäre 423 Malen / Zeichnen, wo die anderen Anleitungen zum Malen und Zeichnen zu finden sind.
- Germanische Religionsgeschichte. Quellen und Quellenprobleme. Hrsg. v. Beck, Heinrich /Ellmers, Detlev /Schier, Kurt, de Gruyter (Reallexikon d. German. Altertumskde. Erg.-Bde 5) falsch bei *544 Christentum*. Richtig wäre die Gruppe *547 Nichtchristliche Religionen* (die eine nicht ganz klare Benennung hat, weil sie Medien über andere als die christliche und die jüdische Religion enthält).
- Der Inhalt der Warenuntergruppe *545 Praktische Theologie* wird sehr eigenwillig verstanden, indem dort über das Thema Verwirklichung des Glaubens in Gottesdienst und Predigt, in der Seelsorge und der kirchlichen Sozialarbeit sowie im Religionsunterricht hinaus auch Bücher über Themen wie Mönchtum und Klöster allgemein, über Befreiungstheologie und Pilgern allgemein zugeordnet sind.

Auch das Register enthält unbefriedigende, vereinzelt falsche Eintragungen:

- Im Register erscheint *Merowinger*, aber nicht *Franken* auf, obwohl es über die Franken und das Frankenreich mehr als zehn Mal so viel Bücher lieferbar sind.
- Das Register enthält auch eine Auswahl von Personennamen, die geistige Strömungen oder historische Epochen geprägt haben. Das erleichtert ohne Zweifel das Verständnis der Warengruppen. Leider lautet eine Registereintragung fälschlich Günter Anders statt richtig Günther Anders.
- Die im Register erscheinenden Begriffe *Asiatische Sprachwissenschaft* und *Asiatische Literaturwissenschaft* gibt es nicht.
- Das Register verweist *Schulkochbücher* auf die Warenuntergruppe *453 Allgemeine Kochbücher / Grundkochbücher*. Die Warengruppen-Systematik selbst legt nahe, dass Schulkochbücher in den Warenuntergruppen *810 Schulbücher* bzw. *830 Berufsschulbücher / Fachschulbücher / berufsbezogene Lehrbücher* zu finden seien – und dort stecken sie auch tatsächlich mit Ausnahme des Schulkochbuchs von *Dr. Oetker*.

Die Liste der Beispiele ließe sich fortsetzen. Zusammengefasst kann man feststellen:

- Die Anzahl der subjektiv falschen Zuordnungen (mangelnde Kenntnis der Sachverhalte, mangelnde Sorgfalt) entwertet die sehr wertvolle klassifikatorische Erschließung.
- Das gedruckte Register enthält sachlich falsche Zuordnungen, fehlerhafte Schreibweisen und ins Leere führende Eintragungen.
- Dringend erforderlich sind ausführliche Klassenbeschreibungen, die über die knappen Klassenbenennungen hinaus Sachverhalte eindeutig zuordnen. Sie können als Hypertext hinterlegt werden und dann zugleich ein umfangreiches Register bilden.
- Die Warengruppen-Systematik, die Sachgruppen des VLB (umfassend 66 mehr oder minder breite Gebiete, Ausschnitt siehe Abbildung 1) und die Schlagwörter im VLB sind nicht aufeinander abgestimmt und nicht miteinander verknüpft.

Überhaupt wäre wohl der ergiebigere Weg, das Titelmaterial automatisch zu klassifizieren. Als Ausgangspunkt wäre ein intellektuell sorgfältig klassifizierter Korpus von Titelwörtern denkbar. Damit bekommt man allerdings den Ansatz der Warengruppen-Systematik nicht in den Griff, viele Themen sowohl in einer der Hauptwarengruppen *5*, *6* oder *7* als auch in einer der beiden Hauptwarengruppen *4* oder *8* unterzubringen, je nachdem ob es sich um fachlich-wissenschaftliche, um populäre Sachbuchdarstellungen oder um Lehr- und Lernmaterialien handelt. Hier könnte helfen, auch Verlag und Reihe als Klassifikationskriterium für die automatische Zuordnung zu berücksichtigen.

Wolfram Henning

Bibliotheksbauten für das Medienzeitalter? Impulse und Konventionen am Beispiel einiger Wettbewerbe [236]

Architektur im Medienzeitalter

Abb. 1: Disney feature animation building, Burbank USA (1994)
Robert A.M. Stern architects / Morris architects

Drei Tendenzen prägen nach den Beobachtungen Otto Riewoldts die Architektur im Medienzeitalter:

- Formal äußert sich Progressivität in comic-inspirierten Spaßbauten oder in dekonstruktivistischen Entwürfen
- Funktional vereinen hybride Bauten unterschiedliche Funktionen unter einem Dach
- Konstruktiv entwickeln sich intelligente Gebäude, die sich selbst steuern; ökonomische, ergonomische und ökologische Anforderungen werden optimiert [237]

In aktuellen Beispielen verschränken sich die drei Phänomene. Kein schlüssiger Beweis findet sich jedoch „für die zwingende Kopplung zwischen Architekturfortschritt und Medienrevolution .... Nicht die digitalen Medien, die nachgebauten Images der Unterhaltungsindustrie erobern als Urban Theme Parks den städtischen Raum." [238]

Aber, aber!, schrillt der Zwischenruf der Bibliotheksingenieure (oder Ingenieurbibliothekare): Haben wir nicht Hohlraumböden für die Nachverkabelung und wenn es sehr gut geht, überkragende Dachkonstruktionen, die für angenehmes Licht an den Bildschirmarbeitsplätzen sorgen?

[236] Überarbeitete Fassung eines Vortrags vom 22. März 2000 auf dem Bibliothekskongress in Leipzig.

[237] Riewoldt, Otto: Bauten für die Zukunft. Architektur im Informationszeitalter. Stuttgart: Deutsche Verlags-Anstalt (1997). Vgl. S. 8 f.

[238] Riewoldt, Otto: S. 9 f.

Blendfreier Bildschirm und doppelter Boden. Sonst keine Neuigkeit? Ist das die bibliothekarische Anregung für eine Architektur der Zukunft? Gibt es das – eine neuartige Bibliotheksarchitektur, die durch neue Bibliotheksprogramme ihre Impulse empfängt? Riewoldt kritisiert den „gediegen-biederen Kanon akademischer Bauten“. [239]

Eindrücke aus vier Wettbewerben

Der berufliche Zufall wollte es, dass ich in den Jahren 1998/99 vier zeitlich nahezu parallele Realisierungswettbewerbe begleiten durfte:
- den Projektwettbewerb für die Kantonsbibliothek Baselland in Liestal
- den Realisierungswettbewerb für die neue Zentralbibliothek der Stadt Ulm
- den Realisierungswettbewerb Bibliothek 21 in Stuttgart
- den baukünstlerischen Wettbewerb für Hauptbibliothek und Zentralverwaltung der Wiener Städtischen Büchereien

In Basel waren Entwürfe von 14 Büros zugelassen, 426 Arbeiten waren es in Ulm, 235 Arbeiten in Stuttgart, 121 Arbeiten in Wien. Schlaglichtartig möchte ich vier Aspekte beleuchten:

- Bibliothekare fordern
- Architekten entwerfen
- Juroren entscheiden
- Politiker entscheiden erst recht

Bibliothekare fordern

In Wettbewerbsauslobungen erwartet man außer dem eigentlichen Raumprogramm eine bündige Darstellung des bibliothekarischen Konzepts, das dem Programm zugrunde liegt – eine bauvorbereitende „Unternehmensphilosophie“. Konzept und Raumprogramm sind die einzigen Möglichkeiten, mit einer anonymen Architektenschar zu kommunizieren, ehe sie sich ans Entwerfen macht. Was fordern wir? Welche Impulse sollen überspringen? Zum *state of the art* gehört heute in jedem Fall ein lebendiger, mit interessanten Angeboten lockender Eingangsbereich, die heftige Betonung von Multimedialität und ein Bibliothekscafé. Darüber hinaus gibt es deutliche Unterschiede.

Baselland – hier handelt es sich um die Umnutzung eines ehemaligen Weinlagers – legt Wert auf Begegnung, geistige Auseinandersetzung, Einzel- und Gruppenarbeitsplätze, Veranstaltungen und Ausstellungen. Das Foyer soll als Piazza ausgebildet werden. Die Hauptnutzfläche beträgt 2.605 m²

Ulm – vorgesehen ist ein Neubau in historischer Umgebung – bietet 13 Thesen zum Funktionswandel der Stadtbibliothek wie Produktionsfaktor „Wissen“, „Elektronische Bibliothek“, Informationsgesellschaft, Vernetzung, Erlebnis. Diese Thesen sind im Anhang der Auslobung eher unauffällig präsentiert. Das Raumprogramm und seine Erläuterungen folgen der Terminologie der dreigeteilten Bibliothek. Um eine Verknüpfung von Thesenpapier und Programm müssen sich die Architekten selbst bemühen. Die Hauptnutzfläche soll 3.490 m² betragen.

---

[239] Riewoldt, Otto: S. 216.

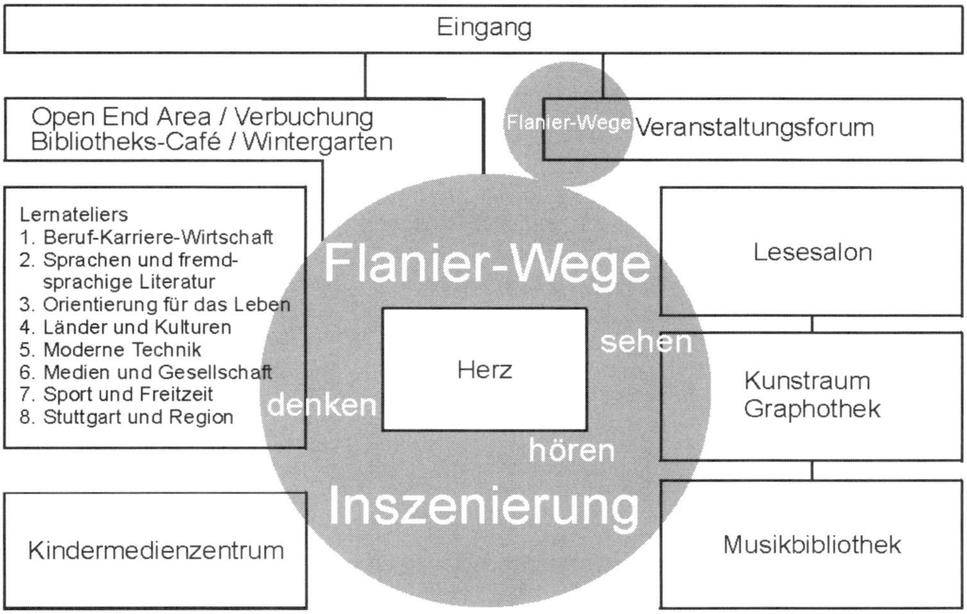

Abb. 2: Bibliothek 21 in Stuttgart, Funktionsschema Publikumsbereiche

In Stuttgart handelt es sich um einen Neubau als Teil des städtebaulichen Großprojekts Stuttgart 21. Das Konzept findet sich in den „16 Punkten" zur Philosophie des Gebäudes und der Bibliothek. Einige Stichworte:

- Basis für die Wissensgesellschaft der Zukunft
- Medienpädagogische Verantwortung
- Innovatives, selbstgesteuertes Lernen
- Literarischer Ort, Zusammenspiel der Künste
- Beitrag im Wandel der Arbeitswelt
- Gastlichkeit

Vorangestellt ist ein hochgemuter Satz:

> *„Die Bibliothek 21 ist einmalig. Sie hat ihre Wurzeln in der Tradition der Bibliotheken – die Bibliothek als Gedächtnis der Welt – und wendet sich reflektierend, provozierend, optimistisch und fantasievoll in die reale und virtuelle Zukunft."*

Einer von 235 Architekten wird ihn überzeugend beantworten.

Ein komplexes Konzept im Gegensatz zu einem überwiegend technologiebasierten Ansatz. Die Verknüpfung zwischen den „16 Punkten" und dem daran anschließenden Raumprogramm ist evident:

Die Hauptnutzfläche ist mit 11.200 m² angegeben.

Die Wiener Auslobung sieht einen Neubau über einer offenen, in einem Graben geführten U-Bahnstrecke am Gürtel vor. Ein Anforderungsprofil in elf Punkte nennt Begriffe wie:

- Lebenslanges Lernen
- Kommunikationsort
- Medienkompetenz
- Begegnung mit Literatur und Kunst
- Brückenschlag zwischen Buch und elektronischen Medien
- Informationsvermittlungsstelle

Der Bezug zwischen diesen Punkten und dem Raumprogramm ist weniger strikt gehalten. Die zur Stadtbücherei Stuttgart angebahnten Kontakte trugen inzwischen zur weiteren Entfaltung der Planung bei. Auch Wien wird einen bis in die Nacht geöffneten Bibliotheksbereich haben (open access area), die „colleges" sind eine Antwort auf die Stuttgarter Lernateliers. Diese Wünsche lagen aber noch nicht den am Wettbewerb teilnehmenden Architekten vor. Mit einer Hauptnutzfläche von 6.085 m² ist das Projekt entschieden zu klein für eine Metropole.

Architekten entwerfen

Welche Impulse der Auslobung werden besonders wirksam? Gibt es kreative, auch unerwartete Antworten auf die Forderungen der Bibliothekare?

Abb. 3: Kantonsbibliothek Baselland,
Liechti Graf Zumsteg Architekten

In Liestal mussten zwei Arbeiten ins Stechen gehen. Der letzten Endes unterlegene Teilnehmer hatte sich unglaublich in das historische Gebäude verliebt, blieb indes in Funktionalität und Tageslichtführung schlüssige Antworten schuldig. Das Büro Liechtii Graf Zumsteg aus Brugg setzte das Programm solide um und überstand sanfte Kritik der Jury wegen einer frech aufs historische Dach gesetzten Laterne („Darf eine Bibliothek so selbstbewusst wirken?")

Unter den 426 Ulmer Entwürfen war, auch durch den Zuschnitt des Grundstückes suggeriert, eine so inflationäre Zahl von „Kisten“ (Juryjargon), dass zur kritischen Bewertung zeitweise ein Unterausschuss der Jury tätig werden musste. Ähnliches galt für „Eier“. Als fantasieanregendes Spielobjekt hatten viele Architekten das Bibliothekscafé ausgeguckt. Kein Geschoß und kein funktionaler Zusammenhang, in dem es nicht auftauchte. In scharfem Kontrast zum langen, schmalen Baukörper des Kölner Büros Minkus & Wolf (1. Preis) stand die erlebnisverheißende Glaspyramide des Büros Gottfried Böhm, ebenfalls Köln (3. Preis). Der Jury-Entscheid war einstimmig, vielstimmig dann aber der Protest aus der Bevölkerung. Die vier Preisträger wurden zur Überarbeitung aufgefordert, der funktional entscheidend verbesserte Entwurf Gottfried Böhms wird nun realisiert.

Abb. 4: Zentralbibliothek der Stadt Ulm,
1. Preis: Minkus & Wolf, Köln

Abb. 5: Zentralbibliothek der Stadt Ulm,
3. Preis: Prof. Gottfried Böhm, Köln, (vor Überarbeitung)

Das schwierige, vielseitig fordernde Stuttgarter Programm ließ viele Architekten an ihre Leistungsgrenze geraten. Das „Herz“ der Bibliothek erwies sich besonders für die Ingenieure unter den Architekten als rechter Stolperstein. Mehrfach wurde das Profil einer öffentlichen Bibliothek mit dem einer Universitätsbibliothek verwechselt, die Göttinger „Lesesaalfinger“ wurden zitiert. Der 1. Preisträger Eun Young Yi aus Hürth/Köln gibt auf die bibliothekarischen Vorgaben unerwartete (und nun die Bibliothek herausfordernde) Antworten, die ihn zum Teilhaber und nicht einfach zum ausführenden Organ der Stuttgarter Konzeption qualifiziert haben. Zur inneren Durchdringung des gläsernen Kubus erläutert Yi:

Abb. 6: Bibliothek 21 in Stuttgart,
1. Preis Eun Young Yi, Hürth/Köln

„Das Bibliotheksgebäude kann von allen vier Seiten betreten werden. Über die Open End Area gelangt man in ‚Herz‘, das Kernstück der Bibliothek. Es wird gleichsam von einer zweiten Fassade umschlossen und liegt als würfelförmiger Raum in der Mitte des Gebäudes, nur durch ein zentrales Oberlicht erhellt.
Das Herz ist in allen Geschossen ringförmig von dem Lesesalon, der Musikbibliothek, dem Kunstraum und der Graphothek umgeben. Sein ‚occulus‘ mündet in einen trichterförmigen Lesesaal. Dieser erstreckt sich über vier Geschosse und verbindet die acht verschiedenen Lernateliers.
Innere Erschließungstreppe und die äußere Fluchtrampe sind als fließende Flanierwege konzipiert. Die Gebäudehülle ist als Doppelfassade aus Glasbausteinen in Betonrahmen und Glasfassade konzipiert, um einen archaischen und gleichzeitig modernen Eindruck zu gewinnen.
Das Forum, das als zentraler Bestandteil der Bibliothek verstanden wird, befindet sich direkt unter dem ‚Herz‘.“
(Ansprache in der Stadtbücherei Stuttgart am 01.07.1999.)

Abb. 7: Bibliothek 21 in Stuttgart,
Eun Young Yi, Schnittmodell

Abb. 8: Hauptbibliothek der Wiener Städtischen Büchereien, Ansicht mit Freitreppe,
1. Preis: Ernst Mayr, Wien

Wien – das wird „die Bibliothek mit der Treppe“. Die große Freitreppe, die größte in Wien (oder Europa?) wurde in Auseinandersetzung mit dem Standort, nicht mit dem bibliothekarischen Programm entwickelt. Allerdings verweist der 1. Preisträger, Architekt Ernst Mayr aus Wien, mit Recht darauf, dass das äußere Erscheinungsbild der Bibliothek die Neugier auf den Inhalt wecken kann. Geht man heute durch den weitgehend fertiggestellten Rohbau, registriert man, dass die akustische Abschirmung gegen die Stadtautobahn funktionieren könnte – und man ist begeistert von Raumvolumina und Tageslichtführung. Einige aufregend-futuristische „Wolkenbügel“-Entwürfe fielen dem Diktum des Statikers zum Opfer: „Das Gestell steht nicht“.

Juroren entscheiden

Einige Beobachtungen zur Arbeit der vier Jurys:

- Wie nach einem variablen, aber stets sorgfältigen Ritual aus einer scheinbar unüberschaubaren Menge von Arbeiten die rund zwei Dutzend Entwürfe herausgefunden werden, die eingehende Erörterung verdienen, ist ein Phänomen für sich.
- Die deutschen Jurys waren strikt nach GRW 1995 besetzt, also stets mit einer Stimme Mehrheit auf Seiten der Fachpreisrichter. Die Wiener Jury war paritätisch besetzt, dafür zählte die Stimme des vorsitzenden Fachpreisrichters doppelt. Die Vorsitzende in Baselland trägt als Kantonsarchitektin auch für die Bauausführung Verantwortung.
- Die Abhängigkeit von Experten kann ein Thema sein. Wenn der Statiker sagte: „Das Gestell steht nicht“, verstummten in Wien betreten alle Fachpreisrichter und alle Sachpreisrichter.
- Unterhaltsam ist die lästernde Jury. „Den Entwurf hat der Briefträger gemacht ... diese Arbeit ist am Küchentisch entstanden ... das macht der nur, weil er so ein schönes Kurvenlineal hat“). Hilfreicher für die Umsetzung bibliothekarischer Vorstellungen ist freilich die „lernende Jury“. Sie begreift und erfragt die Bibliothekskonzeption von Rundgang zu Rundgang genauer und kann schließlich den Unterschied zwischen einer Universitätsbibliothek und einer Stadtbücherei überzeugend nachvollziehen.

Politiker entscheiden erst recht

Politiker entscheiden im Vorfeld. In Stuttgart wie in Wien begegnet das dominierende Motiv der Stadtentwicklung. Flagge zeigen, kulturelle Gegenkraft im kommerziellen Umfeld entfalten – nicht zuletzt diese Chance ließ die Stuttgarter Sachpreisrichter so einmütig für den Entwurf von Eun Young Yi votieren. Die Stuttgarter Standortentscheidung ist übrigen für die Bibliothek mit beträchtlichem Risiko verbunden. Denn der Standort hinterm Bahnhof funktioniert nur, wenn das Gesamtprojekt Stuttgart 21 realisiert wird. Bund, Land, Stadt, Region und Bahn meldeten im Februar 2001 zwar den „Durchbruch“, aber einen beträchtlichen Planungsverzug musste die Stadt Stuttgart hinnehmen, d.h. zwischen Wettbewerbsentscheid und Bibliothekseröffnung dürften etwa sieben Jahre liegen.

Für die Stadt Wien scheint die Bibliothek geradezu das rettende Bauwerk geworden zu sein, um sich aus heftiger unternehmerischer Umklammerung zu lösen. „Mörtel“ ante portas! [240]

Politiker entscheiden nachträglich. Der Oberbürgermeister der Stadt Ulm beglückwünschte in der Stunde der einhelligen Entscheidung die städtischen Sachpreisrichter zur

[240] Vgl. den Beitrag von Alfred Pfoser in diesem Band.

ihrem Mut und forderte sie zur Standfestigkeit auf. Bürgerprotest führte zu einer „Wende um 180 Grad" (Südwestpresse vom 15.07.1999), gebaut wird der überarbeitete 3. Preis.

Die starke Bibliothek

Kann von Wettbewerbsauslobungen im Bibliotheksbau eine architekturprägende Kraft ausgehen? Vielleicht sogar deutlicher denn je.

Im allgemeinen Sinne. Der Wettbewerbssieger von Wien, Ernst Mayr, resümiert:

> *„Ein öffentliches Gebäude in der Stadt kann sich darstellen. Es hat Zeiten gegeben, da musste man sich mit solchen Gebäuden fast verstecken. Aber jetzt gibt es international eine Phase, in der sich Bibliotheken mitten in Brennpunkte oder Problemzonen von Städten setzen... Ich stehe dazu, wenn sich die Stadt einen solchen Bauplatz für eine Bibliothek aussucht, dies auch stolz zu zeigen."* [241]

Im aktuellen Sinne. Das elektronische Zeitalter gibt zwar zu Karikaturen Anlass, die einen Bildschirm auf einem verwahrlosten Grundstück zeigen: und hier sollte eigentlich die neue Bibliothek gebaut werden. Gleichzeitig wächst der Sinn für die Bedeutsamkeit konkreter öffentlicher Orte, an denen sich Menschen begegnen.

> *„Ob vor dem Monitor oder unter dem Datenhelm – wenn der Cybernaut sich von den virtuellen Bildräumen abwendet, soll er sich schließlich wiederfinden in einer gebauten Wirklichkeit, mehr noch ergonomisch und ökologisch mit seiner soziokulturellen wie natürlichen Umwelt versöhnt."* [242]

Eun Young Yis Stuttgarter Kubus bezieht sich auf eine archaische Grundform, auf technologischen Wandel und das im Raumprogramm geforderte „Herz" der Bibliothek:

> *„Die Auslober haben den Begriff ‚Herz' geprägt und von den Architekten die räumliche Umsetzung gefordert, was ich als Anhaltspunkte für die Stellungnahme zur Architektur unserer Zeit genommen habe.*
> *Als das ‚Herz' der Bibliothek wird der archaische Raumtyp Pantheon vor dem Hintergrund unserer veränderten technischen Wirklichkeit neu interpretiert. Zukunft und Geschichte des Menschen wird hier gleichermaßen vergegenwärtigt.*
> *Das ‚Herz' soll ein Ort der Ruhe sein, mit einem fast meditativen Erlebnis.*
> *Und das ‚Herz' soll gleichzeitig ein Ort der Connection sein, ein Ort der Kommunikation im zeitgemäßen Sinne, d.h. mit Anschluss an das Internet und somit den Cyberspace.*
> *Dieser konzeptionelle Gedanke spiegelt meinen Standpunkt zur Architektur der epochalen Übergangszeit zur Jahrtausendwende wider; also von der physischen Kultur zu der medientechnologischen Kultur." (Ansprache in der Stadtbücherei Stuttgart am 01.07.1999.)*

Architektur und Bibliothek gehen bei ihren raumbildenden Überlegungen freilich davon aus, dass sich die „Mediengesellschaft" umfassender als Wissens- und Kulturgesellschaft begreift. Die Bibliothek ist stark, wenn ihre Ansprüche komplex, fantasievoll und genau sind. Der Architekt Arno Lederer erklärte es einmal vor Studenten der HBI Stuttgart: Der Bauherr, der immer nur Schnitzel bestellt, bekommt auch nur Schnitzel serviert.

[241] In: Der Gürtel wird Bibliothek. Ein neues Wahrzeichen für Wien (neue wiener bücherbriefe • spezial) o.J.
[242] Riewoldt, Otto: S. 11.

Abb. 9: Bibliothek 21 in Stuttgart, „Herz“ mit „occulus“, Eun Young Yi

Die Wiener Hauptbibliothek wird voraussichtlich im Frühjahr 2002 eröffnet, in Basel und Ulm geht man vom Jahr 2003 aus, für die Bibliothek 21 in Stuttgart wird das Jahr 2006 genannt.

MEDIEN- UND BIBLIOTHEKSGESCHICHTE

Gerd Schmidt

„The Indecipherable Amen-script": ein Irrweg der Schriftgeschichte?

Mit der Entzifferung der Hieroglyphen durch J. F. Champollion (1822) war ein Rätsel gelöst, das die Gelehrten Europas über Jahrhunderte hinweg beschäftigt hatte. Das alte Ägypten sprach endlich mit eigener Stimme. Gediegene wissenschaftliche Arbeit trat an die Stelle phantastischer Vermutungen und abstruser Spekulationen. Die Aura, welche die „heiligen Schriftzeichen" lange Zeit umgeben hatte, verblasste, aber sie verschwand nicht völlig. Neben den Esoterikern waren es vor allem die Dichter, die das Geheimnis der Hieroglyphen zu bewahren suchten. Dass die Poesie dabei über unterschiedliche Möglichkeiten verfügt, soll im folgenden anhand zweier Beispiele aus der amerikanischen Literatur des 20. Jahrhunderts verdeutlicht werden.

Im vierzehnten Abschnitt seines *magnum opus* „A" schreibt Louis Zukofsky (1904 - 1978):

... I have

exchanged 10 books
I won´t need
(how else afforded)

for The Book
Of the Dead ... [243]

Bei der kostspieligen Anschaffung handelt es sich um die von E. A. Wallis Budge besorgte Faksimile-Ausgabe des ägyptischen Totenbuchs[244]. Der Schluss von Zukofskys „A14" ist von besonderem Interesse:

grave the
black glyphs
new moon

adz
(sail?) -
bird -
lamp
(cruse?) -
gaze

---

[243] Louis Zukofsky: „A". Berkeley 1978, S. 357.

[244] The Book of the Dead. The Papyrus of Ani in the British Museum. By Ernest Alfred Wallis Budge. London 1894/95.
Budge war von 1893 bis 1924 Keeper of Egyptian and Assyrian Antiquities am Britischen Museum. Seine Übersetzung des Totenbuchs fand in der angelsächsischen Welt weite Verbreitung und hat unter anderem James Joyce, Ezra Pound und Conrad Aiken beeinflusst.

(mouth?)
exult
tally
wiggle
exult
tally -
(one:
three)
Sun
eye[245]

Nach Reno Odlin steht hinter dieser Wortfolge ein Zitat aus dem Totenbuch, das Zukofsky in der Einleitung der Faksimile-Ausgabe fand. Budge gibt den Text in Hieroglyphen wieder und übersetzt: „Thou shalt exist for millions of millions of years." Für Odlin bleiben einige Fragen offen: was bedeuten „black glyphs" und „new moon", und woher kommt der bei Zukofsky angefügte Name des Osiris („a very late spelling not part of the sentence, and probably not to be found in Budge"[246])? „Grave the black glyphs" mag jedoch nicht mehr sein als eine Aufforderung zu schriftlicher Fixierung. Bei „new moon" hat Zukofsky möglicherweise ein Schriftzeichen im Blick (Aa 1 nach der Zeichenliste von Gardiner[247]), das zwar innerhalb des Zitats nicht vorkommt, bei Budge aber zweimal kurz hintereinander in unmittelbarer Nachbarschaft erscheint. Akzeptiert man zudem eine doppelte Interpretation des Zeichens N 5 – „Sonne" und (fälschlicherweise) „Auge" -, so entfällt die Notwendigkeit einer Textergänzung, und wir dürfen auf „Osiris" verzichten.

Am Ende von „A14" stände demnach die Verheißung: „Du wirst Millionen von Millionen Jahren leben." Zu fragen wäre allerdings, ob und inwieweit der ägyptische Hintergrund für das Verständnis der Passage überhaupt herangezogen werden muss.

Zukofskys Anweisung „grave the black glyphs" impliziert die Idee der Schrift, die ihrerseits nicht denkbar ist ohne die Intention der Vermittlung sprachlich gefasster Informationen. Die Hieroglyphen sind von ihrem Wesen her keine Bilder, sondern Elemente eines Schriftsystems, sie wollen nicht betrachtet, sondern gelesen werden. Für die ägyptische Schrift ergeben sich dabei spezifische Probleme. Eines von ihnen benennt Zukofsky selbst: er zitiert den ägyptischen Titel des Totenbuchs (*„Pert - / em-hru"*) und schließt daran die Frage: „pronounced // it how?"[248] - ein Hinweis auf die Schwierigkeit, mit einer Schrift umzugehen, die für eine heute nicht mehr existente Sprache konzipiert wurde und sich im wesentlichen auf die Wiedergabe von Konsonanten beschränkt.

Eine weitergehende Berücksichtigung des ursprünglichen Kontexts scheint sich jedoch zu verbieten. Die eigentliche Bedeutung der „schwarzen Glyphen" ist für Zukofkys Gedicht ohne Belang. Die Zeichen – oder genauer: ihre sprachlichen Äquivalente – stehen um ihrer selbst willen da, die Frage nach dem „Sinn" ist zu einer sinnlosen Frage geworden.

Louis Zukofsky gilt in der Geschichte der amerikanischen Lyrik als herausragender Vertreter des „Objektivismus". Definiert man „Objektivismus" als die Fähigkeit, einen Gegenstand in seiner ihm eigenen Wesenheit zu erfassen, so sind Zukofskys Hieroglyphen

---

[245] Zukofsky (Anm. 1), S. 358.

[246] Reno Odlin: „Materials Toward an Essay on Zukofsky´s `A´." Paideuma 9 (1980), S. 553- 554. Vgl. Budge (Anm.2), S. LVII.

[247] Alan Gardiner: Egyptian Grammar, 3rd ed. London 1957 u. ö.

[248] Zukofsky (Anm.1), S. 358.

kaum „objektivistisch": der Dichter zählt auf, was *er* wahrnimmt oder wahrzunehmen glaubt, wobei gegebenenfalls Alternativen genannt und Fragezeichen gesetzt werden. Von daher gesehen sind die Schlußzeilen von „A 14" eher eine subjektive Aussage. Versteht man dagegen „Objektivismus" im Sinne Zukofskys und seiner Dichterkollegen, so ist das Ende von „A 14" eine überzeugende Illustration „objektivistischer" Dichtung. Der „objektivistische" Dichter sieht im Gedicht „a distinct entity that may be appreciated for its own structural, aural, visual, and intellectual qualities rather than as a symbol of some other thing or emotion."[249] Zukofsky sagt einmal: „The word is so much of a psychological thing that its articulation, as against that of other words, will make an object."[250] Der Text als Struktur überlagert das Bewusstsein, dass es sich hierbei um eine Aufzählung bildhafter Schriftzeichen handelt. Der Leser soll sich mit dem Geflecht der aus dem ursprünglichen Zusammenhang gelösten Wörter begnügen: nicht die Verheißung billionenfachen Lebens, sondern das Medium ist die Botschaft.

In andere Zusammenhänge führt das zweite Beispiel. 1923 unternahmen Hilda Doolittle (1886 - 1961) und ihre Freundin Winifred Ellerman – besser bekannt unter dem Pseudonym Bryher - eine Ägyptenreise. Sie besuchten Luxor, Karnak und das Tal der Könige, wo sie die Öffnung des im Jahr zuvor entdeckten Grabes Tut-anch-Amuns miterlebten. Hilda Doolittle verarbeitete ihre Eindrücke in der Novelle „Secret Name: Excavators Egypt." Viele Jahre später widmete sie Bryher den Gedichtzyklus „The Walls Do Not Fall", mit dem sie an „Karnak 1923" erinnerte. Von der Erinnerung an Ägypten geprägt ist auch das Spätwerk „Helen in Egypt", das zwischen 1952 und 1956 geschrieben und im Todesjahr der Dichterin veröffentlicht wurde.

Das Land der Pharaonen war Hilda Doolittle somit aus eigener Anschauung vertraut. Ihr Zugang zu Altägypten unterscheidet sich allerdings von dem der meisten Reisenden, wie er auch unterschieden ist von dem des Wissenschaftlers (obwohl Helen Fairwood – Hilda Doolittles zweites Ich in „Secret Name" - die Rolle einer Mitarbeiterin des berühmten Ägyptologen „Bodge-Grafton" annimmt). Hilda Doolittle suchte die Begegnung mit Mystik und Magie, nicht das Ägypten der Ausgräber und der Bildungstouristen. Ihr, die im Reich der Sterne reiste,[251] hatte Ägypten „ den Traum für das Leben" und „ein Opiat für einen Kuß" zu bieten, „poison brought with knowledge / ... / ritual returned and magic"[252] – wobei freilich auch hier die Warnung gilt: „Be careful, or you'll find what you're looking for."[253]

Am Beginn von „The Walls Do Not Fall" steht der Gegensatz zwischen der grauen, von Bombenangriffen heimgesuchten Stadt - „London 1942" – und „the Luxor bee, chick and hare", die ihr Ziel in Grün, Rosenrot und Lapislazuli verfolgen. Der Blick der Dichterin geht zurück zu den mit Hieroglyphen übersäten Tempelwänden Ägyptens. Sie sind der „steinerne Papyrus", dem die in der Schrift bewahrte Prophezeiung anvertraut

---

249 Twentieth Century Literary Movements Dictionary. Ed. by Helene Henderson and Jay P. Pederson. Detroit 2000, S. 545.

250 Zitiert nach Reinhold Schiffer. „Die Poetik und Lyrik der Objektivisten", in: Die amerikanische Literatur der Gegenwart. Hg. v. Hans Bungert. Stuttgart 1977, S. 94-95.

251 Hilda Doolittle über die Tätigkeit des Schriftstellers: „The fact is writing is the thing – it trains one to a sort of yogi or majic (sic) power ... it is 'travelling in the astral' ..." Zitiert nach Barbara Guest: Herself Defined. New York 1984, S. 269.

252 Hilda Doolittle: „Egypt." Collected Poems 1912-1944. Ed. by Louis L. Martz. Manchester 1984, S. 140-141. Zur modernen „Ägyptosophie" und ihrer Vorgeschichte s. Erik Hornung: Das esoterische Ägypten. München 1999.

253 Nach Burton Raffel: T. S. Eliot Journal 1 (1990), S. 229.

ist.[254] Biene, Küken und Hase als Schriftzeichen begegnen auch in „Helen in Egypt". In „Hermetic Definition" ist der Tempel des Oedipus Aegyptiacus mit Bildern von Vögeln und Bienen geschmückt. Unter den übrigen von Hilda Doolittle erwähnten Hieroglyphen finden sich Falke, Geier und Ibis. Anscheinend sprachen Zeichen, die Tiere – insbesondere Vögel – wiedergeben, die Vorstellungskraft der Dichterin in besonderer Weise an.[255] Mit dieser Vorliebe steht Hilda Doolittle in einer Tradition, die bis ins Mittelalter und die Zeit der Renaissance zurückreicht. Benjamin von Tudela, der Ägypten um 1170 bereiste, berichtet von einem „Marmorgrab, auf dem alle Arten von Vögeln und Tieren aufgemalt sind, alle in uralten Schriftzeichen, die niemand entziffern kann."[256] „Vogelschrift" war eine Bezeichnung für die Hieroglyphen in der mittelalterlichen islamischen Literatur.[257] Im 15. Jahrhundert verfasste Carlo Marsuppini ein Epigramm auf Niccolò Niccoli, dem Ciriaco d´Ancona die Kopie einer hieroglyphischen Inschrift übersandt hatte, in welchem von „unkenntliche(r) Schrift, seltsam aus Tieren gefügt" die Rede ist.[258]

Was immer die moderne Wissenschaft behaupten mag – für Hilda Doolittle waren die „heiligen Zeichen" zunächst und vor allem Bilder und als solche Symbole. In „Helen in Egypt" ist zu lesen:

> *the old pictures are really there,*
> *eternal as the painted ibis in Egypt,*
> *the hawk and the hare.*[259]

Die Deutung der ägyptischen Schriftzeichen als Bildsymbole geht auf die Spätantike zurück. Im 5. Jh. n. Chr. schrieb der Ägypter (!) Horapollon eine Abhandlung über das Thema, die das abendländische Verständnis der Hieroglyphen nachhaltig beeinflussen sollte. Der Autor verbindet korrekte Lesungen mit phantasievollen Erklärungen. Einige Beispiele mögen genügen:

> *Wenn sie etwas Offenes bezeichnen wollen, malen sie einen Hasen: Weil diese Tierart immer die Augen geöffnet hält (I, 26).*
> *Ein Volk darzustellen, das den Befehlen des Fürsten gehorcht, malen sie eine Biene. Diese haben nämlich als einzige Tierart einen König ... (I, 62).*
> *Übrigens bezeichnen sie eine Mutter ..., indem sie einen Geier malen ... Weil es in dieser Tierart keine Männchen gibt (I,11).*[260]

Horapollons Werk wurde 1419 wiederaufgefunden und von den Gelehrten der Zeit begeistert rezipiert. In einer bekannten Passage der „Adagia" faßt Erasmus von Rotterdam zusammen, was die Renaissance von den Hieroglyphen dachte:

---

254 Hilda Doolittle: Trilogy. Cheadle 1973, S. 3.

255 Vgl. Hilda Doolittle: Helen in Egypt. Manchester 1985, S. 16 (Geier), 21 (Hase, Küken, Biene), 264 (Ibis, Falke, Hase). Dies.: Hermetic Definition. Oxford 1972, S. 69 (Vögel, Bienen). Dies.: Palimpsest. Boston 1926, S. 306 (Falke), 321 (Falke, Küken, Geier), 333 (Biene, Küken).

256 Karl H. Dannenfeldt: „Egypt and Egyptian Antiquities in the Renaissance." Studies in the Renaissance 6 (1959), S. 12-13.

257 Ulrich Haarmann: „Das pharaonische Ägypten bei islamischen Autoren des Mittelalters." In: Zum Bild Ägyptens im Mittelalter und in der Renaissance. Hg. v. Erik Hornung. Freiburg / Schweiz 1990, S. 35, 44.

258 Ludwig Volkmann: Bilderschriften der Renaissance. Leipzig 1923, S. 9.

259 Helen in Egypt (Anm. 13), S. 264.

260 Horapollo: Zwei Bücher über die Hieroglyphen. In der lateinischen Übersetzung von Jean Mercier, Paris 1548. Hg. u. übers. v. Helge Weingärtner. Erlangen 1997, S. 63, 83, 47/49.

> *So heißen nämlich die geheimnisvollen Schriftzeichen, die in alten Zeiten viel verwendet wurden, besonders von den ägyptischen Sehern und Priestern. Denn sie hielten es für eine Profanierung, die Mysterien der Weisheit in gewöhnlicher Schrift dem gemeinen Volke preiszugeben, wie wir es tun. Wenn sie daher etwas für wissenswert erachteten, dann stellten sie es mit Bildern von Tieren oder Sachen dar, jedoch so, dass es nicht für jedermann ohne weiteres verständlich war.*

Lesbar war diese Schrift nur für die, welche „die spezifischen Eigenschaften einer Sache, die besondere Wesensart eines Tieres erfasst und voll und ganz begriffen“ hatten.[261] Dem Schreiber, der über diese Kenntnis verfügt, kommt daher eine Vorrangstellung zu. Hilda Doolittle greift den Gedanken auf und gibt ihm eine eigene Färbung: für sie steht der Schreiber noch über dem Priester, „second only to the Pharaoh.“[262] Zu dieser Aussage gibt es eine merkwürdige Parallele aus dem Alten Ägypten. Der Verfasser der Lehre des Cheti rät seinem Sohn, den Beruf des Schreibers zu wählen: „Merke: Es gibt keinen Beruf ohne einen Vorgesetzten, / außer dem Schreiber: der *ist* der Vorgesetzte.“[263] Das Anliegen der amerikanischen Dichterin ist allerdings ein anderes: hier geht es nicht um soziales Prestige, sondern um Sendungsbewusstsein. Der Schreiber hält den Schlüssel zu den Geheimnissen des Universums in der Hand, er ist der Eingeweihte (In „Hermetic Definition“ warten der Schreiber, der Eingeweihte und der Verzweifelte vor der Schwelle des Tempels des Oedipus Aegyptiacus[264]). Ein Brief Hilda Doolittles an Norman Holmes Pearson bestätigt, was der Leser bereits vermutet haben dürfte: mit dem Schreiber ist in Wahrheit der Dichter gemeint, mit dem Pharaoh Gott.[265]

Dichter sind „Träger der geheimen Weisheit“, aber sie gelten auch als „nutzlos“ und „mitleiderweckend“. Doch ist gerade dem Dichter ein besonderer Auftrag gegeben. Griffel, Feder und Schreibpalette überdauern die Zeit, während der Triumph des Schwertes zeitlich begrenzt ist. Hier mag man sich an eine berühmte Kontroverse erinnern, die ihren literarischen Niederschlag im ersten Teil des „Don Quijote“ gefunden hat: den „Discurso de las armas y las letras.“ (I, 38). Für Hilda Doolittle steht der Vorrang des geschriebenen Wortes fest. Der Name der Königin Hatschepsut, den ihr kriegerischer Nachfolger sich bemühte auszulöschen, ist immer noch zu lesen, „circled / with what they call the *cartouche* „[266] (man beachte den Doppelsinn von *cartouche*: „Patrone“ und „Königsring“, mit dem in der ägyptischen Schrift der Herrschername hervorgehoben wird).

Wenn Hilda Doolittle die Hieroglyphen als Bildsymbole auffasste, stellt sich die Frage, welcher Art die Wirklichkeit war, die sich für sie dahinter verbarg. In „Helen in Egypt“ erklärt die Protagonistin: „I would study and decipher / the indecipherable Amen-script.“ Es handelt sich dabei um eine besondere Weise des Entzifferns, ein eher irrationales Begreifen der als unentzifferbar bezeichneten Schrift, die als Ganzes vom Herzen angenommen und umschlossen ist. Horapollons Deutungen helfen hier ebenso wenig weiter wie das heutige Verständnis der Hieroglyphen (auch wenn es einmal heißt: „how did I know the vulture? / why did I invoke the mother?“). Helen „kennt“ die Zeichen, aber ihre Kenntnis ist intuitiv, begründet in einer Erfah-

---

261 Erasmus von Rotterdam: Dialogus cui titulus Ciceronianus. Adagiorum chiliades. Übers., eingel. u. m. Anm. vers. v. Theresia Payr. Darmstadt 1972, S. 475.

262 Doolittle (Anm. 12), S. 15.

263 Die Weisheitsbücher der Ägypter. Eingel., übers. u. erl. v. Hellmut Brunner. München 1991, S.165.

264 Doolittle (Anm. 13), S. 69.

265 Doolittle (Anm. 12), S. VII.

266 Ebd., S. 14, 16, 17.

rung, die für Außenstehende kaum nachvollziehbar ist. Die Notwendigkeit einer „Lesung" wird schließlich überhaupt infrage gestellt: „Let the temple walls flower with 'the indecipherable Amen-script'. It is not necessary to 'read' the riddle. The pattern itself is sufficient and it is beautiful." Was genau mit „the pattern" gemeint ist, bleibt offen.[267]

Helen Fairwood in „Secret Name" fragt sich, was geschehen wäre, wenn sie sich auf das spirituelle Abenteuer im Tempel von Karnak eingelassen hätte: „Yes, certainly, there were heiroglyphs (*sic*), the usual bee and chick ... If she had gone further, would she, fourth dimensional, have followed Rafton, fourth dimensional, up those steps that utterly she had proved, were of another element?" Die Hieroglyphen verweisen auf eine andere Dimension. Sie sind zeitliche Bilder, die zu zeitlosen Bildern in Beziehung stehen. Ihre Parallelen liegen im Bereich des Ewigen.[268]

Gleichzeitig spiegelt sich im Geheimnis der Schrift die menschliche Seele. Hilda Doolittles „Huldigung an Freud" enthält die Schilderung eines seltsamen Erlebnisses, das sie 1920 auf Korfu hatte. An der Wand ihres Hotelzimmers erschien „eine Reihe von Schatten- oder Lichtbildern," unter anderem Kopf und Schultern eines Soldaten oder Fliegers, ein Pokal und ein Dreifuß. Bryher, die auch damals in ihrer Begleitung war, entdeckte zudem einen Kreis „wie die Sonnenscheibe" und darin einen Mann, der das Bild einer Frau in die Sonne zeichnete – für Hilda Doolittle eine Art Zusammenfassung ihrer eigenen Vision, vergleichbar einem Determinativ. In dem Geschauten erkannte Hilda Doolittle eine Bilderschrift - „Greek in spirit, rather than Egyptian" -, die sich jedoch in heutige Begrifflichkeit übersetzen lässt. Freud, dem sie davon berichtete, interpretierte die Erscheinung als Sehnsucht nach Vereinigung mit der Mutter. Die Dichterin selbst verweist auf die Möglichkeit, dass es sich um „den unterdrückten Wunsch nach verbotenen 'Zeichen und Wundern',, - „the desire to be a Prophetess, to be important anyway"- oder um eine Erweiterung des künstlerischen Bewusstseins handeln könne. Wie weit solche Deutungen überzeugen, sei dahingestellt. Aufschlussreich ist immerhin, dass Hilda Doolittle hier von „Hieroglyphen des Unbewussten oder Unterbewussten" spricht, „the hieroglyph actually in operation before our very eyes."[269] Die ägyptische Helena wurde nicht „unterwiesen", aber sie ist den Zeichen näher als der unterwiesene Schreiber: „She herself is the writing."[270]

Darf man die Schriftzeichen Altägyptens - mehr als hundert Jahre nach ihrer Entschlüsselung - noch als rätselhafte Glyphen oder als Träger geheimer Botschaften und Spiegelungen subtiler seelischer Prozesse ansehen? Wir wissen heute, dass die ägyptische Schrift eine komplizierte Mischung aus Laut- und Begriffszeichen ist. Für den Leser ägyptischer Texte führt kein Weg zurück zu Erasmus oder Horapollon. Die Hieroglyphik ist ihrerseits Gegenstand der Forschung geworden. Horapollons „Hieroglyphica" sind ein Schlüsseltext der Ägypten-Rezeption, nicht der Schlüssel zur Geisteswelt Ägyptens.

Das muss noch nicht bedeuten, dass die Dichtung an derartige Vorgaben gebunden ist. Erst in dem Augenblick, da der Dichter die objektiv richtige Lesung der ägyptischen Schriftzeichen in sein Schaffen mit einzubeziehen sucht, unterwirft er sich dem Diktat der Fachwissenschaft. Halten seine Lesungen einer Prüfung nicht stand, so hat dies Konsequenzen auch für den Rang der Dichtung, die sich nicht mit dem Hinweis auf die Freiheit des Künstlers erledigen.

---

[267] Doolittle (Anm. 13), S. 21, 86, 23, 13, 32.
[268] Doolittle: Palimpsest (Anm. 13) S. 333-334. Dies.: Helen in Egypt (Anm. 13), S. 13.
[269] Hilda Doolittle: Tribute to Freud. Boston 1974, S. 41, 45-46, 56, 51, 44, 47.
[270] Doolittle: Helen in Egypt (Anm. 13), S. 22. Vgl. ebd. S. 13-17.

Wenn andererseits die Position der Wissenschaft bewusst ignoriert, der Anspruch des *poeta doctus* nicht erhoben wird, ist der Dichter frei, aus vorgegebenen und imaginären Elementen seine eigene Welt zu schaffen. Zukofskys „black glyphs“ und die „unentzifferbare Amun- Schrift“ Hilda Doolittles sind einer kritischen Hinterfragung entzogen. Sie gehören nicht in die Geschichte der Schrift, sondern sind Teil einer „in sich geschlossene(n) Spielsphäre,“[271] die sie in ihrem Eigenwert legitimiert.

[271] Wolfgang Kayser: Die Wahrheit der Dichter. Hamburg 1959, S. 54.

Konrad Marwinski

Die Kunst, sich eine Bibliothek zu sammeln ...

Immanuel Vertraugott Rothe und seine Grundlage einer auserlesenen Bibliothek (1798)

1. Einleitung

In Rudolf Zacharias Beckers Reichsanzeiger erschien am 3. Februar 1797 unter der Überschrift „Allerhand“ eine Anfrage von Martin Lilia, Direktor des Wittenberger Schulmeister-Seminars, wie es komme, „daß man seit einiger Zeit in öffentlichen Blättern nichts mehr von dem Herrn Dr. Rothe in Camenz angezeigt findet“.[272] Eine Antwort sucht man in den folgenden Nummern vergebens und ist deshalb auf Vermutungen angewiesen, von denen eine sicherlich nicht fehl geht: Der Doktor der Medizin Immanuael Vertraugott Rothe war anderweitig vollauf beschäftigt – das Manuskript des wenig später veröffentlichten, über 500 Druckseiten umfassenden Kompendiums mit Werken für eine private Universalbibliothek, das hier vorgestellt werden soll, nahm seine ganze Aufmerksamkeit in Anspruch. Zudem war er bei seinem Verleger, dem Buchhändler und Schriftsteller Friedrich August Gottlob Schumann[273] (1773 – 1826) in Ronneburg, in argen Zeitverzug geraten war. Das Buch erschien 1798 gleich zweimal in dem Verlag, aber mit abweichendem Inhalt, verschiedenen Titeln und mit unterschiedlichen Vornamen des Verfassers. Ein bibliographisches Kuriosum.

Die Rückseite des Titelblattes enthält eine Nachricht: „Dieser Titel wird nur ad interim beigelegt. Ein anderer Abdruck desselben, (nebst Vorrede, Einleitung und Registern), folgt in 14 Tagen nach.“ Sie erklärt, weshalb lediglich der rein bibliographische Teil des Buches angeboten und verkauft wurde.[274] Auf Seite 416 befindet sich die Kustode Re=, die andeutet, dass nun das Register folgen sollte (was aber nicht der Fall war). Der zweite Vorname des Autors „Fürchtegott“ ist falsch, was in den Bibliothekskatalogen bis heute für Verwirrung sorgt. Zwei Wochen später, im Mai 1798, sah sich das interessierte Publikum mit einem „zweiten“ Werk Rothes konfrontiert:

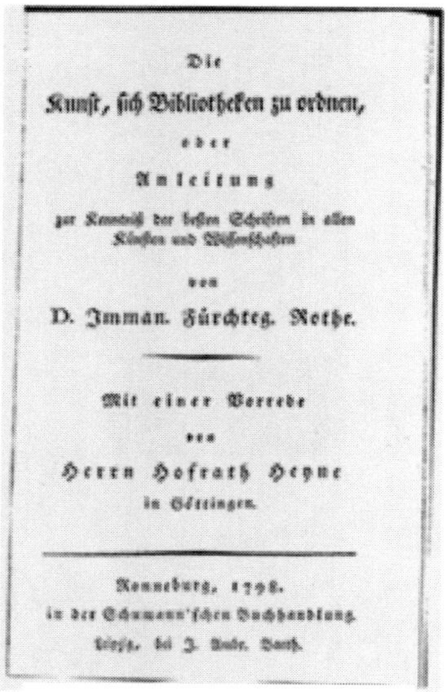
Die
Kunst, sich Bibliotheken zu ordnen,
oder
Anleitung
zur Kenntniß der besten Schriften in allen
Künsten und Wissenschaften
von
D. Imman. Fürchteg. Rothe.
Mit einer Vorrede
von
Herrn Hofrath Heyne
in Göttingen.
Ronneburg, 1798.
in der Schumann'schen Buchhandlung.
Leipzig, bei J. Ambr. Barth.

Titelblatt der ersten Ausgabe

[272] Reichsanzeiger, Gotha (1797) I, Nr. 23 vom 3. Febr., sp. 305.

[273] Vater des Komponisten Robert Schumann.

[274] Vorhanden in der Herzogin Anna Amalia Bibliothek in Weimar. Nach der Zugangsnummer zu urteilen, kam das Buch erst 1943 über einen antiquarischen Ankauf (70 RM) erst in die damalige Landesbibliothek Weimar (Sign.: 16,6: 89 $\underline{^{37}}$). - Otto, Lexikon (wie Anm. 14), gibt bei der Aufführung der Schriften Rothes den in diesem Zusammenhang nicht zutreffenden Hinweis zu 5) Die Kunst sich Bibliotheken zu ordnen: „1800 erhielt es den Titel: Die Kunst sich eine Bibliothek zu sammeln.“

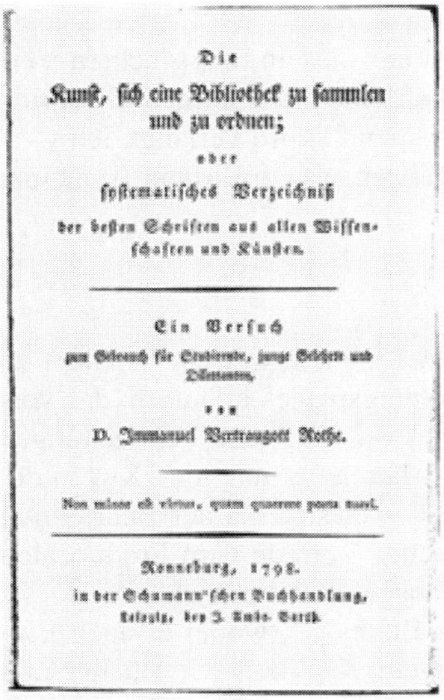
Die
Kunst, sich eine Bibliothek zu sammlen und zu ordnen;
oder
systematisches Verzeichniß
der besten Schriften aus allen Wissenschaften und Künsten.
Ein Versuch
zum Gebrauch für Studierende, junge Gelehrte und Dilettanten,
von
D. Immanuel Vertraugott Rothe.
Ronneburg, 1798.
in der Schumann'schen Buchhandlung.
Leipzig, bey J. Ambr. Barth.

Titelblatt der zweiten Ausgabe

Wer nun aber glaubte, er fände die oben angekündigte Vorrede des berühmten Göttinger Professors der Beredsamkeit und Universitätsbibliothekars Christoph Gottlob Heyne (1729 – 1812) vor, sah sich getäuscht. Statt dessen sind dem bibliographischen Teil eine umständliche Vorrede des Verfassers (S. V – XXXII) und seine „Erklärung der bey Aufführung der kritischen Journale gebrauchten Abkürzungen und Zeichen“ (S. XXXIII – XXXVI) vorangesetzt. Dann folgt der bereits erwähnte bibliographische Teil (S. 1 – 416), der auch mit der Kurztitelbezeichnung „Rothe Kunst Bibl. zu ordnen“ versehen ist. Wie in der ersten Ausgabe, findet sich auf Seite 416 die Kustode Re=, aber statt des zu erwartenden Registers folgen die „Zusätze, Vermehrungen, Verbesserungen, Anzeige der Druckfehler“ (S. 417 – 474), und dann erst schließt sich das alphabetische Register an (S. 474 – 508).[275] Der zweite Vorname Rothes ist mit Vertraugott (statt Fürchtegott)[276] richtig angegeben.

In seiner Vorrede äußert sich Rothe zum Titel des Werkes:[277] „Die Aufschrift meines Buchs: die Kunst sich Bibliotheken zu sammeln, ist Erfindung des Verlegers“, und gibt zu erkennen, dass er mit beiden Titelfassungen nicht einverstanden ist. Die Titel täuschen den Leser, der eine Anleitung zur Sammlung und Ordnung einer Bibliothek erwartet. Das haben bereits die Zeitgenossen kritisch vermerkt, wie z. B. der Rezensent der Neuen Allgemeinen Deutschen Bibliothek: „Ueber die Kunst, Bibliotheken z[u] s[ammeln] u[nd] z[u] o[rdnen] enthält das Buch auch nicht eine Zeile. Bloß der Verleger hat sich diesen Einfall erlaubt; in der Hoffnung vermuthlich, ein paar Käufer mehr durch dergleichen Aufschrift herbeyzuziehn.“ [278] Der gescholtene Verleger beschrieb wenig später den in der Allgemeinen Literaturzeitung eingerückten Titel der Neuerscheinung zutreffender: „Bücherfreunden, welche bey dem Ankaufe neuerer und älterer Bücher nicht das Schlechte mit dem Guten kaufen wollen, welche sich, ohne kostspielige Erfahrungen, ihre Büchersammlung zweckmäßig vervollständigen und ordnen wollen, empfehlen wir ...“[279]. Erst der Untertitel deutet den wirklichen Inhalt der Publikation an. Im übrigen hatte er Rothes Unmut schon durch eigenmächtiges Weglassen des Inhaltsverzeichnisses und auch durch anderweitige Eingriffe hervorgerufen.

Wegen einer Vorrede, so Rothe weiter, habe er an Hofrat Heyne in Göttingen geschrieben, welcher antwortete, „er habe sich nie in diesem Fache gezeiget, daher könne er keine Vorre-

---

275 Nach dem Exemplar der Thüringer Universitäts- und Landesbibliothek Jena (Sign.: Hist. lit. XVIII, o. 58) mit dem Kaufvermerk eines unbekannten Vorbesitzers: Trieste den 21ten Märtz 1807, – Band 51 Xer .

276 In dem Handbuch der medizinischen Literatur (vgl. Anm. 26) ist dieser auf der Haupttitelseite zu „Vertrangott“ verunstaltet worden.

277 Vorrede, S. XXII.

278 Xy in: Neue Allgemeine Deutsche Bibliothek 43 (1799) St. 1, H. 1, Intelligenzblatt Nr. 9, S. 60 – 62.

279 Allgemeine Literaturzeitung, Jena (1799) Intelligenzbl. Nr. 78 vom 26. Juni., Sp. 622.

de schreiben u.s.f. Der Hofrat Hr. Kästner würde eher sich darzu verstehen"[280]. Bemerkenswert, weil allgemeingültig, sind Rothes Schlussfolgerungen aus diesem missglückten Versuch. Er „fand bey reiflicher Ueberlegung eine Vorrede von einem berühmten Gelehrten ganz unnöthig". Das Buch ist nun einmal gedruckt, „ist Bedürfniß, wird verlangt, ich werde darzu von vielen Gelehrten aufgemuntert, ich habe geleistet, was ein Mann in meiner Lage und Umständen leisten kann".[281]

2. Lebensumstände des Verfassers

Im folgenden erfährt der Leser, warum Rothe selbst zur Feder griff, um ein Vorwort zu verfassen. Er wollte das Für und Wider seines Veröffentlichungsplanes erläutern, das vorgelegte Ergebnis selbstkritisch beleuchten und Erklärungen für mögliche Fehlleistungen geben. Sein Vorgehen verstimmte die Rezensenten, wie den bereits genannten „Xy" in der Neuen Allgemeinen Deutschen Bibliothek, der schwankte, wie er sich bei der Beurteilung eines Produktes benehmen sollte, „das laut sehr umständlicher Vorrede dem Producenten höchst sauer geworden, ohne deshalb empfehlungswerther ausgefallen zu seyn".[282]

Zunächst erzählt Rothe dem Leser „die Geschichte des Buchs"[283], wobei er auch Einzelheiten aus seiner Biographie mitteilt. Es gelte als ausgemacht, dass wir Bücher und Schriften brauchen, sie seien nun einmal notwendig und unentbehrlich. Ebenso stehe fest, dass es gute und schlechte Schriften gäbe. Es käme deshalb „außerordentlich viel" darauf an, welches Buch man zuerst lese und studiere:

> *„Sonderlich scheint dieses jetzt Behertzigung zu verdienen, da nicht zu leugnen ist, daß in unsern Zeiten mehr geschrieben wird, als jemals ... Es sind auch ehedem schlechte Bücher geschrieben und gedruckt worden. Aber in unsern Tagen wohl beynahe mehr wie ehedem. Unser Leben ist kurz, die Zeit edel, kostbar, schnell vergehend, unersetzbar, und – des Geldes wenig. Täglich erweitern sich die Wissenschaften und Künste ... Der Mensch ist einmal da, sich Kenntnisse zu erwerben, zu sammeln, sie zu vermehren, zu vervollkommnen. Jeder will doch gern mit seinem Zeitalter fortschreiten. Den Mehresten ist es aber gleichgültig, auf welche Art dies geschiehet. Natürlich wählet man am liebsten den geradesten, leichtesten Weg. Und welcher ist dies nun?"*

Eigene Erfahrungen hatten Immanuel Vertraugott Rothe, der am 24. August 1768 im Dorf Sohra[284] bei Görlitz geboren worden war, bewogen, „diesem Uebel abzuhelfen" und einen Leitfaden durch das Labyrinth der Literatur zu erarbeiten Er stammte aus einer Familie, deren Vorfahren aus Glaubensgründen ihre Heimat in Böhmen und Ungarn verlassen hatten.[285] Sein Vater[286], der ihn durch häuslichen Unterricht auf das Gymnasium vorbereitete

---

280 Vorrede, S. XXII. - Gemeint ist der Göttinger Professor der Naturlehre und Geometrie Abraham Gotthelf Kästner (1719 – 1800). Beide waren gebürtige Sachsen: Heynes Geburtsstadt war Chemnitz, Kästner wurde in Leipzig geboren.

281 Ebenda, S. XXII – XXIII.

282 Xy (wie Anm. 7), S. 60.

283 Vorrede, S. V - VI.

284 Das Dorf Sohra liegt 9 km von Görlitz entfernt, jenseits der Neiße, heute Polen. Nicht zu verwechseln mit der Sorau in der Niederlausitz, Stadt in der preuß. Provinz Schlesien, Regierungsbezirk Oppeln, Kreis Rybnik (1863), heute Polen.

285 Vgl. Lausitzisches Magazin (1792) Stück 21 vom 15. Nov., S. 334.

und dem Rothe in dankbarer Erinnerung sein Werk widmete, habe durch sein Beispiel, seine Anweisung und durch seine Büchersammlung die Neigung, Leidenschaft und Liebe zu den Büchern in ihm geweckt. Es habe ihm nie an Gelegenheiten gefehlt, Bücher zu erhalten, Bibliotheken zu besuchen und Bücher kennen zu lernen. Zu Hause habe er z. B. zusammen mit dem Vater viele gelehrte Zeitungen und Journale gelesen. Er habe „ein Schulmann" werden wollen und deshalb nicht nur „die gewöhnlichen ältern, sondern auch die hebräische und neuern Sprachen" gelernt. Der gelehrte Archidiakonus Gottlieb Christian Giese (1721 – 1788), Besitzer einer großen Bibelsammlung[287], gestattete ihm freien Zutritt zu seiner Bibliothek.[288] Einer Anzeige im „Lausitzischen Magazin" ist zu entnehmen, dass er schon als Gymnasiast mit Vorliebe die „Gelehrten-Geschichte, vorzüglich die Bücher-Kenntniß" betrieb.[289] In Leipzig, wo Rothe seit 1787 zuerst Philosophie, Geschichte und alte Sprachen studierte, sich aber später aus freien Stücken zum Medizinstudium entschloss, hatte er Zugang zu öffentlichen und privaten Bibliotheken und nahm „an allen Lese-Gesellschaften und Leih-Bibliotheken Antheil". Buchhandlungen und Antiquariate besuchte er „fleißig", er versäumte keine Gelegenheit, sich Bücher zu verschaffen. In kurzer Zeit brachte er eine große Anzahl Bücher zusammen, merkte aber bald, „daß es nicht auf die Menge, sondern auf die Güte der Bücher ankomme".

Einen sicheren Führer als Ratgeber und Wertmaßstab fand er nicht. So fasste er noch als Student den Plan, „ein Werk zu schreiben, welches Studierenden, angehenden Gelehrten und Liebhabern der Wissenschaften und Künste zum Leiter beym Bücher-Kauf und bey neuer Sammlung einer Bibliothek dienen könnte". Er verhandelte mit Verlegern, zog Gelehrte zu Rate und besuchte zur Erweiterung seiner Kenntnisse die Dresdner Bibliothek. Er begann seine bibliographischen Arbeiten mit der pädagogischen Literatur, die Philosophie folgte. Beides blieb stecken, „mein sogenanntes Brodfach[290] und andere Umstände rissen mich damals von allen literarischen Arbeiten los". Als Rothe 1791 nach Wittenberg wechselte, wo er 1792 seine Dissertation[291] verteidigte, fehlte es ihm „theils an Zeit, theils an Gelegenheit, Hand ans Werk zu legen". Trotzdem sammelte er weiter, soviel er konnte. Unterstützung fand er durch den Wittenberger Kirchenhistoriker und Professor der Poesie

---

286 Immanuel Gottfried Rothe, 1737 in Berthelsdorf (Oberlausitz) geboren, hatte nach dem Besuch des Görlitzer Gymnasiums Theologie auf den Universitäten Leipzig und Halle studiert, wo er auch als Informator in der Lateinschule des Waisenhauses herangezogen und „1761 als Collega ordinarius und als Hofmeister einiger Edelleute angenommen wurde". 1765 wurde er Konrektor und bald danach Rektor zu Sorau in der Niederlausitz, dann Prediger in den Gemeinden zu Sohra und Sohrneundorf in der Oberlausitz bei Görlitz, starb 1809 in Altwohlau. Neben einer Reihe von theologisch-praktischen Schriften und zahlreichen Zeitschriftenaufsätzen verfasste er auch einige Arbeiten zur Pädagogik und zur Art und Weise des Studierens, Themen, die später auch seinen ältesten Sohn interessieren sollten, wie z. B. Von den Vortheilen der Erziehung der Studierenden (Görlitz 1768); Vom Gebrauch der alten Schriftsteller bey der Bildung des moralischen Characters der Jugend (Görlitz 1770). - Zur Biographie vgl. u. a. Otto, Gottlieb Friedrich: Lexicon der seit 15. Jahrhundert verstorbenen und jetzt lebenden Oberlausitzischen Schriftsteller und Künstler. Bd. 3, Abt. 1, S. 98f. u. 2, S. 787f. (Görlitz 1803) u. Suppl.Bd. (Görlitz 1821), S. 369. – Rothes Mutter war Sophia Benedicta geb. Schirach. – Für Auskünfte danke ich Frau Edeltraud Schnappauf vom Lessing-Museum Kamenz und Herrn Matthias Wenzel von der Oberlausitzischen Bibliothek der Wissenschaften Görlitz.

287 Die Sammlung wurde nach seinem Tode vereinzelt und verkauft.

288 Es ist unklar, ob es sich hier nicht um die Bibliothek der Evangelischen Kirchgemeinde St. Peter und Paul zu Görlitz gehandelt hat, für die Giese zuständig war (vgl. Handbuch der historischen Buchbestände in Deutschland. Bd. 17: Sachsen A-K. Hildsheim 1997, S. 282).

289 Lausitzisches Magazin (wie Anm. 14), S. 334f.

290 Das war die Medizin.

291 De atrophia partiali sive de Ariduris (Vitebergae 1792).

Johann Matthias Schröckh (1733 – 1808).[292]

In Liebenwerda, wo er sich „für einige Zeit" als praktischer Arzt aufhielt, fehlte es ihm zwar nicht an Zeit, aber er war „vollends ganz von der litterarischen Welt abgeschnitten". Hier lernte er die Tochter des Kurfürstl. Sächsischen Land-Accis- und Geleitskommissärs A. Sigmund Beßer kennen, die er am 25. April 1793 heiratete. In Kamenz, wo er wahrscheinlich zunächst privatisierte, hoffte er es besser zu haben, „und war fast noch übler dran". Weil er schon soviel Arbeit und Mühe in sein Vorhaben investiert hatte, hielt er daran fest. Er reduzierte sein Konzept dahingehend, „nur die Bücher auszusuchen, welcher jeder unumgänglich braucht, um eine Wissenschaft oder Kunst zu erlernen". Er machte die Idee publik und fand breite Zustimmung. „Ich las, studierte! Sammelte, was, wo und wie ich konnte!". Für „einige Zeit" besuchte er seine Eltern in Sohra und benutzte von dort aus „mehrere Werke der Görlitzer Bibliothek[293]. Der Herr Dr. Anton in Görlitz war so gütig, mir aus seiner Büchersammlung[294] verschiedene Schriften zu lehnen, ja, als ich nach Kamenz zurückkehrte, sendete er mir sogar dahin Bücher". Wann er seine ärztliche Praxis wieder aufnahm, wissen wir nicht. Durch einen im Mai 1797 verfassten Spendenaufruf für ein Lessing-Denkmal in Kamenz, dessen Veröffentlichung im Reichsanzeiger[295] ihm einigen Verdruss einbrachte, ist bekannt, dass er zu diesem Zeitpunkt seinen Beruf wieder ausgeübte.[296]

Seinen Verleger Schumann fand Rothe „durch Zufall" im Zusammenhang mit einem anderen größeren Verlagsprojekt, zu dem dieser Mitarbeiter suchte. Die günstige Gelegenheit nutzend, bot ihm Rothe ein „Systematisches Verzeichnis der besten Schriften aus allen Wissenschaften und Künsten", von dem hier die Rede ist, und das spätere „Handbuch für die medicinische Litteratur" an. Letzteres übernahm Schumann sofort, er wollte es 1796 der Presse übergeben[297], ersteres auch, „wenn sich hinlängliche Interessenten fänden". Ursprünglich hatte Rothe wohl nur an ein Werk gedacht, „allein das Manuscript schwoll unter der Arbeit so an, daß ich bald sah, beyde müßten getrennt werden". Nun begann der oben erwähnte Wettlauf mit der Zeit. Rothe musste zweigleisig weiterarbeiten. Das zuerst genannte Projekt wurde ausgeweitet und er bestimmte das Manuskript „zu einem besonderen Werke, zum Vorläufer meines größeren litterarischen Verzeichnisses. Daher ist das Buch nicht so ausgefallen, wie es bey einer neuen Auflage erscheinen wird", die, wie wir

---

[292] Vgl. Lausitzisches Magazin (wie Anm. 14), S. 335. – Von Schröckh hat Rothe 5 Werke in die Bücherkunde aufgenommen.

[293] Vermutlich die Bibliothek der Oberlausitzischen Gesellschaft der Wissenschaften.

[294] Der Jurist, Historiker und Sprachforscher und Initiator der Oberlausitzischen Gesellschaft der Wissenschaften Karl Gottlob Anton (1751 – 1818) besaß eine bedeutende Privatbibliothek, die er testamentarisch der Gesellschaft vermachte (1801). Vgl. hierzu Handbuch (wie Anm. 17), S. 284.

[295] Aufruf an meine Landsleute zu Beyträgen, dem großen Lessing in seiner Geburtsstadt Camenz ein kleines Denkmal zu errichten. In: Reichsanzeiger (1797) Nr. 123 vom 30. Mai, Sp. 1225 – 1228. Unterzeichnet: Camens in der Oberlausitz, Rothe, Dr. - Nach Auskunft des Lessing-Museums Kamenz vom 27. März 2001 ist diese Initiative Rothes in Kamenz bisher unbekannt geblieben. Ihr war wohl auch kein Erfolg beschieden, das erste Lessing-Denkmal der Stadt wurde 1863 errichtet, nachdem das Geburtshaus des Dichter beim Stadtbrand von 1842 zerstört worden war.

[296] Noch am 4. Sept. 1797 bezeichnet der Kamenzer Stadtrat ihn unter Bezugnahme auf den genannten Aufruf als „hiesigen Arzt", vgl. Reichsanzeiger (1797) Nr. 239 vom 14. Okt., Sp. 2574f.

[297] Das „Handbuch für die medizinische Litteratur nach allen ihren Theilen; oder Anleitung zur Kenntniß der besten auserlesenen medizinischen Bücher, mit beygesetztem Inhalt, Werth, Jahrzahl, Rezensionen, historischen, biographischen und andern Anmerkungen; in systematischer Ordnung; Ein Versuch zum Gebrauch angehender Aerzte" erschien aber erst 1799 in der von Kleefeld'schen Buchhandlung zu Leipzig (VIII, 664 S.).

wissen, niemals fertig wurde.

Ostern 1797 war Schumann im Besitz des vollständigen Manuskriptes. Aber erst zu Weihnachten begann der Druck, der sich zu Rothes Leidwesen bis Pfingsten 1798 hinzog. Die Vorrede, die mit der Schlussschrift „Dorf Sohra bey Görliz in der Ober-Lausiz, im Monat Mai 1798. Der Verfasser“ versehen ist, hatte er wiederum im elterlichen Hause abgefasst. Nicht ganz zu Unrecht befürchtete er, bei einem verspäteten Erscheinen des Werkes nicht mehr aktuell zu sein: „Hätte ich dieses Zaudern nur geahndet“, beklagt er sich, „wäre es mir nicht darauf angekommen, das Werk nochmals auszuarbeiten, auszufeilen, zu erweitern, zu verbessern, zu vervollkommnen, um es so zu liefern, wie ich es wünschte, und wie es nach und nach werden soll. Das Publikum und die Recensenten, denen beyden ich nun mein Werk auf Gnade und Ungnade übergebe, sehen also, daß ich ganz und gar keine Schuld habe, wenn das Werk späte, minder vollkommen erscheint.“ Gesundheitlich angeschlagen, hoffte Rothe, noch einige Zeit zu leben, in „bessere Verhältnisse [und in eine] sorgenfreyere Lage“ zu gelangen, um aus dem „nur schwachen Versuch“ das seinen Anforderungen entsprechende vollkommene Werk zu gestalten.

3. Rothes Bücherkunde

A. Encyklopädien
B. Methodik
C. Sprachkunde
D. Schreibekunst
E. Buchdruckerkunst
F. Alte Sprachen
G. Neuere Sprachen
H. Kenntniß der Alterthümer
I. Mythologie
K. Archäologie
L. Geschichte
M. Hülfswissenschaften
  a. Geographie
    1. alte
    2. mittlere
    3. neuere
    4. mathematische Geogr.
    5. Astronomie
    6. Statistik
    7. Diplomatik
    8. Heraldik
    9. Chronologie
    10. Genealogie
    11. Münzwesen
    12. Kritik
N. Geschichte an sich
O. Geschichte des Mittelalters
P. Abhandelnde Werke
Q. Neuere und neueste Geschichte
R. Special-Geschichte
S. Geschichte der erloschenen Völker und Staaten
T. Geschichte noch bestehender Völker und Staaten
V. Schriften über besondere Materien
W. Geschichte denkwürdiger Personen
X. Philosophie
Y. Moral
Z. Pädagogik
AA. Staatswissenschaften
BB. Kriegswissenschaften
CC. Gewerbs-Kunde
DD. Mathematik
EE. Naturkunde
FF. Schöne Wissenschaften und Künste
GG. Litterargeschichte
HH. Arzneygelahrheit
II. Rechtsgelahrheit
KK. Gottesgelahrheit

Rothes wichtigste Quelle für die zeitgenössische Literatur und zugleich Vorbild für die Präsentation der Titel war das *Allgemeine Repertorium der Literatur für die Jahre 1785 bis*

1790 (3 Bände, Jena, sp. Weimar 1793 – 1794) des Bibliographen Johann Samuel Ersch (1768 – 1828), das dieser während seiner Jenaer Jahre von 1790 bis 1793 als Mitarbeiter an der Allgemeinen Literatur-Zeitung erarbeitet hatte und später für die Berichtszeit bis 1800 fortsetzte.[298] In der Systematik ging Rothe allerdings eigene Wege:
Sie erfüllte mehr praktische Zwecke und ist gewiss nicht als Grundlage für eine theoretische Auseinandersetzung gedacht, weshalb sie im folgenden auch nicht thematisiert werden soll. Den Komplex „Geschichte" löst Rothe z. B. in selbständige Gruppen auf (M – W), wobei ihm bei der Unterteilung der Hilfswissenschaften (M) insofern ein Versehen unterläuft, als er der Geographie (a) die unterschiedlichsten Untergruppen zuweist, von denen die Ziff. 5 – 12 (vielleicht mit Ausnahme der Statistik) besser mit b – i zu benennen gewesen wären. Die Untergliederung der einzelnen Systematikgruppen erfolgt der Größe des Gebietes angemessen, so dass das Ergebnis überschaubar bleibt. Wer an der richtigen Stelle sucht, findet. Die bibliographischen Beschreibungen Rothes sind bei aller Kürze hinlänglich genau, Erscheinungsort(e) und -jahre, sowie Umfang (Bände, Teile etc.), Format und Preis werden grundsätzlich angegeben. Von den Vornamen der Verfasser erscheinen stets die Anfangsbuchstaben, im Register wurden sie weggelassen. Eine durchgängige Kategorie ist die Bücherkunde. Wo immer entsprechende Literatur vorhanden ist, zeigt er sie in dieser Kategorie an.

Unter formal-statistischen Aspekten ergibt sich nach der Zahl der zugewiesenen Seiten folgende Rangfolge der Fächer mit über 20 Seiten:

Gewerbskunde (CC., 57 S.)
Naturkunde (EE., 55 S.)
Litterargeschichte (GG., 41 S.)
Schöne Wissenschaften und Künste (FF., 41 S.)
Sprachen (F. Alte Sprachen, G. Neuere Sprachen, 32 S.)
Geschichte denkwürdiger Personen (W., 27 S.)
Schriften über besondere Materien [der Geschichte und Zeitgeschichte] (V., 20 S.)

Diese im Geist der Zeit liegende Wichtung sagt nichts über die Anzahl der dort genannten Titel aus. So zählt Rothe mehrfach aus Platzgründen, z. B. an einigen Stellen bei den Schönen Wissenschaften (FF.), nur die Namen von bekannten Autoren auf. Dass die Arzneigelahrheit (HH.) als das eigentliche Fach des Verfassers so unterrepräsentiert ist (5 Seiten), liegt in der Absicht begründet, mit dem genannten Handbuch der medizinischen Literatur[299] ein Spezialnachschlagewerk zu schaffen, an dem er parallel arbeitete und das mit der „Bibliothek" in fortdauernder Wechselwirkung stand, denn dort findet der Leser im ersten Teil unter der Überschrift „Allgemeine Wissenschaften, die einen Arzt, wenn er auf den Titel eines Gelehrten Anspruch machen will, besitzen muß, ohngeachtet sie nicht den eigentlichen Arzt bilden, sondern ihn nur vollkommner machen helfen" auf 152 Seiten einen kurzgefassten Querschnitt aus dem Titelmaterial der entsprechenden Gruppe in der „Bibliothek" vor.

Betrachtet man Rothes Bücherkunde aus den Blickwinkeln des Bibliothekars und des Bibliographen, so ist sie eine empfehlende und zugleich räsonierende Bibliographie, die

---

298 Zu Ersch vgl. Seifert, Siegfried: Johann Samuel Ersch. Ein Bibliograph und Enzyklopädist an der Wende zum bürgerlichen Zeitalter. In: Studien zum Buch- und Bibliothekswesen. Bd. 7 (Berlin 1989), S. 40 – 53, bes. S. 46 – 49.
299 Vgl. Anm. 26.

Studierenden, jungen Gelehrten und Dilettanten gleichermaßen als Leitfaden durch die Literatur zu allseitiger Bildung im Sinne der Aufklärung einerseits und andererseits als qualitativer Ratgeber für den Aufbau einer kleinen, universal ausgerichteten und im wesentlichen auf den Neuerscheinungen des Buchmarktes im 18. Jahrhunderts basierenden Privatbibliothek dienen kann. Zur Abrundung und als Hinweis darauf, dass Wissenschaften und Künste in der zeitlichen Dimension einen viel größeren Raum beanspruchen, als sein „Versuch" zu vermitteln vermag, hat der Autor hier und da auch Standardwerke des 16. und 17. Jahrhunderts aufgenommen, und zwar immer dann, wenn es aus seiner Sicht inzwischen nichts besseres gab. Mit Lob und Tadel hält Rothe nicht zurück, wenn er es für angebracht hält. Er kannte die meisten Werke aus eigener Lektüre und mittelbar aus Rezensionen, deren Quellen er regelmäßig und ausführlich angibt. Nachfolgend einige Beispiele aus der Fachgruppe GG. Litterargeschichte, in der sich unter III. Geschichte des Bücherwesens, 2. Bücherkenntniß auch die „Bibliothekenkunde" (2.a.) findet. Als Einleitungsschriften sind kommentarlos aufgeführt:[300]

- J. G. Schelhorn, Anleitung für Bibliothekare u. Archivare. Ulm gr. 8. 2 Thle. 88 – 91. (2 Thlr.)
- A.L.Z. 88.160. 93.18. A.d.B. 97.2. III.1. Obd. 88.625. T. 88.98.
- A. C. Kayser, über die Manipulation bey der Einrichtung e. Bibliothek u. d. Verfertigung d. Bücherverzeichnisse u.s.f. Bayr. 90. Gr 8. (10 gr.)
- A.L.Z. 90. Int.Bl. 751. 975. 91.2. 313. A.d.B. 102.2. Gth. 90.594. Gtt. 90.1741. N. 90.576"

Unter „2.b. Eigentliche Bibliographie, 2. Nachrichten von gedruckten Werken überhaupt, 1. in systematischer Ordnung" wird zuerst *H. W. Lawätz, Handbuch für Bücherfreunde u. Bibliothekare – auch m. d. Titel: Handbuch zum Gebrauche derj., die sich von der Gelehrsamkeit überhaupt einige Bücherkenntniß zu erwerben wünschen. Halle, gr. 8. 88 – 95* angezeigt und kritisch besprochen:[301]

> *„Ein äußerst weitläufiges, unzweckmäßiges, nach keinem bestimmten Plane, kostspielig gedrucktes Werk ... Der verst[orbene] Krünitz hat eine Vorr. darzu geschrieben. – Des Verf. ganzes Unternehmen wäre sonst ganz beyfallswerth; nur übereilte sich der Verf. Am verdiensteten machten sich Verf. u. Verl., wenn das ganze Werk völlig umgearbeitet erschiene, möglichst vervollkommnet, systematischer eingerichtet ..., sparsamer gedruckt, und der Werth jeder Schrift kurz angegeben würde. Denn ich kann mich jetzt noch nicht von dem Werthe einer Schrift völlig überzeugen, die alle Bücher u. Schriften ohne Auswahl, ohne Bestimmung ihres Werthes u. innern Gehaltes aufgezeichnet enthält. Dieses unterlassen fast alle Verf. Sie häufen Titel u. Citationen auf einander. Dem Gelehrten hilft dies wenig, und dem angehenden Gelehrten, dem Bücherfreunde, dem Liebhaber nutzet es vollends gar nichts. Man muß doch erst die besten, unentbehrlichsten Bücher kennen lernen. Ich schmeichle mir sehr, durch diese Bogen, u. mein großes systemat. Werk diesem Uebel abzuhelfen ..."*

Erschs oben genanntes *Repertorium* hat Rothe als dritten Titel in die Bibliographie-Gruppe aufgenommen und ausführlich gewürdigt, wobei er bemerkt, dass er keine einzige, ihn be-

300 Rothe, S. 374f.
301 Ebenda, S. 376f.

friedigende ordentlich Rezension gelesen habe:[302]

> *„Das Ganze ist systemat. bearbeitet, u. enth. alle Bücher, Schriften, auch einzelne Abh., so daß leicht nichts fehlen wird. Ersch hat die Ausführung des systemat. Registers u. die Einschichtung d. Schriften in die Fächer ..., ja oft auch die Zergliederung einzelner Titel in kleinere Unterabtheilungen ganz alleine mit alle dem Fleiße, der Genauigkeit und Geschicklichkeit ausgeführet, als sich nur von einem Manne erwarten läßt. Ich bin das Werk jetzt bey meinen literar. Arbeiten ganz Zeile vor Zeile durchgegangen, habe es fleißig benutzet – welches ich hier öffentl. freymüthig gestehe, u. wofür ich dem Hrn. Ersch aufrichtig unendlichen Dank zolle – , daher kenne [ich] solches sehr genau. Die Litteratur ist, wie gesagt, äußerst vollständig. Nur wünschte ich, Hr. Ersch befleißigte sich in Anführung der Titel, der Recensionen mehr bey der Forts. des Repert. f. die Jahre 91 bis 95 der Kürze, setzte gleich den Preiß bey, und fügte noch mehrere gangbare gelehrte Zeitungen bey. Bedeutende Fehler habe [ich] nicht gefunden. Nur mit den Registern bin ich nicht hinlängl. zufrieden. Darin habe [ich] Fehler u. Nachläßigkeiten gefunden...“*

Rothe dankte zum zweiten Mal „Hrn. Ersch verbindlichst“, denn einen Teil der Nachweise für die Rezensionen hatte er von ihm übernehmen können. Als er in Leipzig mit der Arbeit begann, wo ihm alle Hilfsmittel zur Verfügung standen, hatte er Rezensionen nicht aufnehmen wollen und deshalb die Nachlässigkeit begangen, sich zwar die guten Werke auszuzeichnen, ihren Inhalt anzumerken „und was ich sonst bemerkenswerth fand, zu excerpiren“, aber die Zeitung, das Journal und dergl. nicht festzuhalten.[303]

In den Zusätzen fügt er noch *A. Burkardt's Anleitung zur Bücherkunde in allen Wissenschaft[en]. Grundlage zu einer auserlesenen Bibliothek in allen Fächern. Bern und Lpz 1797 8. (1 Thlr. 4 gr.)* hinzu.[304] Rothes Urteil, in das er wegen der unverkennbaren Ähnlichkeit des Ansatzes Argumente zu seiner Verteidigung einfließen lässt, fällt negativ aus:

> *„Wer sich dies Buch zum Führer wählet, ist gewiß übel berathen. Das Ganze ist ohne Plan, System und Ordnung. Eine Menge Büchertitel, ohne Wahl, ohne Preiß, oft ohne Jahrzahl, Verlagsort, Format u.s.w. D. Vf. will sich 28 Jahre mit der Bibliographie beschäftigt haben! Er hat schon Recht, daß nicht immer das neueste das beste Buch sey ... In wiefern ich zweckmäßiger gearbeitet habe, als der Vf., mag das Publikum entscheiden. Der Recens. in d. A.L.Z. 97. N. 295 hat schon vor mir den Gehalt und Werth des Buchs entschieden, folglich darf d. Vf. nicht denken, daß ich darum, weil wir einerley Zweck haben, ungünstig von seinem Buche urtheile ... Th. Kempis von der Nachfolge Christi ist des Vfs Lieblingsbuch. Dies denk ich, ist die beste Karakteristik des Vfs, seines Geschmacks, seiner Kenntnisse und Wahl. – Ich habe aber gar nichts dawider, wenn jemand des Vfs Buch zweckmäßiger, als meine Bogen findet. Meine Pflicht ist es zu sagen, was an jedem Buche ist: denn darum schrieb ich.“*

Anschließend behandelt Rothe die Bibliographien in alphabetischer Ordnung (2.2.).[305] Er setzt sich für ein allgemeines Bücherlexikon ein, indem er, die Zielgruppe seines eigenen Werkes über die Verzeichnisse von Weimann, Georgi, Heinsius, Giesecke, Vandenhoeck, Monath, Nicolai und Beygang informierend, wie folgt argumentiert:

---

302 Rothe, S. 378 – 380.
303 Rothe, Vorrede, S. XVI - XVII.
304 Rothe, S. 469f.
305 Ebenda, S. 380 – 382.

> *„Hierher gehören alle Buchhändler-Verzeichnisse, deren es so viele giebt, als Buchhändler sind. Sie haben aber keinen großen Werth; sie geben nur die neuen Bücher an mit beygefügtem Laden-Preise; sie sind aber nicht vollständig, genau u. richtig, sonderlich in Rücksicht der Preise ...*
> *Ich habe eine große Anzahl dergl. Verzeichnisse, die mich aber sehr oft alle verliessen. Es wäre sehr heilsam, nützlich u. löblich, wenn alljährlich ein richtiges Verzeichniß aller wirklich erschienen[en] Bücher u. Schriften mit beygesetztem Preise erschiene. Das allgemeine Verzeichniß neuer Bücher, so zu Lpz. in 4. schon seit langer Zeit jährlich in der Oster- und Michaelis-Messe in der Weimann. Buchhandlung herauskommt, sollte genauer, richtiger u. vollständiger seyn. So kann man sich nie darauf verlassen, u. die Buchhändler schaden sich selber. Da Th. Georgii allgem. Europ. Bücherlexicon, Leipz. Fol. 42. 4 Bde (8 Thlr.) u. 50 u. 55. 2 Bde Suppl. (6 Thlr.) nicht mehr für jetzt zulänglich war, gab 93. in 4. 4 Bde, W. Heinsius, ein allgem. Bücherlexicon heraus (9 Thlr, Schrbp. u. 8 Thlr. Drckp.), welches aber sehr unvollkommen, mangelhaft, unrichtig und falsch in Ansehung der Namen ist ...“*

Trotz der angedeuteten Mängel gelang es aber dem von Wilhelm Heinsius bearbeiteten Mehrjahresverzeichnis (Berichtszeit 1790/92 ff.), sich auf dem Buchmarkt zu behaupten. Rothes Ausführungen gipfeln in dem Satz, dass alle diese Verzeichnisse immer noch ein allgemeines Bücherlexikon „nothwendig u. wünschenswerth“ machten. Das wurde wohl seitens des Buchhandels in ähnlicher Weise empfunden, denn – wie wir wissen – im gleichen Jahr (1798) begann der Hinrichs'sche Halbjahreskatalog[306] zu erscheinen (Berichtszeit 1797 ff.), der im 19. Jahrhundert zum Träger der buchhändlerischen Bibliographie werden sollte. Die Anordnung (alphabetisch und systematisch) entsprach Rothes Vorschlägen, wenn er auch nicht „von einem Gelehrten ausgearbeitet“ worden war.

Mit dem renommierten Buchhändler und Schriftsteller Christoph Friedrich Nicolai (1733 – 1811) und dessen *Verzeichnis einer Handbibliothek der möglichsten Schriften* (4., ganz umgearb. u. verm. Aufl., Berlin 1795) geht Rothe hart zu Gericht, wenn er in den Zusätzen bemerkt:[307]

> *„Nicolai nennt die n. Aufl. s. Verz. e. ganz umgearbeitete u. verm. Aufl. Vermehrt ist sie, aber nichts weniger als nach e. verbesserten Plane bearbeitet. Wie viele gute Werke fehlen nicht! Wie sind sie nicht durch einander geworfen! Unter den vermischten Schriften stehen medicin. Bücher! Wie viele Fächer fehlen gänzlich! Ich wundere mich über Hrn. Nicolai, daß ein Mann, wie er, uns nichts besseres, vollständiger[e]s geliefert hat. Und grade war Nicolai vor vielen Andern d. Mann, welcher uns ein schätzbares Werk liefern konnte, da er in Berlin Büchersammlungen zu nutzen Gelegenheit hat, da er so lange Buchhändler u. selbst Gelehrter ist. Und so eine Schrift erlebt mehrere Auflagen!“*

Bei der Vorstellung von Nicolais *Allgemeiner deutschen Bibliothek* (Bd. 1, 1766 – 106, 1792)[308], dem maßgebenden Rezensionsorgan der deutschen Aufklärung, und deren Fortsetzung merkt Rothe kritisch an:

> *„Die Recensionen [in der Neuen allgemeinen deutschen Bibliothek] sind sehr ungleich, u. tragen oft das Zeichen des Buben auf der Stirne. Mancher verdiente*

[306] Erarbeitet durch die 1791 gegründete Hinrichs'sche Verlags- und Sortimentsbuchhandlung in Leipzig.
[307] Ebenda, S. 381f.
[308] Ebenda, S. 383f.

Mann wird unwürdig behandelt. Nicht selten entschuldigen sich die Recensent., sie hätten keine Zeit gehabt, das Werk recht zu studiren, keine Quellen und weitere Kentniß, um entscheidend zu urtheilen u.s.w. Wie sonderbar! Keiner sollte recensiren, wenn er nicht das Fach ganz inne hätte, worin das Buch einschlägt. Jeder Recens. sollte angeben, was ein Buch enthält, wie die Materie behandelt sey, worin sich das Buch von andern ähnlichen unterscheidet u.s.w.“

Als Rothe in den Zusätzen einige Bücher zur Französischen Revolution aufführt, nennt er auch die Private memoirs relative to the last year of the reign Lewis XVI. by Ant. Fr. Bertrand de Mollewille, m. Bildn., 3 voll. 1797 8. Lond. und läßt so nebenbei seinen Eindruck von der zeitgenössischen Übersetzungspraxis einfließen:[309]

„Wahrscheinlich hat es ein allzeit fertiger Arbeiter aus unsern Uebersetzungs-Fabriken schon verdolmetschet, oder hat es unter seinen Klauen. Denn selten erhalten wir mit Kenntnißen u. Verstande abgefaßte Verdeutschungen. Wie müssen die Ausländer nicht über uns lachen, daß wir so begierig über jedes, auch noch so unbedeutende ausländ. Produkt herfallen. Obiges Werk verdiente eine gute Uebersetzung.“

4. Rothes ferneres Leben und Einsichten aus der Arbeit an der Bücherkunde

Zum Verständnis von Rothes Gedankengängen und seines bibliographischen Werkes ist die Kenntnis seiner Biographie unerlässlich, die leider nur bruchstückhaft überliefert ist. Der erste flüchtige Eindruck, dass sich hier ein noch relativ junger Mann wagemutig auf ein ihm unbekanntes Terrain begeben hat, und muss sich nun mit den Folgen seines Tuns herumschlagen muss, stimmt keinesfalls. Die für die auserlesene Bibliothek bestimmten Werke wurden mit Bedacht ausgewählt und kenntnisreich beurteilt. Sehr persönliche Gründe hatten Rothe nach eigenem Zeugnis bewogen, diesen Versuch nicht noch länger auf seinem Pulte liegen zu lassen: „Zum Unglück wählte ich zu meinem Brod-Fache die Heilkunde. Einen schlimmern Missgriff konnte ich nicht thun.“ Und nun bricht es aus ihm heraus: Es würde gepfuscht und gequacksalbert, der „medizinische Handwerker und Stümper“ dem gelehrten, rationell denkenden, „nach ächten Grundsätzen einer vernünftigen, erfahrungsmäßigen Heilkunde handelnden Arzte so lange vorgezogen, bis endlich auch dieser auf jene niedrige, schmutzige Stufe sich herabzulaßen genöthigt ist, will er nicht darben“. Es schmerze ihn sehr, wenn man ihm seine Jugend vorwerfe, in den Augen der meisten Menschen sei es fast ein Verbrechen, wenn der Arzt noch jung, munter und feurig tätig sei. Es gäbe noch andere Umstände, welche ihm die Praxis verleideten: Er werde spät zu Rate gezogen, der Patient sei nicht aufrichtig, in vielen Fällen könne er kaum lindern, geschweige denn helfen, „wie oft fehlt es nicht am Gelde, um nur die wohlfeilsten Arzneyen zu bezahlen, wenn man auch für seine Mühe und Gänge gern nichts verlanget ... Kurz, so angenehm das Studium der Heilkunde ist, so viele Unannehmlichkeiten und Beschwerden benehmen dem gefühlvollen Arzte alle Lust zur Praxis“.

Möglicherweise hätte er diese ohne weiteres aufgegeben und privatisiert, wie er es späterhin ein- oder zweimal getan hat, aber „bey so bewandten Umständen, die dadurch noch verschlimmert wurden, daß mein Schwiegervater ... meiner Frau beträchtliches mütterli-

[309] Ebenda, S. 428.

ches Erbtheil uns bis auf etliche Thaler muthwillig entriß[310], worauf ich stark rechnete, blieb mir nichts [anderes] übrig, als meine Zuflucht zum Bücherschreiben, dem leidigen gewöhnlichen Erwerbsmittel der jetzigen Gelehrten, zu nehmen". Und hier tat er aus Leidenschaft und Unkenntnis „abermals einen Fehltritt". Er habe nicht mit den Schwierigkeiten gerechnet, denen bibliographische Arbeiten unterworfen sind: „Ich wähnte viel gelesen, excerpiret zu haben. Ich meynte Bücher genug zu kennen, zu besitzen. Meine Gemüthsart machte mir alles leichte. Aber ich betrog mich gewaltig. Noch hätte ich können umkehren. Allein das mochte ich nicht." Die Anlage einer „Übersetzungsfabrik", auch das Abfassen medizinischer Volksbücher wären ihm leichter gefallen, aber daran mochte er sich nicht beteiligen. Es schien ihm angemessener, die schon längst angefangene Bibliographie zu bearbeiten, „wobey ich hinzusetzen muß, daß ich, man nenne es, wie man will, gern etwas Eignes, Nützliches, Notwendiges, Unentbehrliches liefern wollte".

Schwer, sehr schwer sei ihm die Ausarbeitung dieser Bogen geworden. „Viel lieber will ich eine vollständige Litteratur irgend einer Wissenschaft oder Kunst liefern, welche man will, als nur die besten [Schriften] angeben ... Der Geschmack ist zu verschieden, die Kenntnisse und Fähigkeiten der Menschen sind zu relativ und subjetivisch." Auf den Beifall aller rechne er nicht, es genüge ihm schon, wenn er „nur im Allgemeinen ein beyfälliges Zuwinken sehe". Bei einer Neuauflage werde er einige Veränderungen vornehmen und hoffe auf Anregungen.

Rothe lässt den Leser über seine Absichten nicht im Unklaren und baut zugleich der Kritik vor:[311]

> *„Ich schmeichle mir auch, daß mein Werk das leiste, wozu ich es bestimmte. Ich eigne es nämlich Studirenden auf niedern und hohen Schulen, jungen Gelehrten und Liebhabern der Wissenschaften und Künste. Diesen Zweck bitte [ich] Recensenten und das Publikum nicht außer Acht zu lassen. Für Gelehrte schrieb ich nicht. Diese kennen diese Bücher lange. Nur dem wollte ich die besten Schriften angeben, welcher anfängt zu studieren, welcher eine Wissenschaft, eine Kunst gern kennen lernen will, welcher nicht Zeit und Geld hat, alles zu lesen und zu kaufen, welcher gleich das beste Werk wünscht, welcher zu seinem Unterricht und Belehrung sich eine kleine auserlesene Bibliothek anlegen will."*

Er wisse sehr wohl, dass sein Buch diesen Zweck nicht ganz erreiche, deshalb nenne er es auch nur einen Versuch.

Dem begegnete der Rezensent der Neuen Allgemeinen Deutschen Bibliothek mit dem Sätzen: das Verzeichnis enthalte „über sehr viele Zweige menschlichen Wissens eine Menge Büchertitel, und das von solchen, die ein ächter Gelehrter niemals wird missen können. Weit mehr aber fehlen noch, die nicht minder unentbehrlich sind; und ebenso beträchtlich ist die Anzahl derer, die ein Mann von Geschmack und Urtheilskraft in seine Sammlung durchaus nicht aufnehmen darf ..." , und: „Was in aller Welt helfen uns immer neue Versuche, wenn der Waghals am Ende selbst eingestehen muß, daß Alles verunglückte?"[312]

Der Verfasser begründete Fehler bei der Auswahl und Einordnung eines Titels damit, daß er „ohnerachtet aller Mühe und Kosten doch nicht jedes Buch aus eigner Ansicht ken-

---

[310] Rothe ging mit diesem Fall an die Öffentlichkeit: An das Publikum, den Streit mit seinem Schwiegervater betr. (o. O. u. J.)

[311] Rothe, Vorrede, S. XVIII.

[312] Xy (wie Anm. 7), S. 61 – 62.

nen“ könne. „Man erwäge den Ort, wo ich es schrieb, fern von Bibliotheken und Buchhandlungen. Man vergesse nie, daß ich unmöglich in allen Fächern gleich stark seyn kann. Man überlege, daß ich mich gar sehr nur auf meine Kollektanea und mein gutes Gedächtniß verlassen mußte ... Will man keine Lücken haben, muß man alle Blätter lesen. Daher war ich seit meiner Entfernung von Leipzig übel berathen. Selbst hier in Sohra, etwas über eine Stunde von Görlitz, wo es nicht an gelehrten Zeitungen, Journalen u. dgl. fehlet, kann ich sie nur erhalten, wenn sie über ein Jahr als sind.“[313]

Den Benutzern des Buches empfiehlt Rothe, den Band mit weißem Papier durchschießen zu lassen, damit es laufend ergänzt und verbessert werden kann. Es lasse sich auch zu Unterrichtszwecken mit heranziehen: „Daß Lehrer auf niedern und hohen Schulen über dieses Buch Vorlesungen mit Vorzeigung der Bücher, mit näherer Schilderung ihres Werthes, Gehaltes, Inhalts u.s.f. halten möchten, wäre sehr heilsam und ersprießlich für die Jugend.“ Und ein weiteres Mal klingt die Unzufriedenheit mit seiner beruflichen Situation an: „Nichts würde mich mehr freuen, als wenn mein Wunsch mir noch in Erfüllung gienge, irgendwo als Lehrer angestellet zu werden, um selbst darüber Vorlesungen halten zu können. Ich habe von jeher große Lust und Neigung zum Lehr-Stande gehabt. Vielleicht erreiche ich bald meine Absicht. Oder wenn ich Bibliothekar werden könnte. Ich schmeichle mir, alle dazu erforderliche[n] Eigenschaften zu besitzen.“ Dann würden seine begonnenen bibliographischen Werke ungleich vollkommener ausfallen, „als alleweile in meiner beschränkten Lage, gedrängten Umständen und von Kummer, Sorgen, Noth, Verfolgung verursachten traurigen Seelen-Stimmung, die jetzt schon sichtlichen Einfluß auf alle meine Arbeiten, Betragen, Denk- und Handlungs-Art gehabt haben.“[314]

Obwohl Rothe „das Angenehme und Unangenehme solcher Arbeiten“ zu Genüge kennen gelernt hatte, blieb er der Bibliographie, seinem „Steckenpferd“, wie er es selbst nannte[315], treu. Er wollte z. B. eine besondere „Anleitung zur Kenntniß der besten Bücher, Kunstwerke und Musikalien blos für Dilettanten, Frauenzimmer und Ungelehrte“ veröffentlichen, mit der er einzig und allein Belehrung über gemeinnützige Gegenstände, Vergnügen und Unterhaltung bezweckte. Neulich habe er in der Zeitung gelesen, begründete er sein Vorhaben, „daß eine Obrigkeit für ihren Ort eine Volksbibliothek anlegen wollte. Es ward ein Gelehrter gesucht, der die Wahl der Schriften besorgte. Hätten wir nun schon so ein Buch, brauchte kein Gelehrter bemühet zu werden. Viele lesen gern, um ihre Kenntnisse zu erweitern, um sich die Langeweile zu vertreiben, um sich zu zerstreuen, um sich zu belustigen, sie wissen aber nicht immer, was und welches das beste [Werk] ist. Wie leichte, wie oft thun sie nicht bey der Wahl Missgriffe. Welcher Schaden entsteht nicht daher.“ [316]

Rothe hat diesen Plan nicht verwirklicht. Auch seine Wunschträume gingen nicht in Erfüllung, er wurde weder Lehrer noch Bibliothekar. Zwischen 1799 und 1802 finden wir ihn in Görlitz als Redakteur und Herausgeber des wöchentlich erscheinenden Görlitzischen Anzeigers[317]. Von seinen Schriften, die nicht dem medizinischen Fach zuzurechnen

---

313 Rothe, Vorrede, S. XX – XXI.

314 Ebenda, S. XXIV – XXV.

315 Vgl. Handbuch der medizinischen Litteratur (wie Anm. 26), Vorrede, S. [V].

316 Ebenda, S. XXIX.

317 Görlitzischer Anzeiger, oder: Chronik Lausitzischer Angelegenheiten ... Nebst Aufsätzen zur Belehrung und Unterhaltung der Leser über gemeinnützige Gegenstände aller Art (Görlitz und Ronneburg).

sind[318], sollen hier nur solche angeführt werden, in denen er seine philanthropische Idee, den Bildungsstand der „Ungelehrten" zu heben und den mühevollen Weg durch geeignete Anleitung zu ebnen, weiter verfolgt. Dazu zählen der „Versuch einer kurzen Geschichte der Oberlausitz, für Stadt- und Dorfschulen" (Görlitz 1801) und der „Versuch einer kurzen Geschichte der Sechsstadt Görlitz" (2 Hefte, Augsburg 1805). Zwei andere Titel, die seine Biographen nennen, nämlich sein „Sendschreiben an alle Gelehrte, Schriftsteller, Recensenten, Herausgeber der Zeitschriften und kritischen Blätter, Censoren, Buchhändler und Buchdrucker" (Görlitz 1806) und „Wie kommt man durch die Welt? Oder die Kunst, zu einem einträglichen Amte, großen Vermögen und hohen Alter zu gelangen. Ein Blatt für Jedermann" (Ronneburg 1806)[319], lassen aktuelle Meinungsäußerungen Rothes vermuten. Der Verfasser war inzwischen als Königl. Preuß. für das Herzogtum Schlesien und die Grafschaft Glatz approbierter und geschworener Arzt in Parchwitz a. d. O. zu Amt und Würden gelangt, 1812 wurde er ordentliches Mitglied der Schlesischen Gesellschaft für vaterländische Cultur. Er starb am 6. April 1813 „als ausübender Arzt" in seinem letzten Wohnort Herrnstadt in Schlesien im Alter von nur 44 Jahren, 7 Monaten am Nervenfieber (Typhus).

Wir wissen nicht, was aus Rothes privater Büchersammlung wurde, ebenso wenig ist bekannt, welchen Nutzen sein bibliographisches Handbuch stiftete. Die von ihm geschilderten Phänomene gehören zu den Grunderfahrungen, die keinem Bibliographen erspart bleiben. Als ein wissenschaftsgeschichtlich interessantes Zeitdokument ist Rothes Bücherkunde eine jener relativ frühen Auswahlbibliographien, die Bücherliebhaber und Bibliothekare immer wieder verlangten und denen im 19. Jahrhundert noch zahlreiche andere folgen sollten

---

318 Hier verfasste er u. a.: Anweisung zur Verhütung ansteckender Viehkrankheiten und Ausrottung der Rindviehpest, für gerichtliche Ärzte, Polizeibeamte, Landwirte und Fleischer aufgesetzt (Glogau 1810).

319 Vgl. Hamberger/Meusel: Das gelehrte Teutschland. 5. Aufl. Bd. 15 (Lemgo 1811); Otto (wie Anm. 15), Suppl.Bd., S. 369. – Diese Vermutung muss leider offen bleiben, die beiden Schriften standen mir nicht zur Verfügung. K. M.

Michael Knoche

Auf dem Weg zur Sammlerbibliothek

Fragt man nach der Entstehungsgeschichte der großen öffentlichen Bibliotheken, stößt man fast immer auf dasselbe Phänomen, gleich ob man die fürstlichen oder universitären Büchersammlungen betrachtet: Die Bibliotheken sind bis auf die eine große Ausnahme - Wolfenbüttel im 17. Jahrhundert - nicht kontinuierlich aufgebaut und planmäßig vermehrt worden, sondern durch die Integration von Privatsammlungen in großen Schüben gewachsen. Mit Lessing gesagt: „Die meisten Bibliotheken sind *entstanden*: nur wenige sind *angelegt* worden ...“[320]

Ein kurzer Blick auf die Entwicklung der Herzogin Anna Amalia Bibliothek in Weimar[321] soll diese These belegen und zugleich verdeutlichen, in welcher Weise sich die Funktion der Privatsammlungen in der öffentlichen Bibliothek im Lauf der Zeit gewandelt hat.

Als Herzog Wilhelm Ernst von Sachsen-Weimar 1691 den Entschluss fasste, die herzogliche Kammerbibliothek zu einer veritablen fürstlichen Bibliothek auszubauen, veranlasste er den Ankauf verschiedener Privatsammlungen, um rasch zu einem Grundstock an Büchern zu kommen. 1701 wurden 1700 Bände aus dem Besitz des Weimarer Kanzlers Moritz von Lilienheim erworben. 1704 gelang der Ankauf der etwa 6500 Bände umfassenden Bibliothek des Barons Balthasar Friedrich von Logau aus Breslau, eines Sohnes des bekannten Epigrammatikers. 1706 wurden aus der Versteigerung der Bibliothek des holsteinischen Gelehrten Marquard Gude ca. 1000 Druckschriften erworben, darunter seltene Ausgaben griechischer und römischer Schriftsteller aus dem 15. und 16. Jahrhundert. Als Folge der Berufung von Konrad Samuel Schurzfleisch, eines berühmten Wittenberger Universalgelehrten, zum Direktor der Bibliothek ging im Jahr 1722 dessen bedeutende Privatsammlung im Umfang von 8400 Bänden in den Bestand der fürstlichen Bibliothek ein. In Schurzfleischs Privatbibliothek hatten zwei weitere Sammlungen Eingang gefunden: die des Wittenberger Professors und Schriftstellers August Buchner, eines Mitglieds der Fruchtbringenden Gesellschaft, und Teile der Büchersammlung des holländischen Philologen Nicolaus Heinsius.

Nach Abschluss dieser ersten Erwerbungsphase waren also ungefähr 20 000 Bände zusammengetragen und im Weimarer Schloss aufgestellt worden. Fast 90 % des Bestandes machten die gelehrten Privatsammlungen Lilienheim, Logau, Gude, Schurzfleisch aus, die zunächst auch noch unvereinigt nebeneinander stehen blieben und wenig „admiration“ weckten, wie die herzoglichen Kammerräte Alberti und Oppermann damals kritisch bemerkten.[322] Die Professorenbibliotheken vermittelten keinen glanzvollen Eindruck. Nicht die Tatsache, dass sich die Bibliothek überhaupt aus ganz unterschiedlichen Quellen zusammensetzte, sondern die Provenienz dieser Bestände war für eine höfische Institution erstaunlich. Offensichtlich kam es dem Fürsten mehr darauf an, Weimar als Ort auf der

---

320 Gotthold Ephraim Lessing: Sämtliche Schriften. Hrsg. v. Karl Lachmann u. Franz Muncker. Bd. 11. [Reprint] Berlin 1968, S. 319.

321 Ausführlich zur Geschichte der Bibliothek: Herzogin Anna Amalia Bibliothek - Kulturgeschichte einer Sammlung. Hrsg. von Michael Knoche. München: Hanser 1999.

322 Die Kammerräte an den Herzog am 19.1.1723. Zit. nach den Regesten der verlorengegangenen Akten des Thüringischen Hauptstaatsarchivs (ehemals A 11600g).

imaginären Landkarte der internationalen Gelehrtenrepublik einzutragen, als eine repräsentative Fürstenbibliothek aufzubauen.

An der Wende zum 19. Jahrhundert lässt sich in Weimar ein interessanter Wandel der Funktion dieser inkorporierten Sammlungen feststellen. Es fällt auf, dass zunehmend kleinere geschlossene Bücherbestände angekauft wurden. Die Zeit der Erwerbung großer enzyklopädisch angelegter Sammlungen war vorbei, den Bibliothekaren erschienen jetzt Spezialbestände interessant, die das Vorhandene an bestimmten Stellen vertieften. Zu den besonderen Erwerbungen der Weimarer Bibliothek in der Zeit Carl Augusts gehören z.B. die Sammlung Gottfried David Schöber aus Gera mit Meistersingerhandschriften des 14.-17. Jahrhunderts (1779), die Manuskripte zur sächsischen Geschichte aus dem Besitz des Gymnasialprofessors Karl Wilhelm Schumacher (1781), Bekenntnisschriften aus der Reformationszeit des Jenaer Theologen Johann Georg Walch (1782), Literatur zur sächsischen Geschichte des Jenaer Professors Johann Gottfried Müller (1793), 275 Stammbücher des Ulmer Bürgers Christian Ulrich Wagner (1803) und schließlich 1813 noch einmal Meistersingerhandschriften mit dem Gemerkbüchlein des Hans Sachs aus dem Besitz des Nürnberger Gelehrten Christoph Theophil Murr. Außerdem kam nach dem Tod der Herzogin Anna Amalia (1807) ihre umfangreiche und kostbare Privatbibliothek ins Haus sowie Teilbestände folgender Personen aus dem Umkreis ihres Musenhofes: Karl Musäus (1787), Johann Gottfried Herder (1805), Charles Gore (1807), Carl Ludwig Fernow (1808), Christian Joseph Jagemann (1809). Erworben werden also einerseits thematisch profilierte Sammlungen oder aber Nachlässe von Personen, die in enger persönlicher Beziehung zum Herzoghaus standen. Jedoch bleibt fast keine Sammlung als solche erhalten, nicht einmal der Nachlass Anna Amalias. Anders als in der frühen Phase der Bibliotheksentwicklung werden jetzt alle Erwerbungen in den Gesamtbestand eingeordnet.

Im 20. Jahrhundert sind u.a. die Bibliotheken von Franz Liszt, Friedrich Nietzsche und der Familie von Arnim Teil der Herzogin Anna Amalia Bibliothek geworden. Im Gegensatz zu früher wurden diese Bestände geschlossen aufgestellt und als individuelle Einheiten mit eigener Signatur versehen. In diesen Fällen war es weniger der Inhalt der Sammlungen als die Person des Sammlers, die den Ausschlag für die Integration gegeben hat. Über die Sammlung wird die Sammlerpersönlichkeit erkennbar - das ist ein modernes Erkenntnisinteresse der Wissenschaft und ein noch nicht sehr altes Motiv für die Erwerbungstätigkeit der Bibliothek. Friedrich Schillers private Büchersammlung z.B. ist keineswegs pietätvoll zusammengehalten worden, sondern von der Familie in Einzelstücken unbekümmert an Freunde verschenkt worden. Heute ist Schillers Privatbibliothek in Weimar nur noch als Rumpfbestand vorhanden.

Die drei Motive, die im Laufe der Bestandsgeschichte der Herzogin Anna Amalia Bibliothek zutage getreten sind - Erwerbung eines breiten Literaturreservoirs, Vertiefung um Spezialaspekte, Dokumentation der Interessen einer großen Sammlerpersönlichkeit -, sind auch heute noch starke Argumente für die Fortsetzung des Versuchs, wichtige Privatsammlungen in öffentliche Bibliotheken zu holen. Ohne Privatsammlungen droht die Gefahr einer uniformen Politik der „Literaturversorgung“, die unsere öffentlichen Bibliotheken ununterscheidbar macht. Privatsammler treffen wohlabgewogene, gleichwohl subjektive und stark zufallsbedingte Kaufentscheidungen. Durch Kompetenz und Leidenschaft können originelle und differenzierte Sammlungen zustande kommen, die durch das bibliothekarische Akzessionsgeschäft mit seiner primären Ausrichtung auf Benutzerbedürfnisse nie aufgebaut werden könnten.[323]

Tatsache ist, dass heute in Deutschland zahlreiche große und bedeutende private Büchersammlungen nach dem Tod ihrer Besitzer ortlos werden. Üblicherweise wandern sie in den Antiquariats- und Auktionshandel und werden stückweise verkauft. Immer wieder kommt es auch zur Auflösung großer Sammlungen, wie in jüngster Zeit etwa des exzeptionellen Nachlasses von Friedrich von Laßberg als Bestandteil der Fürstenbergischen Bibliothek in Donaueschingen. Die Bücher gehen wieder in den Kreislauf des Handels ein, werden Bestandteil neuer Sammlungen, aber der einstige Sammlungszusammenhang ist verloren, bestenfalls durch einen Auktionskatalog dokumentiert. Keine deutsche Bibliothek stand bereit, um der Bibliothek Laßberg eine Heimstatt zu bieten.

In Deutschland gibt es nur eine einzige erstklassige Adresse für die Aufnahme privater Büchersammlungen: Das Deutsche Literaturarchiv in Marbach/Neckar versteht sich programmatisch als Ort für Schriftstellernachlässe einschließlich der Büchersammlungen und hat dafür die nötigen organisatorischen Strukturen ausgebildet und Magazinkapazitäten geschaffen. Der Reichtum dieser noch jungen Institution auf dem Gebiet der deutschen Literatur des 19. und 20. Jahrhunderts ist bereits unermesslich groß - nach einer nicht einmal fünfzig Jahre dauernden aktiven Erwerbungstätigkeit von geschlossenen Sammlungen.

Aber welche anderen Bibliotheken in Deutschland bemühen sich aktiv um wichtige Privatsammlungen jenseits der Schriftstellernachlässe? Die großen Staats- und Landesbibliotheken stehen gelegentlich zur Verfügung; auch Universitäts- oder Spezialbibliotheken ergänzen ihre Sammlungen ab und zu um spezielle Bestände privater Herkunft. Aber nehmen nicht alle öffentlichen Bibliotheken allenfalls Gelegenheiten wahr und verfolgen weniger eine systematische Strategie zum Erwerb privater Sammlungen? Im deutschen Bibliothekswesen ist keine Institution in Sicht, die dem „Sammlermuseum“ vergleichbar wäre, das Heinrich Klotz im Zusammenhang mit dem Zentrum für Kunst und Medientechnologie in Karlsruhe etabliert hat. Dort wird erstklassigen Privatsammlungen zur Gegenwartskunst ein attraktives Forum geboten.

Fragt man nach der Zurückhaltung der öffentlichen Bibliotheken gegenüber Privatsammlungen, stößt man bei Bibliothekaren auf verschiedene Vorbehalte, die zum Teil sehr praktischer Art sind. Z.B. beziehen sie sich auf die beträchtlichen Erwerbungskosten, die anfallen, wenn eine Sammlung nicht als Vermächtnis oder Stiftung ins Haus kommt, sondern mit einem Mal erworben werden soll. Die Bibliothek Laßbergs wurde z.B. als unverdaubar großer finanzieller Brocken betrachtet. Hinzu kommt das für Bibliothekare ungewohnte Geschäft, mit dem Besitzer einen fairen Marktpreis aushandeln zu müssen. Ein Problem ist auch der häufige Wunsch der Besitzer von Privatsammlungen nach geschlossener Aufstellung ihrer Sammlung. Dieses Ansinnen stößt in öffentlichen Bibliotheken schnell auf Ablehnung, weil Bibliothekare damit die Gültigkeit der eingeführten Aufstellungsordnung infrage gestellt sehen. Schließlich ist der hohe Einarbeitungsaufwand für die schlagartig ins Haus gekommene Menge an Büchern nicht von der Hand zu weisen. Die verbreitete Personalknappheit erlaubt es in den seltensten Fällen, Tausende von Titeln in kurzer Zeit zusätzlich durch den Geschäftsgang zu schleusen.

Diese Vorbehalte sind zum Teil berechtigt, können aber je nach Lage der Dinge auch ausgeräumt werden.

---

[323] Die besten Bemerkungen über Sammlermotive und Sammlerstrategien bei Wulf D. von Lucius: Bücherlust. Vom Sammeln. Köln: DuMont 2000.

Finanzieller Aspekt

Keine Bibliothek verfügt heute innerhalb des Jahresbudgets über eine Reserve für den Ankauf geschlossener Sammlungen. Fast immer müssen bei entsprechenden Angeboten Drittmittel (Stifterverband für die deutsche Wissenschaft, Kulturstiftung der Länder etc.) eingeworben werden. Doch gibt es auch in Deutschland eine gute mäzenatische Tradition, nach der die Besitzer gerade der besten Privatsammlungen ein öffentliches Vermächtnis zu stiften bereit sind. Allerdings müssen sie das Gefühl haben, mit ihrer Sammlung willkommen zu sein.

Aspekt geschlossene Aufstellung

Tatsache ist, dass mehrere aneinandergereihte Privatsammlungen keine homogene und leicht benutzbare Gesamtbibliothek ergeben, dass also das Provenienzprinzip für die Buchaufstellung nur bedingt tauglich ist. Eine Entscheidung über die Art der Aufstellung wird man heute je nach Einzelfall treffen müssen. Über die elektronischen Kataloge ist es leicht, Zusammenhänge virtuell zu dokumentieren. Prinzipiell jedoch sollte eine physisch geschlossene Aufstellung der erworbenen Sammlung möglich sein, gerade wenn es darum geht, spezielle Zugangsweisen und Verwendungsabsichten eines Sammlers zu erhalten.

Aspekt Einarbeitungsaufwand

Als Faustregel kann ein Personenarbeitsjahr für 2500 einzuarbeitende Bücher (Inventarisierung, Formalkatalogisierung, rudimentäre inhaltliche Erschließung, Beschriftung und Codierung für Benutzung) angenommen werden - bei beträchtlichen Schwankungen je nach Material. Bei der bibliothekarischen Bearbeitung ist jede öffentliche Institution auf Drittmittel angewiesen. Sie wird die häufig unterschätzte Dimension der Aufgabe nicht im Handumdrehen bewältigen können. Hilfestellungen, z.B. durch die Deutsche Forschungsgemeinschaft im Fall überregional interessanter Spezialbestände, sind aber grundsätzlich vorhanden, wenn nicht der Sammler den Weg zu Drittmittelgebern weisen oder sogar selbst einen Beitrag zur Erschließung seiner Sammlung leisten kann.

Neben den objektiven Schwierigkeiten bei der Integration privater Sammlungen gibt es auch eine mentale Hürde bei den Bibliothekaren. Sie pflegen häufig eine tiefsitzende Furcht vor „Dubletten" im Bestand. Eine gewisse Überschneidungsrate der neuen gegenüber der vorhandenen Sammlung ist in der Regel unvermeidlich. Daher wollen Bibliothekare am liebsten eine Auswahl aus dem Angebot treffen dürfen, um Ballast im Bestand auszuschließen. An diesem Punkt pflegen Besitzer von Privatbibliotheken weitere Verhandlungen gekränkt abzubrechen.

Natürlich sind besonders in heutigen Zeiten extremer Knappheit öffentlicher Gelder alle Redundanzen zu vermeiden. Aber Mehrfachexemplare historischer Bücher oder bibliophiler Ausgaben sind nicht unbedingt Dubletten, sondern Einzelexemplare, die sich durch besondere äußere Merkmale wie Einband, Besitzvermerke, Exlibris, Widmungen oder auch durch den definierten Ort in einem Sammlungszusammenhang voneinander unterscheiden. Die Herzogin Anna Amalia Bibliothek besitzt z.B. fünf Exemplare der seltenen „Physiognomischen Fragmente" von Johann Caspar Lavater. Alle Exemplare desselben Buches haben eine andere äußere Form und vor allem: eine bestimmte Geschichte. Sie stammen von verschiedenen interessanten Vorbesitzern aus dem Herzoglichen Haus oder sind nachweislich von Goethe ausgeliehen worden.

In den Bibliotheken mit großen historischen Buchbeständen zeichnet sich derzeit ein Mentalitätswandel ab. Die Bibliothekare werden zunehmend mit Fragen von Wissenschaftlern nach der Besitzgeschichte einzelner Bücher des historischen Bestandes konfrontiert.[324] Das Erkenntnisinteresse an den Provenienzdaten ist denkbar vielfältig. Es ist motiviert durch Fragestellungen der Personen-, Institutionen- und Bibliotheksgeschichte (Rekonstruktion von Sammlungen und Buchwanderungen), der Sozial- und Lesergeschichte (Buchbesitz und Lektüre), der philologischen Wissenschaften (Medienübergänge von Handschrift und gedrucktem Buch, z.B. in Form von Marginalien, Brief im Buch etc.), der Kunstgeschichte (Einband und Exlibris) u.a. Hinzu kommen in den Bibliotheken der neuen Bundesländer rechtlich relevante Fragen nach der Herkunft bestimmter Sammlungsteile im Zusammenhang mit Rückführungsansprüchen ehemaliger Besitzer. Daher werden zur Zeit Methoden entwickelt, um in bestimmten Fällen eine Provenienzerschließung zusätzlich zur notwendigen Formal- und Sacherschließung eines Buches möglich zu machen.[325] Die Provenienzen sollen den Blick sowohl auf die Individualität eines Exemplars als auch auf seinen historischen Sammlungs- und Gebrauchskontext erlauben. Mit der gewachsenen Sensibilität für Sammlungszusammenhänge[326] schwindet die Dublettenfurcht in den öffentlichen Bibliotheken, und das Interesse an Privatsammlungen nimmt zu.

Bereits seit 1997 wird an der Herzogin Anna Amalia Bibliothek die Provenienzverzeichnung praktiziert. Bei jeder Gelegenheit, in der ein Bibliothekar ein Buch im Rahmen einer anderen Aufgabe (antiquarische Erwerbung, Verfilmungsauftrag, Ausgabe des Buches an Leser im Lesesaal, Sonderprojekt zur Auswertung historischer Kataloge) in die Hand nimmt, wird die individuelle Provenienz eines Buches den Katalogdaten hinzugefügt. Die Ergebnisse sind im OPAC recherchierbar. Auch ein Instrument wie die Provenienzverzeichnung scheint mir unabdingbar für den Anspruch einer Sammlerbibliothek zu sein.

Die Herzogin Anna Amalia Bibliothek möchte an die in den letzten Jahrzehnten weitgehend abgebrochene Tradition anknüpfen, Privatsammlungen in ihren Bestand zu integrieren. So wie die Herzogliche Bibliothek des 18. Jahrhunderts für bürgerliche Sammlungen offen stand, will die Herzogin Anna Amalia Bibliothek ihre kontinuierliche Erwerbungstätigkeit im Dienst der Forschung zur Literatur- und Kulturgeschichte durch originelle und differenzierte Privatsammlungen ergänzen. Sie möchte wieder eine Heimstatt für herausragende Privatbibliotheken werden. Bislang standen diesem Anspruch die unzulänglichen Magazinverhältnisse entgegen. Ausreichend Platz und gute konservatorische Bedingungen für die Lagerung der Bücher sind natürlich elementare Mindestvoraussetzungen für jede öffentliche Bibliothek, die Sammlerbibliothek sein will. Dieses Problem wird in Weimar spätestens 2004 gelöst sein.

Dabei kommt der Weimarer Bibliothek ihre Funktion als unabhängige Forschungs-

---

[324] Wolfgang Harms: Das Buch im Sammlungszusammenhang. In: Bibliothek und Wissenschaft 33 (2000) S. 50-58.

[325] Jürgen Weber: Provenienzforschung und Buchbearbeitung. In: Deutscher Bibliotheksverband (DBV). Jahrbuch 1998, S. 147-152.

[326] Zahlreiche Bibliotheken des In- und Auslands haben Kataloge zu Handschriften und Inkunabeln mit Provenienznachweisen angelegt. Dennoch steckt - insbesondere in Deutschland - die Erschließung von Provenienzen von Druckschriften noch in den Anfängen. Den besten ersten Überblick bietet das in Kürze erscheinende Gesamtregister zum "Handbuch der historischen Buchbestände in Deutschland". Die erste große deutsche Datenbank mit recherchierbaren Provenienzen ist das Verzeichnis der Drucke des 17. Jahrhunderts im deutschen Sprachraum (VD17 mit mehr als 100.000 Einträgen).

bibliothek entgegen, also eines Bibliothekstyps, der entlastet ist von der Aufgabe, einer übergeordneten Institution, z.B. der Benutzerschaft einer Universität, Fachbehörde oder Kommune zu dienen. In der Bibliothekswissenschaft werden solche Bibliotheken als Forschungsbibliotheken bezeichnet, die darauf abzielen, Wissenschaftlern umfassend günstige Bedingungen für die Arbeit mit Quellenliteratur zu bieten. Das Gewicht, das dem alten Buch in der Bibliotheksarbeit zugemessen wird - von der guten Erschließung durch Kataloge, der Unterstützung der Wissenschaftler bei mehrtägigen Bibliotheksaufenthalten bis hin zur funktionierenden Restaurierungswerkstatt -, der hervorragende Stellenwert der historischen Bestände also, unterscheidet eine Forschungsbibliothek von anderen wissenschaftlichen Bibliotheken. Prototyp in Deutschland ist die Herzog August Bibliothek in Wolfenbüttel.[327]

Für den Sammler kann die „Aufhebung“ seiner Sammlung in einer öffentlichen Bibliothek durchaus reizvoll sein. Der mit so viel Aufwand zusammengetragene Bestand bleibt erhalten, wird vielleicht sogar erstmals nach professionellen Gesichtspunkten erschlossen und stiftet in einem adäquaten Kontext auch nach dem Tod ihres Begründers Nutzen. Manchmal entstehen besonders interessante Ausstellungsprojekte. Im Nebeneffekt steigern sie den Bekanntheitsgrad und Wert der Sammlung.

Öffentliche Bibliotheken, die Privatsammlungen aufnehmen, lassen eine immanente Konkurrenz von Auswahlkriterien zu. Die Erwerbungsentscheidung des Bibliothekars[328] steht der des Sammlers gegenüber. Die individuelle Stärke beider Perspektiven steigert das Literaturangebot qualitativ. Es sind die Sammlungen in der Sammlung, die das Profil alter Bibliotheken so unverwechselbar machen. Achten wir darauf, dass spätere Generationen unsere heutigen Bibliotheken unterscheiden und wiedererkennen können.

---

327 Michael Knoche: Die Forschungsbibliothek. Umrisse eines in Deutschland neuen Bibliothekstyps. In: Bibliothek - Forschung und Praxis 17 (1993) S. 291-300.

328 Ulrike Steierwald: Leitlinien einer bestandsorientierten Erwerbung. Ein kulturwissenschaftliches Konzept der Herzogin Anna Amalia Bibliothek. In: Bibliothek - Forschung und Praxis 22 (1998) S. 200-207.

Boris Volodin

Der Göttinger Bibliothekar Karl Becker und die deutsche Diaspora der Kaiserlichen Öffentlichen Bibliothek zu St. Petersburg

Traditionell wird die Geschichte der Kaiserlichen Öffentlichen Bibliothek von russischen Bibliothekshistorikern als einzigartiges Phänomen der Weltbibliotheksgeschichte betrachtet. Zwar war die sowjetische Periode dieser Bibliothek für die Forscher der Geschichte nicht weniger interessant; dabei wurde der Prozess der Umwandlung dieser Bibliothek in eine der führenden Nationalbibliotheken Europas und in eine der weltgrößten Bibliotheken ausschließlich als Verdienst der russischen Bibliothekare betrachtet.[329]

Ohne Zweifel verdient der Beitrag vieler russischer Bibliothekare zur Entwicklung russischer Wissenschaft, Bildung und Kultur sowie zur Entwicklung des Bibliothekswesens höchste Wertschätzung. Trotzdem erscheint es kaum gerechtfertigt zu sein, die Geschichte der Kaiserlichen Öffentlichen Bibliothek einseitig darzustellen und die Rolle derjenigen Bibliothekare zu unterschätzen, die, aus Deutschland kommend, hier die deutsche Diaspora gebildet haben und damit zur Entwicklung dieser Bibliothek stark beitrugen.[330]

---

329 So schrieb nicht ohne Stolz Olga D. Golubeva, eine der Bibliothekshistorikerinnen, die besonders tatkräftig die Geschichte der Kaiserlichen Öffentlichen Bibliothek des 19.Jhs erforscht, in der Monographie über das Leben und die Tätigkeit Modest Korfs: „Bei der Erforschung des Bibliothekswesens im Ausland vermag Korf von den Erfahrungen der deutschen Bibliotheken nur das Einzigste (Hervorhebung vom Verf.) entlehnen - die Arbeitstische, deren Fläche nicht mit dem Tuch, sondern mit dem Wachstuch, das die Farbe des Mahagoni imitiert, bezogen worden sind, was reißfester und schöner war, als die /Tischdeckungen/, die damals in der Öffentlichen Bibliothek existierten". - Vgl.: Olga D. Golubeva. M.A. Korf. St. Petersburg 1995.S.106-107.

330 Dass sich so eine einseitige Betrachtungsweise der Bibliotheksgeschichte herausgebildet hat, lässt sich nicht nur durch Patriotismus und Ideologie erklären. Hier werden auch Folgen einer bibliothekshistorischen Forschung unter bestimmten methodologischen Standpunkten deutlich. Im Rahmen der vaterländisch orientierten Erforschung der Bibliotheksgeschichte wurden die Entwicklungen ausländischer Bibliotheken - sowohl im Hinblick auf die Gegenwart, als auch im Hinblick auf die Vergangenheit - als eine Summe organisatorischer und technischer Neuerungen betrachtet. Dabei wurde die Bibliotheksgeschichte in der Regel außerhalb des sozial-kulturellen Kontextes dieser oder jener Zeit betrachtet. Dabei war es für die russischen Bibliothekswissenschaftler und Bibliothekshistoriker besonders wichtig, den veränderten gesellschaftlichen Verhältnissen entsprechend – vor allem der Verabschiedung der totalitären Vergangenheit entsprechend -, altgewohnte Forschungsansätze der Bibliotheksgeschichte zu verändern. Auch hier waren die Erfahrungen der deutschen Kollegen nützlich; deren Tradition, Geschichte im jeweiligen zeitlichen Kontext zu betrachten, war nie unterbrochen worden. Von großer Bedeutung für die Überwindung der tendenziösen einseitigen Betrachtungsweise der Bibliotheksgeschichte waren die ins Russisch übersetzten Schriften von führenden ausländischen Bibliothekshistorikern, darunter die Werke von Professor Peter Vodosek. Seine Schriften verdienen deshalb eine Auszeichnung, wie z.B. sein Beitrag „Est' li buduschee u proschlogo?" (Ob die Vergangenheit eine Zukunft hat?). Peterburgskaja bibliotetchnaja schkola. (Petersburgische Bibliotheksschule) 1997 N. 2, S.56-63). Diese Veröffentlichungen haben den russischen Kollegen geholfen, Bibliotheksgeschichte als eine Wissenschaft zu erkennen, die nicht nur an der Sozialgeschichte, sondern auch an der Geschichte des Alltagslebens, an der Wissenschafts-, Kultur- und Bildungsgeschichte orientiert ist. Vodosek hat bewiesen, dass gerade die Anwendung dieser Betrachtungsweise zur Entstehung neuer Kenntnisse und Erreichung bedeutsamer Erfolge geführt hat. Die Möglichkeiten dieser komplexen Betrachtungsweise wurden von ihm am kon-

Die Kaiserliche Öffentliche Bibliothek – am 27. Mai 1795 gegründet und am 14. Januar 1814 eröffnet – ging schon nach sehr kurzer Zeit, nämlich Mitte des 19. Jahrhunderts, in die Reihe der größten wissenschaftlichen Bibliotheken ein. Ihre rasante Entwicklung ist phänomenal. Anfang der 1840er-Jahre wurde diese Bibliothek die Nationalbibliothek Russlands.

Ihrem ersten Direktor Alexej N. Olenin (1763-1843) gelang es, den vollständigen Bestand der russischen Drucke zusammenzufassen, allerdings wurde die laufende Beschaffung ausländischer Literatur zu diesem Zeitpunkt zum Schwachpunkt der Bibliothek.[331] Ein sich nachteilig auswirkender Widerspruch der Bibliothek war auch es, dass in den letzten Jahren unter der Leitung von Olenin die Tendenz beobachten war, zur Arbeit in der Bibliothek viele Gelehrte und Schriftsteller heranzuziehen. Die Bibliothek wurde so mehr und mehr zu einer Art „Mäzenenasyl" der Literaten", was dazu führte, dass einige Mitarbeiter ihre Bibliothekspflichten nicht erfüllten.

Diese Verhältnisse veränderten sich jedoch allmählich, und bereits in den 1860er-Jahren konnte der Bibliotheksdirektor Baron Modest A. Korf (1800-1876) bestätigen, dass die Bibliothek sich Schritt für Schritt „von einer Schülerin zu einer Lehrerin" verwandelte.[332] Die Veränderungen waren in größerem Maße dadurch bedingt, dass in St. Petersburg die deutschen Erfahrungen angewendet wurden, die zum integrierenden Bestandteil des russischen Bibliotheks-Diskurses wurden, Erfahrungen in Bereichen der Bibliothekseinrichtung, Bestandsaufstellung, Katalogführung, Bibliotheksverwaltung, Bestandserwerbung und Leserbedienung.

Der neue Direktor, Dmitrij P. Buturlin (1790-1849), der an Stelle Olenins getreten war und die Bibliothek bis zu seinem Tode leitete, hatte die Prioritäten in der Organisation der Bibliotheksarbeit einschneidend verändert. Vor allem hat Buturlin strenge Anforderungen an das Bibliothekspersonal gestellt. Die Bibliothekare wurden von ihm nicht als Gelehrte, sondern als Mitarbeiter mit bestimmten Dienstpflichten - reinen bibliothekarischen Aufgaben – betrachtet, deren Erfüllung die entsprechenden Dienstinstruktionen zur Pflicht machten.[333] Die Instruktionen galten für die Bereiche Bestandsaufstellung und Katalogführung, d.h. für die Hauptgebiete der Bibliotheksarbeit. Unter Buturlin wurde auch ein Versuch unternommen, alle Bibliotheksmitarbeiter an der Arbeit mit den Bibliotheksbeständen zu beteiligen, um alle im Bestand aufbewahrten Drucke zu katalogisieren. Entsprechend zeigten sich schon zu Mitte 1840er-Jahre positive Veränderungen bei der Bestandsaufstellung und der Bestandsverteilung sowie bei der Zusammenführung der Kataloge für die ver-

kreten Beispiel gezeigt, am Beispiel des Bibliothekswesens Weimarer Republik, einer für die Geschichtswissenschaft meistens schweren und widersprüchlichen Zeitstrecke des Bibliothekswesens Deutschlands (Vgl.: Peter Vodosek: Bibliotetchnoe delo Weimarskoj respubliki (Das Bibliothekswesen in der Weimarer Republik), in: Istorija bibliotek: Issledovanija. Materialy. Dokumenty (Bibliotheksgeschichte: Forschungen. Materialen. Dokumente) Bd. 2. St. Petersburg 1999, S.174-183).

331 Innerhalb der Periode 1811-1849 erwarb die Bibliothek 10.246 Bände, darunter allerdings nur 6.000 – 7.000 ausländischer Bücher; vgl. z.B. Istorija Gosudarstvennoj ordena Trudovogo Krasnogo Znameni Publitschnoj Biblioteki imeni M. E. Saltykova-Schchedrina (Die Geschichte der Staatlichen, mit dem Orden des Roten Arbeitsbanners ausgezeichneten, Saltykov-Schchedrin Bibliothek. Leningrad 1963. S. 32

332 vgl.: Olga D.Golubeva. M. A. Korf. St. Petersburg 1995, S.105

333 Zu Buturlins Zeit war eine der wichtigsten Anforderungen, die an den Bibliotheksmitarbeitern gestellt wurden, Sprachkenntnis. 1843 hatte der Minister der Volksbildung seinen Vorschlag unterstützt, nach dem jeder, der in der Bibliothek als Bibliothekar arbeiten wollte, folgenden Sprachen könne musste: Russisch, Französisch, Deutsch, Latein, Griechisch (oder statt einer von denen - einige orientalische Sprache); der Assistent des Bibliothekars musste Russisch und drei fremden Sprachen kennen.

schiedenen Bestandsabteilungen - Handschriftenabteilung, Estampenabteilung, Russische Abteilung, Abteilung für Geschichte.

Vor allem aber wurden während der Amtszeit von Buturlin für die Arbeit in der Bibliothek deutsche Bibliothekare herangezogen sowie die Gelehrten aus Deutschland, die von der Organisation der Bibliotheksarbeit in besten deutschen Bibliotheken gute Vorstellungen hatten. Gerade Buturlin nahm also die Bibliothekare als Mitarbeiter in den Dienst, die später zu führenden Fachmännern wurden; einige von ihnen wurden Abteilungsleiter:

- 1847 bis 1883: Bernhard Dorn (1805-1881), aus Sachsen-Koburg gebürtig, der in Universitäten Halle, Leipzig und Koburg studiert hatte und damals als Privat-Dozent der Universität Leipzig tätig war;
- 1847 bis 1883: der Preuße Rudolph Mintzlow (1811-1883), Doktor der Philosophie von der Universität Königsberg; etwa zur selben Zeit: Karl Heinrich Ludwig Becker (1821-1883), Angehöriger des Hannoverischen Königreiches und Absolvent der Universität Göttingen;
- 1848 bis 1885: Christophore Friedrich Walter (1809-1886), Angehöriger des Fürstentums Schwarzburg-Sonderhausen, Doktor der Philosophie von der Universität Leipzig.

Anfang 1850er-Jahre beginnt eine der hervorragenden und fruchtbarsten Perioden in der Entwicklung der Bibliothek, die mit dem Namen des neuen Direktors - des Barons Modest A. Korfs - verbunden ist.[334] Zu Korfs Zeit, der selbst seiner Herkunft nach ein kurländischer Deutscher war, hat sich die deutsche Diaspora erweitert. Als idealer Mitarbeiter zeigte sich Dorn - der Leiter der Orient-Abteilung. Erfolgreich leitete Mintzlov die Abteilung für Philosophie und die Inkunabel-, Elseviren- und Aldenabteilung. Walter hat sich große Verdienste als der Bibliothekar für die Abteilung Polygraphie und Recht erworben. Von den Deutschen, die zu Korfs Zeiten als Mitarbeiter angeworben worden waren, war der aus dem Herzogtum Holstein gebürtige Moritz Konrad Posselt (1804-1875) eine besonders herausragende Persönlichkeit. Er hatte an der Universität Heidelberg und an anderen Universitäten in Deutschland studiert und war als Doktor der Philosophie an der Universität Kiel tätig gewesen. Er diente der Bibliothek eine lange Zeit – 1851 bis 1873 - und leitete zunächst die Abteilung für Geschichte und später die Abteilung für Recht.

Unter den neu eingestellten Kollegen deutscher Herkunft waren auch zwei aus den Ostsee-Provinzen Russlands Gebürtige - Egon Berckholz (1817-1885), der in Livland geboren war, vorher an der Universität Dorpat, danach an der Universität Berlin studiert hatte sowie Viktor Amandus Gen (1813-1890), der in Dorpat geboren war und dort gelebt und an der dortigen Universität von 1846 bis 1851 unterrichtet hatte. Obwohl Berckholz in der Bibliothek nur fünf Jahre - von 1856 bis 1861 - gearbeitet hatte, spielte er eine wesentliche Rolle, weil er tatkräftig an der Schaffung der Abteilung „Rossica“ beteiligte: Er beschäftigte sich mit der Zusammenstellung der alphabetischen und systematischen Kataloge für den Bestand dieser Abteilung und leitete diese Abteilung. Gen hat etwas länger gearbeitet - von 1855 bis 1873. Er leitete die Abteilung für Geschichte. Diese beiden Mitarbeiter wur-

[334] Er leitete die Bibliothek von 1849 bis 1861 und ging in ihre Geschichte als der Reformer ein, der diese Bibliothek in eine der weltbesten Bibliotheken verwandelt hat. Wie bekannt ist, hat Korf die materielle Lage der Bibliothek stark verbessert - 1850 war nach seinem Vorschlag die Bibliothek in die Zuständigkeit des Kaiserlichen Hofes übergeben worden, wodurch die Mittel für ihren Unterhalt sich fast verdoppelt hatten.

den von Korf so hoch geschätzt, dass er sie als die „Perlen der Bibliothek“ bezeichnete.[335]

Korf hat die Bibliothek in Hinblick auf die Recherche für die damalige Zeit optimal neu strukturiert. Zu seiner Zeit hat sich die Abteilungsstruktur endgültig herausgebildet und verfestigt. Im Gegensatz zur Systematik von Johann Michael Francke und zu anderen Systematiken der Fachabteilungen, die man in deutschen Bibliotheken anwendete, war die Systematik der Fachabteilungen der Kaiserlichen Öffentlichen Bibliothek viel näher den einzelnen Wissenschaften und Wissensgebieten angepasst. Hier handelte es sich schon um die Schaffung einer wissenschaftlich begründeten Systematik. Jede der Abteilungen stellte eine Bibliothek in der Bibliothek dar, die nicht nur hinsichtlich von Bestandserschließung, Bestandserhaltung und Leserbedienung, sondern auch in bezug auf die Erwerbung, die an den entsprechenden Leserbedürfnissen orientiert war.

In vieler Hinsicht erwiesen sich die deutschen Bibliothekare als die idealen Leiter der wissenschaftlichen Bibliothek mit ihren für die damalige Zeit fortschrittlichen Vorstellungen von der Organisation der Arbeit. Jeder von ihnen trug zu der Verwandlung der Kaiserlichen Öffentlichen Bibliothek - der wissenschaftlichen Bibliothek - in ein Instrument der Wissenschaft bei, besonders jene, die für einzelne Abteilungen der Bibliothek verantwortlich waren, die einzelnen oder mehreren Wissenschaften dienten. Sie machten diese Abteilungen, die Bibliotheken in der Bibliothek, zu Instrumenten konkreter Wissenschaften. Inwieweit ihnen dies gelungen ist, kann man an der Qualität der Arbeitsorganisation, der Sammlungen von Drucken, der Kataloge und der Leserbetreuung ablesen.

Was bisher von der deutschen bibliothekarischen Diaspora insgesamt gesagt wurde, betrifft Karl Becker im besonderen. Er hat im Leben dieser Bibliothek eine herausragende Rolle gespielt, nicht nur, weil er sich als Leiter der Abteilungen für Medizin, Mathematik und Naturwissenschaften und im Dienste dieser Wissenschaften ausgezeichnet hatte. Karl Becker, von Göttingen nach St. Petersburg gekommen, hatten einen weiteren wissenschaftlichen Horizont und besaß die Fähigkeit, den Kosmos der Wissenschaften im ganzen zu ergreifen. Von allen Vertretern der deutschen Diaspora hat deshalb gerade Becker auf die Entwicklung der Bibliothek besonders stark gewirkt.[336]

Zum Unterschied von seinen deutschen Kollegen betrachtete Becker die Bibliothek als einen einheitlichen Organismus, ohne die Funktionen der einzelnen Abteilungen zu vernachlässigen.

Deswegen war es nicht zufällig, dass es gerade Becker gelang, das in der Bibliothek verwendete Klassifikationsschema von Olenin „Opyt novogo bibliografitscheskogo porjadka“ (Versuch der neuen bibliographischen Ordnung) den neuen Anforderungen anzupassen. Dies gelang ihm unter Berücksichtigung der für die damalige Zeit modernen Vorstellungen von der Struktur der Wissenschaft und ihrer Widerspiegelung in der Klassifikation der neuen Wissensgebiete. Er ging davon aus, dass „der heutige Stand der Wissen-

---

335 Genau so hat sie M.A.Korf in einem der Briefe an V.F.Odoevskij gekennzeichnet, der auf Französisch geschrieben worden ist: „Ce sont les perles de la Biblioth`eque“. Zitiert nach: Imperatorskaja Publitchnaja biblioteka... (Die Kaiserliche Öffentliche Bibliothek...), S. 211

336 In einem der Briefe an Odoevskij hat Korf geschrieben: „Herr Becker ist, ohne Zweifel, einer der gewissenhaftesten und nützlichsten unseren Bibliothekare, die sich ohne Lärm, ohne Prahlerei und fast ohne Bezahlung unvergleichlich mehr, als vielen anderen, bemühen“. Zitiert nach: Imperatorskaja Publitchnaja biblioteka za sto let (Die Kaiserliche Öffentliche Bibliothek für 100 Jahre) 1814-1914. St. Petersburg 1914, S. 108; 1873 ist Becker nach Deutschland zurückgekehrt, und zwar nach Karlsruhe, wo er seine wissenschaftliche Tätigkeit fortsetzte. Dort erschienen zwei seine Bücher - „Geschichte des badischen Landes zur Zeit der Römer. N 1. Karlsruhe 1876 und „Versuch einer Lösung der Celtenfrage durch Unterscheidung der Celten und der Gallier“. Karlsruhe 1883

schaft und die Zahl der Schätze der Kaiserlichen Öffentlichen Bibliothek eine Ergänzung dieser Systematiken notwendig machen, die überaus bedeutsam sein müssen“.[337]

Becker hat die Hauptteilungen der Systematik von Olenin aufgehoben, diese ergänzt und differenziert und dazu einen alphabetischen Sachkatalog erstellt. Er kannte ausgezeichnete - sowohl alte als auch neue - bibliographischen Klassifikationen, die in verschiedenen Bibliotheken verwendet wurden. Als Vorbild nahm er die Systematik von Andreas August Ernst Schleiermacher, die ihm als die gelungenste erschien; sie war besonders differenziert - sie bestand aus 12.575 Rubriken - und es gab zu ihr ein sorgfältig zusammengestelltes alphabetisches Sachverzeichnis mit 34.000 Sachwörtern.

Nach einer Versammlung der Bibliotheksmitarbeiter im September 1857 wurde dem Konzept von Becker insgesamt zugestimmt. Es wurde vorgeschlagen, nach der Eintragung nötiger Ergänzungen und Verbesserungen für jeden Mitarbeiter eine Instruktion auszuarbeiten. Obwohl dieser Vorschlag dann doch nicht umgesetzt wurde, hat doch die von Becker durchgeführte Arbeit die in der Bibliothek verwendeten Klassifikationstabellen bedeutsam vervollständigt.[338]

Doch Beckers Interesse galt nicht nur der Systematik und Klassifikation. Er war zutiefst davon überzeugt, dass die meiste Aufmerksamkeit auf die Qualität der Erwerbung der Drucke für den Bibliotheksbestand gerichtet werden müsste. Im Mittelpunkt der Reformen von Korf standen Fragen der Beschaffungspolitik. Dafür erarbeitete Becker einen Entwurf – „Projekt" -, um die Organisation der Anschaffung mit Hilfe eines Erwerbungs- und eines Zeitschriftenkataloges zu verbessern. Der Entwurf wurde 1857 vorbereitet und beeinflusste die weitere Entwicklung der Bibliothek, auch wenn nicht alle Vorschläge angenommen und realisiert wurden.

Unter dem Titel „Proekt usoverschenstvovanija kataloga priobretenij i kataloga periodiki“ (Projekt zur Verbesserung des Erwerbungs- und Zeitschriften-Katalogs") wurde der in deutscher Sprache verfasste Entwurf zur Erörterung der Bibliotheksverwaltung und den Bibliotheksmitarbeitern vorgelegt. Vor der Besprechung dieses Projektes auf der Sitzung des Haushaltskomitees der Bibliothek unter dem Vorsitz von Vladimir F.Odoevskij - dem Stellvertreter des Direktors - die am 4. Februar 1858 stattfand, hatte Becker zahlreiche Ergänzungsmaterialien erarbeitet und Odojevskij vorgestellt.[339]

Während der Ausarbeitung dieses Projekts wurde es Becker klar, dass - zum Nutzen der ganzen Bibliothek - für diesen auf den ersten Blick sehr konkreten, engen Arbeitsbereich ein spezieller Mitarbeiter notwendig wäre, um die Kontrolle im Hinblick auf die neu erworbenen Drucke zu haben. Dabei ging er von einem für die damalige Zeit sehr modernen Verständnis von den Aufgaben eines Bibliothekars aus. Er zitierte F.A. Ebert:

> *„Die Tätigkeit des Bibliothekars gehört jetzt mehr der* Nachwelt *(Hervorhebung von Becker, Anm. d. Verf.) an, für welche er treuer u. verständlicher Depositär seyn muss... für sie sammelte er aus* seiner *(Hervorhebung von Becker, Anm. d. Verf.) u. aus früherer Zeit, was er des Sammelns werth hält...“.*[340]

---

[337] Vgl.: Die Dienstmeldung von K.Becker und V.I.Sobol'schikov an die Direktion der Kaiserlichen Öffentlichen Bibliothek von 28.Juni 1857. - Archiv der Russischen Nationalbibliothek. 1857. N 55.Bl.4.- Rückseite 5.

[338] Vgl: Istoria Gosudarstvennoj ordena Trudovogo Krasnogo znameni...(Anm.3.). S.65.

[339] Seine Einstellung hat Becker in seinem Schreiben an Odoevskij von 19.Januar 1858 begründet. - Archiv der Russischen Nationalbibliothek. R.1. N 60. Verzeichnis N 1. 1858.

[340] Vgl: Archiv der Russischen Nationalbibliothek. R.1. N 60. Verzeichnis N 1. 1858. Hier zitiert Becker Ebert nach der Ausgabe: Ebert F.A.: Die Bildung des Bibliothekars. Leipzig, 1820, S. 9.

Becker richtete seine Aufmerksamkeit deshalb auf das Problem der Erwerbungskataloge, weil gerade hier die Anfechtbarkeit des in der Bibliothek herausgebildeten Erwerbungssystems deutlich wurde.

Natürlich ging es nicht nur um die Kritik am Erwerbungssystems. Es ging auch um die Verbesserungen der Arbeitsabläufe bei der Bestellung und der Verteilung der Drucke unter den verschiedenen Bibliotheksabteilungen.

Die diesbezüglichen Reformen unter der Leitung des Direktors Korf wurden von der deutschen Bibliothekarsdiaspora dankbar akzeptiert, da diese Veränderungen für sie zum selbstverständlichen Niveau der bibliothekarischen Arbeit gehörten.

Der Initiative zur Veränderung der Beschaffungspolitik wurde von Korf vor allem in Hinblick auf die moderne ausländische Literatur eingeführt. Ihm gelang es, den Widerstand von Kaiser Nikolaj I. (1796-1855) zu brechen, der Buchumtausch und den Versand russischer Bücher ins Ausland nicht wünschte. Vladimir F.Odojevskij,1846 bis 1861 Assistent des Direktors, kümmerte sich besonders um die Erwerbung der neuesten ausländischen Veröffentlichungen aus den Bereichen Physik, Chemie, Naturwissenschaften, Mathematik und Geologie, die in der Bibliothek besonders schwach repräsentiert waren.

Bedeutsam sind auch die Veränderungen, die Korf hinsichtlich des existierenden Status des Ehrenbibliothekars durchsetzte. Er führte zwei neue Varianten ein - das Ehrenmitglied und den Ehrenkorrespondent. Zu Ehrenmitgliedern wurden Personen, die „sich Bekanntheit durch die Liebe zu Aufklärung und zur Bibliothek gewonnen hatten". Ehrenkorrespondenten wurden namhafte Bibliothekare und Buchhändler, „von denen durch ihre Bemühungen, Verbindungen und Schenkungen auf nützliche Unterstützung für die Bibliothek erwartet werden kann". Damit gab die Bibliothek ihrer Dankbarkeit für die Finanzhilfe und für die Mithilfe in Hinblick auf den Einkauf von Rara-Drucken Ausdruck. Die Einführung von Ehrenmitgliedern und Ehrenkorrespondenten hat eine wichtige Rolle bei der gesellschaftlichen und kulturellen Integration der Bibliothek in St. Petersburg gespielt. Am wesentlichsten war jedoch, dass sich durch die große Unterstützung der Ehrenmitglieder und Ehrenkorrespondenten die Erwerbung aktueller Bücher aber auch wertvoller älterer Drucke verbessert hatte, was sich insbesondere auch auf die Qualität der fremdsprachigen Bibliotheksbestände auswirkte.

Diese Ehrentitel wurden Staatsmännern, Gelehrten, Bibliographen, und Buchhändlern verliehen, sowohl russischen Bürgern als auch Angehörigen anderer Staaten, darunter auch Deutschen.[341]

Die Verbesserungsvorschläge für ein effektiveres Erwerbungsverfahren entstanden bei Becker aufgrund der Erfahrungen, dass es häufig zu Dublettenkäufen kam, während andere wichtige Bücher nicht gekauft werden konnten. Ursache war ein Verfahren, nachdem Bestellungen und Erwerbungsvorschläge von Bibliothekaren, Lesern und Buchhändlern unkoordiniert durchgeführt wurden. Offenbar war es bisher nicht Interesse der Abteilungen gewesen, Dubletten zu vermeiden.[342]

Auch die ausländischen Bestellungen wurden von niemanden kontrolliert. Lieferzeiten von maximal einem Jahr wurden nicht definiert und überprüft und mancher Titel kam inzwischen als Dublette auf einen anderen Weg ins Haus. Diese Situation war nach Meinung

341 Vgl.: Natal'ja K.Lelikova: Die Ehrenmitglieder und Ehrenkorrespondenten der Kaiserlichen Öffentlichen Bibliothek. In: Publitchnaja biblioteka: ljudi, knigi, zisn' (Die Öffentliche Bibliothek: Menschen, Bücher, Leben). St.Petersburg 1998, S. 29-40.

342 Vgl.: Archiv der Russischen Nationalbibliothek. R.1. N 60. Verzeichnis N 1. 1858. Bl.24.

Beckers auch dadurch erschwert, dass alle Kontakte mit den ausländischen Buchhändlern vom Direktor Korf selbst kontrolliert wurden. Dies bedeutete, dass man bei in jeder Angelegenheit eine Bittschrift bei ihm einreichen musste.[343]

Von der Bibliothek wurden außerdem weder die Preise, noch die Qualität der eingekauften Bücher kontrolliert. Und schließlich wurden gelieferten Bücher von den Mitarbeitern an die Abteilungen der Bibliothek verteilt, die keine Kenntnisse im Bereich der Bibliographie hatten und die Bibliotheksbestände nicht kannten.[344]

Die Bibliothekskollegen stimmten der Idee des Erwerbungskatalogs zu und waren bereit die entsprechenden Arbeiten im Laufe eines Jahres in Gang zu bringen. Außerdem wurde entschieden, dass dafür verantwortliche auch die Leser konsultieren sollte.[345]

Anfang der 1860er-Jahre fing die Bibliothek auch an, den Katalog der fremdsprachigen Neuerwerbungen zu veröffentlichen[346]. Dem Vorschlag von Becker, auf die Führung der Kataloge für jede einzelne Abteilung zu verzichten und einen alphabetischen und systematischen Gesamtkatalog für die ganze Bibliothek zusammenzustellen[347], wurde nicht zugestimmt, gerade auch deutsche hatten sich dagegen ausgesprochen: nämlich Dorn, Mintzlov, Muralt, Berckholz und Gen.[348]

Die Divergenz zwischen den Ansichten von Becker und den Auffassungen seiner Kollegen aus der deutschen Diaspora war auch später zu beobachten. Besonders stark trat sie Anfang der 1860er-Jahre auf, als man sich über Rolle der Bibliothek in der Gesellschaft verständigen wollte. Becker, zusammen mit Sobol'tschikov, meinte, dass die Bibliothek am Leben der Gesellschaft aktiver teilnehmen könnte und müsste und sie infolgedessen breiten Leserkreisen zugänglich sein müsste. Walter, Mintzlov, Posselt und die anderen Vertreter der deutschen Diaspora beharrten auf der Meinung, dass vor allem die zeitenabhängige Funktion staatlicher Bibliotheken als Archive der menschlichen Kenntnisse unabänderlich sein müsste.[349]

Obwohl es Becker auch später nicht gelang, die Kollegen von Gesamtkatalogen zu überzeugen, hat er erreicht, dass einheitliche Katalogisierungsregeln eingeführt wurden, nach denen 1863 bis 1864 alle Bibliotheksbestände und Kataloge überarbeitet wurden. Bisher hatte es bedeutsame Differenzen bei er Erfassung von Monographien, Beiträgen aus Sammelbänden sowie mehrbändigen Titeln gegeben.[350]

Karl Becker war ein der Vertreter der deutschen Bibliotheksdiaspora, die sich damals in der Nationalbibliothek Russlands herausgebildet hatte. Wie die anderen deutschen Bibliothekare - seine Kollegen - hat er die Kenntnisse und die Fertigkeiten des deutschen Bibliothekars, die Erfahrungen im Bereich der Organisation der Arbeit der deutschen wissenschaftlichen Bibliotheken eingeführt. Die Kaiserliche Öffentliche Bibliothek begann sich

---

343 Ebda. Bl.25.

344 Ebda. Bl. 26

345 Im Protokoll war der letzte Leitsatz sogar unterstrichen. Vgl: Archiv der Russischen Nationalbibliothek. R..1. N 60. Verzeichnis N 1. 1858. Bl.24.

346 vgl. z.B.: Istorija Gosudarstvennoj ordena Trudovogo Krasnogo znameni... (Anm.3). S. 111

347 Archiv der Russischen Nationalbibliothek. R..1., Verzeichnis 1., 1858, N 60, Bl. 24.

348 Archiv der Russischen Nationalbibliothek. R.1. N 60. Verzeichnis N 1. 1858. Bl. 24.

349 vgl.: Istorija Gosudarstvennoj ordena Trudovogo Krasnogo znameni... (Anm.3). S. 78.

350 Die von Becker ausgearbeiteten Katalogisierungsregeln waren ins Russische von Arkadij A. Stojkovitsch übersetzt worden und ab 1860 wurden diese Regeln zur offiziellen Katalogisierungsinstruktion, die unter dem Titel „Podrobnye pravila vedenija katalogov Imperatorskoj publitchnoj biblioteki...“ (Ausführliche Regeln der Führung der Kataloge der Kaiserlichen Öffentlichen Bibliothek...) bekannt sind. Nach dieser Instruktion wurden sowohl der Inventurkatalog als auch die alphabetischen und systematischen Kataloge der Abteilungen geführt. Vgl. ebda. S. 102.

zu verwandeln, wobei die Veränderungen von den Abteilungen der Bibliothek ausgegangen waren. In den Abteilungen, für Becker unmittelbar verantwortlich war, hatte er - nach Korf die Wissenschaften „aus jener beklagenswerten Lage herausgeführt, in der sie sich (in der Bibliothek) befanden"; in die selben Abteilungen „brachte er die ausgezeichnetste Ordnung und alle Teile (der Abteilungen) brachte er, soweit es die begrenzten Mittel der Bibliothek zuließen, auf das Niveau der Wissenschaften im Westen".[351]

Jede der Abteilungen der Bibliothek wurde zu einer Art Laboratorium einer Wissenschaft, das so organisiert war, dass es optimal die Bedürfnisse dieser oder jener Wissenschaft befriedigen konnte. Als dies ereicht war und das Modell der deutschen wissenschaftlichen Bibliothek auf dem „Mikroniveau", d.h. auf der Ebene der Abteilungen erfolgreich zu funktionieren begonnen hatte, entstand der Bedarf, die Zusammenwirkung dieser Abteilungen - der Laboratorien einzelner Wissenschaften - in die Wege zu leiten. Und gerade damals wurde der von Göttingen ausgegangene Impuls des „Kosmos der Wissenschaften" wahrgenommen - der Impuls, der in St. Petersburg von dem Gesandten aus der „seligen Republik der Gelehrten" dankbar aufgenommen wurde, um den ganzen Kosmos der Wissenschaften zu ermessen.

Diesen Impuls vermochte Becker im Hinblick auf alle Hauptaufgaben der Kaiserlichen Öffentlichen Bibliothek, vor allem im Hinblick auf die Erschließung der Bestände durch die Kataloge, umzusetzen. Nicht weniger bedeutsam war auch sein Einfluss auf den Prozess der laufenden Beschaffung der in der Welt erschienenen Drucke. Er hat vieles dafür getan, um das Erwerbungsverfahren und damit die Erwerbungsqualität zu verbessern. Er strebte an, dass hier die Vorbilder – aus dem Statut der Universitätsbibliothek Göttingen – für die Erwerbung in die Praxis umgesetzt wurden. Und im Einklang mit dem Vorbild aus Göttingen, der Bibliothek als „Enzyklopädiebibliothek" wollte er den Büchern den Vorzug geben, die dem Fortschritt dienten und „einen einzelnen Schritt vorwärts" taten, den Büchern, die „nicht bloß im Wiederholen, Nachbeten und Compiliren des bereits Bekannten, oder gar Trivialen, bestehen"[352].

In St. Petersburg war das Modell der deutschen wissenschaftlichen Bibliothek bei weitem nicht in vollem Umfang in die Tat umgesetzt worden, was angesichts der grundsätzlich anderen Verhältnisse unmöglich war und auch kaum notwendig gewesen wäre. Nichtsdestoweniger war die Verwandlung der Kaiserlichen Öffentlichen Bibliothek - einer der jüngsten Nationalbibliotheken Europas für die damalige Zeit - in eine der besten Bibliothek dieses Typs, in die Bibliothek, die nach der Qualität ihrer Arbeit mit der besten Nationalbibliothek damaliger Zeit - mit der Bibliothek des Britischen Museums – vergleichbar sein konnte, vor allem deswegen möglich, weil in dieser Bibliothek die Erfahrungen der deutschen wissenschaftlichen Bibliotheken aktiv umgesetzt wurden. In diesem Fall war das Modell der deutschen wissenschaftlichen Bibliothek nicht nur in ein anderes Land und in andere soziokulturelle Verhältnisse übertragen worden. Dieses Modell war, obwohl nicht in vollem Umfang, in der wissenschaftlichen Bibliothek besonderer Art, sogar in der wissenschaftlichen Bibliothek besonderen Typs realisiert, der im Deutschland damaliger Zeit fehlte - in der Nationalbibliothek, die im Hinblick auf die Bürger ihres Landes in vollem Umfang die zwei Hauptfunktionen erfüllte: die Funktion des „Nationalgedächtnisses" (der Sammlung und der Erhaltung des vaterländischen Schrifttums) und die Funktion der

---

[351] vgl.: Imperatorskaja Publitchnaja biblioteka... (Anm.7.). S. 205-206.

[352] Bernhard Fabian, „Der Gelehrte als Leser. Über Bücher und Bibliotheken" (Hildesheim; Zürich; New York 1998), S. 96.

zentralen wissenschaftlichen Universalbibliothek des Landes.

Doch die Kaiserliche Öffentliche Bibliothek hat über ihre Grenzen hinaus gewirkt. Ähnlich wie ihre Hauptkonkurrentin - die Bibliothek des Britischen Museums - hat sie sich als die wahrhafte europäische wissenschaftliche Bibliothek gezeigt, die in höchstmöglichem Umfang ihre Grundfunktionen - die Sammlung und das Erhalten des Schrifttums der Länder und Völker Europas erfüllt.

Giuseppe Vitiello

National libraries: the practice of a symbolic concept (18th – 21st century)

Universal, nation-oriented or functional?

The scope of national libraries has often been formulated within the framework of these three core concepts. A national library is universal because it has to acquire, as extensively as possible, national as well as foreign publications. Thanks to legal deposit and related products, such as national bibliographic services, national libraries have a responsibility for collecting the publishing output of a particular country and recording it for public and/or commercial purposes. And finally, as it fulfils information needs that are of relevance for a nation, a national library is also the hub of library services performed in co-operation with the other libraries of a country.

This threefold concept has not always been the main constituent of the scope of a national library, but has laboriously matured according to historical patterns and cultural traditions that differ from country to country. This article intends to describe the emergence of the concept in four countries (France, Great Britain, Germany and Italy) and the way it has followed different streams of development through symbolic acts, national representations and political visions.

The symbolic use of pre-modern collections

Professional literature about national libraries has usually focused on how the written legacy of a country has been transmitted from past time to present generations. This legacy is often the offshoot of a dynastic library - usually royal, or aristocratic - that became public at a later stage. „At the beginning of the history of the Bibliothèque nationale de France – an occasional pamphlet says – is the great personality of some French kings who were book lovers."[353] Such kings are Louis IX, Charles V, Louis XI and, obviously, François I who introduced the practice of legal deposit with the Montpellier Decree of 28 December 1537. Not far from Montpellier, slightly later, the universal mission of premodern collections had already been prefigured in Konrad Gesner's monumental *Bibliotheca Universalis*: libraries should collect all known publications in Latin, Greek, Hebrew, the three canonic languages of the culture of Renaissance.

In spite of Gesner's ambition, it would have been difficult to find in the 16th century universal collections in humanistic, university and cloister libraries. Most of them were limited in number and scope, even when they did not follow pre-established trends of collection development. According to Burckhardt, books and buildings were the dominant passions of the princes of the Renaissance. Nevertheless, in humanistic libraries, antiquarian and bibliophilic concerns prevailed over qualitative criteria. In the rich dynastic libraries, the museological intention was dominant. Libraries were essential constituents of the *Kunstkammer*, a cabinet where precious relics and rare objects were exhibited, the value of

353 Virginie de La Batut (ed.). Bibliothèque nationale de France. In Connaissance des arts (numéro hors série). Paris: Société française de promotion artistique, 1996, p. 11.

which was more in their number and nature than in their intellectual value.

University and religious libraries, too, were intrinsically selective. University libraries were too modest to have the slightest pretension to go universal. As religious congregations were in many countries monopolistic providers of education, their libraries were larger. The Escorial Library, created in 1567, developed rapidly and after only 20 years already possessed some 18.000 volumes. Nevertheless, the views on collection development of its Jesuit founder, Claude Clément, were „those of a censor and a persecutor, which leads us to the closed attitude of Counter-Reformation."[354] Similarly, Reformation movements also implemented criteria of „safe" reading in their controlled libraries. In his booklet *An die Ratsherren aller Städte deutsches Lands, dass sie christliche Schule aufrichten und halten sollen*, Luther prescribes a set of rules valid for collection development in the *Stadt* or *Gemeinde* libraries. Papist books and scholastic works are excluded, whereas the humanistic literary canon is highly recommended together with the reading of Bibles and all forms of *rechtschaffene bücher*.[355] Jochum has rightly commented that the humanistic-oriented Reformation library „rather than educating people, intends to institutionalise the way in which Reform should educate people."[356]

In the 17th century, the theory of universal libraries is promoted in peripheral intellectual groups rather than at institutional level. In the first half of the century, a circle of philosophers and writers, such as Gassendi, La Mothe le Vayer, and Cyrano de Bergerac, gathered at the home of the Dupuit brothers in Paris. As a result of the scientific discoveries of the 17th century, a deep sense of scepticism animated their conversations. They revised religious tenets and ex cathedra teaching systematically. One of the members of the circle was Gabriel Naudé, a pupil of celebrated heretics in Italy, who developed the concept of the model library of the French 17th century *honnête homme*. In his *Advis pour dresser une bibliothèque* (1627), Gabriel Naudé was the first to claim that library holdings should be universal and not limited by any kind of misconception or prejudice. All principal authors writing on any kind of topic and subject should be present on library shelves together with their interpreters and commentators and their works should be in their original languages: „Bibles and Rabbis in Hebrew, Holy Fathers in Greek and Latin, Avicenna in Arabic, Boccaccio, Dante and Petrarca in Italian".[357] While Renaissance princes had seen in libraries a way of preserving in an ideal place the memory of their actions, Naudé sketched the image of a library as a public place. His idea was that it should not exhibit books for bibliophilic purposes but ought to make them available.

In the 17th century, library practice had preceded theory. The library established by Cardinal Federico Borromeo in Milan contained a wide range of titles, including heterodox books that were kept in a separate room. A library in Oxford was created by Thomas Bodley. He and his librarian, Thomas James, bought books from many European countries and in various languages, including Chinese, at that time spoken by only a few people in Europe - and very likely by nobody in England. Another celebrated library belonged to Cardinal Mazzarino in Paris. Before it was dispersed a few years later, it is said it included 40,000 volumes, half of the European known publications, including 6,000 heretic books.

---

354 Mario Rosa. I depositi del sapere: biblioteche, accademie e archivi. In La memoria del sapere. Forme di conservazione e strutture organizzative dall'antichità a oggi. Bari: Laterza, 1988, p. 165-209; quotation, p. 190.

355 Wolfgang Thauer – Peter Vodosek. Geschichte der öffentlichen Bücherei in Deutschland. Wiesbaden: Harrassowitz, 1990.

356 Uwe Jochum. Kleine Bibliotheksgeschichte. Stuttgart: Reclam, 1993, p. 89.

357 Gabriel Naudé, Advispour dresser une bibliothèque. Leipzig: VEB Edition, 1963, p. 38.

Of course, such examples are not the rule; just as rare is the case of a person in the 17th and 18th centuries possessing large quantities of books. Except for Scandinavian countries, illiteracy was widespread in Europe and concerned 50 % of the adult population, with peaks of 90 % in Southern Europe.[358] Even among wealthy people and members of royal families, library expenses were considered sumptuary rather than educational. Having a rich library was a status symbol and an aristocratic duty; it almost never fulfilled what we would call today the information demand. According to Saint-Simon, Louis XIV had a limited culture and few intellectual curiosities. He could hardly read and write and was so ignorant that any of his courtiers was more learned than him in history and in cultural matters. Nevertheless, the *Roi Soleil* had very likely the richest library in Europe and the most competent librarians.

The explanation for such apparent contradiction lays in the social and mental foundation of the court society. As Elias demonstrated, court society is a complex one and protocol and etiquette played the same role as administration and legislation.[359] Even individual extravagances and squandering was part of the representation that organised the social hierarchy, according to people's rank and categories of peerage. Moreover, the *Roi Soleil* bibliographic lavishness is a political act that aims at overriding rival centres of collectionism. Louis XIV library was to French libraries what Versailles was to the court society – an exclusive place where the royal power monopolised all forms of expression, in particular dissident voices that had been strengthful in the past, and might be strong again. Louis XIV never forgot the *Frondes* that agitated his infancy. During his reign, one after the other, collections belonging to well known free thinkers like the Dupuit brothers or independent aristocrats such as Gaston d'Orléans were integrated into the King's library.[360]

In the course of the 18th century royal libraries opened to the public and made their collections accessible through catalogues and book loans. This was an important step. Nevertheless, opening a library to the public does not necessarily mean that a library is public. The *Ancien Régime* library is the property of a sovereign who grants access to its subjects according to personal and often arbitrary rules. Frederic II of Prussia was a genuine book lover, a champion of Letters and Arts and never grudged resources allocated to the Berlin Royal Library. Nevertheless, he did not hesitate to limit access to its collections and put an end to the practice of lending books. Only between the 18th and 19th centuries, royal libraries gradually became „public" and accessible institutions, state owned rather than personal property. This is when European governments began to put instruction, information and national cohesion at the top of their agendas. In the 18th century, such evolution corresponds to the decline of the court society as a sphere of the public power and the emergence of the state as a category of the political thought. Moreover, as Habermas has demonstrated, it also reflects the emergence of a political public sphere that is a public category in the framework of the private sphere.[361] In other words, public places and institutions (such as private *salons*, cafés, libraries or reading rooms) are the sites where cultural products are regularly exchanged and a public opinion is formed through newspapers and books. Dynastic libraries may still be the property of royal or aristocratic families; notwithstanding, they become a place where written opinions in books are freely imparted and

[358] Carlo M. Cipolla. Istruzione e sviluppo. Il declino dell'analfabetismo nel mondo occidentale. Torino: UTET, 1971.
[359] Norbert Elias. The court society. New York: Pantheon Books, 1983.
[360] Simone Balayé. La Bibliothèque Nationale des origines à 1800. Genève: Droz, 1988.
[361] Jürgen Habermas. The structural transformation of the public sphere : an inquiry into a category of bourgeois society. Cambridge Mass: MIT Press, 1989.

information is readily accessed.

As they were open at regular hours and made available a consistent number of works to the public, royal and aristocratic libraries became a model of knowledge transmission in the face of the growing demand for education. Their popularity was so high that the establishment and development of museums in Germany in the 18th century adopts the „public" model of libraries.[362] Ephemeral pleasure is banned from these public spaces. Therefore, royal and aristocratic libraries promoted a model of cultural policy carried out by absolutist regimes with a view to educating people and spreading enlightened thoughts among the population.

The emergence of national collections

The Revolutionary and Napoleonic years had demolished much of the European *Ancien Régime*. New states emerged after the Vienna Congress with innovative and longlasting features. Political borders in modern states define a nation where governments exert their authority on the whole of the territory without local middlemen. Their authority is rooted in a legal system that applies indiscriminately to all subjects. The historical privileges that had once legitimated parliaments, towns, provinces or individuals left way to a steady administration in charge of applying the law on behalf of „the people."

In order to exert their sovereignity, national governments have to cope with two main cultural problems. The first is to choose a language that is common to all citizens and is used to deal with the national administration. If civil servants are not able to speak to the people whose rights they intend to protect, conflicts and tensions arise. This is why national language, or languages, become literally a state business. The second is to build up consensus among their subjects so that they can identify themselves in the party or in the personalities in the government. Such consensus has not only a legal and economic basis, but presupposes some cultural elements that nurture a sense of belonging and form the core identity of a people. Common myths and stories, and a common language, these are the basic ingredients of the national identity. They are expressed through a narrative that is communicated with shared symbolic marks - flag, anthem, parades, national currency, capital city - and literary and cultural values - myths, heros, folklore.

Set against this background, legal deposit becomes a perfect working tool to affirm the symbolic power of a state. It conciliates the library's need to create a reference collection with the mandate of transmitting the written legacy of a country to the public. What a formidable reservoir of legends, myths, and values are national libraries! What an extraordinary way of re-inventing the cultural tradition by providing evidence of the continuity of national core values along the centuries![363] It is nationalism that creates the nation, and not the other way round, Gellner asserts in a reference work.[364] And legal deposit adapts itself to the renewed needs. In the 16th century it was designed to enrich libraries. From the 17th to the 19th century it was a way of implementing censorship. In the 19th century it will become a means of re-inventing the cultural tradition of a country through the objective of

[362] Henning Bock. *Collections privées et publiques, les prémices du musée public en Allemagne*. In *Les musées en Europe à la veille de l'ouverture du Louvre, actes du colloque (3-5 juin 1993)*, ed. by Edouard Pommier. Paris: Klincksieck, 1995, p. 61-77.

[363] Eric J. Hobsbawm – Terence Ranger (eds.). The invention of tradition. Cambridge: Cambridge University Press, 1983.

[364] Ernest Gellner. Nations and nationalism.Oxford: Oxford University Press, 1983.

building up its historical national collection.

To extend current national attributes in a retrospective vision is important for a state, for it can embody them in primeval and „imagined" communities where citizens find the source of their particular character, the cradle of their national identity, and the rationale to adhere to what Renan called „a daily plebiscite."[365] Re-focussing legal deposit as a way of building up the national collection is functional both to heritage and educational objectives. Through deposited accessions national libraries work on the heart of a nation as they store its written memory and make it available for future generations.

Legal deposit also works on the brain of a nation as it serves the dissemination and the divulgation of the publishing output of a country, thus showing its intellectual supremacy. In the 19th century, national libraries contend with one another for the first place in Europe with respect to budgets, personnel, number of books and quality of holdings. If a national library is an intrinsic component of a state, a powerful national library can only be the expression of a triumphant nation. In 1836, Panizzi used this argument with the members of the parliamentary committee in charge of evaluating the state of the British Museum Library and advocated the need for a budget increase. The same argument was applied by Bonghi, Minister of Public Instruction in the unified Italy, to establish a national library in Rome in 1870, even though Italy had already national libraries in Florence, Turin and Naples.

National libraries in France, Great Britain, Germany and Italy

France. In 1793, the Bibliothèque du Roy in Paris, one year before being renamed Bibliothèque nationale, is in danger. A series of decrees emanated by the Terror during the French Revolution establish that all marks of the *Ancien Régime*, whether in art and architecture or in books, have to be destroyed. Ex-libris, bookplates and thousands of books are under threat. Rumors spread that the library itself will be set on fire. Marat, one of the Terror leaders, said that the French Revolution would dismantle any trace of the previous Kingdom and generate a new viril and virtuous literature. A neologism is also forged to designate such revolutionary iconoclasm: vandalism.

In the same year, however, the Thermidorian wing holds power in France and also intervenes to save threatened library holdings. Old library collections change their paradigm: from venomous elements of corruptions they become the bedrock of the revolutionary virtue. This accomplishment is the work of Abbé Grégoire, an extremely active member of the *Assemblée nationale,* who is considered to be the founder of French modern cultural policy. Grégoire was convinced that art and literature were the fruit of people's sweat and that it was the task of the Revolution to give back to the people what was once confiscated from him. Hence, the notion of cultural good, a national asset for which the government should care and that ought to be made available to the public.

One of the pillars of Abbé Grégoire's theory was the intervention of state in culture.[366] In the recognition that no other entity would be as neutral in cultural policy, the state cannot tolerate any rivals in the governance of cultural heritage and in the expropriation of artistic works of art. According to Grégoire, expropriation was not a matter of appropriation

---

365 Benedict Anderson. Imagined communities. Reflections on the origin and spread of nationalism. 2nd edition. London-New York: Verso, 1991. Ernest Renan. Qu'est-ce qu'une nation? In Ernest Renan. Qu'est-ce qu'une nation? Et autres essais politiques., par J. Roman. Paris: Presses Pocket, 1992, p. 55.

366 Rita Hermon-Belot. L'Abbé Grégoire. La politique et la vérité. Paris, Seuil, 2000.

but rather of re-appropriation: the state - that means „we the people" - would be returned works of art that are the products of people's accomplishment. The state would use them not for individual and sterile contemplation, but as a tool of revolutionary and collective education. On the basis of the anti-vandalic theory, expropriations made by the Revolution are *a posteriori* justified, including the spoils of the wars waged by Revolutionary and Napoleonic armies. This marks the beginning of a massive transfer of works of art and library holdings from occupied countries - that are considered as „lands of slaves", inapt to hold such collections - to French museums and libraries.

Therefore, after a season of vandalism, the French Bibliothèque nationale was to know a period of prosperity and the most extraordinary time of its history. The library was now empowered to „manage abundance."[367] The treasures held in religious and *émigrés* collections in France and libraries in Italy, Germany, Austria and Belgium were plundered and brought to Paris. In 1794 the Bibliothèque nationale had a collection of 300.000 volumes. After the end of the Napoleonic era, when works of art came back to their original countries, it remained the most important library in the world.

United Kingdom. More britannico, the national library of the United Kingdom is not the fruit of revolutionary turmoils or anti-Jesuit campaigns, as is the case in many European countries. A nobleman and learned personality, Sir Hans Sloane, physician and President of the Royal Society, donated his splendid collection to the nation. A sum of 100,000 pounds was raised by a lottery and used not only to remunerate the owner of the outstanding collection, but also to acquire the premises where it was then stored. In spite of such a remarkable start, the British Museum Library was not to take off until the Thirties of the 19th century. When Alexander I, czar of Russia, visited the library in 1814, the model he had in mind was the library in Saint-Petersbourg, created by Catherine the Great on the basis of the transfer from Poland of 400.000 volumes belonging to the rich Zaluski library. Alexander the First was struck by the limited number of volumes he found in the British Museum Library. The principal librarian, Joseph Planta, blatantly replied to the impolite remark of the Czar: „*Sire, tout est payé ici.*"[368]

The way in which the British Museum Library turned into the greatest library in the world is a well known story. The credit goes mainly to a young librarian of Italian origin, Antonio Panizzi, who carried out an energetic campaign in favour of the library among the members of the British Parliament, clearly explaining the advantages to a nation of having a first class library. Even Panizzi, however, would have failed, had he not found a favourable historical context. In November 1830, after having been excluded for almost half century, the whig party holds power in the United Kingdom and adopts a number of bills focused on electoral reform, suppression of slavery, free trade exchange and improvement of miners' working conditions. The cultural and social life was then dominated by the longlasting influence of the *Essay on the principle of population as it affects the future improvement of society*, written by the economist Malthus. Published in 1798, this work attempted to demonstrate that, while the means of subsistence grow at an arithmetical pace, the population of a country increases instead in geometrical progression. Although the theory proved to be wrong, public opinion conjured up hungry masses of workers taking hold of gentry areas and plundering the lands of rich people. The ruling class felt that the infe-

367 Balayé, op. cit., p. 323.

368 Arundell Esdaile. The British Museum Library. A short history and survey. London: George Allen & Unwin, 1946, p. 57.

rior layers of the society should be kept quiet through some kind of productive leisure, and in particular education and training.

Such favourable political climate was determinant to accelerate the positive developments that took place at the British Museum Library. Panizzi, himself a whig-oriented personality, was able to use the appropriate arguments to impress the Committee in charge of inquiring the situation of the library during the parliamentary debate in 1835. The points he made raised much sympathy for they were innovative and straightforward. First point: national information policy. The British Museum Library had to give equal chances to any of its citizens and allow them to have the same learning possibilities as a rich men.[369] Second, national pride. The Library had less conspicuous collections than the equivalent library in Paris, rich of 700.000 volumes. Third, civic attitude: users themselves have to be educated to think that libraries are created for the promotion of studies and of scientific investigation and not for the pleasure of those who keep them. Fourth, national acquisition policy: the Library had to dispose of important collections in English and a large choice of reference books both in English and in foreign languages. And so on.

There is very little that Panizzi did not manage to achieve. He was instrumental in increasing the annual budget of the library to 10.000 pounds yearly. The number of acquisitions tripled. The library was enlarged thanks to the construction of the famous *Reading room*, a model for reading places all over the world. New cataloguing rules and ways of arranging books were adopted. After thirty years, Thomas Watts, Keeper of the Printed books department, could say that the British Museum Library had the best Hungarian library out of Hungary, the best Dutch library out of Holland, briefly the best library in every European language out of the country where this language was spoken.[370]

Germany. Another quite different case of formation of a national library is to be found in Germany. At the end of the 19th century there was little doubt that the only library entitled to play this role was the Imperial Library in Berlin. Founded in 1659, the library had served as royal library and, in the 18th century, as the main Prussian library, before being part of the university of Berlin, created by Wilhelm von Humboldt in 1810. Napoleon's triumph over the Russian army was considered a humiliation for the German *Geist.* Humboldt conceived an ambitious plan for the budding higher education infrastructure in Prussia and called the German intelligentsia, mainly idealistic circles, to converge on the newly born university of Berlin. Fresh blood came to revive the stagnant academy. Fichte, Wolf, Savigny and Schleiermacher were part of the teaching staff. The latter also wrote the new statute of the university library. Needless to say, the new statute conceded a large autonomy to the library and the effects were soon to be seen. In spite of the king's resistence, the first professional librarian, Friedrich Wilken, was appointed thanks to his personal record and competence. This was a splendid time for the library that not only increased enormously its collections, but grew up with a universal scope and the ambition to become among the best in the world. When Wilhelm I received the imperial crown in the Mirrors Room in Versailles in 1870,

369 „I want a poor student to have the same means of indulging his learned curiosity, of following his rational pursuits, of consulting the same authorities, of fathoming the most intricate inquiry, as the richest man in the kingdom, as far as books go, and I contend that Government is bound to give him the most liberal and unlimited assistance in this respect" (quoted by Esdaile, op. cit., p. 96).

370 Philip J. Weimerskirch, Panizzi, sir Anthony. In Encyclopedia of Library and Information Science, vol. 21 (1977), p. 325.

there was no doubt that the Imperial Library in Berlin would become the nation's library.[371]

Collecting or not the whole of the publishing output of German-speaking countries? This question was central for policy-makers in the library field. One of them was Friedrich Althoff, Director of the Department of Arts and Sciences within the Ministry of Interior, who advocated the idea that the Imperial Library should collect all publications from the 25 states of the Federal Imperial Germany. This idea was shared by the powerful German publishers' and booksellers' association that put pressure on the government and requested the creation of a national library. This library would be empowered to receive legal deposit publications and able to generate the catalogue of all German publications – something that the book trade desperately needed.

The Director of the Imperial Library, however, was not in the same wavelength. He had in mind the high standards of academic libraries in Germany, mainstay of research and teaching, that collected mainly university-oriented publications. Exhaustiveness in legal deposit, therefore, was seen more as a burden than an opportunity. The 1885 Imperial Library statute, an Althoff offspring, stated indeed that the library should „collect, as extensively as possible, national and foreign publications."[372], including those issued in Austria and Switzerland. Nevertheless, the Library never implemented extensively this rule, nor compiled the bibliography of German publications. In Althoff's views, the national bibliography not only would have been the German catalogue of traded books, but it would have generated overall savings in the cataloguing operations of German libraries at large. The situation was then at a standstill and no solutions were envisaged in the short term.

The idea of collecting the whole of the German publishing output in a library and of recording it in a general catalogue had been first proposed in the early 19th century by Brockhaus, a successful publisher. Almost one century later, Erich Ehlermann, one of the presidents of the association of the German publishers and booksellers, resumed it with a significant variation: the library would not be in Berlin, but in Leipzig.

In his booklet, *Eine Reichsbibliothek in Leipzig* (1910), Ehlermann went as far as proposing in detail the general features of the library that:

a) had to collect commercial as well as non commercial documents;
b) should enjoy a depository status for all German publications, each German state within the federation should have worked out a new regulation;
c) had to collect the totality of the publications issued in German speaking countries;
d) had to lend books when they were no longer available in the book trade;
e) should be unique, without equivalent in the rest of Germany;
f) should not compile itself the bibliography but should assign this task to the German publishers' association.[373]

The strong links between the German national library and the book trade were clearly prefigurated. Under the pressure of the publishers' and booksellers' association, the Leipzig library (*Deutsche Bücherei*) was built up in a short time, from 1912 to 1916, as a response to the needs of the publishers. After the second world war, when Leipzig became the na-

371 Eugen Paunel. Die Staatsbibliothek zu Berlin. Ihre Geschichte und Organisation während der ersten zwei Jahrhunderte seit ihrer Eröffung 1661-1871. Berlin: Walter de Gruyter, 1965.

372 Rudolf Blum. Nationalbibliographie und Nationalbibliothek. Die Verzeichnung und Sammlung der nationalen Buchproduktion, besonders der deutschen, von den Anfängen bis zum zweiten Weltkrieg. Frankfurt am main: Buchändler-Vereinigung, 1990, p.141.

373 Ibidem, p. 208-209.

tional library of East Germany, the story repeated itself. In 1946, a publisher, Georg Kurt Schauer, and a librarian, Hans Wilhelm Eppensheimer, expressed the idea to create a repository for German publications. The American representative of the Allied forces in Germany accepted their proposal. This was the inception of the German Library in Frankfurt am Main. Since 1991, the Frankfurt library has merged with the Deutsche Bücherei in Leipzig and has officially become the national library of Germany.

Italy. At the moment Italy was unified, the level of literacy of the adult population was quite low. According to official statistics, three out of four Italians were illiterate with peaks of 90 % in Southern Italy. At the same time, in Prussia and in England such percentages were, respectively 20 and 30 %, and 40 % in France and in Austria.[374]

In 1869, a Committee for the „scientific and thematic re-organisation of the libraries of the Kingdom", chaired by count Ciborio, was set up by the Minister of Public Instruction Bargoni. The brief of the government was clear: to create a national library that would act as a cornerstone of the Italian library system. The conclusions drawn by the Ciborio Committee, however, went in opposite directions. Not one, but nine libraries were considered of national relevance by the Committee, for they stored prestigious and rare book collections. Most of them were already national in the pre-unitary Italian states. The reasons alleged by the members of the „technical" Committee were symbolically connotated. Italy had its own distinctive tradition and „neither the geographic configuration nor the *genius loci*, nor the historical series of facts after the fall of the Roman Empire would acknowledge the existence of a dominant town, as is the case of Paris or London, that would reflect the greatness, the power and the big interests of the nation."[375]

In spite of such „professional" arguments, even Minister Bargoni considered that the Committee had gone too far in their historically-oriented vision of national libraries. The first Decree on libraries, that was promulgated in 1869, designated „only" three national libraries with that of Florence having the privilege of being depository for all Italian publications. An academic prejudice had prevented the Imperial Library in Berlin becoming the national library of Germany. Similarly, Italian professionals were too much imbued in historicism to set criteria other than the heritage function as a constituent attribute of a national library. The „technical" argument, however, disguised a truly political problem: the difficulty for the newly established national authority imposing national core values in a state where identities and the sense of belonging were eminently local. This became even more apparent during the second attempt to re-arrange the Italian library system, when Ruggero Bonghi was nominated Minister of Public Instruction in 1874. A fine literate and a strong advocate of national identity, Bonghi's views around libraries were centralistic: having in mind the examples of the French Imperial Library and the British Museum Library, he devised to organise the Italian library system around a central institution, a modern, entirely new library, based in the heart of the young state, its capital city Rome.

Rome had been occupied by royal troops in 1870 at a time when Napoleon III, the great defender of the Papist rule in Rome, was distracted by the French-Prussian war and unable to intervene. The rich and „charismatic" Vatican library, a possible candidate for holding the nation's memory, was on foreign territory, the slim area that still belonged to the Pope.

---

374 Robert A. Houston. In Europa tutti vanno a scuola. In Storia d'Europa. L'età contemporanea. Secoli XIX-XX (vol. 5), ed. by Paul Bairoch and Eric J. Hobsbawm. Torino: Einaudi, 1996.

375 Quoted by Paolo Traniello. La biblioteca pubblica. Storia di un istituto nell'Europa contemporanea. Bologna: Il Mulino, 1997, p. 94.

Bonghi's concept of the new library was simple. He wanted to bring together the collections of the suppressed convents (300.000 printed volumes) and store them in the former college of the Jesus Society in Rome. The newly born Italian national library was inaugurated a few years later. Its beginnings were however in all but name, for the employees were too much absorbed by routine operations of cataloguing and shelving books. Moreover, because of mismanagement, confusion, and lack of professionalism, the library closed its doors for three years before it opened again in 1881. Bonghi again reinforced its role in 1876 when he made the Parliament adopt the second Decree on libraries with national libraries now being in the number of four.[376] Bonghi himself considered that this number was excessive: „no nation, however rich and big it may be, can maintain too many national libraries and make them prosperous and adequate to fulfil the needs of its citizens. To have too many [national libraries] is like to have none."[377]

Nonetheless, even this energetic champion of genuine nationalism and advocate of centralism had to relinquish his vision of libraries and conciliate it with local instances. Nine years after, with Bonghi no longer in office, another regulation would re-adjust his approach. This time, the term „national" was assigned to six libraries; only two, Florence and Rome, were considered „central national" and benefited from legal deposit legislation. Their role was to collect the national publishing output, whereas the „simple" national libraries had a merely regional function. This Decree established the definitive administration of state libraries in Italy for more than one century. Neither the two world wars, nor fascism, nor the advent of a democratic state in 1945 changed such arrangement. The two-headed system of national libraries in Italy, centered in Rome and Florence, with overlapping functions and role, is therefore a historical legacy. It also marks, however, the political failure of governments from the Unification to now to build up a coherent policy of devolution of powers to the regions and the predicament they find themselves in dealing with local and regional identities.

Towards a functional concept of national libraries

Four nations, four identities, four different stories. They give an idea of the variety of the political and cultural drives that brought about the emergence of national libraries in the 19th century. In London, the impulse was mainly educational with the corollary aim to disseminate culture widely; in Paris, the heritage function prevailed over other objectives and was paralleled by a strong identification with the national cultural values represented by the state; in Berlin, the approach was mainly bibliographic and strongly supported by the book trade, in Rome and Florence, the national tradition had to find a compromise with local and regional identities.

To this already multifold variety, more cases of formation of national libraries may be added, each with its own characteristic perspective. The most recent (1994) is that of the Russian National Library in Saint-Petersbourg and the Russian State Library in Moscow contending with each other the title of national library and the subsequent Solomonic decision made by public authorities to assign such title to both. In Bern, a national library only emerged at the end of the 19th century, hardly acknowledged by the German-speaking cantons of Switzerland. Other particular cases are to be found in the Balkans with national li-

[376] They were Florence, Naples, Rome and Turin.

[377] Ruggero Bonghi. La Biblioteca Vittorio Emanuele e i musei. Discorso inaugurale. Roma, 1876, p. 18.

braries on fire (Sarajevo) or utterly empoverished (Pristina) as they represent the threatened identities of groups of population. In the Baltic states, after the fall of Soviet Union, the first symbolic act of the newly born national libraries was to make free the „closed" collections of dissident literature.

Whatever the origin and the circumstances of their formation, it is a fact that after the second world war national libraries were established in almost every European state. The bulk of them were large size libraries, with old and rare books, expressing the historical continuity of the written memory of a nation. Almost all benefited from legal deposit legislation, compiled a national bibliography and acquired a good number of foreign publications. Having the same status as that of national galleries, museums, archives and theatres, they were usually lavishly funded by governments. Most of them were considered to be the national archive of publications and gained an image of antiquarian and conservative institutions that proved to be a burden for their future operations.

A number of comparative investigations were then carried out in order to find out some topical elements and patterns common to national libraries that would eventually promote a model. A pioneer book, written by Esdaile in 1934 and revised in 1957, reviewed the national libraries of the world.[378] Another important event was a Symposium organised by UNESCO in Vienna in 1958.[379] At the end of this process, a definition of national library was issued at the 16th General Conference of UNESCO held in 1970. According to UNESCO, national libraries are:

> *„responsible for acquiring and conserving copies of all significant publications published in the country and functioning as a „deposit" library, whether by law or under other arrangements. They will also normally perform some of the following functions: produce a national bibliography; hold and keep up to date a large and representative collection of foreign literature, including books about the country; act as a national bibliographical information centre; compile union catalogues; publish the retrospective national bibliography."*[380]

This definition was a compromise between those who would have liked to concentrate many of the national information needs into a single institution and those who would limit the role of national libraries, pleading for a more distributed repartition of functions within the library system. In 1966, Humphreys had listed three categories of functions: essential, desirable and inessential.[381] Essential functions were those that were eventually endorsed by UNESCO in its 1970 General Conference. Desirable functions were: interlibrary loan, manuscript archive, research on librarianship. Inessential functions were: international exchanges, the blind library, professional training, and assistance to the other libraries of the country.

This concept, concentrating many functions in a single institution, was elaborated under

---

378 Arundell Esdaile. National libraries of the world. Their history, administration and public services. London: Grafton, 1934; 2nd edition revised by F.J. Hill. London: The Library Association, 1957.

379 UNESCO. National libraries : their problems and prospects. Symposium on national libraries in Europe. Paris: UNESCO, 1960.

380 F.L. Schick. „The International standardization of Library statistics". In UNESCO Bulletin for Libraries, v. XXV, n. 1 (1971), p. 8-9.

381 Kenneth W. Humphreys. „National library functions". UNESCO Bulletin for libraries, 20 (July-August 1966), p. 158-169; also in National libraries, edited by Maurice B. Line and Joyce Line. London: Aslib, 1979, p. 64-75.

the influence of Arab and socialist countries, for which national libraries were the apex of the library system. The UNESCO definition seemed to be so sound that it was re-stated with almost no change in the UNESCO Guidelines published in 1987.[382] Nevertheless, consensus on them was not unanimous. In a report written in 1989, Line, a former director of the British Library, radically re-questioned the radial model of library system, with the national library working as its hub.[383] In the light of information technologies and library networking, he stated, information needs at national level could be fulfilled also by other libraries. The national collection could be dispersed in several repositories. Co-operation with the private sector would be the alternative to individually produced national bibliographies. Single location of remote resources for interlibrary loan could be the business of a national provision system. And so on.

The reason for such a paradigm shift may be found in library automation and in the success of union catalogues in the 1970s and 1980s, that allow tracing books and other materials no matter where they are stored, without necessarily resorting to national library services. The radial model, however, was challenged also because national libraries had been unable to keep up with social transformations and changed tastes of the people. Whereas in the 1970s public libraries had opened themselves to new media and new publics eventually taking the forefront of library development, national libraries' self-representation was still élite- and research-oriented. Even the collection of non-book material was considered as non relevant by national librarians – witness the proliferation in the '70s of specialised institutions such as national Music, Film, Audiovisual Institutes that concentrated the tasks of selecting, depositing and processing non-print material.

National libraries and globalisation

Two decades later, the trend seems to reverse and there is a lot of buzz again about national libraries. Spectacular architectures and grand plants were inaugurated in Frankfurt (1996), Paris and London (1997), Copenhagen (1999). In spite of hardship and budgetary constraints, new buildings also opened in Tallin (1993), Zagreb (1995) and Saint-Petersbourg (1998).

This infrastructural affluence unveils national libraries' aspiration to resume the role of prime movers within a national library system. Many of the specialised archives for non-printed media are now being strictly associated with the work of national libraries. National libraries seem to be the only cultural institutions to be on a firm footing to store also electronic publications. Media convergence, i.e. the coming together of telecommunication, audiovisual and media industries, has been an opportunity for them and their role is emphasised in the new information environment.[384]

Rather than technical, challenges for national libraries are of a more political and economic nature and may be summarised with a single world: globalisation.[385] Globalisation is the most distinctive economic, social and political factor of contemporary societies with overall implications for cultural and educational products. In the cultural field, it coincides

[382] Guy Sylvestre. Guidelines for national libraries. Paris: UNESCO, 1987.

[383] Maurice Line. National library and information needs : alternative means of fulfilment, with special reference to the role of national libraries. Paris: UNESCO, 1989.

[384] Graham P. Cornish. The role of national libraries in the new information environment. Paris: UNESCO, 1991.

[385] I have dealt in detail with this issue in my article „National libraries in the age of globalization", forthcoming in Zeitschrift für Bibliothekswesen und Bibliographie (4/2001).

with the world-wide dissemination of uniform models and patterns behaviour, usually permeated by the entertainment culture of Hollywood blockbusters. For many critical commentators, globalisation means lack of diversification among cultural products and a selection of content that is exclusively dictated by profit concerns.

In the environment that surrounds national libraries some distinctive trends may be noticed. The first is concentration of cultural industries. The world publishing industry is on the way of being in the hands of a few global players. In almost all countries few groups control more than half of the publishing business. Cross border alliances and mergers are taking place at a rapid pace and it may well be that in a few years a handful of companies will control the whole European publishing market. All the more that new technologies are favouring the vertical concentration of global players with the result that a handful of conglomerates may control both the segments of production of cultural content and its distribution to consumers at large.[386]

Another effect of globalisation is linguistic uniformity. The diminished importance of national language(s) is paralleled by the inevitable penetration of the English language in all domains of everyday life. English is spoken by successful people in different countries and cultures and is adopted by the richest countries as the language of international exchanges. It has been estimated that, because of linguistic homogeneisation, 25 languages die every year and that, at the end of the 21st century, only half of the existing 5.000 languages will still be in existence.[387]

The third aspect of globalisation is the decline of the public sphere in the cultural field and the consequent downsizing of support schemes to libraries, documentation and information centres, as a result of cuts in public grants. This will eventually lead to generalized and increasingly commercialized information services. In recent years, the „désétatisation" of public services with a cultural vocation has brought a disengagement on the part of the state in favour of private initiatives.

In the global environment, therefore, especially where the publishing industry of a country is unable to cope with the pervasive aspects of globalisation and disseminate its publications all over the world, national libraries may become the strongholds of national language(s) and culture(s). Their mission in the electronic environment is to protect and to reinforce the position of minority languages. They should diffuse local content into the world arena for native speakers living out of the country and represent pluralistic outlets for channeling cultural products and services in particular where multinational players only make available proprietary and uni-dimensional content.

The key for that is not to create alternatives to the channels created by the publishing trade, but rather to work with it and to sustain the public principle of information in the private sector. Digital national libraries may therefore act as clearing centres for national publications and serve as their electronic distribution outlets, after previous agreements made with right owners and remuneration for authors.

Legal deposit may prove to be highly instrumental for that. Today, publishers hesitate to deposit electronic publications in the recognition that they would not be remunerated for the content they make available. If national libraries work out appropriate arrangements with publishers, the risk of creating „dead collections", deposited for storage purposes only, may be overcome. In those countries where national libraries have a co-ordinating function within the

386 José Afonso Furtado. Os livros e as leituras. Novas ecologias da informaçao. Lisboa: Livros e leituras, 2000.
387 Claude Hagège. Halte à la mort des langues. Paris: Odile Jacob, 2000.

national library system, they could easily lead a consortium of libraries and negotiate for better conditions to access electronic publications on behalf of the other libraries of the country.

If these conditions are fulfilled, the nature of national libraries would be totally re-invented. First, they would be able to create vast repositories of national content in electronic form where copyright issues have been cleared with the right owners. The simultaneous creation and maintenance of content repositories both by the private and public sectors – the model we are now heading toward – is a luxury that can only result in overlapping work and waste of resources.

Second, they should be able to disseminate such content through a network of library consortia on a simplified fee-based tariff system. By complying with copyright regulations and paying producers, such consortia would reinforce authors' rights in the electronic environment. Third, when and where needed, they should establish contacts with a network of sale points where publications available online may be printed locally through print-on-demand techniques and at the payment of an additional fee for value-added services.

National libraries may therefore play a big role in striking a balance between information rich and poor. In contemporary societies, they no longer represent the symbol of a powerful nation-state and its alleged supremacy over the others. Today, they are called to be the champions and the unequivocal defenders of pluralistic expression and cultural diversity – a mission in which they have to re-invent their symbolic function and put it into practice.

Peter Hoare

The Operatives' Libraries of Nottingham: a 19th century radical initiative

In his introduction to Ulrich Hohoff's *Quellen zur Geschichte der Volksbibliotheken in Württemberg und Hohenzollern 1806 - 1918*, Peter Vodosek wrote of the unsatisfactory nature of the sources for the early history and pre-history of public libraries in Germany. This, he said, was partly due to the fact that the earlier 19th-century library movement had no single point of origin. Libraries were rarely civic enterprises but owed their existence to societies or clubs - of many different kinds - or to charitable foundations. He also mentioned the growing interest in adult education in the *Vormärz*, the period before the revolutions of 1848: this arose partly from genuinely philanthropic motives but also as a means of social control.[388] These traits can be seen in England too, though with variations because of the differing social structures.

In this tribute to Peter Vodosek, recognising many years of friendship and encouragement in the field of library history, I shall examine a particular manifestation of library activity in a radical English manufacturing town, which may offer parallels or contrasts to developments in Germany. There were at least 12 'Operatives' Libraries' in Nottingham in the nineteenth century, mostly based in public houses (inns or pubs) in working-class areas. They pre-dated the public library movement but survived for more than fifty years, even operating alongside the Free Public Library. Primary evidence for the operatives' libraries is poor or non-existent, except for a few catalogues and sporadic reports in the town's newspapers. However, something of their nature can be pieced together from different sources, and the libraries have not been entirely ignored by historians. The most valuable study is David Wardle's *Education and society in nineteenth-century Nottingham* (1971), but this does not relate them in any detail to the wider library scene in Nottingham through the 19th century.[389] The present paper is, then, an interim investigation of some of the evidence from a library history perspective, not a definitive history of the operatives' libraries.

Nottingham had a long tradition of dissent from the established church, going back before the Civil War and Commonwealth in the mid-17th century, and its civic society retained a strong non-conformist and Liberal flavour, with much evidence of philanthropy among the industrial magnates. By the early 19th century, its prosperity was based on the hosiery industry (machine-made lace followed later in the century), and like other textile towns further north, it became a focus for industrial unrest during the Luddite movement. This period was captured vividly by Ernst Toller in his powerful Expressionist drama *Die*

388 Quellen zur Geschichte der Volksbibliotheken in Württemberg und Hohenzollern 1806 - 1918. Bearbeitet von Ulrich Hohoff mit einem Beitrag von Peter Vodosek (Stuttgart, 1990).

389 David Wardle, Education and society in nineteenth-century Nottingham (Cambridge, 1971), especially pp. 182-6. For other insights on radical libraries I am indebted to Dr Chris Baggs.

Maschinenstürmer, set in Nottingham 'about 1815'.[390] By the 1830s, this form of unrest had abated but radicalism had not disappeared: Nottingham Castle was burnt in 1831 as a sign of popular opposition to the anti-Reform stance of its owner, the Duke of Newcastle. Notorious slums were developing in the wake of the uncontrolled expansion of industry, some of them close to the town centre. Nottingham was recognised as one of the centres of the Chartist movement, Britain's nearest approach to the 1848 revolutions of continental Europe; in 1847 Nottingham elected Feargus O'Connor as the only Chartist MP ever to sit in the House of Commons. It was the interaction of this widespread radical temperament and the philanthropic enterprises of the middle classes which seems to have given rise to the operatives' libraries.

The Nottingham operatives' libraries were not quite unique, even in being based in public houses. Similar reading rooms existed in Carlisle and were commented on in 1851 in Charles Dickens's magazine *Household Words*; they have also been fully studied in Brian Graham's *Nineteenth century self help in education* (1983). [391] However, the Nottingham situation seems to have been sufficiently unusual to attract comment at a national level. In 1841 the Chartist newspaper *The Northern Star* described Nottingham in the following words:

> *'This is the famous radical town. Reading rooms and libraries abound, though some of them are unfortunately held in public houses.'* [392]

By the 1830s Nottingham was home to several libraries of various kinds. There were commercial circulating libraries, as there had been for nearly a hundred years; these dealt not only in novels but in a range of popular literature. They were mostly located in bookshops in the Market Place or the adjacent streets, like Nottingham Subscription Library in the elegant 18th-century Bromley House on Angel Row.[393] Some professional groups such as lawyers and doctors had also set up specialised societies with libraries. Like the Subscription Library these obviously catered for a moneyed and educated section of society.

The lower classes were not entirely neglected, however. The Artizans' Library, founded in 1824 in Smithy Row, just off the Market Place, was a well-meaning middle-class initiative aimed at a lower stratum of society. It admitted apprentices as well as 'artizans' or skilled craftsmen, and charged a quarterly subscription of 1s. 6d.[394] Its original constitution was based in outline on that of the middle-class Subscription Library, which also supplied its classification scheme and one of its early librarians. It later spawned one or two similar enterprises such as the rather obscure Female Artizans' Library, and the Radford Artizans'

---

[390] Ernst Toller, Die Maschinenstürmer. Ein Drama aus der Zeit der Ludditenbewegung in England. (Leipzig, 1922). The play includes a dramatised version of Lord Byron's 1812 speech to the House of Lords against the death penalty imposed for frame-breaking. An English translation by Ashley Dukes, The machine-wreckers, was published in 1923.

[391] The labourer's reading-room', Household Words, vol. 3 (1851), 581-5. T.Brian Graham, Nineteenth century self help in education - mutual improvement societies. Case study: the Carlisle Working Men's Reading Rooms (Nottingham, 1983).

[392] Northern Star, 6 February 1841.

[393] Bromley House 1752-1991, edited by Rosalys T. Coope and Jane Y. Corbett (Nottingham, 1991). My chapter in this book includes a section on 'The Library's forerunners and competitors' (pp. 7-11) which summarises the Nottingham library scene in the earlier 19th century.

[394] The terms 'mechanic', 'artisan' (or 'artizan') and 'operative', while all implying manual trades, seem to have been applied somewhat differently. The three words are often used together, suggesting that there was a descending social scale with 'operatives' at the bottom.

Library in an inner suburb west of the town centre. By 1868 the Artizans' Library had run into financial difficulties, and its stock and premises (by then in Thurland Street not far from its original home) were taken over as the basis for the Free Public Library, which continues as the City Library today.

In its earlier days, however, the efficacy of the Artizans' Library was restricted by its founders' view of adult education and improved literacy as a means of social control, through the encouragement of 'good' reading and socially-acceptable views. Like many such small subscription libraries throughout the country it allowed nothing inflammatory into its stock, so politics and 'controversial theology' were banned. At the first annual meeting in May 1825 committee members were exhorted to

> *'sacrifice their individual predilections to the general task, and also from carefully avoiding proposing regulations, or ordering books which can in any way wound the feelings or excite the alarms of any Members constituting a body, which present such a variety of sentiments and opinions.'* [395]

Similar social controls seem to have been in force, at least initially, at the Mechanics' Institution, one of the main educational societies of the town throughout the century. The Mechanics' was conceived as a body with primarily educational aims, with lectures and classes as well as a library, but the same limiting principles applied. Its first constitution of November 1837 referred to the need to 'avoid every chance of dissension', hence the rigorous exclusion of 'all matters tending to political or religious controversy'. A provisional committee (wholly middle-class in composition) recommended that

> *'the elevation of the working classes in the scale of moral and intellectual excellence was not only desirable, but essential to the comfort and lasting existence of our social institutions.'* [396]

It is well known that such institutions tended increasingly to attract white-collar workers and craftsmen rather than the lower working classes, and to adopt middle-class attitudes in their ambitious educational and library programmes. This certainly happened with the Mechanics' Institution, and the Artizans' Library seems to have developed in the same way.

It was in fact the failure of the Artizans' Library to cater for the real wants of the 'true' working class (and the patronising tone so often adopted by its committee), that led to the establishment of the first Operatives' Library. George Dawson's evidence to the 1849 Select Committee on Public Libraries, the parliamentary inquiry which led to the Public Libraries Act of 1850, included a remarkable snapshot of what happened:

> *'Do they not admit works of party politics? - In Manchester they do; they admit everything to the mechanics' institutions, but in Nottingham the operatives library was founded because of the exclusion. I have a note of what a working man said about that; he said that he and nine other subscribers to the artisan's library seceded from it because they could not get such books on political and religious subjects as they wished to read. They „clubbed" together and bought Howitt's History of*

[395] Nottingham Artizans' Library, Annual reports and minutes of 1st-17th Annual Meetings, 1825-1841 (Nottinghamshire Archives, M415).

[396] Richard Iliffe and Wilfred Baguley, Victorian Nottingham: a story in pictures. Vol. 14: The Mechanics' Institute [etc.] (Nottingham, 1975), 9.

Priestcraft, and that was the beginning of operative libraries in Nottingham.' [397]

The choice of the first book is significant: William Howitt was a well-known Nottingham writer and publisher, and his *Popular history of priestcraft* (1833) attracted much attention, both positive and negative, at a national level. The break-away had occurred in 1835, two years after its publication: this was eleven years after the foundation of the Artizans' and two years before the establishment of the Mechanics' Institution in 1837 (the Mechanics' however would clearly not have been more liberal in this respect).

George Dawson's account of the secession is enlarged on in a report of the Library's first anniversary dinner in December 1836, published in the *Nottingham Review,* a radical local newspaper:

> *'An outline of its history was given: - the commencement of which was, that a few working men joined for the purchase of Howitt's History of Priestcraft; after which, nine individuals agreed to purchase by small weekly payments, some other approved work; and in a few weeks others expressed a desire to join the infant society. The increase being great, towards the close of last year [1835], the members assembled, and the following resolutions were adopted: - „That being deeply impressed with the importance of knowledge, we resolve to establish a book society, because we believe that as we progress in knowledge, we must advance in freedom, knowledge being the only lever that can raise the working class into a fit condition to possess electoral privileges; and because we believe, that if ever the working classes are admitted into the privileges of the constitution, that knowledge is the safest avenue by which they can enter". Other resolutions were passed for the government of the society; and the members agreed to assist regularly in the business of the library, so that no one either receives or expects any salary.'* [398]

The founders are named in Wylie's *Old and new Nottingham* as 'Mr. W. Brooksbank and five other working men'[399] and indeed Mr Brooksbank and Mr Elsom were elected as president and vice-president at the anniversary dinner. The radical basis for their action was confirmed by the rules of the 'Nottingham Operatives' Library No. 1', as presented in the earliest surviving catalogue of 1843, which gives the foundation date as August 1835. The first rule states:

> *'The objects of this Society are the dissemination of useful and entertaining knowledge; and as politics concern our welfare here, and religion affects our happiness hereafter, and as we believe, no political institution ought to stand that cannot bear examination, and no creed ought to be believed that cannot bear discussion, we, therefore, resolve to purchase works of every description, political and theological, as well as those embracing history, science, and literature.'* [400]

There is more than a hint of Chartist thinking in the original references to electoral privileges and in those of eight years later to political institutions that 'cannot bear examination', but the operatives' library movement outlasted Chartism and was still in existence sixty

397 Minutes of evidence taken before the Select Committee on Public Libraries (London, 1849), 81 (minute 1229).

398 Nottingham Review, 30 December 1836. The stipulation about 'no salary' was not universally applied; some other libraries paid their officials or gave them free membership.

399 W.H. Wylie, Old and new Nottingham (London, 1853), 350.

400 Catalogue of books belonging to the Nottingham Operatives' Library, No. 1 (Nottingham, 1843).

years after it began.

Before long, several other operatives' libraries had followed the example of this first one, which was based in the *Rancliffe Arms,* a public house with a radical (and later explicitly Chartist) reputation, just south of the town centre and on the edge of what became one of the worst slums in Europe; it remained there until nearly the end of the century. [401] The exact sequence of the later foundations is confused, not least because some libraries moved from one public house to another, perhaps reflecting financial or political pressures from the landlords. The numbers which were attached to many of them do not seem to relate exactly to the date of foundation, and different dates are given in some sources. The closure of the libraries is not documented at all, except in a negative way by their disappearance from directories. The following list, derived from a variety of sources which often do not agree, is as full as possible but obviously needs further refinement. [402]

1. *Rancliffe Arms*, Sussex Street, Middle Marsh or Leenside. Founded August 1835 by W. Brooksbank and five (or eight) others, the original seceders from the Artizans' Library, and survived until at least the 1890s.
2. *Seven Stars,* Barker Gate. Founded 27 August 1837 but had moved by 1844 to the *King George on Horseback,* Woolpack Lane (a centre of Chartism, like the *Seven Stars* and the *Rancliffe Arms*). Moved again to the *Golden Ball,* Coalpit Lane (near Beck Street), probably in 1852*;* but also referred to later as being at the *Seven Stars.* (All these pubs were in the old town, near what had become the textile manufacturing area, now known as the Lace Market.) The founders were Messrs. Hart, Mellors, Fox and others; they probably included William Fox, stated to be 'a very poor artisan of Nottingham', whose 'indefatigable but unpaid exertions' also led to the founding of several other operatives' libraries.[403]
3. *Queen Caroline*; later at the *Pheasant* (by 1842)*,* then at the *Alderman Wood* (c. 1848-1879), and again at the *Pheasant* by 1887. (These three pubs, all in Charlotte Street just north of the town centre, were demolished in 1900 to build the Victoria railway station.) Founded 10 March 1836 by Messrs Morgan, Farrow, Palmer and others.
4. Sneinton Operatives' Library, *Queen Adelaide,* North Street, New Sneinton (a new extension of an old village east of the town centre). Founded October 1840 by Henry Norris and five others.
5. Radford Operatives' Library, *White Swan,* Alfreton Road; later moved to the *Pelican Inn,* in Pelican Street, New Radford (both locations are west of the town centre, in a manufacturing suburb). Founded 1844 by Samuel Chettle senior and five others.
6. *Cricket Players,* Hyson Green (a working-class suburb north-west of the town centre). Founded 1840.
7. *White Swan,* Alfreton Road, New Radford (the original home of no. 5, also founded in 1844 - there may be some confusion between the two). Founded March 1844. A stock of 'upwards of 100 volumes' was reported in 1844.

---

[401] E. Peter Bailey, 'Leenside: the churches and a nineteenth-century Nottingham slum', Transactions of the Thoroton Society of Nottinghamshire, vol. 100 (1996), 137-156.

[402] The 'numbered' libraries are helpfully listed, with the names of their librarians, in Francis & John White, Nottinghamshire: history, directory and gazetteer (Sheffield, 1844), 169-170; and in Wylie's Old and new Nottingham, 350-351.

[403] James Orange, History and antiquities of Nottingham (1840), vol. 2, p. 927.

These numbered libraries seem to have formed a conscious union (during the 1840s at least annual gatherings of members and friends of all these libraries were held at No. 1, as the centre of the operatives' library movement). Other operatives' libraries, apparently without numbers, were also listed as early as 1840 in the following pubs, but with no details of their foundation or size.[404]

- *Castle Inn* (Cross Street, near No. 2 at the *Golden Ball*)
- *The Loggerheads* (Narrow Marsh, near No. 1 at the *Rancliffe Arms*)
- Sir John Borlace Warren (Alfreton Road)
- *Lord Rancliffe* (Gedling Street, not far from No. 2 in the *Seven Stars* and *King* George on Horseback)

There was also the *Nottingham Temperance Operatives' Library*, at Smith's commercial coffee house in Houndsgate, in the town centre. This was founded in January 1841 by Mr William Smith and others.

The operatives' libraries were located in public houses close to the main concentrations of factories or workers' housing (some of the pubs are still in existence but most were destroyed in slum clearance or other development schemes). This is further evidence of their being rooted in the working community rather than imposed from outside. The use of public houses is, perhaps, more contentious, but these were the normal places for relaxation and social engagement for most working men, and they were conveniently situated.[405] Some of them, like the *Rancliffe Arms,* were already centres of Chartist or other radical activity, and would have been familiar to the independently-minded operatives who set up the libraries. The existence of a Temperance Operatives' Library, however, shows that not all radicals were comfortable in licensed premises; the Chartist William Lovett argued in 1841 against the use of public houses for the circulating libraries he proposed, which bore many similarities to the operatives' libraries.[406]

The way the libraries operated is, inevitably, rather unclear. Members paid an entrance fee (normally sixpence or a shilling, but occasionally higher), and a weekly subscription of a penny (the Temperance Library only charged a halfpenny) - more manageable than the quarterly subscription of 1s. 6d., payable in advance, which the Artizans' Library charged. The librarian was usually in attendance for an hour on one, two or three evenings a week, and often for two or three hours on Sunday morning. As well as the librarian an 'examiner' was often present to check that books were not damaged (some libraries had real problems with careless handling and had to threaten offenders with heavy penalties). Books had to be returned for a week before Christmas, to allow stocktaking and any necessary repair. A 2d. fine was charged for non-compliance, four times the usual fine for an overdue book.

And what were these books? What was read by these radically-minded operatives? Once again, the evidence is very incomplete. Only four catalogues survive, three from Library No. 1 and one from No. 2, but they show clearly that the libraries were not solely concerned with politics and theology. The loss of all other catalogues is unfortunate, but

404 Orange, History and antiquities of Nottingham, vol. 2, p. 927.

405 J.J. Rowley, 'Drink and the public house in Nottingham, 1830-1860', Transactions of the Thoroton Society of Nottinghamshire, vol. 79 (1975), 72-83; this article also refers to the operatives' libraries.

406 William Lovett and John Collins, Chartism: a new organization for the people (London, 1841), 34-35 and 47-50. See also Lovett's account of coffee-houses in Minutes of evidence taken before the Select Committee on Public Libraries (London, 1849), 176-77 (minutes 2759 ff.).

perhaps not surprising since members of No. 2 were exhorted to bring their copy of the catalogue every time they exchanged books to have them marked off. The committee of Library No. 1 congratulated themselves in 1846, ten years after its foundation, on the achievement of the operatives' library movement, in words which though exaggerated suggest that the benefits were genuine:

> *'Then, the works of our greatest writers were, by their price, sealed books to those who most stood in need of their ennobling influence. Then, the majority of operatives desirous of spending their leisure in reading, could only have that wish gratified, by obtaining at a high charge the loan from some circulating libraries or other, tales, whose mawkish sentimentality or gloomy horror can only result in a morbid state of feeling, and tend to close the avenues of the mind to that knowledge which can have a refining and beneficial influence upon society. Now, we have thousands of volumes of the choicest works in the language placed at the disposal of the sons of toil, and the town swarming as it were with institutions claiming support from the working man, and resting those claims on the liberality of their laws, and the valuable nature of their ultimate objects in a moral and social point of view.'* [407]

A few years before this enthusiastic outburst, the 1843 catalogue of Library No. 1 had listed 169 volumes of history, including two copies of Howitt's *History of Priestcraft,* the original *casus belli* for the secession from the Artizans'. The 150 volumes of biography ranged from Tom Paine, Benjamin Franklin and Robert Emmet to the Duke of Wellington and William IV, but also included Kotzebue's *Memoirs* and lives of the actress Mrs Siddons and the clown Joseph Grimaldi. Over 200 volumes were listed under 'Natural Philosophy, Manufactures, Politics, Theology, &c.' - a broad class of subjects which included Tom Paine's *Age of Reason* and *Political Works* but also Adam Smith's *Wealth of Nations* and a number of practical scientific and technical works. But there were also over 300 volumes of novels, and 250 of poetry and 'Miscellaneous' (essays and other lighter reading); and it was fiction that showed the most rapid growth, doubling in size within ten years and coming to dominate the library by the end of its life. The same picture is seen in the 1857 catalogue, with 943 novels out of 2000 monograph titles, and even more in the 1866 catalogue, with 1516 novels out of fewer than 2500 titles. More striking still is the 1858 catalogue of Library No. 2, with fiction forming 80 per cent of the titles listed (640 works out of 794).

It is clear that leisure reading was in demand and was being catered for - a situation mirrored in many libraries of this kind, and foreshadowing the 'fiction debate' which concerned public libraries for many years in the 19th and 20th centuries. Wylie's list of the operatives' libraries helpfully gives a breakdown of the stock of some of them in 1853: in the three largest libraries fiction formed 31 %, 58 % and 51 % of the total, and in another the 53 % of 'Miscellaneous' probably included much fiction (but the smaller libraries seem to have had quite small collections, numbered in hundreds of volumes).

The heavy use of fiction caused problems, as Library No. 1's annual report for 1849 makes clear:

> *'Wanton mischief has been perpetrated, many of the newest books have lost pages, and most of them in Class C (novels). It is lamentable that working men should thus destroy or injure the property of an institution intended for their sole benefit. [...] If all the members who read the above class, would be as careful of the books as those*

---

407 Nottingham Review, 16 January 1846.

> *who read some of the other classes, the subscriptions would find double the amount they now do, and thus augment considerably the amount of amusement and instruction now obtained; and as this class of readers clamour the loudest for new works, it seems surprising they should not not take better care of the old ones.'* [408]

This sheds new light on the tension between fiction and non-fiction, and also illustrates the way the library tried to respond to the wishes of all its members. It is not clear how the 'clamour' for new fiction relates to the procedure laid down in the Library's rules, which required every suggestion to be voted on at one of the weekly or monthly meetings before it could be purchased - a more democratic method than at the Artizans', where many books were bought by the committee without wide consultation.

At mid-century, however, there was still a good proportion of serious reading as well as novels in most of the operatives' libraries. In addition, the many periodicals subscribed to (and kept in stock) were by no means all 'light reading'. Titles included the information-rich *Penny Magazine* and the *British and Foreign Review,* as well as *Ainsworth's Magazine* and the *Lady's Repository.*

That last title raises the question of how far the operatives' libraries were a male preserve. The great majority of members must have been working men - the extant literature about the libraries is written almost entirely in terms of 'men' and all the officials named were men - but some of the novels and other material, at least, would have attracted female readers too, and it is quite possible that members borrowed books for their wives or daughters to read. What is more remarkable is that Library No. 3, at least, made explicit reference to women and children; at its 1850 annual meeting, the committee reported:

> *'We should open the doors of our institution as wide as possible. The female and juvenile classes claim our special care; the latter will be the people of the future. We have observed them well during the past year, and the books they have read, whilst they have been amusing have been instructive. Many of the wise have said that the forming of the youthful mind depends on the female; if she be well informed, her children will be wise and virtuous. It is our duty to facilitate their desire to obtain information, and guide them in their choice of books; by these exertions we shall make the library useful and truly beneficial.'* [409]

According to another source No. 3 actually had a separate juvenile section in 1855, with books such as *Æsop's Fables, Robinson Crusoe,* and the adventure novels of Mayne Reid (by 1858 these popular works also appear in the catalogue of No. 2, but under 'Novels' rather than in a separate section). This early awareness of children's needs foreshadows the opening in 1882 of the 'Library for Boys and Girls' as part of Nottingham's Free Public Library (the first public lending library for children in Britain); this had its origins in a gift of £500 from Samuel Morley, a local textile magnate, who had noted that 'the working classes are deluged and poisoned with cheap, noxious fiction of the most objectionable kind'. It is not clear, however, that J. Potter Briscoe, the borough librarian, was directly influenced by the work of the operatives' libraries in his innovative thinking. [410]

The regular opening hours also incorporated provision for weekly, monthly and quarterly meetings. At these, books were approved, disciplinary action taken against defaulting

---

408 Nottingham Review, 1 February 1850.

409 Nottingham Review, 1 February 1850.

410 Thomas Kelly, Books for the people: an illustrated history of the British public library (London, 1977), 130-131.

members, and - at least at No. 1 - the officers were to be re-elected quarterly. Other activities also went on: there was often an anniversary dinner and certainly an annual general meeting. In 1842 the members of No. 3 presented a silver snuff-box to their Secretary 'for his very active services', at an annual meeting at which the committee addressed the members in the following inspirational words:

> *'They rejoice that the rising generation are daily becoming more desirous of information, and they hope that your exertions will not be relaxed; that those whose daily bread is earned by labour may find, in becoming members of societies like this, that their cabinets are stored with instruction and delight. They trust, that in gathering the flowers of intellectual knowledge, you will not let them perish in your hands; but that you will distribute them so, so their fragrance may extend to all around; and that you will bear in mind, that in aftertimes, they who still drink of these fountains of knowledge will not be unmindful of those who erected them, but will gratefully pronounce a blessing on your names.'*[411]

Lectures and classes were a feature of the Mechanics' Institution, and there is a suggestion that some of the operatives' libraries also offered educational opportunities of this sort. In 1845 the committee of Library No. 1 had proposed holding lectures jointly with the other operatives' libraries in the neighbourhood. On this occasion, at least, the initiative was unsuccessful:

> *'That project was carried out - five lectures being delivered by the Rev. W. Linwood at the Theatre, and three by Mr Thomas Beggs, at No. 30, Exchange-rooms - and although the subjects were of a popular nature, and treated in every case in a masterly manner, the attendance of members was not such as to warrant us in continuing the responsibility attendant upon so unproductive a matter. The chief cause of failure is, in our opinion, attributable to the high rent we were obliged to pay for the rooms we required.'*[412]

The Artizans' and the Mechanics', of course, had their own property, large enough to accommodate lectures and other functions. The operatives' libraries, on the other hand, relied on using a room in a public house at a low weekly rent to house their books and needed to go elsewhere for larger occasions, presumably having to charge a significant entrance fee which discouraged attendance.

Relationships with these two larger (and less worker-dominated) bodies continued to be uncertain. At its 1848 annual meeting, Library No. 1 reiterated its support for the education of the working classes (several libraries seem to have supported the People's College, founded explicitly to offer schooling to anyone - and still in active existence today as a college of further education), and issued a ringing challenge to their masters:

> *'To the higher and middle classes we would say, - Gentlemen, remember we are the root of the social tree, and if that root is impregnated with poison and death, what is to become of the branches, the leaves, the flowers, and the fruit? In conclusion, when the condition of the labourer is depressed, neglected, and demoralized, the other*

[411] Nottingham Review, 14 January 1842. The use of the word 'information' in a library context is remarkable at this early date.

[412] Nottingham Review, 16 January 1846.

classes of society can rest upon no solid foundation.'[413]

.From their higher social position, both the Artizans' and the Mechanics' regularly lamented their inability to draw in operatives and sought ways of doing this. However, the gap in understanding seems to have been too wide to be easily bridged, as can be seen from the discussion at the Mechanics' annual meeting in 1850, reported at length in the local press. The committee expressed the hope that:

> *'it will be possible to meet the wishes of the operative class on some important particulars,* without any detriment to the substantial interest of the Institution. *Your committee have the satisfaction to express a belief that the operative classes regard the Institution with favour, and that they would cheerfully avail themselves of any increased facilities.'*[414]

The meeting went on to be told about the views of John Evelyn Denison, a local MP and later Speaker of the House of Commons, who was President of the Mechanics' Institution but also a benefactor to some of the operatives' libraries (significantly the speaker was the Town Clerk, William Enfield, hardly a representative of the lower classes). Denison, he said, had called for an expansion of the range of members, for the benefit of the Mechanics' as much as to improve the lot of the operatives. He continued:

> *'Mr Denison had taken another opportunity of sharing the interest he had in promoting this object, by recently inviting a number of the persons connected with the Operative Libraries in the town and neighbourhood, as well as a deputation of the Committee of that institution [the Mechanics'], to meet him for the purpose of discussing and considering in what way that object might best be carried out. Those who were present at that meeting would, he was sure, agree that it was one attended with great interest, and that the addresses delivered by the working men who were present, and the intellect shown by them, fully justified the desire to have them more closely connected with the Mechanics' Institution. These operative libraries had done great good in the town, for although they comprised a great number of works of a light character, as their own library did, still those who had begun by reading works of a light description have been led on to study books of a higher character. These libraries had also a beneficial effect, for he believed they had very much checked, if not in many instances entirely prevented, the reading of books of the lowest, and to young people especially of the most demoralising description. The inhabitants of the town were, he considered, greatly indebted to the libraries for the benefits they had already conferred on the community with which they had been mixed.'*[415]

This meeting between the two sides was not the first: J.E. Denison and Charles Paget, 'two of the more adventurous middle-class leaders', had held a conference in 1846 with representatives of the operatives' libraries, with a view to some kind of co-operation. 'The scheme fell through due to the peculiar bitterness of relations between the classes at that time, but the evidence suggests that the libraries lost some of their political fervour, especially in the 1850s when relations between employer and employed became less hostile.'

---

413 Nottingham Review, 14 January 1848.
414 Nottingham Journal, 1 February 1850. (My italics.)
415 Nottingham Journal, 1 February 1850.

[416] A foretaste of this better understanding - on one side at least - can perhaps be seen in the words of another speaker at the Mechanics' 1850 annual meeting, Mr Richard Enfield, who perceptively made the point that

> *'the Operatives' Libraries established in the town were the more interesting, because they had been established by the working classes themselves. From the classification of the members of the [Mechanics'] Institution they had heard read, it appeared that but few operatives availed themselves of the opportunities the lectures and the library afforded them, and some persons might imagine that the working men of the town of Nottingham were not desirous of acquiring the instruction their Institution offered them. [...] There were, he believed, five Operatives' Libraries, which had been founded by working men themselves, at present in the town. In these, there were about five thousand volumes, while the persons who reaped the benefit from them were about 700. It could not then be stated that there was no wish for reading - no wish for mental improvement. It had been said that „one man could bring a horse to water while five could not make him drink". In their own instance they had found the water, but for some reason or other the operatives would not drink the water they had found them; while, on the other hand, they had found 700 of them drinking other water, their own way. He only wished some arrangements could be made which would induce the mechanics of the town to join the Institution.'*[417]

The longer-term outcome of these hopes and fears is not clear. Later in the century several of the operatives' libraries had apparently closed (at least they were no longer listed in directories), and the Artizans' Library, as has already been noted, sold out to the Borough Council when the Free Public Library was established in 1868. Other operatives' libraries continued to be listed, with the *Alderman Wood* (which had latterly moved to the *Pheasant*) disappearing from directories after 1887; the original Library No. 1, at the *Rancliffe Arms,* continued into the 1890s or conceivably even longer: it is said to have owned 8,000 volumes at this time. The Mechanics' Institution continued to flourish well into the twentieth century, but there is no indication of its relationship with the operatives' libraries. The only survivor from the early nineteenth century is the Subscription Library (now called Bromley House Library), which had always served a different class of society. The days of specifically working-class provision were over.

---

[416] Wardle, Education and society in nineteenth-century Nottingham, 185.
[417] Nottingham Journal, 1 February 1850.

Klaus G. Saur

Das Gesamtverzeichnis des deutschsprachigen Schrifttums 1700 bis 1965

Vorgeschichte

Im Jahr 1974 wurde der Oberbibliotheksrat Dr. Reinhard Oberschelp von der Niedersächsischen Landesbibliothek, der bereits die Niedersächsische Landesbibliographie bearbeitet hatte, in die Bibliographie-Kommission des Vereins Deutscher Bibliothekare berufen. Er überlegte sich, welche Aufgabe eine derartige Kommission haben könnte. Aus den Protokollen der Sitzungen der vergangenen Jahre war immer nur hervorgegangen, dass es sog. Fortschrittsberichte über die Entwicklung der „Deutschen Bibliographie", herausgegeben von der Deutschen Bibliothek in Frankfurt, gab. Irgendwelche weiteren Themen schienen nicht angesprochen worden zu sein. Reinhard Oberschelp war bewusst, dass eine – wenn nicht sogar die – große Aufgabe für eine Bibliographie-Kommission wäre, einen Deutschen Gesamtkatalog aller Bibliotheksbestände zu realisieren. Der erste Start – zu Beginn des Jahrhunderts unternommen – endete bei dem Wort „Beetordnung" und wurde bekanntlich nicht fortgesetzt. Wäre das seinerzeitige Unternehmen fortgesetzt worden, wäre es bei gleichem Arbeitstempo auch heute noch nicht am Ende angelangt. Reinhard Oberschelp stellte bei seinen Untersuchungen außerdem fest, dass es nicht einmal eine Zusammenfassung der Angaben des deutschsprachigen Schrifttums gab. Eine Deutsche Nationalbibliothek existierte erst seit 1912 mit der Deutschen Bücherei in Leipzig, die vom Börsenverein der Deutschen Buchhändler zu Leipzig gegründet worden war und welche die nationalbibliographische Berichterstattung ab 1912 durchführte. Auch diese Bibliographien enthielten nur Nachweise zu Publikationen, die der Deutschen Bücherei vorlagen, und erschienen getrennt nach Buchverzeichnissen, nach Hochschulschriftenverzeichnissen, Schriften außerhalb des Buchhandels und so weiter. Daraufhin entwickelte er einen Plan unter der Überschrift „Gesamtverzeichnis des deutschsprachigen bibliographisch erfassten Schrifttums 1700 bis 1965". Um einen einigermaßen vollständigen Schrifttumsnachweis alleine für die Zeit von 1911 bis 1965 zusammenzuführen, mussten mehr als 100 Bibliographien mit rund 2.000 verschiedenen Alphabeten zusammengebracht werden. Der Zeitraum 1911 bis 1965 war natürlich nicht zufällig gewählt. Das Jahr 1911 markiert den Beginn des Berichtszeitraums der Deutschen Nationalbibliographie, 1966 wurde mit der elektronischen Erfassung begonnen mit der Aussicht, dass dann irgendwann einmal alle neuen elektronisch erfassten Titel in sich kumuliert werden können.

Reinhard Oberschelp arbeitete ein Exposé aus mit der Beschreibung des Materials und mit dem Ziel, ein umfassendes Gesamtverzeichnis in zwei Abschnitten, einmal für 1700 bis 1910, einmal 1911 bis 1965 zu erstellen. Seine Grundidee war, alle Materialien im Rahmen einer Reprokumulation zusammenzuführen. Das heißt, alle vorhandenen Quellen sollten zunächst fotografiert, ausgeschnitten, neu sortiert, dann in eine alphabetische Folge gebracht und veröffentlicht werden. Es war uns durchaus bewusst, dass bei diesem Verfahren, welches die Einträge ohne Neusatz reprographisch wiedergibt, vorhandene Druckfehler beibehalten werden. Anhand diverser Materialien der Niedersächsischen Landesbibliothek in Hannover erstellte Reinhard Oberschelp Mustereinträge und berechnete, dass für die beiden angegebenen Zeiträume jeweils etwa 2,5 Million Titel anfallen würden und dass eine Reprokumulation rund 150.000 Seiten füllen würde. Die Idee war ebenso einfach wie genial. Keine Bibliothek verfügte lückenlos über alle von Reinhard Oberschelp nachgewiesenen Quellen und vor allem hatte keine Bibliothek das Material in einem System oder in einem Alphabet zugänglich. Von der Idee ungemein fasziniert, ermittelte ich anhand der Angaben einen ungefähren Kostenrahmen und einen voraussichtlichen Umfang von etwa 300 Bänden. Meine anfängliche Euphorie wich allerdings völliger Ernüchterung, als ich fünf der bedeutendsten deutschen Bibliotheksdirektoren anrief und ihnen begeistert von diesem Plan erzählte. Die Reaktion war mehr als entmutigend. Alle fünf angesprochenen Koryphäen der Bibliothekswelt rieten dringend ab, hielten das Projekt für unrealisierbar, wiesen darauf hin, dass die jungen Leute dann nicht mehr lernen würden zu bibliographieren, und betonten, dass die Bibliotheken bisher auch ohne ein solches Verzeichnis außerordentlich glücklich gewesen seien. Ihre jeweilige Bibliothek würde ein solches Produkt nicht kaufen.

Mir war deutlich geworden, dass die Mindestinvestition für den ersten Teil etwa 5 Mill. DM betragen würde. Wie konnte ich 5 Mill. DM – die ich nicht hatte – riskieren, wenn die größten Experten so deutlich von einer solchen Publikation abrieten? Aber ich ließ mich immer noch nicht entmutigen und rief Richard W. Dorn, den Seniorchef des Hauses Otto Harrassowitz, an. Ich erklärte ihm in einem knapp 20-minütigen Telefongespräch dieses Projekt und bat ihn um seine Meinung. Die Antwort war eindeutig. Er garantierte mir, 100 Exemplare zu verkaufen. Mit dieser Zusage, die natürlich rechtlich überhaupt keine Verbindlichkeit hatte, war ich bereit, zu starten. Allerdings waren zunächst einmal fünf ganz wesentliche Problemkreise zu klären, bevor der Start wirklich erfolgen konnte, und hätte auch nur eines dieser Probleme sich als unlösbar erwiesen, wäre das Projekt nicht realisierbar gewesen.

1. Die urheberrechtliche Problematik

Da das Konzept auf der reprografischen Übernahme der Vorlagen basierte, bedurfte es der Zustimmung der jeweiligen Rechteinhaber. Für den Zeitraum 1911 bis 1965 waren dies zu mehr als 90 % die Deutsche Bibliothek in Frankfurt, die Deutsche Bücherei in Leipzig, die Österreichische Nationalbibliothek in Wien und die Schweizerische Landesbibliothek in Bern. Mit den Bibliotheken in Wien und Bern konnte sehr schnell eine Übereinkunft getroffen werden, die uns lediglich dazu verpflichtete, ein Freiexemplar zu liefern. Frankfurt war schon erheblich schwieriger. Die Bibliographie wurde herausgegeben von der Deutschen Bibliothek, der Verleger war aber die Buchhändler-Vereinigung GmbH, ein Wirtschaftsunternehmen, das den buchhändlerischen Landesverbänden gehört. Die Buchhändler-Vereinigung neigte zu einer Absage, die Deutsche Bibliothek aber, vertreten durch ihren Generaldirektor Professor Dr. Günther Pflug und ihren Stellvertretenden Generaldirektor Kurt Nowak sahen das Projekt äußerst positiv und stimmten zu. Von Seiten der Deutschen Bücherei war zu Zeiten des Kalten Krieges im Jahre 1975 eine offizielle Genehmigung nicht zu erwarten. Daraufhin informierte ich mündlich den Generaldirektor der Deutschen Bücherei, Professor Dr. Rötzsch, und er bestätigte mir, dass er dies für ein ganz hervorragendes Projekt hielt. Daraufhin dankte ich ihm für die Bestätigung und bestätigte ihm wiederum, dass ich der Deutschen Bücherei zwei kostenlose Belegexemplare nach Fertigstellung übergeben würde. Ob dies bei einer juristischen Auseinandersetzung als Vertragsgrundlage ausgereicht hätte, wage ich auch heute noch zu bezweifeln. Wichtig war: wir hatten uns gegenseitig alles bestätigt und wir konnten arbeiten.

Größere Probleme gab es dann auch noch bei der Realisierung des „Gesamtverzeichnisses 1700 bis 1910", das auf 200 oft vielbändigen Quellen mit Tausenden von Alphabeten basierte, von denen eine Reihe erst im 20. Jahrhundert erschienen war. In einem Fall kam es sogar zu einer Klage gegen uns, die erst in einem mühsam herbeigeführten und kostenintensiven Vergleich beigelegt werden konnte.

2. Die technische Durchführung

Das grundlegende Prinzip basierte darauf, dass alle Titel reprografisch übernommen werden mussten. Wir machten Versuche mit verschiedensten Firmen, die alle ergebnislos blieben. Das Problem lag vor allem in den unterschiedlichen und zum Teil sehr kleinen Formaten der bibliographischen Angaben in den Vorlagen, die das Herauskopieren zunächst unmöglich erscheinen ließen. Ich erinnerte mich dann daran, im „Jahrbuch der deutschen Bibliotheken" die Anzeige einer Firma Norbert Gärtner in Mainz gesehen zu haben, die sogenannte Copyflow-Karten angeboten hatte. Ich suchte die Anzeige heraus, setzte mich mit der Firma in Verbindung und fand die Ideallösung. Diese Firma war in der Lage, sämtliche Vorlagen so zu fotografieren, dass sich anschließend von jedem einzelnen Titel eine Karte im A-6-Format erstellen ließ. Dabei wurden Übergrößen entsprechend verkleinert und zu kleine Texte entsprechend vergrößert. Somit hatte die Redaktion nun für das GV neu rund 3,5 Mio. Titel, für das GV alt rund 5,6 Mio. Titelkarten zur Verfügung. Die Zettel wurden vollständig in einem Alphabet sortiert, die entsprechend zahlreichen Duplikate wurden ausgeschieden, unterschiedliche Angaben wurden überprüft und nach endgültiger Feinsortierung aufgeklebt, um schließlich reproduziert und gedruckt zu werden.

Das Konzept von Reinhard Oberschelp sah vor, sämtliche Angaben unverändert aus den vorliegenden Bibliographien zu übernehmen. Die Redaktion hat sich dann aber der wesentlich größeren Aufgabe gestellt, Sortierfehler zu überprüfen und in den allermeisten Fällen zu bereinigen. So wurde beispielsweise die Serie „Reclams Universalbibliothek" in der Deutschen Nationalbibliographie in Leipzig 50 Jahre lang korrekt unter „Universalbibliothek, Reclam" geführt, während fünf Jahre lang ein Bibliograph auf den originellen aber trotzdem falschen Gedanken kam, sie unter „Reclam" zu führen. Hätten wir nun die Vorlagen vollautomatisch übernommen, wäre in unserem Verzeichnis „Reclams Universalbibliothek" für 50 Jahre unter „U" gestanden, für fünf Jahre unter „R". Bei der Benutzung kann man das heute sehr leicht feststellen: auf jeder zweiten Seite findet sich im Schnitt mindestens ein Eintrag, in dem ein Ordnungswort unterstrichen ist. Dies signalisiert, dass der Titel zuvor nicht korrekt nach Preußischen Instruktionen sortiert war und eine Korrektur vorgenommen wurde. Es musste also erst ein bayerischer Verlag kommen, damit zum ersten Mal für den Zeitraum von 1911 bis 1965 die Preußischen Instruktionen konsequent und durchgehend angewandt wurden.

3. Die Bearbeitung

Wir standen vor der großen Frage, wo das Ganze bearbeitet werden könnte. Die Idee selbst war in der Niedersächsischen Landesbibliothek entstanden. Diese Bibliothek stand kurz vor einem Umzug in neue Räume, so dass auch überlegt wurde, ob man die Redaktion nicht in den alten Räumen der Bibliothek unterbringen könnte. Diskutiert wurde auch, das Werk in Verbindung mit der Bayerischen Staatsbibliothek herauszugeben. Nach gründlichen Überlegungen entschlossen wir uns, innerhalb des Verlages eine Redaktionsmannschaft mit etwa 15 Bibliographen aufzubauen. Die Leitung des Projektes übernahm Willi Gorzny, der sich als Herausgeber des Zeitungsindexes und der Deutschen UNESCO-Bibliographie bereits einen Namen in der Bibliothekswelt gemacht hatte. Die Bearbeitung war ungewöhnlich schwierig, da wir auch die entlegensten Quellen auffinden mussten, da die Titelangaben immer wieder unterschiedlich waren. So wurde häufig festgestellt, dass ein „Handbuch der..." in Leipzig unter dem Titel, in Frankfurt unter dem Herausgeber oder umgekehrt aufgeführt war usw. Auch heute noch ist es absolut unbegreiflich, dass – obwohl das Konzept erst im Januar des Jahres 1975 im Verlag vorlag – im Frühjahr mit den Arbeiten begonnen wurde und bereits am 24. Dezember des gleichen Jahres die beiden ersten Bände im Umfang von über 1.000 Seiten erschienen.

4. Finanzielle Problematik

Das Wort „Verlag" kommt sprachgeschichtlich vom Wort „vorlegen". Das heißt, der Verleger hat die Aufgabe, Geld vorzulegen für Autoren, Bearbeiter und auch häufig für den Buchhandel oder die Kunden. Es wurde bald mehr als deutlich, dass dieses Prinzip hier stark zur Anwendung kommen musste. Die Vorarbeiten waren erheblich und kosteten viel Geld und der Verlag Dokumentation, wie er damals noch hieß, war wirtschaftlich nicht in der Lage, dies alleine zu leisten. Mein damaliger Gesellschafter Dr. Thomas Karger, Inhaber des Karger-Verlages in Basel, sagte mir einen zusätzlichen Kredit über DM 240.000.- zu. Dieser Kredit musste nur zu DM 180.000.- in Anspruch genommen werden, denn schon vor Erscheinen des ersten Bandes kamen zunächst nicht erwartete Vorauszahlungen. Als ein ganz wesentliches Finanzierungsinstrument hatte ich mir ein neues Konzept überlegt. Das GV 1911 bis 1965 in 150 Bänden sollte für DM 108.- pro Band = DM 16.200.- Gesamtpreis angeboten werden. Ich bot zusätzlich einen Vorauszahlungspreis von DM 92.- pro Band an, unter der Bedingung, dass dann die DM 13.800.- in einer Summe bei Erscheinen des ersten Bandes bezahlt werden. Dies war nur ein Rabatt von lediglich 15 % für ein Projekt, das auf fünf Jahre angelegt war, und demnach keineswegs eine sehr attraktive Finanzierung. Da aber für Bibliotheken weniger die Finanzierung und mehr der Etat im Vordergrund steht, gab die vergleichsweise hohe Differenz von DM 2.400.- den Ausschlag und 65 % aller Bestellungen kamen zum Vorauszahlungspreis. Damit war die finanzielle Problematik für dieses Projekt restlos gelöst.

5. Absatzrealisierung

Potenzielle Kunden waren natürlich die Universitäts- und Wissenschaftsbibliotheken insbesondere im deutschsprachigen Raum, aber auch weltweit, weiterhin auch stark die Stadtbibliotheken im deutschsprachigen Raum, Spezialbibliotheken und Antiquariate. Die erste Anzeige mit der Subskriptionseinladung erschien am 30. April 1975 im Börsenblatt für den deutschen Buchhandel. Am gleichen Tag bestellte die Stadtbücherei Mülheim an der Ruhr und die Bibliothek des Instituts für Weltwirtschaft in Kiel. Harrassowitz gab eine erste Bestellung für 50 Exemplare auf und bestellte genau 10 Jahre nach dem vorstehend erwähnten Telefongespräch das 100. Exemplar. Der Erfolg war von Anfang an grandios. Bereits im ersten Jahr verkauften wir 250 Exemplare und schon nach drei Jahren hatten alle Universitäts-, Staats- und Landesbibliotheken in Deutschland, Österreich, Schweiz, Luxemburg und Liechtenstein mit einer einzigen Ausnahme das GV 1911 bis 1965 bestellt. In der Frankfurter Allgemeinen Zeitung erschien ein Artikel, in dem diese fehlende Universität genannt wurde, was nicht zu einer Bestellung, sondern zu einigem Ärger geführt hat. Eine Versandbuchhandlung in Essen-Mülheim rief an und wollte 50 Exemplare verkaufen. Es stellte sich heraus, dass dies der beste Lieferant für Stadtbüchereien in mittleren und kleineren Städten war und 38 Exemplare konnten immerhin über diesen Weg verbreitet werden. Sämtliche Stadtbibliotheken in den Städten mit über 100.000 Einwohnern waren bis auf zwei Ausnahmen nach zwei Jahren komplett versorgt. Aber auch viele kleinere Stadtbüchereien, die bisher kaum über bibliographische Nachschlagewerke verfügten, kauften das GV und hatten damit sämtliche Auskünfte zur Verfügung.

Auch der Auslandsabsatz lief hervorragend. Es kamen sogar Bestellungen aus Papua-Neuguinea, Vietnam und Nigeria. Der US-amerikanische Markt wurde weitgehend durch Harrassowitz bedient und hier war es die University of Michigan in Ann Arbor, die als erste Universität gleich zwei Exemplare orderte – dies nicht aus Versehen, sondern ganz bewusst: einmal für die Zentralbibliothek und einmal für die Germanistik-Abteilung. Ein privater Liebhaber kaufte sich das GV und zahlte es in 60 Monatsraten tapfer ab. Dies veranlasste das Bayerische Fernsehen, bei ihm eine Sendung aufzunehmen, wobei die Recherchen mühsam waren, da sich der Mann wegen seiner hohen Ausgaben für Buchkäufe kein Telefon leisten konnte.

Zahlreiche Antiquariate kauften das GV für Eigenbedarf und ebenfalls erfreulich viele Spezialbibliotheken. Insgesamt konnten 750 Exemplare in Buchform abgesetzt werden und dieser Erfolg setzte sich mit dem „Gesamtverzeichnis des deutschsprachigen Schrifttums 1700 bis 1910" fort. Hier erschienen die ersten Bände im Jahr 1979 und die allermeisten Bibliotheken bestellten es mehr oder weniger automatisch zur Fortsetzung.

Die Sowjetunion hatte vom GV 1911 bis 1965 drei Exemplare mit normalen Bestellnummern bestellt, drei weitere über Messekontingente übernommen. Wir haben daraufhin das GV alt automatisch an die drei Exemplare mit Bestellnummern angehängt, weiter geliefert und unter der gleichen Nummer weiter berechnet. Es wurde auch prompt bezahlt und die Bibliotheken teilten uns später mit, dass sie außerordentlich glücklich darüber gewesen seien, denn sie hätten sonst eine neue Bestellung nie genehmigt bekommen.

1983 reduzierte sich der Absatz erheblich, der Markt war weitgehend bedient worden und es kamen nur noch 6 neue Bestellungen in dem Jahr. Daraufhin haben wir uns entschlossen, eine Mikrofiche-Ausgabe herauszubringen. Von dieser Ausgabe konnten noch einmal rund 250 Exemplare abgesetzt werden, vor allem an Spezialbibliotheken, in einigen Fällen an Universitäten, die für ihre Institute noch nachbezogen, und an zahlreiche Auslandskunden. Auch die einzige deutschsprachige Universität, die das Werk nicht in Buchform gekauft hatte, kaufte nun endlich wenigstens die Mikrofiche-Ausgabe. Zwei Jahre später, nach dem Abschluss des GV 1700 bis 1910, erschien dann auch diese Ausgabe auf Mikrofiche.

Ergänzungen

Ab 1966 liegt den allermeisten Bibliotheken das jeweilige 5-Jahres-Verzeichnis der Deutschen Bibliothek vor, in dem aber bis 1980 nur die Veröffentlichungen innerhalb des Buchhandels berücksichtigt sind. Wir haben deshalb für diesen Zeitraum ein „Gesamtverzeichnis des deutschsprachigen Schrifttums außerhalb des Buchhandels 1966-1980" und ein „Gesamtverzeichnis deutschsprachiger Hochschulschriften 1966-1980" herausgebracht. Beide Verzeichnisse haben die in sie gesetzten Absatzerwartungen in keiner Weise erfüllt. Die Redaktions- und Herstellungskosten waren höher als erwartet, der Absatz erheblich niedriger. Es wurde deutlich, dass der öffentliche Büchereibereich als Käufer für solche Großprojekte aufgrund der Etatsituation weitgehend ausfällt. Auch das Ausland hat wesentlich zögerlicher gekauft, als das bei den ersten beiden großen Gesamtverzeichnissen der Fall war, so dass durchaus ein beachtlicher Teil des Gewinnes, den wir mit den beiden großen Gesamtverzeichnissen erzielt hatten, Verluste der beiden Anschlussprojekte mitfinanzieren musste.

Wirtschaftliche Bedeutung

In der Liste der umsatzstärksten Projekte des K. G. Saur Verlages liegt das „Gesamtverzeichnis des deutschsprachigen Schrifttums" nur an vierter Stelle. Die fünf größten Umsatzbringer bisher waren (in dieser Reihenfolge) das Verzeichnis lieferbarer Bücher, die Biographischen Archive, das Yearbook of International Organizations, das Gesamtverzeichnis des deutschsprachigen Schrifttums (alle Ausgaben) und der British Library General Catalogue of Printed Books (alle Ausgaben).

Trotzdem kommt dem „Gesamtverzeichnis des deutschsprachigen Schrifttums" eine ganz entscheidende Bedeutung für die Entwicklung des Verlages zu.

Beim „Verzeichnis lieferbarer Bücher" handelt es sich um ein Auslieferungsprojekt, das im Verlag der Buchhändler-Vereinigung GmbH Frankfurt erscheint und für das wir die weltweite Vertriebsarbeit leisten. Das Copyright beim „Yearbook of International Organizations" liegt beim Herausgeber, der Union of International Organizations, und die „Biographischen Archive" konnten – sowohl vom finanziellen Rahmen als auch von der inhaltlichen Gestaltung her – überhaupt nur aufgrund der Erfahrungen mit dem „Gesamtverzeichnis des deutschsprachigen Schrifttums" erstellt werden. Das gleiche gilt natürlich für den „British Library General Catalogue of Printed Books", den wir nie hätten verlegen können, wenn wir nicht das erfolgreiche GV vorgelegt hätten. Das GV hat für den Verlag eine enorme wirtschaftliche Bedeutung. Es hat eine erhebliche Umsatzausweitung gebracht und eine Reihe neuer Möglichkeiten eröffnet, die es vorher nicht gegeben hat. In der Bibliothekswelt ist es nach wie vor eines der meistbenutzten Nachschlagewerke. Es gibt bis heute kein elektronisches Verzeichnis, das so konsequent die deutschen bibliographischen Daten von 265 Jahren zusammenfasst, wie dieses GV. Im Signierdienst und für die Auskunft ist es nach wie vor unentbehrlich und wird intensiv benutzt. Eine größere Anerkennung kann es für ein Verlagsprojekt überhaupt nicht geben. Im bibliographischen Unterricht spielt es eine erhebliche Rolle, auch wenn zutrifft, was einer unserer Ratgeber 1975 gemeint hat, dass die jungen Leute es jetzt erheblich einfacher haben, zu bibliographieren. Etwas Sinnvolleres kann ein Verlagsobjekt nicht bieten.

Ein sehr wohlmeinender und liebenswürdiger Verlegerfreund sagte mir 1975 den Bankrott durch dieses unvorstellbare Mammut-Projekt voraus. Glücklicherweise hat er Unrecht behalten, im Gegenteil: die Erträge des GV haben entscheidend dazu beigetragen, dass andere Verlustobjekte diese Prophezeiung nicht wahr werden ließen.

Gesamtverzeichnis des deutschsprachigen Schrifttums (GV) 1911-1965. Hrsg. v. Reinhard Oberschelp. Mit einem Geleitwort von Wilhelm Totok. Bearb. unter der Leitung von Willi Gorzny. 150 Bde. München et al. 1976-1981.

Gesamtverzeichnis des deutschsprachigen Schrifttums (GV) 1700-1910. Vorwort von

Hans Popst und Rainer Schöller. Bearb. unter der Leitung von Hilmar Schmuck, Willi Gorzny und Peter Geils. 160 Bde. München 1979-1986. Nachträge. 1 Bd. München et al. 1987.

Gesamtverzeichnis deutschsprachiger Hochschulschriften 1966-1980. Hrsg. v. Willi Gorzny. 40 Bde. München et al. 1984-1990.

Gesamtverzeichnis des deutschsprachigen Schrifttums außerhalb des Buchhandels 1966-1980. 45 Bde. München et al. 1988-1990.

Gesamtverzeichnis der Übersetzungen deutschsprachiger Werke 1954-1990 (GVÜ)/ Bibliography of Translations of German-Language Publications 1954-1990. Bearb. v. Willi Gorzny. 12 Bde. München et al. 1991-1994.

Joachim Felix Leonhard

Was wird aus dem Wort durch den Ton? – Radio und Hörer: Hineinhören in die Zeit.*

Wahrnehmung erfolgt über *alle* unsere Sinne und ist Aufnahme zwecks Speicherung in unserem Gedächtnis, dem Archiv des Gehirns. Sie bestimmt Inhalt und Form der Kommunikation der Menschen untereinander in Nachricht und Kommentar, im Binnenverständnis von Sender und Empfänger. Und meint dabei keineswegs nur die Beziehung zwischen Rundfunk-Station woanders und Empfangsgerät zu Hause, sondern auch das Verhältnis zwischen Programmmacher und Hörer bzw. Seher. Ein vielfältiges Netzwerk ist im kommunikativen 20. Jahrhundert und seinen Massengesellschaften entstanden; Worte werden in der einen Hemisphäre gesagt und mit Bildern verbunden und in der anderen Welthälfte global empfangen - als Fern-sehen und Fern-hören.

Wir sehen, was wir *wissen* und identifizieren über das Auge, aber wie steht es mit unserem Hören und damit mit einem Sinnesorgan, das wir, im Gegensatz zum Auge, nicht etwa einfach schließen können: Was uns über das Ohr erreicht, ist als Wahrnehmung nicht ausschließlich logisch, sondern, wie Joachim Ernst Berendt bemerkte, ana-logisch. Ja, wir müssen uns die Ohren schon zuhalten, wenn wir Inhalte, Töne, Geräusche, Klänge von uns fernhalten wollen, und was wir hören, setzen wir in Bilder um, überall und nicht nur bei Live-Reportagen der Fußballbundesliga. Wir sollten uns erinnern: bis zur Einführung des Fernsehens war die auf Aktualität bezogene Massenkommunikation neben Presse, gedruckten Medien und Film vehement über den Rundfunk als Hör-funk ausgelegt. Ein massenpsychologisches Phänomen, das ebenso wie audiovisuelle Quellen überhaupt, in der zeitgeschichtlichen Forschung bislang kaum Bedeutung gefunden hat: nicht *was* Goebbels oder Ulbricht sprachen ist nämlich etwa – allein - entscheidend, sondern *wie* ihre Worte inszeniert wurden und wirkten. Aufarbeitung von Geschichte erschließt sich eben nicht nur oder fast ausschließlich über Akten, und Zeitgeschichte ist mehr: mehr als „veritas in actis", da auch die Töne und Bilder in uns gespeichert sind.

Radio, mit den ersten Sendungen vor 75 Jahren, und, nach dem 2. Weltkrieg insbesondere das heutige Leitmedium Fernsehen, sind im wahrsten Sinne des Wortes in die Häuser und das Leben eingetreten, und haben das Wohnen radikal verändert: wo zuvor zunächst ein Radio in schlichter Warenästhetik im Wohnzimmer stand, zog in den 50er Jahren ein

---

* Vortrag zur Eröffnung der Wanderausstellung „Rückkehr in die Fremde?". Remigranten und Rundfunk in Deutschland 1945 bis 1955. - Die Ausstellung, die von der Stiftung Deutsches Rundfunkarchiv Frankfurt am Main/Potsdam angeregt und gemeinsam mit dem Arbeitskreis selbständiger Kultur-Institute e. V. und der Stiftung Archiv der Akademie der Künste (Berlin) organisiert wurde, wurde und wird in folgenden Städten gezeigt: Berlin, Bonn, München, Frankfurt am Main, Magdeburg, Dresden, Stuttgart, Göttingen, Hamburg, Unesco-Weltkulturerbe Kloster Lorsch. Zur Ausstellung sind ein umfang- und materialreicher Dokumentationsband sowie eine CD erschienen: „Rückkehr in die Fremde", 1999. Eine Dokumentation zu einem Thema der deutschen Nachkriegsgeschichte, zusammengetragen von Hans-Ulrich-Wagner mit einem Essay von Peter Steinbach, hrsg. von Barthold C. Witte, Joachim-Felix Leonhard, Wolfgang Trautwein – Berlin 2000, 191 S. – CD hrsg. vom Deutschen Historischen Museum, Berlin, Deutschen Rundfunkarchiv, Frankfurt am Main – Potsdam-Babelsberg, Haus der Geschichte, Bonn, Museumsstiftung Post und Telekommunikation, Bonn, Akademie der Künste, Berlin und AsKI, Bonn (erhältlich bei den genannten Instituten).

televisionärer Hausaltar zwischen Tütenlampen und Nierentischen ein - und die Menschen an, was nicht nur Folgen auf die Innenarchitektur hatte; Radio und Fernsehen haben auf die Gewohnheiten eingewirkt. Anlässlich dieser Ausstellung, die sich erstmals experimentell der Dokumentation deutsch-deutscher Nachkriegsgeschichte an Hand von Rundfunkzeitzeugen zuwendet, gibt es Grund und Anlass zu einer Zeitreise besonderer Art: hören wir hinein in die Zeitläufe.

Was wurde eigentlich aus dem Wort durch den Ton - im Äther?

Die ersten Sendungen des Radios wurden ab dem 29. Oktober 1923 vom Berliner Vox-Haus aus über zunächst abenteuerlich anmutende Antennenanlagen und Empfangsmöglichkeiten ausgestrahlt, deren technische Bezeichnung „Detektor“ schon das Eigentümliche ausreichend beschreibt. Worte wurden in den Äther gesprochen und gesungen – und waren doch nicht Schall und Rauch.[418] Die Vielfalt der Gesellschaft und Kultur der 20er Jahre entfaltete sich in der breiten Vielfalt von Programmen, zwar mit Werbung, aber ohne Schielen auf Marktanteile und Quoten. Wie sagte doch Bertolt Brecht im Jahre 1927 über das Radio: „Die Resultate des Radios sind beschämend, seine Möglichkeiten unbegrenzt. Also ist das Radio eine gute Sache“. Und unnachahmlich die Beschreibung, die Albert Einstein als Festredner zur Funkausstellung am 22. August 1930 von diesem lebendigen Medium gab:

> *„Verehrte An- und Abwesende! Wenn Ihr den Rundfunk höret, so denkt auch daran, wie die Menschen in den Besitz dieses wunderbaren Werkzeuges der Mitteilung gekommen sind. Der Urquell aller technischen Errungenschaften ist die göttliche Neugier und der Spieltrieb des bastelnden und grübelnden Forschers und nicht minder die konstruktive Phantasie des technischen Erfinders. Denkt an Oersted, der zuerst die magnetische Wirkung elektrischer Ströme bemerkte, an Reis, der diese Wirkung zuerst benutzte, um auf elektromagnetischem Wege Schall zu erzeugen, an Bell, der unter Benutzung empfindlicher Kontakte mit seinem Mikrophon zuerst Schallschwingungen in variable elektrische Ströme verwandelte. Denkt auch an Maxwell, der die Existenz elektrischer Wellen auf mathematischem Wege aufzeigte, an Hertz, der sie zuerst mit Hilfe des Funkens erzeugte und nachwies. Gedenket besonders auch Liebens, der in der elektrischen Ventilröhre ein unvergleichliches Spürorgan für elektrische Schwingungen erdachte, das sich zugleich als ideal einfaches Instrument zur Erzeugung elektrischer Schwingungen herausstellte. Gedenket dankbar des Heeres namenloser Techniker, welche die Instrumente des Radio-Verkehrs so vereinfachten und der Massenfabrikation anpassten, dass sie jedermann zugänglich geworden sind. Sollen sich auch alle schämen, die gedankenlos sich der Wunder der Wissenschaft und Technik bedienen und nicht mehr davon geistig erfasst haben als die Kuh von der Botanik der Pflanzen, die sie mit Wohlbehagen frisst.“*[419]

Der Rundfunk berichtete, frei, etwa von der Verleihung des Nobelpreises an Thomas Mann

[418] Zur Programmgeschichte des Rundfunks in der Weimarer Republik vgl. Joachim-Felix Leonhard (Hrsg.), Programmgeschichte des Hörfunks in der Weimarer Republik, 2 Bände, München 1997; zur Rundfunkgeschichte allgemein vgl. Hans Bausch (Hrsg.), Rundfunk in Deutschland, 5 Bände, München 1980. Konrad Dussel, Deutsche Rundfunkgeschichte. Eine Einführung. Konstanz 1999; (Reihe Uni-Papers 9).

[419] Stiftung Deutsches Rundfunkarchiv Frankfurt am Main – Potsdam-Babelsberg, Standort Frankfurt, Archivnummer 2590015; (vgl. Walter Roller. Nr. 946 (Bearb.) Tondokumente zur Kultur- und Zeitgeschichte. 1888 bis 1932. Ein Verzeichnis, Potsdam 1998 (Veröffentlichungen des Deutschen Rundfunkarchivs 15; Roller 1).

am 10. Dezember 1929;[420] im Jahre 1932 (11. April) war Bertolt Brechts „Heilige Johanna der Schlachthöfe“ in Ausschnitten mit Fritz Kortner in der Hauptrolle, neben ihm Helene Weigel, Ernst Busch, Peter Lorre u. a.[421] ebenso im Rundfunk zu hören wie noch 1932 Walter Benjamins Kinderhörspiel „Radau um Kasperl“ (am 9. September)[422]. Paul Hindemiths Oper „Mathis der Maler“ wurde 1933 im Rundfunk gesendet - und bereits 1934 mit Sendeverbot belegt.[423] Bald waren diese Stimmen, waren die Autoren, nicht mehr zu vernehmen, wie in den Bibliotheken ihre Werke entfernt, ins Feuer oder in die Papiermühlen geworfen wurden.[424]

Bezeichnend war, dass Stefan Zweig im Jahre 1933 (12.3.) zwar sein Gedicht „Hymnus an die Reise“ in deutscher Sprache, jedoch schon nicht mehr über einen deutschen Sender, sondern über den Schweizer Rundfunk Bern zu den Hörern bringen konnte: nicht nur im Nachhinein ein Symbol für Abschied und Wegfahrt, die Literatur und Kultur, Freiheit und Demokratie widerfuhr:

> *„Schienen, die blauen Adern aus Eisen,*
> *Durchrinnen die Welt, ein rauschendes Netz.*
> *Herz, rinn mit ihnen! Raff auf dich, zu reisen,*
> *Im Flug nur entfliehst du Gewalt und Gesetz.*
> *Im Flug nur entfliehst du der eigenen Schwere,*
> *Die dir dein Wesen umschränkt und erdrückt.*
> *Wirf dich ins Weite, wirf dich ins Leere,*
> *Nur Ferne gewinnt dich dir selber zurück!*
> *Sieh! bloß ein Ruck, und schon rauscht es von Flügeln,*
> *Für dich braust eine eherne Brust,*
> *Heimat stürzt rücklings mit Hängen und Hügeln*
> *Ein Neues, es wird dir neuselig bewusst.*
> *Die Grenzen zerklirren, die gläsernen Stäbe,*
> *Sprachen, die fremden, sie eint dir der Geist*
> *Unendlicher Einheit, da er die Schwebe*
> *Der vierzehn Völker Europas umkreist.*
> *Und in dem Hinschwung von Ferne zu Fernen*
> *Wächst dir die Seele, verklärt sich der Blick,*
> *So wie die Welt im Tanz zwischen Sternen*
> *Schwingend ausruht in großer Musik.“*[425]

Ab dem 30. Januar 1933 hallten dann die Straßen und Plätze von markigen Worten und vom Klappern der Stiefel wider, wurde insbesondere in den ersten Jahren des nationalsozialistischen Terrors über den Rundfunk gebrüllt und gegrölt, dumpf gedröhnt. In den nächsten 12 Jahren drangen Inhalte an die Ohren - und in die Köpfe, gaben Authentizität

---

[420] Ebenda, Archivnummer C 7419 a; vgl. Walter Roller (1), Nr. 786.

[421] Ebenda, Archivnummer 53.612; Roller (2), Nr. 1321.

[422] Ebenda, Archivnummer 52.12453; Roller (2), Nr. 1453.

[423] Ebenda, Archivnummer F 7588; Irmgard von Broich-Oppert, Walter Roller, H. Joachim Schauss (Bearb.), Tonaufnahmen zur deutschen Rundfunkgeschichte 1924 – 1945, Frankfurt am Main 1972 (Bild- und Tonträger-Verzeichnisse 1), Nr. 236.

[424] Vgl. Ulrich Walberer (Hrsg.), 10. Mai 1933 – Bücherverbrennung in Deutschland und die Folgen, Frankfurt am Main 1983. Joseph Wulf (Hrsg.) Literatur und Dichtung im Dritten Reich, Hamburg 1966; Joachim-Felix Leonhard, Bücherverbrennung, Zensur, Verbot, Vernichtung unter dem Nationalsozialismus in Heidelberg, Heidelberg 1983.

[425] Ebenda, Archivnummer 52.12626;

vor und bauten gezielt neue Wirklichkeiten durch Manipulation und Desinformation auf, die Phantasie durch das im Volksempfänger zu hörende Unerhörte stimulierend: der Volksempfänger hatte die Volksgemeinschaft ebenso ideologisch zu bilden wie die Volksgenossen und der Volkswagen[426]. Zweifel ließ das Regime an solchen Zielen von Anfang an gar nicht erst aufkommen, denn schon bei der Einführung des ersten Parteigenossen in ein Intendantenamt, in Köln am 24. April 1933, erklärte Joseph Goebbels sein unmissverständliches Ziel.

> *„Eine stählerne Romantik, die uns entgegengrüßt aus den siegumwitterten Symbolen dieser Bewegung; die uns entgegenspringt aus jeder Manifestation des geschriebenen oder gesprochenen Wortes des neuen revolutionär-nationalistischen und sozialistischen Deutschland. Das zu verkörpern, das dem Volke nahezubringen, nicht nur das, sondern das Volk in dieser Gewissheit und dieser Gesinnung bis in die letzte Phase zu durchtränken. Die Menschen solange zu hämmern und zu feilen und zu meißeln, bis sie uns verfallen sind: das ist eine der Hauptaufgaben des Deutschen Rundfunks, einer der Hauptaufgaben der Sendegesellschaften, die Sie zu betreuen haben."*[427].

So verflüchtigte sich bald der lebendige Geist der frühen Zeit: die Gleichschaltung bedeutete nicht nur die Ausrichtung des Rundfunks auf den „deutschen Geist", wie der Reichssendeleiter Hadamovsky 1933 meinte: sie bedeutete die Metamorphose zu Zensur, Verfolgung und Vernichtung auf breiter Linie. Die Liste des schädlichen und unerwünschten Schrifttums von 1935 wurde nicht nur ein Index für Bücher, sondern ebenso für Rundfunk, Theater, Film, auch für die Unterhaltung. Bald verboten die Nazis die Auftritte der Comedian Harmonists im Jahre 1935 - und ahmten sie zynisch mit den Drei Rulands nach, einem Gesangstrio, das im November 1938 den Stil der Ersteren zu Hassliedern um die Pogromnacht verzerrte, aber schon 1939 selbst in Ungnade fiel[428].

So dumpf die Übertragungen vom Tag der Kunst 1938 in München, von Parteitagen und anderen Veranstaltungen sein mochten – mit Beginn des Krieges und in dessen Verlauf veränderte der Rundfunk die Tonart in gleich mehrfachem Sinne: an die Stelle dumpfer Marschmusik oder Wortbeiträge, die es nach wie vor - aber nicht mehr so oft - gab, trat zunehmend ein Programm, das als raffinierte Unterhaltung getarnt war, Leichtigkeit bei der Schwere der realen Situation inszenierte und das in den Kriegsjahren ebenso wie eine beispiellose Filmproduktion vom Eigentlichen ablenken - und zum Durchhalten anhalten sollte. Ja, Hitler selbst hatte 1941 angeordnet, für den deutschen Auslandsrundfunk nach England nicht mehr schwere deutsche Marschmusik, sondern englische Musiktitel zu senden, freilich mit neuen Texten und politischen Anspielungen insbesondere auf Winston Winnie Churchill. Was den Deutschen vorenthalten war, produzierte nun entgegen dem allgemeinen Jazzverbot[429] mitten in Berlin Charlie's Orchestra, nämlich jazzige Titel:

---

426 Zur Rundfunkgeschichte im Nationalsozialismus vgl. Ansgar Diller, Rundfunkpolitik im Dritten Reich, München 1980 (Rundfunk in Deutschland, hrsg. v. Hans Bausch, 2).

427 Stiftung Deutsches Rundfunkarchiv, Standort Frankfurt am Main, Archivnummer 2632036; (vgl. Roller (2), Nr. 148).

428 Stiftung Deutsches Rundfunkarchiv, Standort Frankfurt am Main, Archivnummer 52.13837 (vgl. Walter Roller (Bearb.), Tondokumente zur Zeitgeschichte 1933 – 1938, Frankfurt am Main 1980, (Bild- und Tonträger-Verzeichnisse 10), Nr. 899.

429 Dies hatte der Reichssendeleiter Eugen Hadamovsky bereits am 12. Oktober bei einer Intendantentagung angeordnet; vgl. Konrad Dusel/Edgar Lersch, Quellen zur Programmgeschichte des deutschen Hörfunks und Fernsehens, Göttingen/Zürich, 1999 (Quellensammlung zur Kulturgeschichte 24), Nr. 32, S. 134 ff.

„Goody Goody
So you met someone who set you back on your heels -
goody, goody!
So you met someone and now you know how it feels –
goody, goody!
So you gave him your heart too,
just as I gave mine to you;
and he broke it into little pieces –
now, how do you do?
So you lie awake just singing the blues all night –
goody, goody!
So you think that love's a barrel of dynamite –
hooray and hallelujah!
You had it coming to ya,
Goody, goody for him,
goody, goody for me;
and I hope you're satisfied, you rascal you!
Who is that guy who set you back on your heels?
Winnie Churchill!
Who never fought in France and doesn't know how it feels?
Winnie Churchill!
Not a word he said came true,
he is always teasing you.
He breaks the Empire into little pieces –
what are you going to do?
Who lies awake, just dreaming of revenge all night?
Winnie Churchill!
He would like to put the whole world on a barrel of dynamite.
Hooray and hallelujah!
Winnie – You had it coming to ya!
You declared this war
and you will be licked like never before!
Now I hope you're satisfied, you rascal you!"[430]:

Natürlich war dies auch ein Reflex auf die Gegenseite, die von den Sendeanlagen der BBC aus nicht nur ab 1942 Thomas Manns „Reden an die deutschen Hörer"[431], sondern auch Satiresendungen über Hitler, die „Sendungen des Gefreiten Hirnschal"[432] und die Nazis ausstrahlte. Deutschen wurden dabei eigentlich die Ohren zugehalten, weil der Empfang ausländischer Sender unter Strafe stand. In Deutschland selbst stand der Rundfunk freilich im Zeichen des Krieges.

Es gehört zu den Besonderheiten der Mediengeschichte des 20. Jahrhunderts, dass diese

430 Stiftung Deutsches Rundfunkarchiv, Standort Frankfurt am Main, Archivnummer 5014108; Zu Charlie's Orchestra vgl. Horst J. P. Bergmeier, Rainer E. Lotz, Hitler's Airwaves. The Inside Story of Nazi Radio Broadcasting and Propaganda Swing, New Haven, 1997.

431 Die Reden wurden in der Regel an Manns Wohnsitz in Kalifornien aufgezeichnet und auf Schelllackplatten gepresst, sodann nach New York per Flugzeug transportiert und von dort nach London zur Ausstrahlung überspielt. Die Reden von fünf bis acht Minuten Länge wurden später unter dem Titel „Deutsche Hörer! 55 Radiosendungen nach Deutschland von Thomas Mann im Bermann-Fischer-Verlag publiziert (zweite, erweiterte Ausgabe, Stockholm, 1945).

432 Vgl. Hans-Ulrich Wagner, (wie Anm. *), S. 40 f.

vom deutschsprachigen Programm der BBC ausgestrahlten Sendungen ebenso wie die Nachkriegssendungen hätten verloren gehen können, wären sie nicht in Kooperation zwischen BBC und Deutschem Rundfunkarchiv im Jahre 1999 zur Komplettierung der umfangreichen historischen Sammlungen des Deutschen Rundfunkarchivs an dessen Frankfurter Standort verbracht worden[433].

Ähnliche Ergänzungen zu den Beständen aus der Zeit vor 1945 sind im Laufe der Zeit in Kooperation mit vielen anderen Archiven in verschiedenen Ländern erfolgt, wobei stets Kopien erstellt wurden und die Originale am jeweiligen Ort verblieben: Besonders umfangreich wurden die Ergänzungen des audiovisuellen Gedächtnisses mit dem Ende der Ost-West-Konfrontation und der Teilung Deutschlands, als die ARD – und nicht, wie bei vergleichbaren Kulturinstitutionen der Staat - das gesamte und umfangreiche Archiv und Programmvermögen von Hörfunk und Fernsehen der DDR übernahm und es der Stiftung Deutsches Rundfunkarchiv an ihrem jetzigen Standort Berlin, bald im Neubau in Potsdam, zuordnete[434].

Und Informationen waren wesentlich zu Desinformationen geworden, wenn die Sprecher am Radio pathetisch von gar nicht erfolgten Siegen an der Front X, Y berichteten oder wenn, wie am Heiligabend des Jahres 1942, Ehefrauen und Kinder einer Weihnachtsringsendung mit (vermeintlichen) Übertragungen von diversen Kampfplätzen der Wehrmacht an verschiedenen Ecken der Welt lauschten. Eine globale Inszenierung, die in Wirklichkeit in den Studios in der Masurenallee in Berlin zusammengestellt wurde. Nicht Fiktion, sondern Betrug wurde in der emotionalen Stimmung des Heiligen Abends erzeugt, wurde mit Hilfe von künstlichen Hall- und Geräuscheffekten Ferne vorgetäuscht, wo die Betrüger in der Nähe saßen[435].

Nicht nur die Zerstörungen in den eigenen Städten führten aber bald vor Augen, was den langen Ohren verborgen wurde: das Ende des Krieges. Bemerkenswert, wie trotzig-pathetisch der Reichssender Flensburg den letzten OKW-Bericht am 9. Mai 1945 verlas:

> *„(Pausenzeichen) 20.03 Uhr. Reichssender Flensburg und die angeschlossenen Sender. Wir bringen heute den letzten Wehrmachtsbericht dieses Krieges. Aus dem Hauptquartier des Großadmirals, den 9. Mai 1945. Das Oberkommando der Wehrmacht gibt bekannt: In Ostpreußen haben deutsche Divisionen noch gestern die Weichselmündung und den Westteil der Frischen Nehrung bis zuletzt tapfer verteidigt. Seit Mitternacht schweigen nun an allen Fronten die Waffen. Auf Befehl des Großadmirals hat die Wehrmacht den aussichtslos gewordenen Kampf eingestellt. Damit ging das fast sechsjährige Ringen zu Ende. Es hat uns große Siege, aber auch*

---

433 Ein besonderer Dank gilt den Verantwortlichen des deutschsprachigen Dienstes der BBC, die nach Beendigung des Programms im Jahre 1998 das Archiv der Stiftung Deutsches Rundfunkarchiv übergaben. BBC, Stiftung Deutsches Rundfunkarchiv und Deutsches Rundfunkmuseum haben 1999 gemeinsam eine Edition wichtiger Sendungen auf CD herausgegeben.

434 Vgl. Joachim-Felix Leonhard, Der Rundfunk der DDR wird Geschichte und Kulturerbe, in: Dietrich Schwarzkopf (Hrsg.) Rundfunkpolitik in Deutschland. Wettbewerb und Öffentlichkeit, 2 Bde, München 1999, S. 927–977. Zum Deutschen Rundfunkarchiv und seinen Beständen vgl. Joachim-Felix Leonhard (Hrsg.), Deutsches Rundfunkarchiv Babelsberg. Der Neubau des Ostdeutschen Rundfunks Brandenburg für die Stiftung Deutsches Rundfunkarchiv, Frankfurt am Main 2000; ders., Dokumente des Rundfunks – Zeichen der Zeit, in: Buchhandelsgeschichte 1995/4, hrsg. von der Historischen Kommission des Börsenvereins des Deutschen Buchhandels, S. 155-164.

435 Stiftung Deutsches Rundfunkarchiv, Standort Frankfurt am Main

> *schwere Niederlagen gebracht. Die deutsche Wehrmacht ist am Ende einer gewaltigen Übermacht ehrenvoll unterlegen".*[436]

Das war nicht unähnlich der Weise, in der 50 Jahre später ein plötzlich unsicherer SED-Staat sein Ende einräumte und in die Mikrophone stammelte.

Wie aber erfuhr man vom Zeitgeschehen, um es ins eigene Leben einordnen zu können? Sich über die Zeitumstände zu informieren, auch Mut zu fassen und Richtungen zu erkennen, war nicht leicht: Einer immerhin hat Mut zu machen versucht, Thomas Mann am 11. Mai 1945 in der BBC von London aus.

> *„Deutsche Hörer: wie bitter ist es, wenn der Jubel der Welt der Niederlage, der tiefsten Demütigung des eigenen Landes gilt. Wie zeigt sich darin noch einmal schrecklich der Abgrund, der sich zwischen Deutschland, dem Land unserer Väter und Meister, und der gesitteten Welt aufgetan hatte. Die Friedensglocken dröhnen, die Gläser klingen, Umarmungen und Glückwünsche ringsum. Der Deutsche aber, dem von den Allerunberufensten einst sein Deutschtum abgesprochen wurde, der ein grauenvoll gewordenes Land meiden und sich unter freundlicheren Zonen ein neues Leben bauen musste, der senkt das Haupt in der weltweiten Freude. Das Herz krampft sich ihm zusammen bei dem Gedanken, was dies für Deutschland bedeutet. Durch welche dunklen Tage, welche Jahre der Ohnmacht zur Selbstbestimmung oder abbüßenden Erniedrigung, nach allem, was es schon gelitten hat, wird gehen müssen. Und dennoch: die Stunde ist groß, nicht nur für die Siegerwelt, auch für Deutschland. Die Stunde, wo der Drache zur Strecke gebracht ist, das wüste und krankhafte Ungeheuer, Nationalsozialismus genannt, verröchelt und Deutschland von dem Fluch wenigstens befreit ist, das Land Hitlers zu heißen."*[437]*:*

Zeitungen existierten noch nicht, und Veranstaltungen fanden statt, die geleitet waren von Menschen, die Deutsch sprachen und doch die Uniform der Alliierten trugen, die das Land hatten verlassen müssen und die nun wiederkehrten, aber in welches Land? Wohl kaum in das Land, das sie verlassen hatten, eher in ein Gebiet, das ihnen topographisch bekannt war und doch - und irgendwie - fremd. Emigranten begaben sich in Regionen, die jetzt nach dem Verlauf von Flüssen und Autobahnen in Besatzungszonen eingeteilt wurden, und dabei nicht nur territoriale, sondern auch ideologische Basis für die Politikentwicklung der nachfolgenden Zeit bedeuteten. Verschieden waren die Entwürfe und Muster für die Gestaltung von Demokratie und Freiheit, „re-education" zu Werten, die ohnehin nicht einfach zu definieren waren. Und: wie sollten die Menschen denn erreicht werden angesichts zerstörter Verkehrswege und nicht mehr vorhandener Infrastruktur von Presse und Verlagswesen? Schon war begonnen worden, neben anderen Symbolen der NS-Zeit, auch die Volksempfänger zu zerstören, bis man erkannte, dass die gleichen Apparate, zwölf Jahre gleichgeschaltet, jetzt eigentlich nur zur Vermittlung neuer Inhalte „umgeschaltet" zu werden brauchten.

Zu welchen Zielen aber die Deutschen zu erziehen waren und wie dies bei ihnen ankam, macht die schlichte wie eindringliche Ansprache des Landrates des Landkreises Osterholz bei Bremen vom Jahre 1946 deutlich:

---

[436] Stiftung Deutsches Rundfunkarchiv, Standort Frankfurt am Main, Archivnummer 2723099; ediert auf der CD „Kapitulation und Wiederaufbau", hrsg. von der Stiftung Deutsches Rundfunkarchiv, dem Deutschen Historischen Museum und der Bundeszentrale für politische Bildung, 1995, Nr. 9.

[437] Ebenda, Archivnummer 2782362; ed. ebenda, Nr. 13.

„Ich wende mich an die Jugend für die wir Alten bauen und für die wir zu sorgen haben und ich bitte Sie, helft mir dazu, den Weg zurückzufinden von nationalistischer Verranntheit zurück zu einer Weltbürgerschaft, in der das deutsche Volk ein Volk des Friedens, der Arbeit und der Hoffnung auf bessere Zeiten sein wird. Eines Tages wird die Zeit kommen, an dem das deutsche Volk, wenn es arbeitsam, wenn es fleißig, wenn es voller Frieden und voller sozialistischem Gemeinschaftsgefühl ist, wieder aufsteigen wird in der ganzen Welt. Dafür arbeiten wir, darauf hoffen wir und ich bitte deshalb, helft alle mit, zu dem großen Ziel, ein neues Deutschland voller Frieden, Freiheit, Gerechtigkeit und voller Sorge für die Armen und Hilfsbedürftigen zu schaffen.“[438]

Die Hoffnung eines Landrates auf eine Wiedervereinigung in einem – sozialistischen – Deutschland als Gedanke der Zeit, gedanklich nah zu politischen Programmen der Parteien und fern von der Form von Sozialismus, die lange Zeit den Deckmantel für die SED-Diktatur abgab.

Soziale Bindung in der Entwurzelung, die Suche nach Gemeinschaft und – konkret, nach Kindern, Müttern, Vätern – all' dies waren Themen des Rundfunks in der Nachkriegszeit, auch „Hilfestellung“, die vielfach gefragt und benötigt war: dafür stehen zwei Tondokumente des Alltags, nämlich zuerst eine kleine Reportage aus dem Bremer Hauptbahnhof vom Jahre 1946:

„Reporter(Ansage):	*„Lloyd-Gepäckhalle des Bremer Hauptbahnhofs. In wenigen Minuten wird hier ein Transport von Kindern erwartet, die jetzt aus der russischen Zone hierher zu ihren Eltern zurückkehren. Wo kommen diese Kinder jetzt her?*
Krankenschwester:	*Die Kinder kommen aus den russisch besetzten Gebieten, also aus ....,aus sämtlichen.., aus Sachsen vor allen Dingen, nicht.*
Reporter:	*Also aus den Kinderlandverschickungslagern, in die sie damals verschickt wurden.*
Krankenschwester:	*Jawohl!*
Reporter:	*Das ist natürlich eine große Freude für die Eltern, vor allen Dingen da sie ihre Kinder so lange nicht gesehen haben.*
Krankenschwester:	*Ja, selbstverständlich.“*[439]

Dann war da noch eine Sendung, die sehr häufig in den verschiedenen Rundfunkanstalten im täglichen Programm zu hören war und - bei den Vermisstenmeldungen des Roten Kreuzes - dem Suchen und Finden diente:

„Piliza, Manfred, geb. 22.4.42 in Königsberg, letzte Heimatanschrift: Heuhausen / Ostpreußen,
Rüthel, Witold, Pole, 30 Jahre alt, geb. in Warschau, verhaftet im Oktober 44 nach Großrosen gebracht, gesucht von seinem Sohn Rüthel, Piotr!,
Der Soldat Fritz Unruh, geb. am 17.8.1907 in Keitjinen sucht seine Frau Martha Unruh aus Schoschen, Kreis Heiligenbeil. Sie hörten den Suchdienst.“[440]*:*

Kindheit und Jugend stellten sich in Entbehrung und Kargheit nicht selten ohne elterliche Beziehung und häufig auf dem Schwarzmarkt dar, auf dem es Vieles zu veräußern und

---

438 Ebenda, Archivnummer 2833926.
439 Ebenda, Archivnummer 2833929.
440 Ebenda, Archivnummer 2852563.

Weniges zu verdienen gab, Gespräche des Reporters aus dem Alltag belegen dies:

> *„Reporter: Und da stehen sie hier herum an den Ecken. Die Großen mit den dicken Aktentaschen über dem Arm, den durchtriebenen Gesichtern und hier die Kleinen, 9, 10 vielleicht auch 11 Jahre, wie alt mögen sie sein? Und kaum, dass man in ihren Gesichtern noch eine Spur von Kindlichkeit findet.*
>
> *Junge: Eis, Feuerstein, Schokolade.*
> *Reporter: Was kosten denn die Amis bei Dir?*
> *Junge: Sechs*
> *Reporter: Dann gib mir mal zwei. Halt' mal mein Mikrofon so lange, Augenblick.*
> *Junge: Ja.*
> *Reporter: So, 10 und noch einen 2-Mark-Schein, 2 Stück, nich',*
> *Junge: Danke.*
> *Reporter: Was verdienst denn am Tag?*
> *Junge: Och, kommt ganz darauf an, manchmal 20, manchmal 10, auch mehr, janz, wie es kütt (geht).*
> *Reporter: Verkaufst noch anderes?*
> *Junge: Nee!*
> *Reporter: Haste eben Feuer, sag' mal.*
> *Junge: Ja, Moment mal.*
> *Reporter: Schönen Dank. Du rauchst ja schon, sag' mal, wie alt bist Du denn?*
> *2. Junge: 17.*
> *Reporter: En' Kopf hast Du wie 24.*
> *2. Junge: Ja, allerhand mitgemacht, nich'.*
> *Reporter: Andere Sprache hast Du auch, wo kommst Du her?*
> *2. Junge: Aus dem Osten.*
> *Reporter: Und.*
> *2. Junge: Ja, nun, alles verlor'n.*
> *Reporter: Und jetzt?*
> *2. Junge: Jetzt, hier im Westen und nun muss ich ja irgendwas anfangen.*
> *Reporter: Was machst Du für Geschäfte?*
> *2. Junge: Auch Zigaretten, Seife usw., was' grad so geht.*
> *Reporter: Lohnt sich's.*
> *2. Junge. Ja, man lebt von.*
> *Reporter: Arbeit?*
> *2. Junge. Auch, aber bringt nicht viel ein.*
> *Reporter: Na, ja." [441]*

In welchen Lebensumständen sich der Wiederaufbau vollzog und dass Wiederaufbau erst einmal Beseitigung der Trümmer bedeutete, darüber wurde in zahlreichen Rundfunksendungen berichtet. Die Aufarbeitung der politischen Trümmer, nämlich der historischen Verantwortungslast für die 12-jährige Terrorherrschaft, ließ sich dagegen nicht so ertragreich an: in Nürnberg wurde zwar mit den Mitteln des Strafrechtes in den Kriegsverbrecherprozessen historisch-politische Aufarbeitung betrieben und darüber im Rundfunk berichtet[442], aber dass sich zunehmend Verdrängen breit machte, wo das Vergessen nicht möglich sein durfte, war unverkennbar: in Rundfunksendungen debattierten die Köpfe der

---

441 Das macht eine Reportage aus Köln über den Schwarzmarkt und Zigarettenverkauf deutlich; vgl. ebenda, Archivnummer 2783591.

442 Vgl. Hans-Ulrich Wagner, (wie Anm.*), S. 82 ff.

Zeit über die Frage von Schuld und Sühne, von Kollektivschuld, und den Diskussionen über Wiedergutmachung und Erziehung zu Freiheit und Demokratie hörten Tausende von Radiohörern, meist gemeinsam vor dem Apparat zu.[443]

So wie sich im Alltag ab 1948 mit der Währungsreform zugleich Aufwärtstendenzen zeigten und andererseits die Blockade der Sowjets Berlin im gleichen Jahr bedrohte, so bereiteten sich die Deutschen-West und die Deutschen-Ost auf ihre jeweilige Staatenbildung vor. Dabei schenkte man schon damals und nicht erst nach der Wiedervereinigung der Frage der Hauptstadt im Westen besondere Aufmerksamkeit, wie eine Rede aus der Zeit deutlich macht, genauer: hätte verdeutlichen können:

> *„Liebe deutsche Landsleute, liebe Frankfurter Mitbürger, unsere Stadt Frankfurt hat die Nachricht, dass sie zur Bundeshauptstadt gewählt wurde, keineswegs mit dem Gefühl irgendeines Triumphes gegenüber anderen deutschen Städten, die gleichfalls zur Wahl standen, aufgenommen. Sie gibt vielmehr ihrer Freude Ausdruck, dass der Parlamentarische Rat in Bonn nach rein praktischen und sachlichen Gesichtspunkten entschieden und damit dem Wunsche des größten Teiles der deutschen Bürger der Westzonen entsprochen hat.“*[444].

Nein, so ist es nicht gekommen, sondern bekanntlich anders, als es Walter Kolb, der damalige Frankfurter Oberbürgermeister, schon in Vorfreude auf Tonband gesprochen hatte. Zur Ausstrahlung gelangte die in Frankfurt am Main überlieferte Rede gottlob nicht.

Also, Bonn wurde es für die Bundesrepublik Deutschland, und Berlin für die Deutsche Demokratische Republik, als zwei Staaten gegründet wurden und wie Konrad Adenauer bzw. Wilhelm Pieck in ihren Rundfunkreden die das jeweils „neue“ Deutschland für den Westen bzw. den Osten hervorhoben! Zuerst Adenauer in Bonn:

> *„Das Werden des neuen Deutschlands hat sich nach den langen Verhandlungen im Parlamentarischen Rat und den Wahlen zum Bundestag am 14. August mit großer Schnelligkeit vollzogen. Am 7. September hat sich der Bundestag und der Bundesrat konstituiert, am 12. September hat der Bundestag den Bundespräsidenten gewählt, am 15. September den Bundeskanzler. Der Bundespräsident hat mich daraufhin am gleichen Tage zum Bundeskanzler ernannt. Heute, am 20. September, hat er auf meinen Vorschlag, die Bundesminister ernannt. Mit der Konstituierung der Bundesregierung, die am heutigen Tag erfolgt ist, ist auch das Besatzungsstatut in Kraft getreten.“*

Dann in Berlin; Wilhelm Pieck:

> *„Wir stehen heute an der Wende der deutschen Geschichte: Dank der unermüdlichen Arbeit der besten Kräfte des deutschen Volkes und dank der großen Hilfe, die uns die Sowjetregierung erwiesen hat, unternehmen wir den ersten Schritt der staatlichen*

---

[443] Wie im übrigen viele Autoren und Schriftsteller, die seit 1933 verboten und verfolgt worden waren, angesichts fehlender Verlage und Papierherstellung erstmals wieder oder zum ersten Male über den Hörfunk in Gestalt von Features und Hörspielen bekannt gemacht wurden; zum letzteren vgl. Hörspiel 1945 – 1949. Eine Dokumentation, zusammengestellt von Bernd Löw u. Mitw. von Susanne Höschel, Anne Schmidt und Hans-Ulrich Wagner, Potsdam 1997 (Veröffentlichungen des Deutschen Rundfunkarchiv 12; Hans-Ulrich Wagner, „Der gute Wille, etwas Neues zu schaffen.“ Das Hörspielprogramm in Deutschland von 1945 bis 1949, Potsdam 1997, (Veröffentlichungen des Deutschen Rundfunkarchiv 11).

[444] Stiftung Deutsches Rundfunkarchiv, Standort Frankfurt am Main, Archivnummer 2633034 (ed. auf der CD „Hör‘ doch mal hin, hrsg. vom Hessischen Rundfunk und der Stiftung Deutsches Rundfunkarchiv, Nr. 15).

> *Selbständigkeit des deutschen Volkes. Sorgen wir alle in verantwortungsbewusster, loyaler und freundschaftlicher Zusammenarbeit dafür, dass wir uns der Größe der geschichtlichen Aufgaben gewachsen zeigen, und dass wir dereinst vor dem Urteil der Geschichte bestehen können.“*[445]

So wurden Teilung und Trennung manifest: im Jahre 1949 waren dann gleich auch zwei Goethe-Feiern zu veranstalten, in Frankfurt am Main und Weimar, und es ist interessant, dem Preisträger Thomas Mann nicht nur bei seinen Reden in Frankfurt und Weimar zuzuhören, sondern ihn auf dieser Reise, die ja einen besonderen Grenzgang bedeutete, zu begleiten: Im Frankfurter Hauptbahnhof, begleitet von Lokomotivgeräuschen, äußert sich dazu Thomas Mann am 3. August 1949 im Interview mit Gottfried Hoster, einem Reporter des Hessischen Rundfunks, ein eher zufälliges Gespräch und dennoch keineswegs belanglos.

„Thomas Mann:	*Die Lebensverhältnisse sind selbstverständlich wirtschaftlich günstiger in der Westzone, vorläufig, aber der Empfang, den ich persönlich in der Ostzone hatte, sehr ergreifend, ich muss sagen, dass ich nicht bereue, den Besuch in Weimar gemacht zu haben.*
Gottfried Hoster:	*Noch eine kurze letzte Frage: Dürfen Ihre deutschen Leser Sie bald vielleicht endgültig wieder in Deutschland zurück erwarten?*
Thomas Mann:	*Endgültig, das will ich lieber nicht versprechen in meinem Alter, nicht wahr, aber ich hoffe, Deutschland wiederzusehen.*
Gottfried Hoster:	*Dann dürfen wir Ihnen zuletzt noch gute Reise wünschen.*
Thomas Mann:	*Danke.“*[446]

Sechs Jahre später, im Schillerjahr 1955, hatte der gleiche Zeitgenosse neuerlich diesen Grenzgang vorzunehmen und wurde, wie die Resonanz auf Thomas Manns doppelte Preisträgerschaft und die Veranstaltungen in Stuttgart und Weimar zeigen, wieder ein Grenzgänger besonderer Art: Subjekt des eigenen Handelns und doch Objekt der jeweiligen Bemühungen um Vereinnahmung[447].

Radio und Hörer - Hineinhören in die Zeit der 50er Jahre meint auch, die sich verändernde Rundfunklandschaft kennen zu lernen. So schlossen sich im Jahre 1950 die damals 6 Landesrundfunkanstalten zur Arbeitsgemeinschaft der öffentlich-rechtlichen Rundfunkanstalten, der ARD zusammen, der von Anfang an der „Rundfunk im amerikanischen Sektor“, kurz: RIAS attachiert war und der in den 50er Jahren der Saarländische Rundfunk (1955) und der Sender Freies Berlin (1953) beitraten[448]. Letzterer war gleichsam eine Neugründung im „Haus des Rundfunks“ an der Masurenallee gegenüber dem Funkturm, von wo der Berliner Rundfunk, mittlerweile sowjetisch geprägt, aus dem britischen Sektor in den sowjetischen Sektor nach Köpenick ausgewandert war. Von jetzt an funkte es wahrlich

---

445 Vgl. Stiftung Deutsches Rundfunkarchiv, Standort Frankfurt am Main, Archivnummer 2600100 u. 2763427 (Adenauer); Deutsches Rundfunkarchiv, Standort Frankfurt am Main, Archivnummern 2783608, 2783609, 2743191, 2874500 (Pieck); beide Reden sind in Auszügen ediert auf der CD „Wir sind wieder wer“, Nr. 2.

446 Stiftung Deutsches Rundfunkarchiv, Standort Frankfurt am Main, Archivnummer 2742182.

447 Vgl. Hans-Ulrich Wagner (wie Anm.*), S. 130 ff.

448 Zur Geschichte der ARD bzw. ihrer einzelnen Rundfunkanstalten vgl. Hans Bausch, Rundfunkpolitik nach 1945, Zwei Teile, München 1980, (Rundfunk in Deutschland, hrsg. von Hans Bausch, 3,4); Dietrich Schwarzkopf (Hrsg.), Rundfunkpolitik in Deutschland. Wettbewerb und Öffentlichkeit. (Koordination: Deutsches Rundfunkarchiv, 2 Bände, München 1999; vgl. auch „50 Jahre ARD“, hrsg. von der Arbeitsgemeinschaft der öffentlich-rechtlichen Rundfunkanstalten der Bundesrepublik Deutschland (ARD), Koordination: Deutsches Rundfunkarchiv, Frankfurt am Main, 2000.

zwischen Ost und West, hielt der „Kalte Krieg“ Einzug in den Äther: bevor die Fernsehtruhen im Wohnzimmer Einzug hielten, versammelte man sich zum gemeinsamen Hören - und wartete stets, mit beinahe kindlichem Gemüte, zunächst gebannt auf die Rundung und Vollendung des magischen Auges: grünlich und künstlich: Kinder, Mutter, Vater, Großeltern, sie alle hörten manches, was Ihnen bekannt vorkam und doch irgendwie anders klang, wie z. B. ein Lied aus dem Ostberliner Funkhaus Nalepastraße im Jahre 1952.

„Wenn das Thermometer steigt und fast 30 Grad anzeigt,,
ja dann zieht man aus Berlin zum Strand vom Wannsee hin,
Kinder ist das ein Gewühl, Oma kauft ein Eis am Stiel.
und die Planscherei, doch damit ist's jetzt vorbei.
Schließ' die Badehose ein, lass' das Baden lieber sein,
denn der Ami schießt am Wannsee,
wenn die Sonne strahlend scheint
und das Schwesterchen auch weint,
fahre bloß nicht an den Wannsee.
Ich kann schießen, sagt der Ami, wie ich will und wo ich mag,
das erlaubt mir Adenauer ja im Generalvertrag.
Kinder woll'n wir doch mal seh'n,
ob wenn wir zusammensteh'n, nicht die Amis eines Tages baden geh'n.
Will man sich erholen geh'n.
sieht man bloß Kanonen steh'n
und die Amis blitze knall'n in unserm Grunewald,
wer zum Strand will, ist entsetzt, denn da sitzt der Ami jetzt,
doch wir ham parat, für die Brüder einen Rat,
Pack' die Panzerwagen ein, leg' paar Steine noch mit 'rein
und dann 'rin damit in' Wannsee,
denn wir pfeifen auf das Glück, auf 'ne Kugel im Genick,
wir woll'n Frieden: auch am Wannsee,
schließlich zieh'n wir, wenn wir baden, keene Panzerwesten an,
denn Berlin ist nicht Chicago,
unser Bär kein dritter Mann.
Keine Sorgen Hans und Klaus, pack' die Badehose aus,
Ami, geh nach Haus, sonst fliegste raus!“[449].

Die Sängerin war nicht Cornelia Froboess, die dann für viele Jahre Conny hieß, sondern Gina Pressgott. Gebannt folgten die Hörer am 17. Juni 1953 der Reportage des RIAS-Reporters Jürgen Graf vom Potsdamer Platz[450] und vernahmen aus dem Ost-Berliner Rundfunksender eine Reportage über ein Volksfest am Prenzlauer Berg[451]: Verharmlosung zur Beruhigung der Gemüter, Inszenierung staatlicher Normalität.

Eine hohe Fistelstimme klang bald immer öfter über das Radio und drang – später mit Spitzbart als visuellem Erkennungszeichen - auch in das Bewusstsein der Deutschen in Ost und West ein: Kaum jemand erinnert sich an das, *was* Walter Ulbricht, zumal in zum Teil mehrstündigen Parteitagsreden, sagte, wohl, aber, *wie* er sprach: Worte wurden zu Ton in

[449] Stiftung Deutsches Rundfunkarchiv, Standort Potsdam-Babelsberg, Archivnummer 1950064.
[450] Stiftung Deutsches Rundfunkarchiv, Standort Frankfurt am Main, Archivnummer 5500872; die Reportage ist in Auszügen ediert auf der CD „Wir sind wieder wer“, hrsg. vom Deutschen Rundfunkarchiv und dem Deutschen Historischen Museum, Nr. 2.
[451] Stiftung Deutsches Rundfunkarchiv, Standort Potsdam-Babelsberg, Archivnummer DOK 1436/3.

unserem Gedächtnis und unserer historischen Überlieferung, sowie z. B. bei einer Ulbrichtrede in Eisenhüttenstadt:

> *„Im Auftrag der Regierung der Deutschen Demokratischen Republik vollziehe ich die feierliche Namensgebung des Eisenhüttenkombinates in Eisenhüttenkombinat „Josef Wissarionowitsch Stalin“ und die erste sozialistische Stadt der Deutschen Demokratischen Republik erhält den Namen „Stalinstadt““.* [452]

Es war in diesem Schicksalsjahr 1953, als der SED-Sekretär die Umbenennung von Eisenhüttenstadt in Stalinstadt vornahm in einer Rede, von der es zwei Fassungen gibt: während die – kürzere - Ost-Fassung am Berliner DRA-Standort wiedergefunden wurde, war die längere Fassung schon immer in den Frankfurter Sammlungen des Deutschen Rundfunkarchivs vorhanden. Die Erklärung für die unterschiedliche Länge liegt im Reagieren auf die Zeitläufe: Stalin war gestorben, und die sich anschließende Entstalinisierung bedeutete nicht nur einen politischen Einschnitt, sondern schlicht und einfach auch technische Schnitte, und zwar auf den Archivbändern: Tilgen der gröbsten Lobhudeleien.

Das Leben nahm Anfang der 50er Jahre in den sich bildenden beiden deutschen Staaten an Normalität zu: Die Warengesellschaft mit Markt und Wettbewerb im Westen trat in Kontrast zur Bedarfsdeckungsgesellschaft des Ostens, dem Westen wurde das Fremde, bis dahin über vielfältige Kommunikation bekannt, fast vertraut, und es war keineswegs „nur“ Sprachübung, wenn eine Mutter ihrem Töchterchen in einem Werbespot des Jahres 1952 die Vorzüge französischen Weinbrands erläuterte: 36 Sekunden Worte, aber Ton und ein Bild der Gesellschaft:

„Kind:	*Mami, sieh' mal dort: die Schaufenster.*
Mutter:	*Was denn Kleines: da stehen doch lauter Weinbrand- und Likörflaschen.*
Kind:	*Ja, Mami, da ist aber die Flasche, die Du Papi geschenkt hast: Dujardin. (Kind buchstabiert) Du-jar-din.*
Mutter:	*Ach, Du meinst, Dujardin-Weinbrand. Wie kommst Du denn darauf?*
Kind:	*Weil: oft, wenn Papi nach Hause kommt und macht so ein ernstes Gesicht, dann nimmt er die Flasche Du..(Kind buchstabiert wieder)*
Mutter:	*Dujardin.*
Kind:	*und trinkt ein Gläschen und schon wird er lustig um die Nase und zwinkert mit den Augen und sagt „Ach, der ist wundervoll“. Das muss doch was Schönes sein.*
Mutter:	*Da hast Du recht. Dujardin ist auch etwas Schönes. Und wenn Papi sagt: Dujardin ist ein wundervoller Weinbrand, dann stimmt's.““* [453]

Das Fremde wurde zudem im Westen entfremdet, als Männer aus Sizilien, Katalonien und von der Peleponnes nach Berlin, Dortmund und München und in andere Orte kamen, nicht der Sprache ihres neuen Gastlandes mächtig und doch an dessen wirtschaftlichem Aufbau beteiligt. Die Deutschen hörten am Radiogerät – Worte und Inhalte im Ton - Canzone und Sirtaki in Programmen für die Gastarbeiter, die ihrerseits etwas über ihre Heimatländer er-

---

[452] Stiftung Deutsches Rundfunkarchiv, Standort Frankfurt am Main, Archivnummer 2633018; Standort Potsdam-Babelsberg, Archivnummer DOK 115; ein Redeausschnitt ist ediert auf der CD „Wir sind wieder wer“, hrsg. vom Deutschen Rundfunkarchiv und dem Deutschen Historischen Museum, Nr. 2.

[453] Stiftung Deutsches Rundfunkarchiv, Standort Frankfurt am Main, Archivnummer 2864097; der „Werbespot“ ist ediert auf der CD „Wir sind wieder wer“, hrsg. vom Deutschen Rundfunkarchiv und dem Deutschen Historischen Museum, Nr. 2.

fuhren und über ihr Gastland, das zunehmend zweite Heimat bedeutete. Die Deutschen (West) fuhren in überladenen VW-Käfern an den Gardasee und die Adria, wie die Deutschen (Ost) in den Wartburgs nach Bulgarien reisten. Sie reisten in die Fremde, während andere, die aus der Ferne, genauer aus ihrem Exil zurückgekehrt waren, zuweilen das Land wieder verließen: nicht selten aus Enttäuschung über den Verlauf von Politik und Geschichte - und in der Einschätzung, nach Deutschland als in die Fremde zurückgekehrt zu sein.

Was war, was ist *das* Fremde, vor allem *wer* sind Fremde? Über 50 Jahre nach dem Ende des 2. Weltkriegs müssen wir aufpassen, dass aus dem Wort nicht wieder und zunehmend auch Lärm und Getöse werden.

Ulf Scharlau

„...aber etwas ganz Richtiges gibt es nicht.“

Anmerkungen zu den Kernaufgaben
des Bereichs Dokumentation und Archive im Südwestrundfunk

Kernaufgabe - ein schillernder Begriff

Die Pressedokumentation der Hauptabteilung (HA) Dokumentation und Archive (DuA) des früheren Südwestfunks Baden-Baden und - seit Ende 1998 - des fusionierten Südwestrundfunks hat für Redaktionen des Fernsehens im Landesprogramm seit geraumer Zeit eine regelmäßige Dokumentation regionaler Zeitungen und Zeitschriften des Sendegebiets angefertigt. Dieser regionale Dienst, von DuA als unmittelbares Kerngeschäft nicht angesehen, erforderte einen beträchtlichen personellen Aufwand, der, da von der Redaktion erwünscht und bestellt, von dieser in Form einer hausinternen Budgetierung finanziert wurde. Aufgrund von Sparmassnahmen wurde im Herbst 2000 mitgeteilt, „dass die Redaktionen auf diesen Service verzichten werden“. Dies führte nun zur Beschwerde anderer Redaktionen, die Nutznießer der Dokumentation gewesen waren und zur Bitte des zuständigen Direktors an die HA Dokumentation und Archive: „... möchte ich Sie doch herzlich bitten, die Morbus Personalkapazitätsgründe zu korrigieren, aber dies nach Möglichkeit nicht einseitig und zu Lasten des SWR-Kerngeschäfts“.

Im Herbst 2000 war die zum 01.01.2001 von der Kommission zur Ermittlung des Finanzbedarfs (KEF) vorgeschlagene und von ARD/ZDF erhoffte Gebührenanpassung zeitweilig gefährdet, da die Zustimmung hierfür im Landtag von Sachsen ungesichert schien. In den Notplänen für eine Haushaltsgestaltung für diesen - hoffentlich nicht eintretenden - Fall wurden dem Bereich Dokumentation und Archive von unterschiedlichen Seiten zwei sich widersprechende Szenarien nahegelegt: eine angemessene Beteiligung an der dann notwendigen Einsparquote sowie andererseits ein Investieren in DuA, da der Einsparungszwang die Redaktionen und ihre Programmplanungen mehr als je zuvor an das Angebot der Archive würde binden müssen.

Was ist an diesen beiden Vorgängen zu erkennen? Innerhalb der Redaktionen bestehen anscheinend differierende Einschätzungen und Prioritäten über Art und Umfang der Zuarbeiten und Dienstleistungen von DuA, die deren Kernaufgaben als notwendige Voraussetzungen begleiten. Und es wird das, was Kerngeschäft von Dokumentation und Archive ist, ganz offensichtlich fachbereichsintern partiell anders definiert als extern - und wird auch von außen her unterschiedlich bewertet. Freilich wird die Sicht der Redaktionen nach aller Erfahrung stark von der Intensität der von ihnen erwarteten archivischen Dienstleistung fokussiert. Zwangsläufig gehören Redaktionen für Kultur, Hörspiel, Literatur, Musik, Fernsehspiel, Dokumentation, Feature mit zu den intensivsten Nutzern der Archive und deren Serviceangebot. Archivmaterialien sind das Repertoiregut dieser Redaktionsbereiche. Anders liegt dies bei den sogenannten „aktuellen“ Redaktionen: Eine Nachrichtenredaktion, eine Sportredaktion, eine politische Redaktion, deren vordergründiger Programmauftrag die tagesaktuelle Informationsvermittlung und Kommentierung ist, muss nur in Ausnahmefällen auf Archiveinblendungen zurückgreifen. Dies betrifft insbesondere den

Hörfunk. Beim Fernsehen sieht dies buchstäblich anders aus, hier wird auch von den aktuellen Redaktionen tagtäglich Videomaterial als Visualisierung vordergründiger Verbalinhalte benötigt.

Dies bedeutet: die Einschätzung der Kernaufgaben von Dokumentation und Archive sind beim Fachbereich selbst und bei den Redaktionen aufgrund unterschiedlicher Interessenslagen, Prioritäten und Gewichtungen nur zu Teilen deckungsgleich. Es gibt keine eindeutige Definition des Kerngeschäfts von Dokumentation und Archive in Form eines unstrittigen Kodex der innerhalb der Institution Rundfunkanstalt gültig wäre. Wir erkennen von Interessen geleitete Annäherungen aus unterschiedlicher Perspektive. Diese Erkenntnis ist - nota bene - keine Besonderheit des jungen Senders SWR, sondern sie ist medienimmanent. „Aber etwas ganz Richtiges gibt es nicht", lässt Theodor Fontane den alten Stechlin sagen, und diese Weisheit gilt auch in unserem Zusammenhang.

Fusion als Einschnitt

Der Zusammenschluss von Süddeutschem Rundfunk Stuttgart (SDR) und Südwestfunk Baden-Baden (SWF) wurde zum 01. Oktober 1998 Wirklichkeit. Wesentliche Grundbedingungen für die Struktur des Südwestrundfunks regelt der zwischen den Ländern Baden-Württemberg und Rheinland-Pfalz geschlossene „Staatsvertrag über den Südwestrundfunk". Sollten doch mit der Rundfunk- Neuordnung im Südwesten der Bundesrepublik eine Stärkung der Landesidentität beider Länder durch Schaffung landesbezogener einheitlicher Programmstrukturen, mehr landes- und regionalspezifische Programmangebote und zugleich ein sozialverträglicher Standortausgleich erreicht werden.
Hierfür formuliert der Staatsvertrag als wesentliche Vorgaben unter anderem:

- Das Dritte Fernsehprogramm wird auch als Fernsehangebot der beiden Vertragsländer gestaltet.
- Der jeweilige Landesanteil an diesem Programm wird mit 30 % quotiert, während 70 % des Programms als Gemeinschaftsprogramm zu gestalten sind.
- Die beiden ersten Hörfunkprogramme (SWR1) werden jeweils als Landesprogramme für Baden-Württemberg und Rheinland-Pfalz veranstaltet .
- Das zweite Hörfunkprogramm (SWR2) wird als länderübergreifendes Kulturprogramm unter Einschluss landes- und regionalbezogener Inhalte gestaltet.
- Die bisherigen dritten Hörfunkprogramme SDR 3 und SWF 3 werden zu einem länderübergreifenden Pop-Pogramm (SWR3) mit regionalen Fenstern zusammengefasst,
- während die vierten Hörfunkprogramme in Rheinland-Pfalz und Baden-Württemberg als eigenständige Landesprogramme gestaltet werden.

Zugleich werden im Staatsvertrag produktionsrelevante Prämissen fixiert: Landes- und Regionalprogramme sollen grundsätzlich in den jeweiligen Landeshauptstädten bzw. den Regionalstudios produziert werden, während die Programme SWR 2 und SWR 3 aus Baden-Baden kommen. An Baden-Baden als Produktionsort werden zudem die Herstellung des gemeinsamen „Mantels" (70 % des Programmanteils) des Dritten Fernsehens des SWR und die Zulieferung des SWR zu den Gemeinschaftsprogrammen der ARD delegiert. Die aktuelle Berichterstattung erfolgt von beiden Landessendern aus Mainz und Stuttgart.

Die Planungen der DuA-Fachbereiche beider Rundfunkanstalten, die ab 1997 eine Konzeption zur Zusammenfügung der beiden bisherigen Hauptabteilungen Dokumentation und Archive von SDR und SWF zu einem Bereich zu erarbeiten hatten, mussten sich an diesen

Vorgaben orientieren. Hiermit waren die Schwerpunkte künftiger Kernaufgaben an den SWR-Standorten Baden-Baden, Mainz und Stuttgart und in den Studios in nuce bereits vorgebildet.

Personalfragen

Von Anfang an stand fest, dass sich die Planstellen-Zahl im neuen Sender, die sich zwangsläufig zunächst aus der Addition der Planstellen von SDR und SWF ergab, erheblich würde reduzieren müssen, um in der neuen Rundfunkanstalt auf Dauer überhaupt einen nennenswerten Synergieeffekt zu erzielen. Dies verlangte von DuA Strategien zur Einsparung an Personalressourcen bei gleichzeitiger Bewältigung der verbleibenden und der neu hinzukommenden Aufgaben. Erschwert wurde dies für DuA in Stuttgart und Baden-Baden durch eine faktische zusätzliche Einsparforderung, denn neben dem tatsächlichen Abbau von Planstellen musste von diesen Standorten zusätzlich durch Stellenverschiebungen der durch die Programmausweitungen in Mainz entstandene personelle Mehrbedarf im Archivbereich ausgeglichen werden.

Die Planungs-Arbeitsgruppe „Dokumentation und Archive“ von SWF und SDR nahm im Mai 1997 ihre Arbeit auf. Der einvernehmlich verfasste Endbericht mit den Strukturvorschlägen und projektierten Arbeitsaufgaben wurde Anfang Oktober desselben Jahres verabschiedet. Die beiden Gruppenleiter präsentierten im November 1997 in einem fast den ganzen Tag andauernden Gespräch ihre Vorschläge den beiden Geschäftsleitungen von SDR und SWF. Diese stimmten nach intensiver Diskussion allen Vorschlägen zu und gaben deren Umsetzung in Auftrag. Unsere Erwartung, Einvernehmlichkeit als aussichtsreiche strategische Voraussetzung zur Akzeptanz unserer Planungen anzustreben und zu verdeutlichen, war aufgegangen.

Ein Sender - Drei Standorte: Konsequenzen für den D/A-Bereich

Aus den Vorgaben des Staatsvertrages ergaben sich wesentliche Teile der Strukturen der neuen Institution im Ganzen wie auch auf der Ebene der Fachbereiche.

Es wurde eine Hauptabteilung mit drei Standort-Abteilungen in Baden-Baden, Mainz und Stuttgart gebildet. Dabei wurde der Bereich im Sinne der die DuA-Bereiche zunehmend prägenden Trimedialität (Hörfunk, Fernsehen, Print) „interfakultativ“ sowohl der Hörfunk- als auch der Fernsehdirektion zugeordnet. Strukturell wurde der Zuschnitt der Hauptabteilung in neue Organisationsformen durch eine einheitliche Ressortbildung an den Standorten Baden-Baden, Mainz und Stuttgart durchgesetzt. Die Standorte gliedern sich in die an allen Standorten vorhandenen Basisressorts Information und Dokumentation (IuD) Fernsehen / Hörfunk-Wort, Produktionsarchiv Hörfunk/Fernsehen (mit gemeinsamer Magazinverwaltung und bimedialem Programmaustausch sowie mit Zuständigkeiten für Digitalisierung und Bestandserhaltung), IuD Musik (Leichte und Ernste Musik, Notenarchive), IuD Print mit Pressedokumentation und Bibliotheken. Hinzu kommen Standort übergreifend die Ressorts „DuA Online“ sowie „Forschung und Entwicklung (F+E)“, die sich um Online-/Internet-Technologien, multimediale Regelwerksfragen (Stichwort „Metadaten“), um Pflege und Modernisierung der Archivdatenbanken und alle DV-gestützten Anwendungen sowie um Strategien zur Einführung und Fortentwicklung der Digitalisierung in allen Archivbereichen und auf allen Ebenen zu kümmern haben. Als Konsequenzen aus den Strukturüberlegungen der Fusionsarbeitsgruppe Dokumentation und Archive ergab sich für den neuen DuA-Bereich eine Reihe von strategischen und organisatorischen Aufgaben, die anzugehen waren oder zur Zeit oder zukünftig zu lösen sind.

Einige seien beispielhaft aufgezeigt: So muss nach unserer Auffassung das Grundprinzip aller Maßnahmen in DuA des SWR eine weitest gehende Arbeitsteiligkeit sein. Das bedeutet, den Abbau von Doppelarbeit zu Gunsten des Prinzips, möglichst viele dokumentarische Kernaufgaben an einer Stelle so zu organisieren, dass alle Stellen davon den Nutzen haben. Die Geschlossenheit der Bestände an den einzelnen Orten war zu erhalten, denn die Bestände sind historisch gewachsen, sowohl im Umfang als auch in ihrer dokumentarischen Struktur und Erschliessung. Die Aufgaben, Schwerpunkte und Infrastruktur der DuA-Abteilung an den Standorten orientieren sich an dem den einzelnen Standorten zugeteilten Programmauftrag. Die Harmonisierung und Einheitlichkeit der Dokumentationssysteme wurde/wird auch überall dort hergestellt, wo dies noch nicht der Fall gewesen ist. Die Standorte und die Studios des SWR wurden im DuA-Bereich miteinander vernetzt. Dies bedeutet Transparenz der Bestände und schnellen Zugriff von überall im Sender auf alle Informationen und Materialien. Neben dem Programmaustausch innerhalb von ARD, ZDF und dem Ausland, wurde ein hausinterner Programm- und Materialaustausch eingeführt; angestrebt wird für die Zukunft die interne Online-Übermittlung digitalisierter Bestände, dies minimiert den Transport wertvollen Archivguts und reduziert die damit verbundenen Gefährdungen des Materials. Deswegen wird die Digitalisierung der Archivbestände konsequent vorangetrieben. Je höher investiert wird, desto rascher und konsequenter kann der ortsunabhängige Zugriff auf Materialien erfolgen.

Die alltäglichen Kernaufgaben von D/A nach der Fusion

Selbstverständlich waren bereits im SDR und SWF seit vielen Jahren in den Fachbereichen Dokumentation und Archive qualifiziertes Personal auf der Grundlage professioneller Grundstandards tätig, für die zentrale Aufgaben definiert waren. Die „klassischen" Arbeitsfelder von Sammeln, Bewerten/Entscheiden, Erfassen/Dokumentieren, Recherchieren/Informieren, Bereitstellen haben auch in der neuen Institution nichts von ihrer Zentralität für DuA verloren. Sie bestimmen nach wie vor den unabdingbaren Kern der Dienstleistung der Archive und Dokumentationsbereiche im SWR. Dies meint konkret:

- eine inhaltliche Erschließung von Hörfunk- und Fernsehmaterial zur Versorgung aller Redaktionen und Bereiche des SWR nach den Anforderungen der verschiedenen Programme, ihrer Struktur und Programminhalte,
- die Auswahl und Bewertung von Audio- und Videomaterialien nach redaktionellen und archivischen Kriterien, wobei diese durchaus von unterschiedlicher Zielrichtung sein können,
- den Transfer von analogem Ausgangsmaterial auf die digitale Ebene mit dem Ziel einer zur schnellen und von Zeit und Standort ungebundenen Versorgung der Redaktionen sowie zur archivischen Langzeitsicherung der Materialien selbst,
- die inhaltliche Erschließung von in Printform gespeicherten Informationen (Presse, Buch, Illustrationen, Fotos, Manuskripte, Schriftgut) und die Versorgung der Redaktionen/Programme mit Informationen über diese Materialien und mit den Materialien selbst,
- die Informationsbeschaffung aus externen Quellen über Online-Technologien,
- die Akquisition und Erschließung von Hintergrundinformationen, besonders
- von biographischen und terminbezogenen Daten sowie deren Bereitstellung in Inhouse-Informationssystemen,

- die Versorgung der Redaktionen und Programme/Programmplaner mit Profildiensten wie z.B. Themen-, Termin- oder Ereignisvorschauen,
- die Aufbereitung von Informationen aller Art zur automatisierten Versorgung von Redaktion, Moderation und programmbegleitenden Datendiensten wie Digital Audio Broadcast (DAB), Internet, Radio Data System (RDS), Videotext,
- die Weiterentwicklung bestehender und die Entwicklung neuer oder ergänzender Informationssysteme nach den Bedürfnissen des Programms und der Dokumentation; dazu gehört die Auswahl geeigneter externer Informationsangebote,
- die Beratung von Redaktionsbereichen zum Einsatz von Informationssystemen und deren Anpassung an die spezifische Bedürfnisse von Redaktionen,
- die Organisation und Durchführung von Schulungen zu den Informationssystemen sowie die individuelle Benutzerbetreuung und Erarbeitung schriftlicher Dokumentationen, Anleitungen etc.,
- die Entwicklung einheitlicher Dokumentationssprachen und eines einheitlichen kontrollierten Vokabulars zur Indexierung und Recherche,
- die Koordination der DV-gestützten Archiv-Informationssysteme innerhalb des SWR und im Verbund seiner Kooperationspartner; dies schließt die Vertretung der SWR-Interessen in übergreifenden Arbeitsgruppen zur Weiterentwicklung der informatorischen Infrastruktur mit ein,
- die Bedienung von Informationsbedürfnissen außerhalb des SWR z.B. aus der ARD und von dritter Seite (Wissenschaft, Bildung, Hörer etc.) durch konventionelle und digitale Vermittlungswege und schließlich
- die Einschätzung der Repertoireeignung von Produktionen, insbesondere des Fernsehens, für die Bestückung von Spartenkanälen (ARTE, Ereigniskanal „Phoenix“, Kinderkanal u.a.).

Daneben sind Sonderaufgaben zu erledigen, die betriebsbedingt anfallen, aber auch Aufgaben, die durch die Einbindung des DuA-Fachbereichs in die Dokumentations- und Archivwelt ins allgemeine berufliche Umfeld oder im engeren durch die Zugehörigkeit des SWR zur ARD gehören. Hierunter ist eine fachliche Beteiligung in Arbeitsgruppen der ARD, aber auch die Mitarbeit und die Übernahme von Verantwortung in nationalen und internationalen Fachverbänden und Forschungsprojekten zu verstehen.

Besondere Kernaufgabe: Maßnahmen zur Erhaltung der kulturellen und historischen Überlieferung

In den mehr als 50 Jahren der Existenz des öffentlich-rechtlichen Rundfunks in Deutschland ist mit den überlieferten und archivierten audiovisuellen Materialien von Musik, Tondokumenten an gesprochenem Wort, Fernsehbeiträgen und Schriftgut aller Provenienz ein einmaliger Archivbestand entstanden, der die politische, kulturelle, gesellschaftliche, und nicht zuletzt auch die rundfunkpolitische und programmgeschichtliche Entwicklung in den Bundesländern - in unserem Falle also in Baden-Württemberg und Rheinland-Pfalz - und im Verbund der ARD-Rundfunkanstalten und des ZDF in der Bundesrepublik Deutschland einschließlich der vom ehemaligen DDR-Rundfunk produzierten audiovisuellen Überlieferung widerspiegelt.

Es gehört zu einer der Aufgaben des SWR-Archivs an allen Standorten, seine historisch wertvollen Bestände zu erhalten, zu sichern und verfügbar zu machen. Für das Programm liegt der Wert der kulturellen und historischen Überlieferung in der Möglichkeit, auf Dokumente oder gar ganze Sendungen zurückgreifen zu können, deren Inhalte aufgrund von Jahrestagen oder neuer Entwicklungen Aktualität gewinnen. Historisches Archivmaterial ist für Programmvorhaben potentiell stets auch aktuelles Material, das einem kurzen direkten Zugriff unterliegen muss. Im übrigen ist das über fast 50 Jahre archivierte Programmvermögen zunehmend auch für die ausserrundfunkmässige Zweitverwertung (Tonträger, Videokassetten) und als Quellenmaterial für Unterricht, Forschung und Wissenschaft von Interesse.

Aufgaben und Probleme der Digitalisierung

In seinem Roman „Auf der Suche nach der verlorenen Zeit" bemerkt der französische Schriftsteller Marcel Proust: „Das einzige, was sich in Frankreich nicht ändert, ist, dass sich in Frankreich stets etwas ändert." Ist es beim Begriff der Neuen Medien nicht ähnlich? Waren nicht Medien stets neu, zukünftig orientiert und zugleich durch Weiterentwicklungen zumindest in Teilen zum Zeitpunkt der jeweiligen Gegenwart bereits Vergangenheit, bereits präsente Zukunft? Könnte man also sagen, dass das einzige an den Medien statische Kriterium ihre ständige Wandlung sei? Unzweifelhaft ist die Phase der Digitalisierung, in der wir uns gegenwärtig befinden, ein tiefgehender Umbruch, ein Paradigmenwechsel mit technologischen, vor allem aber auch gesellschaftlichen und kulturellen Folgen solchen Ausmaßes, wie sie seit der Erfindung des Buchdrucks und der damit einher gegangenen „Demokratisierung" der Informationsverbreitung niemals mehr so einschneidend unsere Welt geprägt haben.

Wir alle, die wir Teil unserer Informationsgesellschaft und in einer Profession tätig sind, die der Informationsvermittlung dient, müssen zukunftsorientiert leben und denken, vor allem auch im Hinblick auf die Digitalisierung und ihre Folgen. Wir ahnen jedoch nur die Zukunft unseres Berufsfeldes und wissen über sie vielleicht nur wenig, wie sich im nachhinein herausstellen könnte. Wer hätte vor 50, 20, 15, 10 Jahren exakt vorhergesagt, was heute alles möglich ist und in welch rasanter Kürze wesentliche Entwicklungen, vor kurzem noch Utopien, Realität gewinnen würden? Wer von uns will mit Bestimmtheit sagen, was in 10, 20 oder 50 Jahren Stand der Entwicklung sein wird? Nicht allein das Zusammenwirken von uns bekannten Gesetzen, sondern eine Vielzahl von uns im Voraus nur schwer prognostizierbaren und beeinflussbaren rationalen, technologischen, empirischen, aber auch sozialen Möglichkeiten werden unsere Entscheidungen und unser Handeln beeinflussen und lenken, dessen Folgen dann wiederum erst in einer zukünftigen Gegenwart bewertet werden können.

Das zur jetzigen Zeit vordergründige Ziel aller Rundfunksysteme ist die Präsenz im Internet. Auch der SWR strebt diese Technologie neben den konventionellen Medien Hörfunk und Fernsehen als drittes „Standbein" des öffentlich-rechtlichen Rundfunks an. Wir in den Archiven müssen uns realistisch auf diese digitale Zukunft einstellen. Wir arbeiten intensiv daran, diese Zukunft nach bestem professionellem Wissen bereits in unserer Gegenwart anzupeilen. Auch diese zukünftigen Verbreitungswege der Hörfunk- und Fernsehprogramme verlangen die Notwendigkeit der Langzeitsicherung der uns anvertrauten wertvollen Bestände in digitaler Form.

Allein im Stuttgarter Hörfunkarchiv der SWR gelten 16 000 Stunden Eigenproduktion Musik und 70 000 Stunden Eigenproduktion Wort als historisch wertvoll und à la longue in analoger Qualität als potentiell gefährdet und daher digital zu sichern. Denn diese Dokumente sind Unikate, sie sind als einmalig im qualitativen wie quantitativen Sinne anzusehen. Eine Zerstörung von Dokumenten bedeutete unwiederbringlichen Verlust. Das Stuttgarter Fernseharchiv verwaltet 42 000 Stunden unikates produziertes Eigenmaterial. Allerdings: die komplette Digitalisierung dieser Bestände nach heutigen Preisen würde - die Personalkosten nicht eingerechnet - weit über 50 Millionen DM verschlingen - undenkbar, dies zu finanzieren. Und doch, wie ein Kollege aus dem WDR kürzlich sagte, „...die ARD ist zu arm, um sich den Verlust dieser werthaltigen Archivbestände leisten zu können“. In diesem Spagat zwischen dokumentarischer Pflicht und ökonomischer Realität leben wir heute.

Diese durchaus nicht neue Erkenntnis hat die Kernaufgaben im Bereich Dokumentation und Archive des SWR seit der Fusion schärfer definiert. Wir stehen vor der Herausforderung, eine Bewertung unserer Bestände auf einer zusätzlichen Ebene vornehmen zu müssen. Die Aufgabe der Bewertung der Dokumente hat durch den Digitalisierungsprozess eine neue Qualität angenommen, die, wie interne Diskussionen zeigen, durchaus geradezu zu philosophischen Überlegungen über unsere Aufgaben führen können. Was nicht eintreten darf, wäre ein schwankendes „Ja -Aber“, eine Haltung wie: „... es sieht fast so aus als seien die nächsten Jahre die Jahre des Ausstiegs aus dem Ausstieg aus dem Einstieg in den Ausstieg aus der Digitalisierung der Archivbestände, wenn man das so bestimmt und definitiv sagen darf.“ (analog zu Benedikt Erenz in der ZEIT 48/2000 über die Politik zur Kernenergie).

Aspekte der Qualifikation beim D/A Personal

All diese Überlegungen haben Konsequenzen auf die Personalstruktur und auf die notwendige Ausbildung des Personals. Wir arbeiten als Informationsvermittler in einem und für ein Medienunternehmen, dessen eigene Kernaufgabe die Informationsvermittlung ist. Die Dokumentare und Archive des SWR geben Informationen an die Redaktionen weiter, die diese so umsetzen müssen, dass sie - zur Hörerschaft transportiert - von dieser aufgenommen und verstanden und im Vertrauen auf ihre Zuverlässigkeit akzeptiert werden sollten.

Gründliche Recherche, Seriosität in der Auskunftserteilung, Gewissenhaftigkeit und Verantwortungsgefühl sind daher die Grundvoraussetzungen unserer Arbeit. Hierauf müssen sich die Redaktionen verlassen können. Was wir hierfür benötigen, ist der/die gut ausgebildete DokumentarIn und ArchivsachbearbeiterIn, der/die viel wissen muss in der Breite, möglichst viel in der Tiefe und über ein hohes Maß an Kombinationsfähigkeit verfügt. Wir berücksichtigen, wo immer es geht und in die Thematik passt, die individuell vorhandenen Spezialkenntnisse. Doch muss sich jeder Mitarbeiter in den Archiven des SWR zwangsläufig auch professionell mit Themen auseinandersetzen können, für die er oder sie nicht als Experten gelten können.

In der Summe des Individualwissens und der Bündelung und Vernetzung individueller Kompetenz repräsentiert die HA Dokumentation und Archive des SWR ein breites Angebot von Allgemeinbildung, von sozialer und kommunikativer Kompetenz und - seit der Fusion unabdingbar - von Fachkompetenz in der Informationstechnologie und im Bereich Technik und Produktion. Wir können uns keine so weitgehende Abhängigkeit von Experten der Datenverarbeitung und der Bereiche Technik und Produktion leisten, dass wir deren Handeln nicht mehr überprüfen, nachvollziehen und kompetent mitbestimmen können.

Durch „Kundenorientierung“ müssen unsere Mitarbeiter Professionalität und Kompetenz ausspielen und durch diese überzeugen. Denn dies ist die Chance unserer Profession in der Welt von sich leider mehr und mehr ausbreitenden Medien, die nach dem „Quick & Dirty"-Prinzip arbeiten. Dies gilt im übrigen auch für das Programm, dem wir dienen. Der öffentlich-rechtliche Rundfunk kann vorwiegend durch journalistische Solidität und Glaubwürdigkeit seine Zukunft sichern. Das bedeutet durchaus nicht den Verzicht auf leichte Unterhaltung als wesentlichen Teil des Programms, denn auch der öffentlich-rechtliche Rundfunk braucht Akzeptanz in Form von Quote.

Die Qualität bei der Erfüllung unserer Kernaufgaben ist dadurch auch ein Stück Zukunftssicherung unseres Berufsstandes. Sie leistet als Beitrag zu einem qualitätsorientierten öffentlich-rechtlichen Rundfunkprogramm aber auch einen Dienst an der Kultur in unserer Gesellschaft, ein Gegenangebot zu „Big Brother"-Offerten. Denn „nur wo Kultur ist, da lässt sich Schwachsinn aushalten" (August Everding).

Angelika Schütt-Hohenstein

Der Systematische Katalog der Bibliothek für Zeitgeschichte oder The Times They Are A-Changin`

Geschichte und Bedeutung des Systematischen Katalogs der Bibliothek für Zeitgeschichte

Der „Systematische Katalog der Bibliothek für Zeitgeschichte" (SyKa) wurde von 1939 bis 1996 geführt. Er basierte auf einer intensiven bibliothekarischen Inhaltserschließung der Literatur nach klassifikatorischen Gesichtspunkten. Die Systematik wurde Ende der 30er-Jahre eigens für die Weltkriegsbücherei entwickelt; sie wurde an das Sammelprofil und den Bestand dieser Bibliothek angepasst und sollte speziellen Ansprüchen der Literatursuche genügen. In den Jahren nach dem Zweiten Weltkrieg erfolgte der Ausbau der Systematik. Der an sich schon bemerkenswerte Bibliotheksbestand gewann durch den SyKa zusätzlich an Bedeutung. Letztlich bewirkte die Qualität des Bestandes, verbunden mit der Singularität des Sachkatalogs, dass die Bibliothek für Zeitgeschichte überregional als wissenschaftliche Spezialbibliothek Anerkennung erlangte.

Erst etliche Jahre nach Sammlungsbeginn setzte die inhaltliche Erschließung des gesammelten Schrifttums ein. Schritt für Schritt entstand daraus der erste bzw. alte Sachkatalog, der nach Sachgruppen geordnet war und in den 20er und 30er-Jahren als Erschließungsinstrument diente. Eine Sachgruppenübersicht des alten Katalogs ist leider nicht überliefert. Der alte Sachgruppenkatalog genügte angesichts der Ausweitung der Sammelschwerpunkte nicht mehr, so dass man sich zu Beginn der 30er-Jahre entschied, einen neuen Sachkatalog anzulegen. Es wurde ein umfangreiches und differenziertes Klassifikationssystem entwickelt, das ausschließlich auf die bibliothekarische Inhaltserschließung in der Stuttgarter Weltkriegsbücherei zugeschnitten war. Die Verzeichnung im neuen Systematischen Katalog begann 1939. Der alte Katalog wurde aufgelöst, indem die Katalogkarten in den neuen Katalog eingelegt wurden.

Zwar ist der SyKa insgesamt das Werk einer ganzen Reihe von Bibliothekaren, die Anlage des Klassifikations- und Notationssystems muss allerdings ausschließlich als das Werk des Bibliothekars Max Gunzenhäuser gewürdigt werden. Max Gunzenhäuser war von 1921 bis 1977 in der Weltkriegsbücherei bzw. Bibliothek für Zeitgeschichte tätig. Er erwarb in der noch jungen Bibliothek genaueste Bestandskenntnisse, war an der Bestimmung des Sammelprofils beteiligt und wirkte bereits am Aufbau des alten Sachkatalogs mit. Auf dieser Grundlage entwickelte er den SyKa. Seine Veröffentlichungen über Bibliothekskataloge zeigen deutlich, wie er Theorie und Praxis der Katalogführung miteinander zu kombinieren suchte, um für die Bibliothek für Zeitgeschichte einen möglichst optimalen spezifischen Sachkatalog in Zettelform zu entwickeln und zu pflegen[454].

---

[454] Max Gunzenhäuser: Hilfsmittel der Literaturordnung in Zettelkatalogen. Ein rationales Leitkartensystem. In: Nachrichten für Dokumentation. Korrespondenzblatt für Technik und Wissenschaft, Wirtschaft und Vewaltung. 2 (1951), 2, S. 72-74. - Ders.: Einheitliches Format und rationelle Textanordnung auf Schrifttumskarten. Zugleich ein Beitrag zu koordinierter Formal- und Sachkatalogisierung. In: Ebd. 6 (1955), 3, S. 137-140.

Die Grundsätze der hausspezifischen Sachkatalogisierung lassen sich folgendermaßen zusammenfassen: Wie in Bibliotheken allgemein üblich, wurden im SyKa Bücher und Zeitschriften verzeichnet. Darüber hinaus wurde in Auswahl unselbständiges Schrifttum aufgenommen, insbesondere Aufsätze aus Zeitschriften, vereinzelt Aufsätze aus Sammelwerken und zeitweise sogar Kapitel aus Monographien sowie versteckte Bibliographien. Dieser auch für eine Spezialbibliothek hohe Anspruch an den Umfang der Sachkatalogisierung wurde jedoch über die Jahrzehnte recht unterschiedlich erfüllt, das Hauptgewicht jedenfalls wurde durchgehend auf die Inhaltserschließung von Monographien und Zeitschriftenaufsätzen gelegt.

Der SyKa bietet die Möglichkeit, Literatur zu historischen Fragen des 20. Jahrhunderts ausgesprochen differenziert zu ermitteln. Die Bibliothek für Zeitgeschichte sammelte (und sammelt bis heute) sehr umfangreich und mit internationaler Ausrichtung Literatur über die beiden Weltkriege, eingeschlossen die nationale und internationale Geschichte der Kriegsfolgen. Zu den besonderen Sammelschwerpunkten gehört darüber hinaus die Geschichte sämtlicher militärischer Auseinandersetzungen, die seit 1914 weltweit stattfanden, seien es nun Bürgerkriege oder zwischenstaatliche militärische Konflikte. Das Angebot an Büchern, Broschüren und Zeitschriften aus dem Bestand der Bibliothek zur Geschichte der Kriege des 20. Jahrhunderts muss wohl als einzigartig bezeichnet werden. Allerdings sollte der Benutzer seine Erwartungen an den Bibliotheksbestand keinesfalls auf die Kriegsgeschichte bzw. militärische Geschichte beschränken. Internationale Beziehungen und Organisationen, Außenpolitik, außenpolitische Beziehungen und die Innenpolitik einzelner Staaten sowie die Wirtschafts- und Sozialgeschichte gehören ebenso zum Sammelgebiet wie Militärbündnisse und die Sicherheits- und Militärpolitik einzelner Staaten. Die Geschichte des 19. Jahrhunderts wurde zudem als Sammelgebiet eine Zeitlang insofern gepflegt, als Literatur zur Militärgeschichte ab ca. 1866 erworben und verzeichnet wurde. Die Bibliothek für Zeitgeschichte zeichnet sich dadurch aus, dass sie äußerst umfangreich Literatur zur nationalen und internationalen Geschichte seit Beginn des Ersten Weltkriegs sammelt und zur regionalen wie überregionalen Benutzung anbietet. Mit ihrem Gesamtbestand von inzwischen über 300.000 Bänden gilt sie als einmalige Sammlung zur Geschichte und Politik des 20. Jahrhunderts. Durch den SyKa gewann diese Sammlung in den Jahrzehnten nach dem Zweiten Weltkrieg zusätzlich an Bedeutung.

Schon in den 20er-Jahren wurden die Neuerwerbungen nicht nur für die Benutzung vor Ort, sondern auch für die überregionale Literaturversorgung katalogisiert. Die Weltkriegsbücherei war in den deutschen Leihverkehr einbezogen und erlaubte Fernleihbestellungen. Darüber hinaus schuf sie durch die Veröffentlichung sowohl von systematisch geordneten Neuerwerbungslisten[455] als auch von themenbezogenen Literaturzusammenstellungen[456]

- Ders.: Der systematische Katalog der Weltkriegsbücherei. Entwicklung und gegenwärtiger Stand. In: Bücherschau der Weltkriegsbücherei 27 (1955), 1/4, S. 262-271. - Ders.: Die Inhaltsangabe für den Sachkatalog. In: Dokumentation - Fachbibliothek - Werksbücherei. Zeitschrift für technische Archive, Fachbibliotheken, Betriebs- und Volksbüchereien. 11 (1963), 4, S. 141-145. - Ders.: Ein rationales Leitkarten-System für den Sachkatalog. In: Ebd.12 (1964), 4, S. 129-130. - Ders.: Der Systematische Katalog der BfZ/WKB. In: 50 Jahre Bibliothek für Zeitgeschichte Weltkriegsbücherei Stuttgart. Frankfurt/M. 1965. S. 30-60. - Ders.: Einleitung zu den gedruckten Ausgaben des Alphabetischen und Systematischen Katalogs der Bibliothek für Zeitgeschichte. Boston, Mass. 1968. Vol. 1, S. XIII-XVII.

455 Die Zugangsverzeichnisse ordneten die akzessionierten Neuerwerbungen der Bibliothek nach inhaltlichen Kriterien, sie waren in Form eines gedruckten Katalogs eine Teilausgabe des systematisch angelegten Sachkatalogs und wurden als Periodikum herausgegeben. Ab 1924 erschienen die Zugangsverzeichnisse mit dem Titel „Berichte der Weltkriegsbücherei", ab 1934 „Neuerwerbungen der Weltkriegsbücherei", von 1960 bis

quasi gedruckte Katalogauszüge und damit ortsunabhängige bzw. überregionale Recherchemöglichkeiten. Die Weltkriegsbücherei bzw. die Bibliothek für Zeitgeschichte verstand ihre Katalogausgaben immer auch als Angebot für eine überregionale Nutzung ihrer Bibliotheksbestände. In diesem Zusammenhang ist auf die gedruckten Ausgaben sowohl des Alphabetischen als auch des Systematischen Katalogs aus dem Jahre 1968 hinzuweisen, verlegt bei G. K. Hall in Boston[457]. Die gedruckten Gesamtausgaben beider Bibliothekskataloge erlaubten eine Literaturrecherche, die unabhängig vom Stuttgarter Standort durchzuführen war. Wieder aufgegriffen wird das vom Standort unabhängige Rechercheangebot mit der Mikrofichesammlung, die 2001 von K. G. Saur verlegt wurde[458]. Sie hat gegenüber sämtlichen gedruckten Katalogen der Bibliothek für Zeitgeschichte zweifelsohne den Vorteil, ein abgeschlossenes Katalogwerk mit ca. 675.000 Katalogkarten anzubieten.

Der in konventioneller Weise geführte Systematische (Zettel-)Katalog der Bibliothek für Zeitgeschichte stellt eine wirkliche Insellösung dar. Diese wurde seit Ende der 80er-Jahre durch die EDV-gestützten Bibliotheksverbünde zunehmend in Frage gestellt. Die letzten Erschließungsarbeiten nach der einstmals eigens für die Bibliothek für Zeitgeschichte entwickelten Systematik wurden 1996 vorgenommen. Fast sechs Jahrzehnte hatten die Erschließungsgrundsätze des SyKa ihre Gültigkeit. Doch die Zeitläufte bewirkten, dass diese Grundsätze aufgegeben und neue Methoden der Bestandserschließung übernommen werden mussten. Die elektronisch unterstützte Verzeichnung und Recherche von Büchern und Zeitschriften schuf ein völlig verändertes Umfeld und bewirkte in der Bibliothek für Zeitgeschichte die Ablösung sowohl des Zettelkatalogs als auch der Jahresbibliographie.

Eine grundlegende Überarbeitung der Begrifflichkeit des SyKa hätte aufgrund der Entwicklungen der Wissenschaftsfächer Zeitgeschichte und Politik ohnehin erfolgen müssen. Trotz aller Jahrzehnte währenden Katalogpflege stand eine Angleichung an die veränderte Terminologie der Fachwissenschaften noch aus. Darüber hinaus konnten die weltpolitischen Umbrüche nach 1989/90 durch die starre und auch begrenzte Katalogsystematik insbesondere im Länderteil nur unzureichend erfasst werden. Der Aufbau elektronischer Bibliothekskataloge, die über das Internet weltweite Online-Recherchen ermöglichen, lieferte die letztlich überzeugenden Gründe, die zum Abbruch des „Systematischen (Zettel-)Katalogs der Bibliothek für Zeitgeschichte" führten.

Der Aufbau des Systematischen Katalogs der Bibliothek für Zeitgeschichte

Der Aufbau des SyKa, seine hierarchischen Unterteilungen, Systemstellen und Notationen sind von ganz eigener Art und speziell auf die Sammeltätigkeit der Spezialbibliothek zugeschnitten. Zurecht kann man den SyKa als ein ganzes Katalogwerk bezeichnen, das auf einer hauseigenen bibliothekarischen Katalogphilosophie basiert. Grundsätzlich handelt es

---

1997 „Jahresbibliographie der Bibliothek für Zeitgeschichte", womit das Erscheinen eingestellt wurde.

456 In den 30er-Jahren publizierte man die themenbezogenen Literaturzusammenstellungen als Periodikum mit dem Titel „Bibliographische Vierteljahrshefte der Weltkriegsbücherei". Nach dem Zweiten Weltkrieg wurde diese Tradition in Form einer Schriftenreihe fortgesetzt; die „Schriften der Bibliothek für Zeitgeschichte" erschienen in 28 Bänden von 1962 bis 1990.

457 Alphabetischer Katalog der Bibliothek für Zeitgeschichte, Stuttgart. Boston, Mass.: Hall 1968. Vol. 1 - 8; Systematischer Katalog der Bibliothek für Zeitgeschichte, Stuttgart. Boston, Mass.: Hall 1968. Vol. 1 - 11.

458 Systematischer Katalog der Bibliothek für Zeitgeschichte, Stuttgart. Mikrofiche-Edition mit Begleitband. Herausgegeben von der Bibliothek für Zeitgeschichte in der Württembergischen Landesbibliothek. Bearbeitet von Angelika Schütt-Hohenstein. München: Saur 2001.

sich um einen standortfreien und nach klassifikatorischen Gesichtspunkten aufgebauten Sachkatalog, in dem Verfasserschriften, Sammelwerke, Sammelbände, Serien, Zeitschriften, Jahrbücher und in Auswahl auch unselbständige Literatur, überwiegend Zeitschriftenaufsätze, verzeichnet sind.

Der Katalog gliedert sich in drei Hauptteile: den Allgemeinen Sachteil, den Geschichtsteil und den Länderteil. Jeder der drei Hauptteile hat eine spezifische Gliederung und ein eigenes Notationssystem. Die Hauptteile stehen allerdings nicht unverbunden nebeneinander, sondern sind dadurch, dass Systemstellen und Notationen des Allgemeinen Sachteils und des Geschichtsteils im Länderteil gespiegelt werden, miteinander verknüpft. Die obersten Hierarchieebenen haben als Notationen Großbuchstaben mit folgender Zuordnung

– Allgemeiner Sachteil	B - J
– Geschichtsteil	K
– Länderteil	L

Entsprechend der Gliederung in die drei Hauptteile erfolgt die Inhaltserschließung in der ersten Stufe nach den Kriterien Sache, Zeit und/oder Raum. Die weitergehende inhaltliche Erschließung richtet sich nach der bis ins Detail festgelegten Systematik. Innerhalb einzelner Systemstellen sind zusätzlich Schlagwörter vergeben, womit an diesen bestimmten Stellen eine zweite Sacherschließungskomponente aufgenommen wird.

In allen Katalogteilen wird jede Systemstelle von einer Notation und einer verbalen Klassenbeschreibung gekennzeichnet, beides findet sich auf den Leitkarten. Die Notationen sind alphanumerisch zusammengesetzt. Die oben angeführten Großbuchstaben B bis J des Allgemeinen Sachteils stehen für sog. Lebens- oder Themenbereiche. Die weitere Unterteilung folgt den Prinzipien der Dezimalklassifikation und gliedert numerisch von z.B. F 000 bis F 999. Die verbale Klassenbeschreibung erleichtert dem Benutzer, der das Klassifikationssystem nicht im Detail beherrscht, die Orientierung innerhalb einer Notationsgruppe. Darüber hinaus ermöglicht die verbale Klassenbeschreibung als Registereintrag den unmittelbaren Zugang zum gesuchten Sachgebiet. Jede Systemstelle kann wiederum in sich je nach Literaturaufkommen vielfältig untergliedert sein. Untergliederungen wurden vorgenommen nach sachlichen, zeitlichen und räumlichen Gesichtspunkten oder auch formalen Gesichtspunkten, jeweils gekennzeichnet mit Leitkarten.

Im Allgemeinen Sachteil ist die Literatur primär sachorientierten Themenbereichen zugeordnet, d.h. zeitliche und räumliche Aspekte des Literaturinhalts sind für die Erschließung in diesem Katalogteil allenfalls nachgeordnet. Solche sachorientierten Themenbereiche sind z.B. Bibliotheken und Institute, politische Grundbegriffe, allgemeine politische Richtungen, Kriegsrechtsfragen sowie allgemeine Aspekte zu Außenpolitik, Militär einschließlich Waffentechnik, Wirtschaft, Gesellschaft und Geistesleben. Für das grundsätzliche Verständnis des Klassifikationsschemas nicht nur des Allgemeinen Sachteils, sondern des SyKa insgesamt wird darauf hingewiesen, dass die Gliederung des Allgemeinen Sachteils im Länderteil bei jedem Land bzw. jeder Region wiederholt wird und insofern der Allgemeine Sachteil im Sachteil eines jeden Landes/Staates gespiegelt wird.

Im Geschichtsteil werden unter der Notationsgruppe K Ereignisse und Zusammenhänge der Weltgeschichte erfasst. Auf der Grundlage der politischen und militärischen Geschichte werden die Jahrhunderte in historische Abschnitte gegliedert. Diese werden zu Systemstellen erster Ordnung, sind mit den Notationen K 1 bis K 6 gekennzeichnet und werden wiederum nach sachlichen, chronologischen und geographischen oder auch formalen Geschichtspunkten untergliedert. Die inhaltliche Zuordnung der Literatur zu K 1 bis K 6 erfolgt somit primär nach zeitlichen bzw. (welt-)historischen Gesichtspunkten. Entsprechend dem Profil der Bibliothek für Zeitgeschichte liegt der Schwerpunkt sowohl in der Erwerbung als auch in der Literaturverzeichnung auf der Geschichte des 20. Jahrhunderts. Im Katalog ist dadurch das 20. Jahrhundert ungleich differenzierter und umfangreicher untergliedert als frühere Jahrhunderte. Die Anzahl der Systemstellen für die Weltgeschichte ab 1914 und die Menge der verzeichneten Literatur für die Zeit nach Beginn des Ersten Weltkriegs zeigen deutlich, dass die Arbeit der Bibliothek für Zeitgeschichte sich auf den Zeitraum ab 1914 konzentriert.

So wie sich der Allgemeine Sachteil mit seinen Untergliederungen in der Systematik eines jeden Landes/Staates spiegelt, spiegelt sich auch der (Welt-)Geschichtsteil innerhalb des Geschichtsteils eines jeden Landes/Staates. Unter der Geschichte eines Landes werden Ereignisse und Zusammenhänge der jeweiligen Nationalgeschichte verzeichnet. Die Nationalgeschichte wird in Spiegelung des (Welt-)Geschichtsteils periodisiert und die Literatur wird ebenfalls unter den Notationen K 0 bis K 6 verzeichnet. Dabei stehen z.B. K 0 wiederum für die Allgemeine Geschichte/Geschichtswissenschaft, K 3 für die Zeit 1914 - 1918 und K 6 für die Zeit nach 1945. Wenn nationale historische Ereignisse innerhalb des vorgegebenen Schemas herausgehoben werden sollen, erhalten sie im Geschichtsteil des Landes/Staates innerhalb einer Epoche eine eigene Systemstelle bzw. Leitkarte.

Jeder Krieg, gleichgültig ob Weltkrieg, Begrenzter Krieg oder Bürgerkrieg, wird im SyKa in der Regel nicht der National- sondern der Weltgeschichte zugeordnet und mit einer eigenen Systemstelle im (Welt-)Geschichtsteil verzeichnet, z.B. der Erste Weltkrieg mit allen seinen Aspekten unter K 3, der Spanische Bürgerkrieg unter K 4 F 473 oder der Jugoslawienkrieg unter K 6 F 660. Der Erste Weltkrieg als K 3 und der Zweite Weltkrieg als K 5 nehmen im Geschichtsteil insofern Sonderstellungen ein, als sie jeweils wie eine Epoche des 20. Jahrhunderts behandelt und einer Systemstelle erster Ordnung zugeordnet werden. Die Zwischenkriegszeit (= K 4) und die Zeit nach dem Zweiten Weltkrieg (= K 6) als historische Abschnitte des 20. Jahrhunderts, die nicht ausschließlich von einem Krieg bestimmt sind, werden unmittelbar in politische Geschichte unter der Notation E und Kriegsgeschichte unter der Notation F unterteilt.

Bezieht sich der Inhalt eines Buches primär auf eine Region oder ein Land, dann wird das Buch im Länderteil verzeichnet. Anders ausgedrückt: Im Länderteil wird unter der Notationsgruppe L die primär räumlich gebundene Literatur verzeichnet. Literatur über die Innen- und Außenpolitik, das Wehrwesen, die Gesellschaft und Wirtschaft oder die Geschichte eines Landes wird weder im Allgemeinen Sachteil noch im Geschichtsteil, sondern im Länderteil systematisiert. Richtet sich also das Interesse auf die Politik und Geschichte eines bestimmten Landes im 20. Jahrhundert, dann erfolgt die Literatursuche primär im Länderteil des SyKa. Der Länderteil wird in der ersten Ordnungsstufe nach den fünf Kontinenten untergliedert, die nächste Untergliederung erfolgt innerhalb eines Kontinents nach Regionen und Ländern. Im Länderteil ist die umfangreichste und auch wichtigste Unterteilung die eines Kontinents in seine Länder bzw. Staaten. Innerhalb eines Kontinents sind die Länder alphabetisch geordnet, auch die Notationen des Länderteils sind alphanumerische Kombinationen.

Für konkrete Fragestellungen oder Katalogrecherchen, die ohne genaue Kenntnis der Systematik erfolgen, bietet der SyKa in einem gesonderten Teil vier alphabetische Verzeichnisse: ein Sachregister, ein Körperschaftsregister, ein Geographisches Register und ein Personenregister. In der Regel werden in allen vier Registern sowohl die verbalen Klassenbeschreibungen als auch die einzeln vergebenen Schlagwörter für die Eintragungen genutzt. Die Registereintragungen sind mit einer oder mehreren Notationen verknüpft, womit auf die eine Systemstelle oder auf mehrere Systemstellen verwiesen wird, die Literatur zum gesuchten Sachgebiet enthalten.

Im SyKa beginnt jede Systemstelle mit einer Leitkarte, die über die Katalogkarten hinausragt. Auf der Leitkarte befinden sich die zwei Bezeichnungen für die betreffende Systemstelle - die Notation und die verbale Klassenbeschreibung. Damit hat jede Systemstelle zwei Bezeichnungen, die sich allerdings in ihrer Gestaltung und Zusammensetzung grundsätzlich unterscheiden. Die Notation als Kombination aus Buchstaben und Zahlen gibt an, wo die Systemstelle innerhalb des hierarchisch angelegten Katalogs konkret anzusiedeln ist. Bei der Literaturrecherche gibt die Zusammensetzung der Notation Auskunft darüber, wo eine bestimmte Systemstelle innerhalb der drei Hauptteile des Systematischen Katalogs tatsächlich zu finden ist. Die verbale Klassenbeschreibung dagegen fasst die inhaltliche Bestimmung einer Systemstelle in Worte.

Die einzelne Katalogkarte des SyKa resultiert zunächst aus der Titelaufnahme für den alphabetischen Katalog. Auf der Katalogkarte sind die Elemente notiert, die die formale Beschreibung eines Buches oder Aufsatzes umfassen. Zu diesen Elementen gehören der Autorenname, der Titel mit Untertitel, die Auflage, der Erscheinungsort, der Verlag, das Erscheinungsjahr, die Seitenzahl sowie gegebenenfalls der Titel einer Serie oder der Zeitschriftentitel mit Jahrgangsvermerk. Für die alphabetische Einordnung sind die Ordnungsmerkmale gekennzeichnet. Darüber hinaus enthält der überwiegende Teil der Katalogkarten der Bibliothek für Zeitgeschichte Angaben zur inhaltlichen Erschließung der Literatur. In abgekürzter Form ist angegeben, welchen Systemstellen das Buch oder der Aufsatz zugeordnet wurde. Die Systemstellen sind wie Fußnoten unterhalb der Titelbeschreibung aufgelistet. Die von Fall zu Fall vergebenen Schlagwörter sind in der linken oberen Ecke vermerkt. Zur Vervollständigung der Katalogeintragung ist die Signatur vermerkt, die als Standortnummer für die Bestellung der Bücher und Zeitschriftenbände unerlässlich ist. Die Signatur befindet sich immer auf der rechten oberen Ecke einer Katalogkarte.

Die Ausleihe der Bestände der Bibliothek für Zeitgeschichte erfolgt über die Württembergische Landesbibliothek. Für Benutzer der Württembergischen Landesbibliothek wird über die Homepage ein Online-Ausleihsystem angeboten, das u.a. die Selbstbedienungsfunktionen zur Literaturbestellung bereithält. Bestellungen per Fernleihschein über den nationalen und internationalen Leihverkehr sind an die Württembergische Landesbibliothek zu richten, die das Bibliothekssigel 24 hat. Über die Homepage der Württembergischen Landesbibliothek, die Adresse lautet www.wlb-stuttgart.de, erhält man zudem Informationen über Schnelllieferdienste, die kostenpflichtig die direkte Bestellung und Lieferung der gewünschten Literatur ermöglichen. So bietet die Bibliothek für Zeitgeschichte in der Württembergischen Landesbibliothek auch über SUBITO, dem Internet-Lieferdienst der Bibliotheken, die Ausleihe von Aufsätzen und Büchern an.

Fazit und Perspektiven

Die Kooperation zwischen der Bibliothek für Zeitgeschichte und der Württembergischen Landesbibliothek entwickelte sich von 1944/45 bis 1999 in einem Ausmaß, wie man es in der unmittelbaren Nachkriegszeit sicherlich nicht erwarten konnte. Dabei wurde die Kooperation von Seiten der Bibliothek für Zeitgeschichte wohl überlegt auf immer mehr bibliothekarische Arbeitsbereiche ausgeweitet. Die zunehmend engere Zusammenarbeit beider Bibliotheken war für die Bibliothek für Zeitgeschichte angesichts ihrer personellen und finanziellen Spielräume geradezu überlebensnotwendig.

Der Prozess der Kooperation wurde durch die Bibliotheksautomatisierung zusätzlich beschleunigt, denn den großen Aufwand für die unverzichtbare dv-technische Ausrüstung konnte sich die kleine, gleichwohl selbständige Spezialbibliothek nicht leisten. Darüber hinaus brachte die Bibliotheksautomatisierung Kooperationen neuer Qualität mit sich. Bedingt durch die elektronische Datenverarbeitung wurde die bibliothekarische Medienbearbeitung und Medienbereitstellung zunehmend über Verbünde oder Kooperationen vielfältigster Art durchgeführt. So entstand ein völlig verändertes bibliothekarisches Umfeld, in dem Speziallösungen oder gar Innovationen einzelner kleiner Institutionen angesichts der hohen Entwicklungs- und Betriebskosten kaum mehr realisierbar waren.

Bibliothekskooperationen haben allerdings, was das Beispiel der Bibliothek für Zeitgeschichte auch deutlich macht, immer ihre zwei Seiten. Für die einzelne Bibliothek haben sie nämlich sowohl negative als auch positive Aspekte. So ist für die Bibliothek für Zeitgeschichte zunächst sicherlich als Verlust zu verbuchen, dass sie bestimmte Eigenentwicklungen, z.B. ihren SyKa, nicht weiterführen konnte. Als Gewinn ist dagegen zu verbuchen, dass sie bestimmte notwendige Dienstleistung nur über die Kooperation mit der Württembergischen Landesbibliothek anbieten konnte und auch ausschließlich über Kooperationen mit anderen Bibliotheken den Anschluss an Entwicklungen des wissenschaftlichen Bibliothekswesens halten konnte.

Die Bibliothek für Zeitgeschichte geriet damit in die Situation, die grundsätzlich jede noch so notwendige Kooperation unter Bibliotheken mit sich bringt: Eigenentwicklungen und spezifische Traditionen können nur noch bedingt oder gar nicht mehr pepflegt werden. Aber jede Bibliothekskooperation bietet eben auch Chancen, selbst wenn dafür Traditionsbrüche vollzogen werden müssen. So gab die Bibliothek für Zeitgeschichte mit dem hauseigenen SyKa einerseits ein Stück Eigenständigkeit und Unverwechselbarkeit auf, andererseits erhielt sie durch die kooperative Sacherschließung die Chance, im Verbund mit anderen wissenschaftlichen Bibliotheken von nationalen Dienstleistungen zu profitieren und gleichzeitig an diesen nationalen Dienstleistungen mitzuwirken. Darin war darüber hinaus die Chance enthalten, in einer durch Verbünde, OPACs und Internet inzwischen völlig veränderten Informationsstruktur und damit auch Bibliotheksstruktur die hauseigenen Bestandsdaten ohne eigene aufwendige Entwicklungsarbeiten in eine Online-Vernetzung einzubringen und für andere unmittelbar, schnell und umfangreich abrufbar und nutzbar zu machen. Ohne die gesuchte Kooperation hätte die Bibliothek für Zeitgeschichte diese notwendige Entwicklung nicht bewältigen können.

Mit der Integration im Jahr 2000 ist für die Bibliothek für Zeitgeschichte die Frage der Kooperationen keinesfalls abgeschlossen. Über die Württembergische Landesbibliothek ist die Bibliothek für Zeitgeschichte inzwischen ein fester Bestandteil lokaler, regionaler und nationaler Bibliothekskooperationen. In Stuttgart ist sie Teil des BISS (Bibliotheksinformationssystem Stuttgart) und bietet ihre Katalogdaten im StOPAC (Stuttgarter OPAC) an. Auf lokaler Ebene wird sich zudem in naher Zukunft eine noch engere Zusammenarbeit für die Bereiche Erwerbung und Benutzung ergeben. Als regionale Kooperationen sind neben dem Südwestdeutschen Bibliotheksverbund inzwischen ReDI (Regionale Datenbank-Information Baden-Württemberg) und künftig die Digitale Bibliothek Baden-Württemberg erwähnenswert. National tritt neben die überregionale Literaturversorung der DFG beispielsweise die Teilnahme an SUBITO und an der EZB (Elektronische Zeitschriftenbibliothek). Die Bibliothekspolitik der Länder und des Bundes der nächsten Jahre wird Bibliothekskooperationen unterstützen, ja aus finanziellen Erwägungen heraus geradezu fordern.

Die DFG unterstützt ebenfalls den Ausbau der Bibliothekskooperation, was man derzeitig an der Förderung zum Aufbau virtueller Fachbibliotheken verfolgen kann. Die Bibliothek für Zeitgeschichte wird sich darum auch als integraler Bestandteil der Württembergischen Landesbibliothek mit Fragen der Kooperation befassen und in diesen Zusammenhängen möglicherweise die jetzige Sacherschließung wiederum an neuere Entwicklungen anpassen müssen.

Ludwig Delp

Quo vadis Buchwissenschaft

Das Buch ist der einzig dauerhafte, immer, überall, energiefrei und apparatelos, gegenüber jedermann zuverlässig aussagebereite materialisierte Mittler geistiger Werte in dieser Welt, dessen Benutzer aktiv Zeitpunkt, Ort und Intensität seiner Wirkung bestimmt.[459] Das gedruckte Buch besitzt die Merkmale der Identität der Auflage, ist konservander Natur und ein kommerzieller Gegenstand, der den Marktgesetzen unterliegt.[460] Nicht zuletzt setzt das Buch Maßstäbe durch ausgewogene Gestaltung von Satz, Druck und Einband bis hin zum Werk der Buchkunst, erfüllt also auch ästhetische Funktionen.[461]

Es liegt nahe, die außergewöhnlichen Dimensionen des Buches als Aussage seines Autors, als Medium, als gewerbliches, gegebenenfalls auch künstlerisches Erzeugnis, als Gegenstand des Handels- und Rechtsverkehrs, als Beobachtungsgegenstand von Naturwissenschaft und Gesellschaftswissenschaften auf seine Grundlagen zu untersuchen, dadurch wissenschaftliche Erkenntnisse zu sammeln und mit deren Hilfe dem Phänomen „Buch" sichere Stabilität zu geben.

Damit hatten wie 1950 die Notwendigkeit buchwissenschaftlicher Tätigkeit, gleichzeitig aber auch die Notwendigkeit der Pluralform „Buchwissenschaften" begründet.[462] Die seitdem verstrichenen fünf Jahrzehnte haben an unseren Feststellungen nichts geändert, obgleich sich in der Zwischenzeit damals ungeahnte Entwicklungen im Medienbereich vollzogen haben, die zwar den publizistischen Wirkungskreis des Buches eingeengt, dem Nutzer weitere Kommunikationswege gewiesen, aber buchwissenschaftliche Dokumentation und Information noch näher für das geistige Leben existenznotwendig erkennbar gemacht haben. Auch wenn das Buch in bestimmten Sparten Rezessionen auf die Dauer hinnehmen muss, wird immer noch hinreichend Raum und notwendige Wirkung für unser Medium bestehen. Die Neuen Medien haben die Nachfrage eher belebt als unterdrückt;[463] die Statistik der Buchproduktion nennt weltweit steigende Jahresergebnisse.[464]

Mehr als Kanonen habe das Buch die Welt verändert, lehrt ein bekannter Spruch. Dem nachzugehen macht sich die Buchwirkungsforschung anheischig[465]. Die materiellen Voraussetzungen der deutschen Buchproduktion, nicht minder die Kreditpolitik im Verlagswesen nach der Währungsreform waren für die deutsche Nachkriegsbuchwirtschaft nach WW

---

459 Delp, Ludwig: Buch und Wissenschaften. In: Das Buch in Praxis und Wissenschaft. Vierzig Jahre Deutsches Bucharchiv München. Eine Festschrift. Von Peter Vodosek (Hrsg.), S. 776.

460 Schmidt, Wieland: Vom Wesen des Buches. In: Gutenberg-Jahrbuch 1952, S. 197.

461 Delp, Ludwig: Fachvortrag in: Separatdruck zu Band 57 der Buchwissenschaftlichen Beiträge, 8. 24.

462 Vgl. Delp Ludwig: Geleitwort zur 1. Folge der Buchwissenschaftlichen Beiträge. München 1950, S. IV f.

463 Buch und Buchhandel in Zahlen 2000. Börsenverein des Deutschen Buchhandels e.V. (Hrsg.), Frankfurt/Main 2000, S. 31.

464 W. Grebe: Stichwort „Buch". In: Lexikon des gesamten Buchwesens – LGB - Band I, S. 509.

465 Vgl. u.a. Kühnel, Walter: Die Entdeckung des Lesers. Wege der Literatur und Kommunikationswissenschaft zu einer Buchwirkungsforschung. In: Bertelsmann Briefe, Heft 91, Juli 1977, S. 13. Neuerdings Kerlen, Dietrich: Buchwirkungsforschung - Vermessung eines Forschungsfeldes. In: Buchwissenschaft und Buchwirkungsforschung. VIII. Leipziger Hochschultage für Medien und Kommunikation, von Dietrich Kerlen und Inka Kirste (Hrsg.). Leipzig 2000, S. 99 ff.

II von erheblicher wirtschaftlicher Bedeutung[466] und warfen wesentliche volks- und weltwirtschaftliche Fragen auf. Die Existenzsicherung für Künstler und Publizisten wurde mit der Künstlersozialversicherung angestrebt, weil der geistige Schaffensprozess nicht immer ein ausreichendes Äquivalent für die materielle Schaffenskraft bedeute - ein sozialpolitisches, aber auch ein kultursoziologisches, also auch hier ein wissenschaftlich deutbares Problem. Versuche verwandter Art beschäftigen Politiker seit Jahrzehnten, um das noch kapitalistisch anmutende Urheberrecht moderneren Anschauungen anzupassen - hier nun die rechtswissenschaftliche Seite des Buchwesens. Der altbewährten Stagma / GEMA sind zahlreiche Verwertungsgesellschaften zur Wahrnehmung von Urheberrechtsteilen hinzugewachsen, deren Tätigkeiten zur Sozialisierung des Individualrechts der Urheber überleiten könnten. Eine immer wieder aufflammende Erörterung einer Kulturabgabe[467] zielt - nolens volens - in die gleiche Richtung. Das wissenschaftliche Arbeitsgebiet des Verfassers findet rings um das Buch vielfältige Ergänzungen durch weitere Wissenschaftsgebiete, in Sonderheit etwa durch die Geschichts-, Literatur-, sonstige Geistes- und Naturwissenschaften.

Ist eigentlich kaum eine Wissenschaft vorstellbar, die sich nicht mit der Schaffung, der Vermittlung oder der Rezeption geistiger Aussagen auseinandersetzen kann) so ist auch die Vielzahl der Facetten beachtlich, die das Thema „Buch- und Zeitschriftenwesen“ für die wissenschaftliche Forschung bereithält. Vom Autor bis zum Leser durchläuft die schließlich im Buch niedergeschlagene Aussage immer neue Metamorphosen.

Dem Bibliothekswissenschaftler sagen wir mit diesen Reminiszenzen, eingedenk der seit langem erfolgreich tätigen bibliothekswissenschaftlichen Unternehmungen, nichts Neues. Demgegenüber hinken Buchhandel und Verlag mit der Bejahung unabhängiger Buchwissenschaften hinterher. Zwar hat der Börsenverein in den zwanziger Jahren den Lehrstuhl für Buchhandelsbetriebslehre in Leipzig gestiftet, der unter Gerhard Menz bald hohes Ansehen gewann, aber Menz in der ersten Nachkriegszeit Lehrauftrag und Lebensatem nahm. Ungeachtet erneut einsetzender privater Initiativen, aus denen z.B. das Deutsche Bucharchiv entstand, bedurfte es erst der gemeinsamen Planung von Bertelsmann und Börsenverein, mehr als ein halbes Jahrhundert später - nach der politischen Wende - am alten Platz in der Leipziger Universität einen insoweit noch vorbildlosen, neuen Lehrstuhl für „Buchwissenschaft und Buchwirtschaft“ zu etablieren und hierfür aus der Bertelsmann-Führungsriege Dr. Dr. Dietrich Kerlen als Ordinarius zu gewinnen. Weniger einleuchtend war zwar die begriffliche Ausgliederung der Buchwirtschaft aus der Buchwissenschaft; denn der Oberbegriff der Wissenschaft für das Buch umschließt auch die Wirtschaftswissenschaften. Angesichts des Globalauftrags, dem sich Kerlen gegenübersieht, erscheint das Definitionsproblem aber eher als Bagatelle. Wesentlich bedeutsamer ist die wiederholte Veranstaltung der Leipziger Hochschultage für Medien und Kommunikation und die erste Berichterstattung, genauer die jeweilige Selbstdarstellung buchwissenschaftlicher Universitätsaktivitäten in der Bundesrepublik Deutschland in der bereits zitierten, von Kerlen und Kirste herausgegebenen Schrift „Buchwissenschaft und Buchwirkungsforschung“.[468]

---

466 Vgl. Delp, Ludwig. In: Europa-Archiv 1947, S. 537, und in: Börsenblatt für den Deutschen Buchhandel, Leipzig 1948, S. 307.

467 Vgl. Delp Ludwig: Die Kulturabgabe („Le Domaine public payent). Internationale Fragen der Kulturförderung in kultureller, wirtschaftlicher und rechtlicher Betrachtung. Buchwissenschaftliche Beiträge 1. München 1950. - Dieses Thema wurde in den folgenden Jahrzehnten lebhaft diskutiert. Vgl. u.a. Katzenberger, Paul. Diskussion um das „domaine public payment“ in Deutschland. In: Festschrift für Roeber, Georg, 1982, S. 193.

468 Vgl. hierzu die kritische Rezension von Hans-Dieter Kübler in: BuB 53 (2001) 1, S. 71.

Andere Universitätsinstitutionen hatten die Zeichen der Zeit bereits früher erkannt, wie in der erwähnten Schrift nachzulesen ist.

Aloys Ruppel, Mainzer Stadtbibliotheksdirektor, Leiter des Mainzer Gutenberg-Museums, Vorstandsmitglied der Gutenberg-Gesellschaft, begründete Ende der vierziger Jahre das „Gutenberg-Seminar", das sich auch in der Folgezeit weitgehend mit der Frühdruckforschung befasste. Sein Nachfolger Hans Widmann widmete sich dem Buchwesen vom Altertum bis zur Gegenwart. Das Seminar wuchs zum „Institut für Buchwesen" heran, das Hans-Joachim Koppitz als Nachfolger von Widmahn mit Schwerpunkten im Bibliothekswesen und in der Bibliographie, um nur einige Beispiele zu nennen, weiterführte. Stephan Füssel trieb die Entwicklung systematisch voran und änderte, aus Anlass des fünfzigjährigen Bestehens der Mainzer Einrichtung 1997,[469] die Bezeichnung in „Institut für Buchwissenschaft". Dass der Verfasser dieses Beitrags mit Hans Widmann und Hans-Joachim Koppitz, zeitweise auch mit Stephan Füssel, im Gedankenaustausch stand, liegt angesichts der vorausgegangenen Gründung des Deutschen Bucharchivs als Institut für Buchwissenschaften 1947/48 nahe.

1974 hatte Otto Maier „Buch- und Bibliothekskunde" als Haupt- und Nebenfach in die Magister- und Promotionsprüfungsordnungen an der Universität Erlangen aufgenommen. Maier blieb dem Lehrbetrieb auch weiter verbunden, als die von ihm initiierte Professur mit Alfred Swierk besetzt wurde.[470] Es wird von rasch wachsenden Studentenzahlen berichtet, die sicherlich auch auf die thematische Erweiterung des Lehrangebote durch Swierk zurückgingen. Dazu gehörten die seit 1991 vom Verfasser dieses Beitrags beigesteuerten Vorlesungen und Übungen „Das Recht des geistigen Schaffens". Nach der Emeritierung von Swierk besteht derzeit das Kollegium aus Ursula Rautenberg als verantwortlicher Professorin, aus PD Arno Mentzel-Reuters als Bibliothekswissenschaftler, aus Lehrbeauftragten und einem Dipl.-Buchhandelswirt als wissenschaftlichem Mitarbeiter sowie aus dem Verfasser als Honorarprofessor. Sondermittel der DFG stehen für ein Forschungsprojekt über Entstehung und Entwicklung des Titelblatts in der Inkunabel- und Frühdruckzeit zur Verfügung. Seit Sommer 1998 nennt sich auch die Erlanger Institution „Buchwissenschaft". Das derzeitige Lehrangebot behandelt „Digitale Bibliotheken", „Verlagsbetriebslehre", „Geschichte und aktuelle Probleme der wissenschaftlichen Zeitschrift", „Strategien des Verlagsbuchhandels vom 18. bis 20. Jahrhundert", „Grundzüge der Bibliotheksgeschichte", „Der moderne Zwischenbuchhandel", „Konstruktion von Lesekultur im Buchhandel des 19. und 20. Jahrhunderts", „Modernes Buchhandels- und Verlagswesen", „Recht des geistigen Schaffens" und „Einführung in das Desktop Publishing".[471]

Seit dem Wintersemester 1987/88 befast sich das Institut für Deutsche Philologie der Münchner Universität mit der Unterrichtung von Graduierten aus allen universitären Fachrichtungen mit Buchfragen, um günstige Bewerbungen am Arbeitsmarkt zu ermöglichen. Zusätzlich sorgt seit Wintersemester 1996/97 ein Diplomstudiengang für die Ausbildung zum Diplombuchwissenschaftler, allerdings für Absolventen einer abgeschlossenen Aus-

---

469 Ernst Fischer: Buchwissenschaft in Mainz. Ein Porträt in 15 Punkten. In: Buchwissenschaft und Buchwirkungsforschung a.a.O., S. 14 f.

470 Swierk, Alfred: Buch- und Bibliothekskunde an der FAU Erlangen. Rückblick und Perspektiven. In: „Es gibt keine Seligkeit ohne Bücher". Kleine Festschrift zum zehnjährigen Bestehen der Buch- und Bibliothekskunde an der Friedrich-Alexander-Universität Erlangen-Nürnberg von Markus Breitwieser und Marie Kristin Rumland (Hrsg.), Erlangen 1994.

471 Elektronisches Kommentiertes Vorlesungsverzeichnis der Erlanger Buchwissenschaft, Sommersemester 2001.

bildung im Verlag oder Buchhandel. Daneben können von den Studierenden Fremdsprachen, Kommunikationswissenschaften, Wirtschafts- und Werbepsychologie oder Neuere deutsche Literatur gewählt werden. Ein Beirat namhafter Verleger und Buchhändler wirkt bei der Zusammenstellung des Lehrplans mit. Die Seminare werden zu zwei Dritteln von Praktikern aus der Buchbranche bestritten. Aufbaustudiengänge ergänzen das Lehrangebot für Germanisten, Absolventen der philosophischen, philologischen, historischen und pädagogischen Fächer, gleichsam als unmittelbare Vorbereitung zum Einstieg in das Berufsleben. Der gesonderte Diplomstudiengang rundet das vielfältige Angebot ab. Besonders wird Betriebswirtschaft hier mit Buchwissenschaft kombiniert, um damit auch der Forderung der Buchbranche Rechnung zu tragen. Georg Jäger gebührt das Verdienst, diese mehrschichtige, erfolgreiche Ausbildungsstätte für Studenten, Buchhändler und Verleger geplant und verwirklicht zu haben.[472]

Von der Universität Münster werden Überlegungen zum Aufbau eines Studiengangs „Buchwissenschaft" berichtet. Hier soll im Rahmen eines in der theoretischen Konzeption zentralen Kulturbegriffs mit dem Dreieck „Buch, Text und Kultur" in besonderem Maße das komplizierte Verhältnis zwischen den Inhalten und den Medien ihres Transports im Sinne der Konstituierung des Wissens (und nicht nur von Informationen) erforscht und reflektiert werden.[473]

Hans Baier hat in seinem Beitrag „Buchwissenschaft mit Leipziger Profil" den Unterschied zwischen der von Dietrich Kerlen vertretenen vergleichenden Medientheorie und Buchwirtschaftslehre zu ähnlichen buchwissenschaftlichen Studiengängen in der Bundesrepublik hervorgehoben; er meint, dass letztere stärker geschichts- oder literaturwissenschaftlich ausgeprägt seien, beispielsweise in Mainz, Erlangen, München oder Münster.[474] Dies als Kritik anzusehen, wäre sicher verfehlt, werden doch an allen Orten nützliche Dinge für das Medium Buch vermittelt. Die festgestellten Schwerpunkte ergeben sich zweifelsfrei zunächst aus dem Bildungsgang der jeweiligen Lehrkräfte, kennzeichnen aber auch ein gewisses Defizit an interdisziplinärer Kommunikation über das universelle Gesamtthema „Buch".

Dieses Defizit bewog 16 Medienwissenschaftler, am 25. März 1999 die Deutsche Buchwissenschaftliche Gesellschaft zum Zwecke einer universellen Förderung von Wissenschaft und Fachöffentlichkeit im Bereich des Buch- und Zeitschriftenwesens durch buchwissenschaftliche Forschung, Lehre, Dokumentation, Information und Nutzanwendung zu gründen. Dieser Zusammenschluss will die Kooperation buchwissenschaftlicher Institutionen intensivieren, buchwissenschaftliche Studiengänge und Ausbildungseinrichtungen an Hochschulen und Fachschulen fördern, Dokumentation und Information samt Vernetzung buchwissenschaftlichen Forschungs- und Studienmaterials bereitstellen und unterhalten. Dabei betrachtet sich die Vereinigung als Teil einer internationalen medienwissenschaftlichen Gesellschaft.[475] In der ersten ordentlichen Mitgliederversammlung am 16. Juni 2000 in Stuttgart referierten Peter Vodosek über „Buchwissenschaft im Zeitalter der Digitalisierung", Günter Häntzschel über das Forschungsprojekt „Sozialgeschichtliche Aspekte der deutschen Buchkultur in den 50er-Jahren" und Viatcheslav Nourgaliev über

472 Steffen, Kirsten-. Buchwissenschaft an der Universität München - ein aktueller Praxisbericht. :In: Buchwissenschaft und Buchwirkungsforschung, a.a.O., S. 43 ff.

473 Müller-Oberhäuser, Gabriele: Buchwissenschaft in Münster. In: Buchwissenschaft und Buchwirkungsforschung, a.a.O., S. 57 ff, 66.

474 Hans Baier: Buchwissenschaft mit Leipziger Profil. In: Buchhändler heute 12/2000, S. 44.

475 § 1 der Satzung der Vereinigung „Deutsche Buchwissenschaftliche Gesellschaft" vom 25.3.1999.

„Buchwissenschaft im Rußland von heute". Der verlesene Bericht von Mark W. Rectanus über buchwissenschaftliche Unternehmungen in Nordamerika findet seine Konkretisierung durch das ausführlichere Referat von Rectanus vor der 2. Mitgliederversammlung in Leipzig (23./24.3.2001), während Vorträge über „Buchwesen und Wissenschaft in der Schweiz" von Claudia Engler, über „Buchverlagswesen in Ungarn - gestern und heute" von Dorottya Liptak und über „Buchwissenschaftliche Aktivitäten in Großbritannien" von Hans-Jürgen Ehlers weitere Diskussionspunkte lieferten. Winold Vogt berichtete Über „Die Sammlung deutscher Drucke" und Sylvia Wanke über die Online-Aktivitäten im Deutschen Bucharchiv.[476] Es besteht bereits eine wechselseitige Mitgliedschaft zur Gesellschaft für Buchforschung in Österreich.

Diese Bestandsaufnahme des Ist-Zustandes buchwissenschaftlicher Tätigkeit in aller Welt wird zu den Fragen der Gesellschaft nach der umfassenden Konzeption einer Buchwissenschaft überleiten. Dabei werden die bisherigen, keineswegs zahlreichen Stimmen über Buchforschung als Wissenschaft diskutiert werden, ausgehend von den grundlegenden Arbeiten von Alfred Swierk, der Buchwissenschaft als autonome Wissenschaft in der Reihe humanistischer Wissenschaften definiert und in unmittelbarer Nähe zur Kommunikations- und Kulturwissenschaft eingeordnet hat. Es wird auch darum gehen, den Standort der Buchwissenschaft innerhalb der wissenschaftlichen Disziplinen festzustellen und, mit Swierk, die bestehenden Methodenverwandtschaften für ein interdisziplinäres Zusammenwirken zu nutzen.

Die hierüber früher geführten Diskussionen[477] müssen weitergeführt werden.

---

[476] Vgl. Deutsche Buchwissenschaftliche Gesellschaft: Referate und Protokolle 1. 1. Mitgliederversammlung am 16. Juni 2000 in der Hochschule für Bibliotheks- und Informationswesen, Stuttgart. Wiesbaden 2000. Und: Referate und Protokolle 2. 2. Mitgliederversammlung am 23./24, März 2001 gemeinsam mit dem 3. Sächsischen Bibliothekstag in Leipzig. Wiesbaden 2001.

[477] Swierk, Alfred: Was ist und zu welchem Zweck betreibt man Buchwissenschaft? Bemerkungen am Rande eines Jubiläums in Mainz. In: Myosotis 2/97, S. 3 ff, 7. Grundlegend hierzu ders.: Buchwissenschaft. Versuch einer Begriffs- und Standortbestimmung. In: Buchhandelsgeschichte 1989, S. B 64 ff. Bereits die nachfolgende Quellenauswahl zeigt die Vielfalt seitheriger Erörterungen: Meyer-Dohm, Peter: Anlässe und Motive für die Erforschung des Buchwesens. In: Beiträge zur Geschichte des Buches und seiner Funktion in der Gesellschaft. Festschrift für Hans Widmann. Stuttgart 1974. S. 155 - Strauss, Wolfgang: Buchwissenschaft als Gemeinschaftsaufgabe des Buchhandels. In: Lesen und Leben, von Göpfert, Herbert G. u.a. (Hrsg.), Frankfurt/Main 1975, S. 328 - Freitag, Jürgen: Der gegenwärtige Entwicklungsstand der Buchwissenschaft in der UdSSR. In: Börsenblatt für den Deutschen Buchhandel, Leipzig 1975, S.' 410 - Krause, Friedhild: Was ist Buchwissenschaft?. Überlegungen in der Sowjetunion. In: Marginalien Heft 59/1975, S. 93 - Göpfert, Herbert G.: Buchhandel und Wissenschaft. In: Die Begegnung. Autor, Verleger, Buchhändler, Leser. 11. Folge. Berlin 1975/16, S. 127 - Langenbucher, Wolfgang R.: Kommunikationspolitik für das Leben. Bücher schwer zugänglich. Plädoyer für eine „Buchnutzenlehre". In: Börsenblatt für den Deutschen Buchhandel, Frankfurt/Main, Nr. 53/1976, S. 991 - Raabe, Paul: Was ist Geschichte des Buchwesens? Überlegungen zu einem Forschungsbereich und einer Bildungsaufgabe. In: Buchhandelsgeschichte Nr. 8/1976, 8-. IB 319 - Faulstich, Werner (Hrsg.): Kritische Stichwörter zur Medienwissenschaft. Stichwort „Buch". München, S. 48 - Duclaud, Jutta: Verändertes Kaufverhalten und das Konzept? Anmerkung zur erforderlichen Einheit von Buchwissenschaft und -soziologie / neues Bemühen um Kooperation im Zentralinstitut für Bibliothekswesen. In: Börsenblatt für den Deutschen Buchhandel, Leipzig 1986, S. 664 - Kaegbein, Paul: Bibliotheksforschung in der Bundesrepublik Deutschland. Betrachtungen zum Problem ihrer Institutionalisierung. In: Onderzoek in bibliotheek – en Den Haag 1987, S. 54 - Koppitz, Hans- Joachim: Zur Geschichte des Faches Buchwesen an deutschen Universitäten. In: Gutenberg Jahrbuch 1989, S. 387. - Vgl. auch aus früherer Zeit-. - Mey . Peter: Es gibt keine autonome Buchwissenschaft. In: Börsenblatt für den Deutschen Buchhandel Nr. 4/1966, S. 51. - Göpfert, Herbert G.: Wissenschaft vom Buchhandel - Wissenschaft für den Buchhandel. In: Bertelsmann Briefe 52/1967, S. 3 ff.

Die Erörterung über Wesen, Inhalt und Ziele der „Buchwissenschaft“ werden nicht zuletzt auch darüber befinden müssen, ob unter diesem Begriff wirkliche Wissenschaft, Forschung und Lehre betrieben werden soll oder ob der Begriff nur eine wohlklingende Etikette für bestimmte Berufsausbildungsgänge ist, wie sie von anderen Einrichtungen, z.B. durch die Akademie des Deutschen Buchhandels in München, bereits wahrgenommen werden. Dabei wird zu überlegen sein, ob die Fachbezogenheit des Buchwesens ausreichend von Fachleuten aus der Praxis gewährleistet wird, die Abhängigkeiten von gebundenen Interessen bedingen kann. Nur die autonome Wissenschaft ermöglicht und erlaubt es, das Ziel zu verfolgen, das Buch als wohl wichtigstes Medium dieser Welt nach besten Kräften durch objektive wissenschaftliche Forschung und durch die Vermittlung der Forschungsergebnisse auch in der Zukunft zu fördern. Sicherlich kann es nicht der künftige Weg der Buchwissenschaft sein, von abschirmenden Interessenverbänden samt personalen Ausgrenzungen mehr oder weniger beeinflusst zu werden.

BERUF UND POLITIK

Diann Rusch-Feja

Der Beruf ‚Bibliothekar' und die Digitale Aufforderung[478]

Überlegungen über das sich verändernde Berufsprofil

Einführung

Mit der Öffnung des Internets und des danach relativ schnell sich anschließenden World Wide Web wurde es einigen Menschen klar, dass das Internet ein neues Zeitalter eröffnet hatte. Gleichzeitig begann eine andere Ära zu Ende zu gehen. Veröffentlichungsmethoden, -weisen, und -prüfungen nehmen einen neuen Stellenwert an. Der Bibliothekar überschreitet die physischen Grenzen der „Wände" der eigenen Bibliothek und sucht Information, Literatur und relevante Fakten in den Datenbanken und Informationsangebot, die am leichtesten zu ändern bzw. am besten zu bewältigen sind. Durch das Internet sind die Informationsangebote weder von einer Institution noch einer bestimmten Berufssparte abhängig. Im Gegenteil: Wissenschaftler und Universitätsdozenten sind mit den Dienstleistungen der jeweiligen Bibliothek zum guten Teil nicht zufrieden und wenden sich an die mittlerweile besser entwickelten Suchmaschinen im Internet oder die elektronischen Volltexte im Verlagsserver bzw. im PrePrint-Server. Seit dem Anfang der IuK-Kommission der Fachgesellschaften gab es Warnungen, dass die Wissenschaftler anderer Meinung über die Art und Verfügbarkeit der Dienstleistungen waren als die Bibliothekare. In Deutschland führen diese Erkenntnisse zu zwei wichtigen Schlussfolgerungen, die das Berufsbild des Bibliothekars für die Zukunft prägen sollten, nämlich

1. die bestehenden hierarchischen Strukturen im deutschen Bibliothekswesen sowie die Trennung bestimmter Informationsaufgaben nach Bibliothekaren und Dokumentaren müssen verändert werden, und
2. das Berufsbild bezieht sich immer stärker auf spezielle Aspekte des informationsvermittelnden Berufes, wobei die Inhaber dieses Berufs lernen müssen, wie ihr Klientel Information sucht, nutzt, verwendet, zitiert und prüft vor allem in der digitalen, vernetzten Informationsumgebung.

In dieser digital geprägten Umgebung sprengt die bibliothekarische Arbeit die physischen Einschränkungen von komplizierten Regeln, schwindenden Etats sowie ggf. nicht ausreichender Regalfläche. Der Zugewinn an Information über vernetzte Quellen bringt eine neue Art von Erfassungs-, Recherchen- und Beschaffungsmethoden mit sich. Man geht nun nicht mehr nur mit Informationen um, sondern kreiert sie, bereitet sie auf und stellt sie der ganzen Welt zur Verfügung. Publikationswesen, Bibliothekswesen, Informationswissenschaft sowie auch viele technische Berufe (Sekretärin, Statistiker, Rechenzentrumsmitarbeiter etc.) werden ihre Arbeitsmethoden ändern, ihre Zeit effizienter einsetzen und unterschiedliche Methoden, Verfahrensweisen, Work-Flow-Überlegungen etc. in der tägli-

[478] Dieser Aufsatz ist eine ausführlichere Darstellung des Vortrags „Changing Profile in a Changing Environment: The Information Specialist in Germany" am 10. März 2001 in Bologna., Italien, bei der vom British Council gesponserten Tagung „Towards an Information Society for All: A European Perspective" (http://www.britishcouncil.it/tisa/).

chen Arbeit austesten, bei Nutzern beobachten und zum Schluss dieser Phase auch die Ergebnisse auswerten.

Prämisse Nr. 1:

Wenn das Internet eine World Wide Bibliothek ist, brauchen wir dann noch Bibliothekare? Wer hilft den Nutzern bei der Informationssuche, beim Downloading und bei der zeiteffektiven Nutzung elektronischer Fachinformationen? - Natürlich werden Bibliothekare benötigt - aber vielleicht in einer anderen Konstellation bzw. Arbeitsaufteilung, als das bis heute der Fall ist. Ist das Internet wie ein schwarzes Loch in der astronomischen Forschung? Ist die unsichtbare, teilweise undefinierbare Anziehungskraft, die aus dem schwarzen Loch hervorgeht, die bindende Macht des Universums? Und woraus entsteht eine Anziehungskraft in der Informationswelt ähnlich der der Astronomie? Besteht sie aus menschlichem Neugier, Zielstrebigkeit, strukturierten Wissensangeboten, die assoziativ nach Interessensgespür /Feinheiten in viele verschiedene Richtungen weiterleiten und verzweigen? Mindmapping kommt dieser Kraft nahe, weniger aber die starren hierarchischen Strukturen der Bibliotheksregeln und vor allem die strenge Aufteilung der bibliothekarischen Tätigkeiten nach Vergütungsgruppen bzw. nach Berufsgruppen (Dipl.-Bibl., Dipl.-Dok, wissenschaftlicher. Bibliothekar oder Dokumentar etc.).Können Bibliothekare die seit langem bestehenden Strukturen tatsächlich sinnvoll ändern und manche Berufshürden überspringen? Genau wie im Internet, in E-Commerce, in Wissenschaft und Technik wird Innovation und Beweglichkeit gefordert. Die Konsequenz aus der Zurückhaltung sind deutlich: den Zug zu verpassen, den Beruf zu gefährden, die eigene berufliche Motivation zu erdrosseln und die eigene Entwicklung zu verhindern. Aber in welcher Richtung bewegt sich der Beruf am sichersten?

Kein Bibliothekar hat nur mit Büchern zu tun. Es waren immer Zeitungen, Zeitschriften, Pressemitteilungen, Verlagsankündigungen, Konferenzproceedings und amtliche Druckschriften u.a., mit denen der Bibliothekar zu tun hatte. Und eigentlich waren es nicht nur die Formate und Gattungen („Behälter“) der Texte, die vordergründig die Qualität der Bibliothek ausmachten, sondern die Inhalte und ihre Informationsqualität, ihre Aktualität und nicht so sehr die Träger selbst (außer bei Präservierungs- und Konservierungsfragen). So ist dann die neue Bezeichnung „Informationsspezialist“ eher zutreffend als Bibliothekar. Schließlich übernimmt die Informationsvermittlung einen überwiegenden Anteil der Arbeit des Bibliothekars und mit der Zunahme der Nutzung elektronischer Informationsressourcen um so mehr.

Prämisse Nr. 2:

Der Bibliothekar entwickelt sich zum Informationsspezialisten und erfüllt überwiegend Informationsbedürfnisse der Nutzer mit Hilfe verschiedener gedruckter und elektronischer Informationsquellen.

Prämisse Nr. 3:

Ohne Nutzer und ein aktives Dienstleistungsverhältnis zu den Nutzern arbeitet der Bibliothekar in einer Art Büchermuseum, die längst nicht mehr den Anspruch auf Einmaligkeit erheben kann, wie bei den meisten Museen. Darüber hinaus erweitern sich die Informationsvermittlungstätigkeiten auf Bestände und Informationsressourcen, die nicht unmittelbar in einer physischen Bibliothekssammlung oder sogar in der Bibliothek verzeichnet sind. Diese Erweiterung geht über die „Wände“ der Bibliothek hinaus und beruht auf einen gezielten Zugang zu verteilten Informationssammlungen in lokalen, regionalen und überregionalen Netzen und sogar in der gesamten vernetzten Welt.

Neue Tätigkeiten erweitern das Spektrum der bibliothekarischen Tätigkeiten: Mit der Erweiterung der Informationsangebote sind es die Bibliothekare und Informationsspezialisten, die die Benutzerschulung für Informationsnavigation und -evaluationen am Besten durchführen können, da sie die Quellen und ihre Nutzungsbedingungen sowie die Nutzerbedürfnisse am besten kennen. Neue Beschaffungsmethoden (elektronische Dokumentenlieferung nach Auswahl verschiedenster Anbieter, u.a.), nach Lizenzierungsregelungen, Preispolitik und Zahlmöglichkeiten (z.B. Pay-per-view) etc., beeinflussen die Beratung der Nutzer bei der Informationsbeschaffung (eigenständig, vermittelt, etc.). Die Vor- und Nachteile von Zugangsbedingungen statt Besitz der Informationsquellen werden nach den Kenntnissen der Nutzerbedürfnissen und tatsächlichen Nutzungsbeobachtungen erwogen und entschieden. Dafür benötigt der Informationsspezialist Überblick über die verschiedenen Angebote, Preisgestaltung, Verhandlungsgeschick und Austausch (auch Allianzen) mit anderen Berufskollegen.

Die Erweiterung des Informationsangebot bleibt nicht getrennt von den herkömmlichen Beständen, sondern es empfiehlt sich die Integration von Links zu elektronischen Quellen und Volltexten in den Bibliothekskatalogen sowie in Internet- und Intranetangeboten der Bibliotheken. Der Bibliothekskatalog kann zum Instrument der Erstellung nicht nur von Bibliographien mit elektronischen Zusatzwerken, sondern auch von Literaturlisten des institutseigenen Personals, Projektveröffentlichungen und Datenbanken enzyklopädischer Art aufgebaut werden.

Um die hohe Informationsrelevanz und Qualität dieser Dienste zu gewährleisten, ist eine kontinuierliche Nutzungsevaluation erforderlich. Die Informationen sowie die Informationsdienstleistungen selbst unterliegen nun mehr denn je einer Prüfung der Kosten-Nutzen-Relation und der Effektivitätsprüfung.

Die Trainingsrolle der Informationsspezialisten in der Schule, in der Hochschule, in der Spezialbibliothek

In der Schule wird in den nächsten Jahren von Schülern ab 8-9 Jahren Vertrautheit im Umgang mit dem Computer verlangt. Es gibt in Deutschland wenige Computerfachlehrer für die Grundschule, einige für die Sekundarstufen, aber nur äußerst wenige, die sowohl die „Computer Literacy" („Medienkompetenz") als auch die „Information Literacy" („Informationskompetenz") unterrichten können. Zur Zeit ist ein Zustand erreicht, wo diejenigen Lehrer, die Computerunterricht erteilen, oft so unterschiedliche Fähigkeiten unter den Schülern vorfinden, dass sie blutige Anfänger neben Kindern haben, die durchaus größere Fähigkeiten und Computer Literacy besitzen als die Lehrer selbst. In solchen Fällen können Schüler als Mentoren für andere Schüler und sogar für die Lehrer fungieren (je nach Schulklima). Neben dem notwendigen Computer Literacy Kurs für Lehrer (aller Fächer nicht nur die der Informatik) müssen auch Information Literacy Kurse für die Lehrer angeboten werden. Dieses beinhaltet Informationsevaluation, Vertrautheit mit Webdiensten, Prüfmöglichkeiten etc. Auch Aspekte des Informationsmanagements gehören zu den Kompetenzen für die Lehrer insbesondere der Sekundarstufen.

Lehrer und Schulbibliothekar sollten kooperieren, um die Schüler mit den altersgemäßen fachbezogenen Informationsquellen vertraut zu machen sowie mit der Anwendung von Kriterien der Evaluation von Informationen. Hierzu gehören auch Curriculumentwicklung und Aufgaben bzw. Projektbetreuung für Schüler. Fachbezogene Linklisten zu bestehenden Lehrschwerpunkten und Schülerprojekten können die Lehrer unterstützen und den Schülern als Beispiele dienen. Schüler können dann Internetographien (annotierte Linklisten) aufbauen oder eine Bibliographie herkömmlicher Art mit bibliographischen Angabe zu sowohl traditionellen Quellen als auch zu einschlägigen, geprüften elektronischen Ressourcen. Übungen zur Prüfung, Evaluierung und Beurteilung von elektronischen Informationsquellen können von Schulbibliothekaren zur Unterstützung der Lehrer oder mit den Lehrern im Team erstellt und in der Schulbibliothek betreut werden. Außerdem sollte zur Lehreinheit „Vernetzte Informationsquellen" auch Informationsethik unterrichtet werden. Verletzung von Urheberrechten, illegales Kopieren von Bildern, Sound- und Videodateien aus den vernetzten Quellen können kostspielige Konsequenzen haben, abgesehen davon dass es hier um Verhaltensweisen geht, die zwar gesellschaftlich oft akzeptiert oder toleriert werden, aber der persönlichen und später beruflichen Ethik widersprechen.

Auf der Hochschulebene gibt es ähnliche Tätigkeiten, die bisher von den Bibliothekaren nicht ausreichend ausgebaut worden sind: Fachreferenten können die Lehrkräfte und Studenten mit den fachbezogenen Ressourcen und Suchmethoden in verschiedenen Informationssystemen vertraut machen. Sie können annotierte fachbezogene Clearinghouses, Portals und Gateways herstellen, die die Informationssuche erleichtern und ggf. vermeiden, dass kostspielige pay-per-view oder sogar Kauf von Informationseinheiten notwendig sind. In den letzten drei Jahren gibt es in Deutschland konzertierte Projekte in dieser Richtung: neben Einzelprojekten an verschiedenen Bibliotheken und Informationszentren[479] gibt es in Ergänzung zum DFG Sondersammelgebiet auch die SSG-FI (Fachinformation)-Projekte[480], die die einschlägigen vernetzten Informationsressourcen sammeln, für ihre inhaltliche Qualität und Authentizität prüfen und mittels Metadaten in ein der SSG-Sammlung ergänzendes System erschließen. So übernehmen diese Stellen überregionale Informationsaufgaben, die die Informationsvermittlertätigkeiten der Bibliothekare erweitern. Der vom BMBF beauftragten Studie „Nutzung elektronischer wissenschaftlicher Information in der Hochschulausbildung"[481] war ersehen, dass sowohl Studenten als auch Dozenten weder mit den fachbezogenen Informationsquellen in der Bibliothek noch mit den fachbezogenen Internetsammelstellen ausreichend informiert und vertraut waren. Es besteht ein großer Bedarf nach adäquater, fachbezogener Nutzerschulung, die auch von Bibliothekaren erteilt werden kann, und dies wird ausdrücklich von einigen erwünscht. Durch adäquate Nutzerschulung wird der Endnutzer auf vertrauten Zugang und effektive Nutzung von Informationsressourcen nicht nur zur Erleichterung des Studiums vorbereitet, sondern auch für sein späteres Berufsleben. Nutzerschulung beinhaltet nicht nur spezifisches Training in den fachbezogenen Quellen, sondern auch einen begleitenden Service, wobei Updates und Infos über Veränderungen und neue Quellen sowie Vermittlung von wichtigen Informationen über ggf. kostenträchtiges Downloading, Dokumentenbestel-

---

479 Es gibt eine Reihe Projekte, in denen solche Dienste entwickelt werden, darunter z.B. im Rahmen des DFG-Förderprogramms „Verteilte Digitale Forschungsbibliothek" (http://www.dbi-berlin.de/vdbhome/vdbho1.htm) und vom BMBF in Aussicht gestellten „Informationsverbund Bildung – Sozialwissenschaften – Psychologie".

480 Zum Beispiel für die Sondersammelgebiete Geowissenschaften, Mathematik, anglo-amerikanische Geschichte und anglo-amerikanische Literatur an der Niedersächsischen Staats- und Universitätsbibliothek Göttingen. Für ausführlichere Informationen hierzu Das Sondersammelgebiets-Fachinformationsprojekt (SSG-FI) Göttingen, Dokumentation - Teil 1. Berlin: Deutsches Bibliotheksinstitut, 1999.

481 Der Endbericht zu dieser Studie erscheint voraussichtlich im Mai 2001. Für Einzelheiten und eine Zusammenfassung der Ergebnisse, siehe http://www.stefi.de.

lungsmodi etc. den Nutzern zukommen. Der Kosten-Nutzen-Effekt verschiedener Quellen sollte den Nutzern vermittelt werden, genauso die Bedingungen, die evtl. Lizenzverträge bestimmen. (Viel zu oft sind diese den Benutzern gar nicht bekannt!). So ist es die Verantwortung des Informationsspezialisten, Nutzer über die juristischen Aspekte von Lizenzen und Nutzungsbedingungen zu informieren. Auch Informationen wie über Updates usw. können in ein gut aufgebautes Intranet gestellt werden.

Ob im Konsortium oder als Einzelkämpfer, es kommt auf den Informationsspezialisten die neue Aufgabe zu, optimale Nutzungskonditionen für seine Klientel auszuhandeln. Diese können ein elektronischer Handapparat, elektronische Dokumentenlieferung, Sicherung der Autorenrechte, Aufbau eines E-Print-Servers für institutionelle oder spezielle Publikationen etc., beinhalten. Im Rahmen eigener Herstellung von Veröffentlichungen könnte der Informationsspezialist daran beteiligt sein, Eingabemasken für hochschul- oder institutszugehörige Autoren anzubieten, damit die Daten über die Veröffentlichungen gleich in der Bibliotheksdatenbank erfasst werden, so dass sich bei der Spontangenerierung verschiedener Arten von Literaturlisten (Veröffentlichungslisten für ein Curriculum Vitae, Projektveröffentlichungen etc.) in verschiedenen Zitierformaten aus der Bibliotheksdatenbank alle weiteren Updateverfahren erübrigen. Dies ist besonders von Vorteil in einer Forschungsinstitution, wo das Produkt der Forschung in Veröffentlichungen (aber auch Datenvisualisierungen, Präsentationen, Graphiken etc.) mündet.

Die neuen Kompetenzen des Informationsspezialisten

Der Informationsspezialist - auch der Bibliothekar mit neuem Selbstverständnis - hat sich verschiedene IT-Kompetenzen durch Selbstlernen, durch Schulungen, mit Hilfe von Kollegen angeeignet, vor allem Computer Literacy sowie Information Literacy, Programmiersprachen (zumindest HTML, Perl, CGI Scripts). Verschiedene Aspekte von Web-Design werden für die Gestaltung effektiver Navigationshilfen, die Erstellung interaktiver Websites (Intranet) und die Spontangenerierung von Webinformationen und Literaturlisten direkt aus dem Bibliothekskatalog erforderlich sein. Außerdem bietet der Informationsspezialist seinen Nutzern auch die Möglichkeit an, seine Rechercheergebnisse in verschiedenen, universell anerkannten Formaten downzuloaden (z.B. EndNote zur Verwaltung in einer eigenen Literaturdatenbank, Formate, die bestimmten Fachgesellschaftszitierregeln wie APA oder MLA entsprechen, etc.). Weitere Programmierkenntnisse werden ggf. notwendig sein für Schnittstellenforderungen zur Einbindung verschiedener Dienstleistungen für die Hybride Bibliothek und um Z 39.50 Schnittstellen zum Bibliothekskatalog zu ermöglichen. Weiterhin, um eine hybride Bibliothek für die Nutzer zu ermöglichen, werden außerdem Informationsretrievalkenntnisse von Abfragen-Syntax und Fachkenntnisse erforderlich, damit die Abfrage sowohl auf mehreren Ebenen (breit bis hin zu sehr differenziert) als auch in mehreren Sprachen durchgeführt werden kann. Die Definition und Gruppierung von Informationsbedürfnissen spezieller Nutzergruppen wird vorausgesetzt. Links von Suchergebnislisten sollten auf eigenen Bestände zurückführen, vor allem zu elektronischen Dokumenten, zu denen Zugang über die eigenen Bibliothek gewährleistet ist.

Der/die neue Informationsspezialist/in hält sich auf dem laufenden über die neuen Entwicklungen im gesamten Informationsgebiet und ihre Auswirkungen auf die Bibliotheksarbeit. Bibliotheken werden oft von Fachwissenschaftlern und auch anderen Berufsgruppen als unflexibel und begrenzt in ihrem Aktionsfeld kritisiert. Um dieses Bild zu durchbrechen, gibt es eine Reihe von Tätigkeiten, die das Bild des Informationsspezialisten stärken können, vor allem durch die Erstellung neuer Dienstleistungen:

1. Die Rolle der Bibliothek als Verteiler neuer Informationsformen erweitern (elektronische Alerting Dienste, fachbezogene Clearinghouses, Gateways, Portals, elektronische Veröffentlichungen etc.)
2. Neue Dienstleistungen anbieten, die noch nie oder zumindest noch nicht von Bibliotheken angeboten wurden, wie zum Beispiel:
   - Aufbau eines E-Print Servers und elektronischer Archive
   - Erstellung von professionellen spezialisierten Informations-Portfolios inkl. Zugänglichkeitsmodi und Verfügbarkeitsmerkmale
   - Content-Management anbieten wie z.B. Techniken zum Wissensmanagement in der Organisation
   - Web Site Design, Design von Subject Portals etc.
   - Aufbereitung elektronischer Dokumenten durch Hinzufügung standardisierter Metadaten.

Die Einbindung von Metadaten bezieht sich nicht nur auf die Eingabe, sondern auch auf das effektive Sammeln und Display der Metadaten, um schneller und effizienter an präzisere Treffer zu kommen. Metadaten zur Archivierungszwecken und über Nutzungsbedingungen und Preissteuerung werden für bestimmte Informationsprodukte erforderlich sein. Multimediale Anforderungen erfordern Kenntnisse von MPEG7 und anderer Protokolle für die verschiedenen Nichttextformate. Schließlich muss der Informationsspezialist auch mit Techniken vertraut sein, Logfileanalyse, Nutzungsstatistiken, sowie Visualisierung und Ranking der Suchergebnisse auszuführen.

Stärkung des Stellenwerts der Bibliotheksarbeit und der Bibliotheken

Es ist nicht neu zu behaupten, dass auf Bibliothekare und Informationsspezialisten eine Herausforderung zukommen wird. Bestimmte Aspekte ihrer Arbeit werden von den anderen Mitkämpfern in der Informationskette (Verlage, Forscher, Fachgesellschaften) und von verschiedenen Diensten wie Suchmaschinen im Internet in Frage gestellt bzw. übernommen. Gefordert werden Informationstechnologische Kenntnisse und Fähigkeiten, die weit über diejenigen, mit denen man in der Ausbildung zum Bibliothekar ja auch zum Dokumentar ausgestattet ist, hinausgehen. Innovative nachhaltige Lösungen zu den verschiedenen „Informationskrisen" (Auswirkungen der Preisgestaltung von wissenschaftlichen Fachzeitschriften auf die Bibliotheksetats, Schnelligkeit der Beschaffungsmöglichkeiten etc.) in Bibliotheken werden von den Bibliothekaren gefordert. Innovative, kosteneffiziente Alternativen zur kommerziellen Produktion und Dissemination von wissenschaftlichen Forschungsergebnisse kommen aus Bibliotheken (SPARC, etc.). Die Rolle der Bibliotheken ändert sich. Sie haben nicht mehr exklusiv den Anspruch darauf, „Hüterin des gesamten Wissens" zu sein, das in den Seiten von Büchern und Zeitschriften oder gar in Multimedialen Trägern haust. Sondern dieses „Gesamtwissen" verteilt sich in vernetzten Informationsquellen und lässt sich nur virtuell zusammenführen bzw. die Informationssammel- und –bereitstellungstechniken verändern sich rapide. Die Rolle von Bibliotheken, elektronische Volltexte der eigenen Institution webgemäß aufzuarbeiten, mit Metadaten zu versehen, zu archivieren und zugänglich zu machen, kommt auf die Bibliotheken zu. Wenn sie es nicht machen, wer sonst? Fachwissenschaftler ziehen irgendwann weg und nehmen ihre persönliche Websites mit, einige Fachgesellschaften fangen mit solchen Aktivitäten an, können aus finanziellen Gründen nicht garantieren, dass sie diese Tätigkeiten auf Dauer ausführen, Verlage verpflichten sich nur bedingt und möglichst gegen Bezahlung für jeden Zugriff. Bisher waren es Bibliotheken, die die Dauerhaftigkeit von Informationseinheiten gewährt haben. Soll das nun in neuen Strukturen und neuen Technikhüllen nicht auch fortgesetzt werden?

Die Rolle von Bibliotheken bei der Entwicklung neuer Standards

Letztendlich müssen Informationsspezialisten und Bibliothekare auch bei der Entwicklung von Standards für die Gestaltung, Erfassung, Indexierung und Verzeichnung von elektronischen Ressourcen aller Art mitwirken. Bisher waren Bibliothekare immer sehr aktiv bei solchen Gremien, denn eine wertvolle Eigenschaft - der Hang zu Präzision und Detail - kommt in diesen Tätigkeiten den Bibliothekaren zugute. Wo nun durch die verschiedenen Interessensgruppen (oft auch kommerzieller Art) eher als die Bibliothekare in Internetgremien beteiligt sind (z.B. im W3 Konsortium), müssen Bibliothekare und Informationsspezialisten bei der Ausarbeitung von Standardisierungsvorschläge nicht nur mitwirken, sondern auch in verschiedener Hinsicht auch die treibende Kraft dafür sein. Mit der Erweiterung der von Bibliotheken „angezapften" Informationsquellen auf diejenigen im Internet und verfügbar via Internet konfrontiert die Bibliothek / Informationseinrichtung Konkurrenten um die Informationsversorgungsaufgabe. Die Mitwirkung bei der Standardisierungsarbeit kann zwar zeitintensiv sein, ermöglicht aber die Mitsprache in Bereichen, wo vorhandene Informationsquellen und Nachweisinstrumente sonst nicht mehr mit denjenigen in der vernetzten Informationsumgebung kompatibel sind. Sind sie nicht einmal über standardisierte Metadaten und Nachweisregeln in der „Hybriden Bibliothek" (oder über andere Dienste wie Portals etc.) zu verbinden, so wird es zu getrennten Recherchevorgängen kommen, die den Nutzer, der gewöhnt ist, leicht und schnell viele Informationen im Netz vom Schreibtisch aus zu erreichen, evtl. dazu bewegen, traditionelle Informationsdienste zu meiden.

Der Wirtschaftlichkeitsgedanke in Bibliotheken und Informationseinrichtungen

Auf Grund des Zwangs zur wirtschaftlichen Effizienz und um lähmenden Kürzungen entgegen zu wirken, müssen Bibliotheken wirtschaftliche Organisationsformen und konkurrenzfähige Dienstleistungen nachweisen. Informationsspezialisten denken kundenorientiert und prüfen die Wirtschaftlichkeit aller Arbeitsvorgänge und Angebote. Um die Wirtschaftlichkeit der eigenen Dienstleistungen zu prüfen, werden z.B. die Antworten auf folgende Fragen benötigt:

- Welche Produkte und Services werden von der Bibliothek angeboten? Sind sie professionell präsentiert? Erfüllen sie die Informationsbedürfnisse des Nutzerklientels? Steigert sich der Stellenwert der Bibliothek beim Träger, wenn sie Kostendeckungsmodelle (auch wenn zunächst nominal) vorlegt?
- Bei welchen über die Bibliothek angebotenen externen Dienstleistungen darf der Nutzer die Auswahl des Providers treffen? Welche Entscheidungen bleiben im Ermessen des Bibliothekspersonals? Welche finanzielle Konsequenzen werden aus dieser Verteilung sichtbar und was bedeutet dies für den Stellenwert der Bibliothek auf längere Sicht?
- Wie können Kosten/Personal reduziert und gleichzeitig neue Dienstleistungen angeboten werden?

Die letzte Frage ist vielleicht die schwierigste, da verlorenes Personal oft in der Umwandlung von Arbeitsvorgängen resultiert und oft mehr Arbeit für die übriggebliebenen Mitarbeiterinnen bedeutet. So ist dann nur schwer vorstellbar, dass gleichzeitig neue Dienstleistungen entwickelt und angeboten werden können - auch wenn sie zur Stabilisierung und „Rettung" des Stellenwertes der Bibliothek beitragen können. Trotzdem hilft hier eine strategische Prüfung der Notwendigkeit jedes Handgriffs in allen Arbeitsvorgängen, sowie eine Prüfung des Verhältnisses Zeitaufwand für den internen Geschäftsgang gegenüber demjenigen für die Nutzerbedürfnisse. Trotz bibliothekarischen Stolzes über Exaktheit im Detail könnte es sein, dass die Nutzer diese Detailtiefe nicht brauchen und der Personaleinsatz besser für andere Dienstleistungen - insbesondere für diejenigen, von denen der Nutzer am meisten direkt profitiert - zu organisieren ist.

Wirtschaftlichkeit der Bibliothek erhöht sich auch, wenn bestimmte, personalaufwändige Dienstleistungen von anderer Stelle eingekauft werden. Oft wird ein Träger eher Geldmittel für ein sog. Outsourcing-Projekt im Zuge der Personalkürzungen bereitstellen, als dass Hilfskräfte eingestellt werden. Dienstleistungen, die sich zum Outsourcing eigenen, da der Personalaufwand sehr hoch ist, sind Buchbinderarbeiten, Fernleihe durch verschiedene Dienstleistungen (SUBITO, verschiedene Bibliotheken, externe Dienste etc.) und andere mehr. Titelaufnahmen können von zuverlässigen Quellen (anderen Bibliotheken, der DDB, der Library of Congress etc.) übernommen werden und ggf. mit Lokaldaten (institutionseigener Verschlagwortung, Notation und Hinweise) ergänzt werden (wenn dies an sich nicht annähernd so aufwändig ist wie eine Originalkatalogisierung). Eine Entscheidung, ob es Sinn hat, eine Dienstleistung zu kürzen oder zu verändern, liegt oft in der Prüfung, ob diese Dienstleistung für die Nutzer in ihrem vollen Umfang (und damit verbundenen Arbeitsaufwand durch das Bibliothekspersonal) die Kosten-Nutzen-Proportion rechtfertigt. Wären die Nutzer bereit, für diese Dienstleistung einen Kostendeckungspreis zu zahlen bzw. abzuziehen von ihrem fiktiven Anteil des Bibliotheksetats oder könnte die Dienstleistung zu ihrer Zufriedenheit mit weniger Geld, weniger Mühe und ggf. schneller für die Nutzer durch andere Stellen ausgeführt werden? Das Beispiel „Amazon.com / Amazon.de" bietet Vorteile an, die viele Nutzer mittlerweile der Literaturbeschaffung durch die Bibliothek vorziehen. Können sich Bibliotheken diesen Eingriff in ihren traditionellen Arbeitsbereich leisten? Und wie können Bibliotheken mit solchen Dienstleistungen konkurrieren? Vier Gesichtspunkte spielen hier je nach Benutzerbedarf eine Rolle: inhaltliche Präzision der Suchergebnisse, Finanzierungsquelle, Schnelligkeit der Zurverfügungstellung und des geringen Aufwands des Nutzers bei der Beschaffung bzw. zusätzliche Vorteile (z.B. weiterführende inhaltliche Vorschläge aufgrund der individuellen Such- und Kaufergebnisse). Beunruhigend ist jedoch die Vorstellung, dass die Unzufriedenheit mit der Zeitverzögerung durch den bibliothekarischen Geschäftsgang Wissenschaftler dazu veranlassen könnte, zu verlangen, über ihren eigenen Anteil des Etats direkt zu verfügen und benötigte Informationen selbst zu bestellen. In einigen Forschungsinstituten ist diese Vorstellung nicht weit von der Realität entfernt. Auch wenn diese Vorstellung einem unmöglich erscheint, ist die Unzufriedenheit der Nutzer - wenn schon einmal vorhanden - schon sehr reell und entkräftet die Position und den Stellenwert der Bibliothek in der Einrichtung.

Diese Organisationsprinzipien tragen nicht nur zur wirtschaftlichen Effizienz der Bibliothek bei, sondern sie ermächtigen Bibliothekare, bei wichtigen Entscheidungen noch eine maßgebende Rolle zu spielen. Sonst werden Entscheidungen von außerhalb der Bibliothek über Sachverhalte gefällt werden, die die bibliothekarische Expertise oft übersehen, nicht berücksichtigen, nicht mehr interessieren, weil die Bibliothek wieder nur als Finanzobjekt angesehen wird, statt als wichtiger Dienstleister.

Konkurrenzfähige Angebote - Neue Dienstleistungen

In einer Gesellschaft, in der die Tendenz zur Globalisierung immer stärker anwächst, müssen neue Angebote und neue Dienstleistungen von Bibliotheken entwickelt werden, um konkurrenzfähig zu bleiben. Globalisierung bedeutet zusätzlich, dass Verbindungen zu Institutionen mit wichtigen Angeboten und Dienstleistungen gepflegt werden und eventuell gemeinsame Projekte aufgebaut werden. Wirtschaftlich denken bedeutet auch, dass die Erkenntnis, nicht jede Bibliothek kann alles in einem Fach leisten - weder von Arbeitsanfall und Indexierungstiefe her noch von den Kosten und Beschaffungsmöglichkeiten - (abgesehen auch von den Aufbewahrungs- und Archivierungsmöglichkeiten), dazu führt, strategische Allianzen zu bilden und zu pflegen. Dies können Kooperations- und gemeinsame Projekte mit einer Arbeitsaufteilung sein. Ein hervorragendes Beispiel dafür ist in den Bemühungen der IuK-Kommission der deutschen Fachgesellschaften, um zunächst die vernetzte Infrastruktur im deutschen Hochschulwesen auszubauen und zu sichern, danach die IuK-Kommission als Katalysator für weitere Veränderungen im IuK-Bereich zu etablieren, und letztlich (aber nicht desto weniger von Bedeutung), den Anstoß zu geben für das *Dissertationen-Online* Projekt (http://www.dissonline.org), in dem 5-mal 5 Universitäten in Deutschland je in 5 Fachgebieten 5 elektronische Dissertationen pro Jahr bearbeitet und als Grundlage für die Entwicklung von Regelungen für die Abgabe und Gestaltung von elektronischen Dissertationen und Prüfungsarbeiten ausgearbeitet haben sowie einen geeigneten Metadatensatz für diese Art von Hochschulschriften entwickelten. In anderen Kooperations- und gemeinsamen Projekten können Bibliotheken mit anderen Gruppen wie den Fachgesellschaften zusammen arbeiten und "Erstanwender" ("Early Adopters") von neuen Programmen und Service-Leistungen sein. Zum Beispiel können sie sich mit ihren umfangreichen Datenbanken erhebliche Mengen an detaillierten und standardisierten Daten als Testbetten für die Erprobung von Navigationssoftware, IT-Anwendungen und Informationsretrievalprotokollen zur Verfügung stellen. Die Erfahrung als "Early Adopters" und Teilnehmer solcher Projekte - auch internationaler - ergeben nicht nur technologische Vorsprünge, sondern auch das Prestige, an derartigen Projekten mitzumachen und zum Erfolg zu bringen (z.B. NSF-DFG-Projekte etc.). Durch solche innovativen Projekte (wie die Open Archives Initiative, SPARC etc.) können neue Formen von Informationsverarbeitung und neue Entwicklungen, die den Nutzerbedürfnissen entgegenkommen, erprobt und verbessert werden. Durch diese Flexibilität, an innovativen Projekten mitzuwirken, vor allem im wissenschaftlichen Bereich, wächst der Stellenwert der Bibliothek in ihrer Trägerinstitution sowie das Bewusstsein, in ihrem Nutzerkreis, dass die Bibliothek nicht in ihrem traditionellen Aufgabenverständnis befangen bleiben, sondern ihre Aufgaben und Dienstleistungen entsprechend den sich wandelnden Nutzerbedürfnissen gestalten und sogar zu neuen Entwicklungen und deren Akzeptanz (z.B. elektronische Zeitschriften in der Max Planck Gesellschaft) vorantreiben.

Ein weiterer Aspekt, um den Stellenwert der Bibliothek durch ein neues Bewusstsein für Wirtschaftlichkeit im Umgang mit Humanressourcen wie mit Geldmitteln zu steigern, liegt in der kontinuierlichen Evaluierung und Beobachtung der bisherigen Ausgaben und dem Wert der Güter und Dienstleistungen, die dafür erworben wurden. Außerdem ist es eine Notwendigkeit, den Wert einzelner Informationsdienstleistungen für den einzelnen Benutzer wirklich heraus zu finden, und in Planung und Haushaltsregelungen umzusetzen. So wird der Informationswert einzelner Dienstleistungen für ihre Nachhaltigkeit geprüft. Ohne diese Werte wird die Bibliotheksleitung nie wissen, was dem Nutzer wichtig ist.

Nutzerstudien dienen hierzu. In einigen Bibliotheken übernehmen auch Bibliothekspraktikanten Sonderprojekte, wie für z.B. Metadatenentwicklung, Aufbau von E-Print-Servern und Aufbereitung von Textdateien für elektronische Veröffentlichungen. Meist sind dies Projekte, die sonst nicht vom eigentlichen Personal bewältigt werden können. Der Doppeleffekt wird dadurch erzielt, indem das Projekt zu Ende gebracht wird und oft lernen die Teilnehmer (Studenten und Mitarbeiter) dabei gegenseitig voneinander.

Strategische Allianzen und wichtige Kooperationspartner

Neben dem Anschluss an Entwicklungen außerhalb der eigenen Institution braucht die Bibliothek und Informationseinrichtung auch strategisch wichtige Allianzen und Kooperationspartner innerhalb der eigenen Institution. Vor allem die Nutzer der Informationseinrichtung sind die wichtigsten Kooperationspartner. Diejenigen Forscher und Fachkräfte, die in ihrer Arbeit zur Erhaltung der Wettbewerbsfähigkeit der Einrichtung von Aktualität und Umfang des Informationsangebots profitieren, sind wichtige Nutzer, deren Meinung und Interessen an der Entwicklung der Bibliothek und Informationseinrichtung sowie ihrer Dienstleistungen sie zu wichtigen Partnern machen. In einer Forschungsbibliothek sind es die einzelnen Wissenschaftler, in der Universitätsbibliothek sind es die Lehrkräfte. Ihr eigenes Renommee hängt oft von der Aktualität und Bereitstellung der richtigen Literatur und elektronischer Dienstleistungen ab. In Firmen sind es auch die Wissenschaftler, die an der Entwicklung und Erprobung neuer Produkte arbeiten. In Museen und Kunsteinrichtungen besteht es auch aus den Wissenschaftlern und Lehrkräften, die die Informationsmaterialien und Vorträge zu einzelnen Ausstellungen und Stücken vorbereiten. Das Renommee der Einrichtung und der einzelnen Wissenschaftler hängt zwar von eigenem Talent ab, aber nichts desto weniger wichtig sind die Informationsreserven, die die Informationseinrichtung zur Verfügung stellt (und dabei unnötigen Zeit- und Arbeitsaufwand erspart).

Weitere strategische Allianzen sollen mit den Mitgliedern einer möglichen Bibliothekskommission, eines Beratenden Ausschusses oder eines Aufsichtsrats der Informationseinrichtung gepflegt werden. Diese geben die Richtung der Bibliotheks- und Informationspolitik in die Institution weiter und können auch als Advokaten und Multiplikatoren fungieren. Ihre „Pflege“ (Informationsfluss in beiden Richtungen und häufige Kontakte, um die Meinungsbarometer zu erhalten oder neue Ideen von den Nutzern zu hören) ist äußerst wichtig.

Das Rechenzentrum der Einrichtung (oder EDV-Einheit) bzw. alle EDV-Betreuer in der Einrichtung sind wichtige Partner, vor allem beim Problemlösen, aber auch für neue und größere Projekte. Es kann z.B. kein E-Print-Server in ordentlicher Form aufgebaut werden, ohne dass die EDV-Einheit mitmacht und ggf. mitwirkt bei der Gestaltung - nicht nur bei EDV-Fragen, sondern bei allen Aspekten, die den Nutzern zugute kommen sollten. Hier ist auch ein Bereich, wo ggf. bei Kürzungen einige überschneidende Dienstleistungen aus der Bibliothek gestrichen werden können, wenn die EDV bereit ist, diese zu übernehmen.

Wie bereits erwähnt, können die Fachgesellschaft und die IuK-Kommission in Deutschland wichtige Partner sein. Von diesen Gruppen von Wissenschaftlern erhält man eine ausgesprochen ehrliche Meinung und Kritik über die Dienstleistungen, insbesondere im Hinblick auf ihre fachlichen Bedürfnisse bei Recherchen, Informationsaufbereitung usw. Diese sind richtungsweisend und für die Neuorientierung und Bewertung der angebotenen Dienstleistungen äußerst wichtig. Wenn die Bibliothek diese Zielgruppen verfehlt, werden sie ihre Informationen von anderen Quellen direkt beziehen und der Bibliothek / Informationseinrichtung geht ihre Unterstützung verloren. Orientiert sich die Bibliothek / Informationseinrichtung stärker an den tatsächlichen Bedürfnissen dieser Gruppen, so hat sie starke Advokaten, wenn es zu Etatkürzungen kommt. Auch interessierte Verlage / Universitätsverlage, Museen, Kunsteinrichtungen, Archive und andere relevante Forschungs- und Bildungseinrichtungen sind wichtige Partner für die Bibliothek / Informationseinrichtung, um neue Projektpartner zu gewinnen und geteilte bzw. erweiterte Dienstleistungen anzubieten. Die Bildung von Konsortien (regionaler Art, institutioneller Art etc.) zeigt auch, wie ein Zusammenschluss von Bibliotheken und Informationseinrichtungen mehr erreichen kann als einzelne Institute.

Die „politische" Rolle des Bibliothekars / Informationsspezialisten

Wenn er/sie will, kann der/die Bibliothekar/in bzw. Informationsspezialist/in eine wichtige Rolle, sogar eine führende Rolle, in seiner/ihrer Einrichtung übernehmen, indem er/sie den Übergang der Arbeitsvorgänge und Informationsvermittlung in die digitale Informationsgesellschaft angemessen an den inhärenten Bedarf ermöglichen und beschleunigen kann. Seine/ihre fachlichen Fähigkeiten sorgen für den Überblick über die sich verändernden Informationsquellen und -nutzung, so gewinnt er/sie an Urteilsfähigkeit über den Nutzen verschiedener Informationsquellen. Er/sie beschäftigt sich mit den Angeboten und frei verfügbaren Quellen, erreicht einen Überblick und handelt entsprechend den Prinzipien des Informationsmanagements. Die Fähigkeiten, die mit Informationsmanagement verbunden sind, wie z.B. Überblick über das Angebot, Verhandlungsgeschick, Kenntnisse der Entwicklungen und ihre Auswirkungen sowie Übung bei effektivem Management der Informationsressourcen, bilden die Grundlage für eine führende Rolle. Nur so kann auch der/die Bibliothekar/in eine Bewusstseinserhöhung für die Bedeutung von Informationen in tagtäglichen Arbeits- und Lebenssituationen innerhalb und außerhalb der Trägerinstitution erzielen. Sind diese Informationsmanagementfähigkeiten gut etabliert und zeigen auch, dass die Bibliothekspolitik gewinnbringend für die Institution ist, dann wird der Stellenwert der Bibliothek und ihrer Dienstleistungen in der Institution verbessert.

Bis jetzt haben wir vom Informationsspezialisten und Bibliothekaren geredet. Auch wenn diese Berufsbezeichnungen völlig richtig sind, wird aber gleichzeitig anerkannt, dass sich daraus der neue Beruf Informationsmanager / Informationsmanagement entwickelt. Dies ist von ebenso großer Bedeutung wie die Entwicklungen, die sich durch den Wandel zur digitalen Informationsgesellschaft ergeben. Einige der Ausbildungsstätten im Ausland und in Deutschland bieten nun neue Studiengänge an, die sich diese Anforderungen stellen. Das Curriculum ist allerdings noch sehr experimentell und muss die Absolventen doch noch in den meisten Fällen an die bestehenden Arbeitsmarktbedingungen anpassungsfähig machen. Ein weiterer Aspekt bedarf noch Erwähnung: junge Absolventen solcher Ausbildungsgänge kommen schnell in Firmen unter. Anders ist es aber im Öffentlichen Dienst: gerade wo der Bedarf besteht, eine Erneuerung von innen zu verwirklichen, stoßen die jungen Kollegen oft auf angeblich unveränderbare Strukturen und auch wenige dazu motivierende Impulse.

Aber die Veränderungen werden den Bibliotheken vermutlich von außen aufgezwungen: Ohne Berücksichtigung der erstaunlichen Möglichkeiten vernetzter Informationsressourcen wird die Bibliothek und vor allem der/die Bibliothekar/in nicht überleben. Die Aufforderung lautet: mit den Lehrkräften zusammenarbeiten, um ein Curriculum aufzubauen, das die Grundlagen des Auskunftsinterviews bis hin zum Umgang mit der Umstellung des Bibliothekskatalogs auf eine Z 39.50 Schnittstelle bzw. Verbindungen zwischen

Bibliothekskatalogen und anderen Informationsdienstleistungen umfasst, damit die Informations- und Literaturversorgung möglichst umfassend, leicht zu bedienen und präzis ist. Dieses Angebot soll nicht nur den in der Ausbildung stehenden „Anwärtern" zur Verfügung stehen, sondern auch als Fortbildungsangebot angeboten werden. Professionell organisierte und systematische Fortbildungsangebote für bestehende Mitarbeiter in Bibliotheken und anderen informationsvermittelnden Einrichtungen sind nur verstreut und seit der Auflösung des DBI um so weniger sichtbar in der deutschen Bibliothekslandschaft. Hier besteht ein großer Bedarf, den die Fachhochschulen für Bibliotheks-, Dokumentations- und Archivwesen in Zusammenarbeit mit den Berufsverbänden als Aufgabe an sich ziehen sollten.

Ohne die Wende zu neuen Dienstleistungen, neuen Strukturen und zur Entwicklung eines neuen Selbstverständnisses als Informationsspezialist, kann es dazu kommen, dass sich der Stellenwert des bibliothekarischen Berufs weiterhin verschlechtert. Schlüsselqualifikationen[482] müssen einbezogen werden, aber mit Betonung auf Umgang mit neuesten informationstechnischen Entwicklungen, mit mehr Achtung der tatsächlichen und sich rasch verändernden Informationsbedürfnisse der Nutzer und mit größerer Umsicht in Bezug auf eine sich selbst gestaltende Informationsgesellschaft.

Weiterführende Literatur

Bowdon, Russell; Wijasuriya, Donald (Hrsg.): *The Status, Reputation and Image of the Library and Information Profession.* Proceedings of the IFLA Pre-Session Seminar, Delhi, 24-28 August 1992. München (etc.): K.G. Saur, 1994.

Berufsbild und Selbstverständnis der Bibliothekare in Deutschland 1994. Hrsg. von einer Arbeitsgruppe Berliner Bibliothekare. DBI-Materialien, 141. Berlin: Deutsches Bibliotheksinstitut, 1995.

Capurro, Rafael: *Leben im Informationszeitalter.* Berlin: Akademie Verlag, 1995.

Kompetenzen für Spezialbibliothekare des 21. Jahrhunderts. Vorbereitet für den Vorstand der Special Libraries Association (SLA) durch das Komitee für die Feststellung der Kompetenzen für Spezialbibliothekare, Vorsitz: Joanne Marschall; Bill Fisher; Lynda Moulton; und Roberta Piccoli. Deutsche Übersetzung mit ausdrücklicher Erlaubnis der Special Libraries Association von Diann Rusch-Feja und Evelin Morgenstern unter Mitwirkung von Roland Bertelmann. Zusammenfassung der Leitsätze. ... Berlin: Deutsches Bibliotheksinstitut (DBI), 1997. Auch in *Bibliotheksdienst* 31 (4) (1997), 599-609. http://www.dbi-berlin.de/dbi_pub/bd_art/97_04_04.htm

Crosby, Olivia: Librarians: Information experts in the information age. *Occupational Outlook Quarterly.* Winter 2000-01, S. 3-15.

Knowledge Management: A New Competitive Asset. 1997 State-of-the-Art Institute. Special Libraries Association. New York, NY: Special Libraries Association, 1998.

Maguire, Carmel; Kazlauskas, Edward J: Weir, Anthony D.: *Information Services for Innovative Organizations.* San Diego (etc.): Academic Press, 1994.

St. Clair, Guy: Change Management in Action: *The InfoManage Interviews. Industry Leaders Describe How They Manage Chance in Information Services.* Washington, D.C.: Special Libraries Association, 1993.

---

482 Vgl. Sven Grandke; Peter Schmitt; Herbert Emmerich; und Wolfgang Hentschel: Schlüsselqualifikationen in neuen Organisationsformen. Ein Kriterienkatalog für die Praxis. 1998: Deutsches Institut für Normung (DIN), 1998.

Truper-Rehberg, Gerhild: Berufsbild Informationsmanager in der Schule: Gedanken zu einem notwendigen Berufsfeld. *B.I.T.-Online* 4 (2001), 29-34.

Young, Peter R.: Librarianship: A Changing Profession: Questions about the Future of Libraries and Librarianship. In: *Daedalus* Fall 1996, pp. 103-125.

Georg Ruppelt

Lizenz zum Verhandeln

Möglichkeiten der Bundesvereinigung Deutscher Bibliotheksverbände

Von der Pflicht zum Konsens

> *„Verbände sind ein wesentlicher Bestandteil der Demokratie. Verbände sammeln Informationen, Meinungen und Annahmen, diskutieren diese und erarbeiten hieraus in der Diskussion Positionen. In Verbänden werden also aus unterschiedlichen, zum Teil divergierenden Meinungen und Annahmen durch die Behandlung in den Gremien Interessen. Erst auf dieser Ebene der Interessen kann der Dialog mit der Politik beginnen. Verbände haben also einen wesentlichen Anteil an der Entwicklung und dem Erhalt von Pluralismus und Demokratie. Doch Verbände sind nichts ohne die Menschen, die sich in ihnen engagieren.“*[483]

So fasst Olaf Zimmermann die Aufgabe und die Bedeutung von Verbänden kompakt und verständlich zusammen. Olaf Zimmermann ist Geschäftsführer des Deutschen Kulturrates, des Spitzenverbandes der Bundeskulturverbände, – wenn man so will: die Spitze der Spitzen, das Dach der Dächer, die Zusammenfassung der Zusammenfassungen, das Konsensgremium der Konsensgremien. Man kann den Deutschen Kulturrat gut mit der Bundesvereinigung Deutscher Bibliotheksverbände (BDB) vergleichen, die übrigens im Deutschen Kulturrat engagiert mitwirkt, insofern, als beide Verbände Positionen ihrer Mitgliedsvereinigungen, die durchaus unterschiedliche Interessen und Ziele haben können, nach außen zu vertreten haben. Diese Positionen aber müssen vorher innerhalb des jeweiligen Dachverbandes durch Verhandlungen fixiert werden, und zwar im Konsens mit allen Beteiligten.

Diese Aufgabe des Dachverbandes scheint einer Quadratur des Kreises gleichzukommen, wenn man sich nämlich vergegenwärtigt, für welche Vereine und Verbände die BDB das Dach bildet. Die überwiegende Mehrheit der Stimmenzahl der Bundesvereinigung Deutscher Bibliotheksverbände werden durch den Institutionenverband (Deutscher Bibliotheksverband) und die Personalverbände (Berufsverband Information Bibliothek und Verein Deutscher Bibliothekare) gestellt. Weiteres Mitglied ist zurzeit die ekz.bibliotheksservice, ein kommerzielles Unternehmen, dessen Gesellschafter freilich Vertreter der Öffentlichen Hand sind. (Während der Erstellung dieses Beitrages wird die Aufnahme weiterer Mitglieder in die BDB diskutiert.) Mit einiger definitorischer Großzügigkeit und Zudrücken eines Auges könnte der Deutsche Bibliotheksverband (DBV), der rund 2000 Bibliotheken aller Sparten und Größenklassen und deren Träger vertritt, als eine Art Verband der Arbeitgeber bezeichnet werden, während die beiden Personalverbände, nämlich der Berufsverband Information Bibliothek (BIB) und der Verein Deutscher Bibliothekare (VDB) die berufsspezifischen Interessen ihrer Mitglieder, also, wenn man so will, der Ar-

---

483 Olaf Zimmermann: Lobby für die Kultur und Lobby für das Bibliothekswesen – Deutscher Kulturrat und BDB. In: Politik für Bibliotheken. Die Bundesvereinigung Deutscher Bibliotheksverbände (BDB) im Gespräch. Birgit Dankert zum Ende ihrer Amtszeit als Sprecherin der BDB im Auftrag des Vorstandes, herausgegeben von Georg Ruppelt. K.G. Saur, München 2000. S. 115-122; S. 119.

beitnehmer zu vertreten haben. (Der Vergleich ist natürlich nur bedingt richtig, soll aber hier die Konflikt- wie die Konsensmöglichkeiten betonen.)

Vor dem Hintergrund der Tatsache, dass diese beiden großen Gruppierungen durchaus unterschiedliche Positionen einnehmen können, freilich nicht einnehmen müssen, ist es erstaunlich, dass seit über zehn Jahren die BDB effektiv nach innen wie nach außen wirken kann. Erstaunlich vor allem deshalb, weil Beschlüsse der BDB laut Satzung im Prinzip immer im hundertprozentigen Konsens gefällt werden müssen, Entscheidungen von existentiellem Interesse, die ein Mitglied betreffen, nicht gegen dieses Mitglied gefällt werden können. Die Definition von existentiellem Interesse obliegt dabei natürlich den Mitgliedern. Dass der Weg zum Konsens oft sehr mühsam sein kann, belegt die Geschichte der BDB. Sie ist in dem Band „Politik für Bibliotheken" für die Jahre 1989 bis Anfang 2000 beschrieben worden.[484]

In diesem Beitrag geht es aber weder um die Geschichte der BDB, noch um Grundsätzliches, noch gar um ein mit funkelnden Begriffen übersätes bibliothekspolitisches Theoriefirmament, sondern es soll versucht werden, einige Probleme in der bibliothekarischen Verbandsarbeit zu benennen und die Möglichkeiten ihrer Lösung aufzuzeigen.

Bei einer Darstellung von Problemen und Problemlösungen, Ent- und Beschlüssen der BDB ist aber zunächst auf etwas hinzuweisen, was sich wie ein roter Faden durch Geschichte, Gegenwart und Zukunft der BDB zieht und ziehen wird. Alle Kolleginnen und Kollegen im Vorstand der BDB sind durch Wahl demokratisch legitimiert und haben von ihren Wählern eine Lizenz im Zusammenhang mit der BDB erhalten, nämlich die Lizenz zu verhandeln – nicht mehr, aber auch nicht weniger. Dies gilt für die Vorsitzenden bzw. Geschäftsführer der Mitgliedsverbände ebenso wie für den Sprecher und die stellvertretenden Sprecher der BDB. Wenn man nun noch die Konsensverpflichtung laut Satzung der BDB hinzunimmt und die gegebenenfalls unterschiedlichen Interessen der Mitglieder berücksichtigt, so wird schnell klar, dass bestimmte Beschlüsse der BDB einen langen Weg hinter sich haben, bis sie zur endgültigen Beschlussfassung gereift sind. Oft sind diesen Beschlüssen eine Vielzahl von Gesprächen, Briefen, Stellungnahmen, Stellungnahmen zu Stellungnahmen, Entwürfen, sachlichen und polemischen Auseinandersetzungen etc., etc. vorausgegangen. Diese meist langwierigen Entscheidungsprozesse sind besonders für Kolleginnen und Kollegen, die sich das erste Mal in diesem Dachverband engagieren, überraschend, vor allem nämlich dann, wenn sie die in ihrer eigenen Institution oder ihrem Betrieb hierarchisch vorgegebene Struktur akzeptiert haben und mit ihr umzugehen wissen. Gerade aber die Tatsache, dass es Einzelnen oder Gruppierungen nur durch Argumente und Überzeugungsarbeit gelingen kann, den Gesamtverband von der Qualität des eigenen Vorschlags zu überzeugen, macht die Stärke und Dauerhaftigkeit eines Dachverbandes wie der BDB aus. Beschlüsse nämlich sind dann so oft durchgerüttelt worden, dass ein gewisser Verfestigungseffekt entsteht. Vor allem aber werden die Beschlüsse von allen Beteiligten mitgetragen.

Von Konflikten und Kompromissen

Seit Bestehen der BDB waren immer wieder die Struktur und die Finanzen der BDB Grund für kontroverse Diskussionen, ja verbale Konflikte. Erfreulicherweise aber konnte man sich schließlich doch immer einigen und etwa die Frage der Finanzen pragmatisch

---

[484] S. Anm. 1

nach Bedarf und Notwendigkeit entscheiden. Ein besonders aufwendig diskutiertes Problem war seit vielen Jahren das Tagungsgefüge. Die bei diesem Thema erstaunlicherweise oft emotionsgeladenen Diskussionen berührten jahrelang im Prinzip immer nur eine Frage, nämlich die, in welchen Intervallen ein von der BDB ausgerichteter Kongress stattfinden solle. Mit dem gemeinsamen Kongress von BDB und Deutscher Gesellschaft für Informationswissenschaft und Informationspraxis (DGI) in Leipzig im Jahr 2000 kam ein zusätzlicher neuer Spieler an den Pokertisch, von dem zunächst zu befürchten war, dass er die Entscheidungsfindung noch weiter komplizieren würde. Es stellte sich jedoch bald heraus, dass dem nicht so war, sondern dass gerade die Zusammenarbeit mit der DGI die Diskussionen positiv beförderten.

Auf einer außerordentlichen Sitzung des BDB-Vorstandes am 23. Januar 2001 fassten die Teilnehmer einstimmig den Beschluss, in den Jahren 2004, 2007 und 2010 gemeinsame Kongresse zeitnah zur Leipziger Buchmesse und eben dort zu veranstalten. In den Jahren dazwischen werden die Mitgliedsverbände ihre Bibliothekartage oder Jahrestagungen nach eigenem gusto abhalten, wobei jetzt schon vorauszusehen ist, dass es in der Regel gemeinsame Veranstaltungen der Personalverbände wie des Institutionenverbandes sein werden, die damit einem Kongress nicht unähnlich sind. Die Verantwortung für diese Tagungen aber wird bei den veranstaltenden Vereinen und Verbänden selbst liegen.

Ein Außenstehender wird sich kaum eine Vorstellung davon machen können, mit welchem Aufwand dieser Beschluss herbeigeführt werden musste. Wenn man jedoch näher hinschaut, wird bald deutlich werden, dass sich hinter diesen unterschiedlichen Meinungen ein Interessenkonglomerat verbirgt, das zusammengesetzt ist aus finanziellen Erwägungen, Verantwortung gegenüber den jeweils eigenen Mitgliedern und vielleicht auch ein wenig aus je unterschiedlichen Repräsentations- oder Prestigebedürfnissen. Dass die Entscheidung dennoch zustande kam, war nur möglich dadurch, dass, wie bei jedem Kompromiss, nicht jeder alle eigenen Vorstellungen realisieren konnte und auch eigene Interessen einzelner Mitglieder zurückgenommen werden mussten.

Dachverbände und Vereinigungen, die aus Mitgliedern mit durchaus unterschiedlichen Interessenlagen gebildet werden, können leicht der Gefahr ausgesetzt sein, sich vor allem mit eigenen wichtigen oder für wichtig gehaltenen Problemen, kurz: mit sich selbst zu beschäftigen. Dieser Gefahr waren sich BDB-Vorstand wie -Sprecher durchaus bewusst und haben deshalb zu Beginn ihrer Tätigkeit in hohem Maße Dienstleistungen für das Bibliothekswesen, Kooperation mit anderen Gremien und Lobby- und Öffentlichkeitsarbeit in den Vordergrund ihres Engagements gestellt. Dass die BDB auf diese Weise ganz pragmatisch konkrete Leistungen für das deutsche Bibliothekswesen erbringen kann, sei im folgenden an einigen Beispielen aufgeführt.

Zur internationalen Arbeit

Eine der Hauptaufgaben der BDB lag seit Beginn ihres Bestehens in der internationalen Arbeit. Mitglieder der BDB oder von ihr Beauftragte wirkten und wirken etwa in IFLA- oder in EBLIDA-Gremien mit. Auf internationalen Kongressen war und ist die BDB kontinuierlich vertreten. Eine besondere Aufgabe im Bereich der internationalen Arbeit oblag der Bibliothekarischen Auslandsstelle (BA), deren Träger die Bundesvereinigung Deutscher Bibliotheksverbände war. In Paragraph 1 der Geschäftsordnung der BA hieß es u.a.:

> *„§ 1 Aufgaben der Bibliothekarischen Auslandsstelle*
> *1. Die Bibliothekarische Auslandsstelle (BA) ist eine Einrichtung der BDB.*

In ihrem Auftrag fördert sie die persönliche Begegnung, den Erfahrungsaustausch, die Kooperation und die Kontaktpflege zwischen Bibliothekaren und Informationsfachleuten des In- und Auslandes, macht internationale Erfahrungen in Deutschland bekannt und informiert das Ausland über bibliotheksrelevante Entwicklungen in Deutschland. Die Bibliothekarische Auslandsstelle fördert damit den internationalen Dialog und somit eine fruchtbare europa- und weltweite Zusammenarbeit auf dem Gebiet des Bibliotheks- und Informationswesens.

2. *Die ordentlichen Mitglieder der BDB benennen ihre Vertreter, die die BA bilden. Der Vorsitz der BA wechselt unter den BA-Mitgliedern alle drei Jahre.*

Vorschläge der Mitglieder für die fachliche Arbeit gehen an die jeweiligen Verbandsvertreter in der BA und werden so in die Programmarbeit eingebracht. Darüber hinaus können Vorschläge aus der Fachöffentlichkeit im In- und Ausland in die Programmarbeit aufgenommen werden."

Organisation, Durchführung von Austauschvorhaben und Veranstaltungen, also die ganz konkrete täglich Arbeit der BA aber lag in den Händen von erfahrenen und kundigen Mitarbeitern des Deutschen Bibliotheksinstitutes, die im Auftrage der BDB die Geschäfte führten. Durch die Abwicklung des DBI drohte die Auslandsarbeit der BDB zu Beginn des Jahres 2000 wegzubrechen. Nach zahlreichen Verhandlungen, vor allem aber durch den Einsatz vieler engagierter Kolleginnen und Kollegen gelang es der BDB im Jahr 2000, die Arbeit der Bibliothekarischen Auslandsstelle weiterzuführen und neu zu strukturieren. Besonders wichtig und konstruktiv gestaltete sich diese Weiterführung bzw. in einigen Fällen auch der Neubeginn dieser Arbeit dadurch, dass von Anfang an die Zusammenarbeit mit der DGI gesucht wurde und – in diesem Fall vielleicht noch wichtiger – eine enge Partnerschaft mit dem Goethe-Institut aufgebaut werden konnte. Hinzu kommt demnächst auch eine Kooperation mit der Bertelsmann-Stiftung, die sich vor allem im Bereich der Stipendienvergabe auf neue Wege begeben wird.

Dass also die internationale Arbeit der bibliothekarischen Verbände weiter- und teilweise einer neuen Bestimmung zugeführt werden konnte, ist einmal den neuen Kooperationsstrukturen zu danken, zum anderen aber auch der Tatsache, dass die Kulturstiftung der Länder wie das Auswärtige Amt ihr Vertrauen in diese Arbeit weiter unter Beweis stellten, indem sie wie bis dahin entsprechende Projekte förderten und dies auch in Zukunft tun wollen. Vor allem aber ist diese befriedigende Entwicklung dem Engagement einzelner Kolleginnen und Kollegen zu danken, besonders der neuen Vorsitzenden, unter deren Vorsitz sich die Auslandsstelle seit 2001 mit Genehmigung des BDB-Vorstandes auch einen neuen Namen zulegte, nämlich „Bibliothek & Information International".

IFLA 2003

Das für das deutsche Bibliothekswesen wohl wichtigste Ereignis zu Anfang des neuen Jahrhunderts wird zweifellos der Weltkongress der IFLA 2003 in Berlin sein. Mitte der 90er-Jahre hatte sich die BDB um die Ausrichtung von IFLA 2003 in Berlin beworben[485]. Am 21.08.1998 wurde die Entscheidung für Berlin auf der Generalkonferenz in Amsterdam verkündet – ein großer Erfolg für die BDB und damit für das deutsche Bibliotheks-

[485] Vgl. dazu Claudia Lux: Die BDB und die IFLA – ein gelungener Sprung in internationale Gewässer. In: Politik für Bibliotheken, s. Anm. 1, S. 79-87.

und Informationswesen. Erstmals wird nun der bedeutendste bibliothekarische Kongress im vereinigten Deutschland stattfinden. Auch in diesem Fall betrachtete man Ende der 90er-Jahre die Entwicklung um das DBI mit Sorge, die ja dann tatsächlich zu einer von der BDB und ihren Mitgliedern erfolglos bekämpften Abwicklung wurde. Die BDB trat und tritt zwar als Ausrichter und Vertragspartner von IFLA und anderen beteiligten Gremien und Firmen auf, sie war aber zunächst von der Voraussetzung ausgegangen, dass Teile der Planung und Durchführung von IFLA 2003 am DBI erledigt werden würden. Wie sollte es nach der Abwicklung des DBI mit IFLA 2003 weitergehen? Die Sorge der BDB erwies sich erfreulicherweise insofern als unbegründet, als im Jahr 2000 die Stiftung Preußischer Kulturbesitz die Vorbereitung für IFLA 2003 durch Einrichtung eines Generalsekretariates an ihrer Staatsbibliothek sicherte. In Zukunft werden sich auch der Senat von Berlin wie die Zentral- und Landesbibliothek Berlin en gros und en detail an den Vorbereitungen und selbstverständlich auch an der Durchführung des Weltkongresses beteiligen. Nach dem vorher Gesagten ist es nahezu selbstverständlich, dass auch bei diesen Vorbereitungen die DGI und das Goethe-Institut Inter Nationes eng mit der BDB kooperieren.

Kooperationen und Aktionen

Der erste gemeinsame Kongress der Bibliotheks- und Informationsverbände im März 2000 in Leipzig kann man als eine wichtige Initialzündung für verstärkte weitere Kooperationen der beiden Spitzenverbände betrachten. Sichtbar dokumentiert ist der gemeinsame Kongress in einem von beiden Verbänden herausgegebenen umfangreichen Tagungsband.[486]

Es fällt dem Berichterstatter schwer aufzuzählen, in welchen Bereichen der berufspolitischen Arbeit BDB und DGI seither nicht kooperierten. In regelmäßigen Abständen treffen sich der Präsident der DGI und der Sprecher der BDB, um gemeinsame Vorhaben zu planen; sie informieren sich nahezu täglich über aktuelle Anliegen.

Ein besonders erfolgreiches Projekt der Kooperation stellt sich im Bereich der Öffentlichkeitsarbeit dar. Im letzten Quartal des Jahres 2000 installierten BDB und DGI eine Nachrichtenagentur, die ohne großen Aufwand, dafür aber schnell und effektiv in der Lage ist, Nachrichten aus dem Bibliotheks- und Informationswesen innerhalb kürzester Zeit den Medien zu vermitteln. Bibliotheken und Informationsdienstleister wurden aufgefordert, Nachrichten von möglichst überregionalem Interesse per E-Mail an den Sprecher der Bundesvereinigung Deutscher Bibliotheksverbände oder den Präsidenten der Deutschen Gesellschaft für Informationswissenschaft und Informationspraxis zu übersenden. Diese Nachrichten werden gegebenenfalls von diesem oder jenem redigiert, dann an die Geschäftsstelle der DGI in Frankfurt weitergeleitet, von wo aus sie ebenfalls auch per E-Mail an einige hundert Redaktionsadressen von Tages- und Wochenzeitungen, Rundfunk- und Fernsehsendern und auch Fachpublikationen des Bibliotheks-, Informationswesens und Buchhandels verbreitet werden. Diese „Nachrichtenagentur" steht bei Bedarf allen Mitgliedern der beiden Verbände, aber auch ihren weiteren Kooperationspartnern und befreundeten Gremien zur Verfügung. Einer der wesentlichen und schon oft genutzten Vorteile dieses Verfahrens ist die Möglichkeit, auf Aktuelles schnell und flächendeckend zu

---

[486] Information und Öffentlichkeit. 1. gemeinsamer Kongress der Bundesvereinigung Deutscher Bibliotheksverbände e.V. (BDB) und der Deutschen Gesellschaft für Informationswissenschaft und Informationspraxis (DGI), Leipzig, 20. bis 23. März 2000, zugleich 90. Deutscher Bibliothekartag, 52. Jahrestagung der Deutschen Gesellschaft für Informationswissenschaft und Informationspraxis e.V. (DGI) / hrsg. von Georg Ruppelt und Horst Neißer – Wiesbaden: Dinges & Frick, 2000.

reagieren – eine Möglichkeit, die von vielen Bibliotheken mittlerweile oft genutzt wird.

Gemeinsam wird Öffentlichkeitsarbeit in vielfältiger Weise praktiziert, so etwa durch Pressekonferenzen, durch gemeinsame Schreiben an Verantwortliche in Politik und Verwaltung, durch gemeinsame Gespräche mit anderen Verbänden, wie etwa dem Deutschen Hochschulverband. Angesichts der katastrophalen Lage der deutschen Hochschulbibliotheken entschloss sich die BDB Ende des Jahres 2000 aggressiv die Öffentlichkeit von dieser Notlage in Kenntnis zu setzen. Zunächst schrieben der DGI-Präsident und der BDB-Sprecher gemeinsame Briefe an die Spitzen der Bundes- und Landespolitik. Schließlich gelang es ihnen, eine Anzahl kultureller und wissenschaftlicher Verbände dazu zu bewegen, sich den Forderungen von BDB und DGI anzuschließen und eine Resolution an die verantwortlichen Ministerien zu unterschreiben. Diese Gemeinschaftsaktion mit der Bundesvereinigung Deutscher Bibliotheksverbände, dem Börsenverein des Deutschen Buchhandels, der Deutschen Gesellschaft für Informationswissenschaft und Informationspraxis, dem Deutschen Hochschulverband, der Deutschen Literaturkonferenz, dem Goethe-Institut, der Union der Deutschen Akademien der Wissenschaften und dem Verband deutscher Schriftsteller in der IG Medien führten zu einem großen Presseecho, zu Stellungnahmen einzelner Bundes- und Länderministerien, vor allem aber zu einer Beschäftigung des Bundestages mit diesem drängenden Problem.

Nachdem sich der Deutsche Kulturrat dem Anliegen von BDB und DGI angenommen und in einer eigenen Pressekonferenz gemeinsam mit BDB-Vertretern auf die desaströse Lage der Bibliotheken im Januar 2001 aufmerksam gemacht hatte, brachte die FDP-Fraktion einen Antrag in den Bundestag ein, nach dem eine Soforthilfe von 80 Millionen für deutsche wissenschaftliche Bibliotheken bereitzustellen sei sowie pro Jahr 120 Millionen in den nächsten fünf Jahren. Welche Konsequenzen dieser Antrag nach sich ziehen wird, war beim Verfassen dieses Textes noch nicht zu erkennen.

Ein weiteres Beispiel für erfolgreiche Lobby-Arbeit der beiden Verbände zeigt sich in den Aktivitäten im Umfeld der EU-Richtlinie zum Urheberrecht. Gemeinsam mit dem DBV hat hier die BDB über Jahre hinweg und jetzt auch die DGI regelmäßig den Standpunkt der Bibliotheken gegenüber der Politik wie der Öffentlichkeit vertreten. Umfangreiche Aktionen mit Schreiben an die einzelnen deutschen EU-Parlamentarier sind bis zum Tag der Beschlussfassung unternommen worden. Dass die EU-Richtlinie im wesentlichen dann zur Zufriedenheit der Bibliotheken in Europa gefasst wurde, ist EBLIDA, der Zusammenarbeit der Verbände in Deutschland und den kompetenten Stellungnahmen der Rechtskommission des eDBI, vor allem den klaren und juristisch überzeugenden Ausführungen einer Berliner Kollegin zu danken.

Sehr zukunftsorientiert ist die von BDB und DGI gegründete Arbeitsgemeinschaft „Gemeinsames Berufsbild", in der Vertreter aller bibliothekarischen Verbände und der DGI sowie ein Gast des Vereins der Archivare vertreten sind. 1998 wurde die Veröffentlichung „Berufsbild 2000. Bibliotheken und Bibliothekare im Wandel" vorgelegt, die im Jahr 2000 in einer zweiten und um eine englische Übersetzung ergänzten Auflage erschien.[487]

In jedem Fall dürften diese Beispiele zeigen, wie erfolgreich Verbände gemeinsam Lobby-Arbeit im Dienste und zum Nutzen ihrer Mitglieder ausführen können.

---

[487] Berufsbild 2000. Bibliotheken und Bibliothekare im Wandel. Erarbeitet von der Arbeitsgruppe Berufsbild der BDB e.V. unter Leitung von Ute Krauß-Leichert; 2. unveränd. Nachdruck d. dt. Fassung, ergänzt um die englische Version. Wiesbaden: Dinges & Frick, 2000.

Zu Anfang der Kooperationsverhandlungen zwischen DGI und BDB war übrigens auch das Thema Fusion der beiden Verbände Gegenstand der Diskussion. In der heutigen Situation, so jedenfalls die Meinung des derzeitigen BDB-Sprechers, scheint die jetzt gefundene Lösung der engen Kooperation die sehr viel bessere zu sein, weil diese Lösung pragmatisch und effektiv ist. Nicht die Beschäftigung mit Verbands- oder gar Prestige-Problemen, also die Beschäftigung mit sich selber steht im Vordergrund des Handelns, sondern Hauptziel der Kooperationspartner ist die aktuelle und vorausplanende Förderung des Bibliotheks- und Informationswesens.

Noch nicht so umfangreich, aber dennoch in einigen Bereichen bereits sehr erfolgreich, zeigt sich auch die Zusammenarbeit der BDB mit anderen Partnern, die hier nur angedeutet sei. Außer den oben schon beschriebenen Kooperationen mit dem Goethe-Institut und der Bertelsmann-Stiftung finden regelmäßige Gespräche auch mit dem Börsenverein des Deutschen Buchhandels statt. In diesen Spitzengesprächen besteht die Möglichkeit, gemeinsame Standpunkte zu formulieren, aber auch kontroverse Ansichten offen und vertrauensvoll zu diskutieren. Regelmäßige Kontakte, teilweise durch Personalunion der Amtsträger gefördert, werden zur Stiftung Lesen, zur Deutschen Literaturkonferenz, die die Preusker-Medaille für Verdienste um das Öffentliche Bibliothekswesen vergibt, und zum Deutschen Kulturrat gepflegt.

In einer sich wandelnden Welt wird es auch in Zukunft notwendig sein, die vorhandenen Ressourcen gerade auch im Verbandswesen zu bündeln. Die BDB beabsichtigt daher, Gespräche auch mit den Verbänden der Archivare und Museumsfachleute aufzunehmen, um zu untersuchen, ob gemeinsame Standpunkte und Handlungsfelder auch in diesen Bereichen zu einer Kooperation unter den Verbänden führen können.

Mit diesen hier nur beispielhaft aufgeführten Kooperationen, Aktionen und Projekten erfüllt die BDB den Auftrag des umfangreichen Paragraphen 2 ihrer Satzung über Ziele und Aufgaben, dessen erster Satz lautet: „Ziel der BDB ist die Förderung der Kultur und Bildung". Demonstriert werden sollte, dass auch ein Dachverband wie die BDB, der als operatives Mittel zur Durchsetzung der Interessen seiner Mitglieder lediglich eine Lizenz zum Verhandeln hat, damit aber doch über umfangreiche Möglichkeiten verfügt, seine Ziele zu erreichen. Schließlich aber muss gegenüber der Politik und der Öffentlichkeit wie den eigenen Mitgliedern immer wieder darauf hingewiesen werden, dass Bibliotheken und die sie vertretenden Verbände ja nicht im eigenen Interesse handeln, sondern im Interesse der Bürgerinnen und Bürger aller Alters- und Sozialschichten, für die die Bibliotheken da sind.

Klaus-Peter Böttger

Ausbildung und Verbandspolitik - Konsens statt Konflikt

Bibliotheken und Informationseinrichtungen funktionieren in der Grundlage nur mit entsprechend ausgebildetem und qualifiziertem Personal. Ausbildungseinrichtungen haben auf den verschiedensten Ebenen, sei es durch institutionsinterne Einarbeitung, durch die dualistische Ausbildung beim Fachangestellten für Medien- und Informationsdienste, durch Fachhochschul-, Hochschul- oder andere universitäre Studiengänge mit unterschiedlichen Abschlüssen, für diese Qualifikation und deren Qualität Sorge zu tragen. Sieht man von dem situations- und arbeitsplatzbezogenen Anlernen ab, das heute angesichts der stark gestiegenen Anforderungen an eben eine solche Ausbildung nur noch vereinzelt und, wenn überhaupt, hoffentlich nur im einfachen Bibliotheksdienst anzutreffen ist, so unterliegen alle Ausbildungen einem zeitlichen Vorgriff.

Junge, an dem Bibliotheks- und Informationswesen interessierte Leute werden mit einem Vorlauf von 3 bis 4 Jahren auf ein Tätigkeitsfeld ausgebildet, das angesichts der Schnelllebigkeit insbesondere der technologischen Entwicklung beim Beginn der Ausbildung, des Studiums noch nicht abzusehen ist. Lässt man das viel diskutierte Argument des Praxisschocks im Sinne eines komplexen Lernens - vieles von dem, was ich gelernt habe, kommt auf meiner Arbeitsstelle nicht mehr vor - außer acht, so offenbaren sich aus meiner Sicht zwei Problemfelder, die auch auf die bibliothekarische Verbandsarbeit in Sachen Ausbildung zurückgeworfen werden. Zum einen stellt sich die Frage nach der realistischen arbeitsfeldbezogenen Ausbildung erneut: bereitet die Ausbildung - hier wird aus verständlichen Argumenten die dualistische Ausbildung des mittleren Dienstes bewusst ausgeklammert - auf die Realität eines möglichen Arbeitsplatzes in der Bibliothek oder Informationseinrichtung vor? Können die Bibliotheken des Alltags in ihren unterschiedlichen qualitativen Ausprägungen und zuweilen divergierenden Standpunkten des Fortschritts mit den in den zukunftsorientierten Studiengängen vermittelten Inhalten und ihrer fachlichen Ausrichtung auf Bibliotheks- und Medienmanagement sowie Informationsmanagement Schritt halten? So würde die zuweilen erhobene Fragestellung nach einer praxisorientierten Ausbildung einmal invertiert. Dies sollte meines Erachtens nicht als Konfliktpotenzial verstanden, sondern als gemeinsamer Impuls zur Entwicklung des Bibliotheks- und Informationswesens genutzt werden. Wenn Ausbildung und Bibliothek sich einig über die Zukunft sind, insbesondere die Positionierung und Konzeption von Bibliotheken in der Informationsgesellschaft, dann lassen sich in konzertierten, abgesprochenen Aktionen verbandspolitisch und bildungspolitisch Offensiven entwickeln, die beiden von Nutzen sind und Fortschritt bedeuten. Lassen wir dabei selbstbewusst außer acht, dass Impulse außerhalb unseres Einflussbereiches durchaus positive Ansätze enthalten können.

Zunehmend werden Ausbildungs- und Studieninhalte von Fragestellungen geprägt, die vor rund 20 Jahren außerhalb jeglichen bibliothekarischen Denkens lagen: Betriebswirtschaftliche Aspekte, Informationsdesign, Informationstechnik u.v.a.m. Das, was sich Praktiker freiwillig oder zwangsläufig haben betriebsintern oder über Fortbildungsangebote der Verbände aneignen müssen, angefangen von der aufoktroyierten Kosten- und Leistungsrechnung über das outgesourcte Design einer Homepage bis zur Gestaltung bibliothekseigener Werbetexte, all dies bringen Absolventen von Studiengängen wie dem Bibliotheks-

und Medienmanagement bereits in die Praxis mit. Hierbei ist nicht auszuschließen, dass solche Qualifikationen in der Bibliotheksrealität zu Spannungen führen können. Wenn Akzeptanz gegenüber Berufsanfängern nicht ausreichend vorhanden ist, so werden hier fortgebildete BibliothekarInnen mit ausgebildeten Bachelors of Information and Communication konfrontiert, wird jenen ein Spiegel mit den Notwendigkeiten der aktuellen fachlichen Anforderungen vorgehalten.

Grundsätzlich begrüßenswert ist die Erkenntnis, dass sowohl in Vorbereitung auf ein lebenslanges Lernen als auch in Hinblick auf die Qualifizierung des Mitarbeiters als Teil des Organismus Betrieb den Schlüsselqualifikationen zunehmend Gewicht verliehen worden ist.

Die Ausweitungen und Neuorientierungen, die die Hochschule für Bibliotheks- und Informationswesen mit ihren Studienreformen in den vergangenen Jahren vollzogen hat, lässt sich parallel in den Verbandsstrukturen verfolgen. Beide Partner haben die Erkenntnis umgesetzt, dass die Bibliothek und die BibliothekarInnen neue Positionen beziehen müssen bzw. es mit innovativeren Berufsbildern zu tun haben. Nicht ohne Grund oder zumindest nicht aus dem Opportunismus nach neuen Mitgliedern aus nicht originären bibliothekarischen Kreisen haben fast alle Verbände sich mittels Satzungsänderungen Mitte der 90er-Jahre geöffnet, so dass die Sichtweise sich nicht allein auf das Bibliothekswesen bezog, sondern auch Informations- und Dokumentationseinrichtungen und auch die gewerbliche Informationswirtschaft berücksichtigte. Zugegebenermaßen hat man sich aber hierbei auf die ursprünglich bibliothekarischen Ausbildungsstätten konzentriert und eine verbandspolitische Offensive zur Rekrutierung weiterer Mitglieder aus verwandten Bereichen außerhalb dieser Ausbildungen (noch?) nicht gestartet.

Unterstellte Rolf Kluth[488] vor mehr als 30 Jahren der bibliothekarischen Personalvereinigung gegenüber dem Bibliothekenverband allzu leicht berufs- und standespolitische Motive bezüglich Ausbildungspolitik und der Entwicklung entsprechender Maßstäbe, so dürften die entwickelten Formen der Zusammenarbeit dieses Argument entkräften. Insbesondere das Schlagwort, das die Fusionsverhandlungen von VdDB und vba auf dem Weg zum Berufsverband Information Bibliothek begleitete und den grundsätzlichen Wert des neuen Verbandes darstellt, 'sparten- und hierarchieübergreifend', überwindet solche hoffentlich nur noch vereinzelt anzutreffenden Dünkel. Auch wenn die Bundesvereinigung Deutscher Bibliotheksverbände mit ihrer Pflicht zum Konsens, wie Dr. Georg Ruppelt es an anderer Stelle dieser Festschrift bezeichnet, das Forum der grundlegenden Kooperation geworden ist und zukunftsorientierte Publikationen wie das Berufsbild 2000 hervorgebracht hat, so belegen zahlreiche andere Beispiele unterhalb dieses Daches die beiderseitig gewünschte Zusammenarbeit von Ausbildungseinrichtungen und Bibliotheken - an dieser Stelle verzichte ich bewusst auf die Apposition von Theoretikern und Praktikern, da dieses Begriffspaar mir kontraproduktiv gegenüber dem gemeinsamen Intentionen erscheint. Da ist seitens der Berufsverbandes Information Bibliothek (BIB) die Kommission für Aus- und Fortbildung, bezeichnender- und idealer-weise unter dem Vorsitz einer Professorin von der Fachhochschule, die Studieninhalte beobachtet und bewertet und versucht, Hilfestellungen zu bieten, die bei Fragen zu bibliothekarischen Ausbildungsgängen berät und damit prädestinierter Ansprechpartner für Planungen und Weiterentwicklung im Ausbildungssektor ist. Die Kommission organisiert ebenso das Innovationsforum auf den Bibliothekartagen, auf dem Diplom-Arbeiten von Absolventen der Fach- und Hochschulen ausgezeichnet

---

[488] Kluth, Rolf: Grundriß der Bibliothekslehre. Wiesbaden 1970. S. 118

werden, ein Qualitätssiegel für die Hochschule selbst. In der Sektion 7 des DBV, der Konferenz der Informatorischen und Bibliothekarischen Ausbildungseinrichtungen (KIBA), gestaltet sich ein weiteres Forum für die Zusammenarbeit und den gegenseitigen Austausch der Ausbildungseinrichtungen mit den als Gästen geladenen Verbandsvertretern. Dankenswerterweise, sei es als Mitglied oder Gast bei Sitzungen von Studienreformausschüssen oder in Form von erbetenen Stellungnahmen und Statements auf Hearings zu Reformvorhaben, aber auch umgekehrt durch die engagierte Mitgliedschaft von Hochschulangehörigen im Verband, gestaltet sich meines Erachtens die Kooperation von Ausbildung und Verband konsistenter und konsensfähiger als durch den scheinbaren Widerspruch von Theorie und Praxis ausgedrückt. An dieser Stelle ist daran zu erinnern, dass das letzte Berufsbild des Diplom-Bibliothekars an Öffentlichen Bibliotheken des damaligen VBB maßgeblich von an der damaligen Stuttgarter Fachhochschule für Bibliothekswesen tätigen Mitglieder und Professoren überarbeitet wurde.

Theorie und Praxis sind ebenso komplementäre Ergänzungen wie Ausbildung und Verband: verbandspolitisch ist die Ausbildung ein elementares Element und Qualitätsmerkmal, und die Hochschule setzt Qualitäten mit praxis- und arbeitsmarktorientierter Ausbildung, eine Ergänzung, die beiderseits effektiv genutzt werden sollte.

Wolfgang Ratzek

Synergieeffekte durch integrierte Kommunikationspolitik

Einstimmung

In der einschlägigen bibliotheksorientierten Fachliteratur nehmen Themen wie Öffentlichkeitsarbeit, Sponsoring, Kundenorientierung, Dienstleistung oder gar Bibliotheksmarketing zu. Doch fragen wir uns, was kommt davon in der allgemeinen Öffentlichkeit – also bei den (potenziellen) Kunden und in der exklusiven Öffentlichkeit, bei den Medienvertretern, an? Wir können da kaum von einer Erfolgsmeldung reden.

Für den Marketer stellt sich nun die Frage, was läuft da verkehrt? Was könnte verbessert werden? Hinzu kommt noch, dass die Beschäftigungsmöglichkeiten für BibliothekarInnen durchaus als positiv einzuschätzen sind.[489] In den folgenden Ausführungen soll einmal der Aspekt der Kommunikationspolitik näher betrachtet werden, um dann einen Ansatz zur Imageverbesserung von Bibliotheken zu skizzieren. Fangen wir mit einer kurzen Betrachtung über die zwei Gesichter der Kommunikationspolitik an.

Die zwei Gesichter der Kommunikationspolitik

Umgangssprachlich verstanden, bedeutet Kommunikationspolitik etwa folgendes: Alle nach außen gerichteten kommunikativen Aktivitäten von Unternehmen oder Institutionen, um beispielsweise Kunden, Aktionäre, Politiker, Verwaltungen über bestimmte interne Entwicklungen zu informieren. Diese Interpretation kommt dem sehr nahe, was wir unter Werbung oder Öffentlichkeitsarbeit verstehen. Ergänzt sei noch, dass unter kommunikative Aktivitäten sowohl systematisierte Aktivitäten, wie es beispielsweise bei einer kontinuierlichen Pressearbeit der Fall ist, als auch Spontanreaktionen, die sich aus der täglichen Arbeit ergeben, aber auf keiner Konzeption beruhen, was zum Beispiel durch Äußerungen wie „... das könnten wir doch ´mal machen“, zu verstehen ist.

Wir konzentrieren uns hier auf die systematisierte Kommunikationspolitik, um eben, wie im Titel angedeutet, Synergieeffekte zu erzeugen. Deshalb wollen wir einmal festhalten, dass Kommunikationspolitik sowohl in der *Publizistik* als auch im *Marketing* eine Bedeutung besitzt.

Kommunikationspolitik im Sinne der Publizistik meint, stark vereinfacht: Der Kampf um den Zugang zu den (Massen-)Medien. Denn: Wer den Zugang zu den Massenmedien besitzt, übt Macht aus, indem er/sie interessengeleitete Themen auf die Agenda setzt, Gegenöffentlichkeit erzeugt beziehungsweise unterdrückt oder bestimmte gesellschaftliche, kulturelle, politische, wirtschaftliche Strömung fördert beziehungsweise unterdrückt.

In diesem Zusammenhang erhält der sogenannte *Gatekeeper-Effekt* eine besondere Bedeutung (s.u.). Es reicht eben nach meiner Auffassung nicht aus, nur die bibliotheksorien-

---

[489] So berichtet beispielsweise die Direktorin der zlb (Zentral- und Landesbibliothek Berlin), Claudia Lux, dass es zunehmend schwieriger wird, qualifiziertes Bibliothekspersonal zu bekommen. Das gilt übrigens auch für Norwegen, wo AbsolventInnen von der Wirtschaft mit besserer Bezahlung abgeworben werden, s. Ratzek, W.: Bibliotheken in Norwegen. In: Bibliothek – Forschung und Praxis 2/2000, S. 189-195.

tierten Fachmedien zu bedienen, auch die Wirtschafts- und Unterhaltungsmedien[490] müssen bedient werden, um eine breite Akzeptanz zu erreichen. Da jedoch für sowohl Herausgeber als auch Redakteure das Thema Bibliotheken unter ferner liefen rangieren dürfte, gibt es kaum eine ernsthafte Berichterstattung über die Rolle der Bibliotheken in der Informations- und Wissensgesellschaft. Was, wie dieser Beitrag stimulieren will, nicht so bleiben muss.[491]

Kommunikationspolitik im Sinne des Marketing bedeutet dagegen etwas ganz anderes. Im Gegensatz zu anderen Autoren, die Marketing als einen Teilbereich der Betriebswirtschaftslehre sehen und den Trend zu Mathematisierung folgen, wollen wir hier einer Auffassung von Marketing als „Philosophie“ folgen, die neben der Betriebswirtschaftlehre und Informatik auch offen für Erkenntnisse unter anderem aus der Psychologie, Anthropologie, Biologie, Soziologie ist. Der kleinste gemeinsame Nenner zur Erfassung „aller“ Strömungen im Marketing bildet das Marketing-Mix, das sich aus den Submix-Bereichen Produkt-, Preis-, Distributions- und *Kommunikationspolitik* zusammensetzt.

Instrumente der Kommunikationspolitik

Die jeweiligen Submix-Bereiche im Marketing-Mix bieten nun eine Reihe bewährter Instrumente, die es nun gilt, kreativ umzusetzen und weiterzuentwickeln. Für den Submix-Bereich heißt das:

- Public Relations
- Werbung
- Verkaufsförderung (Vkf)
- Persönlicher Verkauf.

Entscheidend jedoch ist, dass die jeweiligen Instrumente aus den Submix-Bereichen zu einem harmonischen Ganzen integriert werden müssen, um Aussicht auf Erfolg zu haben.

Angesicht der Fülle an Literatur soll hier auf eine breite Betrachtung der Submix-Bereiche verzichtet werden. Statt dessen gehen wir kurz auf die Verkaufsförderung und den persönlichen Verkauf ein.

Beim persönlichen Verkauf geht es darum, wie sich BibliothekarInnen gegenüber der Öffentlichkeit im Allgemeinen und gegenüber ihren Kunden im Besonderen „verkaufen“, oder besser: präsentieren. Die häufiger geäußerte Vorstellung, dass BibliothekarInnen die Visitenkarten einer Bibliothek sind, kommt der hier dargestellten Auffassung sehr nahe.

Vor diesem Hintergrund entsteht eine Vision, die sowohl die publizistische als auch die marketingorientierte Kommunikationspolitik gerecht wird. Denn das eine geht nicht ohne das andere. Der Kampf um den Zugang zu den Medien erfordert wirksame Kommunikations-Instrumente[492] zur Zielerreichung, und für die Erreichung von Marketing-Zielen bedarf es des Zugangs zu den (Massen-)Medien. Über diese symbiotische Beziehung müssen wir uns – die im Bereich BDI-Aktiven – im klaren werden, wenn wir das Interesse für unsere Profession und/oder für die BDI-Institutionen steigern wollen.

[490] Im Prinzip gilt das auch für die Fachmedien anderer Fachrichtungen.

[491] Gespräche mit hochrangigen VertreterInnen aus BDI-Institutionen und –Praxis zeigen, dass ein gesteigertes Interesse vorhanden ist.

[492] Im Sinne eines integrierten Marketings muss dann auch Klarheit über die Beschaffenheit/Features Produkt, Preis und Distribution herrschen.

In diesem Zusammenhang wollen wir noch einmal kurz auf den oben genannten Gatekeeper-Effekt eingehen. Wurden früher Gatekeeper eher als Nachrichtenunterdrücker gesehen, so werden die Gatekeeper heute, vor dem Hintergrund der Nachrichtenexplosion durch das Internet, eher als Nachrichtenselektierer gesehen, die analysieren, ordnen und Kontexte schaffen und somit eine Art Sinnstiftung[493] betreiben.

Die folgende Darstellung zeigt das Zusammenspiel dieser beiden kommunikationspolitischen Ansätze.

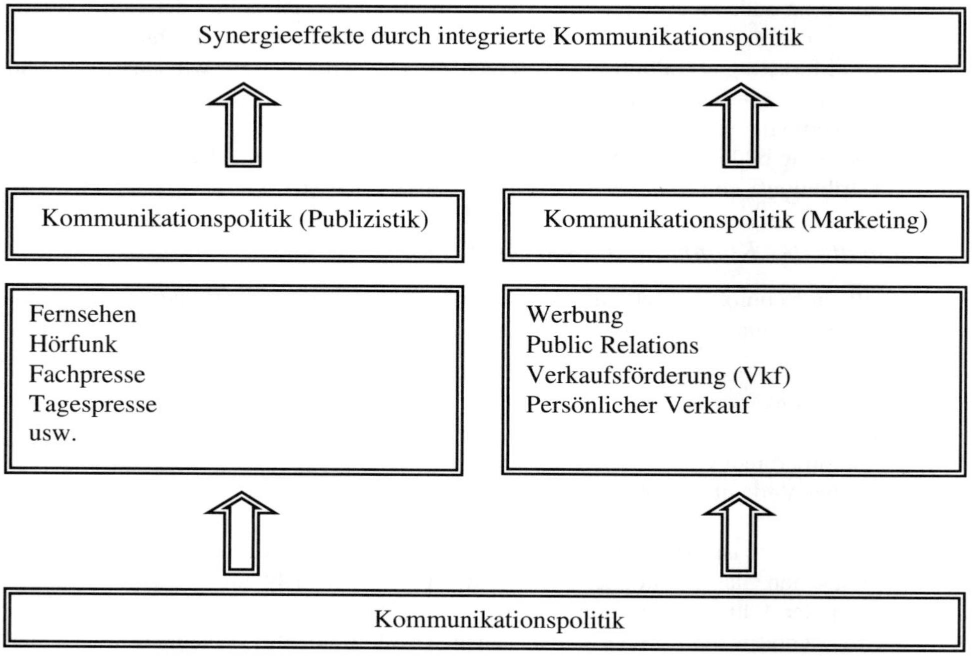

Abb. 1: Die zwei Seiten der Kommunikationspolitik

Bibliotheksmarketing

Gehen wir nun kurz auf das Bibliotheksmarketing ein. Hier soll nicht das gesamte Spektrum[494] dessen ausgebreitet werden, was unter diesem Terminus fällt, sondern lediglich zwei Aspekte herausgestellt werden, die für die weitere Diskussion von Bedeutung sind und die an die vorangegangenen Ausführungen direkt anschließen.

1. Aspekt: Marketing als institutionelle Selbstvermarktungsstrategie

Institutionelle Selbstvermarktung bedeutet, dass jede Bibliothek sich erst einmal selbst (re)präsentiert. Da werden die Produkte – Medien und Dienstleistungen – präsentiert, Prei-

[493] Wohlwissend, dass es in den Print- und TV-Bereich durchaus qualitative Unterschiede gibt. Aber genau das könnte ein Ziel sein, in den überregionalen und internationalen Medien präsent zu sein.

[494] Auch im Bibliotheksmarketing gilt das Marketing-Mix mit seinen Submix-Bereichen. Kommunikationspolitik im Sinne eines integrierten Bibliotheksmarketings ist somit umfassender als nur reine Öffentlichkeitsarbeit.

se (Entgelte) - Mahnungen oder entgeltpflichtige Dienstleistungen - ausgehängt, Distributionswege – Internet oder Fernleihe - organisiert, und last but not least Kommunikation – in Form von Ausstellungen oder Vorträgen – betrieben. Mit diesem Ansatz gelingt es zwar der einen oder anderen Bibliothek sich positiv zu profilieren, aber zwei wesentliche Dinge werden damit nicht erzielt:

- Die Bibliothek kann beispielsweise mit einer Ausstellung oder einem attraktiven Medienbestand nicht als ganzes glänzen, sondern erzielt nur kurzfristige Wirkung, vielleicht auch nur einen fokussierten Effekt („... da gibt´s tolle Software", „... die haben eine breite Auswahl an fremdsprachlicher Literatur" oder „... da kann ich kostenlos surfen").
- Mit den Aktionen wird kein Beitrag für die gesamte Bibliothekslandschaft geleistet.

2. Aspekt: Marketing für Bibliotheken

Der andere Aspekt, der im Bibliotheksmarketing enthalten ist, ist der, den die Marketer generisches Marketing nennen. Ein Marketing für ein gesamtes Cluster[495], in unserem Falle sind das Bibliotheken. Das wirft sofort die Frage nach der Verantwortlichkeit und der Organisation auf. Im Prinzip eine relativ einfach zu beantwortende Frage: Die Interessenverbände wie zum Beispiel IFLA, VDB, DBV, BIB, EUCLID. Was für das individualisierte Bibliotheksmarketing gilt, gilt auch für diesen Bereich, da unternimmt der eine Verband etwas, dann der andere, gelegentlich unternehmen auch zwei Verbände etwas gemeinsam, aber Synergieeffekte ergeben sich kaum, und schon gar nicht auf längere Sicht. Die zahlreichen Kongresse und Tagungen ziehen in der Regel nur Insider an, und die nicht bibliotheksfixierten Medien berichten, wenn überhaupt, nur während der Kongress- oder Tagungsdauer, und dann nur über das Event selbst, nicht aber beispielsweise über die Rolle der Bibliotheken in der Informations- und Wissensgesellschaft in Form einer Sonderbeilage, wie das zum Beispiel während der CeBit, der ITB[496] oder IAA[497] der Fall ist.

Kommunikationspolitischer Aktionsradius

Was in der Werbung *Reichweite* bedeutet, gehört auch in der bibliotheksorientierten Kommunikationspolitik diskutiert: Mit welchen konkreten Kommunikationsmitteln erreichen wir unsere Zielgruppe(n) in optimaler Weise. Oder anders formuliert: Wie ist der größtmögliche Effekt mit einem geringst möglichen Aufwand zu erreichen? In der jetzigen Form, wir gehen darauf gleich näher ein, wird dies nicht optimal erfüllt.

Kampagne für Bibliotheken

Eine Kampagne, so können wir es in einschlägigen Lexika nachlesen, ist eine zeitlich begrenzte Aktion, die bei der Zielgruppe eine Verhaltensänderung herbeiführen soll. Uns ist die Werbekampagne, die Wahlkampfkampagne bekannt, aber auch die Hetzkampagne oder die Imagekampagne. Im Militärwesen ist dieser Begriff ebenfalls nicht ganz unbekannt und steht dort für einen Feldzug. Gelegentlich ist dann auch im nichtmilitärischen Umfeld von einem Werbefeldzug die Rede.

In dem hier aufgespannten Rahmen geht es darum, durch eine gezielte Kommunikati-

[495] Z.B. „Milch macht müde Männer munter", „Made in Germany".
[496] Internationale Tourismus Börse
[497] Internationalen Automobil Ausstellung

onsstrategie eine positivere Einstellung gegenüber Bibliotheken in der Öffentlichkeit, bei Politikern und Medienvertretern herbeizuführen. Das Problem: wir, die im BDI-Bereich Aktiven, besitzen keine Machtinstrumente[498], um diesen Prozess zu forcieren[499]. Erschwerend kommt noch hinzu, dass diese Kommunikationsstrategie Ressourcen personeller und finanzieller Art binden wird.

Konzertierte Aktion

Es liegt also auf der Hand, „alle“ Kräfte zu gewinnen, die an einer Imageverbesserung, oder noch besser: an einer Positionierung des BDI-Bereichs interessiert sind. Angesichts schrumpfender Etats und Bibliotheksschließungen[500] müssten das aus meiner Sicht im Prinzip alle im BDI-Bereich Aktiven sein. Doch ist das so einfach? Da gibt es die historisch gewachsenen Befindlichkeiten gegenüber den anderen BDI-Professionen. Da hegen noch InformationswissenschaftlerInnen gewisse Vorbehalte gegenüber BibliothekarInnen, da gibt es gewisse Vorurteile über die Bedeutung von BibliothekarInnen an Wissenschaftlichen und Öffentlichen Bibliotheken, da bilden Diplombibliothekare und Bibliotheksassistenten eigene Interessenvertretungen.[501] Es gäbe noch eine Reihe anderer Befindlichkeiten aufzulisten, die hier nicht weiter erwähnt werden sollen. Fakt ist, all diese Entwicklungen behindern ein gemeinsames Vorgehen und sind in der Außensicht kaum förderlich für eine Imageverbesserung.

Ebenso wie eine konzertierte Aktion ein abgestimmtes Verhalten des Staates, der Gewerkschaften und der Unternehmensverbände zur Erreichung wirtschaftspolitischer, insbesondere konjunkturelle, Ziele dient, sollten auch die BDI-Aktivitäten unter einem konzeptionellen Dach zusammengeführt werden. Wie wir vom *Bündnis für Arbeit* wissen, gibt es nicht nur Erfolge zu verkünden, aber der Versuch lohnt allemal.

Hans Nerlich, DGI-Geschäftsstelle, kommt in seinem Bericht[502] über die ISI 2000-Tagung zu folgender Feststellung: „Es ist festzustellen, dass man sich in der kleinen Informationsszene auf Grund vieler parallel stattfindender Einzelaktivitäten das Leben schwer macht, ohne die gewünschten Effekte zu erreichen. Eine Bündelung der Tagungsaktivitäten im Bereich der Informationswissenschaft und der Informationspraxis scheint angebracht, vor allem in Hinblick auf eine größere Wirkung nach außen. Damit erhielten auch die Informationswissenschaft selbst ein größeres und ihr zustehendes Forum, in dem sie den notwendigen Rückhalt in der Praxis gewinnen kann. Hier sollten in nächster Zukunft Gespräche unter den Verbänden geführt werden.“ Dieser Vorschlag geht zwar in die richtige Richtung, aber kann nur ein erster Schritt sein, da zum einen nur die Tagungsaktivitäten angesprochen, nicht aber die Einbindung in ein integriertes generisches Marketingkonzept gefordert wird, zum anderen die Informationseinrichtung als Träger der praktischen

[498] Ob beispielsweise das Machtmittel Generalstreik von BibliothekarInnen oder Fachinformationszentren dem Ziel förderlich ist, darf sehr bezweifelt werden.

[499] Wie das beispielsweise in der Gewaltenteilung als Idealfall in demokratisch regierten Staaten der Fall sein sollte: Legislative, Exekutive, Judikative. Wenn das System funktioniert, sieht das verkürzt so aus: Die Regierung erlässt Gesetze, die „Polizei“ überwacht die Einhaltung der Gesetze und „verhaftet“ Gesetzesbrechern, während die Richter diejenigen verurteilt, die gegen Gesetze verstoßen.

[500] Wie dem ÖTV-Magazin für den Bezirk Berlin „dialog 1/2001, S. 8 zu entnehmen ist, wurden „allein im Jahr 1999 (...) 12 Bibliotheken endgültig geschlossen.“

[501] Inzwischen gibt es auch hier eine sehr erfreuliches Umdenken. Die Gründung des BIB oder die Kooperation zwischen dem BDB und der DGI stehen hier stellvertretend.

[502] Nerlich, H.: Informationskompetenz – Basiskompetenz in der Informationsgesellschaft. In: nfd 1/2001, S. 58.

Informationsvermittlung. Wir sind also noch sehr weit entfernt von einem Konzept für eine konzertierte Aktion.

Beispiele für mögliche Ansatzpunkte

Die vertiefte Zusammenarbeit zwischen DGI und BDB böte eine entsprechende Basis, wenn es dann gelänge, die Akteure und Multiplikatoren innerhalb und außerhalb der BDI-Szene zu motivieren.

Ebenso geht die PR-Aktion der DGI „Frag´ Info Profis“ in die richtige Richtung. DGI-Präsident und Direktor der Stadtbibliothek Köln, Horst Neißer, schreibt dazu: „Diese Initiative soll mit ähnlichen Aktionen fortgeführt werden, um die Aufmerksamkeit der Öffentlichkeit (speziell der Medien und Politiker) auf den Berufsstand zu lenken.“[503] Zu bedenken ist dann nur, was bekommen Journalisten (als Repräsentanten der Medien) und Politiker zu sehen, wenn sie auf unseren Berufsstand aufmerksam werden, haben wir uns für diesen Besuch auch schön herausgeputzt (im Börsenjargon ist da von window dressing die Rede).

Die Infobase böte ebenfalls eine jährliche Plattform für eine konzertierte Aktion, zumal die Aussteller selbst auch ein Interesse daran haben müssten, den Kommunikationsradius auszuweiten.

2003 finden in Berlin die IFLA Ratsversammlung und Generalkonferenz statt. Dieses Event bietet gute Möglichkeiten für eine geplante konzertierte Aktion.

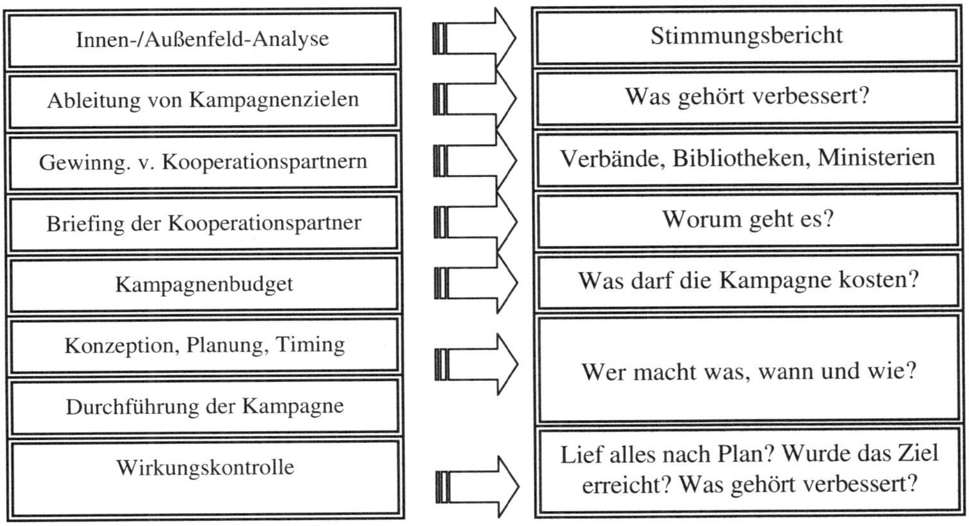

Abb. 2: Ablaufschema einer Konzertierten Aktion

503 Neißer, H.: Der neue DGI-Vorstand ist angetreten. In: nfd 1/2001, S. 3.

Schlusswort

Zwar ist Öffentlichkeitsarbeit in Bibliotheken und das komplexere Bibliotheksmarketing durchaus ein Thema. Die einschlägigen Fachmedien berichten immer wieder darüber. Es gibt eine Fülle von herausragenden Beispielen, dennoch darf die allgemeine Situation als unbefriedigend bezeichnet werden. Aus meiner Sicht, und ich weiß aus zahlreichen Gesprächen, dass ich diese nicht alleine vertrete, fehlt so etwas wie eine konzertierte Aktion zur breiten Akzeptanzförderung des Bibliotheksbereichs, im Prinzip gilt dies auch für den gesamten BDI-Bereich. Um dies zu leisten, bedarf es einer Konzeption, die sowohl auf der Ebene der Interessenvertretungen (Verbände) als auch die Interessen in den einzelnen Bibliotheken sowie der entsprechenden Institutionen in Bund, Ländern und Gemeinden berücksichtigt. In diesem Zusammenhang sollten sich auch die Hochschulen mit bibliothekarischen und informationswirtschaftlichen Studiengängen engagieren.

Vielleicht unerwartet, könnte auch von der ÖTV Unterstützung kommen. Im ÖTV-Magazin für den Bezirk Berlin „dialog“[504] ist unter der Überschrift „Bibliotheken haben eine Zukunft ... oder die Gesellschaft hat keine“ von der 1. Bibliotheksfachtagung die Rede, die unter dem Motto „Zukunft der Bibliotheken – Bibliothek der Zukunft“ stand.

[504] „dialog“ 1/2001, S. 8.

Konrad Heyde

Sich selbst und die Bibliothek im Blick

Zur Motivation bibliothekarischen Handelns

1. Wer sich für etwas Besonderes hält, gibt sich auch gern engagiert.

1.1 Allenthalben gilt Engagement als etwas sehr Positives.

1.11 Mit Engagement verbinden wir Lebendigkeit, Aktivität, Kompetenz, Mitteilsamkeit, Selbstbestimmtheit und Sinnhaftigkeit: lauter positive Attribute.

1.12 Vor allem im Engagement sehen wir (noch vor Wissen und Können) die Bedingung für den Erfolg unseres Tuns.

1.2 Engagement ist eine Haltung, die typisch für uns ist.

1.21 Aber das gilt nicht, weil wir selbst engagiert wären (Engagement ist ohnehin ein eher seltener Zustand, viele geraten niemals in ihn), sondern weil uns Engagement so viel gilt und wir es an anderen bewundern und für uns ersehnen.

1.22 In unserer Vorstellung (in unseren Wünschen) und im Sprachgebrauch ist Engagement allgegenwärtig und hat andere (ältere) Beweggründe, Disponiertheiten, Haltungen verdrängt.

1.221 Weil uns früher gültige Beweggründe verächtlich geworden sind, lassen wir (vor allem und an Stelle aller anderen) nur noch Engagement als Beweggrund gelten.

1.23 Auch wenn wir uns danach sehnen, engagiert zu sein, vermeiden wir Engagement, weil wir uns davor fürchten.

1.231 Engagement befremdet uns; denn der Engagierte erscheint uns als eindimensionales Wesen: aufdringlich, besserwisserisch, eifernd, überheblich, beschränkt.

1.232 Vor diesem peinlichen Zustand hüten wir uns. Um nicht Engagement anheim zu fallen, halten wir zum Engagierten Distanz.

1.24 Unsere Einstellung zum Engagement ist ambivalent.

1.3 Engagement ist zunächst ein militärischer Begriff: Im frühen Barock bezeichnet er das Verhältnis zwischen Söldner und Söldnerführer in jenen privat aufgestellten Truppen, die sich den Stadtstaaten und Fürsten verdingen und aus dem Krieg ein Geschäft machen. Der Begriff wird aufs Theater übertragen, was nahe liegt, weil auch das Theater eine mobile Truppe ist, wie der Söldnerhaufen aus Dahergelaufenen zusammengewürfelt. Wer ein Engagement erhält, also in der Söldner- oder Theatertruppe landet, lässt sich auf ein Vertragsverhältnis ein, das nicht vorgibt, eines zwischen gleichberechtigten Partnern zu sein: Der Söldnerführer/Theaterdirektor engagiert (handelt), der Söldner/Schauspieler wird engagiert (wird behandelt). Die Gage ist als finanzielle Kompensation der durch das Engagement bedingten Entwürdigung gedacht, also dafür, dass der Söldner sich niederkartätschen lässt und der Schauspieler sich vorm Publikum zum Hanswurst macht. - Derartiges Engagement erscheint uns archaisch.

1.31 Wenn wir heute von Engagement sprechen, verstehen wir darunter, sich für etwas zu engagieren.

1.311 Der Engagierte ist Theaterdirektor und Schauspieler zugleich. Er vereint Handeln und Behandelt-Werden in einem Vorgang, im Vorgang des Sich-Engagierens.

1.312 Der Engagierte wählt einen Gegenstand, dem er sich fortan durch sein Tun verpflichtet fühlen möchte.

1.313 Engagement ist der Versuch des leidenden Subjekts, sein Tun (und sich selbst) in einem Projekt zu objektivieren und damit die Angst vor der Freiheit zu überwinden.

1.3131 Engagement betrifft stets das Individuum; sobald es sich um viele handelt, ist es kollektive Unterwerfung.

1.3132 Beim einen und bei den vielen läuft es darauf hinaus, nicht mehr nach dem Sinn zu fragen, sondern sich auf die Methoden zu konzentrieren: der glückliche Fachidiot und die tüchtigen Gefolgsleute. (So mögen es die Diktatoren.)

1.314 Die Tatsache, dass es für den Sich-Engagierenden darauf ankommt, sich zu engagieren, aber der Gegenstand seines Engagements beliebig ist (selbstverständlich widerspricht dem der Engagierte aufs Heftigste), ist das Irrationale am Engagement.

1.315 Das ist das Faszinierende und Schreckliche am Engagement, dass wir mit ihm die gähnende Leere vor uns, die Sinnlosigkeit zu überdecken suchen und wissen, dass es sich um Selbstbetrug handelt, der scheitern wird.

1.32 Engagement erfordert Zwiedenken.

1.321 Der Engagierte ist überzeugt von der Richtigkeit seines Engagements und deshalb von der Wichtigkeit, es auf Dauer aufrecht zu erhalten, und weiß doch, dass sowohl seine Überzeugung schwindet als auch die Dauer nicht gelingt: Engagement ist nicht nachhaltig.

1.322 Wer sich engagiert, tut dies absichtlich. Engagement wird künstlich erzeugt.

1.323 Engagement ist nur zeitlich befristet aufrecht zu erhalten. Die Aufrechterhaltung macht zunehmend Mühe. Die anfängliche Lust am Engagement weicht dem Frust. Wer sich engagiert, muss davon ausgehen, dass das Engagement bald erlischt.

1.324 Das Engagement (und das Glück durch Engagement) ist am stärksten, bevor es in Arbeit ausartet. Wenn Engagement in Arbeit mündet, verschwindet es.

1.325 Man engagiert sich nicht für die Wirklichkeit, sondern für ihre Veränderung.

1.3251 Man engagiert sich für den Anschub, die Initiation eines Projekts, das dann erarbeitet werden muss.

1.3252 Um sich erneut zu engagieren, brauchte man Roboter, die die initiierte Arbeit erledigen.

1.326 Beim Engagement geht es um Sinnfindung.

1.3261 Es ist zu vermuten, dass bei automatischer Erledigung der Arbeit das Anschub-Engagement unterbleibt. Denn der Sinn stellt sich zwar nicht durch (die Qual der) Arbeit ein, wird jedoch in der Zuendeführung eines Projekts gesehen: Den Sinn erwarten wir vom Erfolg, den wir selbst herbeigeführt (erarbeitet) haben – und zwar deshalb, weil unser Handeln dem Risiko ausgesetzt ist: Es hätte auch ein Misserfolg sein können. Für ein Resultat, das ein Roboter erzielt, ist Engagement sinnlos.

1.3262 Wenn die Arbeit schon von Robotern erledigt wird, wäre es nur konsequent, ihnen auch das Initiieren von Projekten (Engagement) zu überlassen. Damit wäre (neben der Produktion) auch die Entwicklung (Geschichte) automatisiert. Dann wäre der Mensch frei, sein Leben in Muse (in Kontemplation, theoretisierend) zu verbringen. Wer sich fürchtet, sich mit sich und der Welt zu beschäftigen (nach dem Sinn zu fragen), verfällt in Engagement, d. h. er begibt sich in eine (Zwangs-)Lage, in der die Frage nach dem Sinn überflüssig ist. (Hierin gleichen sich barockes und gegenwärtiges Engagement.)

1.3263 Wer engagiert ist, wirkt äußerlich vor allem seinem Gegenstand zugetan. Das täuscht; denn Engagement entsteht nicht aus objektivem Interesse, sondern aus subjektivem Bedürfnis. Engagement ist der individuelle Versuch der Sinnfindung, ohne nach Sinn gesucht zu haben, und der Versuch, die Leere des Lebens zu kompensieren, ohne sich mit der Fülle beschäftigt zu haben.

1.3264 Das kann auch schärfer formuliert werden: Der Engagierte ist Egoist.

1.32641 Der Engagierte will es sich bequem machen: Er wünscht sich zwar, groß herauszukommen (ein sinnvolles Leben zu führen), ohne dafür jedoch allzu viel leisten zu müssen.

1.32642 Der Engagierte will sich mit dem halben Leben begnügen; die andere Hälfte, die ihm mühsam erscheint, vermeidet er: Nach dem Engagement muss er die schmerzliche Erfahrung machen, dass das nicht funktioniert.

1.32643 Oft wird daraus keine Erfahrung, weil der Schmerz nur als Schicksalsschlag empfunden und hingenommen („weggesteckt") wird: kein Gewinn, sondern eine Niederlage.

1.33 Der Engagierte registriert den jeweiligen Zustand seines Engagements genau.

1.331 Dazu beobachtet er die Reaktionen seiner Umgebung auf sein Engagement. Vor allem aber richtet er den Blick in sein Inneres: Er belauert das Schwinden des Engagements und seine dadurch ausgelösten Empfindungen.

1.3311 Angst kommt auf: vor dem sich abzeichnenden Desengagement (und dem drohenden Rückfall in die Sinnlosigkeit).

1.3312 Damit tritt das Engagement in seine eifernde Phase, ins Über-Engagement, d. h. in die Phase des verzweifelten Versuchs, das Engagement zu halten.

1.33121 Engagement wird betont, wenn der Motivationsschub schwach wird. In dieser Situation ist die Reklamation von Engagement der Versuch des Sich-Aufraffens: ein Appell an sich selbst, gefälligst motiviert zu sein. Engagement wird vor allem dann reklamiert, wenn es nachlässt.

1.3313 Während der Engagierte zunächst schön und interessant und dann euphorisch erscheint, wird er im Über-Engagement (vor sich selbst und seinen Mitmenschen) hässlich und unerträglich.

1.34 Wenn Engagement schließlich abgeklungen, leergelaufen und misslungen ist, zeigen sich als Folgen der Ent-Täuschung: Zynismus, insbesondere die zynische Abwertung (Verächtlich-Machung) des eigenen beruflichen Umfelds, Betonen von Formalem und Ästhetisierung, also das Unwichtig-Machen (Klein-Machen) der Inhalte der Arbeit, dafür die unverhältnismäßige Aufblähung von formalen und ästhetischen Aspekten.

1.341 Zynismus ist die Haltung, die einem, der schuldig geworden ist, das Weiterleben ermöglicht.

1.342 Den Zynismus des Desengagierten sehen wir und empfinden wir unangenehm. Woraus aber resultiert sein Schuldgefühl? Aus seiner Überheblichkeit?

1.343 Im Engagement und danach geht es darum, sich von der Umgebung abzusetzen. Es geht um Distanzierung und Erhöhung, also darum, sich zu etwas Besonderem zu machen, zu etwas Besserem zu stilisieren.

1.344 Wiederholtes Engagement könnte eine Versuch sein, das Leben additiv mit immer wieder aufs Neue erhofften interessanten Aktivitäten anzufüllen: das Leben als permanenter Wechsel zwischen „himmelhoch jauchzend" und „zu Tode betrübt".

1.35 Wer Engagement bewusst meidet, mag das tun, weil er lieber bei sich bleiben und vernünftig handeln will. Das heißt, er möchte sich die Freiheit bewahren, umfassend über sein Handeln zu befinden und nicht bloß methodisch fit zu sein.

1.36 Engagement ist die Grundlage für die „kleine" Arbeit.

1.361 Durch die Wahl des Gegenstandes, auf den der Sich-Engagierende wirft, schneidet er einen kleinen Teil aus einem komplexen Umfeld für sich heraus. Die Beschäftigung mit diesem Ausschnitt ist thematisch eingeengt und zeitlich befristet.

1.362 Wer als Bibliothekar engagiert handelt, ist nicht in der Lage, seinen Beruf umfassend auszuüben. Er benötigt Unterstützung.

1.363 Der Engagierte arbeitet im Projekt. Das Projekt ist so angelegt, dass seine Notwendigkeit sich aus dem komplexen Umfeld, dessen Ausschnitt es ist, ergibt und dass das Resultat später ins Umfeld eingefügt werden kann. Damit das gelingt, muss das Projekt geplant und vorbereitet und der sich dafür Engagierende eingewiesen und in seiner Arbeit begleitet und überprüft werden

1.3631 Gerade Begleitung und Überprüfung sind wichtig, damit der Engagierte sich vor lauter Engagement nicht „verrennt".

1.364 Darin zeigt sich, dass der Engagierte schon bei der Wahl seines Gegenstandes nicht wirklich frei, sondern sich für einen Vorschlag (Projekt) anderer entscheidet. Er entscheidet sich nicht im Sinne einer Wahl, sondern greift den gemachten Vorschlag auf. Dabei erleichtert der Zustand des Engagiert-Seins, den Projekt-Gegenstand zu akzeptieren.

1.365 Das Projekt ist auch dadurch gekennzeichnet, dass es zwar schade wäre, sollte es zu keinem verwendbaren Resultat führen, dass dies aber auch nicht grundsätzlich schaden würde.

1.366 Engagement ist dort zulässig, wo es nicht so darauf ankommt.

1.3661 Engagement ist Grundlage für freiwillige Mitarbeit, Nischentätigkeit, Projektarbeit, Ehrenamt etc., also für die zwar „kleine" Arbeit, für die der Engagierte jedoch Ernsthaftigkeit (Wichtigkeit) reklamiert. (Diese Einstellung trifft nicht auf jede „kleine" Arbeit zu. Wenn gesagt wird, man „reiße" seinen Job „herunter", dann wird darunter verstanden, dass man die Arbeit ohne Engagement am Gegenstand der Arbeit erledige.)

1.4 Der allgemeinen Wertschätzung des Engagements steht gegenüber, dass es die schwächste Grundlage für das Handeln ist, die es gibt, und deshalb Engagement das Letzte ist, das noch erwartet werden kann.

1.41 So unzulänglich Engagement als Handlungsgrundlage ist, besser als keine Motivation ist es allemal.

1.5 Hinter dem Engagement ist nichts mehr. Nach dem Engagement kommt nichts mehr.

2 Vor dem Engagement liegen all die Motivationen, deren Relikt und kleinste Schnittmenge das Engagement ist: Loyalität, Pflichtbewusstsein, Machtgier, Glaube, Mitleid, Liebe, Fanatismus, Geiz, Geldgier, Besessenheit, Gehorsam, Abhängigkeit, Nationalismus, Rassismus, Sexismus, Höflichkeit, Freundlichkeit etc.

2.1 Diese Motivationen scheinen uns von anderen Menschen, durch die Verhältnisse, durch Ideologien etc., also durch bestimmte Bedingungen (von außen) induziert. Sie können als bedingte Motivationen bezeichnet werden.

2.2 Im Gegensatz dazu können als unbedingte Motivationen die bezeichnet werden, von denen wir den Eindruck haben, sie hätten sich selbst generiert oder seien im betroffenen Individuum entstanden. Diesen Eindruck haben wir vom Engagement, von der Berufung und vom Enthusiasmus.

2.21 Vom Engagement wissen wir, dass dieser Eindruck nicht stimmt; bei ihm handelt es sich um eine durch subjektive Defizite evozierte Sekundärmotivation.

2.22 Von der Berufung wollen wir heute nichts mehr wissen. Sie scheint uns als Handlungsgrundlage nicht zeitgemäß. Möglicherweise folgen wir noch einem Ruf, den wir erhalten, aber ganz gewiss erforschen wir uns nicht mehr danach, ob wir uns zu etwas berufen fühlen. Wer sich auf seine Berufung durch etwas, das ihn gleichsam auserkoren hat (Gott, das Schicksal, die Vorsehung ...), beruft, scheint uns heute auf antiquierte Weise verlogen.

2.23 Enthusiasmus erscheint uns als die positivste der drei unbedingten Motivationen. Er ist nicht antiquiert, sondern durchaus zeitgemäß; er unterliegt keinen emotionalen Wallungen, sondern ist verlässlich; er trägt nicht bloß kurze Zeit, sondern ist auf Dauer angelegt; und er ist nicht verlogen, sondern – wenn auch naiv – offen und ehrlich.

2.231 Allerdings tendieren wir dazu, den Enthusiasten nicht ganz ernst zu nehmen. Denn er enthusiasmiert sich zwar umfassend für sein Gebiet und beansprucht dafür in großem Umfang seine (intellektuellen, emotionalen, zeitlichen, finanziellen) Ressourcen (das nötigt uns Respekt ab); aber mit seinem Gebiet liegt er neben dem, was gewöhnlich als zentral und wichtig gilt und deshalb ernst genommen wird. Enthusiasmus ist die Handlungsgrundlage des Hobbyisten, des Freaks.

2.232 Enthusiasmus wäre (in seltenen Fällen: ist) eine hervorragende Grundlage für bibliothekarisches Handeln.

2.2321 Der Enthusiast, also der Hobbyist, kann von seinem Hobby her zum enthusiasmierten Bibliothekar werden, sozusagen einen Teil seines hobbyistischen Enthusiasmus aufs bibliotheksfachliche Feld ausdehnen; leider gibt es das in nur seltenen Ausnahmefällen (die Glücksfälle für den bibliothekarischen Berufsstand sind).

2.233 Als liege auch die Bibliothek daneben (befinde sich nicht im Mainstream), wird auch der Bibliothekar (von vielen) nicht ganz ernst genommen (hier ist das Maskulinum durchaus angebracht, weil das eher auf Bibliothekare als auf Bibliothekarinnen zutrifft). Das Stück Narrenfreiheit, das damit gegeben ist, könnte als wunderbarer Freiraum für bibliothekarisches Handeln genutzt werden. (Ganz wenige Bibliothekare tun das: Das ergibt dann ein faszinierend erfrischende Agieren.)

2.2331 Bibliothekarischen Enthusiasten müsste es auch hervorragend gelingen, die Engagierten sinnvoll einzuspannen.

3 Bibliothekarische Ausbildung integriert künftige Bibliothekare ins bibliothekarische Berufsfeld und eröffnet ihnen die Teilnahme an der bibliotheksfachlichen Diskussion.

3.1 Da Engagement nicht genügt und Enthusiasmus die Ausnahme darstellt, ist eine reellere Chance für die Motivation bibliothekarischen Handelns die Teilnahme an der bibliotheksfachlichen Diskussion (kommunikative Lust).

3.2 Diese Teilnahme meint die umfassende Teilnahme, mit Blick also auf die ganze Breite der bibliothekarischen Thematik, auch wenn der Einzelne tatsächlich nur über Teilgebiete diskutiert (im Unterschied zum Engagierten, der sich auf einen Ausschnitt fokussiert und alles andere ausblendet, sich also vorübergehend zum Fachidioten macht).

3.21 Teilnahme meint kontinuierliche Teilnahme, nicht nur den punktuellen Versuch oder seltene Anläufe. Sie meint außerdem die Inanspruchnahme der ganzen Breite der formalen Möglichkeiten: vom persönlichen Gespräch über das Diskussionsforum im Internet und das Referat bei Fortbildungsveranstaltungen und Kongressen bis hin zur Publikation.

3.22 Teilnahme heißt, sich (selbst) einzubringen und auf Beiträge anderen zu reagieren.

3.23 Teilnahme setzt voraus, die eigene Arbeit kritisch und neugierig zu betrachten, um in ihr stets aufs Neue Anlässe zu finden, über sie zu reflektieren.

3.231 Voraussetzung für die Teilnahme an der Diskussion im beruflichen Umfeld ist die Diskussion im täglichen beruflichen Umfeld, die als fachliche Basis von den Kollegen in einer bibliothekarischen Arbeitsstätte getragen und stimuliert wird.

3.232 Bibliothekare in One-Person Libraries sind in dieser Hinsicht schwer benachteiligt und durchaus gefährdet, zu verstummen bzw. aus dem Schweigen nicht herauszufinden. Dieses Defizit könnte durch forcierte Beteiligung an der Gremienarbeit kompensiert werde, aber gerade One-Person Libraries bieten personell die schlechtesten Voraussetzungen dafür.

3.3 Die Teilnahme an der bibliotheksfachlichen Diskussion umfasst egoistische und altruistische Momente. Egoistisch sind Bedürfnisse wie: sich darzustellen, sich zu offenbaren (literarische Exhibition), zu verblüffen, zu provozieren, Tabus zu brechen. Altruistisch sind (evtl.) die Bedürfnisse, Bibliotheken zu entwickeln, das bibliothekarische Berufsfeld weiter auszudifferenzieren und mit benachbarten Feldern zu verzahnen, d. h. diese partiell ins eigene Berufsfeld zu integrieren und für das eigene Berufsfeld nutzbar zu machen.

3.4 Das ist nicht jedermanns Sache, da die Teilnahme an der bibliotheksfachlichen Diskussion auch bedeutet, sich öffentlicher Kritik auszusetzen.

3.41 Kritikfähigkeit bemisst sich nicht daran, ob jemand Kritik austeilen kann, sondern daran, wie jemand mit Kritik umgeht.

3.42 Nicht nur der Faule, auch der Ängstliche scheut vor öffentlich geführter bibliotheksfachlicher Diskussion zurück, weil er sich und seiner Sache nicht sicher ist und meint, dies sein zu müssen.

3.43 Aber für den, der teilnimmt, ist es gerade reizvoll, das Risiko einzugehen, weil er sich seiner nicht sicher sein kann (aber auch nicht meint, dies sein zu müssen).

3.44 Wer nicht an der fachlichen Diskussion teilnimmt, mischt nicht nur im beruflichen Umfeld nicht mit (sagt nichts – und es ist zu vermuten, dass er nichts zu sagen hat), sondern hütet sich, sich seiner fachlichen Kompetenz zu versichern und seine Meinungen zu überprüfen. Er läuft Gefahr, (zunächst allmählich und dann immer schneller) sein fachliches Wissen und Können zu verlieren und wieder auf einen vorfachlichen, laienhaften Status zurückzusinken.

3.45 Wer sich isoliert und bedeckt hält, zeigt damit, je länger desto deutlicher, dass er allmählich aufhört, fachlich zu denken und stattdessen zum „Wähnen" übergeht: Dumpfheit statt Klarheit. Zumindest läuft er Gefahr, dass ihm das unterstellt wird.

3.46 Wer sich nicht an der fachlichen Diskussion beteiligt, kann sicher noch (eine Weile) für Teilarbeiten (z. B. im Engagement) eingesetzt werden.

4 Gefragt werden könnte noch, ob die hier betrachteten Motivationen (Engagement, Enthusiasmus, Teilnahme an der fachlichen Diskussion), die nichts spezifisch Bibliothekarisches sind, sondern generell und auch auf andere Berufsfelder zutreffen, von weiteren Gegebenheiten, die typisch für den bibliothekarischen Beruf sind, bibliotheksspezifisch relativiert werden, etwa durch Sammelleidenschaft, die Sehnsucht nach Ordnung (nach einer geordneten und dadurch sicheren Welt),

Welterfahrung aus zweiter Hand (medial, literarisch vermittelt), Introvertiertheit, Verzagtheit, erhöhtes oder auch vermindertes Kommunikationsbedürfnis, Intriganz, das Bedürfnis, andere zu bilden, Abschottung in der „kleinen Welt" einer Bibliothek, nicht nur um sich vor der Rauheit der „großen Welt" in Sicherheit zu bringen, sondern vielleicht auch die Macht, wenn schon nicht in einer großen, dann doch wenigstens in einer kleinen Welt auszuüben. Solche Gegebenheiten schlagen gewiss aufs bibliothekarische Handeln durch und bewirken bibliothekarische Spezifika, aber hier handelt es sich nicht um Motivation, sondern um bibliothekarische Psychopathologie.

PERSPEKTIVEN

Hannelore Jouly

Ist die Fantasie ausgewandert? oder Kreation der Kulturmarke Stadtbibliothek

„Konzepte, Ideen, Vorstellungen - nicht Dinge - sind in der neuen Ökonomie die Gegenstände von Wert." So formuliert Jeremy Rifkin die Zukunft von Unternehmen.

Institutionen der Bildung und der Kultur schöpfen traditionell aus diesen „Nicht-Dingen" und für die „Nicht-Dinge". Sollte sich da eventuell eine neue Beziehung von Wirtschaft und Kultur andeuten?

Wer aufmerksam ist, wird beobachten, wie Trendscouts und Coolhunters unterwegs sind, durch die Welt jetten auf der Jagd nach neuen Konzepten und Ideen. Die Jugendszene wird genauso beäugt wie avantgardistische Kunst oder die konzentrative Kraft des Zen.

Vor kurzem hat ein berühmter Unternehmensberater ein nicht minder berühmtes Museum beraten. Kostenlos. Kostenlos nicht, um ein gutes Werk zu tun, sondern, so die Formulierung des Geschäftsführers, um die eigenen Mitarbeiter durch die Begegnung mit Kunst für andere Arbeitsfelder zu sensibilisieren, zu inspirieren. Einen anderen Weg wählte eine Stiftung, die sich einige Bibliotheksdirektoren auf eine interessante Messe lud, um anschließend in einem Workshop zukunftsträchtige Ideen abzuschöpfen. Charmante Einladungen zum Abendessen in prominente Geschäftshäuser entpuppen sich als gezielte und wohlvorbereitete Ideenschmiede. Dies ist alles höchst legitim, hat weniger dezidiert immer statt gefunden und sei hier ohne jeden Spott berichtet. Im Gegenteil, Kulturarbeiter, Bibliothekare zum Beispiel, könnten stolz sein, nach Ideen befragt zu werden.

„Jener häufig anzutreffende Mangel an Visionen, der unsere Gesellschaft verkümmern lässt, braucht Spurenelemente poetischer Fantasie" (Jóse F.A. Oliver). In diesem Kontext ließen sich Bibliotheken altmodisch und höchst aktuell zugleich als unerschöpflicher Pool für Spurenelemente poetischer Fantasie beschreiben. Die Bibliothek als Jagdrevier für Coolhunters... Wäre das nicht eine gute Formulierung um Leitbilder spannend, lesbar und provozierend zu machen?

Um die Kulturmarke Stadtbibliothek zu entwickeln, muss sich die Bibliothek allerdings selbst als Coolhunter und First Mover bewähren. Den Fundus hat eine Bibliothek in wunderbarer Weise als Ressource im eigenen Haus:

- Bücher und Medien
- Professioneller Zugang zu Informationen der Netzwerke
- Begegnung mit Literaten, Künstlern, Publizisten, Wissenschaftlern im Rahmen des Veranstaltungsprogramms
- Gespräche mit Kunden und Freunden der Bibliothek
- Und... die weitgespannten Kompetenzen, Fähigkeiten, Beziehungen des Kollegiums der Bibliothek

Die Kunst der Bibliotheksleitung wird es sein, Ressourcen zu erkennen und zu pflegen, Netzwerke zu bilden, Ideen und Erfahrungen zu einer zukunftsweisenden Konzeption zu verknüpfen, in der Praxis zu erproben, zu variieren, neu zu kreieren. Dieser nicht endende, anhaltend komplexe Prozess bedarf unterschiedlicher Instrumente. Das informelle Gespräch gehört ebenso dazu wie die Struktur für Wissensmanagement, hinzu kommen Workshops in unterschiedlicher Zusammensetzung und Gedankenflüge im brain-trust. Die Herausforderung an alle ist die Balance zwischen Alltagsmanagement und visionärer, zumindest innovativer Zukunftsentwicklung. Auch das ließe sich Qualitätssicherung nennen. Qualitätssicherung für die Kunden einer Bibliothek, die sich auf Servicekompetenz ebenso verlassen wie auf die Innovationskraft.

„Ganz gleich, wie kreativ und innovativ ihr Unternehmen ist, die einzige Beziehung von Wert, ist die Beziehung zum Kunden“ (Jeremy Rifkin). Mit der Kundenorientierung ist Marketingorientierung verknüpft - wobei in der New Economy die Meinung vertreten wird, dass die Marketingorientierung vor der Produktorientierung stünde. Auch wenn ich diese Meinung nicht ganz teile, gilt, dass gute Produkte, dazu gehören auch gute Ideen, hervorragend vermarktet werden müssen, sonst sind sie schlicht nicht existent.

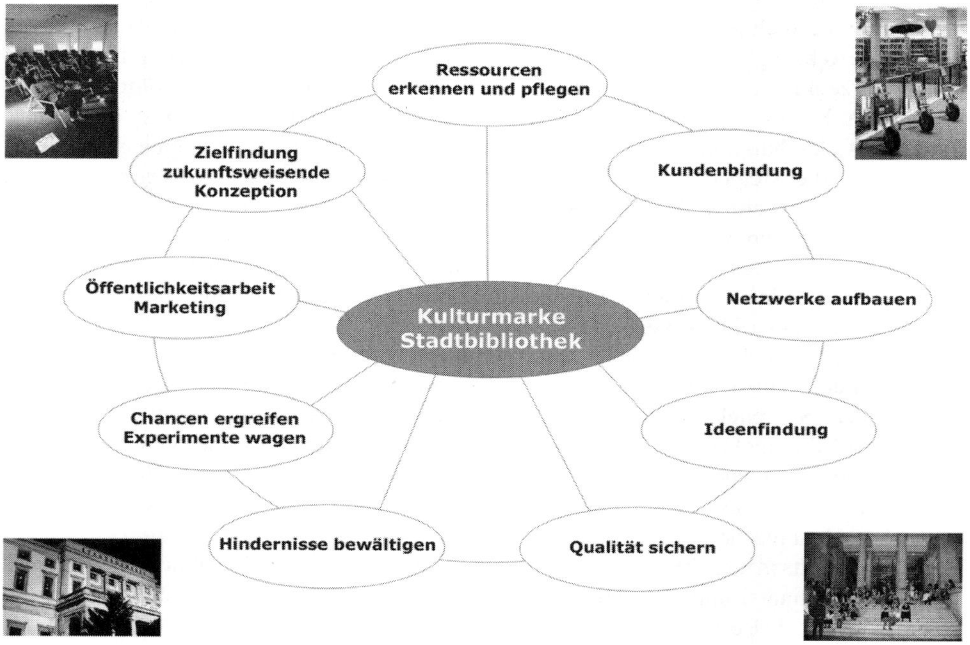

Eine Stadtbibliothek wird nicht ausschließlich an Kundenbindung arbeiten. Mit gleicher Intensität ist die Beziehung zum Geldgeber, zur Kommune also, zu pflegen. Zu reflektieren, darzulegen ist der Nutzen der Bibliothek für die positive Entwicklung der Stadt. Diese Entwicklung ist - abseits der wesentlichen Finanzknotenpunkte der globalen Welt (London, New York, Tokio) - von beträchtlicher Unübersichtlichkeit, schwer begreifbar in hierarchischen Strukturen. Manuel Castells beschreibt die Situation folgendermaßen:

> *„Unsere Gesellschaft errichtet sich rund um die Ströme: Kapital, Information, Technologie, organisatorische Interaktion, Ströme von Bildern, Klängen, Symbolen. Ströme sind Ausdruck der Prozesse dieser Netzwerk-Gesellschaften. In diesem Netzwerk existiert kein Ort aus sich selbst, da alle Positionen durch Ströme charakterisiert werden ... Wohin die Beziehungen zwischen gleichzeitiger Globalisierung und Regionalisierung gehen, steht nicht von vornherein fest.“*

Richard Sennett denkt oder hofft einen Schritt weiter:

> *„Eine der unbeabsichtigten Folgen des modernen Kapitalismus (Flexibilität, Fehlen des Vertrauens und der Verpflichtung, Oberflächlichkeit des Teamworks usw.) ist die Stärkung des Ortes, die Sehnsucht des Menschen nach Verwurzelung in einer Gemeinde."*

Was könnten Qualitäten eines solchen Ortes sein? Qualitäten lokaler Kultur? Vielleicht der Luxus von Entschleunigung, die Vitalität der Face-to-Face Kommunikation, Vertrauen in einen Verbund persönlicher Verantwortung. Und: Optimismus. Optimismus überzeugt, denn die Welt gehört nicht den Bedenkenträgern. Optimistisch ließe sich denn auch postulieren: die Fantasie wird nicht auswandern, solange es lebendige, vitale Bibliotheken gibt, die Experimente wagen und Chancen ergreifen, die zu einer prominenten „Kulturmarke" geworden sind.

Literatur:

Rifkin, Jeremy: Access. Das Verschwinden des Eigentums. 2000
Sennett Richard: Der flexible Mensch. Die Kultur des neuen Kapitalismus. 1998
Castells, Manuel: Space flow - der Raum der Ströme. (Kursbuch Stadt). 1999

Klaus von Trotha

Zum Thema „Wissensgesellschaft“

Auszug aus einer Rede von Herrn Minister von Trotha,
anlässlich der Diplomierungsfeier der HBI am 25. Februar 2000

Liebe Absolventinnen und Absolventen,
Sehr geehrter, lieber Herr Professor Dr. Vodosek,

Sie gehen in eine Berufswelt, die sich mit einer vor Jahren noch unvorstellbaren Geschwindigkeit wandelt.

Um das Jahr 1800 arbeiteten rund 80 % aller Erwerbstätigen in der Landwirtschaft, einhundert Jahre später waren es nur noch 35 %, und heute liegt der Anteil in Deutschland bei ganzen 3 %.

Wir erleben eine kulturelle und technische Revolution im Bereich der Kommunikation. Das Internet hat einen Siegeszug ohnegleichen angetreten. Englisch hat sich wohl endgültig als Weltsprache und „Lingua franca“ der Moderne durchgesetzt. Das Fernsehen vermittelt zur gleichen Zeit die gleichen Worte und Bilder in Berlin und Stuttgart, Kairo und Tokio, Buenos Aires und Vancouver.

Fortschritte in der Menschheitsgeschichte waren immer wissensbasiert. So war die Erfindung des Buchdrucks durch Johannes Gutenberg im Jahr 1453 eine Innovation, ohne die unsere Kultur sich nicht zu der entwickelt hätte, in der wir aufgewachsen sind. Mit der Digitalisierung der Kommunikationsnetze erleben wir eine enorme Aufwertung des Faktors Wissen. Knapp 80 % der deutschen Unternehmen führen nach einer Studie des Internationalen Instituts für Lernende Organisation und Wertschöpfung (ILOI) den größten Teil ihrer Wertschöpfung schon jetzt auf den Faktor Wissen zurück. Wissen ist allerdings nicht nur für die unternehmerische Wertschöpfung von Bedeutung, vielmehr verändert es auch unser persönliches Leben und Arbeiten.

Neue, leistungsfähigere Kommunikationsnetze ermöglichen es, in unterschiedlichen Ländern ansässige Firmen oder Betriebsteile zu vernetzen und wie <u>ein</u> Unternehmen zu führen. Diese kommunikationstechnologische Entwicklung hat dazu beigetragen, dass die wissensbasierten Industrien und Dienstleistungen heute die höchsten Beschäftigungszuwächse überhaupt verzeichnen.

Die Globalisierung war zunächst nur Ergebnis der Anwendung von wissensintensiven Kommunikationsmöglichkeiten. Heute verstärken sich die Trends zur Wissensgesellschaft und zur Globalisierung wechselseitig. Denn im weltweiten „Kampf um Vormachtstellung, Ressourcen, Wohlstand und Beschäftigung ist die Fähigkeit zur Gewinnung und zum Einsatz von Wissen zum entscheidenden Wettbewerbsfaktor geworden“, so die Delphi-Studie von 1998.

Eine eingehende Debatte über das Wissen führen wir erst seit wenigen Jahren. Doch der Zusammenhang und der Unterschied zwischen Wissen und Information ist klar. Während weitergegebenes Wissen für den Empfänger zunächst nur eine Information ist, wird diese durch Aneignung und Verarbeitung zu eigenem Wissen. Informationen sind daher die Bausteine des Wissens. Das Wissen ist abhängig von der Aufnahme- und Verarbeitungsfähigkeit jedes Einzelnen.

Wir stehen am Beginn einer Entwicklung, die deutlich über den Begriff „Informationsgesellschaft“ hinausgeht. Dies war eine zutreffende Bezeichnung für die technologische Seite des Aspekts. Wissensgesellschaft dagegen beschreibt die menschliche Dimension des Wandels. Da nur der Mensch Produzent, Vermittler und Konsument von Wissen sein kann, rückt er in der Wissensgesellschaft in den Mittelpunkt

Charakteristisch für die Wissensgesellschaft ist das hohe Tempo der Wissensvermehrung. Alle 5 bis 7 Jahre verdoppelt sich das weltweit verfügbare Wissen. Die Hälfte davon bleibt nur 3 bis 4 Jahre aktuell und damit wertvoll. Vieles von dem, was Sie heute wissen, wird in 20 Jahren belanglos sein. Vieles von dem, was Sie dann wissen müssen, weiß heute noch keiner. Tucholsky hat dieses Dilemma einmal eindrucksvoll in dem Satz zusammengefasst: *„Wie schön lebt es sich heute ohne den Fortschritt des Jahres 2050.“*

Jeden Tag erscheinen weltweit mehr als 20.000 Publikationen also 100.000 in der Woche. Und in unserer Zeit arbeiten bereits fast so viele Wissenschaftler wie in der ganzen bisher bekannten Menschheitsgeschichte. Das Wachstum des Wissens scheint unendlich. Wissen ist der Rohstoff, der sich durch sich selbst erneuert. Es ist die einzige Ressource, die sich bei intensivem Gebrauch nicht verbraucht, sondern vermehrt.

Das Wachstum des Wissens hat viel mit dem technischen Fortschritt zu tun, mit Mikrochips und Datennetzen. Die Zahl der Computer mit Internetzugang verdoppelt sich weltweit etwa alle 15 Monate. In Deutschland steigt die Zahl der Internet-Zugänge jährlich um mehr als 30 %. Wachstum des Wissens und Wachstum der Netze sind korrespondierende Prozesse.

Inzwischen ist der Satz *„Wissen ist Macht“* allgemein bekannt. Er wurde von Francis Bacon vor Jahrhunderten formuliert. Noch nie war er so bedeutungsvoll wie in unserer Zeit. Wissen wird zunehmend weltweit verfügbar. Die dadurch entstehende Transparenz schränkt den Missbrauch von Macht und „Herrschaftswissen“ erheblich ein und stärkt im Ergebnis die freien Gesellschaften. In China unterlaufen Studierende mit ihrem Internet-Zugang staatliche Zensur und Propaganda. Informationen, die ihnen sonst vorenthalten würden, holen sie sich aus dem Netz.

Immer mehr haben die Chance, dass in Zukunft mehr als je zuvor zählt, was den Menschen als Menschen auszeichnet – seine Fähigkeit, zu lernen, das Gelernte als Wissen weiterzugeben und daraus Konsequenzen zu ziehen. Das, was man von einer Sache denkt, kann nie so zutreffend sein, wie das was man von einer Sache weiß.

Was bedeutet die Entwicklung von der Industriegesellschaft zur Wissensgesellschaft für die Politik und den Hochschulbereich?

Die Politik kann zwar nicht jedem Einzelnen einen sicheren Arbeitsplatz garantieren, aber sie kann dafür Sorge tragen, dass dem Einzelnen gute Bildungseinrichtungen zur Verfügung stehen. Deshalb muss auch in Zukunft in Bildung und Wissenschaft investiert werden und zwar mehr als je zuvor. Denn es gibt im Grunde nur eines, was teurer ist als Bildung, nämlich keine Bildung.

Wenn heute 40 % eines Altersjahrgangs die Hochschulreife erwerben und davon 70 % auch studieren wollen, dann werden wir uns von den hergebrachten Vorstellungen klassischer Akademikerlaufbahnen verabschieden müssen. Noch nicht einmal ein zügiges und erfolgreiches Studium gewährleistet heute eine sichere Karriere. Der einstige Königsweg der akademischen Ausbildung ist in nicht unerheblichem Maß zum Trampelpfad geworden. Zeitverträge, Teilzeitarbeit, freie Mitarbeit und Selbständigkeit prägen das Arbeitsleben. Das bedeutet zwar mehr Risiko für den Einzelnen, aber auch ein Mehr an persönlicher Freiheit. Denn Arbeit und individuelle Lebensplanung werden weit mehr miteinander vereinbar sein.

Es ist auch noch nicht lange her, da gingen 50 % der Absolventen unserer Hochschulen in den öffentlichen Dienst, nur rund 15 % gingen im Laufe ihres Berufslebens in die Selbständigkeit. In Zukunft werden sich diese Verhältnisse gerade umgekehrt darstellen.

Der Übergang zur Wissensgesellschaft stellt die Bildungspolitik vor neue Herausforderungen. Die erste Herausforderung betrifft die *Qualifikationen*, die Bildung in der Wissensgesellschaft vermitteln muss: Wir müssen uns heute bedeutend mehr Wissen aneignen als die Generationen vor uns. Zudem ist einmal erworbenes Wissen immer schneller veraltet und überholt. Fachwissen ist zur leicht verderblichen Ware geworden, auf der das Verfallsdatum schon vorbestimmt ist. Das „Lernen auf Vorrat", das traditionell unser Bildungssystem geprägt hat, kann deshalb den Anforderungen der Arbeitswelt nicht mehr gerecht werden. Die Vorstellung von einer „abgeschlossenen Berufsausbildung" ist schon heute eine Illusion. An ihre Stelle muss das sogenannte „lebenslange Lernen" treten, als Vorsorge des einzelnen und der Gesellschaft im Hinblick auf die Anforderungen der Zukunft.

Eine der wichtigsten Kompetenzen, die das Bildungssystem vermitteln muss, ist deshalb die Fähigkeit, sich Wissen selbständig und auf eigene Initiative anzueignen. In den Lehrplänen unserer Schulen und Hochschulen muss das „Lernen, wie man am besten lernt" einen größeren Stellenwert erhalten.

Angesichts der wachsenden Flut an elektronisch vermittelter Information kommt es auch darauf an, sich Orientierung zu verschaffen, Informationen auszuwählen und zu bewerten. Bill Gates hat dies auf eine schöne Formel gebracht, wenn er sagt: *„Ich habe eine einfache, aber starke Überzeugung", „wie jemand Informationen sammelt, verteilt und nützt, entscheidet darüber, ob er zu den Gewinnern oder Verlierern gehört."*

Hierzu gehört also auch die Fähigkeit, zwischen bedeutsamen und nicht bedeutsamen Informationen zu trennen und aus Informationen „Wissen" zu generieren.

T. S. Eliot hat diese Problematik wunderbar in einem Satz zusammengefasst, wenn er fragt: *„Where is the wisdom I lost in science, where is the science I lost in information, where is the information I lost in data."*

Über grundlegende Fachkompetenz hinaus gewinnen fachübergreifende, sogenannte Schlüsselqualifikationen an Bedeutung. Dazu zählen interdisziplinäres Arbeiten und Flexibilität, Kommunikations- und Kooperationsfähigkeit ebenso wie die Fähigkeit, mit Unsicherheiten umzugehen. Freilich: Schlüsselqualifikationen ohne Fachwissen – das wäre wie Stricken ohne Wolle.

Und noch eines: über die Einübung des Umgangs mit Computern und Netzen dürfen wir die alten Kulturtechniken nicht vernachlässigen. Lesekompetenz und Schreibkompetenz ebenso wie die beiden zugrunde liegende Sprachkompetenz sind durch Computerbeherrschung nicht zu ersetzen. Insofern ist der Satz eines der Pioniere der Computertechnik völlig richtig, wenn er behauptet: *„Zur künftigen Elite wird gehören, wer Kopfrechnen kann"*.

Die Hochschulen müssen nicht nur neue Arten von Qualifikationen vermitteln, sie müssen sich auch für *neue Zielgruppen* öffnen. Dies betrifft vor allem die wissenschaftliche Weiterbildung. Als Weiterbildungsanbieter sind die deutschen Hochschulen bislang kaum in Erscheinung getreten. Ganz anders in den USA und in England: Hier haben die Hochschulen schon längst damit begonnen, gemeinsam mit Partnern aus der Wirtschaft Weiterbildungsprogramme aufzulegen, die im übrigen für die Hochschulen sehr lukrativ sind. Für die deutschen Hochschulen müsste es ein Alarmsignal sein, dass die wichtigsten deutschen Global Players – u. a. DaimlerChrysler, Lufthansa und die Telekom – bereits dabei sind, eigene Corporate Universities aufzubauen, um ihren Bedarf an Weiterbildung für Führungskräfte zu decken.

Schließlich müssen sich die Hochschulen auf einen zunehmenden Bedarf an zeitlich und räumlich *flexiblen, offenen Formen* des Lernens einstellen. Hierfür schafft die Informations- und Kommunikationstechnik einschließlich der computerunterstützten Lehre ideale Voraussetzungen. Dies schließt beispielsweise ein: Studieninformation und -beratung über das Internet, Angebot von Vorlesungsskripten auf dem Server der Hochschule oder virtuelle Seminare. Was für die Unternehmen gilt, gilt ebenso für Hochschulen: Auch sie müssen sich um die Mobilisierung und die effiziente Verwaltung ihrer Wissensbestände bemühen, eben: Wissensmanagement betreiben, und zwar nicht nur in der Forschung, sondern auch in der Lehre.

Es ist schon heute abzusehen, dass der Einsatz neuer Medien in der Lehre bis hin zum Angebot vollständig über Informationsnetze vermittelter Studienangebote künftig wesentlich zur Attraktivität und Profilierung einer Hochschule beitragen wird. In den USA gibt es diese Hochschulen bereits: zum Teil sogar in der Form einer AG, die sogar Gewinn macht.

Wie steht es mit der Leistungsfähigkeit unseres Bildungssystems? Sind wir für das „Informationszeitalter“ gerüstet?

Nur wer sät, kann auch ernten.

An den Exporterfolgen der deutschen Industrie ist abzulesen, dass es um die Qualität unserer Hochschulen nicht so schlecht bestellt sein kann. In den alten Bundesländern hat fast die Hälfte aller Arbeitslosen keine abgeschlossene Berufsausbildung. Die Arbeitslosenquote beträgt bei den Ungelernten rund 20 % und bei den Akademikern 3,5 %. Solche Zahlen sprechen zunächst nicht für eine Ineffizienz unserer Bildungseinrichtungen.

Im bundesweiten Vergleich stehen die baden-württembergischen Hochschulen bestens da. Bei Hochschulrankings belegen sie immer wieder Spitzenplätze.

Es ist jedoch unbestreitbar, dass einige Schlüsselkompetenzen von unseren Schulen und Hochschulen noch viel zu wenig vermittelt werden. Ich denke dabei an die dürftigen Fremdsprachenkenntnisse vieler Absolventen sowie an den mangelnden Praxis- und Berufsbezug von Teilen der universitären Ausbildung. Unser Bildungssystem ist zudem noch viel zu stark auf die umfassende und zeitintensive Erstausbildung zugeschnitten.

Die Aktivitäten unserer Hochschulen auf dem Gebiet des flexiblen, medienunterstützten Lehrens und Lernens sind bislang noch zu schwach ausgeprägt. Hier werden wir mit unserem Förderprogramm „Virtuelle Hochschule“, für das das Land über fünf Jahre 50 Mio. DM bereit gestellt hat, einiges voran bringen. Das heißt jedoch nicht, dass wir in den kommenden Jahren die realen Hochschulen durch virtuelle ersetzen wollen. Ich stimme der Einschätzung von PD. Müller-Böling, einem ausgewiesenen Hochschul-Experten, zu: *„So wie das Büro 2000 nicht papierlos ist, so wird die Hochschule 2010 nicht menschenleer sein.“*

Unsere Hochschulen werden in wenigen Jahren internationaler, interdisziplinärer und stärker an den Bedürfnissen der Berufs- und Arbeitswelt orientiert sein als heute. Weltweit anerkannte Studienabschlüsse nach dem Bachelor-/Master-Modell werden die internationale Anerkennung deutscher Abschlüsse erleichtern und zudem die Attraktivität des Studienstandorts für ausländische Studierende erhöhen.

Regelmäßige Evaluationen werden dafür sorgen, dass die Qualität der Lehre erhalten bleibt oder noch gesteigert wird.

Die von uns institutionalisierte Evaluationsagentur wird diesen Punkt kontinuierlich vorantreiben.

Ich bin der Fachhochschule für Bibliotheks- und Informationswesen dankbar, dass sie bereits frühzeitig einen Master-Studiengang „Informationswirtschaft“ eingerichtet hat.

Dieses Studienangebot ist nicht nur eine hervorragende Ergänzung des bestehenden Angebotes. Dieser Master-Studiengang wird sich auch in das Studienangebot der künftigen *Hochschule der Medien* optimal einfügen.

Ich weiß, dass an Ihrer Hochschule wesentlich weitreichendere Reformüberlegungen verfolgt werden, und ich kann Sie nur ermuntern, den Weg in Richtung Internationalisierung weiterzugehen. Das schließt ein, neben den bestehenden Diplomstudiengängen Bachelor-Studiengänge anzubieten. Unsere Absolventen werden es mit diesen internationalen Abschlüssen in Zukunft leichter haben, sich im zunehmend weltweiten Wettbewerb zu behaupten.

In kluger Voraussicht hat sich die Hochschule für Bibliotheks- und Informationswesen dazu entschlossen, gemeinsam mit der Fachhochschule für Druck und Medien eine neue Hochschule zu bilden. Bereits die vorgesehene Bezeichnung „Hochschule der Medien" macht deutlich, dass sich die neue Hochschule als eine Einrichtung versteht, die einerseits von den Medien und deren Entwicklung bestimmt wird, aber andererseits über ihre Absolventen und ihre Forschungs- und Entwicklungsaktivitäten auch selbst auf den Medienbereich Einfluss ausübt.

Um diese neue Hochschule zu bilden, haben sich die denkbar besten Partner zusammengefunden. Beide Hochschulen, deren historische Wurzeln in den Bereichen Druck und Bibliothek liegen, haben bereits seit langem ihr Studienangebot auf die Anforderungen des Medienbereichs ausgerichtet. Dies geschah an der Hochschule für Druck und Medien in der Erweiterung des Medienbegriffs über die Printmedien hinaus sowie unter dem medienwirtschaftlichen Gesichtspunkt. Die Hochschule für Bibliotheks- und Informationswesen erweiterte ihr Ausbildungsangebot unter Aspekten des Informationsmanagements. Durch die Verbindung beider Einrichtungen zu einer neuen Hochschule der Medien kann somit ein Kompetenzzentrum entstehen, das in Deutschland, aber auch in Europa und darüber hinaus eine einzigartige Stellung einnehmen kann.

Mein Haus hat die Zusammenführung der beiden Hochschulen angeregt und sich von Anbeginn an sehr dafür eingesetzt. Denn der Zusammenschluss fügt sich in den medien- und wirtschaftspolitischen Kontext der Landespolitik hervorragend ein. Die Landesregierung möchte das Profil des Medienstandorts Baden-Württemberg besonders in folgenden drei Bereichen stärken:

- Kompetenz für Konvergenz
- Wissens- und Technologiekompetenz
- Multimedia und digitale Wertschöpfung

Die Hochschulfusion bietet für Baden-Württemberg die großartige Chance, Medienkompetenz auch im Hochschulbereich nach außen noch deutlicher zu machen und das medienorientierte Studienangebot bedarfsgerecht weiter zu entwickeln.

Wenn wir uns für die Schaffung einer Hochschule der Medien einsetzen, ist dies auch vor dem Hintergrund des Arbeitsmarktes zu sehen. Die Informations- und Kommunikationstechnik und die Medienwirtschaft sind zum wichtigsten Wachstumsbereich geworden. Sie spielen eine Schlüsselrolle für die zukünftige Wirtschaftsentwicklung. Weltweit und auch in Deutschland ist die Informationswirtschaft der umsatzstärkste Wirtschaftszweig. Das Weltmarktvolumen erreichte im Jahr 1996 5 Billionen DM, davon entfielen über 400 Milliarden DM auf Deutschland. Die volkswirtschaftliche Bedeutung dieses Bereichs zeigen jährliche Wachstumsraten von 7 bis 8 %, in einigen Segmenten bis zu 15 %. Unternehmen, die verstärkt IuK-Techniken anwenden, erwarten mehrheitlich ein Wachstum ihrer Mitarbeiterzahl. Es wird vermehrt neue Arbeitsplätze für hochqualifizierte Beschäftigte geben, insbesondere auch in den neuen Dienstleistungsbereichen. Im engeren Multimedia-Bereich, zum Beispiel bei Webdesignern und Medienautoren erwarten Fachverbände einen erheblichen Arbeitskräftebedarf, den die derzeitigen Hochschulabsolventen auf Dauer nicht abdecken können.

Die neue Hochschule der Medien soll mit zwei zusätzlichen Studiengängen starten. Einer der beiden geplanten Studiengänge geht auf die Initiative Ihrer Hochschule zurück, nämlich der Diplomstudiengang „Informations-Design“. Bei der Konzeption des Studiengangs sind Sie zu Recht von der Frage ausgegangen: Wie können Unternehmen, öffentliche Einrichtungen oder auch Privatpersonen die Informationsflut so aufbereiten und strukturieren, dass die Interessenten so rasch wie möglich an die für sie wichtigen Information gelangen? Nur strukturierte Informationen werden verwertbares Wissen. In der Fachliteratur wurde der Fall eines Unternehmens bekannt, das zwei Jahre intensiven Arbeitens und Tüftelns daran setzte, um zu erreichen, dass es bei der Abfrage von Internet-Suchmaschinen nicht unter „ferner liefen“, sondern immer an der ersten Stelle zu finden war. Dieser Aufwand – der übrigens zum Erfolg führte – wäre nicht erforderlich, wenn Informationen stärker zielgruppen- und bedarfsgerecht aufbereitet würden. Unter anderem in diesem Problembereich wird der neue Studiengang ansetzen und Lösungen entwickeln müssen.

Dieses Beispiel soll illustrieren, dass wir uns heute in immer kürzerer Folge mit Problemstellungen zu befassen haben, von deren Existenz wir vor nicht allzu langer Zeit noch nichts ahnten. Wir brauchen sehr viel Know-how, um diesen neuartigen Anforderungen gerecht zu werden. Dazu wird die neue Hochschule der Medien durch die Synergie der Kompetenzen einen wesentlichen Beitrag leisten. Der neue Studiengang weist den richtigen Weg.

Die Medienwirtschaft trägt in rasantem Tempo neue Anforderungen an die Hochschulausbildung heran. Eine Hochschule der Medien muss im Zusammenspiel mit der Wirtschaft antizipieren, wo die künftigen Bedürfnisse liegen werden, somit am Puls der Entwicklung bleiben und in Teilbereichen diese Entwicklung selbst mitbestimmen.

Mein Haus setzt sich dafür ein, dass mit der Errichtung der neuen Hochschule der Medien die beiden Stuttgarter Medien – Fachhochschulen nicht nur formal als Institution, sondern auch räumlich zusammengeführt werden. Wir hoffen, dass die Teile der neuen Hochschule, die derzeit noch unter der Bezeichnung „Hochschule für Bibliotheks- und Informationswesen“ firmieren, in etwa vier bis fünf Jahren in einem Neubau auf dem Campus in Vaihingen in unmittelbarer Anbindung an die jetzige Hochschule für Druck und Medien untergebracht werden können. Damit würde auch ein bisheriges Dauerproblem der Hochschule für Bibliotheks- und Informationswesen, nämlich die Unterbringung, gelöst. Das Wissenschaftsministerium ist mit den beiden Hochschulen der Ansicht, dass die räumliche Einheit der neuen Hochschule Grundvoraussetzung dafür ist, damit mit dem Zusammenschluss nicht nur ein neuer Name entsteht, sondern eine neue, innovative Einheit in Lehre, Forschung und Entwicklung.

Unser Altbundespräsident Roman Herzog hat in der viel beachteten Rede vom 26. April 1997 uns allen - und das unterstreiche ich ganz dick - ins Stammbuch geschrieben, er beklage den Pessimismus als allgemeines Lebensgefühl, weil eine von Ängsten erfüllte Gesellschaft unfähig zu Reformen und damit zur Gestaltung der Zukunft werde.

Und in der Tat: ich glaube auch, dass die Welt eher den Optimisten gehört – nicht, weil sie immer recht haben, sondern weil sie positiv eingestellt sind. Selbst wenn sie irren, denken sie positiv. Deshalb erreichen sie etwas, korrigieren Fehler, kommen weiter und haben Erfolg.

Victor Hugo, hat das, was jetzt auf Sie zukommt, in einem ebenso pathetischen wie schönen Satz zusammengefasst, wenn er meint:

> *„Die Zukunft hat viele Namen.*
> *Für die Schwachen ist sie das Unerreichbare.*
> *Für die Furchtsamen das Unbekannte.*
> *Für die Mutigen aber die Chance."*

Liebe Absolventinnen und Absolventen nutzen Sie Ihre Chance!

In diesem Sinne wünsche ich Ihnen alles Gute und der Fachhochschule in Stuttgart auch weiterhin viel Erfolg.

Winfried Gödert

Ein informationstheoretisches Paradigma für bibliothekarisches Handeln

1. Einleitung

Josef Weizenbaum hat anlässlich des Bibliothekartages 1990 in Bregenz einen Vortrag unter dem Thema *Wollen wir noch Menschen in der Bibliothek?* [505] gehalten. Er plädiert in diesem Beitrag dafür, dass Bibliotheken in ihrem Handeln sich nicht ihrer Wertetradition berauben lassen sollten, indem sie sich – etwa im Kontext der Informationstechnik oder des Managements – von überstrapazierten Analogieversuchen und assoziationserheischenden Metaphern blenden lassen. Dabei schließt er mit den Worten: „... die Bibliothek ist ein Instrument der menschlichen Kultur und gehört zur kulturellen Umwelt des Menschen."[506] Inzwischen sind wieder mehr als 10 Jahre verstrichen, die von *Weizenbaum* aufgeworfene Frage hat aber nichts an Aktualität verloren; im Gegenteil, es wird weiterhin und verstärkt die Frage aufgeworfen, ob nicht alles, was man in einer Bibliothek in Erfahrung bringen könnte, längst alternativ oder sogar besser über das Internet abrufbar ist - und das sogar ohne Beachtung lästiger Öffnungszeiten oder anderer Benutzungseinschränkungen?

In eine solche Sichtweise geht entscheidend das Verständnis ein, das man von Information, von Wissen, von Informationsverarbeitung und –vermittlung hat. Es ist daher angezeigt, eine genauere Betrachtung der Möglichkeiten eines solchen Verständnisses vorzunehmen, bevor man sich für eines als Basis bibliothekarischen Handelns entscheidet.

Dieser Weg ist schon mehrfach begangen worden, ohne dass sich bislang im bibliothekarischen Berufsstand ein derartiges Verständnis herausgebildet hätte. Weiterhin ist zu beobachten, dass Grundsatzüberlegungen zum bibliothekarischen Selbstverständnis vielfach von außen formuliert werden, ohne dass sie einen Widerhall in der bibliothekarischen Diskussion finden - in jüngster Zeit erst wieder durch einen Beitrag von *Jürgen Mittelstrass*[507]. Entwicklungen im Bereich der Informations- und Kommunikationstechnik sowie Veränderungen der Mediennutzung bzw. der Rezeptionsgepflogenheiten wird dabei in vielen derartigen Diskussionen ein Einfluss auf die bibliothekarische Aufgabenausübung zugeschrieben, der im Ergebnis zwischen hilflosem Getriebensein und euphemistischen Erwartungen pendelt.

Empirisch lässt sich unschwer feststellen, dass derzeit mindestens die folgenden Bedeutungsbereiche von Information nebeneinander existieren[508]:

---

505 Weizenbaum, J.: Wollen wir noch Menschen in der Bibliothek? In: Bibliotheken mit und ohne Grenzen: Informationsgesellschaft und Bibliothek. Der österreichische Bibliothekartag 1990, Bregenz, 4.-8.9.1990, Vorträge und Kommissionssitzungen. Wien: VÖB 1991. S.85-92. (Biblos-Schriften; Bd.154)

506 A.a.O., S.90.

507 Mittelstrass, J.: Der Bibliothekar als Partner der Wissenschaft. In: Zeitschrift für Bibliothekswesen und Bibliographie 47(2000) H.3, S. 244-253.

508 Vgl.: Janich, P.: Informationsbegriff und methodisch-kulturalistische Philosophie. In: Ethik und Sozialwissenschaften. 9(1998) H.2, S. 169-182.
Capurro, R.: Was ist Information?: Hinweise zum Wort- und Begriffsfeld eines umstrittenen Begriffs. In: Handbuch der modernen Datenverarbeitung. 24(1987) H.133, S. 107-114.

- Die *historische* Dimension (Formen, Gestalt geben, Bilden, Bildung), die auch als etymologische Ableitung des Wortes Information verstanden werden kann
- Die *umgangssprachliche* Dimension (Information verstanden als: Nachricht, Mitteilung, Botschaft Neuigkeit (-swert, -sgehalt) mit ihrer Ausstrahlung in die moderne Medienlandschaft. Ein Charakteristikum dieses Verständnisses ist es beispielsweise, ein Motto wie *Information statt Unterhaltung* zu prägen
- Die *informations-* oder *nachrichtentechnische* Dimension mit der heutigen Erweiterung auf die sog. Informationsverarbeitung innerhalb der Informatik oder Computerwissenschaft bis hin zur Vorstellung von Wissensdarstellung in Wissensbanken innerhalb der künstlichen Intelligenz. Diese Dimension hat entscheidend dazu beigetragen, Information zu quantifizieren, ihr einen materiellen Wert beizumessen und sie als Ressource, als Ware zu betrachten[509]
- Die *biologische* Dimension mit ihrem Verständnis des Erbgutes (DNS) als Informationsträger der Lebensentfaltung[510]
- Die *kommunikative* Dimension als Austausch von Information zwischen Kommunikationspartnern (Mensch-Mensch- oder Mensch-Medium- oder Mensch-Maschine-Dialog)
- Die *kognitive* Dimension als Betrachtung kognitiver mit ihren Prozessen der Sinneswahrnehmung und nachfolgender Verarbeitung im Gehirn. Hierbei spielt der Anstoß zur Informationsverarbeitung zunächst keine Hauptrolle. Er muss insbesondere nicht aus einem Kommunikationsakt hervorgegangen, sondern kann innerhalb der kognitiven Struktur selbstreferentiell erzeugt worden sein.

Obwohl bibliothekarisches Handeln eine lange Tradition in der Mediatorenrolle zwischen Medium und Wissen besitzt, die eine kommunikativ orientierte Generierung von Wissen einschließt, lässt sich als einzig stabile Position derzeit der Rückfall in das informationstechnische Paradigma beobachten. Auch Mittelstrass ist hiervon nicht frei, wenn er unter Aufgreifen einer bekannten Metapher fragt: „Werden wir alle zu Informationsriesen und gleichzeitig zu Wissenszwergen?"[511] Derartige Aussagen sind nur vor dem Hintergrund eines bestimmten Verständnisses vom Anwachsen und vom Verlust, also von einer Quantifizierung von Information und Wissen möglich, das nachfolgend noch näher charakterisiert und hinterfragt werden soll.

Wir können für bibliothekarisches Handeln eine Alternative formulieren: Wollen wir uns für bibliothekarisches Handeln ein informationstechnisches oder ein an der menschlichen Informationsverarbeitung orientiertes kognitives Paradigma zu eigen machen? Zur Beantwortung dieser Frage ist es zweckmäßig, zuvor den Unterschied dieser beiden Sichtweisen zu klären.

Capurro, R.: Information: ein Beitrag zur etymologischen und ideengeschichtlichen Begründung des Informationsbegriffs. München: Saur 1978. 320 S.

509 Vgl. zur Einführung: Topsøe, F.: Informationstheorie: eine Einführung. Stuttgart: Teubner 1974. 88 S. (Teubner Studienbücher)
Shannon, C.E., W. Weaver: *Mathematische Grundlagen der Informationstheorie*. München: Oldenbourg 1976.
Bar-Hillel, Y.: Wesen und Bedeutung der Informationstheorie.
In: *Informationen über Information*: Probleme der Kybernetik. Hrsg.: H. von Ditfurth. Frankfurt: Fischer 1971. S. 9-31.

510 Vgl. z.B.: Eigen, M.: Wie entsteht Information?: Prinzipien der Selbstorganisation in der Biologie.
In: Berichte der Bunsengesellschaft für Physikalische Chemie 80(1976) S. 1059-1081.

511 Mittelstrass, J., a.a.O., S.245.

2. Das informationstheoretische Paradigma im Akkumulationsmodell

Beschreiben wir zunächst das derzeit vorherrschende informationstheoretische Paradigma und seine Anwendung auf materialisierte Informationssysteme. Dieses Modell berücksichtigt alle Arten von Informationssystemen, sowohl die Literaturdatenbanken als auch andere Formen textgebundener Informationssysteme, die heute so populären Multimedia-Datenbanken mit der Integration verschiedener medialer Elemente unter einer Retrievaloberfläche und das World Wide Web.

Das Modell (nachfolgend auch *Akkumulationsmodell* genannt) wird durch nachstehende Abbildung visualisiert und kann durch folgende Punkte charakterisiert werden.
Informationssysteme gemäß des klassischen informationstheoretischen Paradigmas

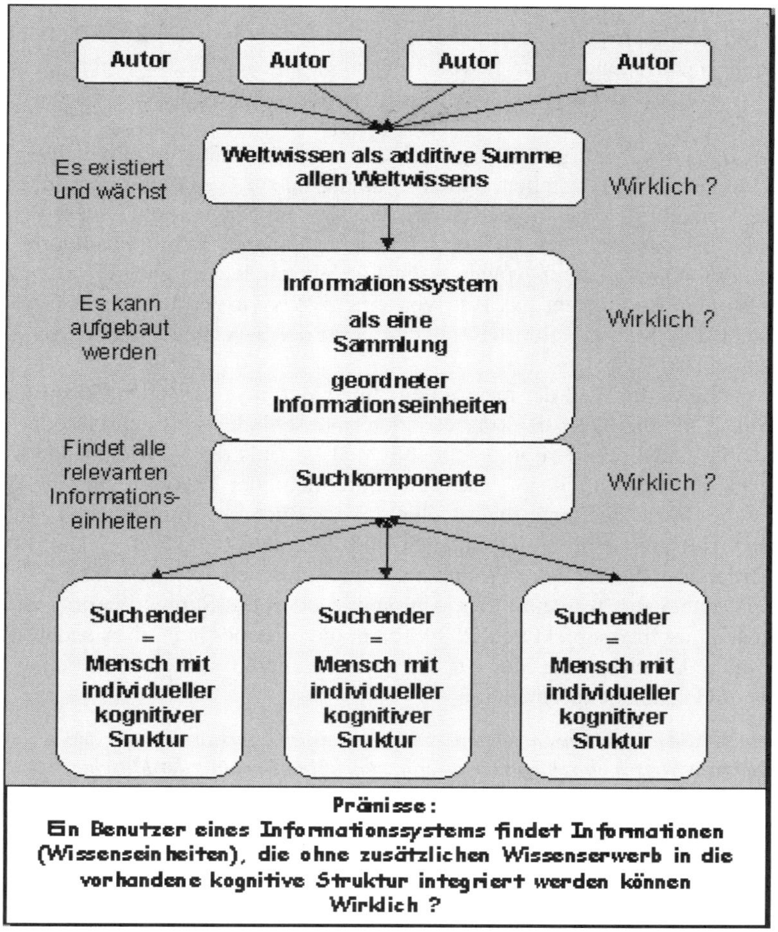

Autoren legen ihr Wissen (oder Teile davon) in Texten oder anderer medialer Form nieder, die der Allgemeinheit zugänglich gemacht werden. Die Summe des publizierten Autorenwissens lässt sich mittels eines Wissensmodells zu einem Weltwissen zusammenfassen, wobei das einfachste Modell das eines additiven Zusammentragens ist. Das so definierte

Weltwissen lässt sich mittels geeigneter Methoden und Verfahren ordnen und in Speichern vorrätig halten. Spezifisches Charakteristikum der Wissensdarstellung in Informationssystemen ist dabei die Aufbereitung in zugriffsfähige Einheiten, sog. *informationelle Einheiten*, die abrufbare Portionierung des Wissens. Die dabei eingesetzten Wissens- und Ordnungsmodelle stimmen mit den als allgemein angesehenen Ordnungsmodellen für das Weltwissen überein. Die Strukturen dieser Ordnungsmodelle kompensieren die zuvor vorgenommene Portionierung des Wissens. Bei geeigneter Konzeption und entsprechendem Ausbaustand enthält das Informationssystem zu einer speziellen Frage mehr Wissen als jeder Mensch. Es lassen sich Methoden und Verfahren entwickeln, die Fragenden mit individuellem Wissen und individuellen Wissensmodellen Zugriff auf das zusammengetragene und geordnet gespeicherte Wissen erlauben. Es sollte möglich sein, den Zugriff so zu optimieren, dass dem Anfragenden das gesamte im Informationssystem zu einer spezifischen Frage enthaltene Wissen als Ergebnis gemeldet wird. Die Ergebnisse des Zugriffs können von den individuell Nachfragenden zur Erweiterung ihres eigenen Wissens genutzt werden, ohne dass zuvor eine Erweiterung oder Modifizierung der kognitiven Wissensbasis erfolgen müsste.

Betrachtet man die vorstehend genannten Punkte hinsichtlich ihrer erkenntnistheoretischen Prämissen, so kann man feststellen, dass als Paradigma zur Gestaltung von Informationssystemen die Vorstellung eines objektivierten Wissens im Sinne von *Poppers Welt 3* benutzt wird. Dabei ist aus einer naturwissenschaftlich geprägten Erkenntnistheorie mit einer Vorstellung von Wahrheitsapproximation die Idee entstanden, es gäbe ein ständiges Anwachsen von Wissen. So entsteht das Bild von einem Wissensvorrat, der zur direkten Nutzung bereit steht. Die Summe aller dieser Ideen ist in der 3-Welten-Theorie von *Karl Popper* zusammengefasst.

Welt 1 wird gedacht als die Welt der materiellen Dinge, der physikalischen Gegenstände und Prozesse, *Welt 2* als die Welt der (insbesondere menschlichen) Erlebnisse oder der psychischen Zustände und Ereignisse und schließlich, *Welt 3* als die Welt der objektiven Produkte oder Ideen des menschlichen Geistes (einschließlich aller Theorien über die Welt und über uns), „die Welt der logischen Gehalte von Büchern, Bibliotheken, Informationsspeichern von Datenverarbeitungsanlagen und ähnlichem“[512]. *Welt 3* kann auch charakterisiert werden als „die Welt der Produkte des menschlichen Teils von *Welt 2*“[513].

Entscheidend ist dabei die Annahme der Autonomie oder Ent-Subjektivierung dieser *Welt 3*, die Existenz einer intersubjektiven Objektivität, die es ermöglicht, dass andere Personen als der jeweilige Urheber diese Idee aufgreifen und weiterentwickeln. So heißt es bei Popper etwa in zwei Gedankenexperimenten:

> *„Experiment 1. Alle unsere Maschinen und Werkzeuge werden zerstört, ebenso unser ganzes subjektives Wissen einschließlich unserer subjektiven Kenntnis der Maschinen und Werkzeuge und ihres Gebrauchs. Doch die* Bibliotheken *überleben und* unsere Fähigkeit, aus ihnen zu lernen. *Es ist klar, dass unsere Welt nach vielen Widrigkeiten wieder in Gang kommen kann.*
> *Experiment 2. Wie vorhin werden Maschinen und Werkzeuge zerstört sowie unser subjektives Wissen einschließlich unserer subjektiven Kenntnis der Maschinen und Werkzeuge und ihres Gebrauchs. Aber diesmal werden* alle Bibliotheken ebenfalls zerstört, *so dass unsere Fähigkeit, aus Büchern zu lernen, nutzlos wird.*

[512] Popper, K.: Objektive Erkenntnis: ein evolutionärer Entwurf. Hamburg: Campe 1993. S.75.
[513] Popper, K.: Auf der Suche nach einer besseren Welt: Vorträge und Aufsätze aus dreißig Jahren. 6. Aufl. München: Piper 1991. S.17.

Wenn Sie über diese beiden Experimente nachdenken, dann wird Ihnen die Realität, die Bedeutung und der Grad der Unabhängigkeit der Welt 3 (ebenso ihre Wirkungen auf die Welt 2 und 1) vielleicht etwas klarer. Denn im zweiten Fall wird unsere Zivilisation jahrtausendelang nicht wieder erstehen."[514]

In diesem Modell entkoppelt sich der Prozess der kognitiven Informationsverarbeitung zum Zwecke der individuellen Wissensgenerierung von einem individualisierten Wissensverständnis.

Die semantischen Einheiten lassen sich in einem Transferprozess - entsprechend der sog. *Pipeline-* oder *Conduit-Metapher*[515] - zunächst aus einer kognitiven Struktur in das Informationssystem hineinspeichern und dann wieder aus dem Informationssystem in die kognitive Struktur des Anfragenden überführen. Auch ein mehrstufiger Prozess, in dem zwischen Autor und Informationssystem etwa noch eine weitere kognitive Struktur steht (z.B. ein Indexierer), die einen Verstehensprozess durchführt und das Ergebnis in einer spezifischen Dokumentationssprache ausdrücken muss, wird in diesem Modell nicht als Anlass genommen, an der prinzipiellen Möglichkeit des Transfers zu zweifeln.

Die zuvor postulierten semantisch abgeschlossener Identitäten werden im Informationssystem einer einfachen Strukturierung zugeführt. In erster Linie erfolgt ein Rückgriff auf 'logische' Begriffsbeziehungen als die intersubjektiv am einfachsten zu vermittelnden. Darüber hinaus finden vermutete oder durch Eigenschaften der Objekte nahegelegte Begriffsbeziehungen (z.B. Subordination, Verwandtschaft) Berücksichtigung. Annahme ist auch hier, dass dies eine Widerspiegelung intersubjektiv gültiger Strukturen ist, da die weitgehendste Implikation der Popperschen Vorstellung vollständige Strukturisomorphie alles Wissenssysteme bedeutet.

Die semantischen Identitäten werden als zeitungebunden betrachtet. Da jedes Wissen zeitgebunden ist, ergeben sich zwei Teilprobleme: Erstens, wie wird die Neuentwicklung von Sachverhalten, von neuem Wissen in das bestehende Informationssystem integriert. Für reine Fakten ist dies durch Berücksichtigung neuer Begriffe (Deskriptoren oder Notationen) noch am ehesten vorstellbar; doch wie verfährt man mit neuen Strukturen? Zweitens, wie geht man mit einem Paradigmenwechsel, mit begrifflichen Fixierungen in der normalen Phase einer Wissenschaftsentwicklung im Kuhnschen Sinn bzw. der revolutionären Phase um[516] (z.B. der Begriff *Materie vor* und *nach* Entwicklung der Relativitätstheorie)?

Für beide genannten Probleme sind bis heute keine befriedigenden Lösungen bekannt. Insbesondere das zweite Problem betont noch einmal die Fragwürdigkeit der Vorstellung, in einem Informationssystem sei Wissen absolut gespeichert und zugänglich.

In Erweiterung *Poppers* Ideen wird die Beschränkung auf 'wahres' wissenschaftliches Wissen, bei dem noch von einem stark konventionalisierten Begriffsgebrauch ausge-

---

514 Ebda., S.111. Für unseren Kontext sei noch festgehalten, dass Bibliothek bei Popper sicher ohne Verfälschung als multi-medialer Wissensspeicher gelesen werden kann.

515 Vgl. z.B.: Fiehler, R.: Kommunikation, Information und Sprache: alltagsweltliche und wissenschaftliche Konzeptualisierungen und der Kampf um die Begriffe.
In: R. Weingarten (Hrsg.), *Information ohne Kommunikation? Die Loslösung der Sprache vom Sprecher.* Frankfurt: Fischer-Verlag 1990. S. 99-128.
Day, R.E.: The „Conduit metaphor" and the nature and politics of information studies.
In: Journal of the American Society for Information Science. 51(2000) no.9, S. 805-811.

516 Kuhn, T.S.: *Die Struktur wissenschaftlicher Revolutionen.* Zweite revidierte und um das Postskriptum von 1969 ergänzte Auflage. Frankfurt: Suhrkamp 1981. 239 S. (Suhrkamp Taschenbuch Wissenschaft; 25)

gangen werden kann, aufgegeben. Es erfolgt für Informationssysteme eine zwanglose - manchmal unreflektierte - Übertragung auf das gesamte Alltagswissen[517]. Konkret bedeutet dies, man geht davon aus, dass eine Fixierung von (kontextunabhängigen) *informationellen Einheiten* (semantischen Identitäten) in externen Speichern, und ein Zugriff auf diese Einheiten in einem Retrievalvorgang zum Zwecke eines Wissenstransfers möglich sind. Für die weitere Diskussion soll der Standpunkt eingenommen werden, dass es nicht möglich ist, *wissenschaftliches* Wissen vollständig von *Alltags*wissen zu unterscheiden, sondern dass es Verbindungen und Übergänge zwischen beiden gibt.

Inzwischen mehren sich die Stimmen, die die Tauglichkeit der Produkte prinzipiell anzweifeln, die gemäß des voranstehenden Modells entwickelt werden. So äußert etwa *F.W. Lancaster*[518]:

> *„What evidence exists that technology has solved the subject access problem? Not much.“*
> *„The improvements that have occured in information handling may be enough to compensate for the growth of the literature but not to* increase *its accessibiblity. Scientists today may have about the same level of access to the literature relevant to their research interests as their counterparts of fifty years ago.“*
> *„The conclusion that emerges most clearly is that, if one wants to know the best things to read on some topic, there is no substitute for consulting an expert, either directly or indirectly (e.g. an expert-compiled bibliography)“.*

Andere Autoren geben bereits Anregungen, in welcher Richtung Lösungsansätze liegen könnten:

> *"In all cases, evaluation of Information Retrieval Systems will suffer from the subjective nature of information. There is no deterministic methodology for understanding what is relevant to a user's search."*[519]
> *„The idea of obtaining subject access to information by being able to visualize an information space, and to navigate through that space toward useful or interesting information, is attractive and plausible. However, this approach to subject access requires additional cognitive processing associated with the interaction of cognitive facilities that deal with concepts and those that deal with space."*[520]

So ist es auch aus dieser Sicht erstaunlich, dass die bibliothekarische Profession mit ihrer langen Tradition einer Mediatorenrolle bei der Wissensakquisition, die Kommunikation und individuelle kognitive Informationsverarbeitung berücksichtigt, nicht bereits nach anderen und vielleicht besseren Modellen für die Informationsübertragung gesucht hat, die

517 Vgl. z.B.: Stock, W.G.: Der Ort der Bibliotheken und Informationszentren in der Informationsgesellschaft. In: Zukunft durch Information: Deutscher Dokumentartag 1995, Fachhochschule Potsdam, 26.-28.9.1995. Hrsg.: W. Neubauer Frankfurt: DGD 1995. S. 305-332.

518 Lancaster, F.W., T.H. Connell u. N. Bishop u.a.: Identifying barriers to effective subject access in library catalogs. In: Library resources and technical services 35(1991) S. 377-391.
Lancaster, F.W.: Has technology improved subject access?
In: Vortrag, International Conference on new Frontiers in Library and Information Services in Taipei, Taiwan, May 9-11, 1991.

519 Kowalski, G.: *Information retrieval systems*: theory and implemetation. Boston, MA: Kluwer Academic Publ. 1997. XIII,282 S. (The Kluwer international series on information retrieval)

520 Allen, B.L.: Designing information systems for user abilities and tasks: an experimental study. In: *Online and CD-ROM review*. 22(1998) no.3, S. 139-153.

z.B. besser Prozesse der Informationsvermittlung beschreiben, die einen Menschen mit individuellem Wissen, individuellen Vorerfahrungen und Fähigkeiten als Adressaten haben.

Im folgenden soll daher ein anderes Modell vorgestellt werden, das aus Sicht des Autor weit besser als Diskussionsplattform für die Entwicklung einer eigenen professionellen Positionierung geeignet ist. Dieses Modell basiert auf Ergebnissen der Sinnes- und Hirnphysiologie, die daher zuvor kurz angesprochen sein sollen.

3. Sinneswahrnehmung und Informationskonstruktion: Prinzipien kognitiver Informations- / Begriffsspeicherung

Ergebnisse der Sinnesphysiologie[521] legen ein anderes Modell zur Erklärung der Informationsübertragung zwischen Menschen und zwischen Menschen und anderen medialen Trägern nahe, als es im Akkumulationsmodell zum Ausdruck kommt: Sinneswahrnehmung erzeugt kein (wie immer auch verstandenes) Abbild von Wirklichkeit, sondern regt kognitive Verarbeitungsprozesse an, die für das Erkennen immer auch Vergleich mit bereits Vorhandenem und Einpassen in die vorhandenen Muster beinhalten. In diesem Sinne ist Sinneswahrnehmung immer auch selektiv:

> *"Das alte Bild eines Stempels aus Stahlstiften, der in eine Lederhaut ein Lochmuster prägt, ist eben keine zureichende Beschreibung dessen, was passiert, wenn ein reizaufnehmendes System - ein Hirn - einem Außen exponiert wird. ... Externe Signalkomponenten werden nicht in das Hirn 'eingedrückt', vielmehr induziert ein Außensignal im System, in das hinein es abgebildet wird, eine Erregung, die sich den vorhergehenden Systemerregungen schlicht überlagert."*[522]

Bezogen auf den Vorgang Informationsverarbeitung heißt dies: Soll die Übertragung gelingen, muss in der kognitiven Struktur bereits ein Schema vorhanden sein, das den Vergleich mit den eingehenden Sinneseindrücken erlaubt, das ein adäquates Verarbeiten gestattet und für Anpassungen zur Verfügung steht.

Es wird häufig davon ausgegangen, dass in Wörtern der Sprache die Bedeutung von Begriffen kodifiziert ist und diese Bedeutung mit der Sprache abgerufen und rekonstruiert werden kann. Definitionen der Begriffe werden dabei als wichtiges Instrument zur Präzisierung oder sogar zur Fixierung der Begriffe – nicht allein in Fach- oder Dokumentationssprachen, sondern ganz allgemein – angesehen[523]. Begriffen wird dabei ein angebbarer Inhalt und Umfang zugeschrieben.

---

521 Zur Einführung in Verbindung mit dem hier dargestellten Thema sei empfohlen:
Hoffman, D.D.: *Visuelle Intelligenz*: Wie die Welt im Kopf entsteht. Aus d. Amerikan. von Hainer Kober. 2. Aufl. Stuttgart: Klett-Cotta 2001. 331 S.
Roth, G.: Das Gehirn und seine Wirklichkeit: kognitive Neurobiologie und ihre philosophischen Konsequenzen. Frankfurt/M.: Suhrkamp 1994.
Edelman, G.M.: *Göttliche Luft, vernichtendes Feuer*: wie der Geist im Gehirn entsteht - die revolutionäre Vision des Medizin-Nobelpreisträgers. 2. Aufl. München: Piper 1995. 396 S.
Oeser, E., F. Seitelberger: *Gehirn, Bewußtsein und Erkenntnis*. 2., überarb. u. erw. Aufl. Darmstadt: Wissenschaftliche Buchgesellschaft 1995. XIV,250 S.(Dimensionen der modernen Biologie; 2)

522 Breidbach, O.: Ein Stoff aus dem die Träume sind?
In: *Ethik und Sozialwissenschaften*. 9(1998) H.2, S. 186-188.

523 Vgl. z.B. DIN 2330: *Begriffe und Benennungen*. Berlin: Beuth 1979.
Dahlberg, I.: Zur 'Begriffskultur' in den Sozialwissenschaften: lassen sich ihre Probleme lösen?.
In: Ethik und Sozialwissenschaften. 7(1996) H.1, S. 3-13.

Schon *Wittgenstein* hat mit seinen Untersuchungen deutlich gemacht, dass Bedeutung von Sprache nicht ohne *Gebrauch* von Sprache gesehen werden kann[524]. Ein Verständnis von Begriffsbedeutung kann somit also ebenfalls nicht ohne den *Gebrauch* von Begriffen entwickelt werden. Dieser Gebrauch ist nun seinerseits wieder abhängig von Personen mit ihrer individuellen Prägung in einem sozio-kulturellen Hintergrund sowie dem aktuellen Verwendungskontext.

Beispiele wie der Begriff *Tisch* zeigen deutlich, wie schwierig es sein kann, eine Definition im obigen Sinne anzugeben. Gleichwohl gelingt es Menschen in der Regel sehr gut, Objekte als Tische zu identifizieren, indem die verschiedenen kognitiven Wissensebenen mit vorangegangenen Lern- und Erfahrungsprozessen zusammenwirken. Die Fähigkeit, Anpassungen an vorhandenen Muster vornehmen zu können, erweist sich in diesem Zusammenhang als wichtiger, als die Vorstellung, man müsse mit fixierten semantischen Einheiten umgehen. Definitorische Fixierung semantischer Einheiten ist im Kontext auch der Verwendungskontext normiert werden muss; eine Beschreibung der Verwendung natürlicher Sprache liefert diese Vorgehensweise nicht [525].

Ein Modell der Übertragung und Rezeption von Information sollte die genannten Faktoren berücksichtigen und sollte erklären können, wie Übertragung und Rezeption von Information im direkten Kommunikationsakt zwischen Menschen, aber auch mit medial externalisierter Information gelingt. Es soll nachstehend skizziert werden[526].

4. Das konstruktivistische Modell der Informationsübertragung und -rezeption

Das vorzustellende Modell sieht Wissensrezeption nicht primär als bloße Übernahme aus Quellen, sondern als kommunikativ generierte kognitive Wissenserzeugung. Dieses Modell versteht die Informationserzeugung und den Informationsaustausch als einen Prozess der strukturellen Kopplung zwischen strukturdeterminierten kognitiven Strukturen und besitzt somit eine kommunikative Komponente, die die Individualität der Partner. Eine zentrale Bedeutung für das Gelingen der Kommunikation bekommt die Möglichkeit zur kommunikativen Rückkopplung ansonsten autonom agierender Systeme. Die charakterisieren-

---

[524] Wittgenstein, L.: *Tractatus logico-philosphicus*: logisch-philosophische Abhandlungen. Frankfurt a.M.: Suhrkamp 1963. 115 S.(Edition Suhrkamp; 12)

Bezzel, C.: *Wittgenstein zur Einführung*. Hamburg: Edition SOAK im Junius Verlag 1988. 151 S, insbes. S.30 ff. (SOAK-Einführungen; 41)

[525] Vgl. Näheres in: Gödert, W.: Externalisierung von Wissen: eine informationstheoretische Betrachtung aus konstruktivistischer Sicht.

In: N. Meder u.a. (Hrsg.), Konstruktion und Retrieval von Wissen: 3. Tagung der Deutschen ISKO-Sektion einschließlich der Vorträge des Workshops „Thesauri als terminologische Lexika", Weilburg, 27.-29.10.1993. Frankfurt/M.: Indeks-Verlag 1995. S. 1-13.

Gödert, W.: Begriffstheorie: Basis einer Theorie von Dokumentationssprachen - Basis zur Erklärung kognitiver Informationsverarbeitung.

In: Ethik und Sozialwissenschaften. 7(1996) H.1, S. 25-28.

[526] Vgl. zum Modell: Gödert, W. u. H.-D. Kübler: Konzepte von Wissensdarstellung und Wissensrezeption medial vermittelter Information: Plädoyer für eine kommunikationstheoretische Betrachtungsweise.

In: Nachrichten für Dokumentation 44(1993) S. 149-156.

Gödert, W.: Grundlegung einer konstruktivistischen Informationstheorie und ihre Konsequenzen für die Gestaltung von Informationssystemen.

In: *Die digitale Revolution*: Deutscher Dokumentartag 1996, Neue Universität Heidelberg, 24.-26.9.1996. Hrsg.: W. Neubauer. Frankfurt a.M.: DGD 1996. S. 351-365. (DGD-Schrift: DOK-9)

den Punkte des konstruktivistischen Modells können im Unterschied zum Akkumulationsmodell wie folgt beschrieben werden.

Kognitive Informationsverarbeitung muss als ein Prozess gedacht werden, der in mehreren Schritten verläuft: über die Gesamtheit aller Sinnesorgane wahrgenommene Impulse werden im Gehirn einer Verarbeitung unterzogen, die aus Vergleichen mit vorhandenen Mustern des Gedächtnisses, dem Anpassen an diese Muster bzw. dem Aufbau neuer Muster besteht. Dabei werden insbesondere nicht allein Fakten akkumuliert, sondern es sind immer auch Strukturen beteiligt - vorhandene oder aufzubauende, in die ggf. Fakten eingepasst werden. Dabei ist es interessant, dass es anscheinend einen aus der Evolution überkommenen Hang zur Formgebung gibt, der jeden kognitiven Prozess begleitet[527]. Es ist keineswegs trivial, eine Vorstellung dafür zu entwickeln, wie viele Fakten erworben werden müssen, um eine neue Struktur anzulegen bzw. zu verfestigen. Sicher scheint nur zu sein, dass beide Teile - Fakten wie Strukturen - in einem ausgewogenen Verhältnis zueinander stehen müssen.

Kognitive Informationsverarbeitung muss jedoch nicht immer durch Sinneswahrnehmung von außen angestoßen werden, sondern kann auch intern erzeugt werden. Menschen verarbeiten Informationen also nicht allein auf Grund eines bewussten Bedürfnisses, sondern ständig. Kognitive Informationsverarbeitung kann nicht abgeschaltet werden.

Für die Gesamtheit dieser Vorgänge besitzen Menschen eine phylogenetisch erworbene Veranlagung, die im Laufe des ontogenetischen Entwicklungsprozesses ausgefüllt und gefestigt werden muss. Insbesondere erwachsene Menschen beginnen in der Regel einen Vorgang kognitiver Informationsverarbeitung stets mit einem bereits vorhandenen Hintergrund und als Lebewesen innerhalb einer kulturellen und sozialen Gemeinschaft teilen sie diesen Hintergrund - zwar nicht in jedem Detail, aber doch in gewisser Übereinstimmung - mit vielen anderen Menschen. Dies muss man beachten, wenn man nun sagt: kognitive Informationsverarbeitung ist Informationserzeugung. Kognitive Abbilder von Umwelt entstehen durch eine individuelle Wirklichkeitskonstruktion. Erkannt wird nur, was die bereits angelegten kognitive Muster zu erkennen gestatten.

Der hiermit beschriebenen Auffassung wird häufig entgegengehalten, sie sei solipsistisch, d.h. sie lasse keinerlei inter-individuellen Kommunikations- oder Verständigungsprozesse zu; jeder sei Gefangener seiner eigenen kognitiven Welt. Diesem wichtigen Einwand kann begegnet werden mit mehreren Eigenschaften kognitiver Strukturen. Menschen sind Lebewesen, die biologischen Regeln unterliegen. Hierzu gehört, dass jede Form von Erstarrung, das unbedingte Festhalten an festen Schemata sowohl das Individuum als auch die Art gefährdet. Jeder autonome biologische Organismus verfügt über die Fähigkeit, auf (zumindest kleine) Veränderungen zu reagieren. Diese Eigenschaft des Gehirns beschreibt die Neurophysiologie als *Plastizität*, sie ist verantwortlich für das Einpassen von Neuem in bereits vorhandene Strukturen. Des weiteren leben Menschen in Sozialgemeinschaft und sind für die Erhaltung ihrer Art auf ein Funktionieren dieser Sozialgemeinschaft angewiesen. Solipsistisches Verhalten kann also allenfalls in Ausnahmen innerhalb einer Gemeinschaft toleriert werden. Jedes Mitglied der Gemeinschaft ist für sein eigenes Leben auf den Austausch Kommunikationspartnern angewiesen. Somit wird verhindert, dass die sich individuell entwickelnden Strukturen, die Konstruktionen von Wirklichkeit zu sehr voneinander abweichen.

---

[527] Calvin, W.H.: *Der Strom, der bergauf fließt*: eine Reise durch die Evolution. Aus dem Amerikan. von Friedrich Griese. 4. Aufl. München: dtv 1998, S.260.

Durch verschiedene Prozesse der individuellen Ontogenese, der Entwicklung des Kleinkindes mit vorwiegendem Bezug auf die Eltern, den Aufbau erster sozialer Gemeinschaften spätestens in Kindergarten oder Schule, den nachfolgenden Lernphasen in der schulischen oder beruflichen Ausbildung, dem Eintauchen in berufliche und private Umfelder, der Zugehörigkeit zu Vereinen oder (fach-) wissenschaftlichen Gruppen bildet sich eine Vielzahl von Bereichen heraus, die als Bezugsrahmen für Kommunikationssituationen genutzt werden können[528]. Neben den schon geschilderten Beispielen gehören zu diesen Bezugsrahmen auch soziale, kulturelle oder ethnische Bereiche, die jeweils in der ihnen eigenen zeitlichen Dimension verstanden werden müssen.

Ohne die nonverbale Kommunikation vernachlässigen zu wollen, ist für die Mehrzahl aller Kommunikationsvorgänge die Sprache das wichtigste Medium. Insofern muss bei einer Betrachtung von Information auch die Rolle der Sprache einbezogen werden. Wir wissen alle, dass es Sprachsituationen gibt, die trotz allen Bemühens um Kommunikation nicht zu einer gelungenen Verständigung führen. Wie kann man testen, ob ein Informationsaustausch über einen verbalen Kommunikationsakt erfolgreich verlaufen ist oder nicht? Allein das Bekunden des Kommunikationspartners *Ich habe verstanden*, ist nicht immer ausreichend. Zur Beantwortung dieser Frage kann auf die genannten Bezugsbereiche zurückgegriffen werden. Der einfachste Test verläuft über die Aufforderung zu einer Handlung, deren Richtigkeit direkt und sofort verifizierbar ist, z.B. *Gib mit bitte den Salzstreuer*. Mit Durchführung dieser Handlung erlernt oder vertieft man das Konzept *Salzstreuer* (z.B. die Formvielfalt, die wichtigsten Erkennungsmerkmale) und kann dieses abstrakte Konzept in künftigen Handlungs- oder Kommunikationssituation mit analogem Bezugsrahmen verstehen oder auch selbst einsetzen. Das Leben ist voll von solchen Ereignissen, die im Laufe der Jahre zu einer Beherrschung von immer mehr Konzepten in verschiedensten Bezugsrahmen führen und in der Folge auch Kommunikation mit sprachlich repräsentierten abstrakten Konzepten ohne Bezugnahme auf Handlungstests erfolgreich machen können. Schwierig wird es immer dann, wenn man mit ganz neuen Konzepten oder bekannten Konzepten in neuen Bezugsrahmen konfrontiert wird, für die noch keine kognitiven Schemata aufgebaut wurden, z.B. Begriffe eines neuen und fremden Fachgebietes, ein Aufenthalt in einem anderen Kulturkreis.

Es wurde schon gesagt, dass jeder Mensch die in seiner kognitiven Struktur enthaltenen Muster im Laufe der Zeit, der Heranwachsens und des späteren Lebens anlegt und ständig benutzt. Diese Muster geben die Bezugsrahmen ab, in denen alle Verarbeitungsprozesse stattfinden. Eine grobe Typisierung dieser Bezugsrahmen – nachfolgend Referenzbereiche genannt – kann wie folgt angegeben werden[529].

---

[528] Piaget, J.: Biologie und Erkenntnis: über die Beziehungen zwischen organischen Regulationen und kognitiven Prozessen. Frankfurt: S. Fischer 1974.

[529] Vgl. für ähnliche Ansätze z.B. auch: Sandkühler, H.J. (Hrsg.): Wirklichkeit und Wissen: Realismus, Antirealismus und Wirklichkeits-Konzeptionen in Philosophie und Wissenschaften. Frankfurt/M.: Lang 1992. S.11ff.

Luft, A.L.: Zur begrifflichen Unterscheidung von 'Wissen', 'Information' und 'Daten'.

In: R. Wille und M. Zickwolff (Hrsg.): Begriffliche Wissensverarbeitung: Grundfragen und Aufgaben. Mannheim: BI Wissenschaftsverlag 1994. S. 61-79.

Fleck, L.: Entstehung und Entwicklung einer wissenschaftlichen Tatsache: Einführung in die Lehre vom Denkstil und Denkkollektiv. Mit einer Einleitung herausgegeben von L. Schäfer u. T. Schnelle. Frankfurt: Suhrkamp 1980.

Referenzbereich der inter-individuellen Gültigkeit

Mit inter-individueller Gültigkeit ist der weitestgehende Anspruch auf Überprüfbarkeit verbunden. Dieser Referenzbereich korrespondiert daher am weitestgehenden mit den Vorstellungen einer Abbildung von Wirklichkeit. Daher kommt als Strukturierungsmittel nur die Logik mit ihren Gesetzen in Frage, da allein mit einem definierten Logikkalkül ein Wahrheitsbegriff eingeführt werden kann. Es lassen sich damit sicher nicht alle Wissensstrukturen, sondern prinzipiell nur ein Ausschnitt derselben abbilden; schon allein aus dem Gesichtspunkt, dass logischen Gesetzen die Dimension Zeit abgeht, die kognitiven Strukturen eigene Form der episodischen Erfahrung damit also nicht abbildbar ist.

Referenzbereich der ent-individualisierten Gültigkeit

Dieser Referenzbereich wird für jeden von uns durch die langjährige Sozialisation in Schule und Ausbildung geschaffen. Darüber werden Strukturen angelegt, die fast schon als inter-individuell erscheinen, die sich bei näherem Hinsehen häufiger aber doch als eine von mehreren Möglichkeiten herausstellen. Hinzu kommt der Bereich der Außenwelt-Erfahrung, der unsere Fähigkeit zur Lebensbewältigung konstitutiert.

Referenzbereich der fachlich ent-individualisierten Gültigkeit

Je länger die Zeit der Ausbildung dauert, je größer das Ausmaß der individuellen Spezialisierung (etwa innerhalb einer beruflichen Tätigkeit) ist, desto kleiner wird die Gruppe derer, die über die gleichen Wissensstrukturen verfügt, mit denen aber auch am ehesten eine problemlose Verständigung über fachliche Fragestellungen des Gruppeninteresses möglich ist. Außerhalb dieses Referenzbereiches unterliegt man den gleichen Bedingungen wie alle anderen.

Referenzbereich der kommunikativ vereinbarten Gültigkeit

Dieser Referenzbereich ist - da am weitesten von den klassischen Vorstellungen des Abbildens von Wirklichkeit entfernt - am schwierigsten für die Strukturierung von Informationssystemen mit unbestimmten Nutzergruppen zu nutzen. Es wäre erforderlich, alle an der Vereinbarung beteiligten kognitiven Strukturen am Planungsprozess zu beteiligen. Für den Aufbau lokaler Informationssysteme ist dies noch vorstellbar, für globale Datennetze wird man in erster Näherung nur die Berücksichtigung statistisch ermittelter Durchschnitte ins Auge fassen können. Allerdings lässt sich eine Notwendigkeit zur Überprüfung einmal fixierter Strukturen mit der Anpassung an veränderte Gruppeninteressen ableiten.

Referenzbereich des individuellen episodischen Gedächtnisses

Dieser Referenzbereich scheint sich nun ganz und gar jeder Kodifizierung für den Aufbau von Informationssystemen zu entziehen. Umgekehrt dürfte gerade dieser Bereich für die individuelle Akzeptanz eines Informationssystems eine große Rolle spielen. Man kann an dieser Stelle durchaus Assoziationen ziehen zu individuellen Gepflogenheiten beim Anlegen eines Zettelkastens oder anderen Formen des sog. kreativen Chaos, das auch durch noch so bunte grafische Oberflächen von (ansonsten starren) Windows-Datenbanken nicht ersetzt werden kann.

Weitere eindrucksvolle Beispiele für die Kontext- und Werte-Verhaftetheit der Informationspräsentation liefern etwa Werbeanzeigen. Manche dieser Anzeigen geben zusätzlich Anlass, die zu Grunde Werte in interkulturellem Kontext zu betrachten. Information in globalem Raum bekommt so eine weitere Konnotation, nämlich die Frage nach den Möglichkeiten einer kulturell invarianten Präsentation von Information. Es gibt bereits Beispiele, dass ein und dasselbe Produkt selbst im deutschsprachigen Raum unterschiedlich beworben wird.

In unserem Diskussionszusammenhang taucht das Verhältnis von Information und Wissen auf, das heute gerne auch im Zusammenhang des Informations- oder Wissensmanagements diskutiert wird. Eine tiefere Diskussion dieses Verhältnisses kann hier nicht gegeben werden; auch ist eine tiefschürfende Analyse des Wissensbegriffs, wie sie etwa von *Wolfgang Cramer* vorgelegt wurde[530], hier nicht reproduzierbar.

Die vorangegangene Diskussion um das Akkumulationsmodell hat gezeigt, dass die Vorstellung eines gebrauchsfähigen Instant-Wissens mit ausgelagerten Wissens-Einheiten und Strukturisomorphie zwischen Sender und Empfänger nicht ausreichen kann. Besonders deutlich hat eine solche Position *Vilem Flusser* zum Ausdruck gebracht:

> *„Elektronische Gedächtnisse sind bequemer als zerebrale informierbar, sie haben eine größere Lagerkapazität, sie können die in ihnen gelagerten Informationen besser bewahren, die einzelnen Informationen sind von dort bequemer abberufbar, und man kann unschwer die Informationen von einem Gedächtnis auf ein anderes übertragen."*[531]

Solche Vorstellungen geben zwar ein Leitbild für das Verständnis von Wissen als verwertbarer Ressource, wie es derzeit im Kontext des Wissensmanagements aufgegriffen wird, eine vollständige Beschreibung des Wissensbegriffs ist so nicht zu erlangen[532].

Von zentraler Bedeutung ist es, Wissen nicht allein im Kontext der Aufgabenstellung des rationalen Problemlösens anzusiedeln, sondern als Voraussetzung für Handeln in all seinen Facetten. Dies bedeutet, Wissen als Gesamtphänomen mit seinen einzelnen Differenzierungen in z.B. Fakten- und Strukturwissen, in formale, episodische oder prozedurale Formen des Wissens wahrzunehmen. Diese Formen dürfen schließlich für einen kognitiven Erkenntnisprozess nicht unabhängig voneinander gedacht werden, sondern müssen immer in Wechselbeziehung zueinander gesehen werden[533]. Das heißt, Wissen hat eine Beziehung zu allen vorhandenen Mustern, die sich als Ergebnis kognitiver Informationsverarbeitung gebildet haben und die zum Vergleich, zur Anpassung an Vorhandenes und zur Selektion, allgemein also zur Bewertung des Momentanen herangezogen werden. Wissen ist somit immer bewertete Information. Wissenverar-beitung greift also ständig auf Klassifikationsprozesse zurück, in denen Vergleich, Anpassung und Selektion eine wichtige Rolle spielen. Erst das Zusammenspiel von Wissen in seinen verschiedenen Erscheinungsformen mit zur Verarbeitung anstehender Information – die nicht notwendig über Sinneseindrücke kommen muss, sondern auch selbst generiert sein kann – lässt ein vollständiges Modell der kognitiven Informationsverarbeitung und Rezeption entstehen. Damit

---

[530] Cramer, W.: *Grundlegung einer Theorie des Geistes*. 3. Aufl. Frankfurt: Klostermann 1975. 105 S. (Philosophische Abhandlungen; 14)

[531] Flusser, V.: Gedächtnisse.
In: Philosophien der neuen Technologie. Hrsg.: Ars electronica. Berlin: Merve Verlag 1989. S. 41-55.

[532] Vgl. z.B. die Diskussion bei: Kübler, H.-D.: Jenseits von bits und bytes: un(v)ermessliches Wissen. Ein Diskussionsbeitrag zu Aufgaben und Qualifikationen von 'Informationsmanagement'.
In: nfd Information - Wissenschaft und Praxis. 51(2000) H.2, S. 95-101.

[533] Von W.H. Calvin stammt beispielsweise die interessante Hypothese, dass sich die menschliche Sprache im Zusammenhang mit einer Verbesserung des Sequenzierungsvermögen bei der Steuerung gezielter Würfe von Faustkeilen herausgebildet hat.
Vgl. Calvin, W.H. a.a.O., S.451 ff.

ist Wissen im hier verwendeten Verständnis Wissen des erkennenden Subjekts und nicht ein funktional verstandenes, für die Operationalisierung oder Mehrwertbildung betrieblicher Strukturen verstandenes, von Menschen entkoppeltes Wissen.

Kommen wir nun zu der Frage, wie sich im Rahmen des vorgestellten Modells Übertragung und Rezeption medial gebundener Information vorstellen lässt.

Für die Externalisierung und spätere Rezeption von Wissen in und aus diversen Medien ist keine direkte kommunikative Rückkopplung möglich. Daher müssen hierfür zusätzliche Strukturen geschaffen werden, die als möglichst optimale Simulation der vielfältigen Gruppen-Interaktion dienen müssen. Hierfür kann die Modellierung von Wissensgemeinsamkeiten gemäß vorstehend angegebener Referenzbereiche eine Orientierungshilfe sein.

Eine Erklärung, wie Wissenserwerb aus Medien möglich ist, für die keine zwischenmenschliche Kommunikationssituation hergestellt werden kann sähe dann wie folgt aus. Zunächst sei festgehalten, dass mit Medien sowohl die vertraute Fixierung von Text in schriftlichen Dokumenten als auch die Speicherung von Bildern und Tönen bis hin zur multimedialen Fixierung auf elektronischen Datenträgern gemeint ist. Ein solcher Speichervorgang wird als Externalisierung kognitiver Information verstanden, bei dem nicht allein Zeichen oder Daten, sondern immer Elemente verschiedenster Bezugsrahmen mit niedergelegt werden müssen. Ein Rezeptionsvorgang wird in diesem Modell nur gelingen, wenn im Rezipienten Elemente in der kognitiven Struktur angelegt sind, die mit dem oder den Bezugsrahmen der medial externalisierten Information korrespondieren. Jede Form medialer Externalisierung unterliegt ihren eigenen Gesetzmäßigkeiten. Jede Stufe in der Entwicklung von Sprechkultur über Schriftkultur bis hin zu einer sich möglicherweise entwickelnden Multimedia-Kultur beinhaltet veränderte Anforderungen an den Externalisierungs- und Rezeptionsvorgang.

Schon dem Medium Schrift wurde Einfluss auf die Bedeutung des Niedergelegten zugesprochen:

> *„Schrift dient u.a. der Erweiterung des begrenzten menschlichen Gedächtnisses. Sie ermöglicht eine zusätzliche, externe Speicherung, die ihrem Inhalt nicht neutral gegenübersteht, sondern ihm einen spezifischen Charakter gibt.“*[534]

Gleiches wird doch für andere Formen medialer Fixierung von Information erst recht gelten. Sicher darf man auch hierbei den Faktor Zeit nicht unterschätzen. Das Medium Buch mit all seinen Möglichkeiten (Layout von Text und Bild) ist uns nicht zuletzt deshalb so vertraut, weil es Zeit genug hatte, sein Potenzial für Darstellung und Rezeption von Information zu entfalten. Man kann auf der Grundlagen neurophysiologischer Befunde vermuten, dass die Kulturtechnik Lesen in enger Verbindung zum vorhan-denen neurophysiologischen Potenzial steht, das sich im Evolutionsprozess auch zur Ausübung anderer Fähigkeiten herausgebildet hat, die Zeit-gesteuerte Koordination erfordern[535]. Man kann weiter vermuten, dass die Entwicklung eines entsprechenden neurophysiologischen Koordinations-Potenzials zur Verarbeitung gleichzeitig darge-botener multimedialer Reize einen nicht näher bestimmbaren Zeit-raum in Anspruch nimmt. Erwartungen an beschleunigte

---

534 Weingarten, R.: Die Verkabelung der Sprache: Grenzen der Technisierung von Kommunikation. Frankfurt: Fischer 1989. S.18.
Vgl. auch: Hasebrook, J.: Multimedia-Psychologie: eine neue Perspektive menschlicher Kommunikation. Heidelberg: Spektrum Akademischer Verlag 1995. XII,330 S. + 1 CD.

535 Vgl. wieder: Calvin, W.H. a.a.O., S.451 ff.

Rezeptions- und insbesondere Lernvorgänge aus multimedialen Quellen werden aus dieser Sicht also stark zu relativieren sein.

Zu allen Zeiten wurde das Anwachsen der Menge an Information geklagt, die es zu verarbeiten gelte. Wir lächeln heute darüber, wenn Goethe darüber klagte, welche Mengen an Büchern alljährlich erscheinen. Wenn uns etwas Probleme bereiten könnte, dann nur der zeitliche Druck, den wir uns selbst im Umgang mit den neuen medialen Erscheinungsformen machen und die damit verbundenen Relativierungen des eigenen Wis-sens. Es wird immer wieder vom schnellen Veralten des Wissens, gar von seiner Halb-wertzeit[536] gesprochen. Bei solchen Aussagen ist das Verständnis von Wissen bereits auf seine – z.B. in Produktionsprozessen - verwertbare Form reduziert und es wird häufig vergessen, dass es erworbenes (Erkenntnis-)Wissen gibt, das für alle nachfolgenden Prozesse der kognitiven Informations- und Wissensverabeitung Gültigkeit behält.

Gestiegen ist insbesondere in unserer Zeit die Zahl der Signale und Reize, denen wir ausgesetzt sind. Ob allein deswegen Informationsmengen wachsen, hängt doch stark vom Verständnis dessen ab, was wir als Information ansehen. Merkwürdigerweise leiden wir doch nicht darunter, dass z.B. Tag für Tag am Bahnhof einer großen Stadt viele Menschen sind, die uns ganz viel Wissen vermitteln oder Erfahrungen weitergeben könnten. Nicht die Zahl der Quellen oder die Menge der Daten erzeugen Rezeptionsdruck, sondern Rahmenbedingungen, die wir uns selbst setzen oder in die wir von anderen gesetzt werden. Insofern hat kompetenter Umgang mit Informationsquellen auch etwas mit Selektion zu tun, die notwendigen Kriterien dafür müssen vielleicht aber erst noch in einem längeren zeitlichen Prozess erworben werden.

5. Konsequenzen für bibliothekarisches Handeln

Welchen Nutzen kann man aus den vorstehenden Überlegungen ziehen? Ein Nutzen kann darin bestehen, dass bibliothekarisch Handelnde ein Fundament bekommen, wenn sie sich nicht allein als Bereitsteller von Daten innerhalb einer informationstechnischen Infrastruktur verstehen wollen, wenn sie dem Kontext von Wissen, seinen Übertragungs-, Vermittlungs- und Rezeptionsbedingungen verpflichtet bleiben wollen. Ein weiterer Nutzen kann im Erkennen bestehen, ob in Diskussionen um die Rolle des Bibliothekars ein neues informationstheoretischen Paradigma eingebracht wird oder ob gemäß des traditionellen Akkumulationsmodells argumentiert wird. Erst der paradigmatische Wechsel im Verständnis von Information im Prozess der Rezeption und der Wissensgenerierung ermöglicht eine veränderte und zukunftsweisende Rollenbeschreibung, die sich frei macht von einem Wissensverständnis, das rein funktional oder zur Erzeugung wirtschaftlicher Mehrwerte gesehen wird – die derzeit typische Sichtweise im Informations- oder Wissensmanagement – und den Menschen in den Mittelpunkt der Betrachtung von Informationsverarbeitung stellt.

An anderer Stelle wurde bereits der Zusammenhang zwischen bibliothekarischem Handeln und dem Fortschrittsgedanken thematisiert[537]. Das hier vorgestellte informationstheo-

---

[536] Umstätter, W.: Die Skalierung von Information, Wissen und Literatur.In: *Nachrichten für Dokumentation.* 43(1992) H.4, S.227-242.

[537] Gödert, W.: Fortschritt und Automatisierung in Bibliotheken: verändern sich Ethos und Verantwortung?. In: *Bibliothek - Kultur - Information*: Beiträge eines internationalen Kongresses anläßlich des 50jährigen Bestehens der Fachhochschule für Bibliothekswesen Stuttgart vom 20.-22.10.1992. Hrsg. P. Vodosek u.a. München: Saur 1993. S.174-185. (Beiträge zur Bibliotheksgeschichte: Bd.8)

retisches Modell als Paradigma für bibliothekarisches Handeln zu nehmen, kann auch einen Beitrag dazu leisten, sich nicht allein in einem Strom genetischen Fortschritts zu bewegen, sondern normative Fortschrittsgesichtspunkte zu berücksichtigen, um erhaltenswerte bibliothekarischen Werte zu erhalten.

Viel ist derzeit von Informationskompetenz die Rede. Diese wäre im vorliegenden Kontext ja wohl nicht nur zu verstehen als die Kenntnis von Ressourcen und der zu nutzenden Instrumente. Unter Berücksichtigung der klassischen Mediatorenrolle und unter der Voraussetzung, dass ein Teil der zukünftigen Entwicklung der Bibliotheken so beschrieben werden kann, dass die eigenen Bestände immer weniger eine dominierende Rolle für diese Mediatorenfunktion spielen, dass über das Internet zugängliche Informationsquellen eine immer größere Bedeutung bekommen, so wären ja auch Fähigkeiten und Kenntnisse eingeschlossen, unter welchen Voraussetzungen Wissenserwerb aus externen Quellen möglich ist, wie solch ein Wissenserwerb abläuft. Idealerweise sollte in einem Informationsvermittlungsprozess explizit berücksichtigt werden, ob es ausreicht, nur Fakten und Daten zu übermitteln oder ob erst noch der Erwerb von strukturellem Wissen erforderlich ist.

Nicht unbedenklich stimmt es allerdings, dass unter Bibliothekaren eine Neigung vorhanden ist, sich selbst in den Bereichen nach Einfachstlösungen zu sehnen, in denen bereits Kinder den Einsatz differenzierter Werkzeuge beherrschen. Diskussionen um professionelles Selbstverständnis müssen immer auch mit dem Blick auf ein Niveau geführt werden, dass man erreichen oder mindestens nicht unterschreiten will.

Es sei daran erinnert, dass gerade die Entwicklung um das Internet und World Wide Web 2 Phänomene hervorgebracht haben, die die bibliothekarische Mediatorentätigkeit von 2 Seiten her in die Zange nehmen. Zum einen werden Fähigkeiten des Recherchierens, etwa die Benutzung der einschlägigen Suchhilfsmittel des Web, zunehmend an einen immer größeren Kreis von Personen erworben. Die populäre PC-Presse ist voll von Artikeln wie: „Alles finden im Web"[538] mit entsprechenden Hinweisen, im allgemeinen Ausbildungskontext werden von der politischen Seite entsprechende Kenntnisse als Allgemeinqualifikation propagiert[539]. Zum anderen setzen gerade die technischen Möglichkeiten des Internet die Klientel der wissenschaftlichen Bibliotheken in die Lage, die Aufgabe des Nachweises der für sie relevanten Informationsquellen selbst zu organisieren. Zahlreiche Projekte zur Erstellung von Subject Gateways liefern dafür einen Beleg[540]. Zum Glück sind an einer Reihe von Projekten auch Bibliotheken beteiligt. Die Gefahr, dass die Wissenschaft den ehemals an die Bibliotheken abgetretenen Auftrag in die eigene Tätigkeit zurückholen könnte, ist damit aber so lange nicht im Grundsatz gebannt, wie die Bibliotheken sich nicht eine neue Position in ihrer Mediatorenfunktion gesucht haben.

538 So z.B. in: PC-Welt 2000, H.8, S.104.

539 So hat z.B. der Ministerpräsident des Landes Nordrhein-Westfalen laut einer Zeitungsmeldung vom 14.4.2000 geäußert, dass Internet-Recherchen künftig zu einem zentralen Unterrichtsinhalt an Schulen werden sollen.
In: Kölnische Rundschau Nr.89 vom 14.4.2000, S.rma01a.

540 Vgl. zum Überblick die Beiträge in: Online information review. 24(2000) no.1.

Blaise Cronin

The Virtues and Vices of Virtual Life

Introduction

In October 1992, I was invited by Prof. Dr. Peter Vodosek to deliver a keynote address at the 50th anniversary of the Fachhochschule fuer Bibliothekswesen in Stuttgart. The event was imaginatively conceived and impressively organized - a tribute to all involved. That fond memory is just one reason why I am so pleased to be able to contribute to this *Festschrift* in honor of Dr. Vodosek, who, for many years, has been a fine ambassador for both his institution and the profession. The title of my 1992 presentation was *Educating librarians for an information society* (Cronin, 1993). In this short paper I want to develop aspects of that presentation and examine more closely the driving forces which affect not just the world of professional information praxis but the institutional structures associated with the production, distribution and archiving of information resources. My focus is not technology (tools, artifacts, platforms, instruments) but the broader social ramifications of the so-called digital revolution. My remarks will concentrate on the Internet and the World Wide Web, using recent developments and trends to highlight some of the behavioral and socio-cultural implications of global internetworking. I shall briefly explore five spheres of activity in order to illustrate the highly nuanced nature of socio-technical change. These five areas are: (i) electronic commerce; (ii) distributed learning; (iii) digital scholarship; (iv) virtual libraries; (v) online access systems. But first a little (recent) history to set the scene.

Leading Indicators of Post-industriality

There is a voluminous literature devoted to the informatization of society. It comprises many different genres, ranging from the utopian to dystopian (e.g., Bell, 1973; Schiller, 1987; Negroponte, 1995; Noble, 1999). Much of the early discussion foregrounded the tools associated with the advent of large-scale computerization. Leading indicators of the putative information society typically included data on PC shipments, global chip manufacturing volumes, telecommunications traffic, proliferation of commercial online databases, rates of office automation, as well as hardware/software performance measures (e.g., processing power, price/performance ratios). They told a good story. Today these kinds of data are supplemented by, *inter alia*, various measures of Web access and Internet use. The macro level shifts are also striking: by way of illustration, America's industrial output weighs about the same as it did 100 years ago, even though real GDP (Gross Domestic Product) is 20 times higher, reflecting the higher knowledge content of contemporary goods and services (*Fortune*, March 2, 1998, p.46).

Labor force statistics on changing occupational roles and ratios across sectors also revealed the pace and nature of underlying change. Notable among these were the pioneering analyses of national accounts data by Machlup (1962) and Porat (1977) that sought to quantify the growing significance of information-related and knowledge-based activities in the overall economy. In aggregate, these figures provided compelling evidence of structural transformation within late capitalistic societies and helped legitimate the idea of the information society.

Others were quick to recognize the deeper significance of the first generation indicators and associated trend lines. Bell (1973) provided a path-breaking analysis of the conditions of post-industriality, though some of his axial assumptions and inferences continue to be challenged. Poster (1990, pp. 24-25), for instance, has accused him of deploying the „rhetoric of totalization" to assert rather that prove that knowledge and information „are the leading variables of society". More recently, the National Research Council (1994) highlighted the importance of fine-grained analyses, at both the industry sector and enterprise levels, of the impacts of information technology investments on organizational performance. The Council found that productivity, though important, was not a sufficient measure of the benefits accruing to an organization from its investments in information systems and technology. It recommended that other elements of performance, such as quality, flexibility, convenience, variety, responsiveness and reliability, be factored into the equation, and that greater attention be given to pass-through benefits felt at the customer/consumer level. In other words, we need to take account of social forces and human factors in trying to grasp the organizational (and societal) implications of information technology.

Social theorists, with diverse academic backgrounds, have greatly expanded the frame by moving beyond simple quantification of instruments/tools and analysis of the first-order effects of computerization to developing a richer understanding of the matrix of socio-cultural forces and factors which influences the adoption and use of information and communication technologies in environments of all kinds (e.g., Kling, 1996). However, the notion of 'information society' continues to be hotly contested by some (e.g., Webster, 1995), while others lament the ahistoricality of much of the writing on the subject (Black, 2001).

Internetworking Trends

With the advent of populist networking has come the need for a deeper understanding of how global computing and asynchronous communication affect social relations, behavioral norms and group values. Thus, my focus is less on what might be termed the *means* of cultural production than on emerging *modes* of cultural production: how and why do people use information technology and communication system the way they do? Why do users ignore much of a software package's functionality? Why do they deploy tools for purposes that were unintended (if not always unimagined) by the designer? How do context, local situations, group values, and professional norms shape the way in which technologies are used, configured, and incorporated into daily life? The key issue is not the productive capacity, cost-performance ratio or functionality of a particular technology, but the ways in, and purposes for, which individuals and groups actually use it. Presumably, the designers and builders of the Internet had little idea that their invention would be used by school children to communicate with their peers in another country, while the creators of the Web had little reason to imagine that pornographic sites would be among the most technically-sophisticated and profitable places on the Web (Cronin and Davenport, 2001). Nor could we have imagined that Internet addiction would so quickly achieve clinical status (Umiker-Sebeok, 1997; Wallace, 1999). The uses, benign and malign, serious and silly, to which the

Internet and Web have been put show convincingly how linear and deterministic models of the impact of computers on society can miss so much of import and skew our appreciation of the phenomena under scrutiny.

Both the Internet and (even more so) the Web continue to exhibit spectacular growth (Kahn, *et al.*, 1997). Together they (Internet/Web) constitute a fertile site, anthropologically speaking, in which to examine emerging social practices, such as the formation of virtual communities and the development of electronic markets. It has recently been estimated that some 610 billion emails are sent annually in the USA (*Economist*, 2000). The Web is a powerful example of a ubiquitous and convivial communications medium, used by a rich cross-section of society for diverse purposes. To provide an historical (*sic*) perspective, from mid-1993 to the beginning of 1997, the number of Web sites grew from less than 200 (of which 1.5 % were commercial in nature) to an estimated 650,000 (of which 60 %+ were commercial). Today, there are approximately 25 million web sites in existence. The number of Internet hosts continues to grow exponentially and the estimated number of Web users worldwide is 300 million, with a forecast of one billion by 2005 (see: www.iconocast.com). Recently, the first UCLA Internet Report (2000) was published by the UCLA Center for Communication Policy. It will provide a useful benchmark for further annual surveys of Internet users and non-users in the USA.

Geo-demographics

The demographics of the Internet and Web, though constantly evolving, show clearly that access and use are neither universal nor egalitarian. There is evidence of social stratification and disarticulations within and between countries (Park, 1997): for instance, disposable income and educational levels are closely associated with use, while ease of access (and, by extension, use) vary enormously from country to country as a function of technological, economic and socio-political conditions (Cronin & McKim, 1997). Indeed, there is a reasonably strong correlation between a nation's ranking on the UNDP's Human Development Index (a composite measure which includes adult literacy and education participation rates) and the number of Internet hosts *per capita* (Press, 1997). Early field studies of Internet use among US households showed that use was age-related (male teenagers are the most Internet-active sub-group) and gendered—males are more frequent users than females (Kraut, 1996). In recent years, however, the (gross) gender difference has virtually disappeared in the USA, though gender-specific patterns of use persist (The UCLA Internet Report, 2000).

Within geographic regions, very different use profiles can be found. To take a non-Western example, comparison of Internet data for Taiwan and Japan shows that home-based use is far more common in the former (72 %) than in the latter (44 %), where office/home use is split evenly. The surveys were conducted in 1996 by the Institute for Information Industry and Market Development Center in Taiwan (http://www.psd.iii.org.tw/ inews/focus/isurvey/ isurvey.htm) and by NIKKEI in Japan (http://www.nikkeibp.com/ RESEARCH/NMM/9607/ nmm13-44.html). Greater similarity is to be found in terms of the purposes for which Taiwanese and Japanese individuals use the Internet: in both countries, recreation is the dominant category (42 % and 53 %, respectively) followed by work-related use (32 % and 37 %, respectively). As in North America, usage in Taiwan has been associated strongly with gender and age: users are 87 % male, though female participation rates are growing more rapidly, while 74 % of users are aged 30 or less.

Socio-technical Change

The Web is having an impact on many aspects of contemporary life, in some cases challenging long established assumptions and practices. Cyber-space affords multiple opportunities to explore the ways in which social practices and relationships are molding and being molded by information technology. I now consider five virtual spheres to show what a social shaping of technology perspective entails.

Electronic commerce

Online selling via the Internet was a US$500 million business in 1996. Estimated values of Net-based business transactions for 2000 fell within the range US$7-20 billion (e.g., Rao, *et al.*, 1998; *Wired*, 1998). The general trend, however, is unmistakable, seasonal and other trading blips notwithstanding. The emergence of electronic commerce has caused us to revisit traditional assumptions relating to market entry/exit barriers, customization, branding, globalization, pricing, inventory management, distribution, market research, advertising, security, privacy and trust. Businesses, large and small, are working hard to understand the peculiarities of virtual markets and the changing demands, expectations and behaviors of both established and new customer segments. This is not business as usual propelled by greater computing power: it is a novel business forum, whose properties are still dimly grasped. Online trust is a case in point. Organizations of all kinds are trying to better understand how trust (a key variable in effective customer relations management) is constituted and sustained in online transactions. They are also beginning to recognize that the Web is a powerful medium for allowing disgruntled customers or shareholders to mobilize support and challenge the reputation or business practices of a firm (Crush, 2001).

Online and distributed learning

The rapid rise of online education and distributed (or network-based) learning as a major focal area in higher education is a response to three major trends: digitalization, demographics and deregulation (Cronin, 1998). By digitalization I mean the mix of technologically-linked developments which facilitate and promote online learning—wide-area networking, distributed computing, collaboration technologies and digital libraries. Central to all of this are the Web and Internet, the delivery platforms of choice. Demographic and lifestyle shifts are also powerful change drivers. In North America and elsewhere (e.g., some Pacific Rim nations) the character of the student body is changing in terms of geodemographic composition, lifecycle learning needs, expectations, aspirations and mobility. These shifts have major supply side implications, as capacity is stretched and student demand for flexible educational products and services grows. At the same time, the *de facto* monopoly exercised by old-line institutions of higher education is being challenged by new entrants, including corporate universities and virtual universities, as well as a growing number of consortia. Progressive deregulation is also a feature of the higher education marketplace. Employers are looking for evidence of competencies and proof of learning, and are correspondingly disenchanted with the traditional seat/time-based metrics used in academia (e.g., Norris, 1997). Once again, the Web is changing the prevailing dynamic between provider and consumer and forcing us to fundamentally rethink many of our standard operating assumptions. In all of this, it is important to maintain „a socially-driven technology agenda" (Agre, 1997).

Digital scholarship

The Internet has not simply made it easier for authors to distribute their ideas to both general and specific audiences; it has challenged the notion of what it means to publish. On the one hand, there is rapid growth in the number of electronic journals, newsletters and magazines, and, more recently still, the emergence of electronic books. Major academic publishers such as Wiley InterScience are migrating their scholarly journals to the Web (see: http://www.interscience. wiley.com/). On the other, authors, individually or collectively, can now bypass the traditional vetting, publication and archival processes by mounting their own works on a Web site, e-print archive, or distributing them via listserv. Vanity publishing has taken on a new meaning in the online age. Posting and electronic pre-printing (think of the Los Alamos National Laboratory Physics Archive established by Paul Ginsparg) are new modalities available to those frustrated with the constraints of the traditional peer-review process (and related reward system) within academia. It is argued by some that Web-based publishing in fact induces greater transparency into the scholarly communication process by supporting open/deep peer review, thus ensuring that poor quality work will ultimately be exposed for what it is. However, peer-review, the backbone of science and scholarship, is medium-independent, and the growth of digital publication (think of ventures such as PubMed Central or CrossRef, researcher-sponsored and publisher-driven initiatives, respectively, designed to increase access to the scientific literature) is not incompatible with the maintenance of rigorous peer review procedures. Here, as before, what we are witnessing is a re-conceptualization of conventional practices and the possible reshaping of community norms and behaviors as the result of a major technological innovation. This is not simply a case of using distributed computing power to improve efficiency (e.g., time-to-market) or cut production costs: rather it constitutes a reengineering of the publishing value chain and also of the relationships between the principal stakeholders.

Virtual libraries

The effects of the digital revolution on library services may well include disintermediation, deprofessionalization and demassification. Increasingly, users will be able to access dispersed digital collections using a variety of intelligent interfaces, search engines, recommender systems and push technologies. In theory, the intermediary (the professional librarian) will be displaced by intelligent information agents and knowbots, or, alternatively, become an unseen presence working in the background. One consequence of disintermediation may well be progressive deprofessionalization of the traditional roles and functions performed by librarians. A less extreme (and, frankly, more plausible) scenario posits that disintermediation will trigger a process of remediation, as the intermediary community creates new value-adding roles (e.g., validators, integrators, quality controllers, negotiators) within the virtual organization (Fallis, 2000). A case in point is the proposed Collaborative Digital Reference Service, a 60-institution consortium which will offer librarian-mediated 24-hour, global electronic reference services at no cost to users. Members of the collaboration, which will be hosted by the Library of Congress, include the national libraries of Australia and Canada and the university libraries of Harvard and Cornell.

From the user's point of view, digitalization should translate into demassification; in other words, a move away from the concentration of cultural assets in a single location (the typical research library model) to easily accessible, but physically remote, knowledge bases (Luke, 1997). However, displacement scenarios downplay social aspects of digital library design and use. Social learning occurs in (physical) libraries as users collaborate and interact with librarians and their peers around terminals, catalogs and similar institutional resources. How are these kinds of (non-programmable) activities to be replicated and supported in the dematerialized, digital library of tomorrow? The technical challenges facing digital library architects are, in some respects, more tractable than the socio-cultural design problems which have yet to be solved.

Online access systems

In the USA, public libraries are the principal means whereby citizens access the storehouse of recorded knowledge. Currently, almost 100 % of public libraries in the USA are connected to the Internet (up from 21 % in 1994), though there is considerable regional variation in the quality of provision, according to surveys by the National Commission on Libraries and Information Science (NCLIS). In some cases access is mediated/controlled; in others, members of the public can log on to the Internet/Web unaided and unrestricted. Among public library staff, there is considerable variation in frequency of Web use: almost 34 % of staff in 1997 never used the Internet, while 5 % used it 100 or more times a week (NCLIS, 1997). In addition to grassroots developments, the federal government has been extremely active in building a large and rich Web presence for its many departments and agencies. More generally, these kinds of initiatives contribute to the idea of dialogic (or digital) democracy, something which appeals greatly to many Americans (Katz, 1997). Indeed, in both Europe and the USA, there is considerable (and growing) interest in developing tools to support electronic government and tele-democracy (*Communications of the ACM*, 2001).

Cyber-communities

Common to an understanding of each of the five virtual worlds sketched above is the idea of community, however evanescent or ill-defined some electronic collectivities may appear. The rise of global networking has highlighted the idea of electronic community in striking fashion (e.g., Rheingold, 1993). The catalytic effect of networking can be seen in the proliferation of online groups and „communities of practice" (Wenger & Snyder, 2000) mobilized around a bewildering array of topics and issues, ranging from the socially enlightened to the superficial. Whether it is the venerable Well (Whole Earth 'Lectronic Link), the world of MUDs and MOOs, or 'blue chip' list publishing (Bennahum, 1998) the common denominators are self-formation, shared identity/purpose, dispersed membership, self-governance. The upside of this trend is a strengthening of civil society, as citizen groups and new social movements become increasingly active within and across national boundaries. There remain, though, questions relating to the creation and persistence of both trust and group cohesiveness in exclusively electronic communities. A downside of pervasive networking is the rising threat of 'information warfare' and 'netwar', as terrorists, transnational criminals, ethno-nationalists and others, such as political radicals or counter-cultural groups, challenge the *status quo* and the rule of law by exploiting networked technologies in support of their military, political or ideological agendas (Denning, 1999).

Conclusion

The effects of global networking on social cohesiveness and notions of statehood illustrate just how potentially far-reaching are the changes being wrought by the Web and Internet on our daily lives. The incorporation of networking technologies into our work and domestic environments is already having an effect on existing social systems and value structures. For example, membership of an electronic community may dissipate the traditional sense of community, and, in extreme cases, result in value conflict and even weakening of national sovereignty. The Web's ease-of-use has opened up a Pandora's box of dubious delights, which, in the USA, at least, is taxing prevailing definitions of free speech and public decency. The tension between constitutional rights and public morals has been thrown into relief by the Web, and has raised, in turn, a host of legal and jurisdictional issues which were surely not envisaged by Tim Berners-Lee and his colleagues when they developed the World Wide Web.

There are other examples. The diffusion of electronic mail into the work place has provided lower status employees, organizational dissidents and others with the means to mobilize support and challenge established bases of cognitive and positional authority, a trend which finds its echo at the wider political level. Monolithic structures do not cope easily with cyber guerrillas: Net warriors can thrive despite massive resource asymmetricalities, a far cry from the realities of conventional warfare. Information warfare, broadly defined, will likely become a feature of 21st century life (Cronin & Crawford, 1999). Such are just a few of the unintended social consequences of a blockbuster technology—the Internet—which was designed originally as a packet switching network to facilitate communication and file transfer between selected computer scientists and members of the US research community. As you can see, we are only beginning to come to grips with the social ramifications of the digital revolution.

References

Agre, P. (1997). *The Internet and education.* Available at: http://communication.ucsd.edu/pagre

Black, A. (2001). The Victorian information society: surveillance, bureaucracy, and public librarianship in 19th-century Britain. *The Information Society*, 17(1), 63-80.

Bennahum, D.S. (1998). The hot new medium is ... Email. *Wired*, 6(4), 104-126.

Bell, D. (1973). *The coming of post-industrial society: a venture in social forecasting.* New York: Basic Books. (see also the special anniversary edition with a new foreword, 1999).

Beniger, J.R. (1986). *The control revolution: technological and economic origins of the information society.* Cambridge, MS: Harvard University Press.

Communications of the ACM (2001). Special issue devoted to e-democracy. 44(1).

Cronin, B. (1993). Educating librarians for an information society. In: Vodosek, P., Blum, A, Henning, W. & Vogeler, H. (Eds.). *Bibliothek-Kultur-Information.* London: K.G. Saur, 15-27.

Cronin, B. (1998). The electronic academy revisited. *Aslib Proceedings*, 50(9), 241-254.

Cronin, B. & Crawford, H. (1999). Information warfare: its application in military and civilian contexts. *The Information Society*, 15(4), 1999, 257-263.

Cronin, B. & Davenport, E. (2001). E-rogenous zones: positioning pornography in the digital economy. *The Information Society*, 17(1), 33-48.

Cronin, B. & McKim, G. (1997). The Internet. In: Courier, Y. & Large, A. (eds.). *World information report 1997/98*. Paris: Unesco, 240-256.

Crush, P. (2001). Out to get you. *Management Today*, November, 9-95, 97.

Denning, D.E. (1999). *Information warfare and security*. Reading, MA: Addison-Wesley.

The Economist (2000). Quantifying information., Byte counters. 21 October, 154.

Fallis, D. (2000). Veritistic social epistemology and information science. *Social Epistemology*, 14(4), 305-316.

Kahn, R., *et al.* (1997). The evolution of the Internet as a global information system. *International Information & Library Review*, 29(2), 129-151.

Katz, J. (1997). The digital citizen. *Wired*, 5(12), 68-82, 274—275.

Kling, R. (1996). (ed.). *Computerization and controversy: value conflicts and social choices*. New York: Academic Press. 2nd.ed.

Kraut, R., *et al.* (1996). The HomeNet field trial of residential Internet services. *Communications of the ACM*, 39(12), 55-63.

Luke, T. (1997) *Discourse and discipline in the digital domain: political economy of the virtual university*. November 1997. Available at: http://www.nzii.org.nz/Papers/Tim_luke/virtual_uni_part1.html

Machlup, F. (1962). *The production and distribution of knowledge in the United States*. Princeton, NJ: Princeton University Press.

National Commission on Libraries and Information Science. (1997). *1997 National survey of US public libraries and the Internet*. Washington, DC: NCLIS.

National Research Council. (1994). *Information technology in the service society: a twenty first century lever*. Washington, DC: National Academy Press.

Negroponte, N. (1995). *Being digital*. New York: Knopf.

Noble, D.F. (1999). *The religion of technology: the divinity of man and the spirit of invention*. London: Penguin.

Norris, D.M. (1997). *Revolutionary strategy for the knowledge age*. Ann Arbor, MI: SCUP.

Park, S.G. (1997). „Disarticulations" in the information society: barriers to universal access to information highways in developing countries. *International Information & Library Review*, 29(2),189-199.

Porat, M.U. (1977). *The information economy: definition and measurement*. Washington, DC: US Department of Commerce.

Poster, M. (1990). *The mode of information: poststructuralism and social context*. Chicago, IL: University of Chicago Press.

Press, L. (1997). Tracking the global diffusion of the Internet. *Communications of the ACM*, 40(11), 11-17.

Rao, H.R., *et al.* (1998). Marketing and the Internet. *Communications of the ACM*, 41(3), 32 34.

Rheingold, H. (1993). *The virtual community: homesteading on the electronic frontier*. New York: HarperPerennial.

Schement, J.R. & Curtis, T. (1997). *Tensions and tendencies of the information age: the production and distribution of information in the United States*. Transaction Press: New Brunswick, NJ.

Schiller, H.I. (1986). *Information and the crisis economy*. Oxford: OUP.

The UCLA Internet Report (2000). *Surveying the digital future.* Los Angeles, CA: UCLA Center for Communication Policy.
Umiker-Sebeok, J. (1997). The semiotic swarm of cyberspace: cybergluttony and Internet addiction in the global village. *Semiotica*, 117, 2/4, 239-297.
Wallace, P. (1999). *The psychology of the Internet.* Cambridge: Cambridge University Press.
Webster, F. (1995). *Theories of the information society*. London: Routledge.
Wenger, E. & Snyder, W. (2000). Communities of practice: the organizational frontier. *Harvard Business Review* (January/February), 139-145.
Wired. (1998). Watching the predictors. 6(3), 80.

Holger Nohr

Wissensmanagement

Wissen wird zum Fokus betrieblichen Managements

Was verbindet so unterschiedliche Unternehmen wie Hoffmann-LaRoche, Siemens, Deutsche Genossenschaftsbank, 3M, Hewlett-Packard, Ernst & Young, Herlitz oder Skandia? Diese und andere weltweit agierende Organisationen haben das Wissen ihrer Mitarbeiter, ihrer Kunden, ihrer Lieferanten sowie die Angebote externer Informationsdienstleister zu einem zentralen Element ihrer Unternehmensstrategie und ihrer Unternehmenskultur gemacht. Unter dem Stichwort Wissensmanagement (Knowledge Management) verändern sie die organisatorischen und technischen Rahmenbedingungen, um von den Mitarbeitern innerhalb des Unternehmens erarbeitetes Wissen in der Organisation zu verteilen und auf breiter Basis zu nutzen, genauso wie das Wissen ihrer Kunden und ihrer Lieferanten. Ziel ist es, durch eine bessere Nutzung von Wissen einerseits zu Produktivitäts- und Qualitätssteigerungen sowie zu einer höheren Kundenorientierung zu gelangen und andererseits durch einen kontinuierlichen Innovationsprozess einen dauerhaften Wettbewerbsvorteil zu erringen.

Das Wissen bestimmt zunehmend den Wert dieser Unternehmen. Die Bewertung der Unternehmen, insbesondere an der Börse, basiert immer weniger auf den physischen und finanziellen Anlagen (tangible assets) eines Unternehmens, sondern auf dem Glauben der Marktakteure an die Fähigkeit, ein bestimmtes Geschäft in der Zukunft profitabel zu betreiben. Diese Fähigkeit beruht auf den sog. intangible assets (Eustace 2000) – dem Wissen über Technologien und Prozesse, Märkte und Marktteilnehmer, Produkte und Dienstleistungen usf. sowie auf der Qualität der Beziehungen eines Unternehmens zu seinen Kunden, seinen Lieferanten und anderen stakeholdern. Das Management von Wissen begründet diese Fähigkeit.

Wissensmanagement ist jedoch keineswegs nur ein Thema für die großen Konzerne. Klein- und mittelständische Unternehmen (KMU) stehen heute – dank des Internet und der durch diese technische Innovation ausgelösten grundlegenden Veränderung des Marktgeschehens – ebenfalls in einem globalen Wettbewerb, der zusätzlich geprägt ist durch permanente Innovation und eine zunehmende Geschwindigkeit. Auch für sie gilt: Wissen um Märkte und Produkte, um die Konkurrenz und um neue technische Innovationen, um den Wandel in der Bedürfnislage und im Lebensgefühl der Kunden und Wissen um Marketingstrategien ist zum bestimmenden Produktions- und Wettbewerbsfaktor geworden. Mehr noch als die Großunternehmen, sind Klein- und Mittelbetriebe auf ihre intellektuellen Fähigkeiten angewiesen, um im Wettbewerb bestehen zu können. Wettbewerb braucht Wissen – in allen Branchen.

Zudem ist Wissensmanagement nicht nur ein Thema für den privatwirtschaftlichen Sektor. Auch in der öffentlichen Verwaltung insbesondere der Städte und Gemeinden ist der effektivere und effizientere Umgang mit dem Wissen eine wichtige Voraussetzung für Kundenorientierung und für bürgernahe Dienstleistungen.

Die Triebkräfte für die stetig wachsende Bedeutung des Wissens fasst North (1999) folgendermaßen zusammen:

- Den strukturellen Wandel von arbeits- und kapitalintensiven zu informations- und wissensintensiven Aktivitäten im Wirtschaftsgeschehen
- Die Globalisierung der Wirtschaft verändert die internationale Arbeitsteilung
- Die Informations- und Kommunikationstechnologien ermöglichen und beschleunigen preiswerte Transaktionen und schaffen weltweite Informationstransparenz

Wissensmanagement beschäftigt sich mit den Möglichkeiten der Einflussnahme auf die Wissensbasis eines Unternehmens. Unter der Wissensbasis eines Unternehmens werden alle Daten und Informationen, alles Wissen und alle Fähigkeiten verstanden, die diese Organisation zur Lösung ihrer vielfältigen Aufgaben in einer zunehmend komplexeren Wirtschaft benötigt. Der Schlüssel für die Wettbewerbsfähigkeit und die Innovationskraft eines Unternehmens liegt heute in der Fähigkeit begründet, diese Humanressourcen (Mohr 1997) zielgerichtet zu bewirtschaften, d.h. Wissen zu erwerben (Organisationales Lernen) oder neues Wissen zu entwickeln, dieses Wissen adäquat innerhalb der Organisation bereitzustellen (Wissenstransparenz und –verteilung) und schließlich in strategische Konzepte und operative Handlungen umzusetzen (Wissensnutzung). Diese Aufgaben verlangen als Voraussetzung die Bestimmung relevanten Wissens, die Formulierung von Wissenszielen der gesamten Unternehmung. Nach Von Krogh und Venzin (1995) können die Aufgaben an das Wissensmanagement folgendermaßen zusammengefasst werden:

- Erschließen von Wissen (Erfahrungen, Best Practices) für alle, die dieses im Rahmen ihrer organisationalen Rolle benötigen
- Verfügbarmachen von Wissen am Ort und zur Zeit der Entscheidung
- Erleichtern des effektiven und effizienten Entwickelns von neuem Wissen (bspw. F&E-Aktivitäten, Lernen auf der Basis von historischen Fällen)
- Sicherstellen, dass jeder in der Organisation weiß, wo Wissen verfügbar ist
- Umsetzen dieser Kompetenzen in neue Produkte und Dienstleistungen

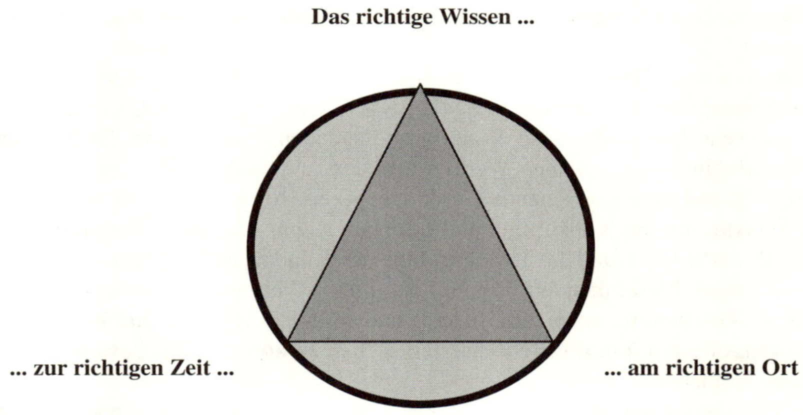

Aufgaben und Ziele von Wissensmanagement

Was genau Wissensmanagement in einem konkreten Unternehmen ausmacht, wie es gestaltet wird, welche Strategien und welche Methoden verfolgt werden, ist dabei für jede Organisation unterschiedlich und muss individuell ermittelt werden. Unter einer eher technologischen Perspektive reichen die Ansätze vom intranet-basierten Dokumentenmanagement, der Anwendung von Groupware-Systemen und Knowledge Mapping-Techniken über web-basierte Diskussionsforen oder virtuellen Communities, web-basierten Lern- und Trainingssystemen bis hin zu den integrativen Wissensportalen (Borowsky/Scheer 2001) für die Mitarbeiter. Aus einer organisatorischen Perspektive betreffen die Veränderungen die internen Strukturen und Abläufe. Hier setzt sich die Parallelisierung ehemals sequentieller Abläufe und die Einführung von Projektorganisation neben oder sogar anstelle der traditionellen Linienorganisation immer deutlicher als dominantes Muster durch. Daneben gewinnen auf einer häufig eher informellen Ebene sogenannte Wissensgemeinschaften (Communities of Practice) eine wachsende Bedeutung. Analog zu den Unterschieden in der Unternehmensstruktur und der Unternehmenskultur und ausgerichtet auf die jeweiligen strategischen Ziele entwickelt jedes Unternehmen seine eigene individuelle Konzeption für ein Wissensmanagement.

Fokus der Bemühungen um das Management von Wissen sind die Geschäftsprozesse des Unternehmens. Den Mitarbeitern wird zur Lösung ihrer Aufgaben in den jeweiligen Prozessen das benötigte Wissen zur Verfügung gestellt. Neben den transaktionsorientierten Informationen aus den ERP-Systemen stellen Wissensmanagement-Tools die benötigten Möglichkeiten zur Wissensbereitstellung und –bearbeitung zur Verfügung. Ziel ist es, Wissen, Wissensressourcen und –träger mit den Geschäftsprozessen zu verbinden. Wissensprozesse bilden keine neuen und eigenständigen Prozesse, sie ergänzen und bereichern die Geschäftsprozesse.

So groß die Unterschiede in der Ausprägung in einzelnen Unternehmen auch sein mögen, die Erfolge des zielgerichteten Managements von Wissen sind nachweisbar. So spart etwa der amerikanische Öl-Konzern Chevron durch sein Knowledge Managementprogramm jährlich rund 150 Millionen Dollar ein, weil das Wissen um die Möglichkeiten der Energieeinsparung in der Produktion weltweit zwischen allen Werken ausgetauscht wird. Dieser Wissensaustausch über Best Practices basiert auf einer Visualisierung von Wissen und Wissensträgern in sog. Wissenslandkarten (Knowledge Maps; Nohr 2000a). Der Pharma-Konzern Hoffmann-LaRoche reduzierte durch Wissensmanagement in der Erforschung und Entwicklung neuer Medikamente den Time-to-Market-Zeitraum um einige Monate. Jeder Tag der Verzögerung mit der ein Medikament auf den Markt gebracht werden konnte, bedeutete einen Einnahmeausfall von rund 1 Million Franken. Beratungsunternehmen wie Ernst & Young, McKinsey oder Andersen Consulting vertreiben wissensintensive Dienstleistungen, die ohne ein umfassendes Wissensmanagement kaum denkbar wären. Die Bewirtschaftung der Ressource Wissen ist bei diesen Beratungsunternehmen unabdingbare Grundvoraussetzung für die Leistungserbringung (Nohr 2000b). Erfolgsstories gibt es viele, aus unterschiedlichsten Unternehmen. Alle führen Kosteneinsparungen, Einnahmezuwächse, Produktinnovationen, höhere Kundenzufriedenheit oder kürze Entwicklungszeiten auf einen jeweils organisationsspezifischen Ansatz des Managements von Wissen zurück. Eine betriebswirtschaftliche Messung, Bewertung und Darstellung des intellektuellen Kapitals eines Unternehmens – also der immateriellen Vermögenswerte – ist bislang nur in Ansätzen und noch unzureichend methodisch entwickelt. Da aber gerade diese immateriellen Vermögenswerte heute über die Leistungsfähigkeit und die Zukunftspotenziale eines Unternehmens entscheiden, werden zuverlässige

Bemessungs- und Bewertungsmethoden dringend benötigt (Kaps/Nohr 2001; Eustace 2000; Picot/Scheuble (2000). Erste Unternehmen beginnen die verfügbaren Bewertungsmethoden anzuwenden und in der Konsequenz auch ihre Darstellung in den Geschäftsberichten zu verändern.

Nach einschlägigen Untersuchungen ist die Wertschöpfung der Unternehmen bereits heute zu ca. 50 bis 90 % von der Bewirtschaftung des Wissens der Unternehmung abhängig. Damit ist Wissen bereits heute der wichtigste *Produktionsfaktor* für eine Vielzahl der Unternehmen (Stewart 1998), mit einer noch wachsenden und weitaus höheren Bedeutung in der Zukunft. Wir sprechen daher von diesen Unternehmen bereits als *wissensbasierte Unternehmen* (Kurtzke/Popp 1999) und von einer *wissensbasierten Unternehmensführung* (North 1999).

Während jedoch 96 % der Unternehmen Wissensmanagement für „wichtig" oder sogar „sehr wichtig" halten, geben lediglich 15 % der in einer Untersuchung befragten Unternehmen dem eigenen Management des Produktionsfaktors Wissen eine „gute" oder gar „sehr gute" Note (Felbert 1997; Ohlhausen et al. 2000). In einer kürzlich in Stuttgarter Unternehmen jeder Branche und jeder Größenordnung durchgeführten Befragung stellte sich heraus, dass es in den meisten Unternehmen heute noch keine geregelte Zuständigkeit gibt und kein eigener Etat für diese Managementaufgabe existiert. Auch ist die Vorstellung über Aufgaben und Ziele von Wissensmanagement meist ausgesprochen vage. Den oft zitierten Erfolgsstories steht eine Vielzahl von mehr oder weniger ziellosen und wenig gesteuerten Ansätzen der Bewirtschaftung der Ressource Wissen gegenüber. Dabei wird die Einführung entsprechender informationstechnischer Werkzeuge (Datenbanken, Groupware, Dokumenten-Managementsystemen usf.) im Kern mit Wissensmanagement gleichgesetzt. Den qualitativen Sprung vom Informationsmanagement hin zum Wissensmanagement muss eine große Zahl von Unternehmen erst noch vollziehen. Unternehmen, die diesen Sprung nicht vollziehen, werden im Wettbewerb die Verlierer sein.

Wissensmanagement ist *die* Zukunftsaufgabe für Unternehmen jeder Größenordnung und jeder Branche. Die Bewältigung dieser Zukunftsaufgabe entscheidet über die Wettbewerbs- und Innovationsfähigkeit (nicht nur) der deutschen Wirtschaft. Vielfach fehlen jedoch noch die Methoden für den Umgang mit der Ressource Wissen und für eine erfolgreiche, wissensorientierte Unternehmensführung. Diesen methodischen Werkzeugkasten zu entwickeln, wird für die nächsten Jahre das Thema Wissensmanagement prägen. In der Lehre und Forschung im Studiengang Informationswirtschaft an der Fachhochschule Stuttgart – Hochschule der Medien (HdM) werden diese methodischen Kenntnisse vermittelt und weiterentwickelt.

Was macht Wissensmanagement erfolgreich? Auch wenn Effekte wie bei Chevron oder Hoffmann-LaRoche sicher nicht pauschalisiert werden können, so lassen sich doch an den diversen Fallbeispielen in deutschen wie in internationalen Unternehmen einige wichtige Erfolgsfaktoren ablesen. Bei allen in der Praxis erfolgreichen Projekten lassen sich drei wesentliche Bestandteile des Wissensmanagement identifizieren:

a) eine offene, zum Wissensaustausch anregende Unternehmenskultur (eine „wissensfreundliche Kultur"),
b) organisatorische Strukturen und Bedingungen, die den Austausch von Wissen begünstigen sowie
c) leistungsfähige, auf die Anforderungen des jeweiligen Unternehmens zugeschnittene Informations- und Kommunikationssysteme zur Unterstützung des Wissensmanagements.

Diese drei Bestandteile sind jeweils unabdingbare Voraussetzung für ein erfolgreiches Wissensmanagement. Sie bilden die notwendigen Rahmenbedingungen für die Bewirtschaftung von Wissen. Wissensentwicklung, Wissensaustausch und Wissensanwendung sind Prozesse, die durch Informations- und Kommunikationssysteme unterstützt, jedoch keineswegs allein bewerkstelligt werden können. Wenn Wissen in diesem Sinne als ein Prozess verstanden wird, sind unternehmenskulturelle und –organisatorische Voraussetzungen erfolgsentscheidend für Wissensmanagement.

Über diese Rahmenbedingungen hinaus lassen sich grundsätzlich konkrete Wissensmanagement-Strategien nach Hansen, Nohria und Tierney unterscheiden in die Ansätze der Kodifizierung und der Personalisierung (Hansen et al. 1999). Beide Vorgehensweisen treten meist gemeinsam auf, jedoch dominiert innerhalb einer Organisation die jeweils eine oder andere Strategie – abhängig von den definierten Wissenszielen.

Die *Kodifizierungsstrategie* versucht das Wissen von Personen – zunächst den eigenen Mitarbeitern – „abzuschöpfen" und anschließend mit informationstechnischen Werkzeugen (Datenbanktechnologien usf.) zu speichern und zu verteilen. Wissen wird in diesem Ansatz mit Information gleichgesetzt, das Wissensmanagement weitgehend mit dem Informationsmanagement. Ziel dieser Strategie ist die Wiederverwertung von explizitem Wissen (Information) in analogen Situationen und Problemstellungen. Die gespeicherten Informationsobjekte sind Dokumente im weitesten Sinne (Lessons Learned, Best Practices usf.)

Die *Personalisierungsstrategie* geht hingegen von der weitgehend einmaligen Expertise einzelner, hochqualifizierter Mitarbeiter aus. Das Wissen dieser Personen gilt als nicht kodifizierbar, insbesondere da ihre Expertise bei neuen Problemstellungen aufgaben- und projektorientiert zu neuen Lösungsstrategien führen soll. Diese Wissensmanagementstrategie ist bemüht, Experten innerhalb und außerhalb des Unternehmens zu identifizieren und verfügbar zu machen. Informations- und kommunikationstechnische Werkzeuge dienen dieser Aufgabe, indem sie bspw. die Experten für bestimmte Aufgaben nennen (bspw. über Yellow Pages oder Wissenskarten) und einen kommunikativen Kontakt (bspw. über Mailing-Systeme, Video-Konferenzen oder Net-Meeting-Systeme) ermöglichen.

Hansen, Nohria und Tierney berücksichtigen in ihrer Darstellung nicht eine dritte, zunehmend an Bedeutung gewinnende Strategie des Managements von Wissen: die *Sozialisierungsstrategie*. Wissen wird in dieser Strategie als ein gemeinsames „Gut" einer Gruppe von Menschen erkannt, die in einer sog. Wissensgemeinschaft oder Community of Practice gemeinsam durch Interaktion Wissen erarbeiten und weiterentwickeln (Wenger/ Snyder 2000; North/Romhardt/Probst 2000). Wissensgemeinschaften entstehen häufig neben den eigentlichen Organisationsstrukturen des Unternehmens oder sogar über dessen Grenzen hinweg. Wissensmanagement hat hier die Aufgabe, solche Communities zu fördern und für eine sinnvolle Nutzung des erzeugten Wissens in der Gesamtorganisation zu sorgen.

Nachdem in der Vergangenheit immer wieder der Versuch unternommen wurde, organisatorische Probleme durch den Einsatz von Informationstechnik zu lösen, setzt sich nun die Erkenntnis durch, dass die einzelnen Mitarbeiter bzw. Gruppen von Menschen und ihr Wissen für den nachhaltigen Erfolg im internationalen Wettbewerb von entscheidender Bedeutung sind. Damit wird der Übergang vom Informationsmanagement zum Wissensmanagement vollzogen und zugleich erstmals eine korrekte Auffassung von Wissen in der Unternehmenspraxis zugrunde gelegt. Weggeman stellt eine Definition von Wissen auf, die eindeutig konstruktivistische Züge trägt und damit dem Charakter von Wissen gerecht wird:

> *„Wissen (W) ist eine persönliche Fähigkeit, die als Produkt der Information (I), der Erfahrung (E), der Fertigkeit (F) und der Einstellung (E) angesehen wird, die einem Individuum zu einem bestimmten Zeitpunkt zur Verfügung stehen; W = I x EFE." (Weggeman 1999, S. 41)*

Die Frage ist nicht, „Wer ist der bessere Wissensmanager, der Mensch oder der Computer?". Die Frage, auf die eine ausgewogene Antwort gefunden werden muss, lautet vielmehr „Wie gelingt es, Mensch und Technologie für das Management von Wissen erfolgreich gemeinsam einzusetzen?" Die Implementierung eines Wissensmanagement hat daher immer beide Elemente zu berücksichtigen: die Mitarbeiter und die Informationssysteme des Unternehmens. Thomas Davenport beschreibt dies als ein hybrides Wissensmanagement:

> *„Human beings my be expensive and cantankerous, but they are quite accomplished at certain knowledge skills. When we seek to understand knowledge, to interpret it within a broader context, to combine it with other types of information, or to synthesize various unstructured forms of knowledge, humans are the recommended tool. These are the types of knowledge tasks at which we excel, and we should be employed for these purposes.*
> *(...) For the capture, transformation, and distribution of highly structured knowledge that changes rapidly, computers are more capable than people. They are increasingly useful – though still a bit awkward – for performing these same tasks on less structured textual and visual knowledge. (...)*
> *Given this mixture of skills, we need to construct hybrid knowledge management environments in which we use both humans and computers in complementary ways. (...) When we are compiling computerized databases of organizational knowledge, we need to include „pointers to people"." (Davenport 1998)*

In vielen Organisationen – privaten wie öffentlichen – sind allerdings noch kulturelle und organisatorische Barrieren zu überwinden, damit Wissenserwerb und Wissensaustausch tatsächlich einen wertvollen und funktionierenden Beitrag für den Erfolg der Organisation leisten kann (McDermott/O'Dell 2000). Noch herrscht vielfach die Mentalität des Herrschaftswissens vor – Wissen ist Macht! Wissensmanagement bedarf einer an der Notwendigkeit des Wissensaustauschs orientierten Veränderung der Unternehmenskultur (Rosenstiel 2000). Die Wissensorientierung eines Unternehmens wird entscheidend durch die kulturelle Offenheit bestimmt, mit der Wissen – ohne Ansehen der hierarchischen Stellung im Unternehmen – ausgetauscht wird (Zimmerl/Zwingmann 2000). Und es bedarf auch eines Anreizsystems, in dem Beurteilungs-, Entlohnungs- und Prämiensysteme auf das Wissensmanagement ausgerichtet sind. Dabei spielen neben den klassischen materiellen Anreizen (Entlohnung, Prämien) die immateriellen Anreize eine zunehmend größere Rolle (North/Varlese 2001). Zu diesen zählen u.a. Karriereaussichten, Partizipation, Arbeitsinhalte oder der über interne Anerkennung erreichte Status im Unternehmen. Die Akzeptanz und die Bereitschaft, Wissen wirklich zu teilen, hängt bei den Mitarbeitern ganz entscheidend von diesen Rahmenbedingungen ab. Eine solche „wissensfreundliche Kultur" wird nicht durch Verlautbarungen – quasi per Dekret – geschaffen, sondern durch einen entsprechenden Führungsstil und durch das Vorleben einer solchen Kultur durch das höhere Management.

Die Mitarbeiter, aber vor allem auch das gesamte Unternehmen sollten in die Lage versetzt werden, vom Wissen einzelner Einheiten zu profitieren. Um dies zu erreichen, sind organisatorische Veränderungen notwendig. Insbesondere sind abteilungsübergreifende, fallweise zusammengestellte (und häufig dezentral und virtuell arbeitende) Teams oder die Förderung und Unterstützung sich bildender Wissensgemeinschaften (Wenger/Snyder 2000; North/Romhardt/Probst 2000) ebenso unabdingbar, wie neue, auf den Wissensaustausch ausgerichtete Beurteilungs- und Entlohnungssysteme. Gleichgültig, ob im Kern eines Wissensmanagement-Programms eine Kodifizierungs-, eine Personalisierungs- oder eine Sozialisierungsstrategie verfolgt wird, Informations- und Kommunikationssysteme sind und bleiben wichtige Werkzeuge für das Wissensmanagement. Keine der vorgestellten Wissensmanagement-Strategien kommt außerdem ohne eine angemessene Erschließung und Verteilung von Wissen aus. Wissensrepräsentation ist eine notwendige Voraussetzung für den erfolgversprechenden Einsatz von Informationssystemen zur Unterstützung von Wissensmanagement. Die Funktionalität und die Akzeptanz von Wissensportalen hängt entscheidend von aussagefähigen Metadaten und übersichtlichen Taxonomien ab.

Der Kodifizierungsansatz setzt auf einen dokumentbasierten Wissensaustausch. Es geht darum, Wissen in einer geeigneten Weise zu dokumentieren, zu speichern und im Bedarfsfalle wieder zu verwenden. Typische Informationsobjekte sind Projektberichte, Lessons Learned, Checklisten, Protokolle, Marktstudien, Präsentationen, Frequently Asked Questions (FAQs) usf. Diese Formen von Dokumenten sind durch ihre weitgehend unstrukturierten Informationen charakterisiert. Nur eine genaue inhaltliche Analyse und Erschließung kann diese Informationen zu einem späteren Zeitpunkt wiederauffindbar machen. Zu diesem Zwecke können bspw. Kategorisierungssysteme, visuelle Strukturierungen oder ausgefeilte automatische Volltextindizierungsverfahren eingesetzt werden.

Der Personalisierungsansatz benötigt technologische Unterstützung zum kommunikativen Wissensaustausch (E-Mail-Systeme, Diskussionsforen usf.) und zur Identifikation der benötigten Experten. Die Einrichtung von „Yellow Pages" oder „Wissenslandkarten" für ein Unternehmen ist in dieser Strategie nur der erste Schritt. Neben der Erreichbarkeit (kommunikative Funktion) müssen auch die organisatorischen Zuständigkeiten und die fachlichen Kompetenzen der einzelnen Mitarbeiter transparent gemacht werden. Durch die Vermeidung anonymer Speicherung erhält dokumentiertes Wissen erst seinen Wert.

Der Sozialisierungsansatz benötigt auf technischer Seite bspw. Groupware- oder Team-Memory-Systeme sowie virtuelle Knowledge Communities. Auch das in den Wissensgemeinschaften erarbeitete Wissen muss letztlich dokumentiert und erschlossen werden, damit es der Gesamtorganisation dauerhaft zur Verfügung gestellt werden kann.

Das Spektrum der Techniken, die für Wissensmanagement eingesetzt werden, reicht von Messaging-Software über Workflow-, Groupware- und Dokumenten-Managementsysteme bis hin zu klassischen Client-Server-Datenbankanwendungen. Eine wirklich neue Qualität auf dem Sektor der IT-Produkte stellen sog. „Organizational-Memory-Systeme" (Lehner 2000) oder die Wissensportale (Borowsky/Scheer) dar. Sie sind die eigentlich ersten originären Tools für das Wissensmanagement, die auch konzeptionell an der wissensbasierten Strategie eines Unternehmens ausgelegt sind. In zunehmenden Maße wird auf Internet-Technologie als Basis-Technologie zurückgegriffen. Neben dem einfachen Zugang über universelle Browser spielt vor allem die schnelle Implementierung auf der Server-Seite eine entscheidende Rolle. Zudem bietet sich auf dieser Plattform die Chance, viele Einzeltechnologien mit ihren jeweiligen Funktionen zu einem integrierten Wissensmanagement-Tool zu integrieren. Dabei spielen Inhalte eine größere Rolle als Design oder Layout, wobei allerdings Usability und ein Corporate Design angestrebt wird.

Welche Basis-Technologie und welche konkreten Werkzeuge auch immer eingesetzt werden, notwendig bleibt in jedem Falle eine strukturierende und organisierende Erschließung der gespeicherten Informationsobjekte.

Wissensmanagement ist also ein organisatorischer, kultureller und technologischer Managementansatz, der die veränderten Wettbewerbsbedingungen beherrschbar machen soll. Wissen und damit auch ein effektives Management dieser Ressource ist erfolgskritisch für die Zukunft der Unternehmen. Die konkreten methodischen Werkzeuge für ein Wissensmanagement sind vielfach noch unzureichend vorhanden. Hier liegt die Herausforderung auch für Forschung und Lehre.

Literatur

Borowsky, Rainer; Scheer, August-Wilhelm (2001): Wissensmanagement mit Portalen. In: Information Management & Consulting 16 (2001) 1, S. 62-67

Davenport, Thomas H. (1998): Some Principles of Knowledge Management http://www.bus.utexas.edu/kman/kmprin.htm

Eustace, Clark (2000): The Intangible Economy: Impact and Policy Issues; Report of the European High Level Expert Group on the Intangible Economy. Enterprise Directorate General, European Commission

Felbert, Dirk von (1997): Einsatz, Gestaltung und Nutzen unternehmerischen Wissensmanagements. In: Wissensmanagement / Hrsg.: H. Hill. Köln: Heymanns. S. 108-118

Hansen, Morten T.; Nohria, Nitin; Tierney, Thomas (1999): Wie managen Sie das Wissen in Ihrem Unternehmen?. In: Harvard Business Manager 21 (1999) 5, S. 85-96

Kaps, Gabriele; Nohr, Holger (2001): Erfolgsmessung im Wissensmanagement mit Balanced Scorecards. In: nfd Information – Wissenschaft und Praxis 52 (2001) 2, S. 89-97 und 52 (2001) 3 (im Druck)

Kurtzke, Christian; Popp, Petra (1999): Das wissensbasierte Unternehmen: Praxiskonzepte und Management-Tools. München: Hanser

Lehner, Franz (2000): Organisational Memory: Konzepte und Systeme für das organisatorische Lernen und das Wissensmanagement. München: Hanser

McDermott, Richard; O'Dell, Clara (2000): Overcoming the „Cultural Barriers" to Sharing Knowledge. Houston: American Productivity & Quality Center (http://www.apqc.org/free/articles/km0200)

Mohr, Hans (1997): Wissen als Humanressource. In: Humankapital und Wissen: Grundlagen einer nachhaltigen Entwicklung / Hrsg.: G. Clar, J. Doré und H. Mohr. Berlin: Springer. S. 13-27

Nohr, Holger (2000a): Wissen und Wissensprozesse visualisieren. Fachhochschule Stuttgart (Arbeitspapiere Wissensmanagement; 1/2000)

Nohr, Holger (2000b): Einführung von Wissensmanagement in einer PR-Agentur. Fachhochschule Stuttgart (Arbeitspapiere Wissensmanagement; 3/2000)

North, Klaus (1999): Wissensorientierte Unternehmensführung: Wertschöpfung durch Wissen. 2. Auflage. Wiesbaden: Gabler

North, Klaus; Romhardt, Kai; Probst, Gilbert (2000): Wissensgemeinschaften: Keimzelle lebendigen Wissensmanagements. In: IO Management 7/8, 2000, S. 52-62

North, Klaus; Varlese, Nadja (2001): Motivieren für die Wissensteilung und die Wissenentwicklung. In: Wissensmanagement 3 (2001) 1, S. 43-46

Ohlhausen, Peter; Rüger, Marc; Grote, Petra (2000): Wissensmanagement heute – Untersuchungsergebnisse bei deutschen Unternehmen. In: Wissensmanagement 2 (2000) 3, S. 55-58

Picot, Arnold; Scheuble, Sven (2000): Die Rolle des Wissensmanagements in erfolgreichen Unternehmen. In: Wissensmanagement: Informationszuwachs – Wissensschwund? Die strategische Bedeutung des Wissensmanagements. Hrsg.: H. Mandl und G. Reinmann-Rothmeier. München: Oldenbourg. S. 19-37

Rosenstiel, Lutz von (2000): Wissensmanagement in Führungsstil und Unternehmenskultur. In: Wissensmanagement: Informationszuwachs – Wissensschwund? Die strategische Bedeutung des Wissensmanagements. Hrsg.: H. Mandl und G. Reinmann-Rothmeier. München: Oldenbourg. S. 139-158

Stewart, Thomas A. (1998): Der vierte Produktionsfaktor: Wachstum und Wettbewerbsvorteile durch Wissensmanagement. München: Hanser

Von Krogh, G.; Venzin, M.: Anhaltende Wettbewerbsvorteile durch Wissensmanagement. In: Die Unternehmung 49 (1995) 6, S. 417-436

Weggeman, Mathieu (1999): Wissensmanagement: Der richtige Umgang mit der wichtigsten Unternehmensressource. Bonn: MITP-Verlag

Wenger, Etienne C.; Snyder, William M. (2000): Communities of Practice: warum sie eine wachsende Rolle spielen. In: Harvard Business Manager 22 (2000) 4, S. 55-62

Zimmerl, Oswald; Zwingmann, Nina (2000): Bewusstsein schaffen für den Wissensmanagement-Prozess. In: Wissensmanagement 2 (2000) 4, S. 10-14

Stefan Grudowski

Knowledge Management – Neues Konzept für Bibliotheken?

Ausgangspunkt der folgenden Überlegungen ist, dass die Industrie, insbesondere die Großunternehmen, ein neues Wissenskonzept entwickelt haben, das sich durchgesetzt hat, das sog. Knowledge Management. Da öffentliche und wissenschaftliche Bibliotheken sich als informations- und wissensvermittelnde Institutionen begreifen, liegt es nahe, das Konzept Knowledge Management auch bibliothekswissenschaftlich zu durchdenken. Aus der Sicht des Verfassers sollten die Bibliotheken und ihre Wissenschaftler dem Konzept Knowledge Management mehr Aufmerksamkeit zuordnen. Sie müssen der Frage nachgehen, was Bibliotheken von dem Knowledge Management der Industrie lernen oder konzeptionell übernehmen können. Zusätzlich ist aber auch notwendig, die Unterschiede des unternehmerischen und bibliothekarischen Wissensverständnisses klarzustellen.

Weitere wichtige Fragen, müssen zukünftig geklärt werden:

- Können die Bibliotheken auch Knowledge Management ihren Kunden anbieten?
- Könnte Knowledge Management ein neues Bibliotheksmodell werden?
- Inwieweit betreiben Bibliotheken bereits Knowledge Management ohne den Begriff zu verwenden?
- Wie verändert sich der Wissensbegriff in der Wissensgesellschaft und damit auch das Image der Bibliotheken?

Die Forschung und Lehre zur Beantwortung dieser Fragen ist an der HBI bereits im Gange (vgl. Bereiter 2000, Grudowski 2000, Grudowski 1999, Grudowski/Jünke 1999, Hütter 2000).

1. Das Knowledge Management-Verständnis der Industrie

Vergegenwärtigen wir uns zunächst das Verständnis des Knowledge Management und des Wissensbegriffs in der Industrie, um beurteilen zu können, ob es auf die Bibliothek übertragen werden kann.

Seit ca. fünf Jahren bemühen sich Industrie, Institutionen, Staat und Politik und ähnliche Unternehmungen, teilweise unterstützt durch Experten aus den Unternehmensberatungen, ihr Wissen – genauer gesagt ihr „Wissenskapital" – stärker als früher auszuschöpfen. Nach einer aktuellen Untersuchung stehen sogar das Wissenskapital eines Unternehmens und die Bewertung des Marktwertes des Unternehmens an der Börse durch Analysten in einem kausalen Zusammenhang (Jonasch/Somerlatte). Information und Wissen ergänzen damit erheblich die klassischen betrieblichen Ressourcen. Daraus hat sich die kommunikative Funktion, das sog. Knowledge Management, in den Unternehmungen entwickelt. Knowledge Management bedeutet nach dem klassischen Managementansatz, den Einsatz der Ressource Wissen möglichst optimal zu planen, zu organisieren, durchzusetzen und zu kontrollieren.

Aus der Sicht des Unternehmens ist der qualifizierte Mitarbeiter, insbesondere der Spezialist und Experte der wichtigste Wissensproduzent und Wissensspeicher. Somit rückt durch das Konzept Knowledge Management der Mensch, „last not least" der Bibliothekar und Dokumentar, in den Mittelpunkt der Informations- und Wissensverarbeitung, während in den achtziger Jahren noch die Informationstechnik vorrangig war. So spielen zahlreiche technikzentrierte Konzepte der achtziger Jahre wie z.B. wie MIS (Managementinformationssysteme), Künstliche Intelligenz (wissensbasierte Software-Implementierungen) und Real-time Systeme (zeitnahe Datenübertragung und –analyse), Datamining (automatisierte Informationsverdichtung) heute eine Nebenrolle. Auch das konservative Verständnis des homo oeconomicus wird durch ein erweitertes modernes Wissensverständnis erweitert: Nicht mehr allein zweckrationales Wissen ist für die Unternehmen entscheidend, sondern zusätzlich auch wertrationales und lebensweltliches Wissen (vgl. Ulrich 87).

Wissen lässt sich aus der Sicht des unternehmerischen Knowledge Management´s, wie es in der Industrie Anwendung findet, in vier Klassen einteilen:

- Das Fachwissen der Mitarbeiter
- Das Faktenwissen der Mitarbeiter
- Das Erfahrungswissen der Mitarbeiter
- Das unternehmenskulturelle bzw. lebensweltliche Wissen der Mitarbeiter

Beim Vermittlungsprozess dieser Wissensarten setzt das betriebliche Knowledge Management sehr stark auf die menschliche Wissenskommunikation. Unternehmenskultur, organisationales Lernen und der klassische Managementansatz sollen den Wissenserwerb und –austausch der Mitarbeiter fördern. Beim betrieblichen Knowledge Management nimmt der Mensch bzw. Mitarbeiter die zentrale Rolle bei der Wissensproduktion, -kommunikation und –speicherung ein. Man geht davon aus, dass Wissen in komplexer Form nur der Mensch kommunizieren kann. Zudem existiert im Unternehmen das formelle und informelle bzw. offizielle und inoffizielle Wissen. Weiter unterscheidet man das implizite und explizite Wissen. Außerdem unterscheidet man zwischen dem objektiven, subjektiven und intersubjektiven, von den Organisationsmitgliedern geteiltem Wissen. Im Grunde genommen sind hier alle Erkenntnisse der Wissenssoziologie (vgl. Bühl, 1984) auf das Unternehmen zu übertragen. Wissen ist daher nach dem Knowledge Management-Konzept ein sehr komplexer Begriff und sehr stark personenorientiert. Zudem ist zum Verständnis des Knowledge Management ein psychologisches Verständnis darüber notwendig, wie Menschen das Wissen verarbeiten.

Während früher in der betrieblichen Fachinformationsabteilung nur das Wissen im Vordergrund stand, welches in der wissenschaftlich-technischen Fachliteratur oder im betrieblichen Schriftgut repräsentiert ist, beschränken sich moderne Ansätze heute nicht mehr auf das schriftlich fixierte Wissen, sondern begreifen als Objektbereich auch das Erfahrungswissen und das intersubjektiv geteilte lebensweltliche Wissen der Mitarbeiter, was schriftlich nur sehr beschränkt festgehalten werden kann. Deswegen sind in Großunternehmen Expertendatenbanken ein wichtiger Bestandteil des Knowledge Management ´s geworden. In den großen Konzernen, in denen mehrere tausend Mitarbeiter im In- und Ausland beschäftigt sind, geht ohne Expertendatenbanken der Überblick verloren, wer über welches Expertenwissen verfügt. Es gibt Fälle in denen die Unternehmensführung Probleme hat, den richtigen Experten zu finden, um an ihn Aufgaben zu delegieren. Expertendatenbanken sind ein Beispiel dafür, wie man die „Köpfe" bzw. Mitarbeiter mit ihren personifizierten Wissen dokumentiert und den Wissensaustausch zwischen den Mitarbeitern unterstützt.

Bei dem bisher Beschriebenen besteht ein wesentlicher Unterschied zum bibliothekarischen Wissensbegriff, der sich nur auf das Wissen beschränkt, welches in gedruckten oder elektronischen Medien gespeichert ist. Während bei der Bibliothek das Wissen im Vordergrund steht, das in der Literatur niedergeschrieben ist, ist es in Unternehmen das Wissen, welches die Mitarbeiter als „Human Ressource" verkörpern.

Für ein Unternehmen ist die Frage nach strategisch und operational relevantem Wissen entscheidend. Das heißt, welches Wissen, in welcher Form abrufbar, verschafft der Organisation einen Wettbewerbsvorsprung? Zum Handwerkszeug des Knowledge Managers gehört, Fach-, Erfahrungs- und Faktenwissen zu bewerten, dokumentarisch zu erarbeiten und zu organisieren - i.S.v. systematisieren, ordnen, speichern und verwalten. Diese Zielsetzung schließt die Auswahl und Gestaltung geeigneter Wissensrepräsentations- und Wissenspräsentations-Techniken mit ein. Wissen dokumentieren und handlungsorientiert präsentieren heißt die Leitmaxime der praktischen Informationsarbeit – dokumentieren alleine reicht nicht mehr aus!

Wo sind in der Praxis die ersten Tätigkeitsfelder des Knowledge-Managements zu finden, die dies umsetzen? Dazu möchte ich einige bereits praktizierte Beispiele aufführen.

1.1. Knowledge Management als Bestandteil des Projektmanagements in Unternehmen

Hier werden Projekte des Unternehmens hinsichtlich der Gründe ihres Erfolges oder Scheiterns dokumentiert. Das Ziel ist, im Rahmen eines Projekts gesammeltes Wissen zu dokumentieren, bevor die Projektmitarbeiter sich neuen Projekten widmen oder in ihre Linienfunktion zurückkehren. Bei Projekten im Wiederholungsfall kann dann später auf dieses Wissen zurückgegriffen werden. Dazu gehört die Dokumentation von wichtigen Unterlagen, wie zum Beispiel Projektplänen, Workshop- und Projektberichten, aber auch die Dokumentation, wer an dem Projekt mitgearbeitet hat und welches Erfahrungswissen und Ratschläge er für spätere Projekte einbringen kann. Des weiteren wird ein sog. „Debriefing" durchgeführt, bei dem Projektmitarbeiter nach ihrer jeweiligen Projekterfahrung gefragt werden. Hierbei wird das Erfahrungs- und Methodenwissen direkt abgefragt und zusammengefasst schriftlich festgehalten - eine neue Form der Wissensakquisition.

1.2. Konzeption und Implementierung von „Virtuell-Corporate-Libraries" als Aufgabe der betrieblichen Bibliothek

Es wird wohl keinen Großkonzern geben, der nicht über eine seiner Größe entsprechenden Bibliothek verfügt. Wichtige Aufgaben, wie Literaturbereitstellung, Document-Ordering und Literaturrecherchen bleiben erhalten. Jedoch wächst der Wunsch der Mitarbeiter, Informationen mit dem Computer vom eigenen Arbeitsplatz recherchieren zu können. Deswegen werden momentan Überlegungen hinsichtlich digitaler bzw. virtueller Bibliotheken, die auf die Bedürfnisse von Unternehmen und Instituten ausgelegt sind, aktuell. Eine virtuelle Bibliothek im Unternehmen schafft neuartige „Links" über Internet mit Informationslieferanten der Unternehmensumwelt und zwischen verschiedenen betrieblichen Standorten. Sie trägt damit der Globalisierung bzw. der globalen Nachfrage von Information der Mitarbeiter eines international agierenden Konzerns Rechnung. Die „Virtuell-Corporate-Library" stellt für Unternehmen eine revolutionäre Aggregations-, Vernetzung- und Digitalisierungsform von betrieblicher Fachinformation dar (Vgl. dazu das Werk von Stielow (Hrsg.) 1999).

1.3. Aktiver Wissensaustausch als Ziel der Informations- und Unternehmenskultur

Hier wird der Wissensaustausch in der betrieblichen Fortbildung thematisiert. Auch werden Techniken, wie die Benutzung von Internet und Intranet, die zum Wissensaustausch genutzt werden sollen, geschult. Das wichtigste hierbei ist jedoch eine geeignete Informationskultur im Unternehmen zu prägen. Intelligente Analysen der Wissensstruktur eines Unternehmens oder Investitionen in die Informationstechnologie bringen nichts, wenn das innere Einverständnis für das Teilen und das zu eigen machen von fremden Wissen bei den Mitarbeitern nicht vorhanden ist. Beispielsweise fördert die häufig geäußerte Überzeugung „Wissen ist Macht“ nicht das Weitergeben und Kommunizieren von Wissen. Denn diese Überzeugung führt dazu, dass Mitarbeiter und Vorgesetzte ihr Wissen individuell für sich behalten, um damit auch die Macht des Wissens im persönlichen Besitz zu halten. So müssen die Symbole, Werte und Normen der Informationskultur, die u.a. zu „Informationsritualen“ führen, interpretiert und mit den Zielen des Knowledge-Managements abgestimmt werden (vgl. S. Grudowski 1998).

1.4. Wissensakquisition als Aufgabe der betrieblichen Fachinformationsabteilung

Fachinformationsabteilungen werden immer mehr zu Einkäufern und Rechercheuren von Information. Durch Knowledge Management wird die Vielseitigkeit der Wissensarten und Wissensquellen bewusster. Dies führt dazu, dass die Fachinformationsabteilung nicht nur in Literatur und Datenbanken recherchiert oder sie diese Medien einkauft, sondern auch andere Medien zur Wissensakquisition nutzt. Neue Formen sind z.B. die Erschließung von Industriemessen und -tagungen hinsichtlich Experten und Firmen, die nützliches Wissen für das Unternehmen bereitstellen könnten. Das Management des Fachwissens bedeutet in aktueller Sicht nicht allein die Recherche des Wissens, sondern die weitergehende Aus- und Weiterverarbeitung in Form der anspruchsvollen Präsentation und Verdichtung.

1.5. Speicherung, Auswertung und Recherche von Dokumenten, die Erfahrungswissen enthalten, als Aufgabe der betrieblichen Dokumentation

Auch „die gute alte Schriftgutverwaltung“ ist in moderner technischer Form am Knowledge-Management beteiligt. In moderner Form wird sie ergänzt durch die Methode der Wissensextraktion, die es ermöglicht, Wissen aus dem Schriftgut „herauszuziehen“.

2. Knowledge-Management als neues Bibliothekskonzept?

Die Bibliothek und ihre Bibliothekare sind bis heute mitführend bei der Entwicklung der größten und besten Katalogisierungssysteme und dem Information Retrieval. So sind und waren sie es, die sich in erster Linie mit der Ressource Wissen und deren zielgruppengerechter öffentlicher Vermittlung in der Vergangenheit, aber auch in der Zukunft professionell beschäftigen.

Allerdings ist bei der Bibliothek das Wissensspektrum schmaler als beim Knowledge-Management-Ansatz bei Unternehmen. Denn die Bibliothek konzentriert sich auf das Fach- und Faktenwissen. Im Vergleich fällt auf, dass die Bibliothek kaum Erfahrungswissen und lebensweltliches Wissen vermittelt. Dies liegt natürlich daran, dass sie sich hauptsächlich nur auf das Wissen konzentriert, das in der Literatur publiziert ist und »bibliothekarisch« erschlossen werden kann. Wissen zugänglich zu machen, heißt in der »klassischen« bibliothekarischen Sicht, Literatur bereit zustellen oder zumindest deren Standort nachzuweisen, so dass für den Benutzer nach der Relevanzentscheidung die Beschaffung der Literatur möglich ist.

Aus moderner Sicht bieten sich nun aber auch für die Bibliothek neue Möglichkeiten,

Wissen abzuspeichern und zugänglich zu machen. Im Blickfeld dafür stehen die modernen elektronischen Medien, in denen Wissen im Internet repräsentiert werden kann.

Neben der Wissensvermittlung mit Hilfe gedruckter oder elektronischer Informationsdienste ist im betrieblichen Alltag die *interpersonelle Informations- bzw. Wissensvermittlung* entscheidend (vgl. oben). Nach einem modernen Managementverständnis spielt der Manager die Rolle des Wissensvermittlers und er muss zur perfekten Beherrschung dieser Rolle eine spezielle Fachkompetenz erwerben. Auch hier kann die Bibliothek für sich selber internes Knowledge-Management betreiben, um das Fach- und Erfahrungswissen der eigenen Mitarbeiter zu vergrößern.

Durch gut erschlossenes Wissen der Gesellschaft Macht für Innovationen zu verleihen, ist eine der Leitmaximen der Bibliothekare. Viel bibliothekarisches Methodenwissen, wie beispielsweise die Thesauruserstellung, Präsentationstechnik von Information im Internet, Informationsrecherche, betriebliche Dokumentation und die formale sowie inhaltliche Erschließung – um nur einige zu nennen – ist durch das Knowledge Management direkt anwendbar. Die wissenschaftliche Auseinandersetzung mit dem Thema Knowledge Management bietet auch der Bibliothekswissenschaft, insbesondere den Öffentlichen Bibliotheken, die Möglichkeit, ihre Rolle in der Wissensgesellschaft neu zu entdecken, darzustellen und auszuweiten. Bibliotheken könnten aktiver werden, indem sie eine Rolle als Produzent von Wissen spielen, indem sie Wissen organisieren sowie auswerten, Information bündeln und auf neuartige Weise präsentieren. Ihre öffentliche Rolle könnte dadurch gestärkt werden, dass sie neben Autoren und Verlagen Wissen im Sinne der Dokumentations- und Kommunikationswissenschaft produzieren und öffentlich, zur allgemeinen Bildungsvervollkommnung kommunizierbar machen. Das bedeutet, dass öffentliche Bibliothekare ihre öffentliche Wissenskommunikation nicht mehr auf die Vermittlung von Wissensträgern eingrenzen, sondern selber aus diesen Wissensträgern und Medien Wissen generieren und produzieren und weitergeben. Auch könnten zukünftig Öffentliche Bibliotheken eine öffentliche Institution zur Wissensproduktion und -vermittlung für Interessengruppen, z.B. für Bürgerinitiativen oder Volkshochschulen werden, die über das Internet sowohl Wissen dokumentieren wie publizieren wollen. Bibliotheken könnten die Zukunftsrolle des „Offenen Kanals" im Internet und beim elektronischen Publizieren „für Jedermann" spielen.

3. Bibliothekarisches Knowledge Management zur Unterstützung der Kommunalverwaltung?

Die Öffentliche Bibliothek kann die Kommunalverwaltung mit Knowledge Management unterstützen, indem sie den Wissensaustausch innerhalb der Verwaltung und zwischen Verwaltung und Bürger durch Knowledge Management effizienter macht. Für die Bibliothekare Öffentlicher Bibliotheken steht neben dem beruflichen Fachwissen, welches im betrieblichen Knowledge Management besonders wichtig ist, das kulturelle (vgl. Bühl, 1984), historische und „lebensweltliche Wissen" (vgl. Berger, Luckmann 1990) zusätzlich im Vordergrund[541]. Im folgenden sollen einige denkbare Ansätze des bibliothekarischen Knowledge Management skizziert werden.

3.1. Knowledge Management mit einem bibliothekseigenen Internetserver?

---

[541] Anzumerken ist, dass diese Wissensarten zwar analytisch zu trennen sind, in der praktischen menschlichen Wissensverarbeitung jedoch stets eine enge Verwobenheit darstellen.

Die Öffentlichen Bibliotheken können sich in das Knowledge Management der Kommunalverwaltung über das Medium Internet einbringen. Sie können zum einen über einen eigenen WWW-Server der Bibliothek, der Stadt oder der Gemeinde eine Publikationsplattform für Wissen anbieten. Wenn Bibliothekare das Know-how im Bereich Knowledge Management und Internetpublizieren nutzen und entwickeln, können sie wichtige Aufgaben der Bürger- und Verwaltungsinformation fachkundig übernehmen. Sie würden damit einen entscheidenden Beitrag zur kommunalen Informationsinfrastruktur liefern und sich durch derartige Zusatzleistungen für die Finanzverwaltung besser „rechnen".
Auch die Hilfeleistung der Bibliothek für Gewerbe und Kleinindustrie, beispielsweise bezogen auf deren Interesse an Produkten der Konkurrenz im weitesten Sinne, kann durch Rechercheleistungen im „Überlebenswettbewerb" durch Transparenz ihres Marktes für diese von Wettbewerbsvorteil sein.

Die Bibliothek könnte auch beispielsweise in Zusammenarbeit mit anderen Stadtarchiven und Museen, Heimatwissen und Geschichtswissen „ihrer" Region anhand von Hypertexten, Grafiken, Landkarten, Animationen, Musik und Videos als multimediales Dokument auf CD-ROM und im Internet anbieten, sogar über Verlage vermarkten.

Zudem könnte sie eine wichtige Bildungsaufgabe übernehmen: Sie könnte die Bürger pädagogisch an diese neuen Wissensnutzungsformen heranführen und in die Nutzung der neuartigen internetbasierten Bürgerinformationssysteme einführen.

3.2. Der Bibliothekar in einer zusätzlichen Funktion als Knowledge Manager?

Der Bibliothekar sollte zu seinen bisherigen „klassischen" Aufgaben zukünftig zusätzliche neue Funktionen ausfüllen. Er würde so auch zum Informationsfachmann, vielleicht sogar zum Wissensmanager „seiner" Kleinstadt oder ländlichen Gemeinde werden. Der Bibliothekar muss dann aber fachkundig sein sowohl im dokumentarischen Bereich als auch im Bereich des elektronischen Publizierens. Damit sind die Bibliothekare mit ihrem Fachwissen im Bereich Bibliotheks-, Dokumentations- und Informationsmanagement direkt angesprochen. Bibliothekare müssen hinsichtlich des Knowledge Managements aber erkennen und akzeptieren, dass es bei ihrer Arbeit um mehr geht, als um die Vermittlung bzw. Bereitstellung von Büchern, Dokumenten, CDs, Videofilmen und Internetarbeitsplätzen für die Nutzer ihrer Bibliothek. Bei bibliothekarischem Knowledge Management geht es vielmehr darum, Wissen aus diesen Medien zu extrahieren, zu komprimieren und mit anderem recherchierten Wissen zu kombinieren, dieses weiterzugeben und evtl. auch zu publizieren. Mit anderen Worten drückt es Elisabeth Niggemeyer (1996) folgendermaßen aus: „Zur Umsetzung einer solchen Vision muss sich das Rollenverständnis einer Bibliothek ändern. Zur historischen Aufgabe, Literatur zu sammeln und anzubieten, kommt nun das Knowledge Management, d. h. elektronische Daten zu analysieren, zu sammeln, zu speichern und anzubieten. Das impliziert Innovation, was zwangsläufig zu Strukturveränderungen in der Bibliothek führt. Knowledge Management führt Bibliotheken aber auch in die absolute Abhängigkeit von Netzinfrastrukturen, EDV-Ausstattung (Hardware) und Softwaretechnologie".

Diesbezüglich heißt es, dass Bibliothekare das Internet nicht als reines Recherchemedium ansehen und pädagogisch ihren Nutzern erschließen, sondern es auch für ihre eigene Wissensorganisation als Publikationsmedium nutzen. Wissen im Internet zu dokumentieren und eigene „Wissensprogramme" zu gestalten und dies als Herausforderung und revolutionäre Chance des Bibliothekars zu begreifen, bedeutet „bibliothekarisches Knowledge Management". Die Leitdevise könnte lauten: Von der Literaturbibliothek zur Wissensbibliothek.

4. Die Öffentlichen Bibliotheken als digitales Archiv des Wissens?

Das wohl größte bibliothekarische Knowledge Management-Projekt läuft momentan in der Library of Congress der USA. Es trägt den Namen „National Digital Library"[542] und soll die Bibliothek zum weltgrößten digitalen „Archiv des Wissens" wachsen lassen. Das Projekt soll die Bibliothek medial mit Hilfe von Internet-Datenbanken, CD-ROMs und DVDs modernisieren. Ziel ist das gedruckte Wissen in digitales Wissen zu transferieren und für den weltweiten Zugriff zu erschließen. Dazu sollen Bücher, Gemälde, Manuskripte und Photographien, evtl. auch Filme und Musik in den Bibliotheken der USA digitalisiert werden. Es werden rund eine Million Dokumente pro Jahr eingescannt. Die Library of Congress zeigt damit, wie eine Bibliothek die „Informationsautobahn" nutzt, indem sie Menschen den Reichtum an Wissen in neuer digitaler Form über das Internet zugänglich macht.

Zugleich dient die rund hundert Jahre alte, im Stil der italienischen Renaissance nachempfundene Bibliothek als am Menschen orientierter Ort der Wissensvermittlung: An den Mahagoni-Sekretären mit glitzernden Messinglampen sitzen Nutzer an ihren Notebooks. Die neu eröffneten Lesesäle sind an Eleganz kaum zu übertreffen. Unter restaurierten Decken von 1897 und den hohen Fenstern stehen Bücherregale im alten Stil. Die Bibliothek kann „Knowledge Management in Hochkultur", aber auch einen traditionellen, ästhetischen Ort der menschlichen Wissensrezeption vermitteln.

Die British Library digitalisiert mit Hilfe von Spezialkameras und Bildbearbeitungssoftware gefährdete Sammlungen mittelalterlicher Handschriften und macht sie einer breiteren „Internetöffentlichkeit" zugänglich. Wissenschaftliche Studien mit Faksimiles werden öffentlich, mit den empfindlichen Originalen wäre das nicht möglich. So bedeutet bibliothekarisches Knowledge Management, dass ästhetisches, historisches und kulturelles Wissen aus wertvollen Altbeständen elektronisch recherchierbar einer breiten Öffentlichkeit zugänglich gemacht werden kann.

5. Zukünftige Entwicklungen

Knowledge Management fängt für die Bibliothek da an, wo sie mit anderen Wissensinstitutionen zusammenarbeitet und dabei ihre Medienkompetenz und ihre Medieninfrastruktur zu Verfügung stellt. Der Öffentliche Bibliothekar könnte sich dabei als Fachmann für Wissenspräsentation einbringen. Zum anderen würde der Bibliothekar als Informationsfachmann/ -frau bzw. Dokumentar anderen Institutionen bei der Wissenspräsentation als Fachmann beratend helfen.

Diese Darstellung war nur ein Anriss um aufzuzeigen, welche Entwicklungen in der Verbindung und Anwendung des Begriffes Knowledge Management und Bibliothek in Zukunft erwartet, ja vielleicht gefordert werden.

Die HBI-Stuttgart berücksichtigt in der Ausbildung der Bibliothekare und Informationsspezialisten diesen neuen Weg in die Zukunft. Damit haben die Abgänger der Hochschule in ihrer zukünftigen bibliothekarischen Tätigkeit, sei es in der Öffentlichen Bibliothek, der wissenschaftlichen Bibliothek oder seien es bibliothekarische und informationswissenschaftliche Tätigkeiten in Industrie, Institutionen, in Staat und Politik, das zeitgemäße

542 Vgl.: http://www.loc.gov

Rüstzeug.

Literaturangaben

Berger, P. L. / T. Luckmann, welche von Alltags- und Jedermannswissen in der Alltagswelt sprechen, anstatt von lebensweltlichem Wissen. Beide Begriffe sind jedoch synonym zu verstehen. Vgl. dazu die Erörterung von H. Plessner 90, Vorw., S. XV, von P. L. Berger / T. Luckmann: Die gesellschaftliche Konstruktion der Wirklichkeit. Eine Theorie der Wissenssoziologie. 5. Aufl. Frankfurt am Main 1990.

Bereiter, Markus: Inwieweit betreiben Öffentliche Bibliotheken Knowledge Management? Analyse und Interpretation von Ansätzen des Knowledge Managements aus der Literatur hinsichtlich eines neuen Dienstleistungsangebots der Öffentlichen Bibliotheken. Diplomarbeit bei Prof. Dr. Grudowski an der Hochschule für Bibliotheks- und Informationswesen Stuttgart. Stuttgart 2000.

Bühl, Walter L.: Die Ordnung des Wissens. Berlin 1984, S. 77 ff..

Grudowski, Stefan: Knowledge Management in der Industrie - und wo bleibt das Knowledge Management der Öffentlichen Verwaltung und der Bibliotheken? In: Buch und Bibliothek 2000, Nr. 4, S. 310-314.

Grudowski, Stefan: Knowledge Management - Know How der HBI gefragt. In: HBI aktuell, Heft 1, 1999. S.26-27.

Grudowski, Stefan / Martin Jünke: Knowledge Management durch Dokumentation und Archivierung bei der EXPO 2000 Hannover GmbH. In: HBI aktuell, Heft 2, 1999. S. 35-39.

S. Grudowski: Informationsmanagement und Unternehmenskultur. 2. Aufl. Stuttgart 1998.

Hütter, Bernhard: Start des neuen Master-Studiengangs „Bibliotheks- und Medienmanagement“.. In: HBI aktuell, Heft 2, 2000. S.12-13.

Ronald S. Jonasch / Tom Sommerlatte: Innovation: Wie erfolgreiche Unternehmen Werte schaffen. Landsberg/ Lech 1999, Kapitel 7.

Niggemeyer, Elisabeth: Der multifunktionale Benutzerarbeitsplatz. Zitiert nach der Internetdokumentation: Weiter auf dem Weg zur virtuellen Bibliothek! Bibliotheken nutzen das Internet. Erste INETBIB-Tagung in der Universitätsbibliothek Dortmund vom 11. - 13.3.1996. Fortbildungsveranstaltung für Mitarbeiter/-innen in Bibliotheken im Rahmen des Fortbildungsprogramms des Hochschulbibliothekszentrums Nordrhein-Westfalen, veranstaltet von der UB Dortmund in der UB Dortmund. Seitenzahl: Internetpage

Stielow (Hrsg.): Creating a virtual library: A how-to-do-it manual for librarians. New York 1999.

Ulrich, Peter: Transformation der ökonomischen Vernunft. Fortschrittsperspektiven der modernen Industriegesellschaft. 2. Aufl. Bern u. Stuttgart 1987.

Volker Wehdeking

Literaturwissenschaft – Kulturwissenschaften – Medien. Eine dokumentationsrelevante Annäherung im Informationszeitalter

Eine bibliotheksrelevante Entwicklung auf dem literaturwissenschaftlichen Feld (Bourdieu) im kulturwissenschaftlichen Kontext zielt auf die möglichst aktuelle, durch Hypertext und vielfältige Rechercheparameter verfeinerte elektronische Dokumentation von Sprache, Literatur und Film (als Literaturverfilmung) in Bibliotheken und Archiven bei zunehmender Kooperation in internationalen Verbundsystemen. Die digital erfassten Bestände (vor allem nach Titeln, segmentweise auch im Volltext) erlauben den externen Zugriff auf große Sammlungen unter vielfältigen Forschungsperspektiven im World Wide Web. Für Literaturwissenschaftler und Kulturforscher sind griffige Beispiele für die neuen, anspruchsvollen Forschungsmöglichkeiten in der elektronischen Erschließung des *Deutschen Literaturarchivs* in Marbach (DLA) im System *KALLIAS*, für die Linguisten im *Institut für deutsche Sprache* (IDS) Mannheim im System *LEXIS* und im *MMB-Browser* im Multimedialen Lesesaal der *Deutschen Bibliothek* in Frankfurt am Main gegeben, der auch die Neuen Medien einbezieht.

Sprach-, Literatur-, und Filmdokumentation in Archiven und Mediotheken erlauben einen orientierenden Forschungseinstieg, der dem erweiterten Medien- und Kulturverständnis im Informationszeitalter entspricht. Durch den jeweiligen OPAC und die oben beispielhaft genannten Datenbanken, homologen Rechercheinstrumente ist der anspruchsvolle Benutzer nicht mehr auf das Einarbeiten in bzw. Lokalisieren von heterogen, nach Fachsystematiken und Klassifikationen aufgestellten Beständen großer Teilbibliotheken (etwa in UBn) angewiesen. Eine Einbettung von „Literatur im Medienspektrum" (die auch populäre Genres und Massenmedien berücksichtigt) und eine Annäherung in gegenseitiger, interdisziplinärer Bereicherung an die Kulturwissenschaften sind durch solche digitalen Schlagwort- und Parameterrecherchen kein Problem mehr. Dass hier dennoch von einer gegenwärtigen, durchaus fruchtbaren, 'Krise' des fachdisziplinären Selbstverständnisses gesprochen werden kann, belegt die folgende kurze Problemskizze und - pars pro toto - mustergültig die integrative und facettenreiche Studie der Konstanzer Anglistin (und Ägyptologin) Aleida Assmann: *Erinnerungsräume. Formen und Wandlungen des kulturellen Gedächtnisses* (München 1999).

Die Folge-Problematik einer zunehmenden Tendenz zur Einbettung der Literaturwissenschaft in die Kulturwissenschaften (im „cultural turn" der letzten Jahre), dass es sich auch wissenschaftstheoretisch um eine Zusammenschau heterogener, oft weit auseinanderliegender Wissenschaftsgebiete handelt, ist auf der Dokumentationsseite noch am ehesten überbrückbar. Die Debatte kann hier nur ansatzweise summiert werden. So gibt Dirk Matejovski zu bedenken:

> *„Wenn wir uns wirklich inmitten eines durch die Medien induzierten gesellschaftlichen und anthropologischen Umbruchs befinden, dann müssen die Kulturwissenschaften medienwissenschaftliche Fragen aufgreifen und Spezialfälle kultureller Überlieferung wie Literatur und Kunst medienwissenschaftlich durchdringen. Ein*

> *solches Programm ist aber nicht ganz leicht einzulösen, denn im Gegensatz zu Psychologie, Soziologie und Ethnologie, um nur die letzten großen Importparadigmen zu nennen, bietet sich in der Medienwissenschaft keine verfestigte Disziplin zur Rezeption an. [...] Betont man den technischen Aspekt der Kommunikation, dann wären Physik, Nachrichtentechnik, Informationstheorie und Kybernetik zuständig. Geht man auf die gesellschaftlichen Kontexte der modernen Massenkommunikation ein, dann sind Fächer wie die Publizistik und Soziologie zu nennen. Fragen der Medienwirkung fallen in das Ressort der Psychologen, Pädagogen und Demoskopen. Gegenüber dieser disziplinären Ressortierung führte eine Medienwissenschaft eher ein Schattendasein." (Matejowski 1996, 255)*

Solchen Einwänden gegenüber einer innovativen, aber fachwissenschaftlich „nomadischen Form des Nachdenkens über Medien" möchte ein integrativer Medien- und Literaturwissenschaftler wie Werner Faulstich auch das literarische und mentalitätsbezogene „Kulturelle Gedächtnis", dessen Krise gegenüber dem „Speichergedächtnis" und seinen digitalen „Aufschreibesystemen" (Assmann 1999, 409-413) heute gesehen wird, dennoch mit einem integrativen Ansatz einbeziehen, der auch der textorientierten Literaturwissenschaft in ihrer Mentalitäts- und Geschichtsdimension entgegenkommt:

> *„Eine dritte, neuere Fachrichtung (Medienwissenschaft) definiert 'Medium' ähnlich als Kommunikationsmittel, akzentuiert aber gegenüber der Publizistik zwei andere Aspekte: erstens die Funktion und Bedeutung der Medien in der gesamten Gesellschaft, zweitens die Geschichte der Medien und ihrer Entwicklung von den Anfängen bis heute, d. h. sie charakterisiert sich durch einen integrativen und einen historischen Ansatz." (Faulstich 1991, 16)*

Auch die jüngste literaturwissenschaftliche Diskussion plädiert für eine fachwissenschaftlich 'offene Leitmetaphorik', wenn sie Kultur nicht als „Gebäude oder Gemälde, sondern vielmehr als Gewebe (textum) mit Löchern und offenen Rändern" wahrnimmt, die gleichzeitig ganz unterschiedliche Muster in einer „Kultur als Makrotext" wahrnimmt:

> *„Anders als Paradigmen lösen Leitmetaphern einander nicht ab, vielmehr akzentuieren sie je für sich Schwerpunkte kulturwissenschaftlicher Orientierung. Gegenüber dem Soliditätspostulat der Gebäude- und dem Mimesisanspruch der Bildmetaphorik, erfasst die Textmetapher zum einen die viel beklagte Diffusion des kulturellen Feldes, zum anderen impliziert sie komplexe Bedeutungsproduktion: Kultur als Textum. Damit wird der Textbegriff weniger substantialisiert als erneut auf sein metaphorisches Potential hin geöffnet. Überdies bietet der Konnotationsrahmen der Textmetapher die Möglichkeit, funktionale Beziehungen zu beschreiben: kulturelle Fäden zu verbinden, Kulturmuster zu konfrontieren, Beziehungsnetze herzustellen und Knotenpunkte zu markieren. [...] Das kulturwissenschaftliche Paradigma entspricht einem solchen perspektivischen Pluralismus. Sie situiert die klassischen Gegenstände der Literaturwissenschaft in einer neuen Rahmung, die den Horizont des Textes überschreitet: Mentalitäts-, Alltags-, Medien- und Sozialgeschichte bzw. historische Anthropologie wären nur einige dieser Bezugsrahmen. Der Beitrag der Literaturwissenschaft wäre noch deutlicher zu bestimmen. Die klassischen Debatten über Kulturgeschichte und Kulturwissenschaften sind von anderen Disziplinen geführt worden: von Philosophen, Soziologen, Historikern und Ethnologen, und von ihnen gingen auch die neueren Impulse aus." (Friedrich 1999, 568-570)*

Im folgenden sollen die eingangs angeführten IT-Recherchetools an verschiedenen deutschen Wissenschaftsinstitutionen als Beispiele für gelungene Lösungen auf der Dokumentationsseite dieser neuen Kontextualisierungsfragen von Literaturwissenschaft präsentiert werden.

1. Dokumentation Linguistik Deutsche Gegenwartssprachentwicklung in Archiven

Das *Institut für Deutsche Sprache (IDS)* in Mannheim stellt lexikologische und lexikographische Textkorpora für die Untersuchung der deutschen Gegenwartssprache bereit und verbindet einige auch für die Gegenwartsliteratur besonders interessante Wortschatzbereiche mit dem Einsatz neuer Software zur Online-Abfrage (COSMAS, LEXXIS, Wendesprache und -Kommunikation / Wende-Bibliografie). Zudem werden Tondokumente zur gesprochenen deutschen Sprache umfassend archiviert

Das IDS als universitätsnahe Stiftung des bürgerlichen Rechts hat 109 Mitarbeiter und 60 Gastwissenschaftler im Jahr, gibt vier wichtige Zeitschriften heraus (darunter *Studien zur deutschen Sprache*), stützt sich auf eine umfangreiche Bibliothek mit 75.000 Einheiten und 300 laufenden Zeitschriften und Textkorpora mit 200.000 über COSMAS abfragbaren Textwörtern. Dieser Reichtum soll auf die Erschließung der Tonarchivalien und die Analyse der Gesprochenen Sprache ausgedehnt werden: COSMAS II soll sprachstatistische Analysen mit neuen Datenverarbeitungssystemen ermöglichen, darunter LEXXIS. Dies soll den Wortschatz der deutschen Sprache umfassend dokumentieren und unter sehr flexiblen Recherchemöglichkeiten (komplexe Querschnittssuchen nach Lexemen, nach unselbständigen Wortbildungselementen oder Wörtern) analysieren. So sollen Fremd- und Lehnworte, Synonymenbildung, Neologismen und Epochenquerschnitte wie jener nach 1989/90 im Wendewortschatz (also auch literaturwissenschaftlich relevant) vielschichtig erschlossen werden. Beispiele wären Lemmata-Recherchen zum Wendewortschatz (Stichwort: „Sozialistisches Lager", „Langzeitarbeitslose") sowie Intranet-Einblicke in den Korpus des Gesprochenen Deutsch in Regiolekten. Die Erstellung einer CD-ROM zur Wendebibliografie ist mittlerweile abgeschlossen und COSMAS sowie LEXXIS / IDS lassen Online Recherchen im Internet bereits im begrenzten Rahmen zu. Auf mittlere Sicht soll ein Projekt „Die Grammatik mit der Maus" (GRAMMIS = Grundlagen eines grammatischen Informationssystems) mittels einer Schnittstelle zwischen lexikalischen Datenbanken und grammatischen Hyperdokumenten Korpusbelege zwischen Lexikon und Grammatik abfragbar machen: nach Wortarten, Komplementen, Supplementen, Verbalgruppen und Linearen Strukturen. Entstehen sollen mittels Hyperlinks themenspezifische Lern- und Informationssysteme zur Grammatik und Kommunikation. LEXXIS erlaubt Suchoptionen zur Bedeutung, Grammatik, Geschichte, Form, Kritik, und Dokumentation deutscher Gegenwartssprache. Dies lexikographische Konzepts (mit künftig 300.000 Lemmata), kann Corpora-Recherchen von COSMAS II einbeziehen und ermöglicht sowohl semantische Klassifizierungen wie Forschungsprojekte zu Neologismen und Fremdwörtern.

Generell ist am Beispiel dieser innovativen Sprachinstitution zu sagen, dass die Medienkompetenz der Bibliotheks- und Firmennutzer immer mehr durch multimediale Angebote auf dem Gebiet von Sprachentwicklung, Autorkompetenz und Analysen der Sprachbasis mit Implikaten für die Gegenwartsliteraturentwicklung gefördert wird. Solche Medienkompetenz wird dadurch zunehmend für Laien verfügbar. Die Nachfrage an dieser Schnittstelle zwischen Sprache und Literatur wird durch die multimedialen CD-ROM-

Verlagsangebote zweier linguistischer Hilfsmittel für Sprach- und Übersetzerkompetenz sowie Autorkompetenz im Bereich Fiktionaler Literatur belegt: das *Duden Oxford Großwörterbuch Englisch* in Verbindung mit dem *Deutschen Universalwörterbuch* (auf CD-ROM, Software Windows) wendet sich mit über 150.000 Worterklärungen und Englisch-Deutschem Vokabular an einen breiten Benutzerkreis wie an den Fachübersetzer. Und der Reclam-Verlag bietet neben einer Reihe von Hörbüchern, CD-ROMs und Audio-CDs zu klassischen und modernen Autoren neuerdings ein „Elektronisches Reimlexikon" mit 50.000 Reimwörtern (Herbst 1999, DM 49.90) zur Stärkung der Medien- und Autorkompetenz im Umgang mit Gegenwartsliteratur. Die Online-Verfügbarkeit der lexikographischen IDS-Textkorpora erweitert die Möglichkeiten zum Erwerb der Schlüsselqualifikation *Formulierfähigkeit* an der Schnittstelle von Sprachentwicklung, Literaturtrends und Autorkompetenz.

2. Dokumentation Literatur im Medienverbund in Archiven und Mediotheken

Mediendokumentationsstellen im literarischen Bereich beinhalten neben dem Archivieren und Erschließen von Nachlässen, Erstdrucken, Werkausgaben, Briefen und Autographen von Schriftstellern auch das Sammeln von deren internationaler Rezeption im Presse- und Nachrichtenbereich, aber auch im multimedialen und audiovisuellen Umfeld. Wort-, Ton-, und Bilddokumente werden mit einer breiten Palette technischer und informationstechnischer (IT) Serviceleistungen archiviert und vermittelt. In Mediotheken wie dem Karlsruher *Zentrum für Kunst und Medien* (ZKM) wird dagegen die geschriebene und gesprochene Wortkunst im Medienspektrum von Spielfilm, Fernsehfilm, Hörspiel, Videokunst, Sprech- und Musik-CDs sowie multimedialer CD-ROMs gesammelt und vermittelt. Spezielle Hör- und Bildkabinen und audiovisuell ausgelegte Arbeitsplätze unterstützen diese multimediale Kunstrezeption. In den Nationalbibliotheken in Frankfurt, Paris und London lädt das reiche Angebot im Multimedia-Lesesaal für den Bereich Literatur im Medienspektrum hinsichtlich Recherchierbarkeit, Umfang und Nutzerkomfort zu Vergleichen ein.

2. 1. Deutsches Literaturarchiv Marbach a. N. (DLA)

Das bereits im Intranet Marbach verfügbare und Ende 2001 auch als OPAC dem externen Zugriff zugängliche Katalogformat „KALLIAS" und die dahinter stehenden Archivalien im Bestand und Software-Aufbau lohnen einen näheren Blick, ist hier doch ein Recherchetool in einer avancierten Annäherung von Fiktionaler Literatur an ihren Kultur- und Medienkontext gelungen. Die Archivfunktion von Marbach wird durch eine intensive Vermittlung (Öffentlichkeitsarbeit) in Ausstellungen in die Pflicht gestellt, über moderne Speichermedien wie CD-ROM hinaus - wegen deren Verfallszeit nach ca. 20 Jahren - ihre Ton- und Bildträger auf konventionelle Bänder zu überspielen und auf lange Sicht verfügbar zu halten. Dies stellt die Raum- und Lagerkapazität des Hauses vor große Probleme, die zu einem Anbau in den 90er-Jahren führten.

KALLIAS führt in einem benützerfreundlichen Format, im Textteil dem RAK-Format der DB angenähert, im Medienteil laienverständlich, die Bestände der Handschriftenabteilung, Bibliothek und des Archivs mit seinen reichhaltigen Rezeptionsdokumenten im Medienverbund zusammen. So können etwa die Bilddokumente zu Autoren (vom Foto bis zum Ölportrait), die weiteren Kunstdokumente (etwa eine Totenmaske oder Plastik), die Rezeption in einer Pressedokumentation und in Zeitungsausschnittsammlungen durch das Einstiegsformat von *Kallias* zusammengeführt und an die RAK-konforme Titelaufnahme der Werke, sowie die typischen Autographenbestände in Kästen und Briefsammlungen im Katalogformat online angeschlossen und so im Intranet, - bald auch ferngenutzt im OPAC - zusammengeführt werden.

In der Marbacher DLA-Medienabteilung (mit allein 7 Mitarbeitern in der Pressedokumentation) wurden die Non-Book-Materialien, die Pressedokumentation und Zeitungsausschnittssammlung (international), die Ton- und Bildträger von und über die Autoren in über 1000 Kästen archiviert und als zweite Quelle zu den Autor(inn)en neben den Beständen der Handschriftenabteilung gesammelt. Zum Beispiel umfasst allein die Sammlung Thomas Bernhard in diesem Bereich 78 Ordner und Kästen, die Schiele-Sammlung umfasst Dokumente seit 1903, seit 1955 wird im DLA die gesamte deutschsprachige Literatur dokumentiert. Die Hauptquelle des Pressearchivs ist die eigene Auswertung von 50 Zeitungen und Zss. (von über 1000 laufenden Zss. in der DLA- Bibliothek), darunter 55 % fremdsprachige Quellen, etwa die *New York Times Book Review* oder die *NY Review of Books* und das *Times Supplement*. Marbach kooperiert hier eng mit dem *Dokumentationszentrum für Neuere Österreichische Literatur* und dem *Literaturhaus Wien* sowie der *Akademie der Künste Berlin* zu Akademieautoren.

Der breite Kulturansatz bedingt das Archivieren auch des kulturellen Umfelds bis hin zur Philosophie und Theologie in einer Sammelstruktur nach dem Prinzip der Mehrfachablage, da die Materialien zugleich an verschiedenen Stellen relevant sind. Die Mappenarbeit erlaubt das flexible Ausscheiden. Die Bildabteilung muss z. B. wegen der intensiven Ausstellungstätigkeit jedes neue Bild zum Autor fünffach kopieren. Auch lässt sich nicht abschätzen, ob ein Übersetzer und Kritiker später zur Weltliteratur gehören wird, weshalb es Mappen zu Debütanten, jungen Autoren und „Großautoren“ gibt, z. B. 200 Mappen je zu Hermann Hesse und Thomas Mann. Die Feinordnung nach „Weltbild“ und „Wirkungsgeschichte“ führt zu einer immer feineren Mappensystematik (die „Ursystematik“ in Marbach umfasste nur zwei Seiten), der über drei Millionen Textausschnitte. Hinzu kommt eine umfangreiche Theaterprogrammsammlung die mit theaterwissenschaftlichen Sammlungen und Museen in Düsseldorf (Dumont-Lindemann), München (Theatermuseum), an der Universität Köln (Theaterwiss. Institut) und an der Österreichischen Staatsbibliothek sowie Ostberlin die über 350 Theater im deutschsprachigen Raum mit Programmen erfasst. Das Digitalisieren und Scannen der Nachlassbestände ist daher ebenso zentral für die weitere Archivierung, wie eine Namennormdatei und das neue elektronische Katalogformat *KALLIAS*.

KALLIAS stützt sich auf eine relationale Standard-Datenbank auf einem zentralen Server (vorzugsweise Oracle unter UNIX oder WindowsNT) mit dem Resultat hoher Datensicherheit, Performance und Offenheit. Das aDIS-Datenformat wird anwendungsbezogen so definiert, das Felder für Verweisungen multipel fungieren; aDis generiert automatisch die SQL-Statements und Hilfstabellen, die relational notwendig werden. Maskenbasierte Datenpflege und lesefreundliche Darstellung im sog. „Zeigemodus“ stützen mehrfach nutzbare Informationen (zu Personennamen etc.), komplexe Bestandshierarchien und Querverbindungen (auch abteilungs-übergreifend) zu den Objekten über die Hyperlink-Funktion. Die feine Struktur des bestehenden Systematischen Katalogs wird durch *KALLIAS* weitergeführt: Sachschlagwörter können mit einer Basissystematik, Elementen aus der Personen- und Körperschafts-Normdateien, Werktiteln sowie einem Form- und Autorenschema zu sog. 'Systematikketten' verbunden werden. Sie ermöglichen im OPAC neben der Suche nach Einzelelementen auch die hierarchische, systematische Präsentation des Bestandes. Links zwischen (auch audiovisuellen) Archivbeständen, Bild- und Handschriftenabteilung, Werktiteln und 'Objekten der Kunst' ermöglichen eine dem Bestand vorzüglich angemessene multimediale Verknüpfung und spiegeln so die innovative Kontextualisierung von Literaturwissenschaft durch Medien- bzw. Kulturwissenschaft (multimediale Materialien zur Rezeption und Produktion der Werke, vgl. Kramski 1999, 165-179).

In der Hörfunk- und Fernseh-Ms-Sammlung gleicht das DLA aus, was an historischem Bewusstsein in den Funkarchiven mangelt. Allein die Tonbandaufzeichnungen von Hausveranstaltungen umfassen Mitschnitte von über 300 Dichterlesungen. Von Hörfunk- und TV-Sendungen sowie Interviews zu Autor(inn)en muss ebenfalls ein Mitschnitt erstellt werden. Eigene Studio- und Schneideräume helfen diese enorme Sammelaufgabe zur deutschen Gegenwartsliteratur bewältigen. Die Abrufbarkeit von *Kallias* und Homepages des DLA und der Schillergesellschaft im Internet sind daher wesentliche Hilfsmittel in der Vermittlung.

2. 2. Literatur im Medienverbund im Multimedialesesaal in Frankfurt a. M.

In der *Deutschen Bibliothek* in Frankfurt mit ihren über 7.037.000 Einheiten aus Druckwerken und Tonträgern, umfassend gesammelt seit 1913 (in Kooperation mit *der Deutschen Bücherei Leipzig)* sind die belletristikrelevanten, digitalen Multimediaangebote im Lesesaal besonders interessant für einen Dokumentationsvergleich mit Paris und London. Hinzu kommt das Sondersammelgebiet Exilliteratur zwischen 1933 und 45 mit einer intensiven Ausstellungs- und Vermittlungsaufgabe.

Das *MMB*, ein *Multimedia-Bereitstellungssystem* der *Deutschen Bibliothek* steht den Benutzern mit der Eröffnung des Neubaus (vom Stuttgarter Architekturbüro Arat, Kaiser und Kaiser) seit 1997 zur Verfügung. Gemeinsam mit der Firma CSC Ploenzke entwickelt, ermöglicht das System die Sammlung, Archivierung und Bereitstellung elektronischer Medien an 40 Arbeitsplätzen im Multimedialesesaal. Der Online-Katalog ist mit den digitalen Publikationen, also auch mit CD-ROMs oder im Netz vorinstallierten digitalen Publikationen (etwa Nachschlagewerke) direkt gekoppelt, die gewünschten Medien werden über einen farbig hervorgehobenen Hinweis auf dem Nachweisbildschirm angeklickt, und die Vollinformation ist alsbald verfügbar. Die Multimedia-Endgeräte mit den leistungsstarken Grafik- und Soundkarten lassen über das *MMB* einen kontrollierten Zugang zum Online Katalog, zu elektronischen Publikationen und dem Internet zu, so dass Katalog und digitale Publikationen gekoppelt werden und das Arbeiten mit WWW-Umgebung (den Internet-Werkzeugen über die Toolbar) möglich wird.

1. So lassen sich vom OPAC Titeltreffer ausdrucken oder auf Diskette herunterladen.
2. etwa 300 vorinstallierte CD-ROMs werden multimedial nutzbar, vor allem Nachschlagewerke, Bibliographien, Wörterbücher und Fachhandbücher
3. CD-ROMs, Disketten und andere elektronische Datenträger aus DB-Beständen, die im OPAC aufgelistet sind, aber nicht im MMB installiert, können selbständig für die Nutzung installiert werden
4. Im Internet lassen sich zusätzliche Informationen (außerhalb der DB-Bestände) ermitteln und Dateien ausdrucken oder downloaden
5. Schließlich lassen sich Daten in einem persönlichen *Workspace* bis zu 5 MB für spätere Nutzung abspeichern

Um diese Funktionen zusammenzuführen, wurde ein spezieller *MMB*-Browser entwickelt, der sie auf einer Oberfläche vereint, die nicht im WWW zur Verfügung steht. Das komfortable Arbeiten mit über 300 audiovisuellen (über die Grafik- und Sound-Karte multimedialen) und mit Filmstrips, Animationen und Bilddokumenten zu einer Fülle von Informationen verdichteten Multimedia-Angeboten im entsprechenden Lesesaal macht auch die Angebote im Literatur- und Filmbereich, ob in Lexika oder auf CD-ROM, in kaum bisher so gebotener Breite und mit Notebook-Funktion länger reservierbar zugänglich. Anhand von Beispielen aus dem Filmographie-Bereich, etwa die 100.000 *Filmindex*-Titel des British Film Institute über die SIFT-Datenbank im Internet, oder das filmographisch reichhaltige Internet-Angebot des amerikanischen *Scriptorama* (www.us.imbd.com), das hier bereits über MMB als Multimedia-Bestand für den Lesesaal eingearbeitet war, konnte ich mich von der Informationsdichte überzeugen, die auch den Gegenwartsliteraturbetrieb intensiv recherchieren lässt. Die komfortable Schlagwortrecherche der Buchbestände über die Datenbank Bibliodata mit der gut eingeführten Retrievalsprache *Messenger* ist hier eine weitere Hilfe der DB.

2. 3. Bibliothèque Nationale de France (Bercy-Viertel, Paris)

Die vor einer Dekade als Projekt des jungen Architekten Perrault wegen ihrer genialen Einfachheit hochgelobte, „sehr große Bibliothek" Mitterands, die mit der Transparenz jener vier winkelförmigen Glastürme über einem Gartenrechteck, dem die Lesesäle zugeordnet sind, auch Benutzerzugänglichkeit versprach, ist heute zu einem von den Parisern kaum angenommenen „Katastrophenbau" geworden (StZ 9.7.1999). Modernste IT-Systeme sollten die als Mediathek konzipierten Bestände der elf Millionen Einheiten per OPAC und Internet fernkonsultierbar machen (z. B. über www.catalogue.bnf.fr/80/servlet/autorite für Autorenanfragen) und es ließe sich nach einem Besuch dort zugespitzt sagen, dass die Fernkonsultation effizienter ist als die Forschung direkt in diesem Mammutbau mit seiner vierstündigen Wartezeit auf eine Buchbestellung und seiner Lage, einen Kilometer von der Neuen Metro-Endstation entfernt inmitten Lagerschuppen, Kornmühlen und tristen Industriehalden.

Die hohen Benutzergebühren und die unpersönliche Benutzereinweisung kommen hinzu. Die umständliche, fehleranfällige Benutzerführung durch die Terminals, die ungewohnte, sprachlich diffizile und Übung voraussetzende Schlag- und Stichwortrecherche schienen dem optimalen Ausschöpfen der Multimediabestände im Lesesaal Kulturwissenschaften natürliche Grenzen zu setzen, ungeachtet eines hohen technischen Standards der Bildschirm- und Laptop-Arbeitsplätze, darunter einige für die audiovisuellen Bestände, und trotz der Opulenz roter Wand-zu-Wand-Teppiche, eleganten Mobiliars und gut sortierter Lesesaalnachschlagewerke.

2. 4. The British Library London

Die zentrale Innenstadtlage des neuen, riesigen St. Pancras Gebäudes der *British Library* des Architekten-Jungstars Sir Colin St. John Wilson mit dem nüchternen Appeal der Klinkerfassaden, die sich den Nachbargebäuden, besonders der nahen Kirche und dem Bahnhof anpassen, 1998 für 1, 6 Milliarden Mark vollendet, hat seine Glanzpunkte eher im Inneren. Dort läuft ein Glasgehäuse mit Handschriften, Inkunabeln und ledergebundenen Folianten als „The King`s Library" und „Showcase" über alle sechs Stockwerke mit 65.000 Bänden aus der Sammlung König Georgs des III. und IV. Die großzügige, lange Theke der offenen Cafeteria wirkt elegant.

Allerdings weist der unmittelbar integrierte *Bookshop* auf der linken Seite des Eingangsplatzes mit über 5000 Titeln und die benachbarte Ausstellungs-Galerie auf den betont öffentlichkeitsnahen, benutzerfreundlichen Aspekt in der Tradition der Englischen Public Libraries - Zugänglichkeit für jedermann - in der Nationalbibliothek hin. Für die Benutzung der 12 Millionen Bände, 8 Mio. Dokumente und 40 Mio. Zeitschriftenbände gibt es 1200 Benutzerplätze, die verschiedenen Wissenschaftszweige sind auf fünf Ebenen mit Lesesälen angeordnet (die Geisteswissenschaften haben im 1. und 2. Stock den Lesesaal, s. Abb. 2). Der komfortabel elektronisch per OPAC und im Internet erschlossene Bestand schließt viele Multimedia-Materialien (CD-ROMs) mit ein. Die Benutzerplätze sind modernst elektronisch ausgelegt, besonders reichhaltige Zeitschriftenbestände flankieren die Nachschlagewerke. Hat man den für jede Recherche notwendigen Benutzer-Code über den elektronisch lesbaren Ausweis eingegeben, eröffnet die Schlag- und Stichwortrecherche im Intranet vielschichtige Suchanfragen (hierarchisch und nach engem SW, per Name, Titel, Thema, Verlag, Jahr, Signatur u.a.). Die Qualität der Multimediaerschließung kann sich allerdings nicht auf dem Niveau der DB hinsichtlich der MMB-Browser-Funktion vergleichen.

Am Ende noch eine Bemerkung - bei aller Euphorie gegenüber den blickerweiternden Möglichkeiten von digitaler Recherche im gemeinsamen Feld von Literatur, Kultur und Medien - zur gegenwärtigen Tendenz, im Zeichen von Globalisierung, Europa-Denken und Internet, die bilateralen Kulturinstitutionen, etwa zwischen Frankreich und der Bundesrepublik, drastisch zu reduzieren. Der Germanist in Valenciennes, Jérome Vaillant, schreibt angesichts der bevorstehenden Schließung des Goethe-Instituts in Lille, die Argumente liefen darauf hinaus, am Beginn des 21. Jhs. „sei es ein Gebot der Stunde, das ‘Netz der Kultureinrichtungen’ zu modernisieren: Das Internet biete ausreichende Möglichkeiten, die staatlichen Institutionen zu ersetzen.“ Der Kulturwissenschaftler warnt davor, es hier zu einer bequemen Entfremdung kommen zu lassen, und plädiert für den regional unterstützten Fortbestand gewachsener Beziehungen in Kulturhäusern, da auch deutsch-französische Beziehungen „täglich neu begründet werden“ sollten, „und sei es nur bei den jüngeren Generationen“, bevor es zu beobachteten Stereotypen im Fremdbild und neuen „Vertrauenskrisen“ kommt (J. Vaillant, FAZ 16. 3. 2001). Dem kann sich der Autor nur anschließen.

Film- und Literaturhäuser der Großstädte (für das Stuttgarter Literaturhaus im Boschareal ist die Eröffnung Herbst 2001), und die Literaturveranstaltungen großer Universitäten sowie Kulturbrücken bildender Institute wie das „*Maison Heinrich Heine*“ in Paris und das „*Centre de recherches sur les pays de langue allemande à l` époque contemporaine*“ in Lille erlauben andererseits eine europäische und internationale Horizonterweiterung für Fragen der Gegenwartsliteraturentwicklung. In einer Zeit, wo die Digitale Bibliothek Fernkonsultationen größter Bibliotheksbestände und Aufsatzdatenbanken erlaubt, ist die kulturelle Verortung solcher kommunikativer Brückenfunktion keinesfalls überflüssig geworden, sondern fast ein notwendiges Pendant.

Literaturhinweise

Aleida Assmann: Erinnerungsräume. Formen und Wandlungen des kulturellen Gedächtnisses. München 1999, S. 149 ff. und 408 ff.

Werner Faulstich: Medientheorien. Göttingen 1991

Udo Friedrich: „Konkurrenz der symbolischen Ordnungen“. In: Mitteilungen des Deutschen Germanistenverbandes. Themenheft „Germanistik als Kulturwissenschaft“, 46 (1999), 4, S. 562-572

Renate Glaser, Matthias Luserke (Hg.): Literaturwissenschaft - Kulturwissenschaft. Positionen, Themen, Perspektiven. Opladen 1996

Heinz Werner Kramski: „Kallias - Integrierter Katalog des Deutschen Literaturarchivs Marbach. In: Sichtungen. Archiv - Bibliothek - Literaturwissenschaft, 1999, S. 165-179

Dirk Matejovski: „Von der Sinnstiftung zum Informationsdesign? Die Kulturwissenschaften in den neuen Medienwelten. In: D. Matejovski, F. Kittler (Hg.): Literatur im Informationszeitalter. Frankfurt a. M. 1996, S. 252-271

Ansgar Nünning: „Kulturwissenschaft". In: A. Nünning (Hg.): Metzler Lexikon Literatur- und Kulturtheorie, Stuttgart 1998, S. 299-302

Jérome Vaillant: „Der schlechte Freund. Für einen Kulturvertrag mit Frankreich". In: FAZ, 16. 3. 2001

Siegfried Schmidt

Die Katholische öffentliche Bücherei (KÖB): Auslaufmodell oder fit für die Zukunft?

Oder: „Nur was sich ändert, bleibt"

Zu den Grundzügen der Entwicklung des Katholischen Büchereiwesens von den Anfängen bis in die jüngere Zeit liegen inzwischen etliche Beiträge in der Fachliteratur vor[543]. Aus Borromäusbüchereien und Pfarrbüchereien vergangener Tage ist in Rezeption und als Reaktion auf innerkirchliche Veränderungen durch das Zweite Vatikanische Konzil Mitte der 60er-Jahre die Konzeption der Katholischen öffentlichen Bücherei (KÖB) entstanden. Dieses Konzept sieht Büchereien katholischer Träger sowohl als Element einer lebendigen Pfarrgemeinde als auch als Beitrag der Kirche zum Öffentlichen Bibliothekswesen insgesamt an, dessen Netz sie verdichten und ergänzen, bzw. in manchen Regionen überhaupt erst schaffen. Zugleich definiert es diese als Einrichtungen, die allen Menschen in ihrem Einzugsgebiet offen steht und Angebote macht.

Gründe für eine neue Positionsbestimmung katholischer Büchereiarbeit

Fast drei Jahrzehnte bis in die 90er-Jahre hinein war diese Konzeption im ganzen erfolgreich und im Kern unbestritten. Zwar nahm seit den 60er-Jahren die Zahl der örtlichen Büchereien kontinuierlich ab, doch wuchsen gleichzeitig die Bestände stetig an und die Ausleihzahlen Katholischer öffentlicher Büchereien verdoppelten im Zeitraum 1971 bis 1998 von 13,86 Mio. auf 27,49 Mio.[544] Insgesamt konnte die katholische Büchereiarbeit so durchaus ihren Platz in der Bibliotheksszene behaupten. In diesem Büchereityp befanden sich 1997 13 % aller Medien

543 Als ältere Gesamtdarstellung immer noch grundlegend ist der Beitrag von Leo Koep und Alfons Vodermayer: Die katholischen Volksbüchereien in Deutschland: Borromäusverein und St. Michaelsbund. In: Handbuch des Büchereiwesens / hrsg. von Johannes Langfeldt. – 2. Halbbd. – Wiesbaden : Harrassowitz, 1965, S. 387-42. – Jüngere Zusammenfassungen sind im Umfeld der Feier des 150. Vereinsjubiläums 1995 erschienen, z.B. die Beiträge von Hans Maier und Norbert Trippen im Sammelband: Bausteine für eine lesende Kirche : Borromäusverein und katholische Büchereiarbeit ; Festgabe für Erich Hodick. – Mainz : Grünewald, 1996. – Unter den Darstellungen, die sich mit einzelnen Zeitabschnitten befassen, seien hier exemplarisch genannt: Dalton, Margaret: The Borromäus Verein: Catholic Public Librarianship between 1845 and 1933. In: Library and Culture 31(1996), S. 409-421. - Für die Zeit von 1900-1933 vgl.: Asselmann, Andrea: Volksbüchereiarbeit im Spiegel der Zeitschrift „Borromäus-Blätter / Die Bücherwelt" (1903-1933). In: Bibliothek. Forschung und Praxis, 19(1995), S. 322-361. – Die beste Zusammenfassung über den Verein während des Nationalsozialismus liefert das Kapitel „Public Librianship and the Catholic Church" des Buches von Margaret Stieg: Public Libraries in Nazi Germany. – Tuscaloosa, Univ. of Alabama Press, 1992, S. 194-215.- Zu den Nachkriegsentwicklungen, schwerpunktmäßig zum Wandel des Selbstverständnisses der Katholischen Büchereiarbeit der 60er- und 70er-Jahre, vgl.: Schmidt, Siegfried: Katholische öffentliche Büchereien – Schnittstellen zwischen lesender Kirche und säkularer Gesellschaft. In: Bibliothek. Forschung und Praxis, 21(1997), S. 307-325.

544 1971 vgl. Schmidt (Anm. 1), S. 325; 1998: Die Jahresstatistik 1998 der Katholischen Büchereiarbeit. In: KÖB 13(1999), H. 4, S. 6-7.

und es wurden 8 % aller Ausleihen Öffentlicher Bibliotheken erzielt.[545]

Inzwischen sind allerdings verschiedene innerkirchliche, gesamtgesellschaftliche und bibliotheksfachliche Entwicklungen zu beobachten, die immer nachdrücklicher die Frage aufwerfen, ob das bisherige Selbstverständnis und Konzept katholischer Büchereiarbeit sich auch in Zukunft als tragfähig erweisen wird, und die letztlich in ihrer Summe eine erneute Positionsbestimmung katholischer Büchereiarbeit erforderlich machen.
Im Kern sind dies:

- Inhaltliche und strukturelle Erosionsprozesse in der katholischen Kirche, die der herkömmlichen, an die örtliche Pfarrgemeinde gekoppelten Katholischen öffentlichen Bücherei mehr und mehr den Nährboden entziehen: Traditionell war und ist die KÖB in den vergangenen Jahrzehnten auf der Ebene der Pfarrgemeinden organisiert und strukturell verankert. *Katholische öffentliche Bücherei – Grundausstattung der lebendigen Gemeinde,* so lautete ein Grundsatzpapier der katholischen Büchereiarbeit der 70er-Jahre.[546] Der moderne Gemeindebegriff, der in der katholischen Kirche dem Paradigmenwechsel des Zweiten Vatikanums zu verdanken ist und der den Laien viele Möglichkeiten zu einem aktiven Gemeinschaftshandeln eröffnete, ist längst an seine Grenzen gestoßen: Allen Bemühungen einer Gemeindepastoral zum Trotz nimmt der Gottesdienstbesuch stetig ab, schwinden die Mitgliedszahlen in kirchlichen Vereinen, gestaltet sich die Glaubensweitergabe an kommende Generationen immer schwieriger. Es kommt zu einer einer Vergreisung und Milieuverengung der Gottesdienstgemeinden.[547] In etlichen Diözesen sind inzwischen zudem Strukturreformen in Gang gekommen, die faktisch auf die Verschmelzung mehrerer einst eigenständiger Pfarrgemeinden zu – was die Fläche und die Zahl der theoretisch zugehörigen Mitglieder betrifft - „Groß"gemeinden mit oft mehr als 10.000 Katholiken hinauslaufen. In der Erzdiözese Köln ist beispielsweise beabsichtigt, dass die bereits jetzt zu Seelsorgebereichen verbundenen Pfarreien bis Ende 2002 eine Entscheidung treffen, entweder eine Pfarreien-Gemeinschaft bzw. einen Pfarreien-Verbund zu bilden oder sich zu einer Pfarrgemeinde zusammen zu schließen.[548]
- Innerkirchliche Legitimationszwänge, die bei schwindendem gesellschaftlichen Einfluss und engerer Finanzdecke alle Aufgabenbereiche und „Dienstleistungen" der Kirche einer Prioritätendiskussion unterwerfen. Analog zur katholischen Erwachsenenbildung muss sich die Büchereiarbeit zunehmend in bezug auf ihren Anspruch, einer allgemeinen Öffentlichkeit dienen zu wollen, rechtfertigen und den pastoralen oder seelsorgli-

---

[545] Das Bibliothekswesen der Bundesrepublik Deutschland : ein Handbuch / von Engelbert Plassmann und Jürgen Seefeldt. – 3., völlig neu bearb. Aufl. – Wiesbaden : Harrassowitz, 1999. – Vgl. S.145-146.

[546] Katholische öffentliche Bücherei : Grundausstattung der lebendigen Gemeinde / hrsg. von der Arbeitsstelle der Katholischen Büchereiarbeit in Deutschland. Bonn, Oktober 1975, [8. Bl.].

[547] Vgl. hierzu: Ebertz, Michael N.: Erlesen glauben – Glauben erlesen : für eine Kommunikationspastoral der Zwischenräume. In: Lesen im Austausch : eine pastorale Gemeinschaftsaufgabe / hrsg. von Ludwig Muth. – Freiburg : Herder, 1999. – S. 71-100; vgl. S. 72-73. – In den deutschen Bistümern sank die Zahl der Gottesdienstteilnehmer unter den Katholiken von etwa 45 % 1960 auf unter 20 % 1995. Bereits 1987 waren 45 % der Gottesdienstbesucher älter als 60 Jahre, obwohl diese Altersgruppe in der Gesamtbevölkerung „nur" 26 % ausmachte. – Diese Zahlen aus Ebertz, Michael N.: Erosion der Gnadenanstalt? – Zum Wandel der Sozialgestalt von Kirche. – Frankfurt a.M.: Knecht, 1998. – 384 S. – Vgl. S. 317 und 333ff.

[548] Kooperation im Seelsorgebereich : Arbeitshilfe zum Schreiben des Erzbischofs von Köln vom 6. Juni 2000 / Hrsg.: Hauptabteilung Seelsorge im Erzbischöflichen Generalvikariat Köln. Köln 2000. 70 S.

chen Charakter ihrer Arbeit herausstellen.[549]

- Diese Tendenz steht in Wechselwirkung mit einer fortschreitenden Säkularisierung und einer Differenzierung der Gesellschaft in verschiedene, gegen einander abgegrenzte Binnenräume. In einer künftigen Gesellschaft, in der Kirche und Staat noch stärker von einander getrennt sein werden als heute, werden Kirche und Religion primär zur Privatsache ohne öffentliche Bezüge. Zwar werden da, wo gegenwärtig die Mittel in kommunalen Haushalten knapp sind, nicht selten Kooperationsmodelle mit kirchlichen Trägern erwogen und realisiert oder gar einzelne kommunale Bibliotheken, z.B. vermeintlich überflüssige Zweigstellen eines großstädtischen Systems, zur wohlfeilen Übernahme angeboten. Die mühsam erstrittene Anerkennung der kirchlichen Büchereien, einen Beitrag zum gesamten Bibliothekswesen leisten zu wollen, wird vermutlich aber von gesellschaftlicher Seite spätestens nach einer Konsolidierung der kommunalen Haushalte erneut stärker hinterfragt werden. Tatsache ist, dass gegenwärtig das eingespielte Staat-Kirche-Verhältnis in Deutschland von verschiedenen Seiten kritisch befragt, deutlich attackiert oder doch zumindest skeptisch beäugt wird: „Für die einen bedeutet das bestehende Verhältnis von Staat und Kirche in Deutschland eine unzulässige Einschränkung der Freiheit des weltanschaulich neutralen Staates, für die anderen steht es der gebotenen Freiheit der Kirchen im Wege".[550]
- Die beständig klammen Kassen der Kommunen in den letzten beiden Jahrzehnten und eine fehlende gesetzliche Verpflichtung zum Betrieb einer Öffentlichen Bibliothek haben nicht nur vielerorts zu einer Leistungseinschränkung und zu einem Leistungsabbau geführt, sondern auch zur Folge gehabt, dass Öffentliche Bibliotheken als Kulturbetriebe in allgemeine Privatisierungsüberlegungen kommunaler Leistungen einbezogen wurden. Noch überwiegen Modelle, die für die Bibliothek eine Budgetierung vorsehen oder diese als kommunalen Eigenbetrieb fortführen; privatwirtschaftlich organisierte Öffentliche Bibliotheken bilden einstweilen noch eine sehr kleine Gruppe. Aber: „Es bleibt abzuwarten, in welchem Maße die gegenwärtige Welle der Privatisierung kommunaler Leistungen das öffentliche Bibliothekswesen erfasst und ob sich das Verhältnis von Regel und Ausnahme gar auf die Dauer umkehren wird".[551]
- Alle bibliothekspolitischen Planungspapiere der Nachkriegszeit bis hin zu *Bibliotheken 93* gehen davon aus, dass im Bereich der allgemeinen Literaturversorgung kleine wie große Bibliotheken einen universalen Sammelauftrag haben und Medien zu allen Themengebieten für die gesamte Bevölkerung des Einzugsgebietes bereit halten. Heute erscheint eine solche Sichtweise zunehmend problematisch, wenn nicht gar überholt: Zu komplex, differenziert und kulturell vielfältig stellt sich die Gesellschaft mit ihren zahlreichen Milieus, Interessengruppen, Schichten und Ethnien dar, zu unüberschaubar und gigantisch präsentiert sich das Medien- und Buchangebot, als dass es mit kleineren Beständen gelingen könnte, eine enzyklopädisch ausgerichtete Grundversorgung der gesamten Bevölkerung zu leisten. Statt einer *Informationsbibliothek* oder einer *Bibliothek für alle* liegen Akzentuierungen und Spezialisierungen im Trend. Angesichts begrenzter Ressourcen und vielfältiger Anforderungen im Dreieck von Information, Kultur und Bildung – also der Diskrepanz zwischen dem theoretisch Möglichen und

---

549 Vgl. z.B.: Leuninger, Ernst: Büchereiarbeit als pastorales Handeln. In KÖB 12(1998), H. 1, S. 2-17 und: Schmidt, Siegfried: Katholische öffentliche Büchereien als pastorale Orte. In: Stimmen der Zeit, 217(1999), S. 117-129.

550 Ruth, Ulrich: Staat und Kirche heute. In: Herder Korrespondenz 53(1999), S. 163-165. – Siehe S. 163 –164.

551 Das Bibliothekswesen ... (Anm. 3), S. 33.

dem faktisch Machbaren - ist die Öffentliche Bibliothek heute gezwungen, sich zu profilieren und zu positionieren: ein Nachdenken über Prioritäten im Rahmen der Diskussion um ein eigenes Leitbild, inhaltliche Schwerpunktbildungen durch Kabinette, Themenbibliotheken oder Nachbarschaftsbibliotheken, Zielgruppenorientierungen in Form von Jugend-, Eltern- oder Familienbibliotheken sind Ergebnis dieses gewandelten Bibliotheksverständnisses und führen zur Diversifizierung des Erscheinungsbildes Öffentlicher Bibliotheken.[552]

– Und schließlich sei auf den raschen Umbruch der Medienlandschaft und auf die wandelnde Rolle der Bibliotheken innerhalb der Medienszene verwiesen. Ging es für Öffentliche Bibliotheken bis in die 90er-Jahre hinein zunächst einmal vor allem darum, die Datenverarbeitung für verschiedene Arbeitsabläufe zu nutzen und in rascher Folge neue Trägermedien (Kassette, CD, Video, CD-ROM) zu adaptieren und – trotz knapper Erwerbungsmittel – sinnvoll in das Angebot zu integrieren, so stellt das Internet diese vor ganz neue Herausforderungen: Nunmehr geraten auch Öffentliche Bibliotheken in den Sog der Automatisierung, Digitalisierung und Virtualisierung ihrer Bestände, Angebote und Dienstleistungen. Sie müssen sich fragen, was sinnvoller Weise weiterhin vor Ort auf herkömmlichen Print-, audiovisuellen oder elektronischen Trägermedien angeboten wird und welche Informationen und Medienangebote besser *just-in-time* aus dem Netz beschafft werden. Wiederum sind es die kleinen Bibliotheken, die auf diese Herausforderungen aufgrund begrenzter personeller und finanzieller Ressourcen kaum angemessen reagieren können und die – wenn sie mit diesen medialen Entwicklungen Schritt halten wollen – in Zukunft gezwungen sein werden, Wege der Vernetzung, Integration und Schaffung größerer Betriebseinheiten zu gehen, die weit über bisherige Formen der Zusammenarbeit und Kooperation hinausgehen. In Ländern, deren Bibliothekswesen weiter entwickelt ist, z.B. in den Niederlanden, werden in dieser Hinsicht viel weitreichendere Lösungsansätze diskutiert.[553]

Die KÖB vor einem Aufbruch ins Ungewisse

Bis heute sind Katholische öffentliche Büchereien in ihrer überwiegenden Mehrzahl kleine und kleinste Einrichtungen geblieben. Der durchschnittliche Bestand der rund 4.300 Einrichtungen lag 1998 bei 4.260 Medien, die 1,5fach umgesetzt wurden.[554] Auch wenn über einen längeren Zeitraum gesehen die Büchereien im Schnitt größer geworden sind – 1971 lag der durchschnittliche Medienbestand bei 1.740 Einheiten, 1990 bei 3.730 Einheiten[555] – und mancherorts auf dem Wege vertraglicher Regelungen in Gemeinden, Klein- und Mittelstädten deutlich größere Bibliotheken in katholischer Trägerschaft entstanden sind: ganz überwiegend sind diese Bibliotheken immer noch deutlich entfernt von Größenordnungen, wie sie in den bibliothekspolitischen Grundsatzpapieren als Mindest-

552 Zur Leitbilddiskussion vgl. Umlauf, Konrad: Leiten + Bilden = Leitbild : Das Bibliotheksleitbild: Inhalt – Funktion – Anforderungen – Erstellung – Umsetzung. In: BuB 51(1999), S. 98-105. – Zu den Themen- und Nachbarschaftsbibliotheken vgl. das Projekt der Bertelsmann-Stiftung „Bibliotheksfilialen – Optimierung von Angebot und Organisation“: www.bertelsmann-stiftung.de/project.

553 Vgl. hierzu Brandorff, Günter: Niederlande : Modelle zur Neustrukturierung. In: BuB 52(2000), S. 270-271.

554 Die Jahresstatistik 1998 ... (Anm. 2)

555 1971 vgl. Schmidt ... (Anm. 1, S. 325); 1990 siehe: Katholische Büchereiarbeit – Jahresstatistik 1990. In: KÖB 5(1991), H. 4, S. 14 – 15.

norm für eine Bibliothek 1. Stufe deklariert wurden. Auch mit der Aktualität der Bestände steht es vielerorts nicht zum besten, da die Erwerbungsmittel im statistischen Durchschnitt zu gering sind: In etlichen Diözesen verfügen die Büchereien seit Jahren über weniger als eine Mark je vorhandenem Medium für Neuanschaffungen.[556] Bei einem durchschnittlichen Preis von DM 30,- je Buch können also die Bestände noch nicht einmal innerhalb einer Generation komplett erneuert werden. An einen Einstieg in kostenträchtige neue Medien, wie etwa CD-ROMs, ist unter diesen Umständen gar nicht zu denken. Dieser qualitative Aspekt einer unzureichenden Bestandserneuerung wiegt schwerer als die bloße Quantität der Bestände. Die mangelnde Finanzkraft hat natürlich in der Summe auch Folgen für die räumliche Unterbringung, die Einrichtung und technische Ausstattung vieler Büchereien; nicht selten unterbleiben hier notwendige oder überfällige Investitionen. Der erforderliche Einstieg in die EDV ist ebenfalls oft nicht möglich, weil es am Geld mangelt. Und schließlich sei noch auf die strukturelle Schwäche einer unzureichenden horizontalen Vernetzung und vertikalen Verflechtung der örtlichen Katholischen öffentlichen Büchereien hingewiesen: Ohne Zweifel sind in den letzten Jahrzehnten viele Formen der Zusammenarbeit der Büchereien auf lokaler Ebene entstanden und punktuell auch entsprechende Strukturen und Einrichtungen auf überörtlicher Ebene entwickelt worden: Dass es den Verantwortlichen in der katholischen Büchereiarbeit jedoch nicht gelungen ist, jene Modellvorstellungen konsequent und in der Fläche umzusetzen, die 1971 in dem richtungsweisenden Grundsatzpapier *Struktur der katholischen Büchereiarbeit* niedergelegt wurden und die sich als Leitlinien für eine zukunftsorientierte Weiterentwicklung des katholischen Büchereiwesens begriffen, muss nach wie vor als ein wesentliches Defizit katholischer Büchereiarbeit benannt werden.[557]

Solchen Schwächen stehen aber nach wie vor auch besondere Merkmale als Stärken gegenüber, auf die katholischen Büchereien zu Recht – zum Teil auch im Unterschied zu Öffentlichen Bibliotheken anderer Träger - verweisen können:

Durch ihre traditionelle Anbindung an die Pfarrgemeinden sind Katholische öffentliche Büchereien bis heute nahe bei den Menschen geblieben, d.h. es gibt sie in Wohnvierteln, Stadtteilen, einzelnen Dörfern innerhalb von Großgemeinden, wo keine andere Bibliothek in der Nähe verfügbar oder in einem vertretbaren Zeitaufwand erreichbar ist. Für weniger mobile Menschen, insbesondere für Kinder bis in die Grundschulzeit hinein, sind sie oft der erste und einzige Zugriffspunkt auf Buch- und Medienbestände jenseits der im Elternhaus, im Kindergarten oder in der Grundschule verfügbaren Angebote. Der weitaus größte Anteil der Mitarbeiterinnen und Mitarbeiter dieser Büchereien engagiert sich aus ganz

556 Unter den nordrhein-westfälischen Diözesen gelang es in den 90er-Jahren nur im Erzbistum Köln, die Erwerbungsmittel der Büchereien durch verschiedene Maßnahmen nachhaltig zu verbessern: Hier standen 1998 DM 1,60 je Medium gegenüber DM 0,86 je Medium (1991) zur Verfügung. Im Bistum Münster stiegen die Mittel in diesem Zeitraum von DM 1,07 auf DM 1,18; in den übrigen drei Diözesen Paderborn, Aachen und Essen sind sogar Rückgänge zu verzeichnen und zwar in Paderborn von DM 1,15 auf DM 1,06 je Medium, in Aachen von DM 1,01 auf DM 0,78 je Medium und in Essen von DM 0,86 auf DM 0,63 je Medium; die Finanzausstattung der Katholischen öffentlichen Büchereien des Ruhrgebietsbistums ist unter den hier verglichenen Diözesen somit als besonders prekär zu bezeichnen. – Zahlenwerte ermittelt aus den Jahresstatistiken 1990 und 1998. Siehe: Die Jahresstatistik 1998 ... (Anm. 2) und Katholische Büchereiarbeit – Jahresstatistik 1990 ... (Anm. 13).

557 Struktur der katholischen Büchereiarbeit. Bonn 1971. Unter anderem veröffentlicht in: Das neue Buch 16(1971) S. 297-308. – Näheres zu den Modellvorstellungen dieses Textes und zu den tatsächlich realisierten Formen der Zusammenarbeit, vgl. Schmidt, Siegfried: Katholische öffentliche Büchereien – Schnittstellen .... (Anm. 1) S. 322.

unterschiedlichen Motiven heraus ehrenamtlich. Die Zahl der ehrenamtlichen Tätigen, zu 90 % Frauen und zu 10 % Männer, ist in den letzten Jahren kontinuierlich angewachsen und beschränkt sich keineswegs vornehmlich auf ältere Menschen und Jugendliche. Wohl kaum ein anderer Dienst einer Pfarrgemeinde kann – einer aktuellen Erhebung zufolge - heute auf eine in ihrer Altersstruktur so ausgeglichene, junge Mitarbeiterschaft verweisen, wie die katholische Büchereiarbeit.[558] Und wer diese ca. 30.000 Frauen und Männer, die sich in KÖB's bundesweit engagieren, vorschnell als unprofessionell abqualifiziert, der übersieht die vielfältigen Qualifizierungs- und Fortbildungsangebote für die Ehrenamtlichen, der negiert den vielfältigen beruflichen und persönlichen Erfahrungshintergrund und die hohe Motivation, den diese in ihr Büchereiengagement einbringen. Ein gutes Büchereiteam ist zugleich auch eine *pressure group* für die Bücherei und sorgt für eine gute Einbindung in die örtlichen Strukturen der Kirchen- und Zivilgemeinde. Nicht zuletzt aufgrund der ehrenamtlichen Mitarbeiterinnen und Mitarbeiter liegt ein überproportional hoher Anteil der Öffnungsstunden der Büchereien werktags in den späten Nachmittagsstunden, an Samstagen und Sonntagen. Katholische öffentliche Büchereien sind mir ihren Angeboten schwerpunktmäßig also dann präsent, wenn ein Großteil der Bevölkerung keiner Berufstätigkeit nachgeht. Aus langjähriger eigener Erfahrung weiß der Autor dieses Beitrages, welche Bedeutung dabei insbesondere der in KÖB's vielerorts üblichen Sonntagsöffnung zukommt, ein Angebot, das in kommunalen Bibliotheken aus vielfältigen Gründen nur höchst selten anzutreffen ist: Die KÖB St. Rochus in Bonn-Duisdorf beispielsweise bietet ihre rund 9.000 Medien an drei Werktagen mit insgesamt 6 Öffnungsstunden und sonntags mit zwei Öffnungsstunden (in der Zeit von 10 – 12 Uhr) an. Von 14.650 Ausleihen im Jahre 2000 entfielen auf die Sonntage 6400 Entleihungen; die beiden sonntäglichen Öffnungsstunden schlugen also mit rund 44 % aller Ausleihvorgänge zu Buche. Zum überwiegenden Teil nutzen sonntags Mütter und Väter (!) mit ihren Kindern die Bibliothek.[559] Die Nutzer rekrutieren sich dabei nur zu einem kleinen Teil aus der Gottesdienstgemeinde. Die KÖB erreicht mit ihren Medien überwiegend Fernstehende und Nicht-Gemeindemitglieder. Sie ist ähnlich wie z.B. ein konfessioneller Kindergarten ein Angebot der Kirche, das über das eigene Milieu hinaus eine Verbindung zu Menschen, die in anderen Lebenszusammenhängen stehen, schafft.

Zukünftige Formen katholischer Büchereiarbeit auf örtlicher Ebene

In Umbruch- und Krisenzeiten haben Aussagen und Prognosen über die Zukunft von Ideen, Konzeptionen und Institutionen Konjunktur. So wundert es auch nicht, dass in den vergangenen Jahren in Gremien, Fachvorträgen und Aufsätzen vermehrt über das Selbstverständnis und die Perspektiven katholischer Büchereiarbeit nachgedacht wurde[560]. Bishe-

---

[558] Vgl. Rolf Pitsch: Ehrenamtlich und erfolgreich : Ehrenamt wird stärker zum Thema der öffentlichen Debatte. In: KÖB 13(1999), Heft 4, S. 2-6 und ders.: Lobbyarbeit für das Ehrenamt : Was kann die Büchereiarbeit zum Thema beitragen? In: KÖB 15(2001), Heft 1, S. 6-12.- Nach den auf S. 7 publizierten Daten zum Alter von rund 18.500 Ehrenamtlichen in der Katholischen Büchereiarbeit betrug 1999 der Anteil der Jugendlichen bis 18 Jahre 21,7 %, der 19 –30-Jährigen 10,8 %, der 31 – 40-Jährigen 16,5 %, der 41 – 50-Jährigen 19,3 %, der 51 – 60-Jährigen 14,0 % und der über 60-Jährigen 17,8 %.

[559] Alle Zahlenangaben aufgrund einer eigenen Auswertung der Daten des Statistikheftes der ÖB St. Rochus, Bonn-Duisdorf für das Jahr 2000. Der Autor kann sich dieses Urteil erlauben, da er seit rund 10 Jahren ehrenamtlich in dieser Bücherei tätig ist und 1x pro Monat den Sonntagsdienst ausübt.

[560] Im Arbeitsbereich des Borromäusvereins wird z.B. gegenwärtig ein Leitbild für Katholische öffentliche Büchereien entwickelt. – Vgl. hierzu: Ganter, Lothar: Warum unsere Arbeit wichtig ist : „Leitbild KÖB". In KÖB 14(2000), H. 4, S. 2-9.

rigen Positionsbestimmungen haftet allerdings der Mangel an, dass einzelne Aspekte einer im ganzen komplexen Ausgangslage zu einseitig untersucht und in ihren Folgewirkungen beschrieben werden. Hier soll nun der Versuch einer Gesamtschau unternommen werden:

Zentraler Punkt der Überlegungen scheint mir dabei zu sein, dass es künftig *die* Katholische öffentliche Bücherei – im Sinne einer weithin einheitlichen Ausprägung und eines nahezu identischen Erscheinungsbildes nach außen – nicht mehr geben kann, wenn die Katholische Büchereiarbeit in einem nennenswerten Umfang fortbestehen will. Vielmehr muss sich notwendigerweise eine Entwicklung hin zu verschiedenen Formen vollziehen.[561] Die dabei entstehende Binnendifferenzierung und Pluralität der Büchereien katholischer Provenienz sollte als Chance, nicht als Gefahr begriffen werden. Vier größere Formkomplexe lassen sich dabei vorläufig von einander unterscheiden:

1. Form

Eine erste mögliche Form kann dabei durchaus weiterhin die „herkömmliche" KÖB als Bibliothek für alle (oder viele) mit einem inhaltlichen Medienangebot für Gemeindemitglieder und alle Interessierten im Einzugsgebiet der Bücherei, für die unter Umständen die Aufgabe der allgemeinen Literaturversorgung übernommen wird, sein. Diese Form ist aber an drei Grundvoraussetzungen gebunden:

- an hinreichend leistungsfähige, finanzstarke und lebendige katholische Gemeinden als Träger und Rückhalt für die Büchereien
- an ein gesellschaftliches Umfeld, das die Katholischen öffentlichen Büchereien in ideeller und materieller Hinsicht fördert, da die finanzielle Kraft des Trägers in der Regel nicht ausreichend wird, die angesichts des Wandels der Medienlandschaft und der Informationsgesellschaft notwendigen Investitionen allein zu tätigen
- an eine offene, in der Tradition des Zweiten Vatikanums stehende, dialogbereite Kirche, die sich nicht als Gegensatz zur Moderne sondern als Teil einer notwendigerweise differenzierten und vielgestaltigen Gesellschaft begreift.[562]

Wo diese Rahmenbedingungen gegeben sind, funktioniert das Modell „KÖB", so wie es sich in den vergangenen Jahrzehnten herausgebildet hat, auch weiterhin mit sehr guten Ergebnissen. Nur, diese Rahmenbedingungen sind inzwischen - bezogen auf die Gesamtfläche der Bundesrepublik – nur noch in wenigen Regionen und Bundesländern, die man vielleicht als Hochburgen des Katholizismus bezeichnen kann, einigermaßen hinreichend erfüllt: Man mag da in erster Linie an viele Teile Bayerns denken; der bayerische Anteil an Gesamtleistungen katholischer Büchereiarbeit ist in der Vergangenheit kontinuierlich angewachsen.[563] Außerhalb Bayerns trifft diese Situation am ehesten auf ländlich-

561 Die Einsicht, dass es „... die Katholische öffentliche Bücherei ... jetzt überhaupt nicht mehr gibt", sondern, dass je nach den örtlichen Gegebenheiten unterschiedliche Differenzierungen geboten sind, äußerte Hans Schachtner, der frühere Direktor des bayerischen Sankt Michaelsbundes, bereits 1968. – Vgl.: Schachtner, Hans: Isolierung oder Kommunikation in der Büchereiarbeit. In: Vorträge des 50. Bibliothekarskurses 30. September – 4. Oktober 1968. Bonn 1969. (Werkhefte zur Büchereiarbeit; 15) S. 1-11. – Vgl. S. 9.

562 Näheres zum Zusammenhang zwischen der Entwicklung der katholischen Büchereien und dem Weg, den die Kirche gehen wird, siehe in: Schmidt, Siegfried: Katholische Büchereiarbeit in einer künftigen Kirche. In: Bausteine für eine lesende Kirche ... (vgl. Anm. 1), S. 140 – 151. Siehe insbesondere S. 146 – 149.

563 Mit einigem Stolz weist Erich Jooß, Direktor des Sankt Michaelsbundes im jüngsten Jahresbericht des Verbandes auf die gegenüber den Büchereien im Arbeitsgebiet des Borromäusverein überdurchschnittlich guten Leistungen hin: „Auch in diesem Vergleich schneidet der Sankt Michaelsbund hervorragend ab. So

kleinstädtische Regionen des Münsterlandes und des Oldenburger Landes zu.

Immer muss man bei dieser Erscheinungsform katholischer Büchereiarbeit befürchten, dass die Voraussetzungen brüchig werden, so dass das Modell KÖB auch hier in Zukunft zunehmend in Frage gestellt werden könnte: Folgt man pessimistischeren religionssoziologischen Untersuchungen zur Lage der Kirche, so muss man beispielsweise konstatieren, dass die Erosion und Milieuverengung der Pfarrgemeinden in diesen Zentren des Katholizismus gegenüber anderen Region zwar zeitlich verzögert, im ganzen aber in ähnlicher Weise und letztendlich mit gleichem Ergebnis abläuft.[564] Zugleich ist auch hier die Gefahr einer schwindenden gesellschaftlichen Akzeptanz kirchlicher Einrichtungen oder eines Rückzuges der Kirche aus gesellschaftlichen Aufgabenfeldern gegeben.

Das lässt zum einen vermuten, dass es auf längere Sicht immer weniger herkömmliche KÖB's geben wird und die im folgenden beschriebenen alternativen Formen mehr und mehr an Bedeutung gewinnen werden. Zum anderen ist zu erwarten, dass bei schwindender innerer Kraft und Gestaltungsmöglichkeiten der Kirche und sinkenden Geldmitteln solche KÖB's selbst einem Säkularisationsprozess unterliegen, der auch die Aufgabe der Trägerschaft zur Folge haben kann[565]. Und sind nicht künftig dort, wo statt der Einbindung einer Öffentlichen Bibliothek in eine Kommunalverwaltung privatwirtschaftliche Organisationsformen für Bibliotheken an Bedeutung gewinnen, Beteiligungsmodelle gemeinsam mit anderen gesellschaftlichen Gruppen, etwa innerhalb eines „e.V's." denkbar?

2. Form

Schon in den 60er-Jahren hat Hans Schachtner darauf hingewiesen, dass es dort, wo Katholische öffentliche Büchereien im Wettbewerb und in räumlicher Nähe zu Bibliotheksangeboten anderer Träger stehen, anderer inhaltlicher Konzepte bedarf, als dort, wo eine KÖB auch die Aufgabe einer allgemeinen Literaturversorgung übernimmt. Schachtner dachte unter Wettbewerbsbedingungen für die KÖB allerdings zuvorderst an eine gemein-

---

beträgt der Entleihumsatz pro Medium im Borromäusverein 1,37, im Sankt Michaelsbund dagegen 1,75. Während der Borromäusverein 3.053 Mitgliedsbüchereien aufweist, betreut der Sankt Michaelsbund 1.184 Büchereien. Das sind 27,94 % aller katholischen Einrichtungen in der Bundesrepublik. Bei den Entleihungen indessen verbucht der Sankt Michaelsbund 12.002.383 gegenüber 15.581.618 beim Borromäusverein. In Prozentzahlen ausgedrückt: der bayerische Verband leistet 43,51 % aller Entleihungen innerhalb der katholischen Büchereiarbeit der Bundesrepublik . Neben den konzertierten Anstrengungen der Diözesanstellen und der Landesfachstelle ist das nicht zuletzt auf die kontinuierliche Förderung durch den Freistaat Bayern und die Einbindung der Kommunen in den Sankt Michaelsbund zurückzuführen. Bücher[ei]politische Weichenstellungen, die hier schon vor Jahrzehnten getroffen wurden, erweisen sich damit nach wie vor als sinnvoll und zukunftsweisend." Vgl.: www.st-michealsbund.de/f_3zahlen/htm (Stand: 18.03.2001).

564 Nimmt man beispielsweise den sinkenden sonntäglichen Gottesdienstbesuch als Indikator für eine abnehmende Bindung der Mitglieder an ihre Kirche, so lässt sich in allen Diözesen Deutschlands ein stetiger Rückgang als Trend feststellen. Allerdings liegt der prozentuale Besuch im ländlich-katholisch geprägten Diözesen immer höher als in konfessionell-gemischten städtischen Gebieten. So lag in der Diözese Münster 1970 der Gottesdienstbesuch noch etwa bei 50 % in der Diözese Essen hingegen bei 30 %. 1995 hatte sich dieser Wert in der Diözese Münster auf rund 20 %, in der Diözese Essen auf ca. 15 % reduziert. – Vgl. Ebertz, Michael N.: Erosion der Gnadenanstalt ... (Anm. 5), S. 336.

565 Es sei an dieser Stelle z.B. auf frühere Entwicklungen in den Niederlanden hingewiesen. Aus dem Nebeneinander von kommunalen und kirchlichen Büchereien entstanden in den späten 60er und frühen 70er-Jahren fast überall gemeinschaftliche Bibliotheken. Damit verbunden war eine als „Dekonfessionalisierung" bezeichnete Tendenz, das konfessionelle Element in der niederländischen Gesellschaft immer weniger in eigenen Strukturen festzulegen.- Vgl.: Meyer, Antje: Die öffentliche Bibliothek in den Niederlanden : Zielsetzungen seit 1960. In: BuB 39(1987), S. 310 – 325; siehe insbesondere S. 313.

deinternen Einrichtung.[566] Katholische öffentliche Büchereien, die sich heute in einer solchen Situation befinden und die zudem noch von geringer Größe sind und nur über begrenzte Ressourcen verfügen, sollten beherzt und mit dem nötigen Mut zum Experiment jene Konzepte der Zielgruppenorientierung und / oder inhaltlichen Spezialisierung auf ihre Verhältnisse hin übertragen, die, wie beschrieben, gegenwärtig als allgemeiner Trend im Bibliothekswesen festzustellen sind. Bezogen auf die je unterschiedliche örtliche Situation sind verschiedene Ausprägungen denkbar: hier eine Kinder- und Jugendbibliothek, dort eine Familien- oder Seniorenbibliothek, anderenorts vielleicht ein Literaturcafé oder – in Zusammenarbeit mit einem benachbarten Jugendzentrum - ein Internet-Café. In der Praxis haben solche Spezialisierungen oder Umwandlungen mancherorts längst stattgefunden.[567] In offiziellen Papieren zur katholischen Büchereiarbeit wird aber immer noch viel zu fest und starr am Paradigma der KÖB als *öffentlicher Bücherei für alle* festgehalten und übersehen, dass jemand, der mit stark begrenzten Ressourcen allen alles bieten will, kaum jemand zufrieden stellen kann.[568]

Eine solche Spezialisierung und Einnischung bietet gerade den durchschnittlichen KÖB`s die Chance einer Profilierung und einer Attraktivitätssteigerung. Sie scheint gerade auch in jenen katholisch geprägten Großstädten ein probates Mittel zur Entwicklung und Zukunftssicherung der Büchereiarbeit zu sein, wo auf engem Raum bisher additiv „nur eine Fülle von nebeneinander stehenden Büchereien existieren".[569] Gefordert ist allerdings eine Überwindung des Kirchturmdenkens. Denn eine konzeptionelle Abstimmung unter benachbarten und künftig voraussichtlich unter gemeinsamen Verwaltungsstrukturen arbeitenden Pfarrgemeinden ist geboten. So könnte z.B. an einem Standort weiterhin eine normale „KÖB" beibehalten werden und in einer Nachbargemeinde eine auf eine Zielgruppe hin spezialisierte Bibliothek geschaffen werden oder es könnte eine Konzentration und Bündelung der Aktivitäten auf einen Standort hin erfolgen

3. Form

In einer zunehmend säkularen Gesellschaft, die für die Kirche nur noch klar umrissene Aufgabenfelder und Räume übrig lässt, ist die Verlockung groß, sich als Kirche auf das „Kerngeschäft" seelsorglich-pastoraler und sozialer Aufgaben zu beschränken und sich aus

---

566 Schachtner, Hans: Isolierung oder Kommunikation ... (Anm. 20), S. 9.

567 Ein aktuelles Beispiel aus dem Kölner Umland: Die kleine Pfarrgemeinde St. Nikolaus in Kürten-Dürscheid hat ihre Bücherei durch einen Jugendtreff mit Internet-Café ersetzt: „In einem Regal stehen einige religiöse Standardwerke und liegen mehrere katholische Zeitschriften aus. Sie erinnern daran, dass in den Räumen ehemals die Pfarrbücherei untergebracht war. ‚Diese hat sich schon lange nicht mehr gelohnt', weiß Vanessa (20) zu berichten." Vgl.: ‚Oase' für Jugendliche : in Dürscheid wird das Internet-Café von St. Nikolaus eröffnet. – In: Kirchenzeitung für Erzbistum Köln, Jg. 2001, Nr. 12 vom 23.03.2001, S.32.

568 Im Grundsatzpapier „5 Voraussetzungen für die Katholische öffentliche Bücherei" (Bonn : Arbeitsstelle der Katholischen Büchereiarbeit, 1993) wird als erste Voraussetzung postuliert, dass die KÖB eine „Bücherei für alle" ist. Vgl.: Schmidt, Siegfried: Fünf Voraussetzungen für die Katholische öffentliche Bücherei : Sachausschuß III der BAG stellt weiteres Grundsatzpapier fertig. In: KÖB 7(1993), H.2, S. 1-7. - Eine ähnliche Sicht vertritt auch Rolf Pitsch, Direktor des Borromäusvereins, wenn er ein einheitliches Erscheinungsbild katholischer Büchereiarbeit und Katholischer öffentlicher Büchereien zeichnet und beispielsweise schreibt, dass eine möglichst breite inhaltliche Auffächerung der Bestände erforderlich sei, „... diese bestehen im Allgemeinen zu einem Drittel aus Sachliteratur, Belletristik und Kinder- beziehungsweise Jugendliteratur", zunehmend ergänzt durch Nichtbuchmedien. – Vgl. Pitsch, Rolf: Menschendienlichkeit als Maßstab : zur Situation der katholischen Büchereiarbeit. In: BuB 52(2000), S. 365-368. – Zitat S. 367 – 368.

569 Schachtner, Hans: Isolierung oder Kommunikation ... (Anm. 20), S.9

anderen Aktivitäten, etwa der Bildung und Kultur, zunehmend zurück zu ziehen.[570] Bezogen auf die katholische Büchereiarbeit birgt diese Entwicklung Chancen und Gefahren zugleich:

Auf *überörtlicher, regionaler und diözesaner* Ebene sind katholische Büchereien, die sich auf Medienangebote religiösen, seelsorglichen und katechetischen Inhalts spezialisieren oder hier zumindest deutliche Akzente setzen, notwendige und sinnvolle Einrichtungen. Diese können zugleich anders konzipierte Büchereien vor Ort in ihrer Arbeit unterstützen. Weitere Synergien sind z.B. denkbar, wenn zusätzlich religiöse oder religiös intendierte Medien zum Verkauf angeboten werden oder eine Verschmelzung einer AV-Medienstelle und einer Bücherei erfolgt. Bislang gibt es nur wenige Beispiele derartiger Einrichtungen, die ohne hauptamtlich beschäftigtes Fachpersonal nicht denkbar sind, z.B. die Regionalbüchereien im Bistum Aachen, das Medienzentrum in Paderborn oder der Medienverleih des Bistums Dresden-Meißen in der Dresdner Hofkirche.[571] Zur Stärkung der katholischen Büchereiarbeit insgesamt wäre es notwendig, wenn künftig solche katholische Medienzentren oder –läden in kleineren Diözesen zumindest auf Bistumsebene, in größeren Diözesen aber auch auf regionaler Ebene geschaffen werden. Dort, wo Katholiken eine kleine Minderheit innerhalb einer weitgehend konfessionslosen Umgebung bilden, also in den östlichen Bundesländern und in den nordwestdeutschen Diasporagebieten sind solche Einrichtungen wohl auf Dauer überhaupt die einzig sinnvolle Erscheinungsform organisierter katholischer Büchereiarbeit.[572]

Auch auf *örtlicher* Ebene erscheint eine deutliche pastorale Akzentuierung katholischer Büchereiarbeit zunächst einmal verlockend. Verspricht diese doch angesichts des wachsenden Legitimationsdrucks eine höhere Akzeptanz bei kirchlichen Entscheidungsträgern. Innerhalb des herkömmlichen KÖB-Konzeptes ist eine solche Buchpastoral jedoch nur begrenzt möglich, da diese Form katholischer Büchereiarbeit einer ausgewogenen Balance „zwischen innerem Auftrag und eigenständigem Profil auf der einen und Offenheit und Weltbezogenheit auf der anderen Seite“ bedarf. Hinsichtlich ihrer pastoralen Bedeutung sind dabei die verschiedenen Zielsetzungen einer KÖB von unterschiedlicher Gewichtigkeit: „Im inneren Kern das Bemühen um die Lebendigkeit des Wortes, um den Bau von Brücken zu den Glaubenserfahrungen anderer und um den Dienst für die pastoralen Dienste, in einer zweiten Schicht Angebote mit einem christlichen Profil, die die religiöse Dimension angemessen berücksichtigen und offen für zentrale Fragen des menschlichen Lebens sind, in einer dritten, äußeren Schicht Offerten, die aus einem ganzheitlichen Men-

---

[570] „Die Akzeptanz der Kirchen als Sozialkirche und die Akzeptanz der Kirchen als Passagenritenkirche scheinen die beiden Nahtstellen zu sein, auf die sich die Integrationskraft auch der katholischen Kirche in Deutschland weitgehend reduziert, worüber also ihr Funktionieren als eine soziale Einheit noch einigermaßen sichergestellt wird“. Aus: Ebertz, Michael N.: Erosion der Gnadenanstalt ... (Anm. 5, S. 135).

[571] Vgl.: Hupbach, Heide: Medienverleih Bistum Dresden Meißen. In: KÖB 10(1996), H. 4, S. 30-33.

[572] Katholische öffentliche Büchereien existieren in den neuen Bundesländern kaum und es ist nicht zu erwarten, dass sich dies in Zukunft ändern wird. Eine im vergangenen Jahr in Potsdam neugegründeten Arbeitsgemeinschaft Katholische Büchereiarbeit im Erzbistum Berlin meldet Kontakte zu 28 Büchereien in Gemeinden, Krankenhäusern und Schulen; eine sehr geringe Zahl angesichts der Tatsache, dass zu diesem Bistum immerhin die Großstadt Berlin gehört. Auch im neu entstandenen Erzbistum Hamburg ist katholische Büchereiarbeit auf Gemeindeebene quasi nicht existent. Das Diasporabistum Hildesheim meldete im Statistikjahr 1998 73 Büchereien mit 118.000 Medien und 94.000 Ausleihen. Das entspricht indiskutablen Kleinstbeständen von lediglich 1.600 Medien und 1.300 Ausleihen / Jahr pro Bücherei. – Zum Erzbistum Berlin vgl.: Falkenhagen, Andreas: Katholische Büchereien zwischen Havel und Oder, Rügen und Potsdam : ein Jahr Arbeitsgemeinschaft Büchereiarbeit im Erzbistum Berlin. In: KÖB 15(2001), H. 1, S. 29 – 33.

schenbild heraus den einzelnen in seinen verschiedenen Bedürfnissen und Lebenswirklichkeiten ansprechen wollen“[573].

Eine zu starke Konzentration auf diesen inneren Kern birgt die Gefahr einer Engführung und möglicherweise auch einer Rückkehr zu Überholtem in sich. Ginge man diesen Weg, so entstünden ebenfalls spezialisierte katholische Büchereien, denen jedoch im Unterschied zu den unter 2. beschriebenen zielgruppen- und themenorientierten Büchereien keine sonderliche Wirkung beschieden sein wird und die daher kaum tragfähig sein werden:

Eine vorrangige Indienstnahme der KÖB als Mittel der Verkündigung und Seelsorge wird diese in eine Pfarrbücherei rückverwandeln. Mit einem auf Beschränkung, Prävention und Reglementierung angelegten Bestand könnte nur eine kleine Minderheit innerhalb des eigenen Milieus erreicht werden.[574] Eine Beschränkung des Bestandes auf religiöse und religionspädagogische Medien führt vor Ort zu einer Fachbibliothek, die ebenfalls nur wenige Nutzer mit speziellen Interessen erreicht.[575]

Keine Lösung scheint ebenfalls zu sein, wenn einzelne Medien in der örtlichen Bücherei in ihrer Bedeutung zu stark hervorgehoben und zugleich funktionalisiert werden, wie es etwa Horst Patenge für die Erzählende Literatur vorsieht, wenn er schreibt: „Das gemeinsame Interesse der Büchereibesucher ist auf eine Bereicherung ihres Lebens gerichtet, und sie billigen der Literatur und den katholischen Büchereien hierbei eine Kompetenz zu“.[576] Diese Sichtweise steht im Widerspruch zu einer zunehmend multimedialen Wirklichkeit nachwachsender Generationen. Die Einforderung einer permanenten Gesprächs- und Zeugnisbereitschaft über das Gelesene überfordert die MitarbeiterInnen und NutzerInnen zumeist gleichermaßen und verkennt, dass häufig ein auf Eskapismus, Entspannung oder Unterhaltung ausgerichtetes, ‚absichtsloses' Lektürebedürfnis zum Griff nach Erzählender Literatur in der Bücherei führt. Und wenn die Bewertung der eigenen Arbeit von gezählten Ausleihen zu den erreichten Menschen hin verändert werden soll, dann wird – vielleicht in Unkenntnis bibliothekshistorischer Zusammenhänge – eine bedenkliche Nähe zum überkommenen Konzept der klassischen Büchereipädagogik Hofmann'scher Prägung hergestellt. Wer eine örtliche Bücherei in diesem Sinne mit einiger Konsequenz transformiert, wird eine Einrichtung schaffen, die vor allem für ältere Nutzerinnen mit einem mittleren und höheren Bildungsniveau interessant sein dürfte, insgesamt aber nur eine geringe Wirkung haben dürfte.

Es ist schon paradox: Die bisherige große Offenheit der Bestände und die Reichweite der örtlichen KÖB über die Kerngemeinde hinaus offeriert gute Ansatzpunkte für eine Lese- und Buchpastoral. Werden diese Anstrengungen jedoch innerhalb der örtlichen Bücherei intensiviert, so geht diese Offenheit verloren und die Reichweite der Bücherei wird eingeschränkt.

4. Form

Da trotz vermehrter Anstrengungen in der Gemeindepastoral der Erosionsprozess kirchlicher Strukturen immer weiter fortschreitet und somit die Grenzen des Modells „Pfarrgemeinde“ als örtliche, territoriale Einheit der katholischen Christen offenkundig geworden

---

573 Vgl.: Schmidt, Siegfried: Katholische öffentliche Büchereien als pastorale Orte ... (Anm. 7), S.120-121.

574 Schmidt, Siegfried: Katholische öffentliche Büchereien – Schnittstellen ... (Anm. 1), S. 324.

575 Schmidt, Siegfried: Katholische öffentliche Büchereien als pastorale Orte ... (Anm. 7), S.120.

576 Patenge; Horst: Von Kirchengemeinden, Milieus und pastoralen Zwischenräumen : zukunftsweisende Gedanken zur Büchereiarbeit in der Kirche. In: KÖB 14(2000), H. 1, S. 2- 5. Zitat S. 3.

sind, suchen inzwischen manche Pastoraltheologen nach neuen Wegen in der Seelsorge, die nicht ohne Konsequenzen für eine bisher weitestgehend an Gemeindestrukturen gebundene Büchereiarbeit bleiben werden.

Der Freiburger Pastoralsoziologe Michael N. Ebertz ist ein profilierter Vertreter dieses Ansatzes.[577] In seinen soziologisch fundierten Analysen kommt er zu dem Schluss, dass zwar in der modernen Erlebnisgesellschaft die klassischen, durch Herkunft, Bildung und Religionszugehörigkeit bestimmten Milieus nicht mehr existieren, dass man aber dennoch sehr wohl immer noch unterschiedliche Milieus benennen kann, die sich im Hinblick auf Konsum, Genuss und ästhetische Kategorien unterscheiden und die sich teilweise scharf von einander abgrenzen lassen. Ebertz charakterisiert dabei das Niveau-, Harmonie-, Integrationsmilieu-, Unterhaltungs- und Selbstverwirklichungsmilieu näher. Zugleich vertritt er die Ansicht, dass Pfarrgemeinden heute vor allem ältere Menschen mit unteren und mittleren Bildungsabschlüssen erreichen, mithin also vor allem im Harmonie- und Integrationsmilieu präsent sind. Ein Aufbrechen dieser Verengung scheint kaum möglich zu sein, da zwischen den einzelnen Milieus ästhetische Ausschlusskriterien wirksam sind („Gemeinden sind oft fidele Altenclubs und frönen eine Biederkeit, die abstoßend wirkt") und innerhalb der Milieus die Selbsterhaltungstendenz erkennbar ist, neue Kräfte nur innerhalb ihresgleichen zu suchen und zu rekrutieren.

Als Ergebnis dieser Analyse fordert Ebertz, dass Kirche in der Pastoral nicht immer und vorrangig in gemeindlichen Kategorien denken, handeln und planen sollte. Wenn Kirche nicht zu einer Subkultur degenerieren will, wenn sie den Prozess der Dispersion des Religiösen aufhalten will, wenn sie die Plünderung ihrer Traditionen verhindern will, dann muss sie selbstaktiv außerhalb der Gemeinden Zugänge zu den anderen Milieus finden. Ebertz spricht sich daher für eine *Pastoral der Zwischenräume* aus, die unabhängig und neben der herkömmlichen Gemeindepastoral neue Orte und niederschwellige Zugangsmöglichkeiten für jene bieten soll, die sich nicht dauerhaft an eine Gemeinde binden wollen. Bereits existierende Zwischenräume sind für ihn beispielsweise die Autobahnkirchen, die Telefonseelsorge und die City-Pastoral. Aber auch für die Lese- und Buchpastoral als Teil einer Kommunikationspastoral sieht Ebertz einen Platz innerhalb einer Pastoral der Zwischenräume.

Die Frage, wie katholische Buch- und Büchereiarbeit jenseits des herkömmlichen Gemeindebezuges im Kontext einer Pastoral der Zwischenräume aussehen könnte und welche Formen sie dabei entwickeln könnte, ist bisher noch weitgehend unbeantwortet geblieben. Auch Ebertz hat bislang vor allem Rahmenbedingungen und Thesen zur Lese- und Kommunikationspastoral formuliert. Dabei geht er insgesamt von einer starken Adressatenorientierung und Milieudifferenzierung der Aktivitäten aus und fordert zudem eine Professionalisierung, Vernetzung, Ressourcen- und Qualitätsorientierung der Arbeit.[578]

Vielleicht können diese beiden Beispiele katholischer Buch- und Büchereiarbeit als erste konkrete Ansätze neuer Formen in dieses nicht gemeindebezogene pastorale Konzept eingeordnet werden:

Mit erheblichem personellen und finanziellen Aufwand hat der Borromäusverein

---

577 Die Ausführungen der folgenden beiden Abschnitte nach: Ebertz, Michael N.: Erlesen glauben ... (Anm. 5), S. 72ff.

578 Ebd., S. 95-97. – In ähnlicher Weise äußerte sich Ebertz während eines mündlichen Vortrages in der Katholischen Akademie ‚Die Wolfsburg' in Mülheim / Ruhr zum Thema „Lesen und kommunizieren – Katholische öffentliche Büchereien als Orte einer Kommunikationspastoral der Zwischenräume" im Rahmen des 38. Diözesantages der Katholischen öffentlichen Büchereien im Bistum Essen am 22.10.2000.

zusammen verschiedenen Büchereifachstellen in den vergangenen Jahren ein „proliko“[579] betiteltes, aus verschiedenen Einzelelementen bestehendes literarisches Fortbildungsprogramm erarbeitet und dessen Umsetzung propagiert. Proliko will ein wachsendes Bedürfnis vieler Menschen nach nicht-informierender Sprache, nach literarischen Texten aufgreifen, wobei in den Angeboten kaum die Interpretation oder wissenschaftliche Auseinandersetzung mit Literatur eine Rolle spielt, sondern es im Kern darum geht, eigene Lebens- und Glaubenserfahrungen an literarischen Texten zu spiegeln und zu reflektieren.[580] Auch wenn proliko in den Büchereien ansetzt und gezielt Mitarbeiterinnen und Mitarbeiter und Nutzerinnen und Nutzer der Katholischen öffentlichen Büchereien zu rekrutieren sucht, handelt es sich letztlich um ein Angebot, dessen Programme auch gänzlich unabhängig von Büchereien und Gemeindestrukturen – etwa im Rahmen der Katholischen Erwachsenenbildung – durchgeführt werden können Im Sinne der Ebertz'schen These, dass die Pastoral der Zwischenräume, nicht für oder gegen die Gemeindepastoral, sondern *neben* ihr arbeitet, dürfte es auch klüger sein, die herkömmlichen KÖB's nicht mit proliko-Angeboten zu überfrachten. Proliko kann insgesamt als ein sehr konkreter Impuls verstanden werden, mit dem sich die Katholische Büchereiarbeit für eine bestimmte Zielgruppe bereits jetzt in die Konzeption der Pastoral der Zwischenräume einbringen kann. Eine spannende Frage für die Zukunft wird sein, ob es bei diesem einen Impuls bleiben wird, oder ob die Katholische Büchereiarbeit die innere Kraft und die Kreativität besitzen wird, völlig andere Konzeptionen für andere Zielgruppen zu entwickeln.

Für einiges Aufsehen sorgte in Bonn die Schließung der KÖB der zentral gelegenen Münsterpfarrei im Dezember 2000. Da hier geradezu exemplarisch eine Entwicklungslinie katholischer Büchereiarbeit von einem Ortsverein des Borromäusvereins über eine Pfarrbücherei, dann eine zunehmend inhaltlich spezialisierte Katholische öffentliche Bücherei hin zu einem allerdings noch wenig konkreten Ansatz der Buch- und Literaturarbeit innerhalb einer neu zu schaffenden City-Pastoral deutlich wird, lohnt es sich, das Beispiel ein wenig ausführlicher darzustellen:[581]

Bereits 1846, ein Jahr nach der Gründung des Borromäusvereins, gab es in dieser Innenstadtgemeinde einen Ortsverein. Dieser war Keimzelle einer Vereinsbücherei, die kurz nach der Wende zum 20. Jahrhundert auch Nichtmitgliedern offen stand. Die Bücherei erlebte ihre Blütezeit zwischen dem Ersten und dem Zweiten Weltkrieg und erzielte hier pro Jahr zwischen 30.000 und 40.000 Ausleihen bei rund 10.000 Büchern Bestand.[582] Doch auch in der Nachkriegszeit bis in die neunziger Jahre hinein konnte die Bücherei immer noch ihren Platz in der Bonner Bibliotheksszene behaupten, obwohl längst die leistungsfähige Zentralbibliothek der Stadtbücherei in ihre Nähe gerückt war. Ihre 30.000 Ausleihen pro Jahr erzielte sie vor allem mit literarisch anspruchsvollen Leserinnen und Lesern und mit solchen, die – oft über Generationen hinweg zur Benutzerschaft gehörend –

---

579 Das Kunstwort „proliko“ steht für „Projekt literarische Kompetenz“.

580 Zu proliko vergleiche einführend: Patenge, Horst: „ProLiKo“: Abkürzung mit viel Gewicht : Projekt Literarische Kompetenz als neues Weiterbildungskonzept. In: KÖB 13(1999),H.3, S. 2-6. – Ders.: Die Entdeckung der Leselust : fünfzehn Monate Projekt Literarische Kompetenz (ProLiKo). In: KÖB 14(2000), H.4, S. 15-18.

581 ‚Den Menschen nicht nur ins Gesicht schauen' – Citypastoral in Bonn. In: Pressedienst des Erzbistums Köln (PEK) : Berichte und Reportagen / Hrsg. Presseamt des Erzbistums Köln. 23.03.2001, S. 2-3. Ferner: Ein Treffpunkt der Generationen schließt seine Türen : Münster-Bücherei ; älteste Bonner Bücherei weicht der City-Pastoral. In: Bonner Generalanzeiger vom 18.12.2000.

582 Die genannten Daten und Zahlen und Daten wurden anhand der im Borromäusverein aufbewahrten Statistikkarte des Ortsvereins Bonn, Münsterpfarrei, ermittelt.

die persönliche Ansprache und Beratung der hier tätigen Mitarbeiterinnen und Mitarbeiter schätzten.

Äußere Zwänge und eine andere Gewichtung in der Pastoral nach einem Wechsel in der Gemeindeleitung sorgten für das „Aus" der bisherigen Münsterbücherei nach 155 Jahren: „Die bisherige Bücherei wird zu einem Standort der City-Pastoral. Münsterbasilika und Kreuzgang sind ein ‚europäisches Monument'... Wir wollen diese Orte nicht nur als kunsthistorische Objekte oder als ‚Muss' einer Sightseeing-Tour sondern als geistliche Orte verstehen wahrnehmen zu lernen. Das ist unser pastorales Leitziel ... Diese Aufgabe kann durch Präsentationstafeln, geistliche Kunst, ausgewählte Musik, durch ein Literaturangebot, durch Sitzmöglichkeiten erfüllt werden".[583] Anstelle einer KÖB soll also künftig katholischerseits in der Bonner Innenstadt ein eng begrenztes Medienangebot mit anderen Kunstformen vernetzt präsentiert und durch eine personale Kommunikation zur Nutzung vor Ort vermittelt werden.

Schlussbemerkung

Katholische Büchereiarbeit in Deutschland hat in ihrer mehr als 150-jährigen Geschichte viele Wandlungen und Häutungen erfahren. Die Chance besteht, dass sie auch heute die zur Existenzsicherung notwendigen Transformationsprozesse vollzieht. Hierzu müssen die in der Verantwortung Stehenden innovative Prozesse zulassen, fördern und bereit sein, für Modellprojekte auch finanzielle Mittel umzuschichten. Eine angemessene personelle Ausstattung und Leistungsfähigkeit der Fach- und Zentralstellen ist eine notwendige Voraussetzung für die Steuerung und Begleitung solcher Prozesse. Da wo wirtschaftliche Sachzwänge den Ton angeben, sind kaum Impulse für zukunftsträchtige Entwicklungen zu erwarten.

Im Hinblick auf die eingangs gestellte Frage nach der Zukunft des Katholischen öffentlichen Büchereiwesens dürfte deutlich geworden sein, dass diese nur dann gesichert zu sein scheint, wenn für eine längere Umbruchszeit verschiedene Typen und Formen von Büchereien katholischer Provenienz nebeneinander gleichberechtigt existieren. Die herkömmliche KÖB, jenes Erfolgsmodell katholischer Büchereiarbeit der letzten Jahrzehnte auf Gemeindeebene, wird dabei allerdings immer seltener anzutreffen sein.

583 Schumacher, Winfried: Münster-Bücherei : mit neuem Gesicht und Gewand am alten Ort ; Information für die Leserinnen und Leser der Münster-Bücherei. [Faltblatt der Gemeinde St. Martin, Bonn]. Sept. 2000. [4 S.] - Zitat auf S. 3.

Veröffentlichungen von Peter Vodosek

Quellen:
Dokumentationsdienst Bibliothekswesen DOBI : Online-Datenbank / Hrsg.: Ehemaliges Deutsches Bibliotheksinstitut und Die Deutsche Bibliothek, Deutsche Bücherei Leipzig. - Berlin : Ehem. Dt. Bibliotheksinst. 10 (1993) - 17 (2000),3
Berichtszeit 1992/93 -1999/2000
Zugang via WWW, Adresse: http://dbix01.dbi-berlin.de:6100/DBI/login.html
Und verschiedene weitere Bibliothekskataloge

2000

Fortsetzung folgt: Auf dem Weg zu einer Medienhochschule, Teil II. // In: HBI aktuell. - Stuttgart. - 2000,1, S. 6 - 7
Resümiert das Voranschreiten der Fusion der beiden Stuttgarter FHs, für die bereits ein Gesetzentwurf vorliegt, mit dessen Verabschiedung im Sommer 2000 gerechnet wird. Nicht Schritt mit der erhofften Wirkung der bahnbrechenden Gründung hält der geplante Neubau, der nicht zum Sept. 2001, sondern nunmehr 2004 fertiggestellt werden soll. Die vorgesehenen Stellen für die empfohlenen „zeitnahen" Studiengänge werden erst 2004 bis 2006 realisiert, d. h., daß Absolventen frühestens 2008 zur Verfügung stehen. Das ist kein Schritthalten mit dem sich rasant entwickelnden Medienbereich. Mit der Einführung des BA-MA-Modells und neuen Studieninhalten im WS 2000/2001 will die HBI ein wichtiges Innovationspotential in die neue HS einbringen. (tr)

1999

Auf dem Weg zu einer Medienhochschule - Chancen und Risiken. - Ill. // In: HBI aktuell. - Stuttgart. - 1999,1, S. 6 - 12
Das BaW-Ministerium für Wissenschaft, Forschung und Kunst überraschte am 19.01.1999 mit einer Pressemitteilung, nach der es die Zusammenlegung der Stuttgarter FHs zu einer Medien-FH erwäge. Seit 1991 wurden derartige Überlegungen angestellt, aber aufgrund des unlösbaren Problems der gemeinsamen räumlichen Unterbringung immer wieder zurückgestellt. Jetzt wird diese nicht mehr als Voraussetzung angesehen. Die HBI steht hinter dem Vorhaben, wenn es politisch und finanziell abgesichert wird. Im Anschluss an den o.g. Beitrag sind Resolutionen beider FHs unter der Überschrift „Eine bundesweit einzigartige Medien-Fachhochschule" abgedruckt. (tr)

Bibliotheken in der literarischen Darstellung : [Referate des Seminars „Bibliotheken in der Literarischen Darstellung", das vom 10. bis 11. Oktober 1994 in der Herzog-August-Bibliothek Wolfenbüttel stattgefunden hat] / hrsg. von Peter Vodosek und Graham Jefcoate. - Wiesbaden : Harrassowitz, 1999. - 235 S. - (Wolfenbütteler Schriften zur Geschichte des Buchwesens ; 33)
darin: Bibliotheksgeschichte in Deutschland : ein Überblick

„Die Bücherhallenbewegung". // In: Das bewegte Buch : Buchwesen und soziale, nationale und kulturelle Bewegungen um 1900 / [Leipziger Arbeitskreis zur Geschichte des Buchwesens]. Hrsg. von Mark Lehmstedt und Andreas Herzog. - Wiesbaden : Harrassowitz, 1999. - 429 S. - (Veröffentlichungen des Leipziger Arbeitskreises zur Geschichte des Buchwesens : Schriften und Zeugnisse zur Buchgeschichte ; 12)

Geschichte des Bibliothekswesens der DDR : [vom 6. bis 8. Mai 1996] / hrsg. von Peter Vodosek und Konrad Marwinski. - Wiesbaden : Harrassowitz, 1999. - VI, 196 S. - (Vorträge der ... Jahrestagung des Wolfenbütteler Arbeitskreises für Bibliotheksgeschichte ... ; 9) (Wolfenbütteler Schriften zur Geschichte des Buchwesens ; 31)

Hochschullandschaft im Umbruch : neue Studienstrukturen im Fachhochschulereich. - 8 Anm. - 10 Lit. // In: Buch Bibl. - Bad Honnef. - 51 (1999),4, S. 245 - 147
Mit der Novellierung des HRG 1998 erhalten die HSn. die Möglichkeit, Bachelor- und Masterstudiengänge zu erproben. Motive für diese Reform dürften die geringe Akzeptanz deutscher Studienabschlüsse im Ausland, mangelnde internationale Vergleichbarkeit, lange Studienzeiten sein. Modularer Aufbau gepaart mit einem Leistungspunktesystem soll national und international Vergleichbarkeit und gegenseitige Anrechenbarkeit ermöglichen. Die Regelung gilt für HSn. und FHn. gleichermaßen. In BaW sollen bereits zum 01.01.2000 die neuen Hochschulgesetze in Kraft treten; zur ggw. Diskussion im FH-Bereich, Schlussfolgerungen für die HBI Stuttgart. U. a. gibt es unterschiedliche Auffassungen zu der Frage, ob für eine Übergangszeit neben BA-/MA-Studiengängen der Diplomstudiengang beibehalten werden sollte. Gewaltige Schwierigkeiten insbes. im Hinblick auf den öffentlichen Dienst sind bei der Positionierung der neuen Abschlüsse auf dem Arbeitsmarkt zu erwarten. Kontrovers diskutiert wird, ob bereits vor der Änderung des Hochschulsystems Tarif-, Beamten-, Besoldungsrecht sowie weitere rechtliche Grundlagen geändert werden sollten oder nicht zeitlich umgekehrt über den Druck der Absolventen mit den neuen Abschlüssen Gesetzesänderungen bewirkt werden sollten. - Auch wenn sich Diplomstudiengänge vielleicht noch einige Jahre in einer Nische halten können, sollte der Bibliothekssektor doch einmal versuchen, an der Spitze des Fortschritts zu marschieren. (St)

Die internationale Dimension : die HBI Stuttgart und ihre Auslandsbeziehungen. - 9 Anm. // In: Bücher, Menschen und Kulturen : Festschrift für Hans-Peter Geh zum 65. Geburtstag / hrsg. von Birgit Schneider ... Unter Mitarb. von Edith Gruber ... - München : Saur, 1999. - S. 344 - 353
Aktivitäten in folgenden Bereichen werden beschrieben: Mobilität der Hochschullehrer, studentische Mobilität, Partnerschaftsverträge, europäische Mobilitätsprogramme, europäische Forschungs- und Entwicklungsprojekte, Mitgliedschaft in internationalen Organisationen, BOBCATSS. Probleme bestehen in der organisatorischen Betreuung der Auslandsbeziehungen, da sie aufgrund fehlender Stellen dafür verteilt wahrgenommen werden muss. (tr)

Zwischen Philanthropismus und Sedativ: >>Die Bücherhallenbewegung<<. - 33 Anm. // In: Das bewegte Buch : Buchwesen und soziale, nationale und kulturelle Bewegungen um 1900 / [Leipziger Arbeitskreis zur Geschichte des Buchwesens]. Hrsg. von Mark Lehmstedt und Andreas Herzog. - Wiesbaden : Harrassowitz, 1999. - (Veröffentlichungen des Leipziger Arbeitskreises zur Geschichte des Buchwesens : Schriften und Zeugnisse zur Buchgeschichte ; 12). - S. 397 - 407
In den meisten bisherigen Darstellungen zur Bücherhallenwegung sind die bibliotheks-, bildungsgeschichtlichen und erwachsenenpädagogischen Bezüge detailliert herausgearbeitet, vernachlässigt wurde der allgemeinpolitische und sozialgeschichtliche Kontext. Hier

wird versucht, die Wurzeln zu ergründen und die sozialen Entwicklungen, die schließlich deren vielversprechende Anfänge bewirkten, darzustellen. Äußerungen der Begründer der Bücherhallenwegung und des Staates (Erlasse) beweisen, dass die Bücherhallen für sozialpolitische, staatserhaltende und nationale Ziele instrumentalisiert (z. B. Nörrenberg) werden konnten. Gegenstimmen wurden nicht nur aus dem Bereich der Arbeiterbewegung, sondern auch der Kirchen laut. Außerdem wird dargelegt, in welcher Form die Bücherhallenwegung in der Tradition des Philanthropismus der Aufklärung verhaftet ist (Reyer in Wien). (tr)

1998

Dem Andenken Hermann Waßners : *2. Sept. 1922 - [verstorben] 3. Dez. 1997. // In: Buch Bibl. - Bad Honnef. - 50 (1998),2, S. 75
H.W., eine derjenigen Persönlichkeiten, die 1960 - 1985 in vielen Bereichen des ÖB-Wesens der BRD, insbes. im Ausbildungsbereich, einflussreich gewirkt haben. Legte die Grundlagen für die heutige Bedeutung der HBI Stuttgart. Engagement in zahlr. Überregionalen Gremien, von denen hier einige genannt sind. (St)

Bericht über die ALA Annual Conference. // In: Bibliotheksdienst. - Berlin. - 32 (1998),8, S. 1434 - 1439
25.06.-01.07.1998, Washington. Erste ALA-Jahrestagung mit umfassendem internationalen Anspruch. 20 000 Teilnehmer, erst 400 ausländische. 2 300 Veranstaltungen, die wichtigsten werden skizziert. Themenkreis Bb als weltumspannendes Ganzes, Rolle der IuK-Technik dabei. Bibliotheksdienstleistungen für Immigrantengruppen mit unterschiedlichem kulturellen Hintergrund. Veränderungen der Curricula in der BID-Ausbildung, 19-Mrd.-Dollar-Programm 1994-1998 der Kellogg-Foundation „Human Resources Information Systems Management“ kam insbes. Entwicklung neuer Curricula und Fernstudienkursen zugute. Experimentierfreudigkeit der Ausbildungsstätten ist beneidenswerterweise nicht durch Ministerien und Vorschriften behindert. Round Table zum Thema Informationsfreiheit im Kalten Krieg, Auswirkungen des McCarthyismus auf Bb. Rückblick auf bibliotheksfachliche Leistungen der letzten 50 Jahre, vielfach Verdienste P. Kaegbeins hervorgehoben. Vorträge zu Auswirkungen des Konzentrationsprozesses auf dem Medienmarkt auf den freien Ideen- und Meinungsaustausch. - Besucher empfanden Anwesenheit ausländischer Gäste und deren Meinungsäußerungen als ausgesprochen anregend. Wäre zu hoffen, dass die Nachfolgerinnen der letzten ALA-Präsidentin deren neue internationale Linie fortsetzen. (St)

HBI Stuttgart: Kooperation mit „Freunden der Hebräischen Universität Jerusalem“. // In: Buch Bibl. - Bad Honnef. - 50 (1998),8, S. 465
Verein „Freunde der Hebräischen Universität Jerusalem in Baden-Württemberg e. V.“, gegr. 1997. Eines der Aktivitätsschwerpunkte ist ein Mobilitätsprogramm unter Einbeziehung der HBI. Beidseitiges Stipendienprogramm der NB Jerusalem, zugl. UB der Hebräischen Univ., und der HBI zunächst WS 1998/99. Als förderungswürdig anerkannt die Fortsetzung eines mit der Diplomarbeit „ShoaNet“ an der HBI begonnenen Projekts, an dem die Hebräische Univ. und das Jad Vashem Archiv Interesse signalisiert haben. Anregung, der Verein möge Diplomarbeiten finanziell unterstützen, die Vor-Ort-Recherchen erfordern. (St)

„Der Mensch lebt nicht von Information allein" : Kulturmanagement in der bibliothekarischen Ausbildung. - 11 Anm. // In: Bibliotheksmanagement – Kulturmanagement : Vorträge und Berichte / 24. Österreichischer Bibliothekartag, Congreß Innsbruck, 3. - 7.9.1996. Vereinigung Österreichischer Bibliothekarinnen und Bibliothekare. [Red.: Maria Seissl]. - Wien : Vereinigung Österr. Bibliothekarinnen und Bibliothekare, 1998. - (Biblos-Schriften ; 168). - S. 99 - 109
Konzept des Wahlpflichtfaches Kulturmanagement ab Sommersemester 1996 im Rahmen der Studienreform an der HBI Stuttgart.

1997

Das Bibliothekswesen der Weimarer Republik. - Ill. - 14 Lit. // In: Börsenbl. Dtsch. Buchh. - Frankfurt a.M. ; Leipzig. - 164 (1997),76: Buchhandelsgeschichte. - 3, S. B142 - B146
Es werden Entwicklungslinien des Bibliothekswesens in der Weimarer Republik dargestellt. Nach dem Ersten Weltkrieg waren die Errungenschaften und das internat. Ansehen der WBb auf einem ersten Tiefpunkt angelangt, und die Probleme in den 15 Jahren der Weimarer Republik sind überwiegend seine direkten und indirekten Folgen. Auf der Substanz der Vorkriegsjahre konnte aufgebaut werden, die Strukturen blieben erhalten. In der extremen finanziellen Notsituation wurden Institutionen und Steuerungsinstrumente für die WBb in Gang gesetzt, die sich bewährt haben und in neuer Qualität bis heute genutzt werden. Die Lage der ÖBb, die sich seit den 90er Jahren vielversprechend mit meistens nichtkommunalen Trägern entwickelt hatten, gerieten mangels finanzieller Mittel in eine prekäre Lage; sie wurden durch den sog. Richtungsstreit noch zusätzlich belastet. Trotzdem konnten Fortschritte und Errungenschaften der ÖBb, wie sie von den beiden Kontrahenten Hofmann und Ackerknecht ins Leben gerufen worden sind, nicht übersehen werden. Das Bibliothekswesen war dennoch durch externe und interne Faktoren so geschwächt, dass es sich der Nazi-Ideologie nicht zu widersetzten vermochte, die schließlich zum moralischen, intellektuellen und materiellen Niedergang der Bb führte. (tr)

„Der eine wartet, daß die Zeit sich wandelt, der andere packt sie kräftig an und handelt" : Zukunftsperspektiven der HBI. // In: HBI aktuell. - Stuttgart. - 1997,2, S. 4 - 5
Wie für alle HS ist auch für die HBI schwierig, dem „Zeitgeist auf den Fersen zu bleiben". Mit der Studienreform von 1995 hat sie den Rahmen geschaffen, mittelfristig auf fachliche Entwicklungen zu reagieren. Endgültig kann der Erfolg nach zwei Jahren noch nicht beurteilt werden. Entscheidend war, dass an der Differenzierung nach Studiengängen festgehalten worden ist. Seit Anfang 1997 Arbeit an einem Konzept für Fortbildungsaktivitäten der HBI. Vielfach behindern rechtliche Grundlagen eine bedarfsgerechte, kreative Gestaltung von Zusatz- und Aufbaustudiengängen. Die HS fällt seit vielen Jahren mit ihren Forschungs- und Entwicklungsaktivitäten für das Fach auf. Eine starke Bündelung ist erforderlich, noch mehr Außenwirkung muss erzielt werden. (tr)

Ein kompliziertes Verhältnis? : wissenschaftliche und öffentliche Bibliotheken. - Referat gehalten am 22.1.1996, Symposium „Eine Zukunft? Wissenschaftliche und öffentliche Bibliotheken". - 16 Anm. // In: Wissenschaftliche und öffentliche Bibliotheken. CD-ROM und Online. Kinder und Jugendliche / hrsg. von der Einkaufszentrale für Bibliotheken. Red.: Henner Grube u. Angelika Holderried. Mitarb.: Anja Jeandrée ...). - Reutlingen,

1997. - (ekz-konzepte ; 5). - S. 26 - 31
In der ersten Hälfte des 19. Jh. setzten sich Bibliothekare für Zugang jedes wiss. Gebildeten zu den wiss. Büchersammlungen ein. In der zweiten Hälfte waren Persönlichkeiten mit gleichem beruflichen Hintergrund Gründungsväter des öffentlichen Bibliothekswesens. Die Bücherhallenbewegung ist ohne deren Beteiligung nicht vorstellbar. Der Richtungsstreit und das von Walter Hofmann entwickelte Konzept „Autonomie der volkstümlichen Bücherei" führte zu einer den Berufsstand spaltenden Auseinandersetzung zwischen ÖBb und WBb. Mit der Preußischen Bibliotheks-Prüfungsordnung vom 24.09.1930 wurde getrennte Ausbildung der Diplom-Bibliothekare durchgesetzt. Das Verschwinden wiss. StBb nach 1964 und Fusion mit ÖBb führte teilweise zu heftigen Auseinandersetzungen. Über die Bedeutung der Tutzinger Erklärung, des Bibliotheksplans von 1969 und 1973. Es besteht begründete Hoffnung, dass ÖBb und WBb aufeinander zugehen. (F.K.)

1996

Behrends, Elke: **Technisch-wissenschaftliche Dokumentation in Deutschland von 1900 bis 1945 : unter besonderer Berücksichtigung des Verhältnisses von Bibliothek und Dokumentation** / mit einem Geleitw. von Peter Vodosek. - Wiesbaden : Harrassowitz, 1996. - VIII, 336 S. - (Buchwissenschaftliche Beiträge aus dem Deutschen Bucharchiv München ; 51). - Zugl.: Berlin, Freie Univ., Diss., 1994

EUCLID: Veranstaltungen in Kopenhagen. // In: Bibliotheksdienst. - Berlin. - 30 (1996),1, S. 121 - 124
6. Board Meeting, 20.11.1995 und Mitgliederversammlung. Einzelheiten aus Bericht des Vorsitzenden. EUCLID hat 44 Mitglieder aus 21 Ländern, zwei assoziierte, fünf korrespondierende Mitglieder. Europaweite Übersicht über Zulassungsvoraussetzungen für BID-Studiengänge erstellt. Mitarbeit an EU-Projekt, in dessen Rahmen Erhebung gegenwärtigen Angebots und Bedarfs an Fortbildung vorgenommen wird. Homepage für Internet geplant. Ergebnisse der Vorstandswahlen. - Internationale Tagung „Improved Practice and Integrated Skills in the LIS-Field". Analysierte Erfordernisse zeitgemäßer Ausbildung von Informationsfachkräften. Ziele: traditionelle Ausbildungen in forschungs- und entwicklungsorientierte Studiengänge umzuwandeln; Informationstechnik in Curricula zu integrieren; Integration von Theorien, Methoden, Erfahrungen aus verwandten Feldern zu fördern; Konzept für „multifunktionale Informationsarbeit" zu entwickeln, Paradigmenwechsel hin zu aktiverer Haltung in der Informationsvermittlung vorzuschlagen. (St)

„Liebesgrüße aus Moskau" : Peter Vodosek und Wolfram Henning besuchten Rußland. - Ill. // In: HBI aktuell. - Stuttgart. - 1996,1, S. 24 - 25

1995

„Anfänge" - Beziehungen zwischen Stuttgart und Leipzig in den letzten 50 Jahren. - 15 Anm. // In: Bibliothekarisches Studium in Vergangenheit und Gegenwart : Festschrift aus Anlaß des 80jährigen Bestehens der bibliothekarischen Ausbildung in Leipzig im Oktober 1994 / hrsg. von Engelbert Plassmann und Dietmar Kummer. - Frankfurt a. M. : Klostermann, 1995.

- (Zeitschrift für Bibliothekswesen und Bibliographie : Sonderh. ; 62). - S. 151 - 158
Über die Verbindung der „Mutter" Büchereischule Leipzig zur „Tochter" Büchereischule Stuttgart seit ihrer Gründung am 01.10.1942. Leiterin wurde Luise Kolb, die in Leipzig einen Ergänzungslehrgang absolviert hatte. Nach Stillegung der Büchereischule Stuttgart November 1944 ging sie an die Büchereischule Leipzig. 1946 wurde sie wiederum Leiterin in Stuttgart und beendete auf Betreiben Erwin Ackerknechts 1960 ihre Arbeit in der Schule. 1970 kaufte das damalige Süddeutsche Bibliothekar-Lehrinstitut den Nachlass Walter Hofmanns von dessen Sohn Hans Eberhard Hofmann, der lange Jahre Leiter einer Zweigstelle der StB Stuttgart war. Seit 1983 nahm die FH Bibl. Stuttgart Kontakte zur FS für Bibliothekare „Erich Weinert" in Leipzig durch Studienfahrten wieder auf. Mai 1990 besuchten 25 Fachschüler und Dozenten der Leipziger FS für Bibliothekare und Buchhändler Stuttgart. Juni 1991 lieferte FH Bibl. das juristische Hintergrundmaterial für Übergangsphase vom Fachschul- zum Fachhochschulstatus in Leipzig. Es besteht ein Klima kollegialer Sympathie, das zu vielfältigen informellen Kontakten geführt hat. (F.K.)

EUCLID: 5. Boardmeeting in Bratislava. // In: Bibliotheksdienst. - Berlin. - 29 (1995),1, S. 90 - 91
18./19.11.1994. - Bericht des Vorsitzenden und folg. Beratungsthemen: red. Fertigstellung des EUCLID-Directory, das weit detailliertere Informationen über Mitgliedshochschulen bieten wird als andere Nachschlagewerke; Erarbeitung eines Prospektes über EUCLID; Entwicklung gemeinsamen „Statements of goals and objectivs of LIS-education" incl. „Guidelines to professionals ethics" für Lehrpersonal an HSn. des BID-Bereiches. (St)

„Die öffentliche Bibliothek ist die nothwendige Ergänzung der öffentlichen Schule" : die Freie Bibliothek & Lesehalle in Frankfurt am Main, die Bücherhallenbewegung und die Volksbildung am Ende des 19. Jahrhunderts. - Ill. - 20 Lit. // In: Buch Bibl. - Bad Honnef. - 47 (1995),2, S. 143 - 149
Festvortrag anlässlich des 150-jährigen Bestehens der StB Frankfurt am Main, da hier 1845 die erste VolksB gegründet wurde. Der Vortrag bezieht sich auf die am 23.09.1894 als selbständiger Verein errichtete Freie Bibliothek & Lesehalle. Mit vielen Zitaten werden der Stand der Volksbildung beschrieben sowie die Entstehung der Bücherhallenbewegung mit ihren Zielen (Zurückdrängung der Sozialdemokratie, Ausbau der Wirtschaft mit Hilfe einer Verbesserung der Volksbildung). Oft wird Constantin Nörrenberg zitiert, der die ÖB als einzig sicheren Weg sah, dem Arbeiter Lektüre zu bieten, die nicht sozialdemokratisch ist. Bezüge zur Comenius-Gesellschaft als zweitem großen Bildungsverein, der die Bücherhallenbewegung mittrug und zu seinem Anteil an Neugründungen in Frankfurt werden hergestellt, damalige Grundsätze für die Begründung freier öffentlicher Bb dargestellt. (Po)

Stand und Perspektiven der Fachhochschulen. - Tab. - 4 Anm. // In: Die Krise zum Umdenken nutzen - Zukunftsperspektiven öffentlicher Bibliotheken : ein Symposium der Bertelsmann-Stiftung, 18. - 19. Mai 1994 / Elmar Mittler ; Bettina Windau (Hrsg.). - Gütersloh : Verl. Bertelsmann-Stiftung, 1995. - S. 75 - 85

Stuttgarter Hochschule unter neuem Namen. // In: HBI aktuell. - Stuttgart. - 1995,1, S. 1 - Zur Umbenennung von Fachhochschule für Bibliothekswesen Stuttgart in Fachhochschule Stuttgart - Hochschule für Bibliotheks- und Informationswesen, Abk. HBI.

Zur Geschichte der Öffentlichen Bibliotheken in Österreich : [die Beiträge des Sam-

melbandes gehen größtenteils auf Vorträge beim Symposium „Geschichte des Öffentlichen Bibliothekswesens in Österreich“ zurück, das vom 12. bis 14. September 1994 im Bundesinstitut für Erwachsenenbildung, Strobl, stattfand] / hrsg. von Alfred Pfoser und Peter Vodosek. - Wien : WUV-Univ.-Verl., 1995. - 216 S. - (BVÖ-Materialien ; 2)
darin: Zur Geschichte des Öffentlichen Bibliothekswesens : ein Forschungsbericht (Schwerpunkt Deutschland)

Zur Geschichte der Öffentlichen Bibliotheken in Österreich /
hrsg. von Alfred Pfoser und Peter Vodosek
BVÖ-Materielien : Wien, Büchereiverband Österreichs, 1995 ISBN 3-901639-01-2

1994

Deutsche und osteuropäische Ausbildungsstätten : eine Chance zur Kooperation. – 3 Lit. // In: Z. Bibl.wes. Bibliogr. - Frankfurt a. M. - 41 (1994),1, S. 107 - 112
188 HSn. der Bundesrepublik unterhalten in 23 mittel- und osteuropäischen Staaten Kooperationsbeziehungen mit 405 HSn. und 65 außeruniversitären Forschungsinstituten, davon drei FH Bibl. Kooperationswünsche, -möglichkeiten und -realitäten der deutschen FH Bibl. mit osteuropäischen HSn. und Univ. Auf Grund der bedrückenden Defizite ist eine Hilfestellung von Seiten der deutschen bibliothekarischen und dokumentarischen Ausbildungsstätten von ganz besonderer Bedeutung. Man sollte wenigstens Lehrmaterialien austauschen oder sie schlichtweg unilateral zur Verfügung stellen. Einige Beispiele für bisherige Aktivitäten: FH Hamburg/FB B und Information führte Gedankenaustausch mit Gästen aus Osteuropa; FH Hannover/FB BID Kooperation mit Univ. Budapest und Warschau; FH für Bibliotheks- und Dokumentationswesen Köln Kontakte zu Univ. Breslau und Prag und HS für Kultur in Minsk; FH Bibl. Stuttgart Partnerschaft mit Pädagogischer HS Szombathely/Lehrstuhl für Bibliothekswissenschaft, intensive Beziehungen zu Rußland, Bibliotheksschulen in Ungarn, Slowakei und Ukraine erhielten Dubletten aus HSB. (F.K.)

FHB Stuttgart : Kontinuität und Wandel. // In: Buch Bibl. - Bad Honnef. - 46 (1994),3, S. 211 - 212
Kurzer Jahresbericht für 1993. Vorhaben einer grundlegenden Studienreform werden zu einem Modell für die Ausbildung in verschiedenen Informationsberufen weitergestaltet, zur Erweiterung des Fächerspektrums zunächst Ausbau in Richtung Medizinische, Wirtschafts- und Medieninformation. Weiterhin ungelöste und neue Probleme bei der Frage der Unterbringung. Reform des Studienganges Wissenschaftliche Bb erst im Herbst 1994. FH Bibl. ist gesuchter Ansprechpartner für Länder, die vor der Neustrukturierung vergleichbarer Studiengänge stehen. (Po)

FHB Stuttgart : „Unwirtschaftlich, veraltet und am Bedarf vorbei“? : zur Denkschrift '94 des Landesrechnungshofes. - 3 Lit. // In: Buch Bibl. - Bad Honnef. - 46 (1994),12, S. 993 - 996
Der Rechnungshof beschäftigte sich in zwei Abschnitten mit der FH Bibl., Kritik wurde in der Presse hochgespielt. Drei Punkte wurden herausgegriffen, rückläufige Bewerberzahlen, Verwaltungsaufwand, Fusion mit anderen FHn. In Auseinandersetzung mit der Kritik wird begründet, dass zurückgehende Bewerber nichts mit nicht mehr zeitgemäßen Ausbildungsinhalten zu tun haben, dass es eigentlich zu begrüßen ist, keine Überlastquote mehr zu fahren. Alle sechs Jahre wurde der Studiengang ÖBb reformiert, für die neue

Reform fehlen rechtliche Änderungen. Ein hoher Verwaltungsaufwand entsteht durch die untragbare Unterbringung in zwei weit voneinander entfernten Gebäuden. Die weitere Polemik richtet sich auf die Forderung, die Ausbildung zum Diplom-Bibliothekar für den Bereich der WBb auf ein verwaltungsexternes Fachhochschulstudium umzustellen und statt fünfzig jahrgangsweise nur acht bis zwölf Studienanfänger aufzunehmen. (Po)

„... in freiester Weise zugänglich?“ : Stadt und Bibliothek - Literaturversorgung als kommunale Aufgabe im Kaiserreich und in der Weimarer Republik. - 1 Lit. // In: Buch Bibl. - Bad Honnef. - 46 (1994),8, S. 675 - 676
Thema der 8. Jahrestagung des Wolfenbütteler AK für Bibliotheksgeschichte, 02.-04.05.1994 in der HAugB. Am Anfang der neueren Geschichte des städtischen Bibliothekswesens stehen die privaten Initiativen des liberalen Bürgertums, die von Vereinen gegründeten und die von Stiftern und Mäzenen geförderten wissenschaftlichen und volkstümlichen Bb, die später von Städten übernommen wurden - eine große Tradition der Kommunen, die gegenwärtig nicht leichtfertig aufs Spiel gesetzt werden sollte. Der erste Teil der Tagung gab einen Überblick über Bb in Städten unterschiedlichen Typs (z. B. Leipzig, Frankfurt am Main, Lübeck, Berlin-Charlottenburg), der zweite Teil befasste sich mit Bauten für StBb im Kaiserreich. (Po)

Neuorientierung: die Fachhochschule für Bibliothekswesen Stuttgart reformiert ihre Studiengänge. // In: Bibliotheksdienst. - Berlin. - 28 (1994),9, S. 1401 - 1405

Die Wiedervereinigung Deutschlands : Probleme und Konsequenzen für Bibliothekswesen und bibliothekarische Ausbildung. - Lit. // In: Libri. - Copenhagen. - 44 (1994),1, S. 1 - 13
Kritische Bestandsaufnahme des Bibliothekswesens der ehemaligen DDR sowie Darstellung und Würdigung der offiziellen Kontakte und Planungen, die das Zusammenwachsen der beiden Bibliothekssysteme zum Zweck haben. Weiterer Themenschwerpunkt ist die Bibliothekarausbildung in beiden Teilstaaten und die Lage der BLI in Leipzig, Berlin, Potsdam und Sondershausen nach der staatlichen Einigung. (Jo)

Zum Stand der bibliotheksgeschichtlichen Forschung. - 13 Anm. // In: Gutenberg-Jahrb. - Mainz. - 69 (1994), S. 307 - 310
Zum unbefriedigenden Stand der Theoriediskussion um den Inhalt der Bibliothekswissenschaft. Die bibliotheksgeschichtliche Forschung ist der Teil der postulierten, ansonsten vagen Bibliothekswissenschaft, deren Prägung durch diese aber obsolet ist. Als bibliothekshistorische Forschung wird die historische Untersuchung aller Phänomene verstanden, die mit Bb in Verbindung stehen. Die Instrumentarien und institutionelle Anbindung. Die Übersicht über die Leistungen ergab in den letzten beiden Jahrzehnten Zunahme der veröffentlichten Untersuchungen. Aufgabe der nächsten Jahre wird es vor allem sein, die deutsche Bibliotheksgeschichte nach 1945 neu zu schreiben. (tr)

1993

Ausbildung im europäischen Rahmen : neuere Entwicklungen und Tendenzen. - 9 Anm. // In: Z. Bibl.wes. Bibliogr. - Frankfurt a. M. - 1993, Sonderh. 55. - S. 57 - 69
Überblick über europäische Kontakte bibliothekarischer Ausbildungsstätten. Stellungnahme zum Abschnitt „Strukturierung und Implementierung von europäischen Aspekten in die Lehre“ aus dem Abschlußbericht der BDB-Arbeitsgruppe „Ausbildung im europäi-

schen Rahmen“. Zur 1991 von Ausbildungseinrichtungen aus 14 europäischen Ländern in Stuttgart gegr. EUCLID. Dokumente und Fakten zur europäischen Dimension im Bildungswesen. (tr)

Bibliothek - Kultur - Information : Beiträge eines internationalen Kongresses anläßlich des 50jährigen Bestehens der Fachhochschule für Bibliothekswesen Stuttgart vom 20. bis 22. Oktober 1992 / hrsg. von Peter Vodosek in Zusammenarbeit mit Askan Blum ... - München [u. a.] : Saur, 1993. - 362 S. : graph. Darst. - (Beiträge zur Bibliothekstheorie und Bibliotheksgeschichte ; 8). - Literaturangaben / [rezensiert von]: Gudrun Laubach. // In: Buch Bibl. - Bad Honnef. - 46 (1994),1, S. 98 u. 100

Bibliothekshistorische Projekte : ein Seminar in Wolfenbüttel. - 4 Lit. // In: Buch Bibl. - Bad Honnef. - 45 (1993), S. 60 - 61
Alljährlich seit 1975 wird ein Bibliothekshistorisches Seminar an der HAugB veranstaltet, die Tagung vom 09.-11.11.1992 umfasste sechs große Themenblöcke mit 24 Beiträgen, um abgeschlossene bibliotheks- und buchhistorische Projekte vorzustellen und bekannt zu machen sowie künftige Projekte und die Vergabe von wissenschaftlichen Arbeiten und ihre Realisierungsmöglichkeiten in Form von Projekten zu diskutieren. Über verschiedene bereits abgeschlossene oder am Anfang stehende Projekte und über die Planung des Wolfenbütteler Arbeitskreises für Bibliotheksgeschichte wird berichtet. (Po)

Chronik der Fachhochschule für Bibliothekswesen Stuttgart. - Anm. // In: Bibliothek - Kultur - Information : Beiträge eines internationalen Kongresses anläßlich des 50jährigen Bestehens der Fachhochschule für Bibliothekswesen Stuttgart vom 20. bis 22. Oktober 1992 / hrsg. von Peter Vodosek in Zusammenarbeit mit Askan Blum ... - München [u. a.] : Saur, 1993. - S. 309 - 360

Drittes Board-Meeting von EUCLID in Sheffield. - 1 Anm. // In: Bibliotheksdienst. - Berlin. - 27 (1993),7, S. 1036 - 1038
07./08.04.1993. - Ständig wachsende Mitgliederzahl, aus Deutschland sind allerdings erst die FHB Stuttgart und Hamburg beigetreten. Behandelte Themen: Weiterarbeit am Handbuch der EUCLID-Mitglieder, das ein- bis zweiseitige Profile der Mitgliedshochschulen bieten soll. Vorbereitung der ersten Mitgliederversammlung und Fachtagung in Barcelona. (St)

Die Entwicklung des Bibliothekswesens in Deutschland 1945-1965 : [Vorträge der 6. Jahrestagung des Wolfenbütteler Arbeitskreises für Bibliotheksgeschichte vom 2. bis 4. April 1990 in der Herzog August Bibliothek] / hrsg. von Peter Vodosek und Joachim-Felix Leonhard. - Wiesbaden : Harrassowitz, 1993. - 500 S. - (Wolfenbütteler Schriften zur Geschichte des Buchwesens ; 19) / [rezensiert von]: Hartwig Lohse. // In: Mittbl. Verb. Bibl. Landes Nordrh.-Westfal. - Bad Honnef. - 44 (1994),3, S. 355 - 361 / [rezensiert von]: Dieter Schmidmaier. - 2 Lit. // In: Buch Bibl. - Bad Honnef. - 46 (1994),9, S. 826 - 827

Erste EUCLID Council and General Conference in Barcelona. - 1 Lit. // In: Bibliotheksdienst. - Berlin. - 27 (1993),10, S. 1565 - 1568
21.-22.08.1993, Barcelona. - Mitgliederversammlung erörterte u. a. folg. anstehende Aufgaben: „Education for Information“ als mögliche offizielle EUCLID-Plattform; Prüfen der Möglichkeit des Sponsoring von HSn. in ost- und südosteuropäischen durch Ausbildungsstätte in bessergestellten Ländern; Fertigstellung des Handbuches der Mitgliedshochschulen; mittelfristig Entwicklung von Kriterien für die Evaluierung von BID-Studiengängen der Mitgliedshochschulen. Überblick über Referate zu den Fachkongress-Themen:

FuE-Situation, FuE-Projekte sind für in vielen Ländern eingeführte Hochschul-Evaluation von eminenter Bedeutung; nationale und regionale Kooperationsmodelle zwischen Lehr- und Forschungseinrichtungen im BID-Bereich; TEMPUS-Programm der EG, Erfahrungen und Ergebnisse. (St)

„International Interdependence and Information Education“ : Jahrestagung der Association of Library and Information Science Education ; (ALISE). // In: Bibliotheksdienst. - Berlin. - 27 (1993),4, S. 502 - 504
19.-22.01.1993, Denver, 200 Teilnehmer. ALISE, ein Zusammenschluss aller amerikanischen und kanadischen HSn. mit Studiengängen im BID-Bereich. Hauptsächlich Bericht von Beobachtungen von Relevanz bezüglich Kontaktpflege zwischen amerikanischen/kanadischen und deutschen HSn. Mangelhafter Informationsstand über die Entwicklung innerhalb der EG. Interesse der USA an Internationalisierung bezieht sich fast ausschließlich auf Südamerika, bestenfalls noch auf Länder der Dritten Welt, allerdings war in Kongressgesprächen die Neigung zu erkennen, stärkere Kontakte in Richtung Europa und insbesondere Deutschland zu knüpfen. Auf „Research“ wird im BID-Bereich großes Gewicht gelegt; jedoch zeigte sich, dass der Begriff weiter definiert ist als „Forschung“, beispielsweise von deutschen FHSn. geleistete Projektarbeit bereits als „Research“ gelten würde - eine Erkenntnis, die Vorurteile ggü. der Ausbildungsqualität in Deutschland abbauen helfen kann. Das Bestreben größtmöglicher Integration praktischer und theoretischer Ausbildung an deutschen FHSn. traf insbesondere deshalb auf großes Interesse, weil in den USA zu großes Gewicht auf höhere Abschlüsse gelegt, die praxisnahe Undergraduate-Ausbildung vernachlässigt wurde. Befremden ggü. der universitären Situation in Deutschland, den nur rudimentär vorhandenen Möglichkeiten des Studiums von Bibliotheks- und Informationswissenschaft, die von Universitäten getrennt verlaufende Ausbildung des höheren Dienstes. (St)

Neuorientierung : Auftrag und Arbeit des Senatsausschusses „Studienreform“. // In: FHB aktuell. - Stuttgart. - 1993,2, S. 1 - 2
Zur längerfristigen Planung und Vorbereitung einer Studienreform an der FHB Stuttgart wurde am 10.02.93 vom Senat ein Ausschuss Studienreform gebildet. Er soll neue Ansätze für alle Studiengänge finden, orientiert am aktuellen Stand des Fachwissens, national und international, an den Anforderungen der Berufspraxis und des Arbeitsmarktes, an den hochschulpolitischen Rahmenbedingungen und den Ressourcen der FHB. Dabei sollen verschiedene Modelle diskutiert werden. (tr)

Öffentliche Bibliotheken 1945 - 1965. - 6 Anm. // In: Die Entwicklung des Bibliothekswesens in Deutschland 1945-1965 / hrsg. von Peter Vodosek und Joachim-Felix Leonhard. - Wiesbaden : Harrassowitz, 1993. - S. 425 - 428

Von der Büchereischule zur Fachhochschule : ein historischer Überblick. - Ill. . - (50 Jahre FHB Stuttgart). // In: Buch Bibl. - Bad Honnef. - 45 (1993), S. 112 - 116, 118 - 119
Die FH Bibl. Stuttgart hat sich, was Lehrkapazität und Ausstattung betrifft, zur größten deutschen HS für das Berufsfeld BID entwickelt, Oktober 1992 50jähriges Bestehen. Der Überblick schildert die einzelnen Etappen: 1942 - 1944 „Büchereischule Stuttgart – Fachschule für Volks- und verwandte Büchereien“ (Ausbildung 2 Jahre), 1946 „Süddeutsche Büchereischule“ (auf 3 Jahre erweiterte Ausbildung), 1965 „Süddeutsches Bibliothekar-Lehrinstitut“ mit dem Status einer Höheren Fachschule (ab 1968 6 Semester theoretisches

Studium, Ausbildungskonzeption „Stuttgarter Modell"), 1971 in den Fachhochschul-Bereich übergeleitet. Seit Gründung nur für Studium künftiger Bibliothekare für den Dienst an ÖBb zuständig, 1984 Angliederung des Fachbereichs „Wissenschaftliche Bibliotheken", 1988 Studiengang „Dokumentation" und Reform des Musikbibliothekarischen Zusatzstudiums, 1992/93 mit Hilfe der FH in Leipzig Studiengänge mit Fachhochschulcharakter etabliert, weitere Kontakte zu verwandten Ausbildungseinrichtungen verschiedener europäischer Länder genannt. (Po)

1992

Ausbildung im europäischen Rahmen. - 5 Anm. // In: Neue Techniken im Informationswesen - neue Trends in der Ausbildung : Beiträge zur Jubiläumsveranstaltung „10 Jahre Fachhochschule für Bibliotheks- und Dokumentationswesen in Köln". - Köln : Greven, 1992. - S. 183 - 191

Bundesvereinigung Deutscher Bibliotheksverbände / Arbeitsgruppe Ausbildung im Europäischen Rahmen: Abschlußbericht / Bundesvereinigung Deutscher Bibliotheksverbände (BDB), Arbeitsgruppe Ausbildung im Europäischen Rahmen / Bundesvereinigung Deutscher Bibliotheksverbände (BDB), Arbeitsgruppe Ausbildung im Europäischen Rahmen. Red.: Peter Vodosek. Berlin: Dt. Bibliotheksinst., 1992. - 41 S. Literaturverz. S. 38 - 41. - ISBN 3-87068-417-8

Bibliotheken während des Nationalsozialismus / hrsg. von Peter Vodosek und Manfred Komorowski. - Wiesbaden : Harrassowitz

Vorträge eines Bibliothekshistorischen Seminars des Wolfenbütteler Arbeitskreises für Bibliotheksgeschichte vom 25. bis 27. September 1989 in der Herzog-August-Bibliothek. - 1992. - 300 S. - (Wolfenbütteler Schriften zur Geschichte des Buchwesens ; 16)

Board-Sitzung von EUCLID in Bozen. - 1 Anm. // In: Bibliotheksdienst. - Berlin. - 26 (1992), S. 1703 - 1704
04.-06.09.1992. Vorstand plante nächsten Newsletter. Weiterarbeit an Informationsblättern über die einzelnen (53) MitgliedsBb, geplant als Loseblattsammlung. Vorbereitung der 1. Generalkonferenz 1993. (fv)

1990

Geschichte der Öffentlichen Bücherei in Deutschland / Wolfgang Thauer und Peter Vodosek. - 2., erw. Aufl. - Wiesbaden : Harrassowitz, 1990. - 216 S. / [rezensiert von]: Manschatz, Hans-Christian. // In: Leipziger Jahrb. Buchgesch. - Leipzig. - 3 (1993), S. 389 - 392

Buch und Bibliothekswissenschaft im Informationszeitalter : internationale Festschrift für Paul Kaegbein zum 65. Geburtstag / herausgegeben von Engelbert Plassmann, Wolfgang Schmitz, Peter Vodosek
Beteiligt: Paul Kaegbein ; Engelbert Plassmann ; Wolfgang Schmitz *1949-* ; Peter Vodosek. Erschienen: München ; New York : K.G. Saur, 1990. Umfang: 485 p. : ill. ; 25 cm. Anmerkung: Contributions in German and English with summaries in English and German. „Bibliographie Paul Kaegbein 1948-1989": p. 425-463. Includes bibliographical

references. ISBN: 3-598-10915-6, Schlagwörter: *Library science ; Libraries / History ; Bibliography / Methodology ; Books / History

Quellen zur Geschichte der Volksbibliotheken in Württemberg und Hohenzollern 1806 1918. Ein Sachthematisches Inventar. Bearbeitet von Ulrich Hohoff mit einem Beitrag von Peter Vodosek / Hrsg. von der Landesarchivdirektion Baden-Württemberg Band 40 Stuttgart : Kohlhammer, 1990. - 357 S. : Ill.

Das Buch in Praxis und Wissenschaft: 40 Jahre Deutsches Bucharchiv München ; eine Festschrift / hrsg. von Peter Vodosek. Wiesbaden : Harrassowitz, 1989. - VIII, 850 S. : Ill., graph. Darst.. (Buchwissenschaftliche Beiträge aus dem Deutschen Bucharchiv München ; 25). Literaturangaben. - ISBN 3-447-02901-3

Volksbibliotheken in der Spätaufklärung / Peter Vodosek 1988
Mit Ippesheim, Rappershausen u. Eichfeld; Hinw. Oberbayern.. - In: Bibliotheken und Aufklärung / hrsg. von Werner Arnold ... . - Wiesbaden. - S. 135 - 175. - (Wolfenbütteler Arbeitskreis für Bibliotheksgeschichte: Vorträge des ...Jahrestreffens des Wolfenbütteler Arbeitskreises für Bibliotheksgeschichte ; 4). - (Wolfenbütteler Schriften zur Geschichte des Buchwesens ; 14)

Peter Rosegger – Anmerkungen zur Rezeptionsgeschichte aus bibliothekshistorischer Sicht / hrsg. von Peter Vodosek
(Sonderdr. aus „Fremd gemacht“? Der Volksschriftsteller Peter Rosegger; Herausgegeben von Uwe Baur, Gerald Schöpfer und Gerhard Pail) : Böhlau Verlag Wien : Köln . Graz, 1988

Hinweise zur Vorbereitung und Durchführung von Fortbildungsveranstaltungen / hrsg. von d. Fortbildungskomm. d. Dt. Bibliotheksinst. Red.: Peter Vodosek. Berlin, 1987. - 48 S. : graph. Darst. (Arbeitshilfen zur Fortbildung. ; 2.) ISBN 3-87068-362-7

Wolfenbütteler Arbeitskreis für Bibliotheksgeschichte. Jahrestreffen (3rd : 1984 : Herzog August Bibliothek)

Staatliche Initiative und Bibliotheksentwicklung seit der Aufklärung / herausgegeben von Paul Kaegbein und Peter Vodosek. Wiesbaden : Harrassowitz, c1985. x, 238 p. : ill. ; 24 cm.

Das Studium an der Fachhochschule für Bibliothekswesen Stuttgart
Informationsbroschüre / [Red.: Peter Vodosek]. - Stand: 1. 1. 1985. Stuttgart, 1985. - 24 S. : Kt.

Auf dem Weg zur öffentlichen Literaturversorgung: Quellen u. Texte zur Geschichte d. Volksbibliotheken in d. 2. Hälfte d. 19. Jh. / hrsg. u. kommentiert von Peter Vodosek. Wiesbaden : Harrassowitz, 1985. - 219 S. (Buchwissenschaftliche Beiträge aus dem Deutschen Bucharchiv München ; 14) ISBN 3-447-02534-4

Der Diplom-Bibliothekar für den Dienst an Öffentlichen Bibliotheken: Informationsbroschüre über das Studium bei der Fachhochschule für Bibliothekswesen Stuttgart / Vodosek, Peter u.a. [Hrsg.]. Beteiligt: Peter Vodosek. Körperschaft: Fachhochschule für Bibliothekswesen Stuttgart / Fachbereich Bibliothekswissenschaft. Erschienen: Stuttgart : Fachhochschule f. Bibliothekswesen, 1982. Umfang: 16 S.

Bibliothekswissenschaft, Musikbibliothek, soziale Bibliotheksarbeit : Hermann Waßner zum 60 Geb. / hrsg von Peter Vodosek ... Wiesbaden : Harrossowitz, 1982. - 391 S. : Ill. ISBN 3-447-02258-2

Bibliothekswissenschaft, Musikbibliothek, soziale Bibliotheksarbeit: Hermann Waßner zum 60. Geburtstag / hrsg. von Peter Vodosek*. Wiesbaden : Harrassowitz, 1982. - 391 S. : Portr.

Andeutungen über Bibliotheken als Fördermittel des Gewerbefleißes und allgemeiner Volksbildung – Karl Benjamin Preusker
(Sonderdr. aus Wolfenbütteler Schriften zur Geschichte des Buchwesens; Band 8 : Hamburg, Ernst Hauswedell & CO. , 1982)

Bibliotheken im gesellschaftlichen und kulturellen Wandel des 19. Jahrhunderts / Referate des 1. Jahrestreffens des Wolfenbütteler Arbeitskreises für Bibliotheksgeschichte vom 24. Bis 26. April 1980 in der Herzog August Bibliothek) : Hamburg, Ernst Hauswedell & CO. , 1982 hrsg. von Gerhard Liebers und Peter Vodosek

Zur Entwicklung des bibliothekarischen Berufs als Frauenberuf Beteiligt: Peter Vodosek. In: Bibliothek : Forschung und Praxis. - München : Verl. Dokumentation, ISSN 0341-4183, Bd. 5 (1981), Nr 3, S. 231-244

Bibliotheksgeschichte als wissenschaftliche Disziplin: Beitr. zur Theorie u. Praxis ; Referate d. 7. Fortbildungsseminars für Bibliothekare, vom 23.-25. Jan. 1979 in d. Herzog-August-Bibliothek Wolfenbüttel / hrsg. von Peter Vodosek. Hamburg : Hauswedell, 1980. - 169 S. (Wolfenbütteler Schriften zur Geschichte des Buchwesens ; 7.) ISBN 3-7762-0204-1

Bibliotheksgeschichte im angloamerikanischen Bereich / hrsg. Peter Vodosek
(Sonderdr. aus Wolfenbütteler Schriften zur Geschichte des Buchwesens; Band 7, 1980; In Zusammenarbeit mit dem Wolfenbütteler Arbeitskreis für Bibliotheksgeschichte herausgegeben von Paul Raabe) : Hamburg: Ernst Hauswedell & CO.

Öffentliche Bibliotheken und kommerzielle Leihbibliotheken. Zur Geschichte ihres Verhältnisses vom Ende des 18. Jahrhunderts bis zur Gegenwart von Peter Vodosek
In: Die Leihbibliothek als Institution des literarischen Lebens im 18. Und 19. Jahrhundert Organisationsformen, Bestände und Publikum. Arbeitsgespräch in der Herzog August Bibliothek Wolfenbüttel 30. September bis 1. Oktober 1977 / hrsg. von Georg Jäger und Jörg Schönert : Hamburg, Ernst Hauswedell & Co. , 1980

Vorformen der öffentlichen Bibliothek / zsgest. u. eingel. von Peter Vodosek. - 1. Aufl., Wiesbaden : Harrassowitz, 1978. - 149 S. (Beiträge zum Büchereiwesen : Reihe B ; 6) ISBN 3-447-01908-5

Thauer, Wolfgang: Geschichte der Öffentlichen Bücherei in Deutschland / Wolfgang Thauer ; Peter Vodosek. - 1. Aufl. Wiesbaden : Harrassowitz, 1978. - 163 S. ISBN 3-447-01947-6

Stoffpläne zu den bibliothekswissenschaftlichen Fächern des Pflichtstudiums / im Auftr. d. Fachbereichs für Bibliothekswissenschaft zsgest. von Peter Vodosek. Fachhochschule für Bibliothekswesen Stuttgart : Berlin : Dt. Bibliotheksverb., 1977. - 100 S. (Schriftenreihe der Bibliothekar-Lehrinstitute : Reihe C ; 3) ISBN 3-87068-643-x

Die sozialethische Motivationen bei Eduard Reyer. – Ein Beitrag zu den Erklärungsmodellen der Bücherhallenbewegung / hrsg. Peter Vodosek
(Bibliothekarische Arbeit zwischen Theorie und Praxis – Beiträge zum bibliothekarischen Fachwissen und Berichte über Bibliothekarische Aktivitäten / herausgegeben von der Fachhochschule für Bibliothekswesen Stuttgart : Stuttgart, 1976

Eduard Reyer : 1849 – 1914, Berlin : Dt. Bibliotheksverb., 1976. - 78 S. : 1 Portr. (Biobibliographien. ; 5.). ISBN 3-87068-384-8

Arbeiterbibliothek und Öffentliche Bibliothek: zur Geschichte ihrer Beziehungen von d. ersten Hälfte d.19. Jh. bis 1933. Berlin : Dt. Bibliotheksverb., 1975. - 64 S. ([Schriftenreihe der Bibliothekarinstitute / B] ; 2). ISBN 3-87068-602-2

Eine Leihbibliothek der Goethe-Zeit: das „Königl. Privilegierte neue Leseinstitut“ d. Carl Friedrich Kunz zu Bamberg / Peter Vodosek 1973. In: Jahrbuch des Wiener Goethe-Vereins . - Wien. - 77 (1973), S. 110 - 133

Lucas Cranach d.Ä. und seine Zeit von Peter Vodosek
In: Lucas Cranach der Maler und seine Zeit / Hrsg. von Mitteldeutschen Kulturamt e.V.; Bonn, 1972

Der Roman als Zukunftsvision. Große schriftliche Hausarbeit zum Diplom-Examen beim Süddeutschen Bibliothekar-Lehrinstitut angefertigt in der Zeit vom 15. März bis zum 25. April 1965 von Dr. Peter Vodosek

Das Emblem in der deutschen Literatur der Renaissance und des Barock von Peter Vodosek. In: Jahrbuch des Wiener Goethe-Vereins ; hrsg. Robert Mühlher ; Band 28 : Wiener Verlag des Goethe-Vereins , 1964

König Maximilian I., die Erbländer, das Reich und Europa im Jahre 1503 Dissertation vorgelegt von Peter Vodosek. Graz, Univ., Diss., 1963. p. Maximilian Römisch-Deutsches Reich, Kaiser, I. | g.Deutschland | p.Habsburger | s.Erblande | z.Geschichte 1503

Verzeichnis der Autorinnen und Autoren

Dr. Franz Berger
Direktor der Universitätsbibliothek Bozen
Freie Universität Bozen
Sernesistraße 1
I 39100 Bozen
E-Mail: franz.berger@unibz.it

Prof. Dr. Maria E. Biener
Hochschule für Bibliotheks- und Informationswesen
Wolframstr. 32
70191 Stuttgart
E-Mail: Biener@hbi-stuttgart.de

Prof. Dipl.-Ing. Askan Blum
Prorektor der Hochschule für Bibliotheks- und Informationswesen
Wolframstr. 32
70191 Stuttgart
E-Mail: Blum@hbi-stuttgart.de

Dipl.Bibl. Klaus-Peter Böttger
Vorsitzender des Berufsverband Information Bibliothek e.V. (BIB)
Stadtbücherei Mülheim an der Ruhr
Friedrich-Ebert-Str. 47
45468 Mülheim/Ruhr
E-Mail: Klaus-Peter.Boettger@stadt-mh.de

Ingrid Bußmann
Stv. Direktorin Stadtbücherei Stuttgart
Konrad-Adenauer-Str. 2
70173 Stuttgart
E-Mail: ingrid.bussmann@stuttgart.de

Prof. Dr. Rafael Capurro
Hochschule für Bibliotheks- und Informationswesen
Wolframstr. 32
70191 Stuttgart
E-Mail: Capurro@hbi-stuttgart.de
www.capurro.de

Blaise Cronin, Ph.D, DSSc.
School of Library and Information Science
Dean & Rudy Professor of Information Science
Editor, Annual Review of Information Science & Technology
Indiana University, Bloomington
Email: bcronin@indiana.edu
http://www.slis.indiana.edu/Faculty/cronin.html

Prof. Dr. Ludwig Delp
Gründer und Leiter Deutsches Bucharchiv München
Von-der-Tann-Str. 5/1
80539 München

Professor John Feather
Loughborough University
Department of Information Science
Ashby Road
Loughborough, Leicestershire LE11 3TU
E-Mail: Featjohn@aol.com

Dr. Arend Flemming
Vorsitzender des Vorstandes Deutscher Bibliotheksverband (dbv)
Direktor Städtische Bibliotheken Dresden
Freiberger Straße 33
01067 Dresden
E-Mail: flemming@bibo-dresden.de

Prof. C. Olivia Frost
The University of Michigan
School of Information
304 West Hall
550 East University Ave. Ann Arbor, Michigan 48109-1092
E-Mail: cfrost@umich.edu

Dr. Helmut Gamsjäger
Büchereien der Stadt Linz
Museumstr. 15
4020 Linz
E-Mail: Helmut.Gamsjaeger@mag.linz.at

Prof. Winfried Gödert
Fachhochschule Köln - Fachbereich Bibliotheks- und Informationswesen
Claudiusstr. 1
50678 Köln
E-Mail: Winfried.Goedert@fh-koeln.de

Henner Grube
ekz.bibliotheksservice GmbH
Bismarckstr. 3
72764 Reutlingen
E-Mail: Henner.Grube@ekz-bibliotheksservice.de

Prof. Dr. Stefan Grudowski
Hochschule für Bibliotheks- und Informationswesen
Wolframstr. 32
70191 Stuttgart
E-Mail: Grudowski@hbi-stuttgart.de

Dr. Hagmann
Ministerialdirektor Ministerium für Wissenschaft, Forschung und Kunst Baden-Württemberg
Königstr. 46
70173 Stuttgart
E-Mail: hag@mwk-bw.de

Ole Harbo
Mitglied des Hochschulrates der Hochschule der Medien in Stuttgart
EUCLID
Ehem. Rektor Royal School of Librarianship
Birketinget 6
2300 S Copenhagen
E-Mail: OH@db.dk

Prof. Dr. Horst Heidtmann
Hochschule für Bibliotheks- und Informationswesen
Wolframstr. 32
70191 Stuttgart
E-Mail: Heidtmann@hbi-stuttgart.de

Prof. Wolfram Henning, M.A.
Hochschule für Bibliotheks- und Informationswesen
Wolframstr. 32
70191 Stuttgart
E-Mail: Henning@hbi-stuttgart.de

Dipl.Bibl. Konrad Heyde
Staatliche Fachstelle für das öffentliche Bibliothekswesen
Breisacher Straße 84
79110 Freiburg
E-Mail: fst@fr.fachstelle.bib-bw.de

Peter Hoare
21 Ouncle Drive, Wollaton Park
Nottingham NG8 1BN
E-Mail: p.hoare@virgin.net

Prof. Dr. Dietmar von Hoyningen-Huene
Vorsitzender der Rektorenkonferenz der Fachhochschulen in Baden-Württemberg
Rektor der Fachhochschule Mannheim - Hochschule für Technik und Gestaltung
Windeckstr. 110
68163 Mannheim
E-Mail: hoy@fh-mannheim.de

Dir. Ian M. Johnson
School of Information and Media
The Robert Gordon University
Garthdee Road
Aberdeen AB10 7QE
E-Mail: I.M. Johnson [imsij1945@yahoo.co.uk]

Hannelore Jouly
Direktorin Stadtbücherei Stuttgart
Konrad-Adenauer-Str. 2
70173 Stuttgart
E-Mail: hannelore.jouly@stuttgart.de

Dr. Michael Knoche
Direktor Herzogin Anna-Amalia-Bibliothek
Platz der Demokratie 1
99423 Weimar
E-Mail: Knoche@weimar-klassik.de

Mária Kovács
Berzsenyi Dániel Tanárkepzö Föiskola
Könyvtár-Informatikai Tanszék
Károlyi G. tér 4
H-9701 Szombathely
E-Mail: pami@kit2.bdtf.hu

Prof. Dr. Joachim-Felix Leonhard
Vorstand Deutsches Rundfunkarchiv
Bertramstr. 8
Postfach
60320 Frankfurt/Main
E-Mail: ubach@hr-online.de

Dr. Konrad Marwinski
Thüringer Universitäts- und Landesbibliothek
Ernst-Abbe-Platz 2
7743 Jena
E-Mail: fkm@uni-jena.de

Prof. Dr. Elmar Mittler
Niedersächsische Staats- und Universitätsbibliothek
Platz der Göttinger Sieben 1
37073 Göttingen
E-Mail: mittler@mail.sub.uni-goettingen.de

Prof. Holger Nohr
Hochschule für Bibliotheks- und Informationswesen
Wolframstr. 32
70191 Stuttgart
E-Mail: Nohr@hbi-stuttgart.de

Gabriele Ott-Osterwold
Leiterin der Graphothek der Stadtbücherei Stuttgart und Ausstellungsleitung
Konrad-Adenauer-Str. 2
70173 Stuttgart
E-Mail: gabriele.ott-osterwold@stuttgart.de

Dr. Christoph E. Palmer
Staatsminister Baden-Wuerttemberg
Richard-Wagner-Strasse 15
70184 Stuttgart
E-Mail: christoph.palmer@baden-wuerttemberg-media.de

Dr. Mihály Pálvölgyi
Berzsenyi Dániel Tanárkepzö Föiskola
Könyvtár-Informatikai Tanszék
Károlyi G. tér 4
H-9701 Szombathely
E-Mail: pami@kit2.bdtf.hu

Prof. Andreas Papendieck
Eberhardstr. 33
73760 Ostfildern
Papendieck@hbi-stuttgart.de

Dr. Alfred Pfoser
Wiener Städtische Büchereien
Skodagasse 20
1080 Wien
E-Mail: pfo-stb@m13.magwien.gv.at

Prof. Dr. Wolfgang Ratzek
Hochschule für Bibliotheks- und Informationswesen
Wolframstr. 32
70191 Stuttgart
E-Mail: Ratzek@hbi-stuttgart.de

Dr. Georg Ruppelt
Ltd. Bibliotheksdirektor Herzog August Bibliothek
Postfach 13 64, 38299 Wolfenbüttel
E-Mail: ruppelt@hab.de
Sprecher der Bundesvereinigung
Deutscher Bibliotheksverbände e.V. (BDB)
Straße des 17. Juni 114, 10623 Berlin
E-Mail: bdb@bibliotheksverband.de

Dr. Diann Rusch-Feja
Max-Planck-Institut für Bildungsforschung
Bibliothek und Wiss. Dokumentation
Lentzeallee 94
14195 Berlin
E-Mail: ruschfeja@mpib-berlin.mpg.de

Prof. Dr. h.c. mult. Klaus G. Saur
Verleger
K.G. Saur Verlag
Ortlerstr. 8
Postfach 70 16 20
81373 München
E-Mail: info@saur.de

Prof. Dr. Ulf Scharlau
Südwestrundfunk
Neckarstr. 230
Postfach 10 60 40
70190 Stuttgart
E-Mail: Ulf.Scharlau@swr-online.de

Prof. Dr. Uwe Schlegel
Gründungsrektor der Hochschule der Medien
Rektor der Fachhochschule Stuttgart - Hochschule für Druck und Medien
Nobelstr. 10
70569 Stuttgart
E-Mail: Schlegel@hdm-stuttgart.de

Dr. Siegfried Schmidt
Borromäusverein e.V.
Wittelsbacher Ring 9
53115 Bonn

Prof. Dr. Gerd Schmidt
Im Gärtle 20
79104 Freiburg i.Br.

Dr. Angelika Schütt-Hohenstein
Bibliothek für Zeitgeschichte
Konrad-Adenauer-Straße 8
70173 Stuttgart
Postfach 10 54 41
70047 Stuttgart
E-Mail: hohenstein@wlb-stuttgart.de

Prof. Ingeborg Spribille
Hochschule für Bibliotheks- und Informationswesen
Wolframstr. 32
70191 Stuttgart
Spribille@hbi-stuttgart.de

Paul Sturges
Reader in Libraries in Social Development
Department of Information Science
Loughborough University
Ashby Road
Leicestershire LE11 3TU
E-Mail: R.P.Sturges@lboro.ac.uk

Prof. Dr. Frank Thissen
Hochschule für Bibliotheks- und Informationswesen
Wolframstr. 32
70191 Stuttgart
Thissen@hbi-stuttgart.de

Minister Klaus von Trotha
Minister für Wissenschaft, Forschung und Kunst Baden-Württemberg
Königstr. 46
Postfach 10 34 53
70173 Stuttgart

Prof. Dr. Konrad Umlauf
Humboldt-Universität zu Berlin
Philosophische Fakultät I,
Institut für Bibliothekswissenschaft
Dorotheenstr. 26
10117 Berlin
E-Mail: konrad.umlauf@rz.hu-berlin.de

Giuseppe Vitiello
Council of Europe
Programme Advisor
Electronic Publishing, Books and Archives
Palais de l'Europe - Conseil de l'Europe
F - 67075 Strasbourg France
E-Mail: giuseppe.vitiello@coe.int

Dr. Boris Volodin
Nalitchnaia ul. 33-47
199406 Sankt Petersburg
E-Mail: niob@nlr.ru

Prof. Volker Wehdeking, Ph.D.
Hochschule für Bibliotheks- und Informationswesen
Wolframstr. 32
70191 Stuttgart
E-Mail: Wehdeking@hbi-stuttgart.de